Van Gogh and the Avant-Garde

Along the Seine

Van Gogh and the Avant-Garde

Edited by Bregje Gerritse and Jacquelyn N. Coutré

With contributions by Jena K. Carvana,
Charlotte Hellman, Joost van der Hoeven,
François Lespinasse, Teio Meedendorp
and Richard Thomson

The Art Institute of Chicago
Van Gogh Museum, Amsterdam
THOTH Publishers, Bussum

Along the Seine

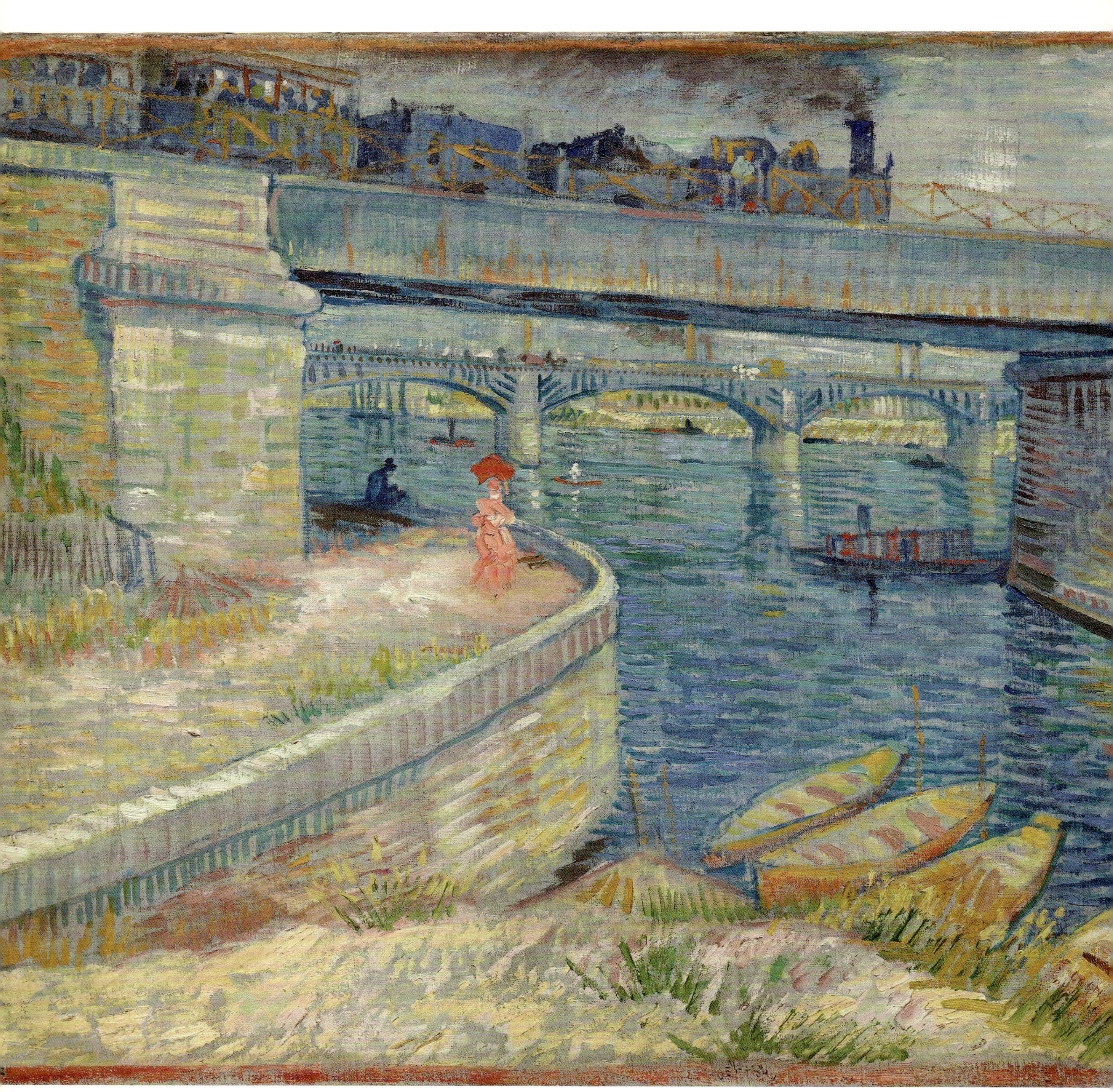

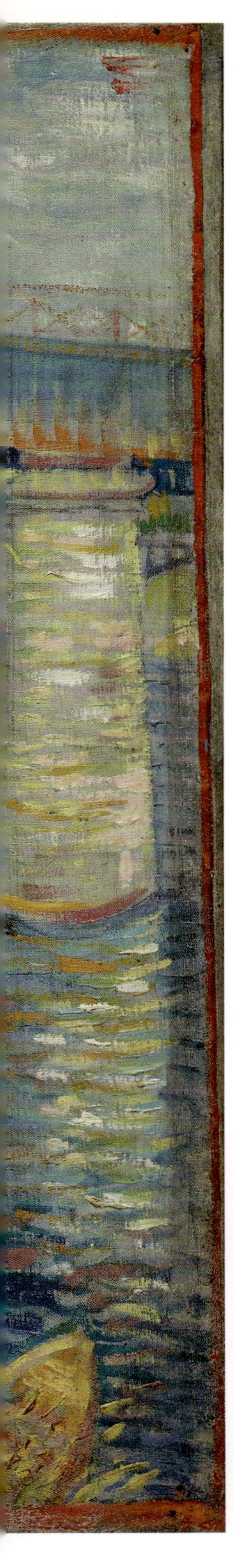

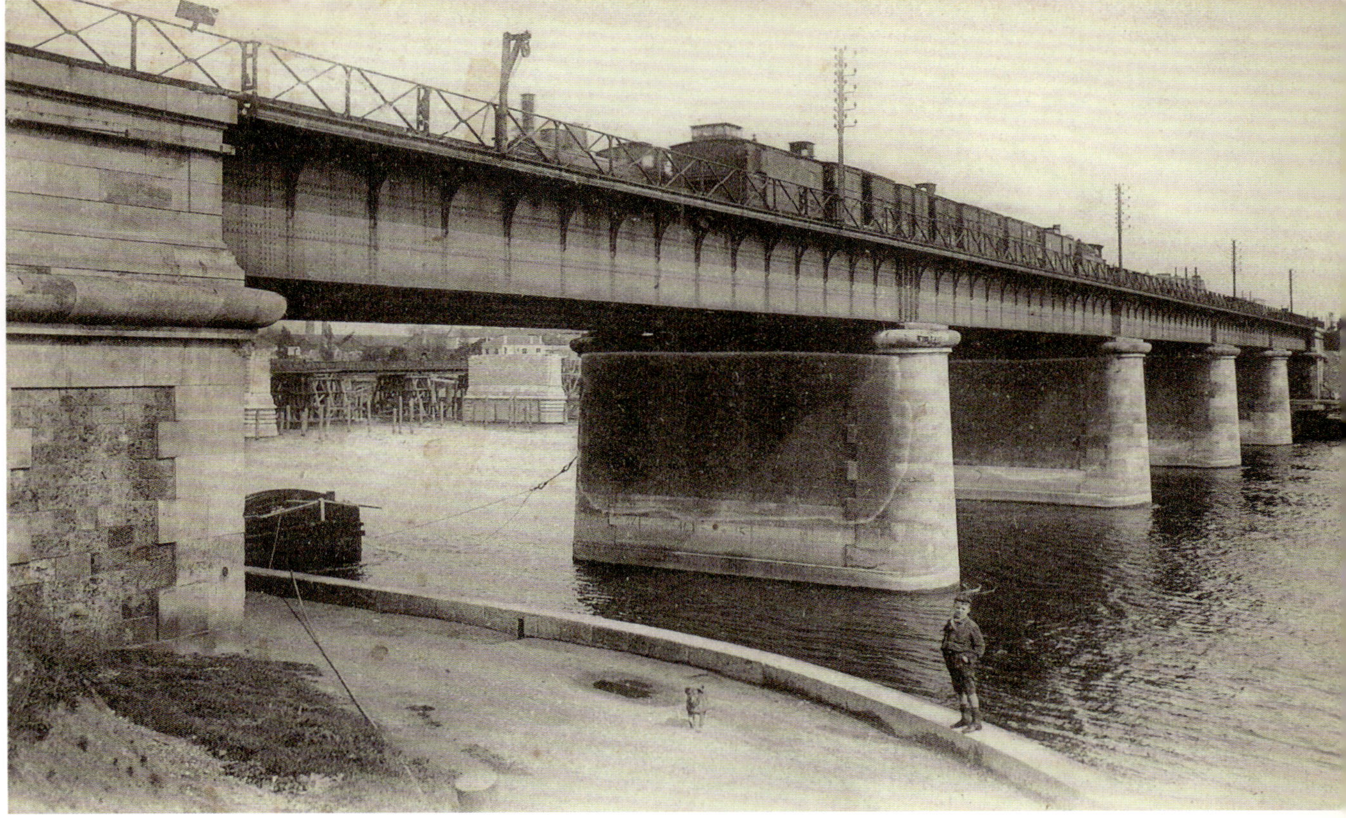

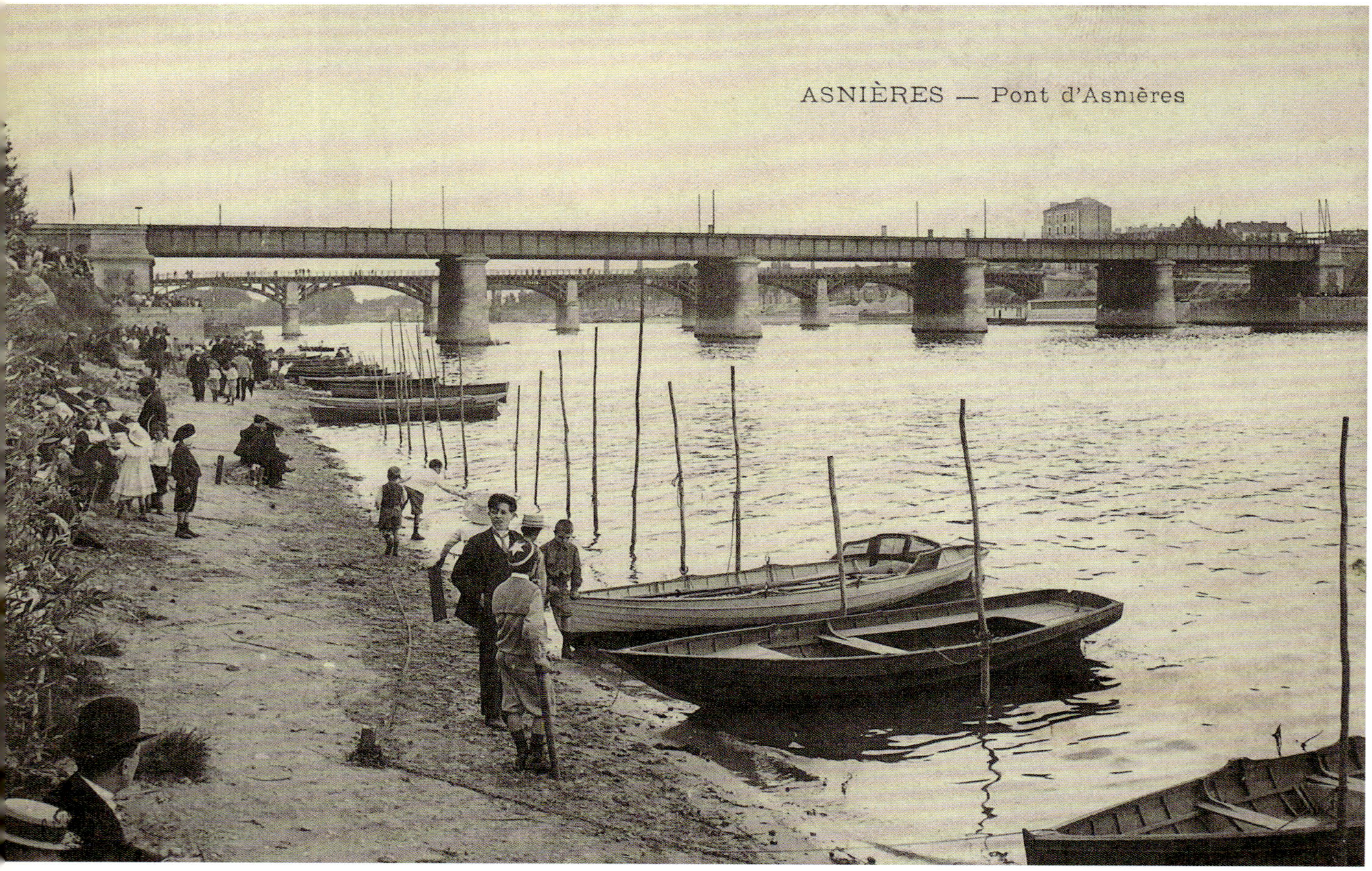

ASNIÈRES — Pont d'Asnières

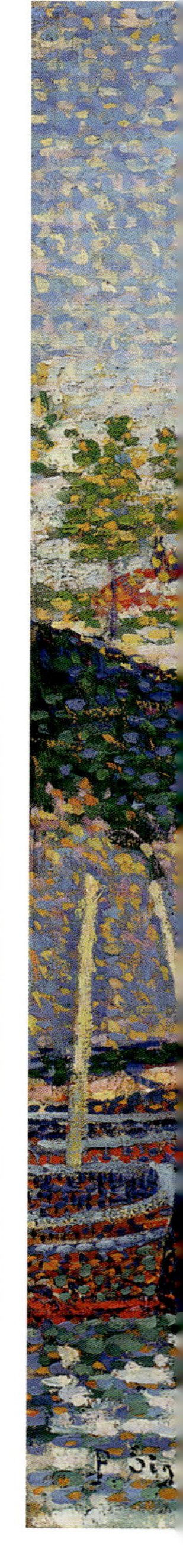

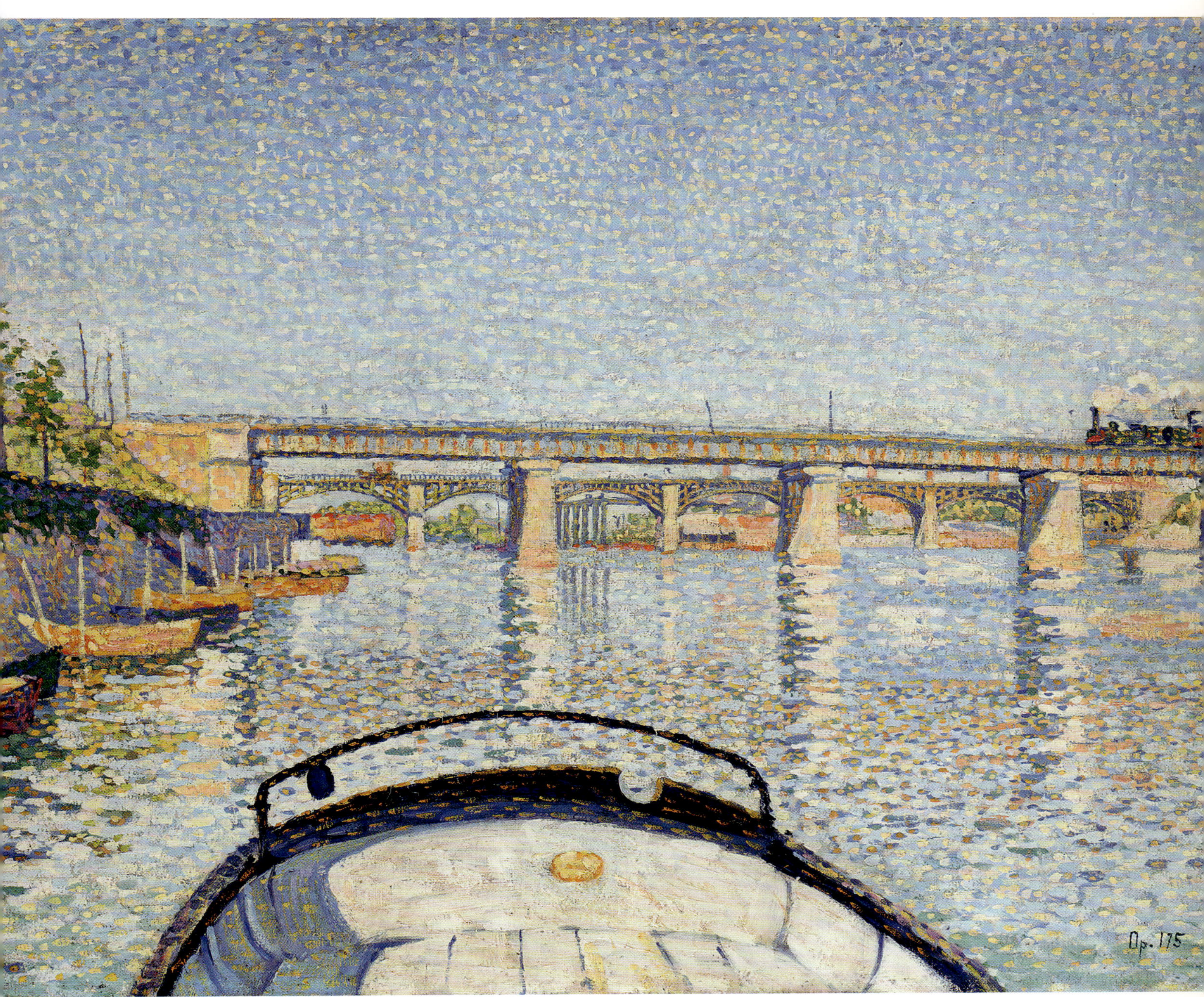
Пр. 175

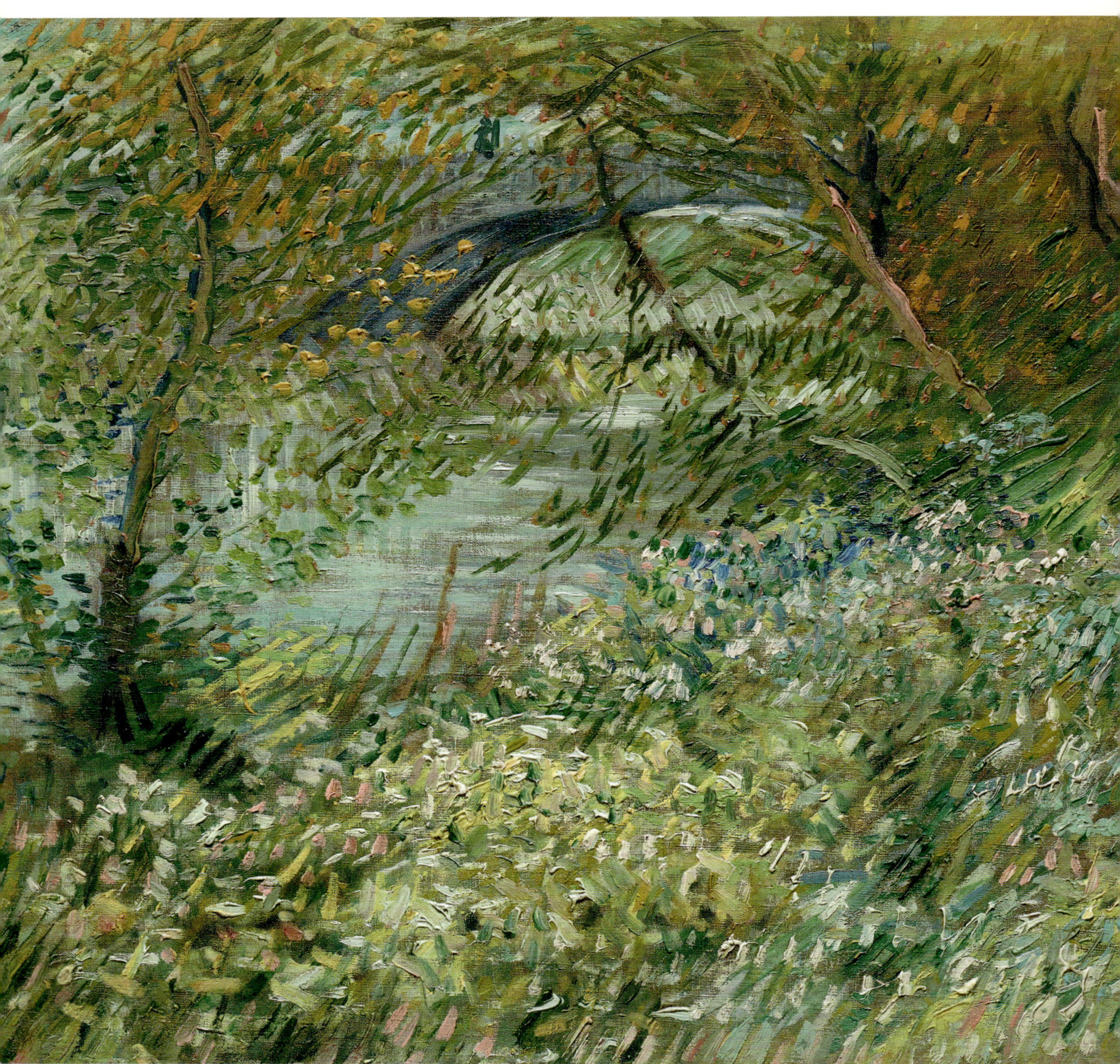

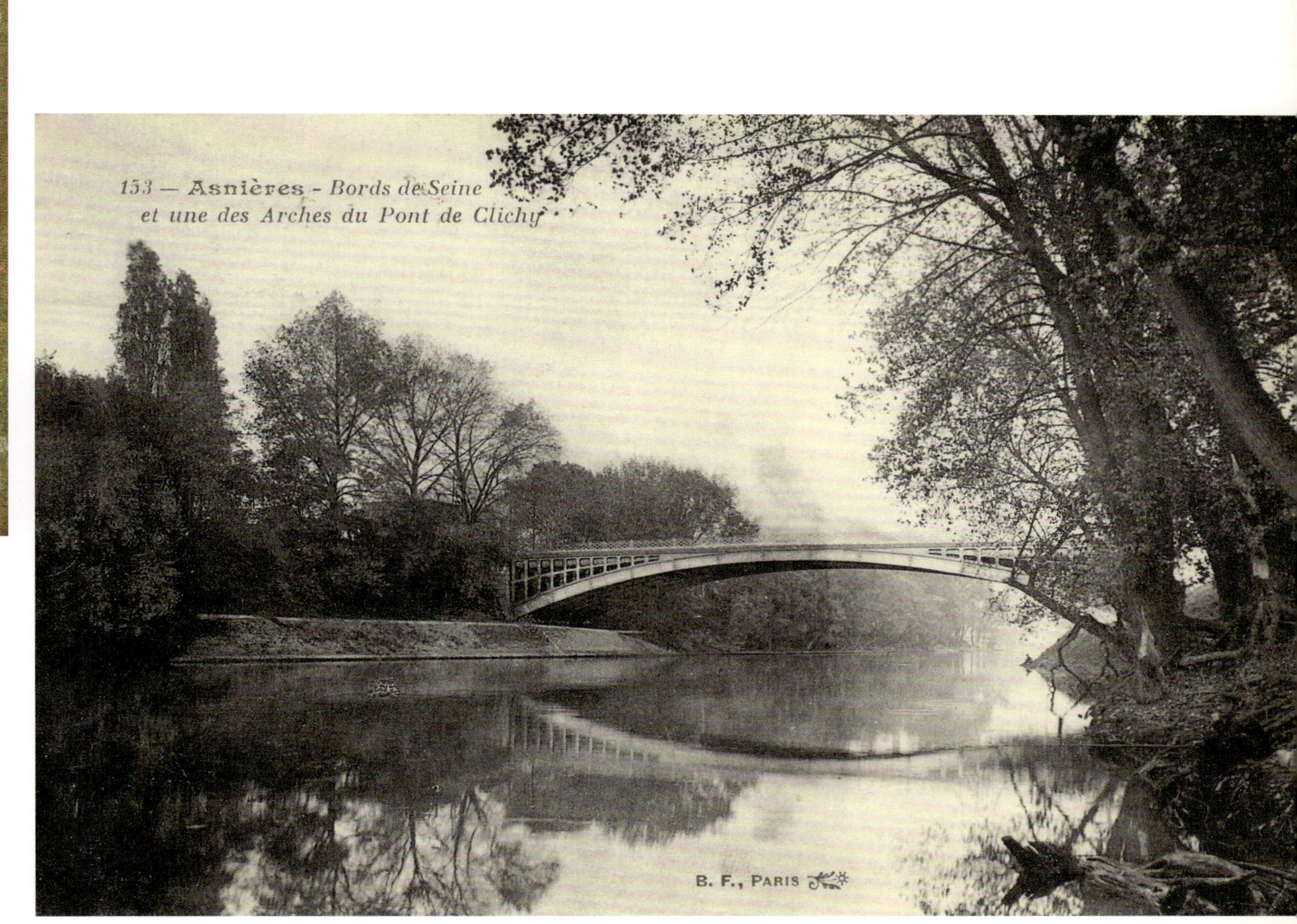
153 — Asnières - Bords de Seine
et une des Arches du Pont de Clichy
B. F., PARIS

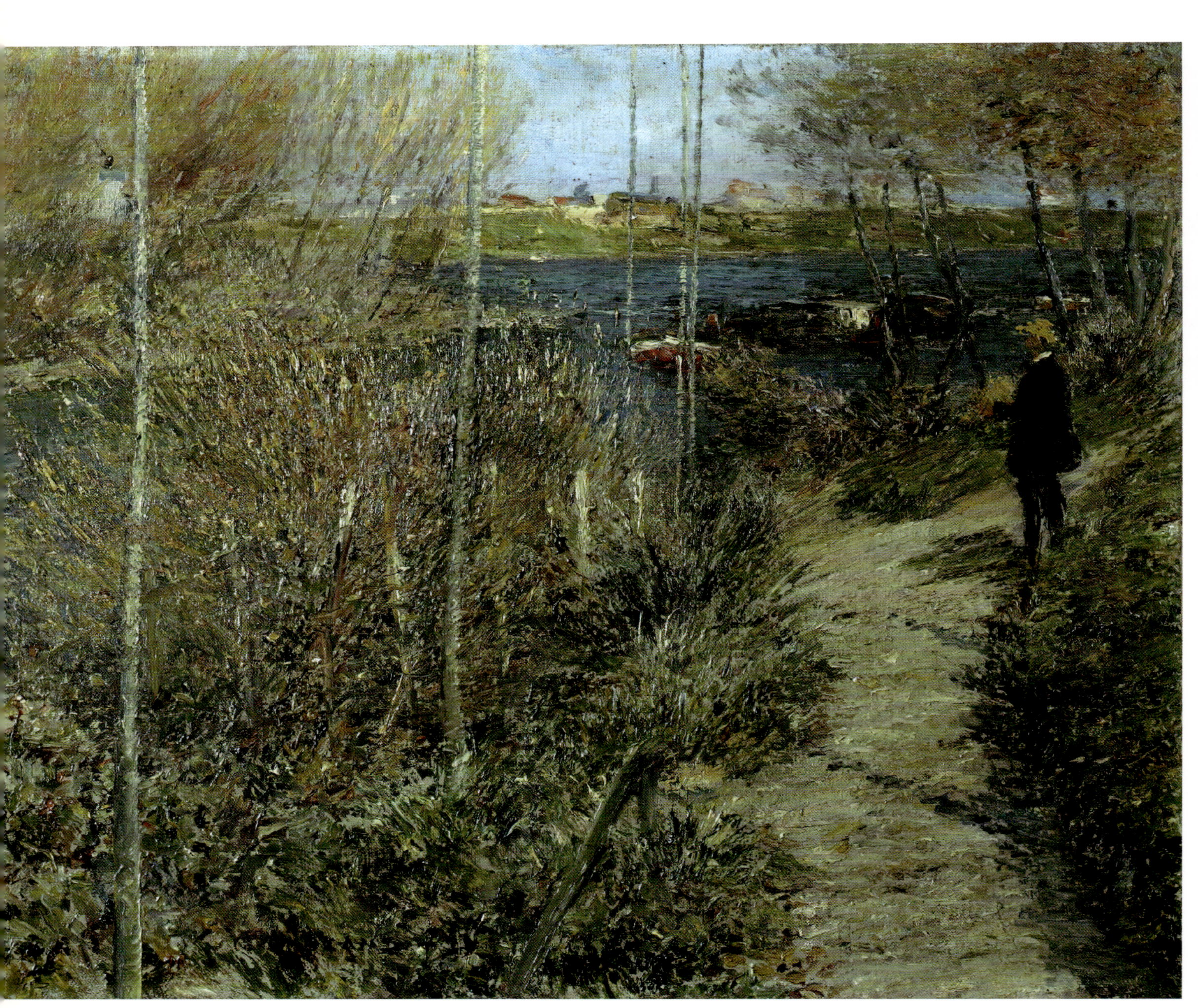

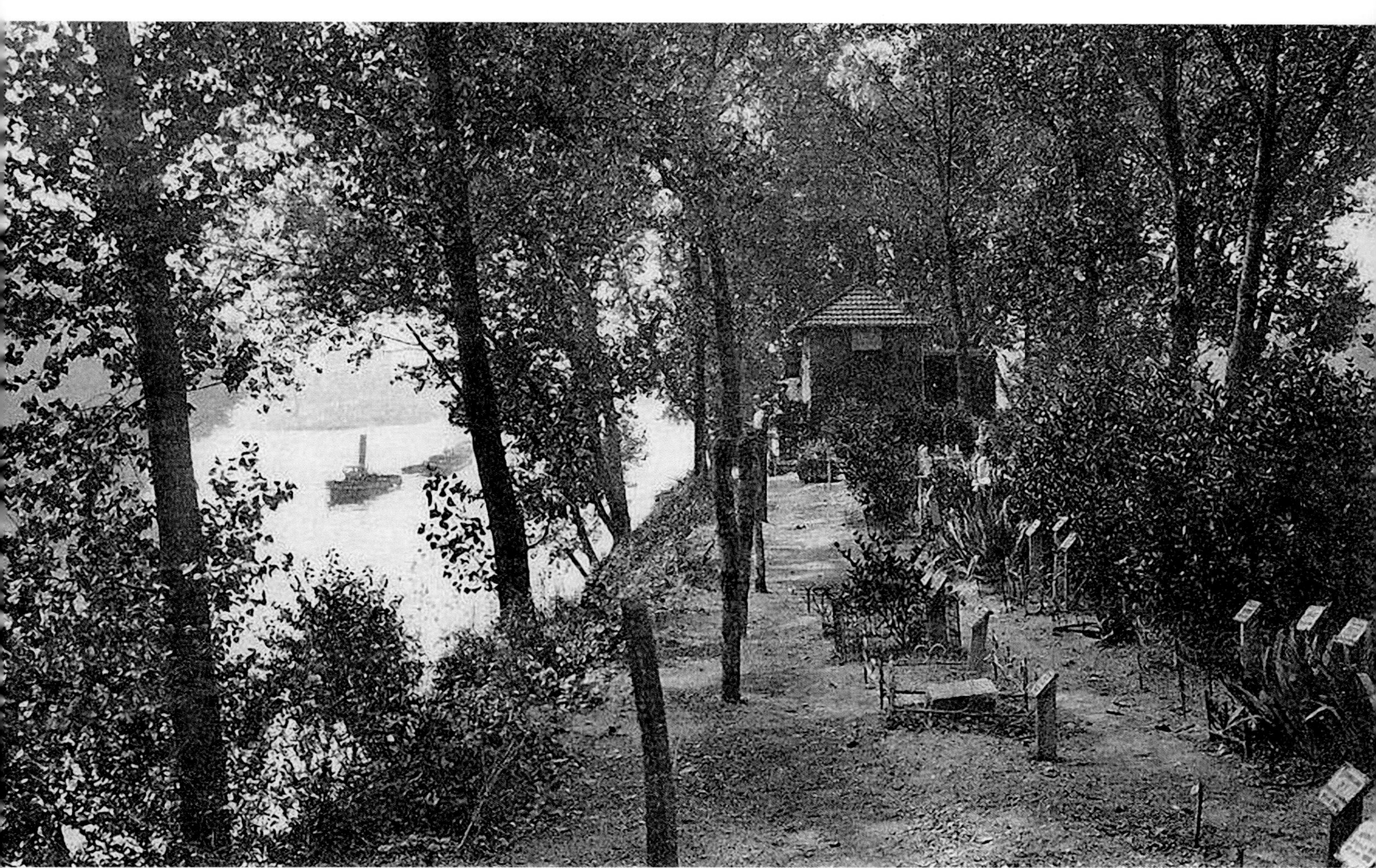

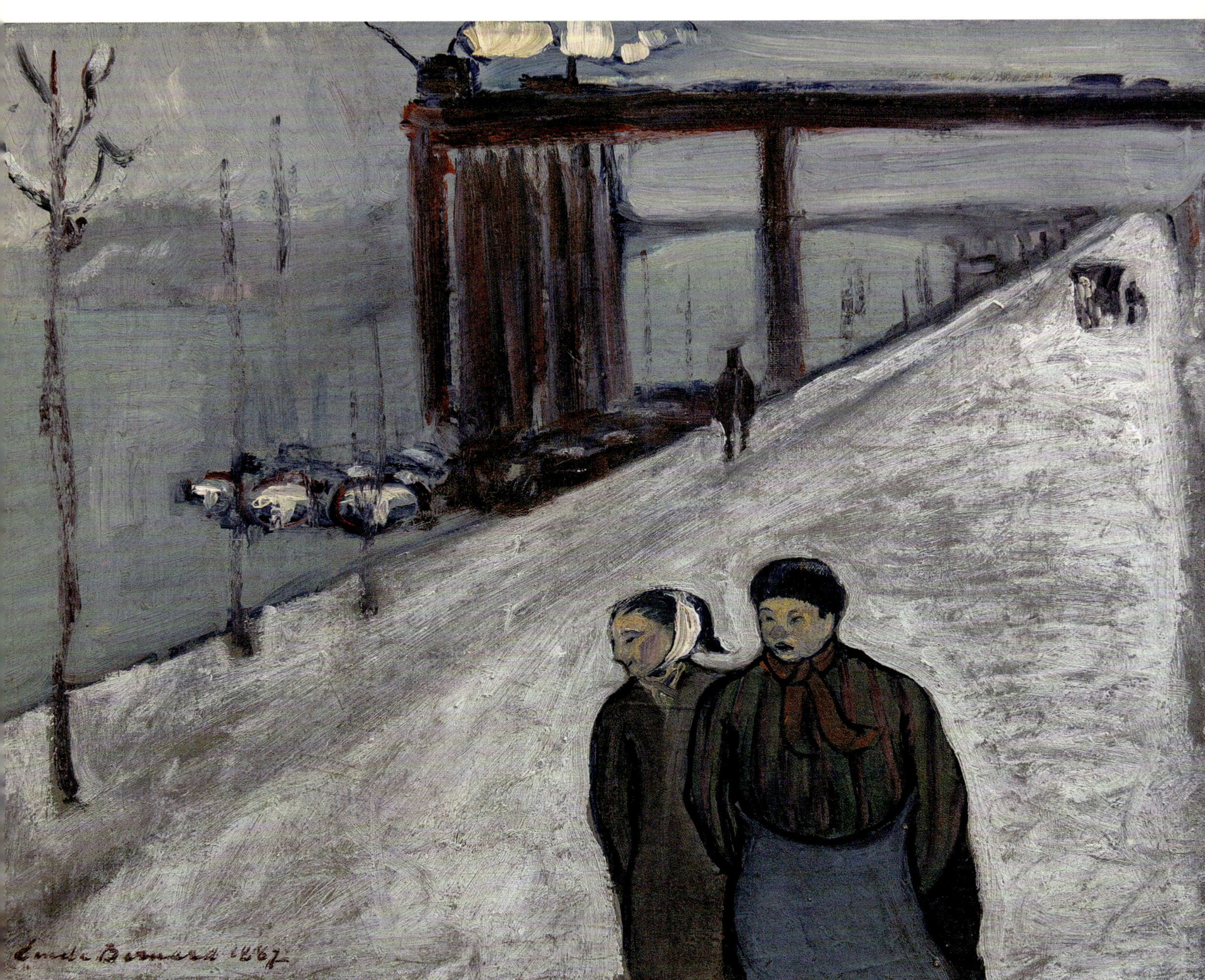
Emile Bernard 1887

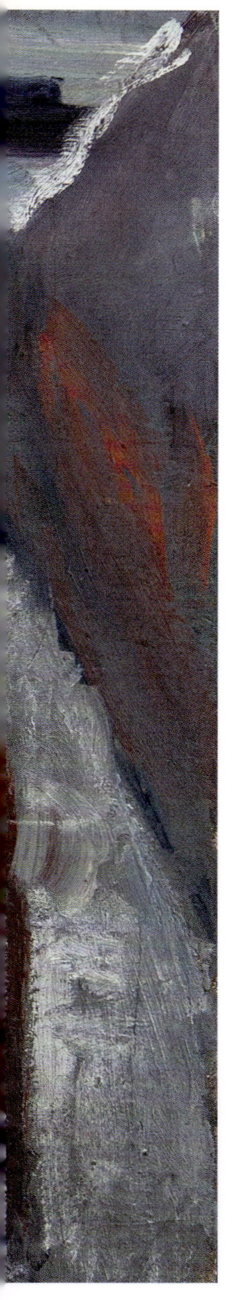

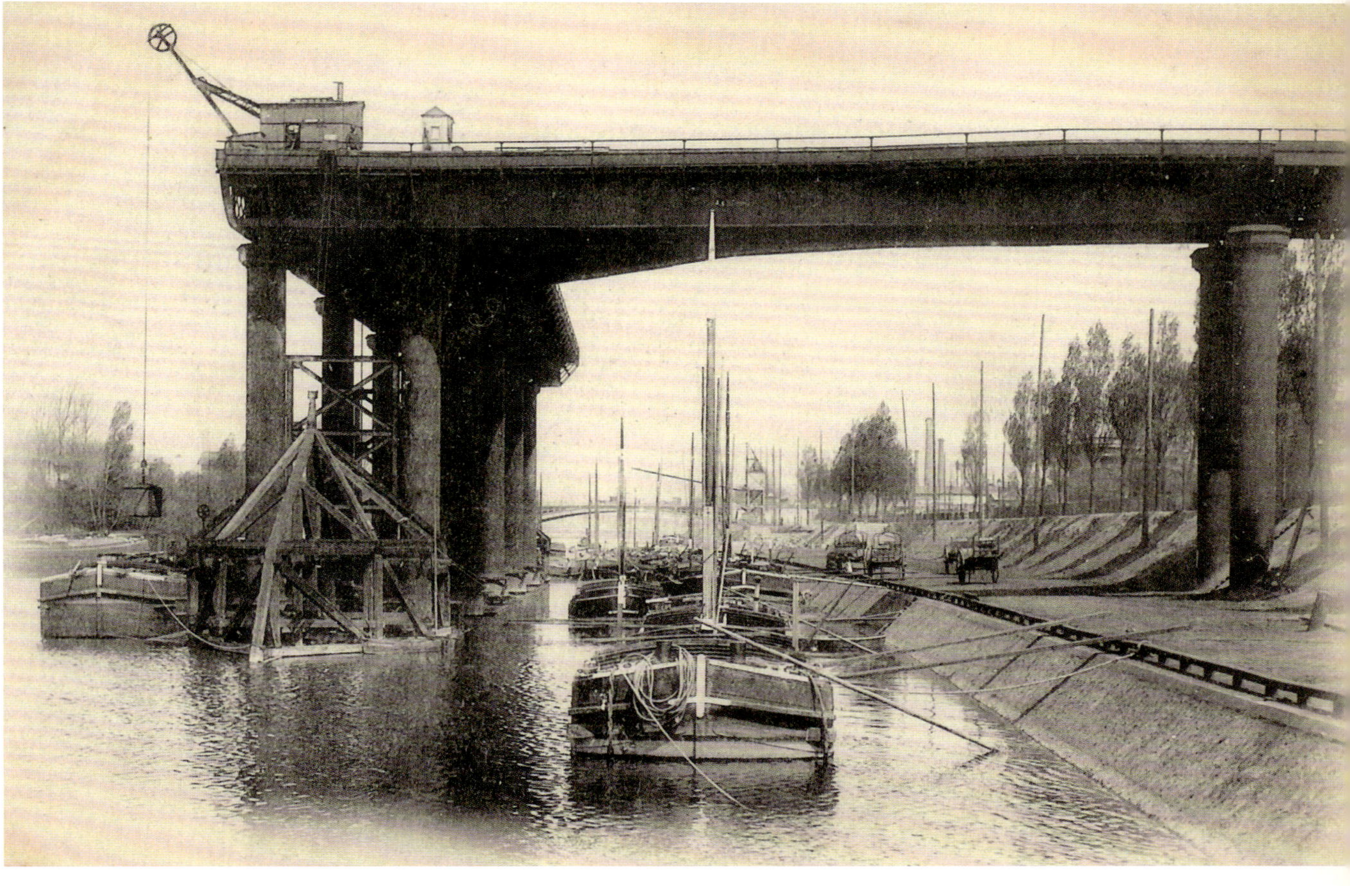

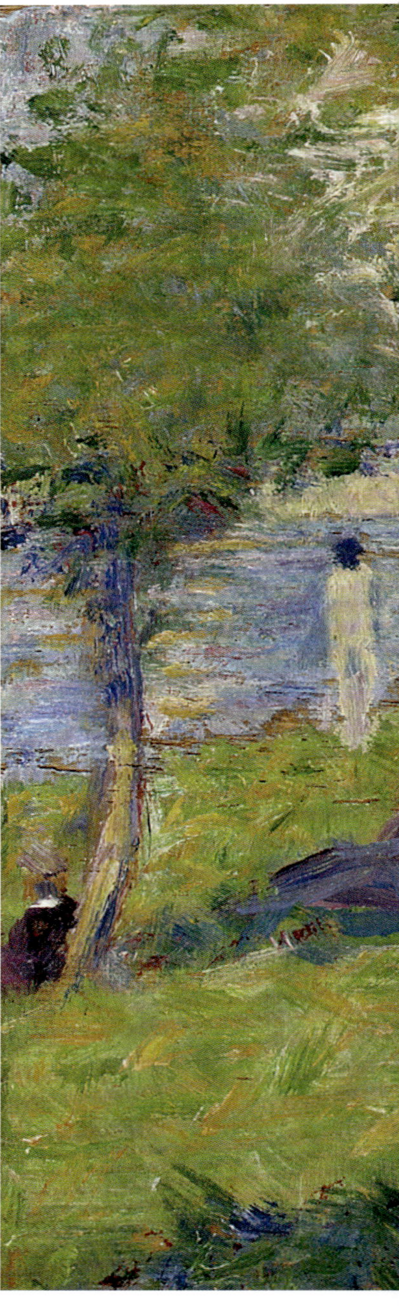

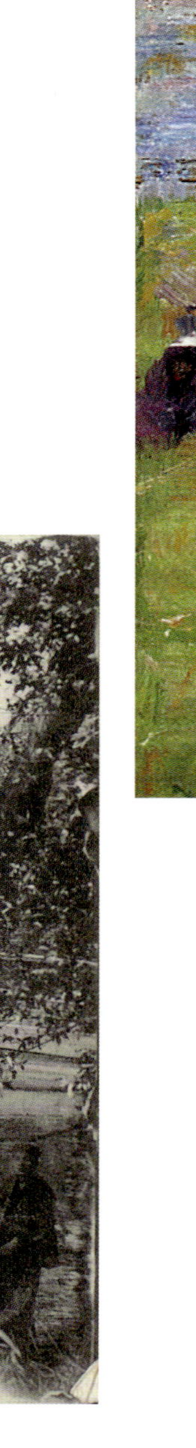
14. COURBEVOIE
Les Bords de la Seine - L'Ile de la Jatte

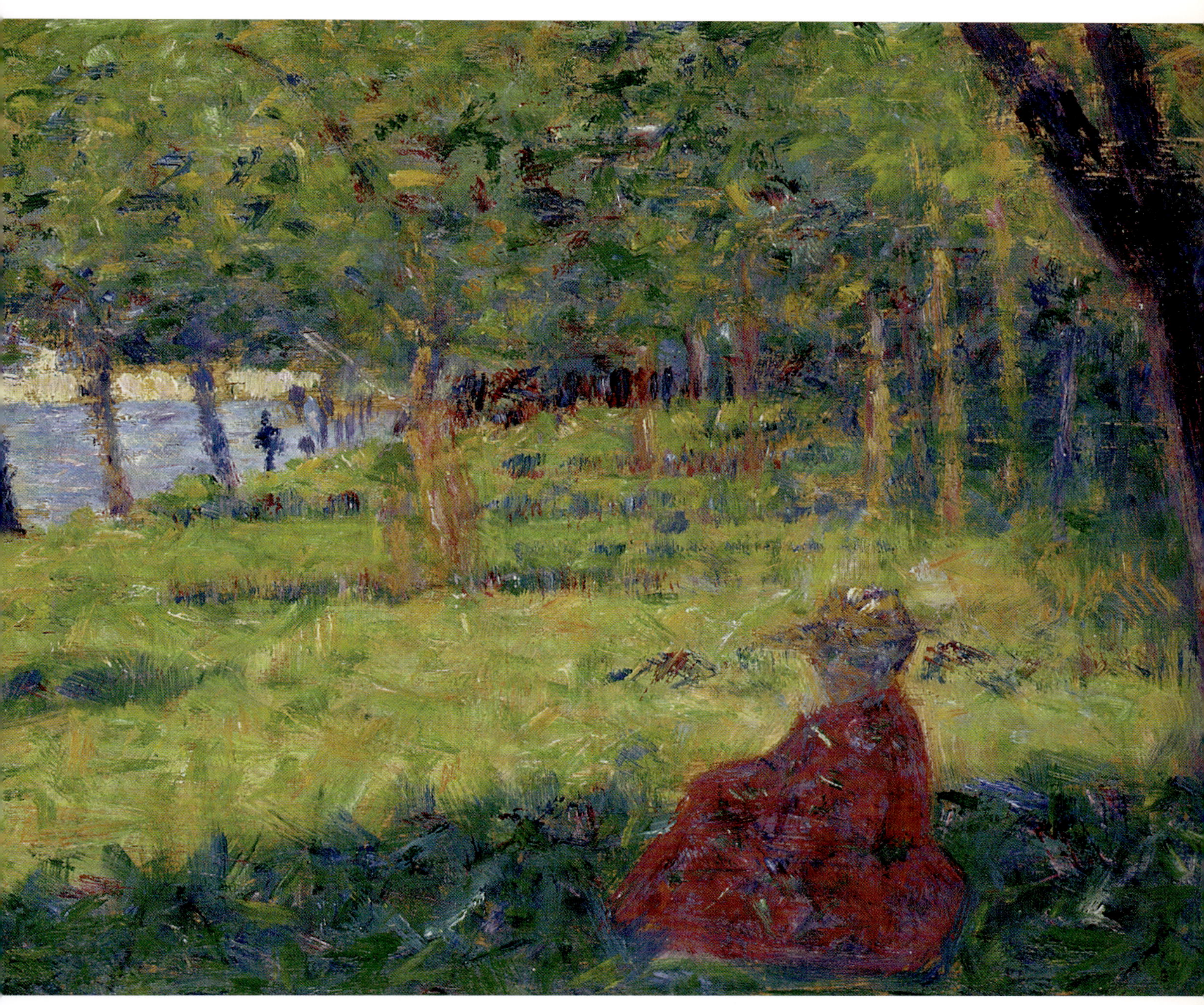

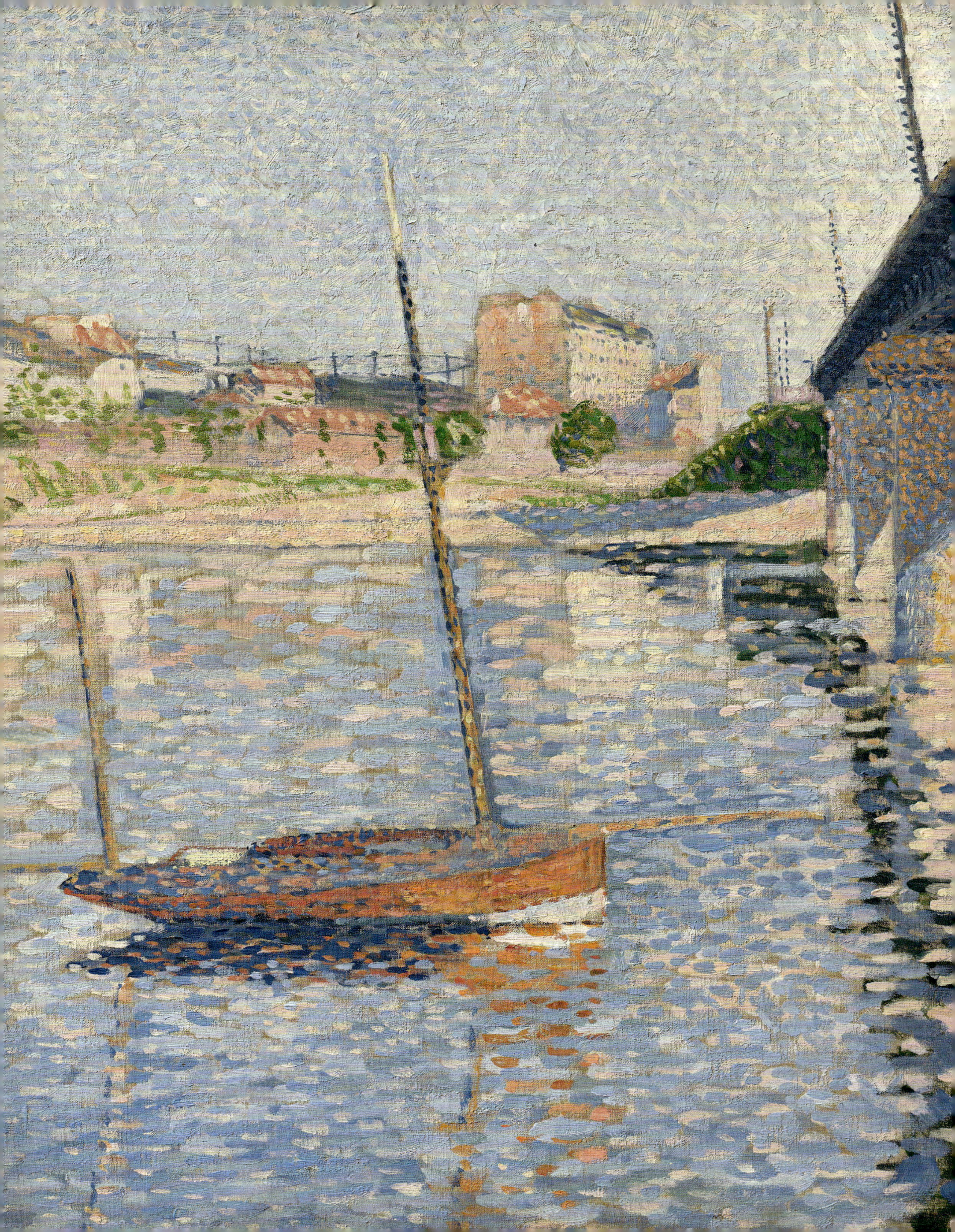

Contents

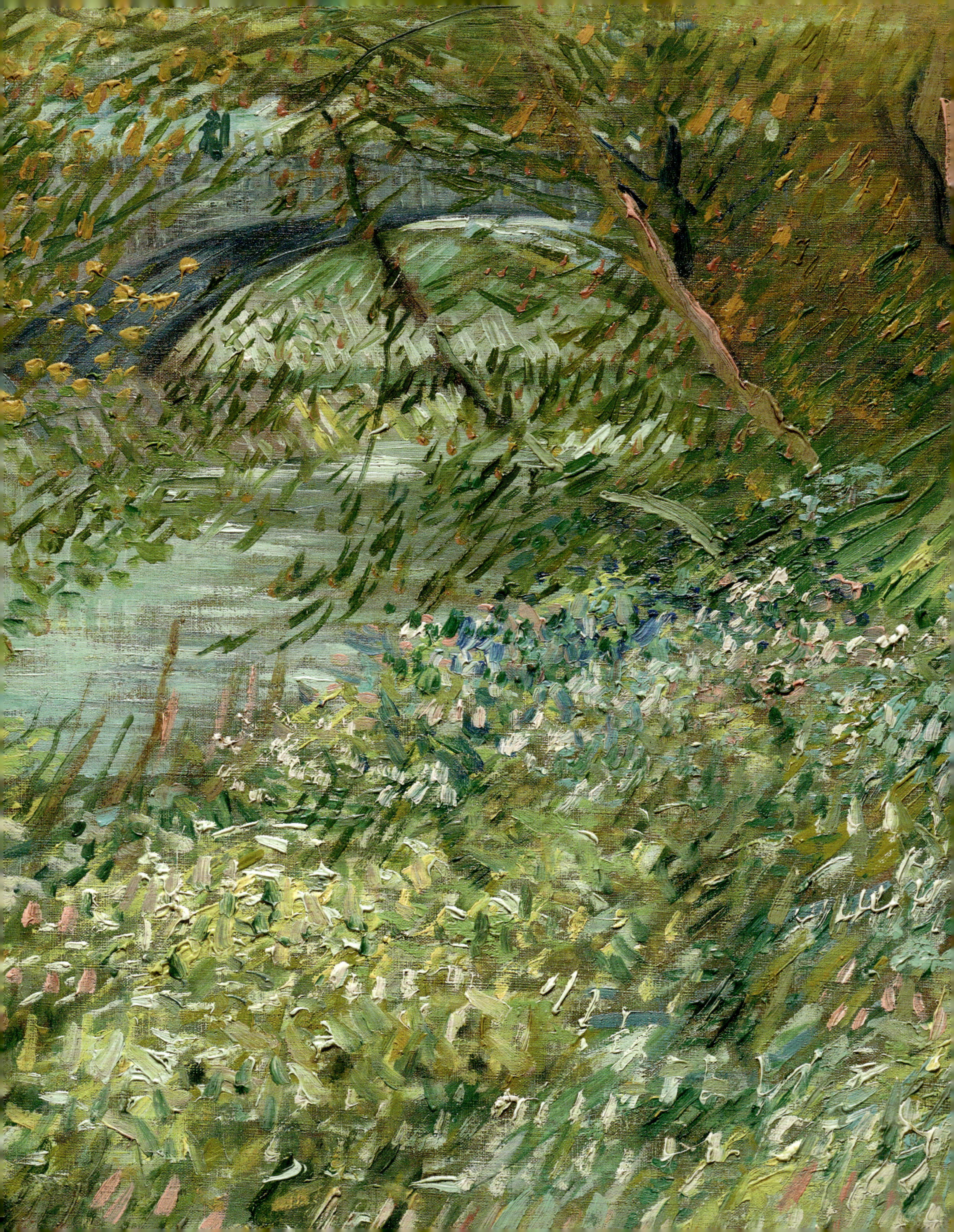

Published on the occasion of the exhibition:

Van Gogh and the Avant-Garde: The Modern Landscape
The Art Institute of Chicago
May 14–September 4, 2023

Van Gogh Along the Seine
Van Gogh Museum, Amsterdam
October 13, 2023–January 14, 2024

Directors' Foreword

The suburb of Asnières (now known as Asnières-sur-Seine), located along the river Seine about three miles outside of Paris, is hardly a household name in Europe or North America. The villages associated with the Impressionists—such as Claude Monet's Argenteuil, Pierre-Auguste Renoir's Chatou, and Alfred Sisley's Bougival—are located further downstream where the countryside has retained its idyllic charm. More closely attached to the metropolis, Asnières and its environs industrialized during the mid-nineteenth century to satisfy the demands of cosmopolitan Parisians. During the 1880s, five ambitious artists—Vincent van Gogh, Georges Seurat, Paul Signac, Emile Bernard, and Charles Angrand—ventured there to paint. Seurat famously traveled to the island of La Grande Jatte in 1881 to sketch. Signac's and Bernard's families moved to the area in 1880 and 1884, respectively. They, in turn, inspired Angrand and Van Gogh to venture outside of the city walls in pursuit of new terrains to use as subjects of their artistic explorations. Asnières profoundly influenced each of these five artists in their revolutionary reconsiderations of color and brushstroke.

Although it has long been observed that this diverse group of painters decided to work in the unassuming suburbs northwest of the city—not only Asnières, but also Clichy, Courbevoie, Gennevilliers, La Grande Jatte, Levallois, and Saint-Ouen—this publication and exhibition are the first to investigate why and to what effect. Over the course of the second and third quarters of the century, the construction of railroad bridges, factories, and boating clubs along the Seine increased at a rapid pace, as an enormous public works project transformed Paris and forced working-class citizens to relocate to the more affordable suburbs. These communities were fundamentally shaped by the modernization of Paris, and artists focused on industrialization as their motif: the iron railroad bridges, the factory smokestacks, and the promenading figures associated with the changing concept of recreation. Before arriving in Paris, Van Gogh described the stimulating tension between city and country, and the radical contradictions increasingly visible along the Seine indeed helped to generate new ideas about color mixtures, the separation of brushstrokes, and how to achieve maximum luminosity on the canvas.

Originally conceived by Maite van Dijk, then Senior Curator of Paintings at the Van Gogh Museum in Amsterdam, since 2021 Director of Museum MORE in Gorssel, this exhibition and catalogue have been developed with great enthusiasm and expertise by Bregje Gerritse, Researcher at the Van Gogh Museum, and Jacquelyn N. Coutré, Eleanor Wood Prince Associate Curator at the Art Institute of Chicago, with the assistance of Art Institute Curatorial Associate Jena K. Carvana. The Van Gogh Museum and the Art Institute have collaborated on several projects, yet this is the first jointly curated exhibition in more than twenty years. Given the Van Gogh Museum's outstanding collection of works by Van Gogh and his contemporaries and the Art Institute's collection strength in works by Seurat—foremost the epic *Sunday on La Grande Jatte—1884* and the many Conté crayon and oil studies for it—the partnership is a natural one for the exploration of this topic.

We are particularly grateful for the generous support of the Vincent van Gogh Foundation, as well as that of major lenders, including the Musée d'Orsay, Paris; the National Gallery, London; and numerous other museums and galleries around the world. We also deeply appreciate the kindness shown by the many collectors who have lent to this show, including those who wish to remain anonymous. A significant number of the works in the exhibition remain in private collections, and without the enthusiastic participation of these lenders, the project would not have been possible. In Chicago, lead support is provided by The Kenneth C. Griffin Charitable Fund. Major support is provided by the Shure Charitable Trust, the Jentes Family, the Pepper Family Foundation, Julie and Roger Baskes, The Manitou Fund, and Margot Levin Schiff and the Harold Schiff Foundation. Additional funding is provided by the Jack and Peggy Crowe Fund, the Suzanne and Wesley M. Dixon Exhibition Fund, and The Regenstein Foundation Fund. Members of the Luminary Trust provide annual leadership support for the museum's operations, including exhibition development, conservation and collection care, and educational programming. The Luminary Trust includes an anonymous donor, Karen Gray-Krehbiel and John Krehbiel, Jr., Kenneth C. Griffin, the Harris Family Foundation in memory of Bette and Neison Harris, Josef and Margot Lakonishok, Robert M. and Diane v.S. Levy, Ann and Samuel M. Mencoff, Sylvia Neil and Dan Fischel, Cari and Michael J. Sacks, and the Earl and Brenda Shapiro Foundation. In Amsterdam, we are indebted to The Ministry of Education, Culture, and Science of The Netherlands, and to our principal partners the VriendenLoterij, ASML, and DHL for their generous support. We also extend our thanks to exhibition partners Van Lanschot Kempen and The Sunflower Circle.

We hope that this catalogue and exhibition illuminate these five artists in new ways, making evident that their vibrant landscapes, which draw upon the dynamism of the Seine and its surrounding areas, not only capture the modernity of the suburban environment but also the growing modernism of their painting practices. Their experiences in Asnières emboldened these artists to broaden their understanding of painting—what it can picture, how and where it can be made—in ways that would shape not only their own respective styles and techniques but also those of subsequent nineteenth- and twentieth-century artists whom they inspired. Only by leaving the city and stepping into its suburban environs could they have charted the new directions that changed the trajectory of modern art.

James Rondeau
President and Eloise W. Martin Director
The Art Institute of Chicago

Dr. Emilie E. S. Gordenker
Director
Van Gogh Museum, Amsterdam

Lenders to the Exhibition

The directors and exhibition curators of both institutions are extremely grateful to all museums, collectors, and anonymous lenders for their generous loans:

The Art Institute of Chicago

The Ashmolean Museum, University of Oxford

The Baltimore Museum of Art

The Courtauld, London

Dallas Museum of Art

Larry Ellison

Emil Bührle Collection, Zürich

Hasso Plattner Collection

The Israel Museum, Jerusalem

Kelvingrove Art Gallery and Museum, Glasgow

Kunsthalle Bremen

Leeds Art Gallery

The Metropolitan Museum of Art, New York

Musée départemental du Prieuré, Saint-Germain-en-Laye

Musée des Beaux-Arts de Brest

Musée d'Orsay, Paris

Musée du Louvre, Paris

Musée Petit Palais, Geneva

The Museum of Modern Art, New York

The Museum of Modern Art, Saitama

National Galleries of Scotland, Edinburgh

The National Gallery, London

National Gallery of Victoria, Melbourne

The Nelson-Atkins Museum of Art, Kansas City

P. & N. de Boer Foundation, Amsterdam

Royal Museums of Fine Arts, Brussels

Saint Louis Art Museum

Solomon R. Guggenheim Museum, New York

Tate, London

Andrew S. Teufel

Uehara Museum of Art, Shimoda

Van Gogh Museum, Amsterdam

Vincent van Gogh Foundation

Virginia Museum of Fine Arts, Richmond

Von der Heydt-Museum, Wuppertal

The Whitworth Art Gallery, University of Manchester

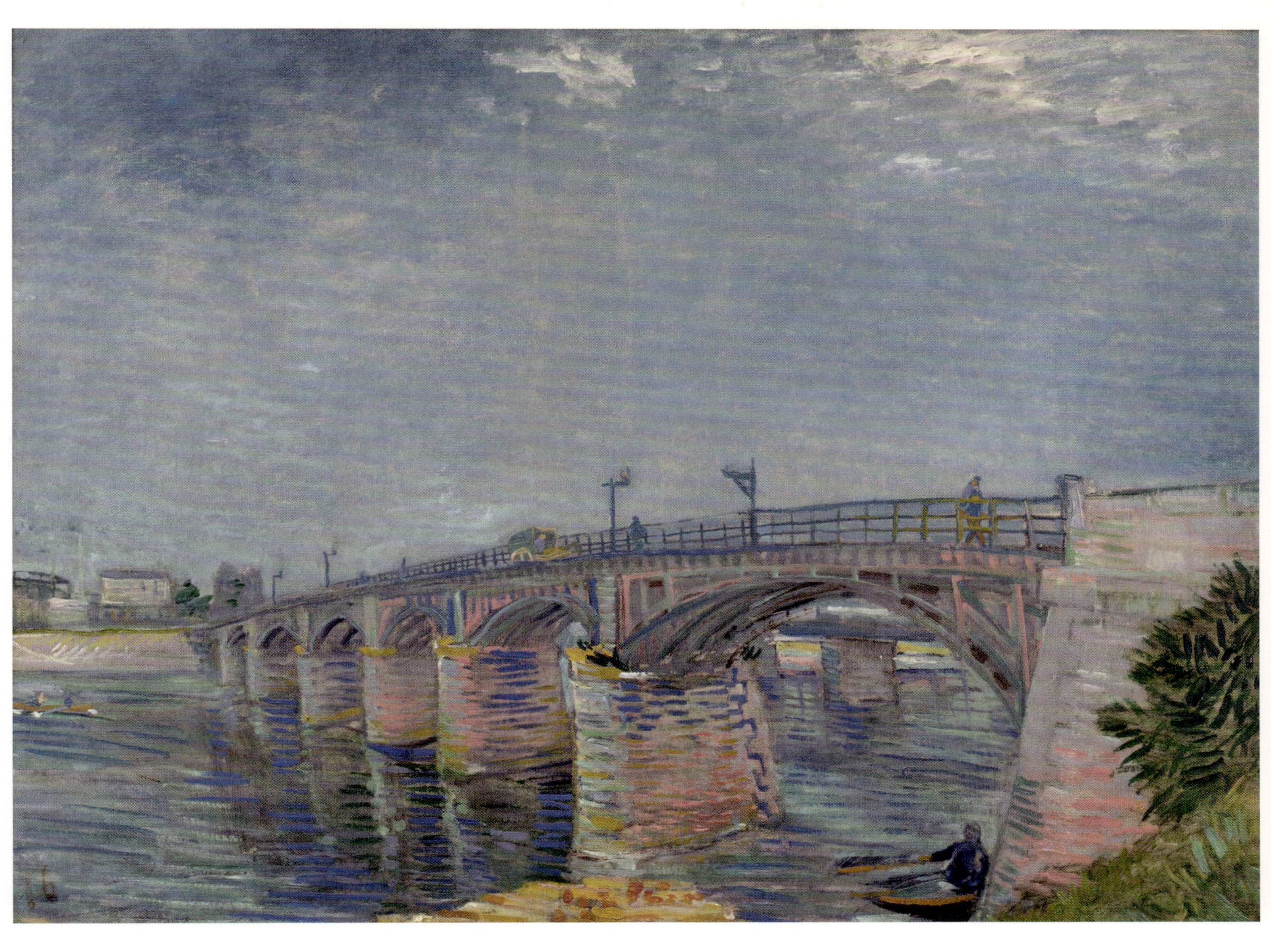

1 (cat.) Vincent van Gogh
View of the Pont d'Asnières, 1887
Oil on canvas, 54.3×73.3 cm
Private collection, Larry Ellison

FIVE ARTISTS ALONG THE SEINE: AN INTRODUCTION

JACQUELYN N. COUTRÉ AND BREGJE GERRITSE

And when I painted landscape in Asnières this summer I saw more color in it than before.

—Vincent van Gogh to his sister Willemien van Gogh, late October 1887 [574]

In a lengthy letter to his younger sister in late fall 1887, Vincent van Gogh (1853-1890) made a passing but powerful reference to his experience painting outside of Paris. It was written several months after his visits to the suburb of Asnières in the spring and summer, and therefore incorporates reflections upon what he learned from these excursions. Notably, he specified that, in contrast to the still lifes and portraits that occupied his attention within the city walls, he focused on landscape at Asnières **(2,3,4)**. Equally striking is his association of this suburban location with a sharpened appreciation for color, a visual element that had challenged him and would continue to play a role in his artistic development after his move to Arles in 1888. His remarkable *Fishing in Spring, the Pont de Clichy (Asnières)* **(51)** demonstrates his understanding of sumptuous color—particularly evident in the lush young leaves adorning the tree branches along the river and the pink flowers dappling the far grassy bank—and reveals a radical shift away from the sober palette associated with his earlier realist years in Holland. Here, in Asnières, he fully embraced the vibrancy of complementary colors. As the artist did not compose letters to his brother, Theo, while he lived with him in Paris, only seven of the more than nine hundred letters that survive mention this suburb. This one from the fall of 1887, however, attests to the powerful effect this location had on Van Gogh's progression as an artist, as Bregje Gerritse's essay in this volume explores.

Asnières and the northwestern suburbs fueled a hotbed of artistic innovation for Van Gogh and other artists in the

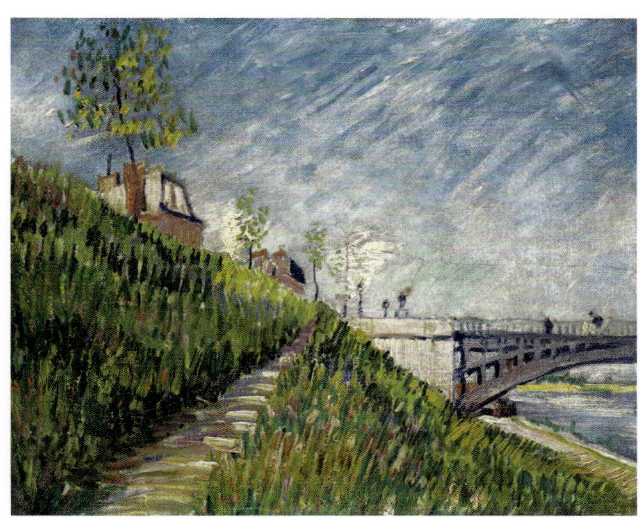

2 (cat.) Vincent van Gogh
Banks of the Seine with the Pont de Clichy, 1887
Oil on canvas, 30.5×39 cm
Private collection

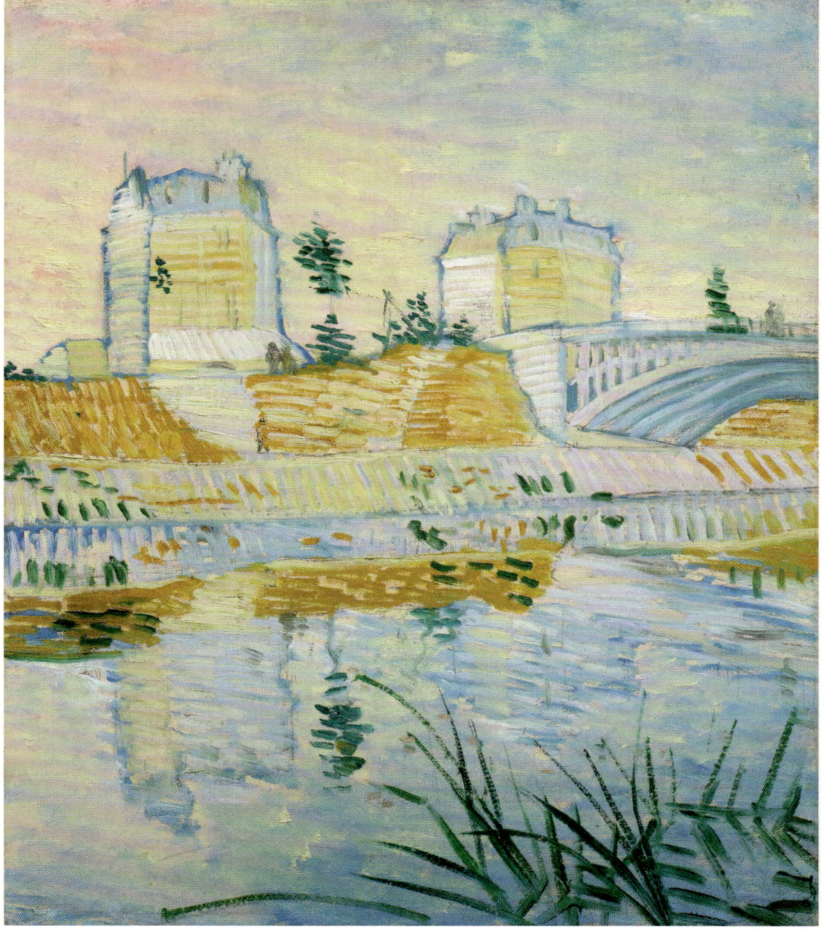

3 Vincent van Gogh
The Seine with the Pont de Clichy, 1887
Oil on canvas, 55×46 cm
Private collection

1880s, as Jacquelyn N. Coutré traces in the essay that follows. Georges Seurat (1859-1891), discussed here by Richard Thomson, was the first to paint here in the early 1880s. By 1884, he had completed his *Bathers at Asnières* **(66)** and had submitted it unsuccessfully to the official, juried Salon, the most important annual art exhibition in France. In this work, Seurat's application of paint in short strokes and his prominent depiction of smokestacks and a railroad bridge in the distance laid a foundation for new ways in which these artists would approach painting. Inspired by this technique, Paul Signac (1863-1935) would work with Seurat to refine Pointillism, which used small dots and dashes of contrasting colors juxtaposed to produce daring luminosity, as Charlotte Hellman details. Meanwhile, Emile Bernard (1868-1941) briefly experimented with this style before adopting the flat color planes defined by thick outlines of Cloisonnism, as is explained by Joost van der Hoeven. François Lespinasse outlines how Charles Angrand (1854-1926) shifted from an Impressionist palette and manner to one inspired by Seurat during this time. While working in Asnières and its surroundings during the 1880s, each artist was considering and assimilating new manners of representation according to their own artistic personalities. Although they would have never conceived of themselves as a coherent group, they were unified by their pursuit of new, modern painting styles. It was through their technical experimentations and unfamiliar subject matter in and around these Parisian suburbs, as well as their exchange with each other, that these artists developed their own approaches to painting.

By the time all five artists started to engage with Asnières and its neighboring villages, Ogden Rood had

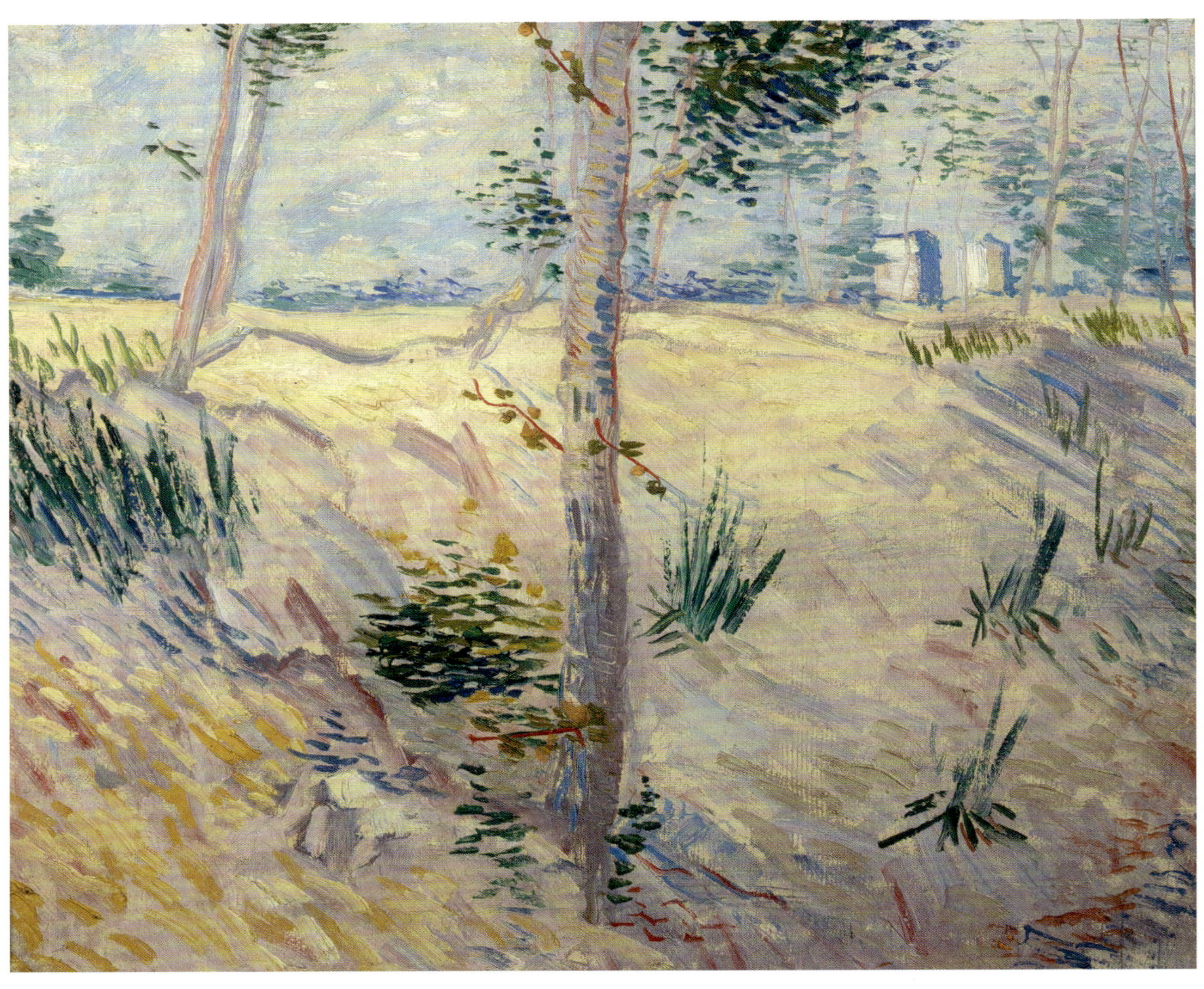

4 (cat.) Vincent van Gogh
Bank with Trees, 1887
Oil on canvas, 37×45.5 cm
P. & N. de Boer Foundation, Amsterdam

published *Théorie scientifique des couleurs* (1881), the French translation of his *Modern Chromatics* from two years earlier. It articulates how color was perceived through the experience of vision, an "optical mixture" of color. Rather than blending pigments on a painter's palette, Rood's text prompted artists to place small dots of pure, complementary hues next to each other on the canvas, so that they would be merged by the viewer's eye. This theory built on Michel Eugène Chevreul's 1839 treatise *De la loi du contraste simultané des couleurs et ses applications*, which argued that the juxtaposition of complementary colors creates a vibrancy unrivaled by other color theories.

Grounded in these scientific models, Seurat's approach to color differentiated itself significantly from the subjective and fleeting "impressions" recorded by Claude Monet and Pierre-Auguste Renoir, a characteristic that appealed to other artists working in this area. Seurat's trials with color can be seen as early as 1883, when broken brushstrokes and intense color contrasts appear in his *croquetons* (small painted sketches) for *Bathers at Asnières* **(66)** and other studies **(5)**. Crucial to his pioneering of the Divisionist, and eventually Pointillist, techniques were these northwestern suburbs and the river Seine, which offered up myriad colors in its ever-changing surface. Although Seurat's early *croquetons* show the greatest color contrasts and most starkly fragmented brushstrokes along the riverbanks, paintings such as his *Seine at Courbevoie* **(69)** reveal the power of these pure, unblended colors laid down in dashes and dots not only to create astonishingly fresh colors but also to capture the water's surface as it responded to shifts in sunlight, wind, and other atmospheric effects. Yet what made these places more than just landscapes for Seurat and, later, Signac—the artist responsible for disseminating this "new art"—was the glorious light, surfaces, and colors they found in nature.

Ultimately, this exciting period at Asnières represented a passing moment in time: by 1891, Van Gogh, Seurat, Signac, Bernard, and Angrand had moved beyond this site and the experimental way of painting it inspired. Van Gogh and Seurat, perhaps the most innovative of the group, had both died by this time. Angrand abandoned painting and resigned himself to drawing in Conté crayon for approximately fifteen years. Bernard, who had rejected the manner of Seurat and Signac as early as 1887, started to look to older painters like Odilon Redon and Paul Cézanne, and focused his line of inquiry on the essentials of Symbolism. Signac continued to develop his personal form of Divisionism, albeit on the Mediterranean coast, far removed from the suburbs that inspired him in his youth. The moments of connection and technical experimentation between these divergent artistic personalities, although short-lived—as the essays and artworks in this compelling catalogue and exhibition demonstrate—led to innovation that would inspire generations of artists to come. ■

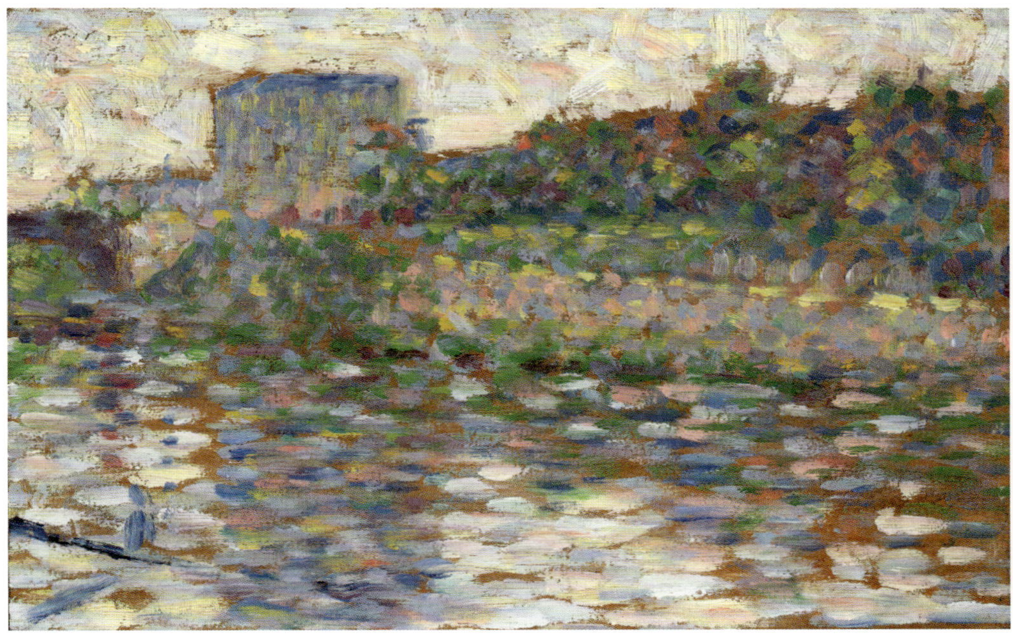

5 (cat.) Georges Seurat
The Seine at Courbevoie, 1883–84
Oil on panel, 15.5 × 24.5 cm
Van Gogh Museum, Amsterdam (purchased with support from the Vincent van Gogh Foundation and the Rembrandt Association, with the additional support from the Prins Bernhard Cultuurfonds)

“AGGRESSIVE, INDUSTRIAL, AND BOURGEOIS ALL AT THE SAME TIME”: THE CULTURAL LANDSCAPE OF ASNIÈRES IN THE 1880S

JACQUELYN N. COUTRÉ

Writing in 1856, on the cusp of major transformations to Paris and its surrounding areas, the anonymous writer B.-R. observed in his guidebook that the suburbs were sites of "astonishing contrasts." He noted that the lush green landscape is juxtaposed with patches of arid earth "bald like the head of an old man," and that "[factory] chimneys poking up like obelisks" loomed over the village streets, which were "covered with their black smoke." Factories, "establishments of a totally modern kind," also dotted the terrain. His description of these areas as "aggressive, industrial, and bourgeois all at the same time," a poignant evocation of these rapidly changing suburbs in the middle of the nineteenth century, captures their identity.[1] Though B.-R.'s highly visual commentary was published in the 1850s, his assessment rang true for the rest of the century.

The five artists at the heart of this exhibition—Vincent van Gogh, Georges Seurat, Paul Signac, Emile Bernard, and Charles Angrand—focused their intentions on these suburbs, specifically Asnières and its environs to the northwest of Paris. Familiarity with this area and its proximity to the capital, combined with tensions noted above within the landscape itself, must have drawn these painters to the region in the 1880s. Signac and Bernard had family ties to the locality: Signac's widowed mother lived in Asnières between late 1880 and 1889, and Bernard's parents had moved to the suburb in 1884 **(6)**. Van Gogh may have known of the area from his stay in Paris in 1875 as an employee of the art firm Goupil & Cie, which had a factory in Asnières **(7)**, though his brief painting campaign there in the spring of 1887 suggests that he considered it as an artistic destination only after he discovered the work of Signac, Seurat, and Angrand. Ease of access likely also encouraged the selection of this area: the distance of about three miles between Montmartre and Asnières was easily achieved on foot **(8)**, as Van Gogh **(9,10,11)**, Signac, and Angrand did, or by ferry for such destinations as the Ile de la Grande Jatte, as Seurat would do.[2]

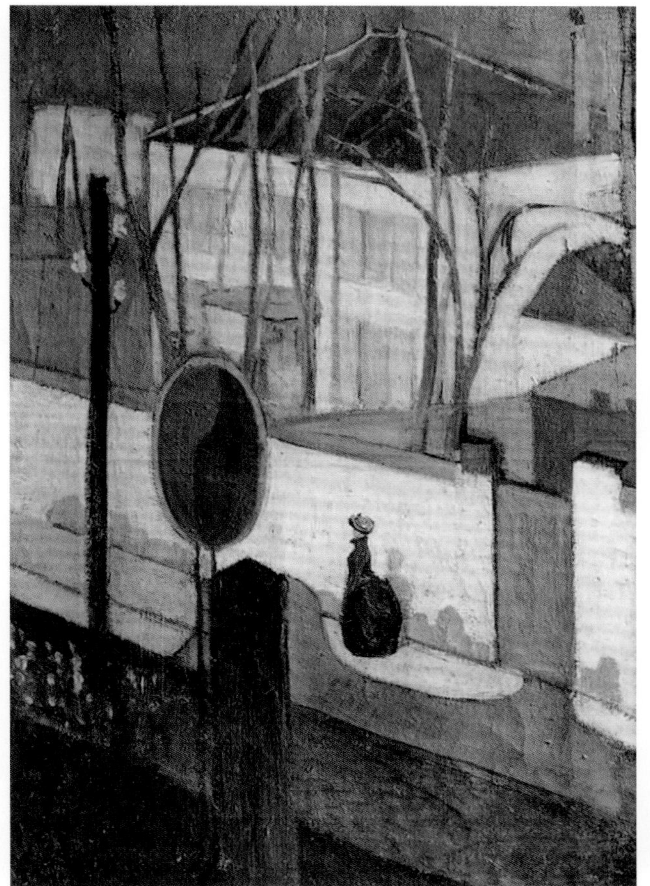

6 Emile Bernard
The House of Emile Bernard's Parents at Asnières, 1887
Oil on canvas, 53 × 37.5 cm
Location unknown

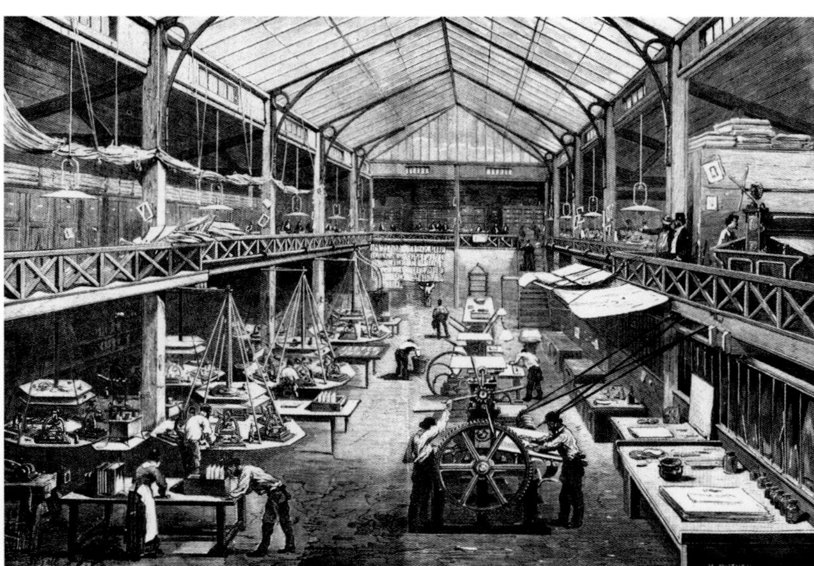

7 H. Dutheil
"Photographic Studios of Goupil & Cie in Asnières," 1873
Wood engraving, from *L'Illustration*, April 12, 1873
Musée Goupil, Bordeaux

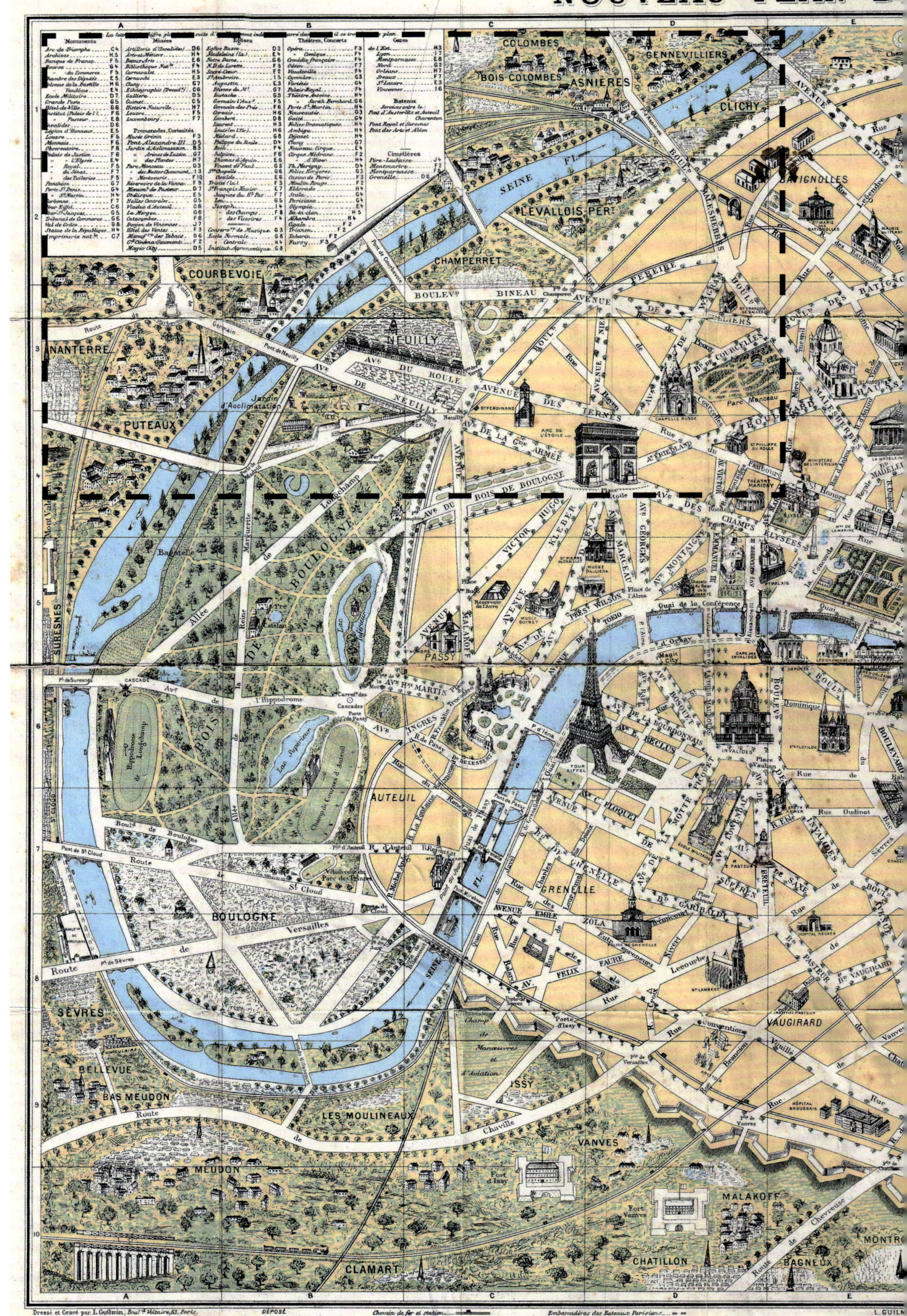

8 L. Guilmin
New Map of the Monuments of Paris, 1890

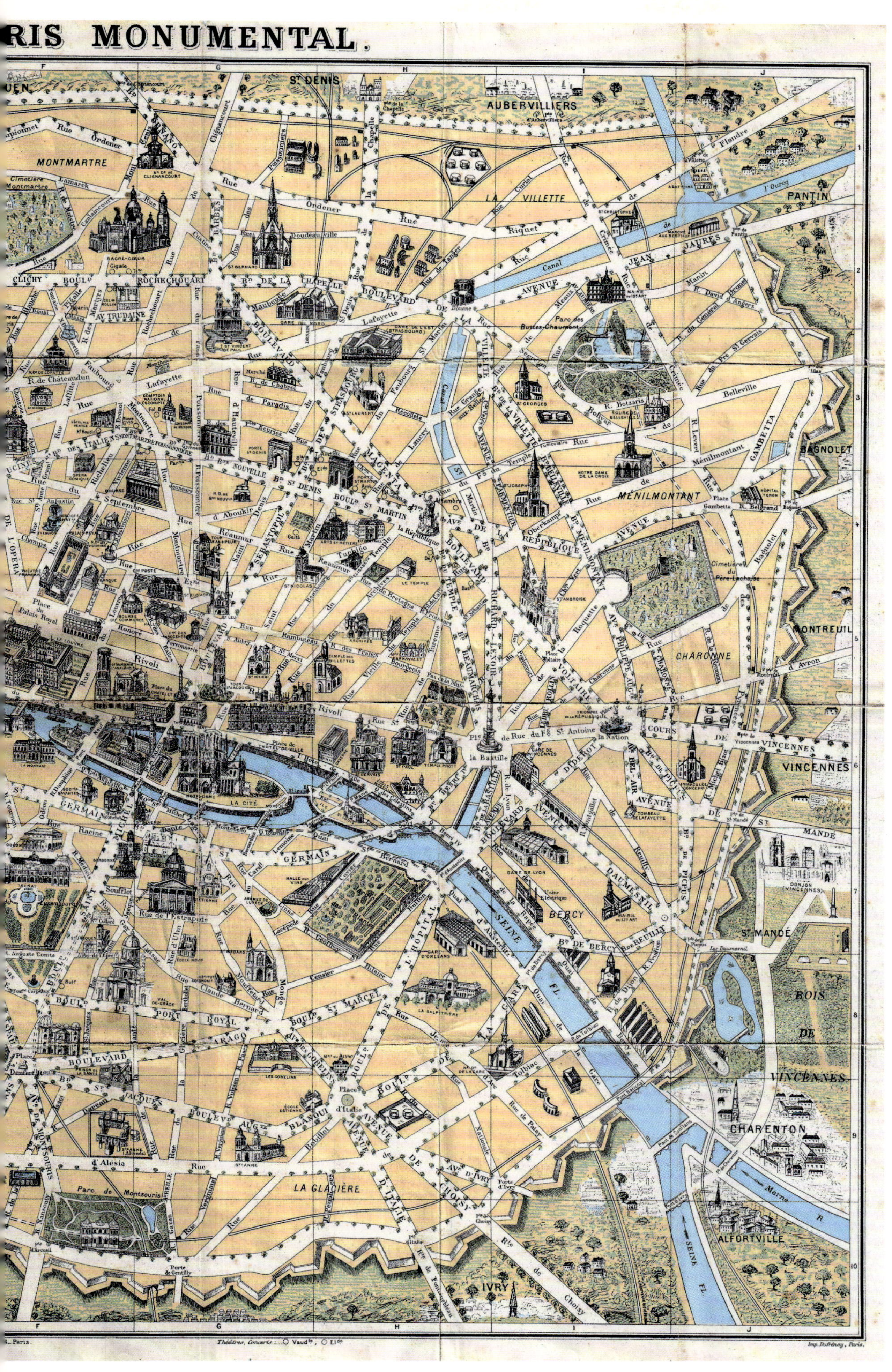
RIS MONUMENTAL.
ST DENIS
AUBERVILLIERS
MONTMARTRE
LA VILLETTE
PANTIN
Parc des Buttes-Chaumont
BAGNOLET
MÉNILMONTANT
Cimetière du Père-Lachaise
MONTREUIL
CHARONNE
la Bastille
la Nation
VINCENNES
LA CITÉ
SEINE FL.
BERCY
ST MANDÉ
BOIS DE VINCENNES
CHARENTON
ALFORTVILLE
IVRY
LA GLACIÈRE
Parc de Montsouris
Imp. Dufrénoy, Paris.

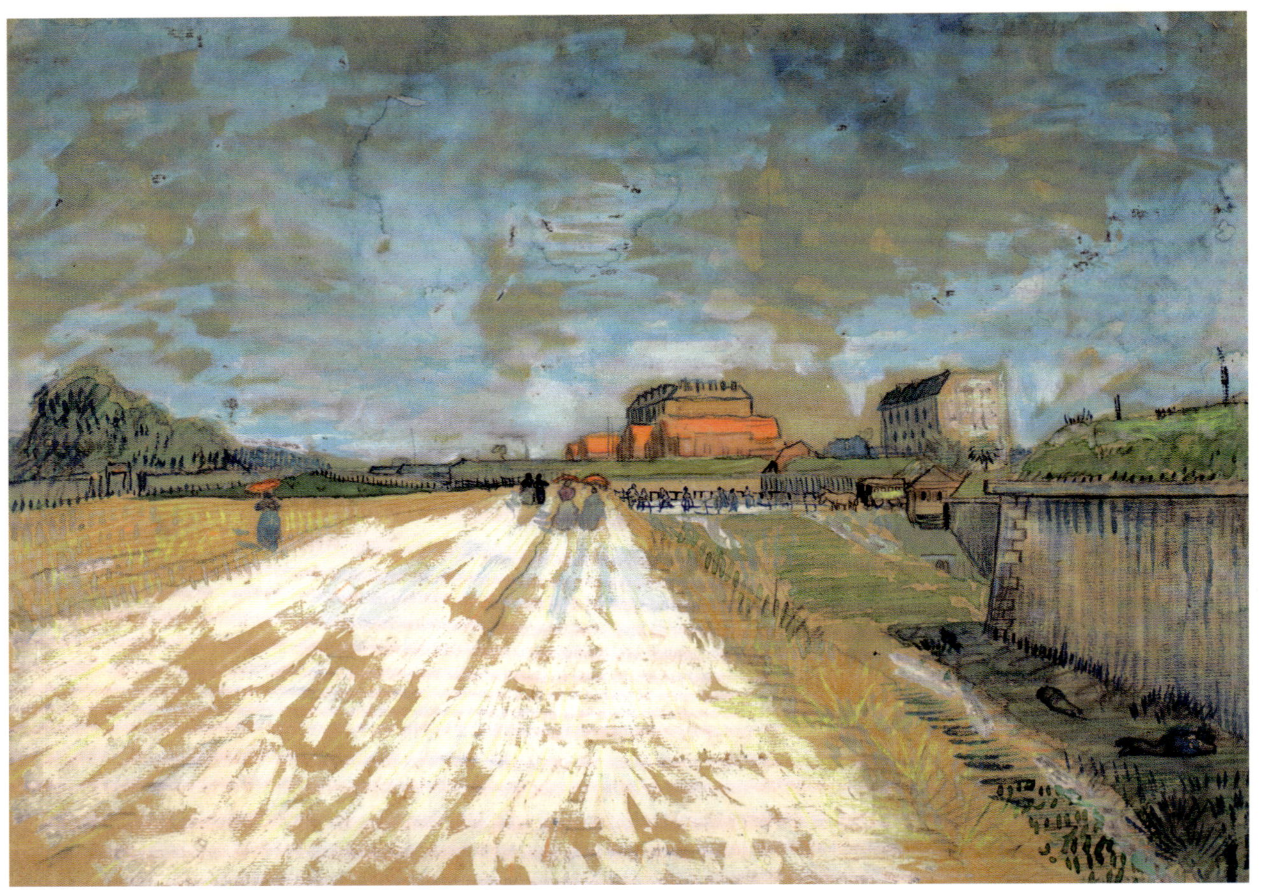

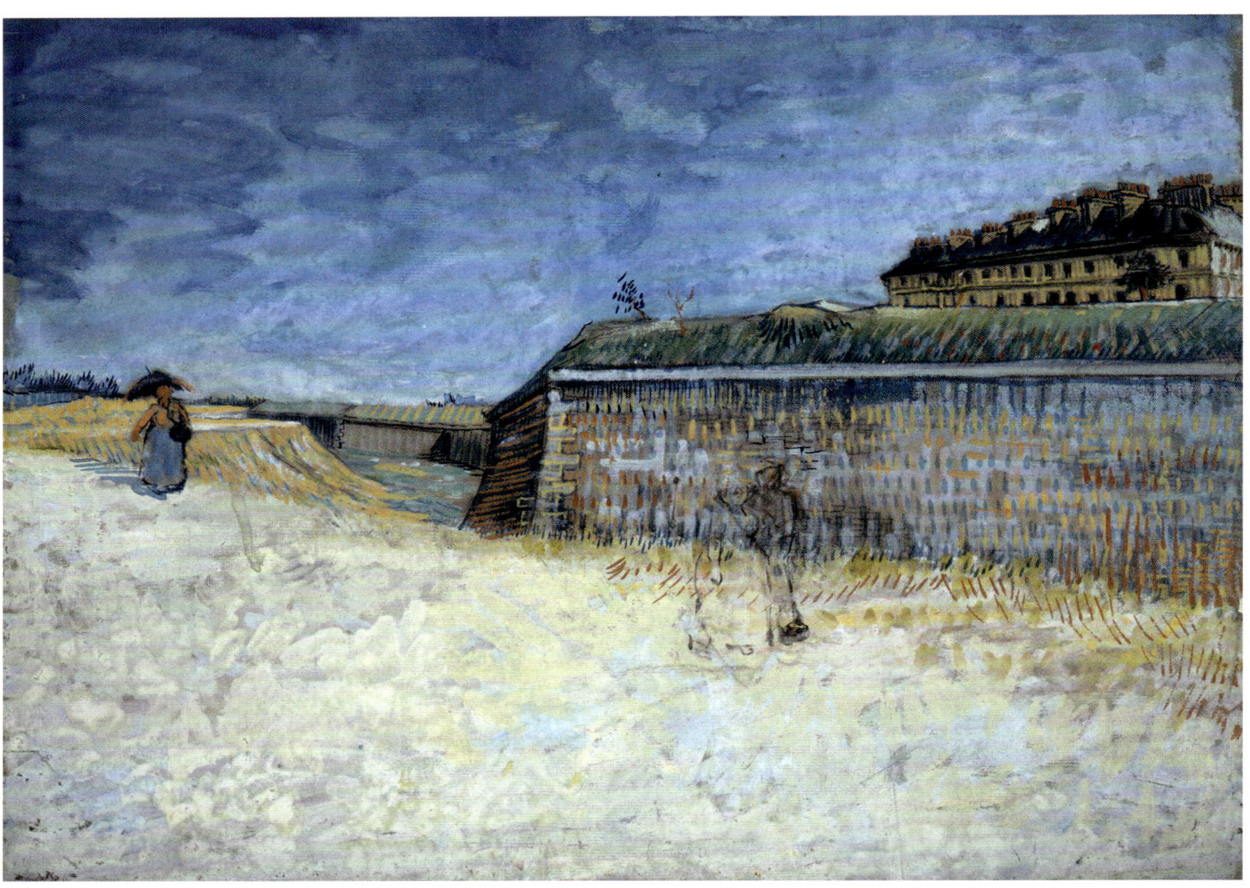

9 (cat.) Vincent van Gogh
Gate in the Paris Ramparts, 1887
Pencil, pen and ink, watercolor, on paper, 24.1 × 31.6 cm
Van Gogh Museum, Amsterdam (Vincent van Gogh Foundation)

10 (cat.) Vincent van Gogh
The Fortifications of Paris with Houses, 1887
Pencil, chalk, watercolor, and bodycolor on paper, 38.7 × 53.4 cm
The Whitworth Art Gallery, The University of Manchester

Ultimately, it must have been the striking contrasts of industry and nature, labor and leisure, as observed by B.-R., that lured these experimental artists to areas outside of the city. Such tensions fueled creativity, as Van Gogh wrote to his brother Theo from Antwerp shortly before moving to Paris: "How the bringing together of extremes gives me new ideas—extremes, the countryside as a whole and the bustle here [in the city]."[3]

In the decade that these five artists were taking the northwest suburbs as their subject, the outskirts of the city remained physically and psychologically distinct from Paris but ever in dialogue with it. This essay explores the cultural topography of these suburbs: how they distinguished themselves from each other and what the visiting Parisian would have recognized in each in the 1880s. It offers, in conjunction with "Postcards Along the Seine" by Teio Meedendorp (p. 50), some historical perspective on the choices that these artists made in terms of their subjects—whether they focused on signature sites or allowed their gaze to be more wide-ranging. In short, this essay argues that place was fundamental to these artists' development and their efforts to transcend the Impressionists, to achieve a more scientific, and thereby physically imitative, landscape.

Le Nouveau Paris: Boulevards, Railroads, and Sewers

Changes within Paris profoundly affected the character of the areas beyond the city limits in the nineteenth century. Starting with the country's shift from monarchy at the beginning of the century to republic by its end, the city's environment was ever-evolving in response to extreme political upheaval. At the heart of this change was the figure of Louis-Napoléon Bonaparte (r. 1848–52 as president), later Napoleon III (r. 1852–70 as emperor), a singularly powerful leader who imposed his vision for a modern city on its citizens.[4] Although his plans sought to elevate Paris to a level of sophistication and efficiency that was

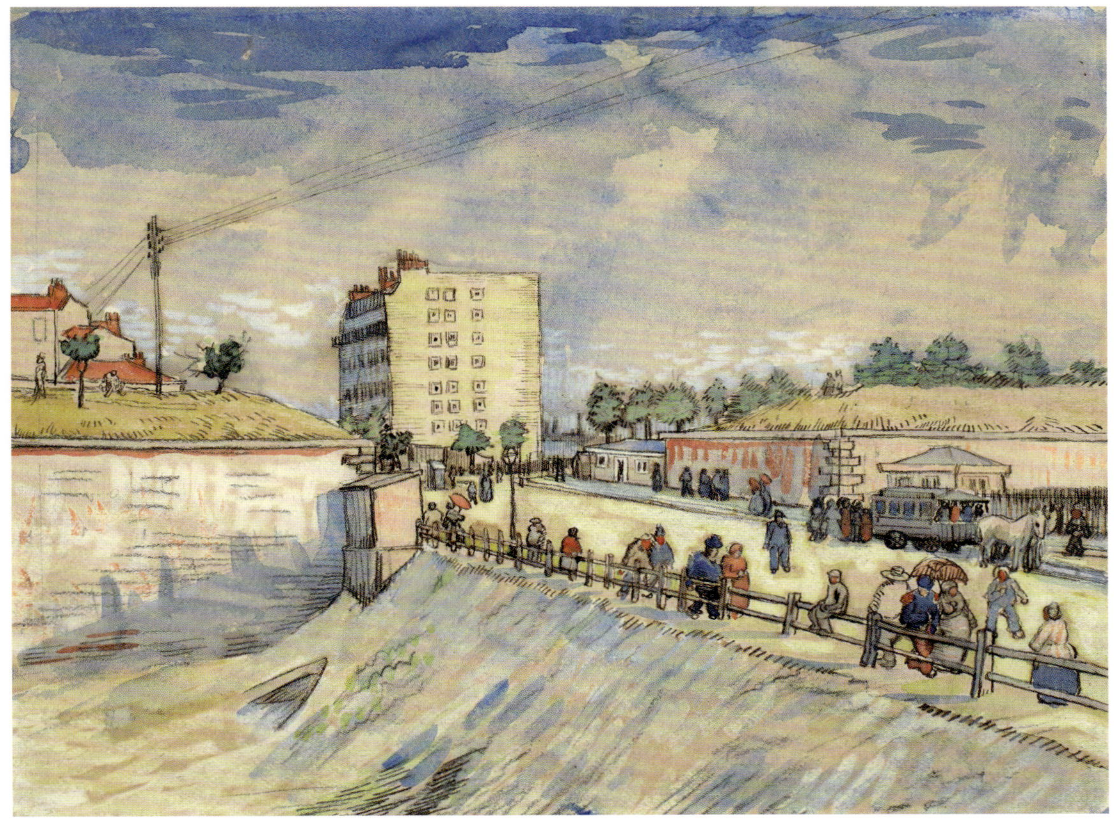

11 (cat.) Vincent van Gogh
Road Running Beside the Paris Ramparts, 1887
Pencil, black chalk, watercolor, brush and (oil) paint, pen and ink, on paper, 39.7×53.8 cm
Van Gogh Museum, Amsterdam (Vincent van Gogh Foundation)

unrivaled in Europe, the implementation of his ideas had enormous consequences for the northwestern suburbs in the third quarter of the century. The city's impact upon the suburbs in the 1880s was acute thanks to the boulevards, the railroads, and the sewers that ran beneath both.

In his desire to enhance the grandeur of the city, to turn it into a "city of marble" as Augustus did for Rome, Napoleon III launched a program of architectural and infrastructural modernization between 1853 and 1870, by which point more than 2.5 billion francs had been spent on the campaign. He selected Georges-Eugène Haussmann (1809–1891) as his prefect of the Seine to oversee "les grands travaux" (the great works), which aimed to improve traffic circulation in the increasingly crowded city, expand green spaces and sites of recreation, and augment the quality of life of its residents. The city's medieval neighborhoods, defined by their narrow and winding streets that were so easily blockaded during the revolutionary moments of the reign of Louis-Philippe (r. 1830–48), were decimated to make space for a more regular urban structure organized around large, radiating boulevards. More than three times the width of their predecessors, these boulevards were lined with more than 17,000 new gas streetlamps, 46,000 new trees, and thousands of new residences known as Haussmannian apartment buildings: seven-story blocks erected in a pale limestone with rectangular windows and prominent cornices and balconies **(12)**. As a result of Haussmann's renovation, more than 20 percent of the city's streets were rebuilt, but to affect such change, more than 27,000 buildings had to be razed, resulting in the

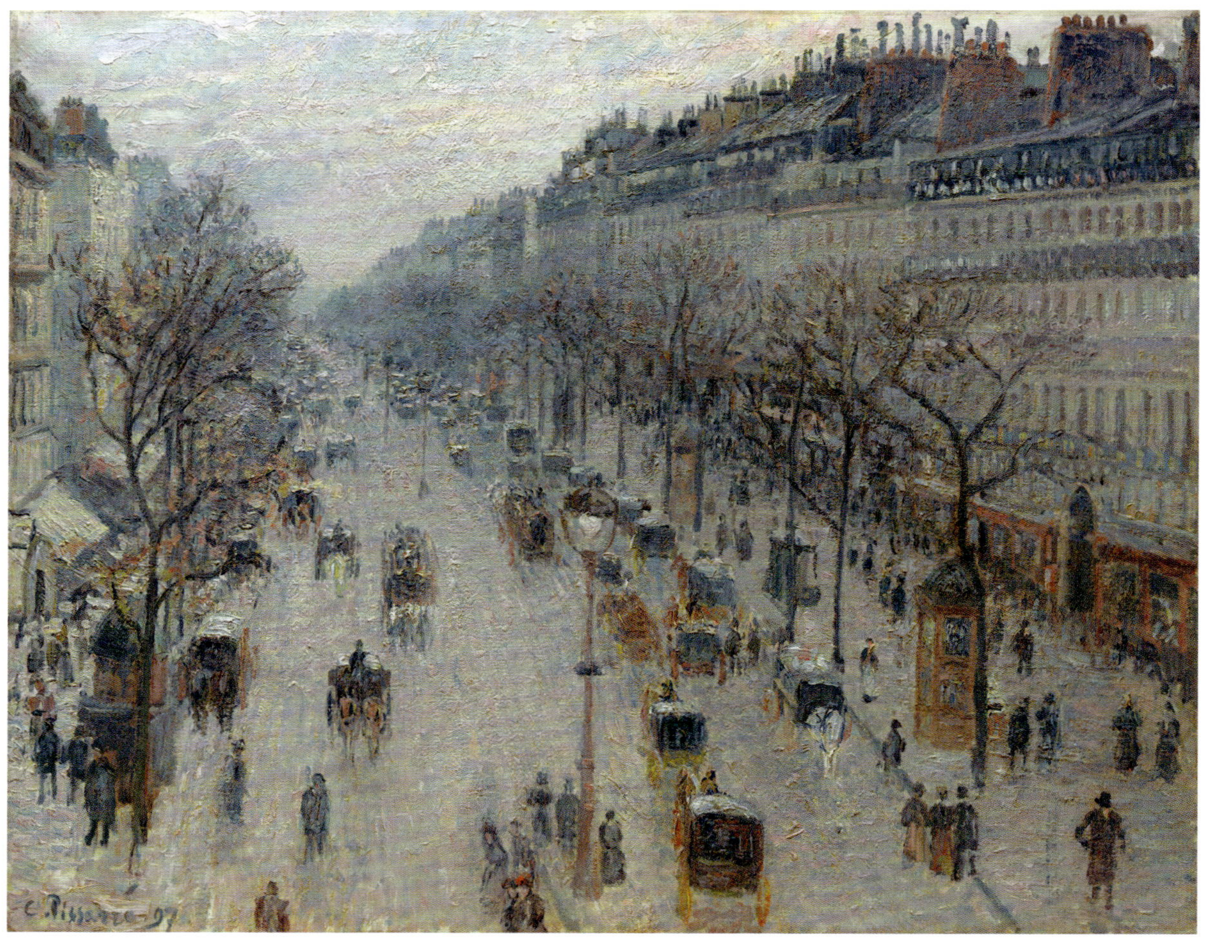

12 Camille Pissarro
The Boulevard Montmartre on a Winter Morning, 1897
Oil on canvas, 64.8 × 81.3 cm
The Metropolitan Museum of Art, New York
Gift of Katrin S. Vietor, in loving memory of Ernest G. Vietor, 1960

displacement of about 350,000 people to the suburbs.[5] This major relocation of the lower classes may have been an intentional side effect of these urban developments: it supported Haussmann's desire to concentrate both factories and their workers outside of the city.[6]

To facilitate the flow of peoples from city to suburb and back again, two large train stations, the Gare de Lyon and the Gare du Nord, were constructed in 1849 and 1866, respectively. The impact of the railroad, established in the late 1820s for commercial transport between Paris and the Upper Loire, was transformative in the Second Empire. What started with the construction of a modest 14 miles of railroad tracks by 1830 expanded exponentially to 14,664 miles of track by 1880.[7] The first passenger line in the country, connecting Paris to Saint-Germain-en-Laye, was inaugurated on August 21, 1837, with its first stop at Asnières.[8] By 1883, there were passenger railroad stations in Clichy, Asnières, Courbevoie, Colombes, and Bois-Colombes **(86)**, which also served the suburbs of Neuilly and Gennevilliers **(13,14)**.

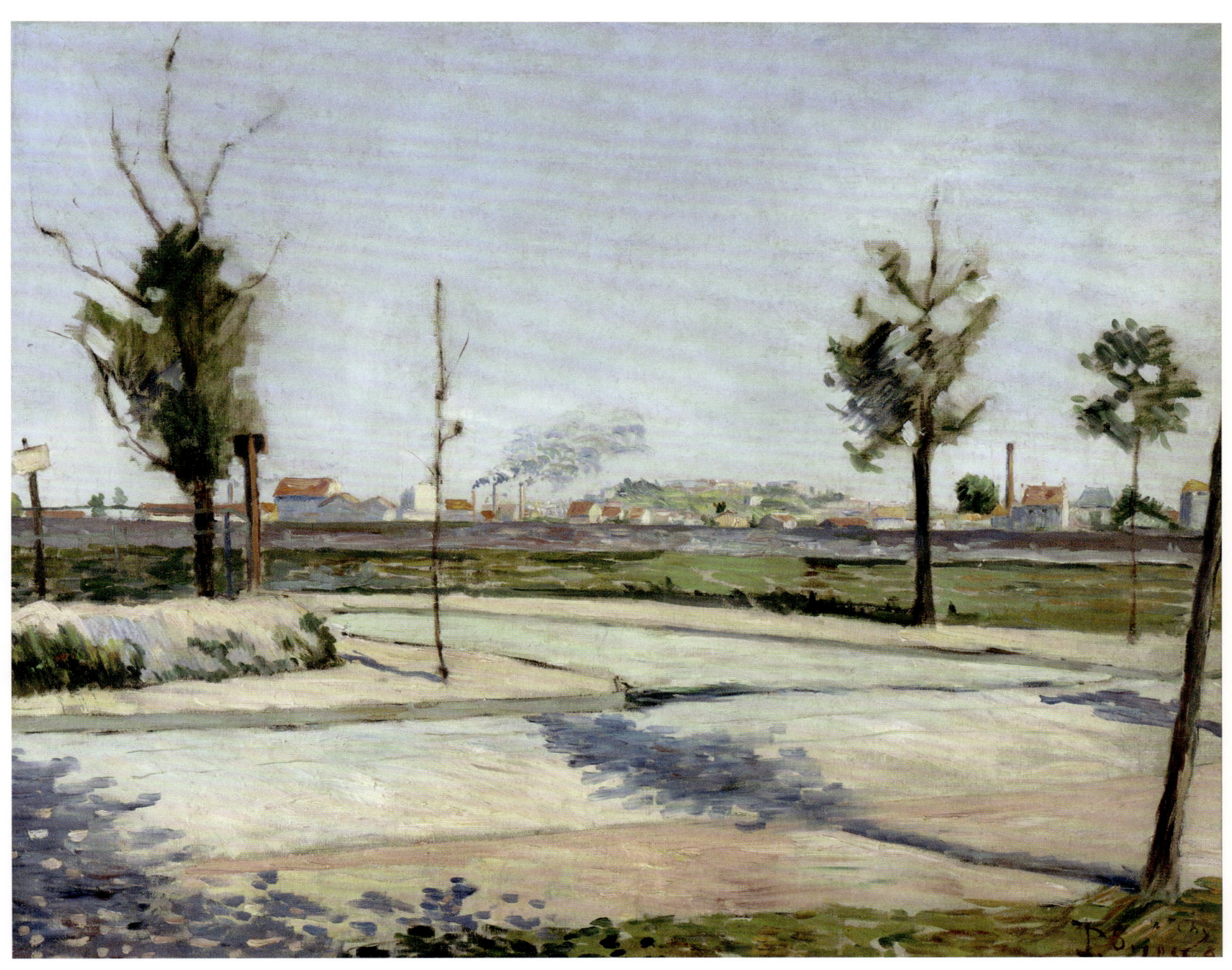

13 (cat.) Paul Signac
Road to Gennevilliers, 1883
Oil on canvas, 73.5×92 cm
Musée d'Orsay, Paris, acquired in 1968

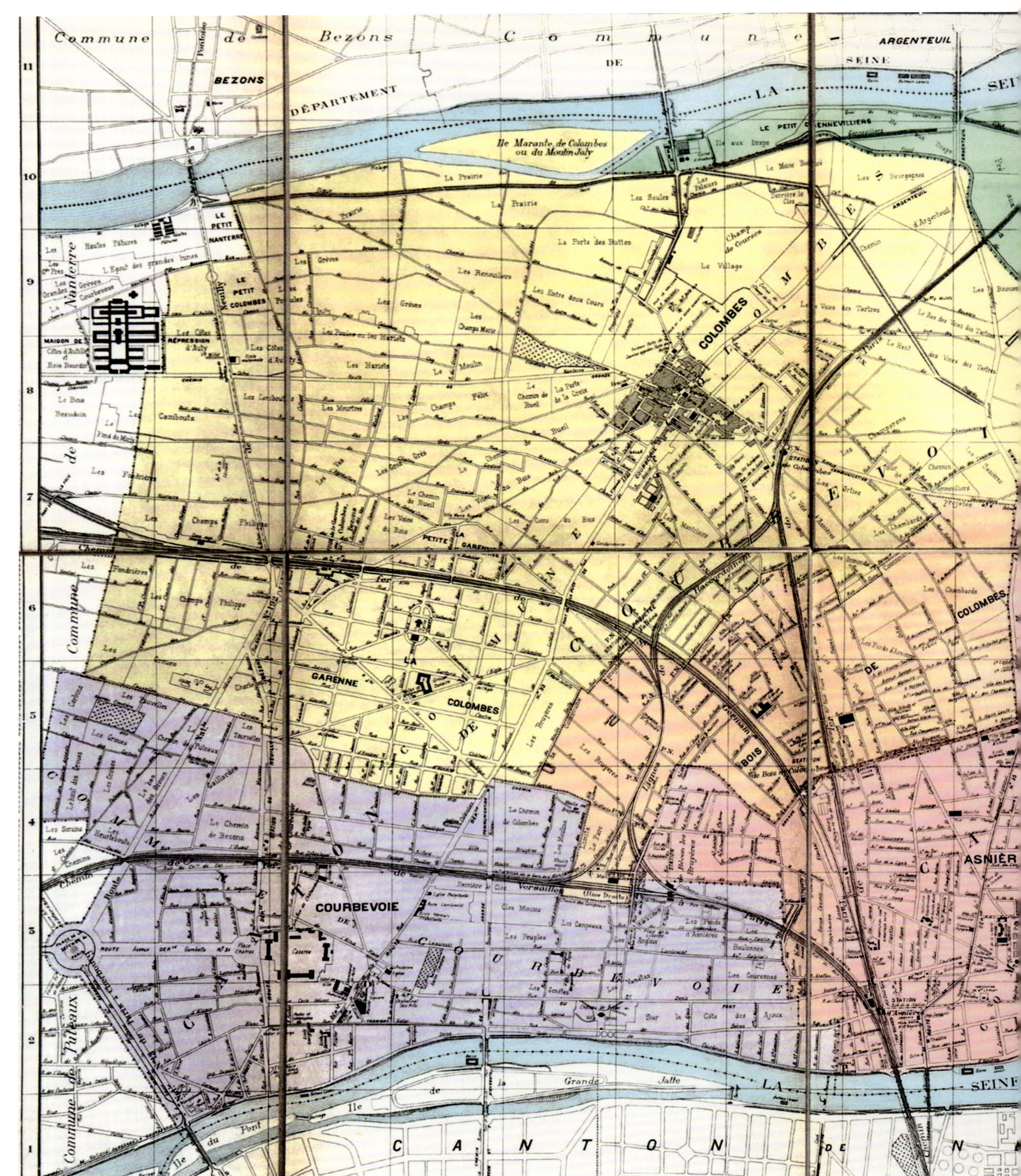

14 L. Balouzet
Map-Guide to the Municipalities of Asnières, Gennevilliers, Colombes, and Courbevoie, 1896
Archives Municipales, Asnières-sur-Seine

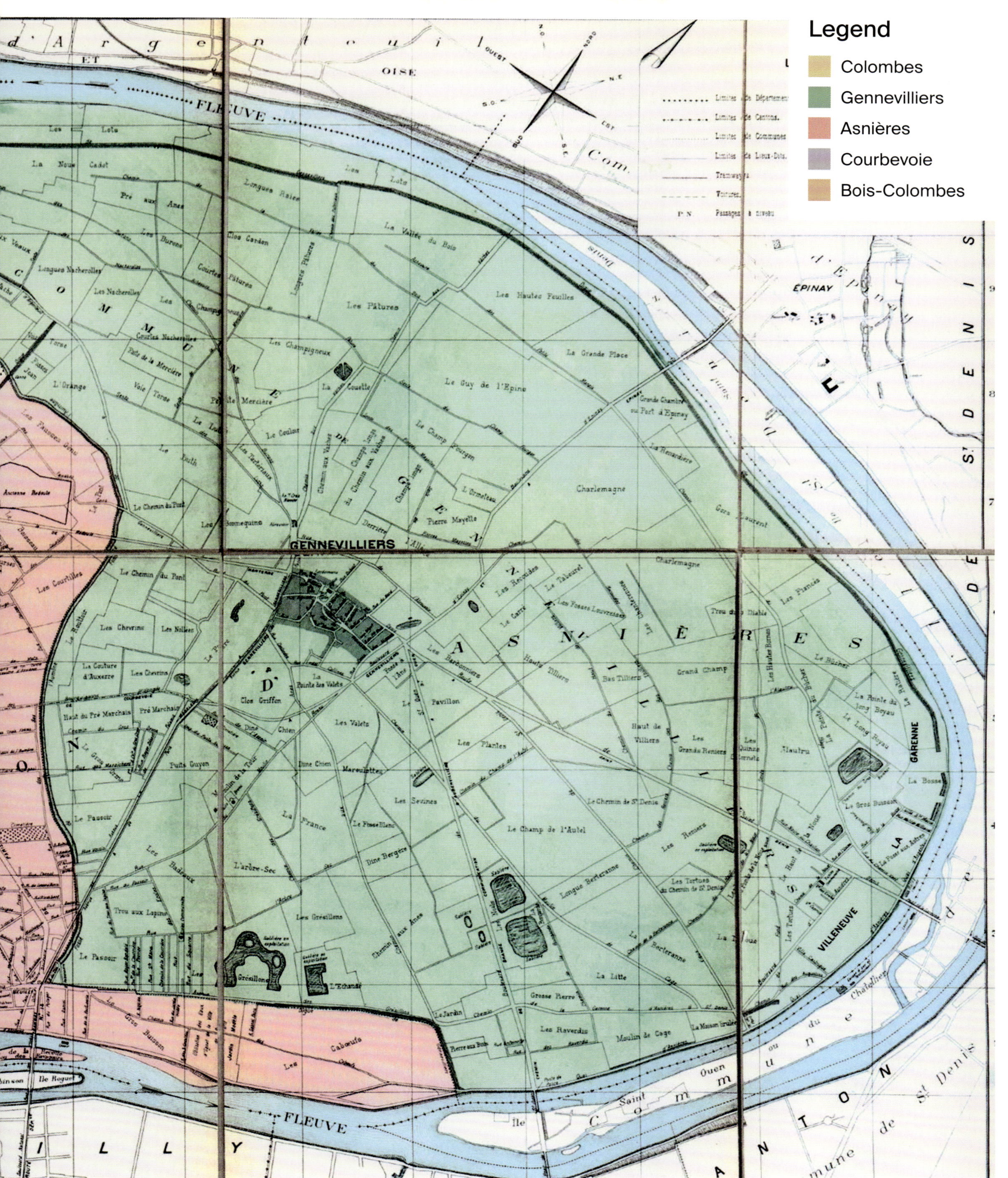
Legend
Colombes
Gennevilliers
Asnières
Courbevoie
Bois-Colombes
FLEUVE
GENNEVILLIERS
EPINAY
VILLENEUVE
GARENNE
Les Lots
La Vallée du Bois
Les Hautes Feuilles
Les Pâtures
La Grande Place
Le Guy de l'Epine
Charlemagne
Le Champ de l'Aulel
Les Grésillons
Cloe Griffon
L'arbre-Sec
La France
Les Valets
Pavillon
Grand Champ
La Litte
Grosse Pierre
Les Ravendis
Moulin de Cage
La Maison Brulée
Ile Roguet
FLEUVE
Saint Ouen

These passenger trains were affordable and efficient, thereby offering expanded possibilities for residents of the suburbs who sought work in the city, and encouraging Parisians to make day trips to the suburbs **(15,16)**. A second-class round-trip ticket from the Gare Saint-Lazare **(17)** to the station in Asnières in 1881 cost 70 centimes (cents) in second class—80 centimes on Sundays and holidays—while a first-class ticket was only 40 centimes more during the week.[9] Equally appealing was the speed at which the steam-powered train could travel: it could make the 12-mile journey from Paris to Le Pecq, near Saint-Germain-en-Laye, in 30 minutes, whereas an omnibus could take five times as long.[10] Some contemporary guidebooks, such as Adolphe Joanne's *Les Environs de Paris illustrés* of 1881, offered all necessary information regarding ticket prices and times of departure as a comprehensive guide to the suburban experience. The title selected for Emile de La Bédollière's 1861 "amusing and varied" guidebook, *Histoire des environs du nouveau Paris*, illustrated by Gustave Doré, indicates how much Paris had expanded because of the railroad: the city had truly become "a new Paris" through it, encompassing the surrounding areas as part of its larger identity.[11] The railroad bridge at Asnières **(121)**, for example, illustrates how powerfully the railroad "animated" and "mobilized" the landscape, as was observed as early as 1863,[12] but also how it created a vital and undeniable lifeline to the city itself, advancing the porosity between city and suburb.

While the author Emile Zola praised the winding Seine as "this soul of Paris" ("cette âme de Paris") for the life that it brought to the city,[13] the waterway had become a major part of the unified sewer system that Haussmann implemented. Prior to 1850, a patchwork of sewer pipes could be found in certain Parisian neighborhoods. Other districts relied solely on the nightly clearing of latrine reservoirs, which resulted in an inelegant and putrid caravan of carts hauling waste to a storage tank north of the city. Between 1833 and 1876, the total extent of sewer pipes increased from 9 to 480 miles.[14] But Haussmann envisioned a more sophisticated trajectory than a storage tank as a way station for the dumping of waste in a distant forest: he wanted the sewer system to dispose of the wastewater outside of the city, at a site with an appropriate incline so that it would remain above the flood stage. In 1861, the Collecteur générale d'Asnières, the location into which eleven smaller sewage collection points from across the city were channeled, was constructed at Clichy. Within four years of its creation, more than 100,000 cubic meters of wastewater (dirty street water, laundering waters, factory and public bathroom waters) passed through this channel.[15] While this was an amenable solution for Parisians, the residents of Clichy found themselves enduring the concentrated stench and visible contamination of the river that previously had been dispersed throughout the city. The municipality eventually requested that the city

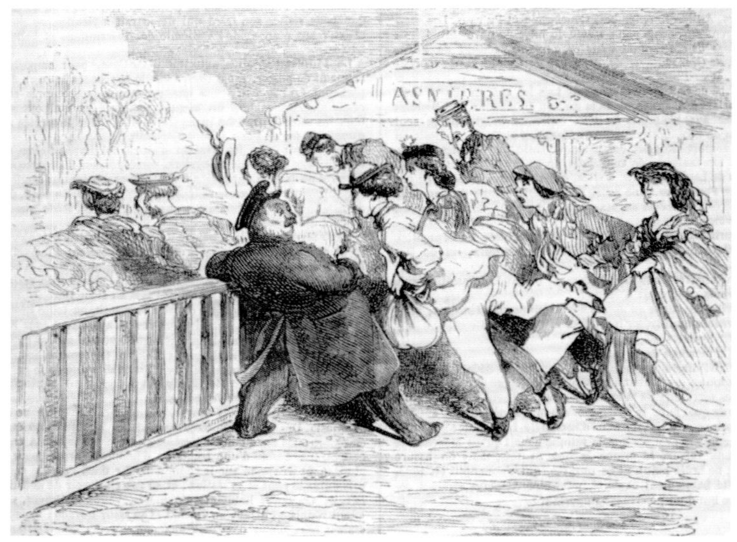

15 Gustave Doré
Arriving in Asnières, from Emile de La Bédollière, *Histoire des environs du nouveau Paris*, Paris 1861, p. 133

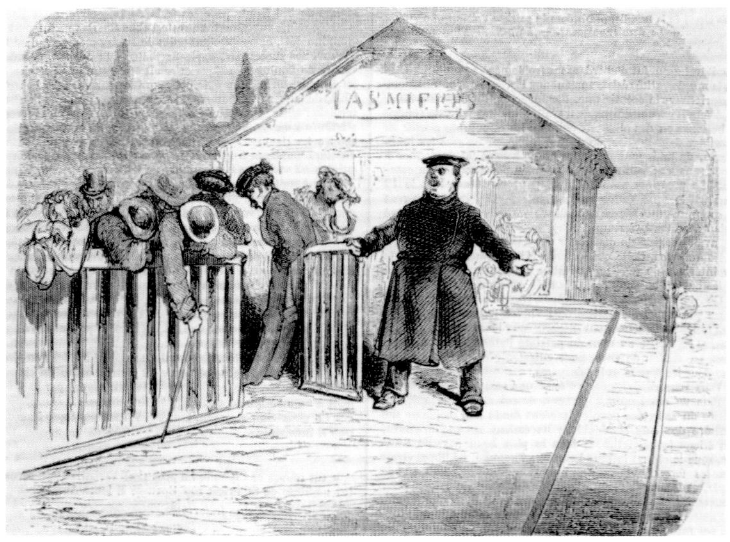

16 Gustave Doré
Returning to Paris, from Emile de La Bédollière, *Histoire des environs du nouveau Paris*, Paris 1861, p. 141

direct the waters from this diversion point to the growing fields of Gennevilliers. Between 1872 and the early 1910s, the wastewater of Paris fertilized a one-hectare "model garden" in this suburb as a pioneering study in the salubrious disposal of wastewater.[16] While Haussmann likened his sewer system to that of imperial Rome, which was described as "the most noteworthy achievement of all [in the city],"[17] the citizens of the suburbs struggled with the unglamorous consequences of Haussmann's innovations, including the pollution of the Seine.

At the same time that Haussmann's efforts sought to elevate Paris to new standards of modernity, they impacted the fringes of the city in powerful ways. Although the suburbs—facilitated by railroad access and a new sewer system that further intertwined its infrastructure with that of the city—grew more integrated into the urban fabric of the region, the renovation of Paris meant that the working classes were driven out, forcing many to take up residence in the suburbs and prompting an overall population shift. These developments helped to shape not only a new city but also a new set of suburbs, whose identities were inherently complex and contradictory, given that they arose not only from the priorities of nearby Paris but also from long-entrenched community cultures. The changes resulting from developments in Paris at mid-century brought more attention to these locations, with their personalities being profiled in numerous guidebooks, local newspapers, and histories of the city.

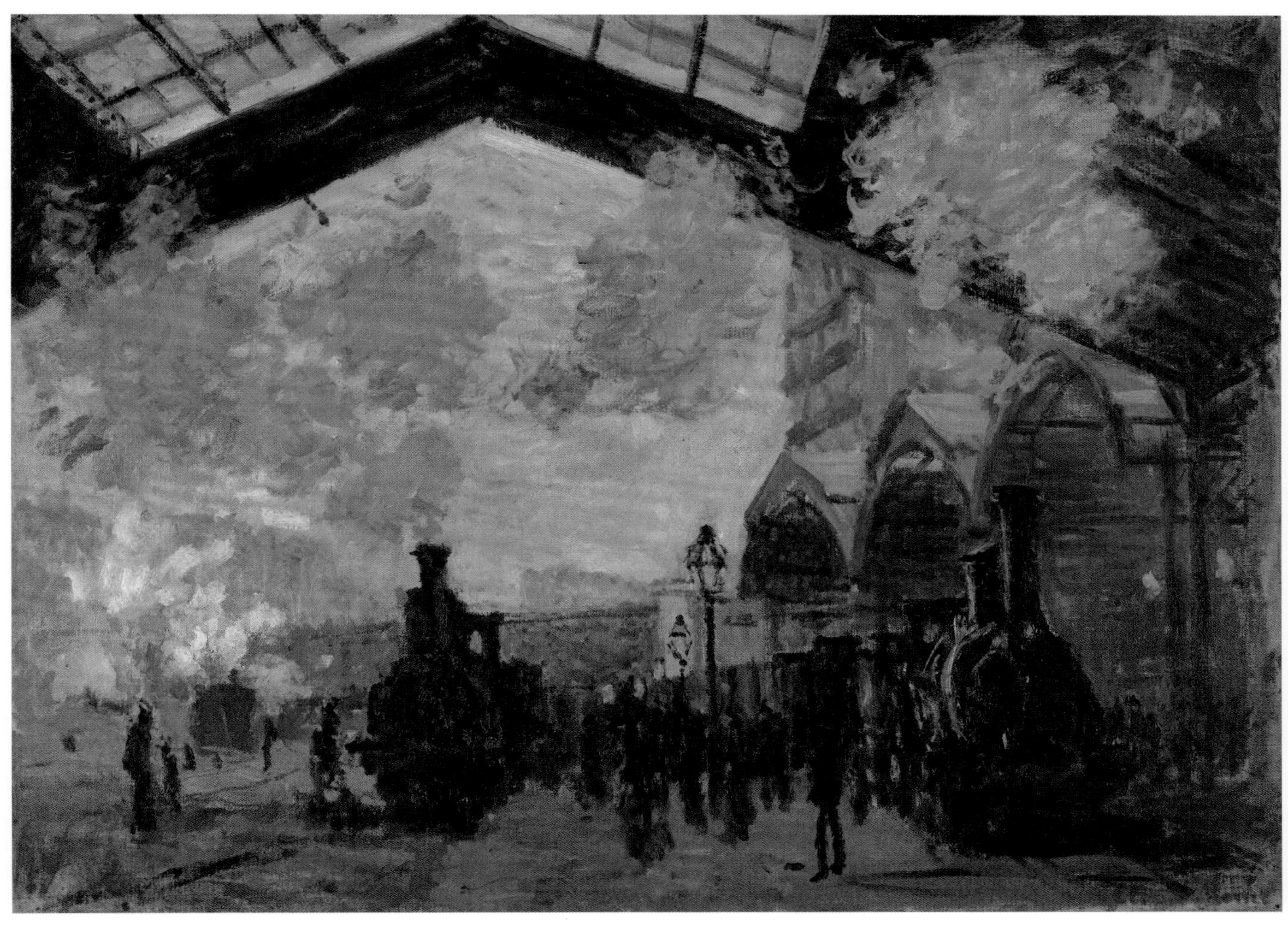

17 Claude Monet
The Gare Saint-Lazare, 1877
Oil on canvas, 54.3×73.6 cm
The National Gallery, London

Autour d'Asnières: The Terrain of a New Avant-Garde

Van Gogh, Seurat, Signac, Bernard, and Angrand were far from the first artists to find inspiration in the French countryside near Paris in the nineteenth century. Claude Monet, as well as Gustave Caillebotte, Pierre-Auguste Renoir, and other Impressionists, gave birth to modern landscape painting, marked by clear signs of contemporary life.[18] Monet's generation of painters located themselves further downstream than their successors: the villages of Argenteuil, Bougival, Vetheuil, and other locations offered idyllic, lush landscapes and numerous leisure activities like boating, fishing, and strolling, with minimal industrial intrusion. The images that they depicted, such as Monet's *Railroad Bridge at Argenteuil* **(18)**, reflects a harmonious vision of humankind integrated into its environment: a pair of dapper gentlemen gaze at two sailboats passing calmly through a forest of columns supporting a railroad bridge. Yet the iron bridge is transformed into a marble-like stylobate elevated above the water, while the train itself—hardly visible but for the tops of its brown cars—disappears into robust plumes of smoke that comingle with vigorous clouds. The train here becomes assimilated into the landscape through its form and coloring.

As suggested above, however, the suburbs that clung most immediately to the city's periphery presented heightened contradictions, which sparked the creativity of ambi-

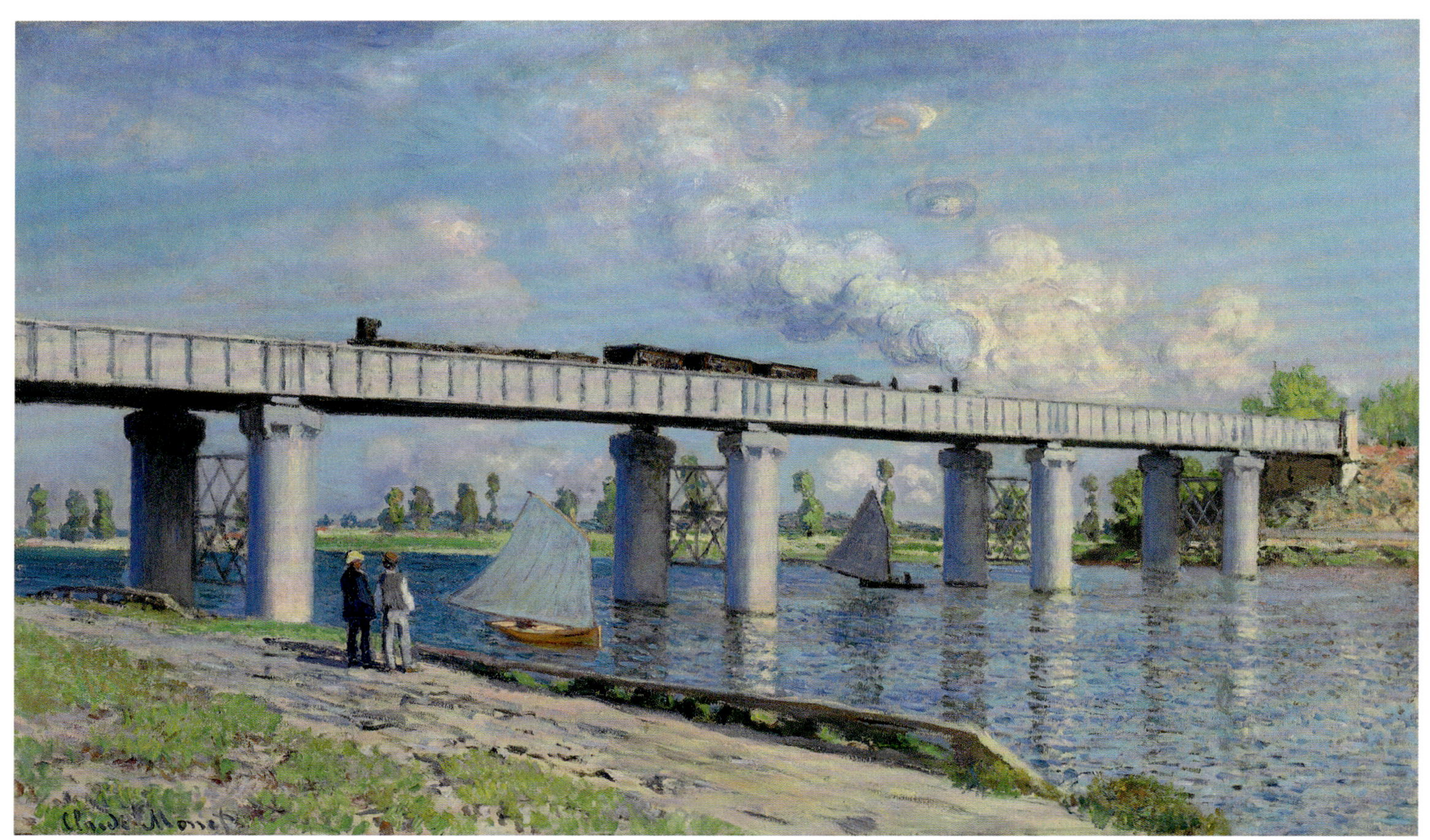

18 Claude Monet
The Railroad Bridge at Argenteuil, 1873
Oil on canvas, 58.2 × 97.2 cm
Private collection

tious painters searching to push the boundaries of painting. Among the desirable areas for them were Asnières and its surroundings: Clichy, Courbevoie, Levallois, and the islands of La Grande Jatte and Saint-Ouen **(19)**. Seurat was the first of the five to seek out these suburbs, taking day trips to La Grande Jatte in 1881. Signac and Bernard made their very first paintings in Asnières in 1882 and 1884, respectively. Signac later investigated the town of Bois-Colombes in 1885–86, while Angrand explored the Ile des Ravageurs for the first time in 1885, going as far as Saint-Ouen **(128)**, with its smokestack-laden skyline, by 1886. Van Gogh worked in the area of Asnières and Clichy during a three-month period in the spring of 1887. By 1888, most of these painters had ceased their activities in the area around Asnières, with the exception of Bernard **(124,125)**.

Asnières: Sunday Site of Leisure

Located across the Seine from Paris, Asnières attracted revelers and day-visitors because of its curated variety of leisure activities. The historian Louis Barron likened the picturesque character of the chestnut- and poplar-lined streets to "a distant province," speculating upon the reason that artists were attracted to it.[19] The area was known for its beautiful villas and country houses, owned by the likes of the Duchess of Brunswick and the marquise de Parabère.[20] The suburb had a substantial population of 15,200 in 1886,[21] a fact that was facilitated by its presence on the train line.[22] With Asnières as the second stop on the train from the Gare Saint-Lazare by the 1880s, it was a natural destination for those commuting into the city for work, as well as a popular destination for those living in the metropolis. As writer Alexis Martin warned in 1894, local residents hid themselves in their homes on Sundays, when the cafés and restaurants of the village were overtaken by Parisians.[23] The locale was recognizable for its double bridges over the Seine to Clichy: a pedestrian one comprising seven wooden arches flanked by two tollhouses,[24] and a railroad bridge

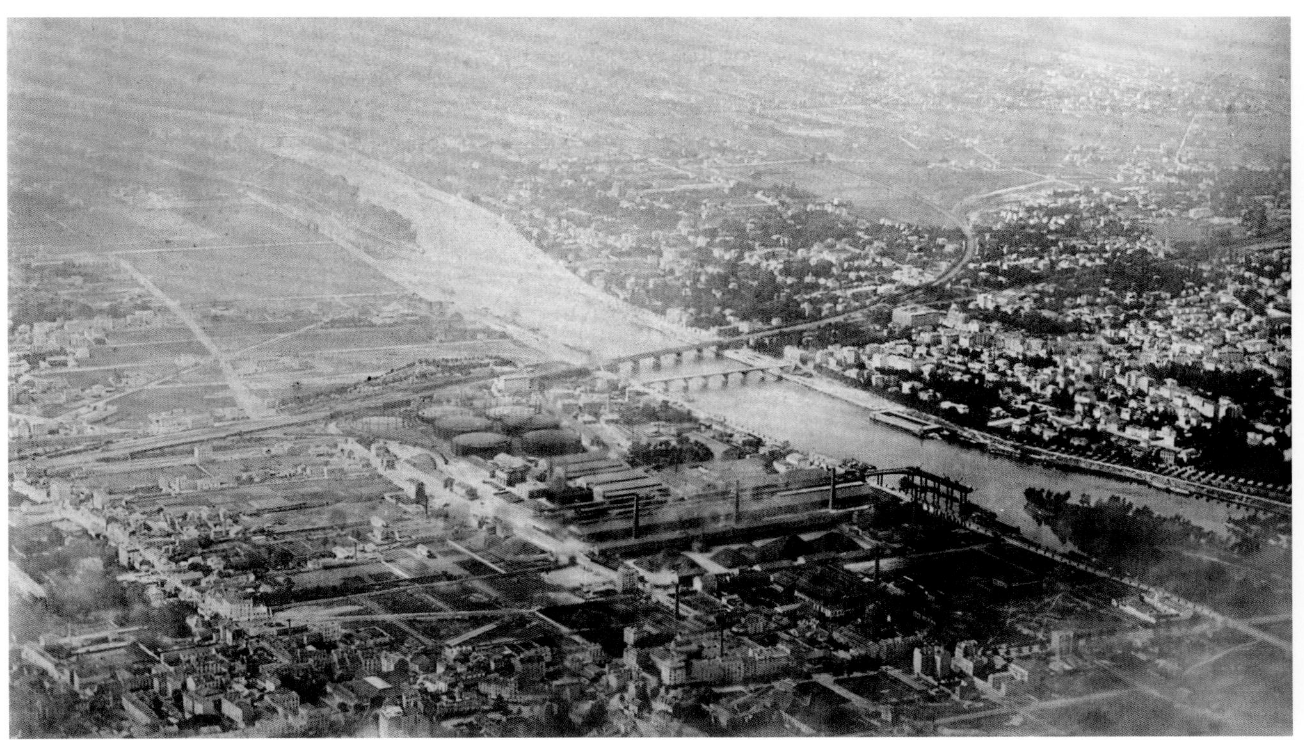

19 Aerial photograph of Asnières taken from a balloon by Commandant Fribourg, June 27, 1885
Archives Municipales, Asnières-sur-Seine

with five spans across stone piers, frequently seen in the background of paintings **(48)**.[25] This latter bridge, reconstructed in 1852 after a design by Ernest Goüin, was the first large sheet-metal bridge to be erected in France.[26] Guidebook author Adolphe Joanne even highlighted the viewing experience from the pedestrian bridge connecting Asnières to mainland Clichy, praising the views of Mont Valérien, the Bois de Boulogne, the Arc de Triomphe, and other areas of Paris.[27]

This "holy city of boating" was the site of the Cercle nautique, an exclusive club devoted to rowing based on the British model **(20)**.[28] Membership was typically restricted to middle-class men residing in the city, as significant monies were required for ownership of a vessel, the necessary clothing, and the membership and registration fees, the latter of which could cost as much as 100 francs per year.[29] The distinctive costume of white flannel pants, a white shirt, and a straw hat with blue border **(61)** was an essential component of this performance of leisure, one that the Englishman John Arthur sought to develop into a more elite activity for Parisians at Asnières.[30] As writer Emile de La Bédollière noted in 1861, "Asnières was made fashionable by Parisian boaters, but one could also say that Parisian boaters were made fashionable by Asnières."[31] This chicness was inherently connected to the rowing club, the likes of which brought young men and women to these suburbs to enjoy the outdoors, partake in good food, and engage in amorous flirtations,[32] as noted in a polka penned in 1886: "The nice women boaters / adore love and balls / They go to Asnières, / Suresnes, Bougival . . ."[33] Even those who did not sail would have come to promenade along the banks of the Seine and to watch the famed regattas **(114)**.

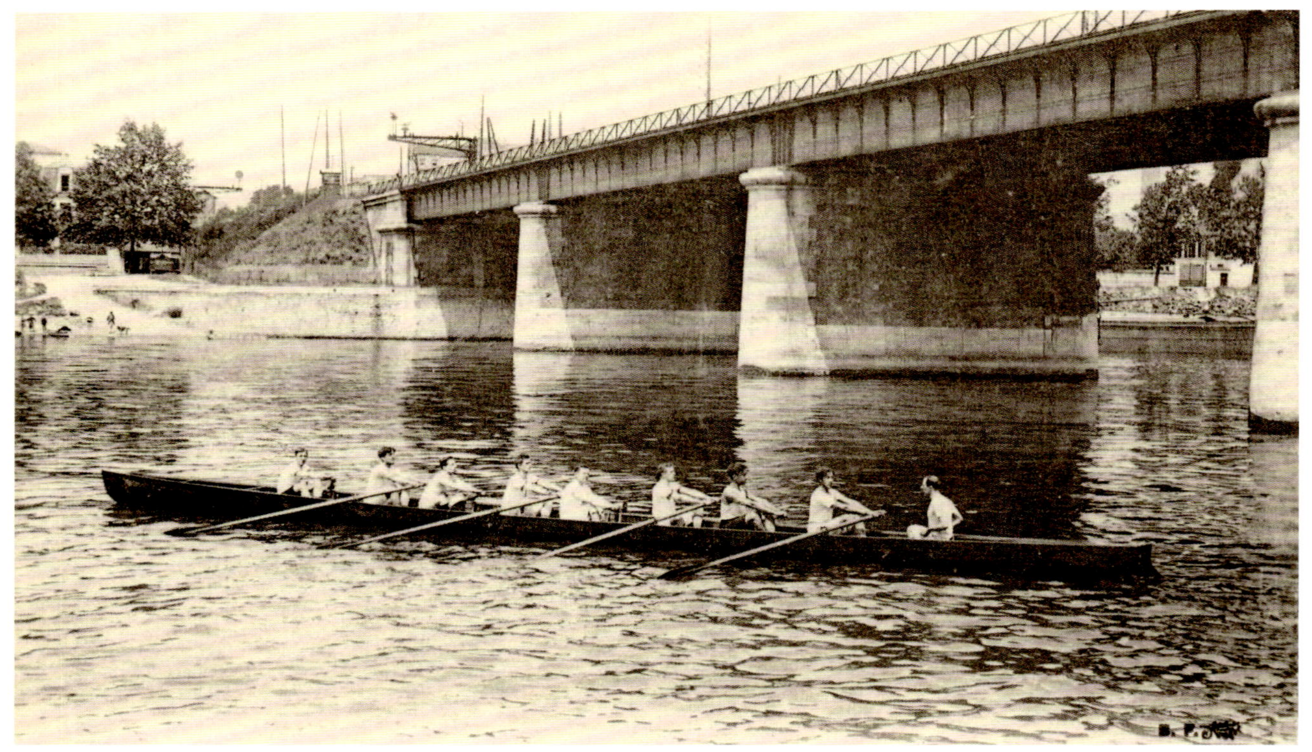

20 *A Team from the "Rowing-Club" at the Pont d'Asnières*, c. 1900
Archives Municipales, Asnières-sur-Seine

In addition to being a destination for avid boaters, Asnières boasted many sites of leisure and entertainment **(21)**. Numerous café-restaurants such as the Sirène, located along the quay, and the Rispal (close to the Pont de Clichy)—both painted by Van Gogh **(22,23,38)**—offered charming dining options for visitors to the suburb.[34] On a more sophisticated scale, the eighteenth-century Château Voyer d'Argenson (built for the minister of foreign affairs René-Louis de Voyer, marquis d'Argenson) was converted into a restaurant in the middle of the nineteenth century, and it was the site of weekly balls themed around such concepts as "fête Chinoise" or "fête des Roses." These soirées were elegant and festive affairs, with fireworks and modern gas lights illuminating the grounds in the nighttime hours.[35] The availability of outdoor space also made Asnières a destination for light sport, such as swimming, promenading, shooting, and horseback riding. Physical competitions, however, were especially common forms of exercise and community building. Several issues of *La Gazette de Neuilly et de Courbevoie* from the 1880s advertise day-long gymnastics competitions, with teams participating from Paris and the surrounding suburbs. Such contests sought to promote friendly competition while maintaining physical fitness in the wake of the Franco-Prussian War. Whether at restaurants or on the field, leisure and community defined Asnières.

According to Barron, Asnières's gaiety contrasted greatly with the mournful Clichy and Levallois,[36] but the

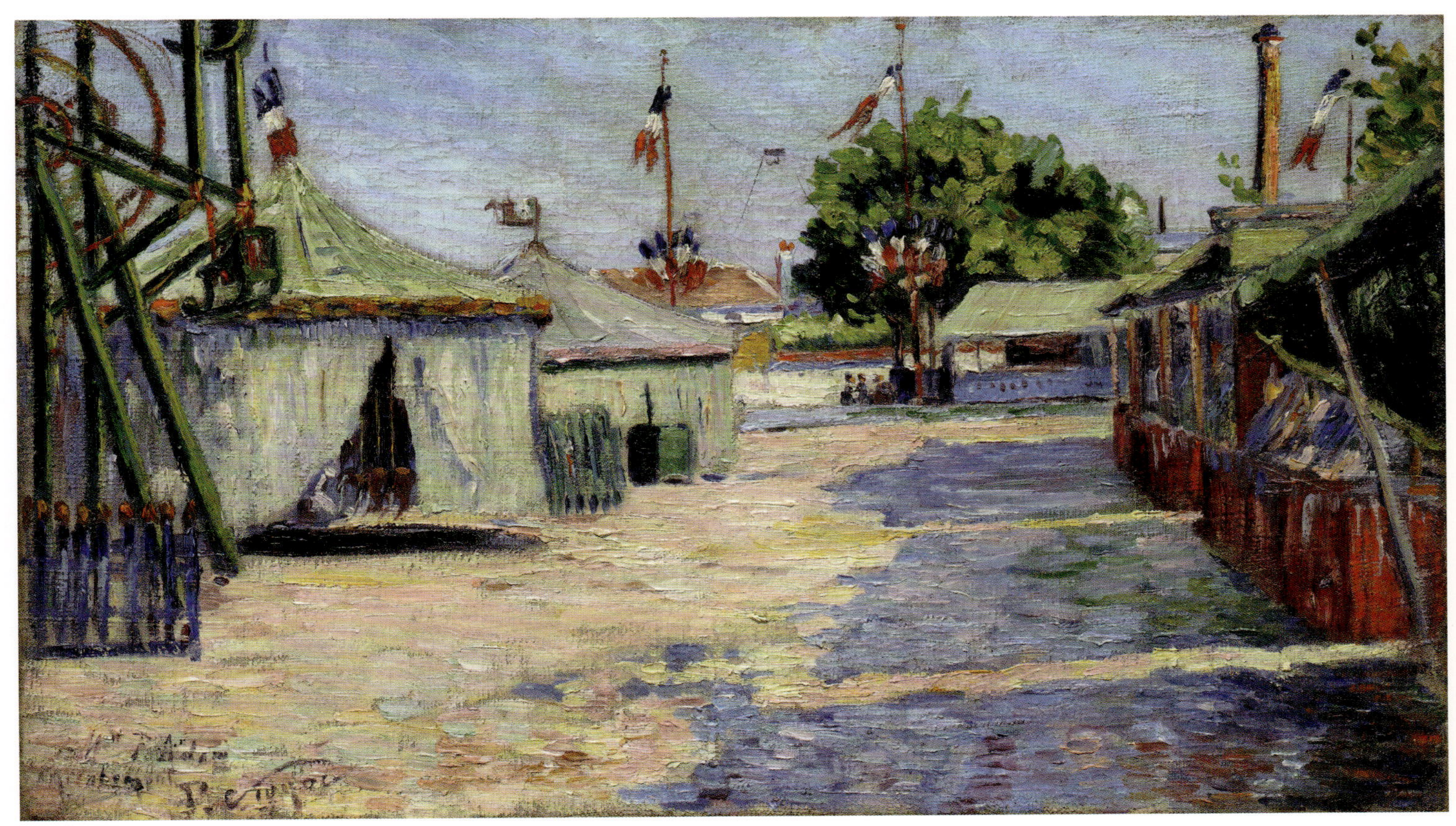

21 (cat.) Paul Signac
The Festival at Asnières, 1884
Oil on canvas, 26.7×45.5 cm
Private collection

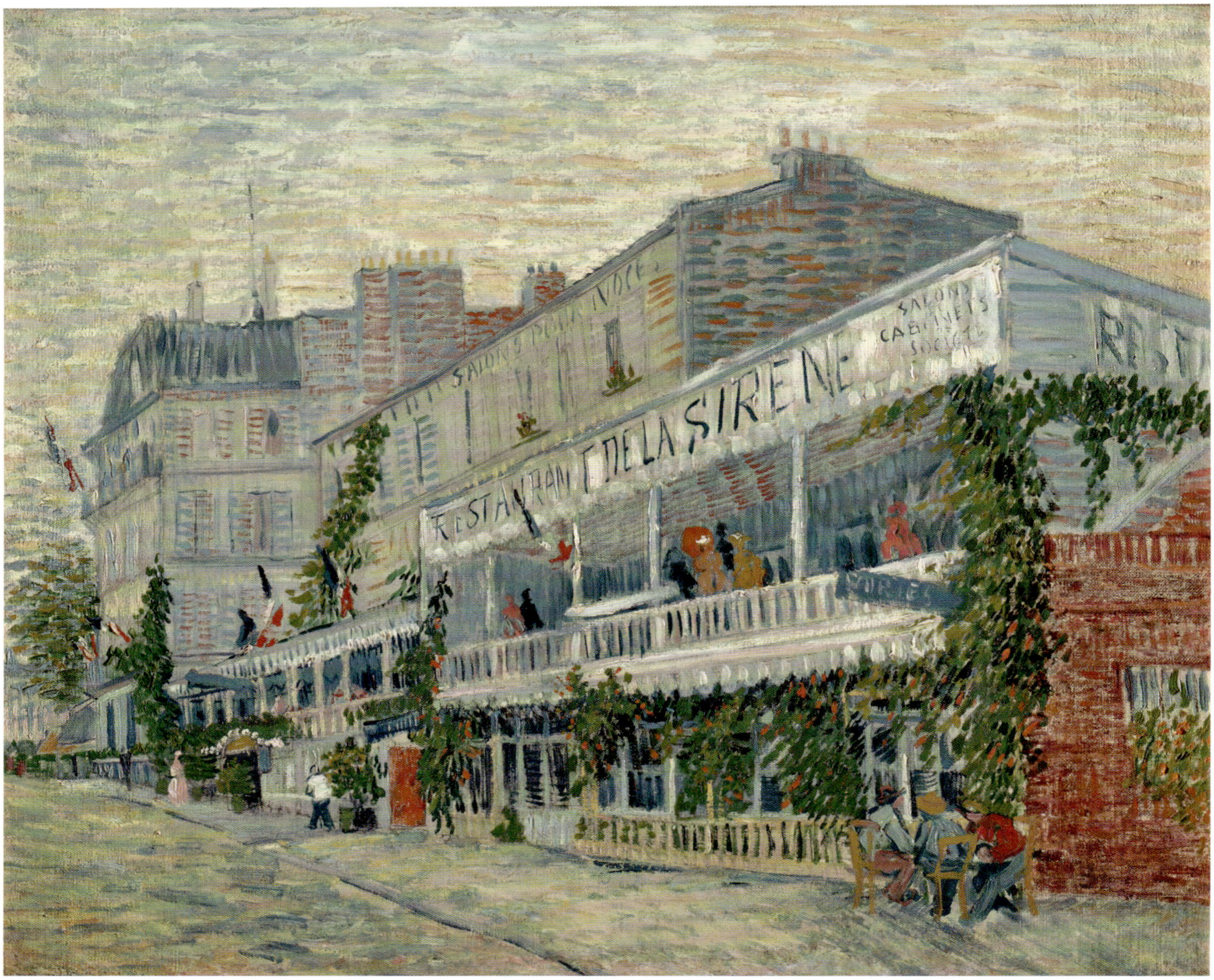

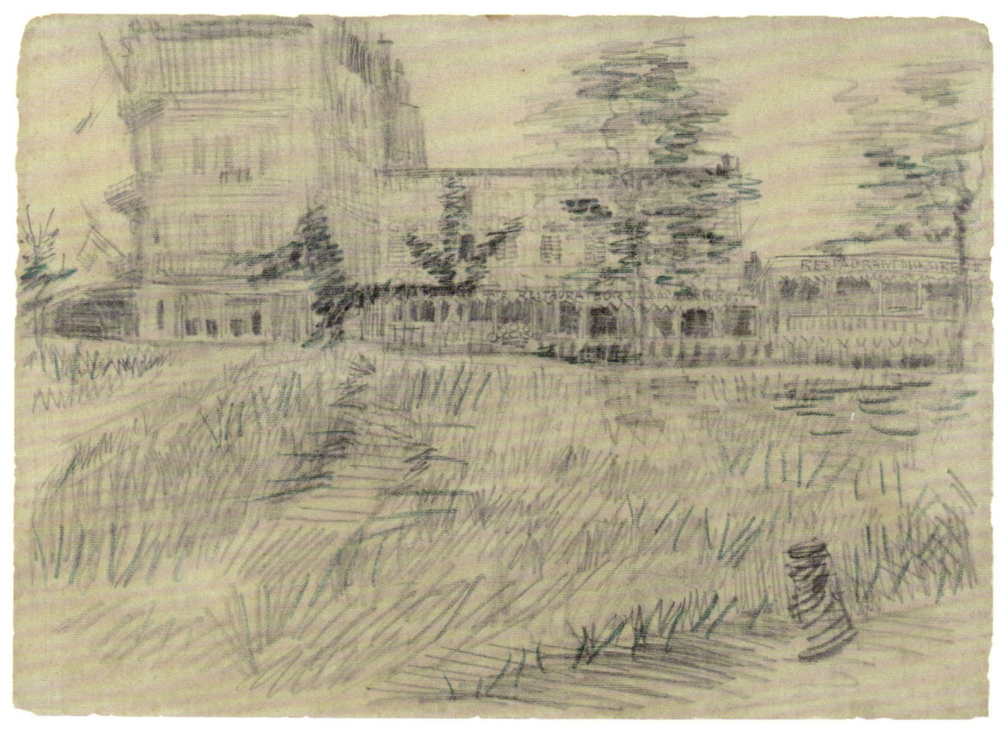

22 (cat.) Vincent van Gogh
The Restaurant de la Sirène at Asnières, 1887
Oil on canvas, 54.5 × 65.5 cm
Musée d'Orsay, Paris, bequest of Joseph Reinach, 1921

23 (cat.) Vincent van Gogh
Restaurant de la Sirène at Asnières, 1887
Pencil and chalk on paper, 39.8 × 53.8 cm
Van Gogh Museum, Amsterdam (Vincent van Gogh Foundation)

character of the suburb was more complex than this assessment acknowledges. Commercial industry operated in this area, including a small Louis Vuitton factory built in 1859 **(24)** and Goupil & Cie's factory for photographic reproductions erected in 1869 **(7)**. The suburb had at least one laundry boat **(35)**,[37] a floating washing facility that was typically located near a bridge or bank to facilitate client access. Such boats had arrived in these suburbs during the time of Louis XVI and were major polluters of the Seine because of the indigo blue and starch used for brightening textiles. In spite of these intrusions upon the recreational character of Asnières, the distilled character of the suburb in the 1880s remained that of the frivolity as described by Edmond and Jules de Goncourt in their novel *Manette Salomon* of 1867: "The summer arrived and Anatole switched from painting to leisure, the joys of the water, the Parisian passion for boating. . . . Enjoying the day, the fatigue, the intoxication, the free and vibrant open air, the glitter of the water, the sun beating down, the gleaming flame of everything that dazes and dazzles in these flowing promenades, the almost animal inebriation of life imparted by a great seething river, blinded by light and good weather."[38]

Clichy: Proletariat Paradise

Directly across the Seine from Asnières, that haven of leisure and frivolity, was the heavily industrialized Clichy. In his profile of the area, De La Bédollière did not mince his words: "It is a city of business rather than pleasure."[39] The land here was especially open and undeveloped, and it was closer to Paris than Asnières. Also, as in all the suburbs, rents were cheaper than in the city, and there were no taxes on materials to build factories and workshops. The population of Clichy increased significantly in the third quarter of the nineteenth century, reaching 24,230 inhabitants by 1881 as workers from Brittany and Auvergne arrived to work in its flourishing industries.[40] Like Asnières, Clichy was identified with its bridges: the three iron arches of the Pont de Clichy, which was inaugurated on November 20, 1869, and rebuilt in 1871 after the Prussian invasion, connected Clichy to the Ile Robinson, the Ile Robinson to the Ile des Ravageurs, and the Ile des Ravageurs to Asnières.[41]

The industrial character of Clichy had been developed as early as the eighteenth century, when numerous bleaching enterprises were established along the banks of the river.[42]

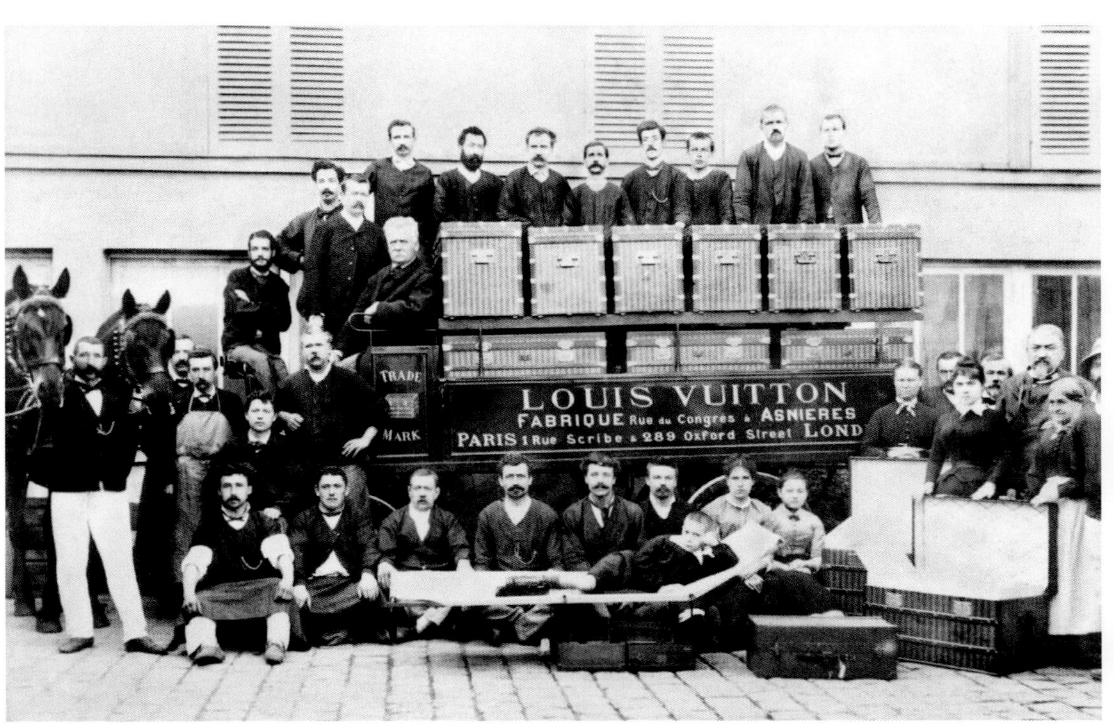

24 Louis, Georges, and Gaston-Louis Vuitton (lying down on a trunk-bed) pose with factory workers in front of a horse-drawn delivery van, Asnières, 1888
Photograph
Archives Louis Vuitton Malletier, Paris

In the nineteenth century, the area was home to a dozen factories that manufactured soap, chemicals, zinc white,[43] and starch, among other products. Most prominent among these was the country's largest facility for the production of stearic candles, the Stéarinerie et Savonnerie de Clichy, founded by Jean Cusinberche and relocated to Clichy by his son in 1850.[44] Not only could the plant produce 40,000 candles a day,[45] but it also possessed a connection to the art world: the famous chemist and color theorist Michel Eugène Chevreul, whose theories influenced Seurat and Signac in terms of developing a scientific approach to color, worked at this plant after discovering stearic acid, an additive that prevented candles from dripping, smoking, and releasing strong odors. The plant was so highly regarded that when the statesman Charles, duc de Morny, sought to host a reception for the emperor and his consort in 1862, he asked the company to produce candles with hand-painted portraits of Napoleon III and Empress Eugénie as gifts for the guests.[46] The factory of the Imprimerie Paul Dupont was also a prominent site on the bank of the Seine as of 1861. Occupying two hectares of land, it was here that the company developed its famed ability to print in color, which, by 1880, was a spectrum of fifteen to twenty different hues.[47]

Equally famous was the prominent gas facility, la Société de Gaz de Paris, located on 19 hectares of land along the banks of the Seine. Recognizable from a distance for its seven signature steel structures designed by Gustave Eiffel's studio in the mid-1870s **(25)**, this enormous and highly visible facility produced gas in service of the citizens of the French capital, not the residents of Clichy. Each tank (or gasometer) had the capacity to store 30,000 cubic meters of natural gas, which was procured for municipal lighting and heating through the gasification of coal. Large cranes along the water served to transport containers of coal that had arrived via the Seine into the plant **(26)**.[48] By 1900, this site would be the most important of the nine gas factories surrounding Paris, creating 325 million cubic meters of gas per year.[49]

Other commercial industry could be found in Clichy at this time. Three glassworks had been established in the second half of the century; Louis-Joseph Maës moved his glassworks to Clichy from Boulogne in 1842. Maës's glass

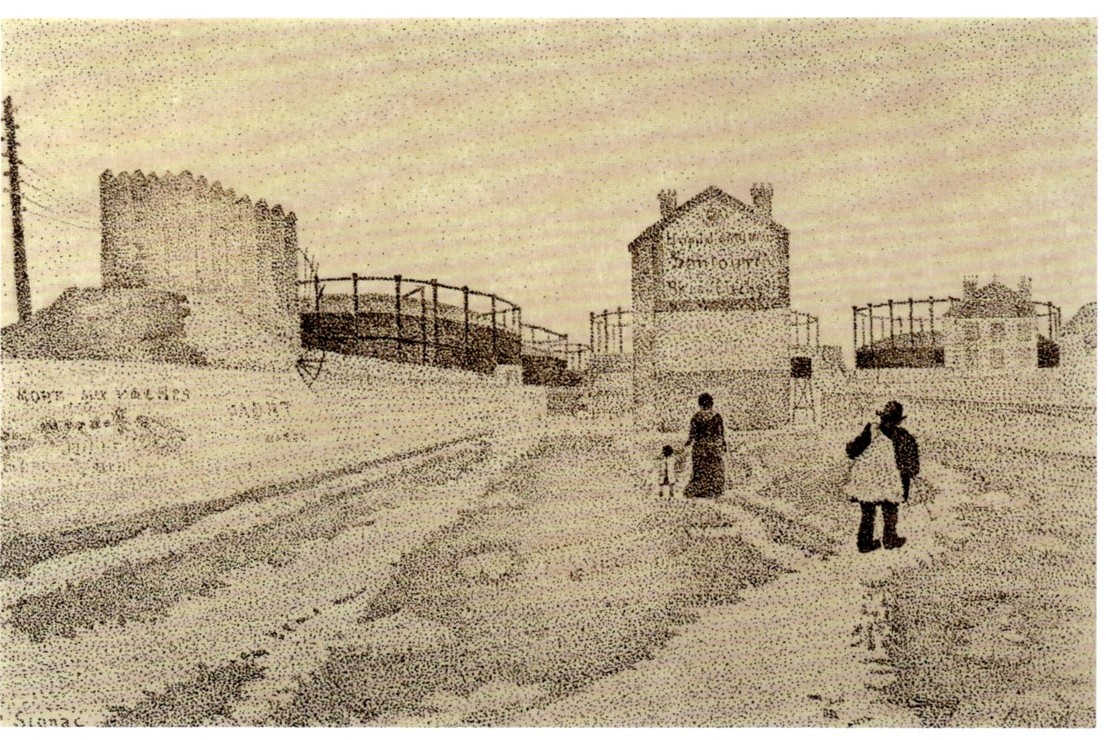

25 (cat.) Paul Signac
The Gas Tanks at Clichy, 1886
Pen and iron gall ink over graphite on Japan paper on cardboard, 24.5 × 36.6 cm
Lent by The Metropolitan Museum of Art, Harris Brisbane Dick Fund, 1948

was highly prized for its brilliant color and sophisticated design, earning it the grand prize at the 1850 Great Exhibition in London.[50] Maës also established a school for the training of glassblowers to ensure that the firm's innovative processes continued to contribute to the renown of Clichy, greater Paris, and France. Unable to continue the family business, his two sons rented the company warehouse to the Sèvres glassworks, creating the Cristalleries Sèvres et de Clichy réunies, which would later be destroyed by fire in 1895. The second glassworks, founded by Louis Appert in Paris in the 1830s, moved to Clichy in 1876 and remained there until 1936. Appert specialized in large-scale glass for windows and clocks, while also producing fine vases and pitchers with highly ornamental surfaces. The third, the Verrerie du Pont de Clichy **(27)**, was situated on 12,000 square meters of land near the bridge. Like the Appert glassworks, it followed a commercial direction, fabricating vessels and utensils for scientific laboratories, and reflectors for omnibuses and carriages, as well as bottles and siphons for carbonated water. The factory had 150 employees in 1866; it closed down in the early twentieth century.[51]

While the heavily industrialized character of Clichy may have dissuaded Parisian tourists from frequenting the area, some authors found beauty in its commercial production. In 1861, De La Bédollière celebrated the "majestic" presence of the candle factory extending along the Seine, with the "remarkable harmony" of its steam engines, through which a "perfectly regulated energy" was produced.[52] Such beauty in the efficiency of industry must have also appealed to the five artists considered here.

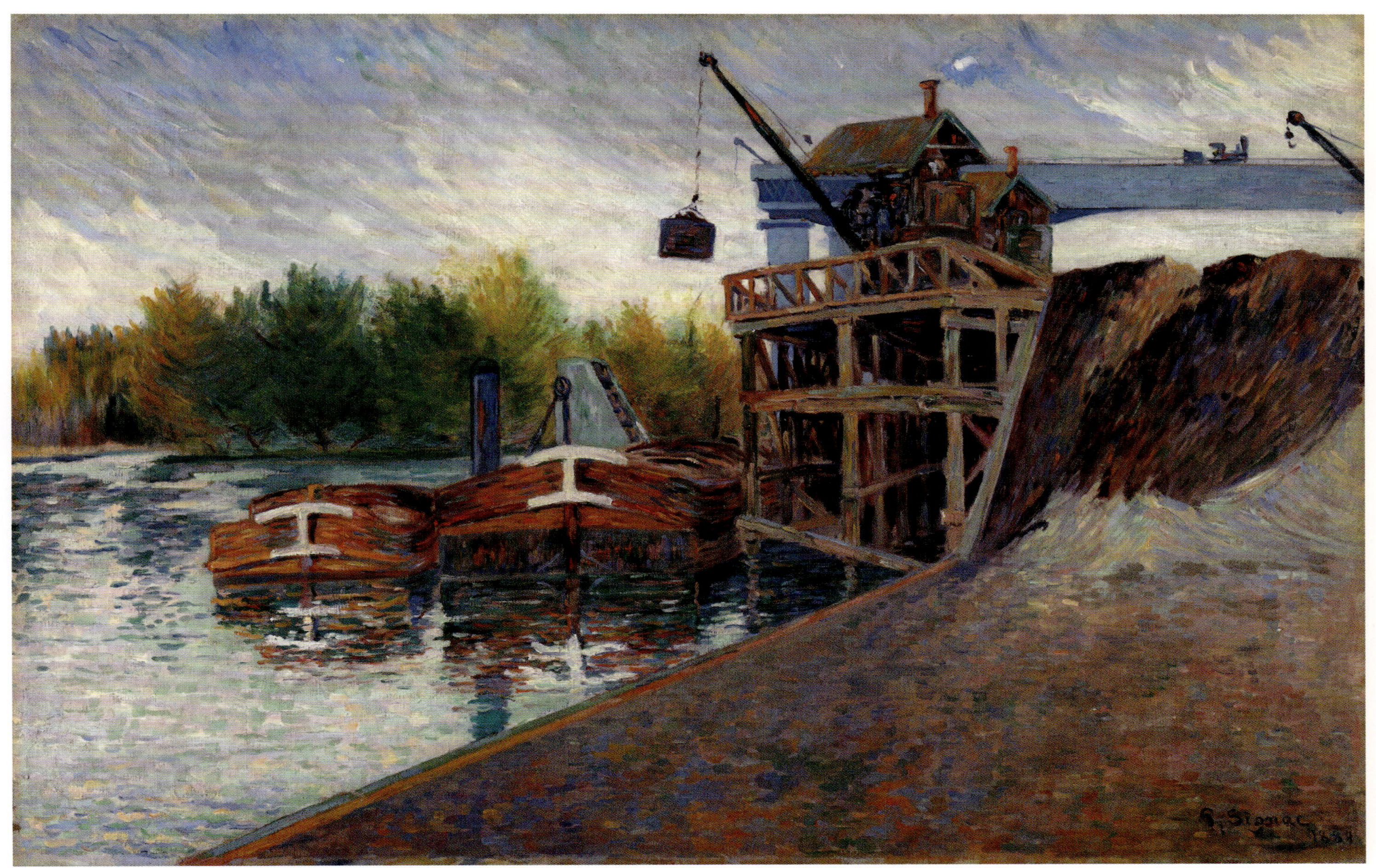

26 (cat.) Paul Signac
Coal Crane, Clichy, 1884
Oil on canvas, 59×91.4 cm
Lent by Glasgow Life (Glasgow Museums) on behalf of Glasgow City Council. Presented by the Trustees of the Hamilton Bequest, 1946

La Grande Jatte, Levallois, and Courbevoie: Relaxation and Entertainment on a Small Scale

La Grande Jatte was a beloved destination because of its bucolic charm and lush greenery. The island, which was originally two discrete islands joined together during the rule of Louis-Philippe, was linked to the mainland by the Pont Bineau and to Courbevoie by the Pont de Courbevoie, first in 1869 and then again in 1877, after its destruction by the Prussians. Prior to this time, it had been accessible only by boat. In 1884, steam-powered ferries were introduced that took passengers from Levallois-Perret on one side of the Seine to Asnières on the other, with a stop at the island.[53] By the time that Angrand was painting on La Grande Jatte in the mid-1880s, weekend visitors were so plentiful that he wrote to his parents that he could work there every day except for Sundays because of "the number of people promenading, which I don't like having at my back while I work."[54]

Since the Seine was cleaner here than at Clichy, La Grande Jatte was a favorite destination for aquatic sports, primarily swimming and fishing but also boating, as well as outdoor dining. The island was dotted with small cafés called *guinguettes*, so named for *guinguet*, a bitter, cheap wine produced from grapes grown at Courbevoie.[55] The *guinguettes* offered a festive dining experience: in addition to serving wine and beer, their menus listed a variety of fish, and the seafood (*le matelotte*) and rabbit (*le gibelotte*) stews were popular. They often had large halls for organized

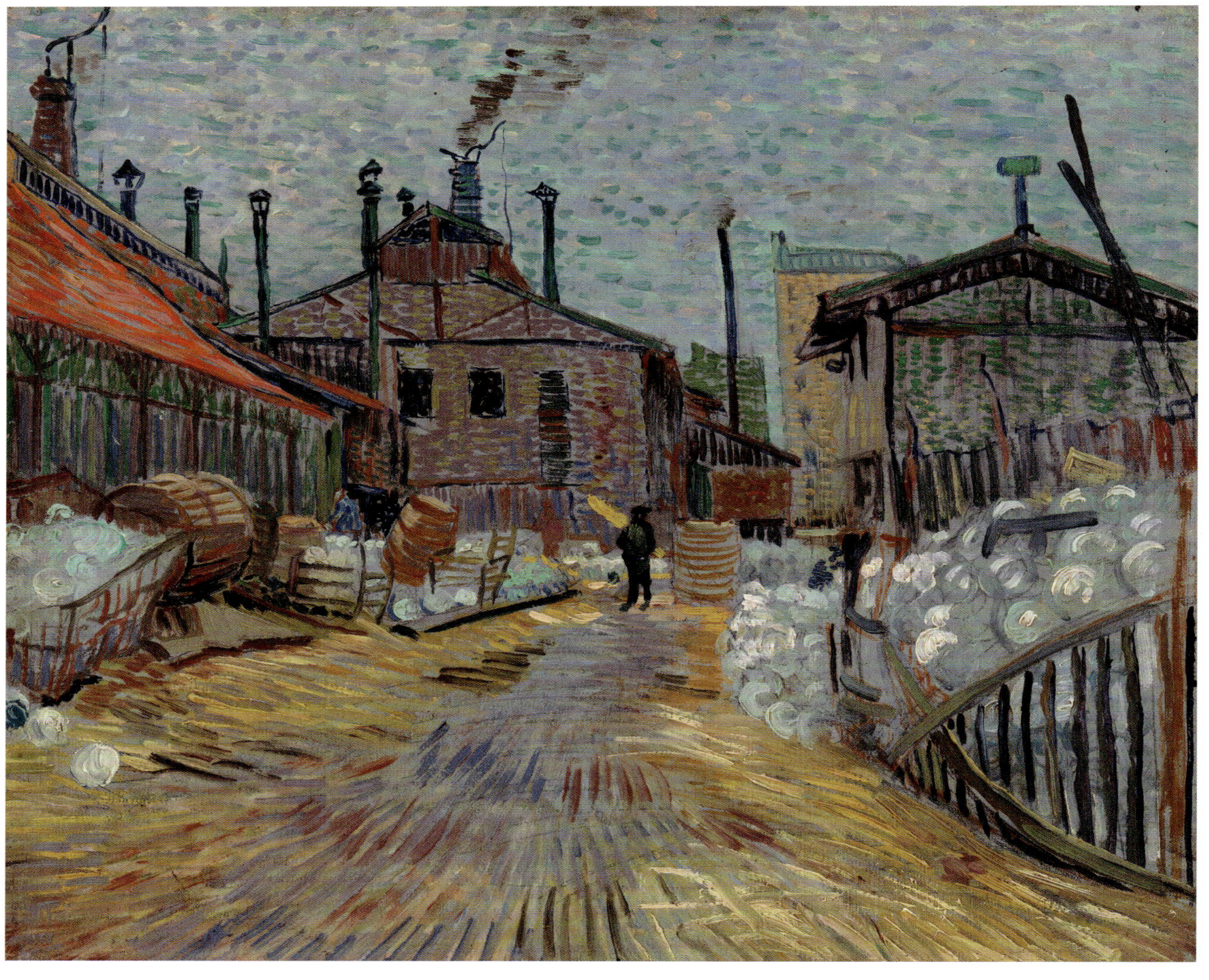

27 Vincent van Gogh
The Factory, 1887
Oil on canvas, 46 × 55.6 cm
Barnes Foundation, Philadelphia

balls and concerts. Parisians would come to dance polkas, waltzes, and quadrilles, and to listen to the captivating notes of the accordion as they feasted. These spots mainly served the boating crowd, as they were located near the boat houses on the smaller branch of the Seine. While *guinguettes* could be found on the periphery of most towns from the eighteenth century on, those on La Grande Jatte cropped up in the 1860s due to the population shift resulting from Haussmann's urban renewal project.

Opposite La Grande Jatte on the Parisian side of the Seine, Levallois, which had a population of more than 35,000 in 1886, saw the growth of factories and industrial sites after the 1860s. Most notable among them were, as of 1867, the studios of Gustave Eiffel, whose glorious tower was fabricated along the banks of the Seine through the efforts of more than one hundred workers. Several perfumeries, including Parfumerie Oriza and the Parfumerie du Globe and Savonnerie du Lion, established themselves there in the 1860s and 1870s. Other factories created paint, athletic equipment, and household goods, while several businesses located there imported desirable comestibles such as tea, rice, and pepper.[56] Levallois was particularly known for its wine merchants—of which there were more than 120 in 1860—as the founder of the village had owned a bistro and was closely connected with the wine trade.

Courbevoie, in contrast, the third stop on the train line from the Gare Saint-Lazare, with just over 13,000 inhabitants in 1881,[57] was distinguished by its beautiful seventeenth- and eighteenth-century houses, churches, and gardens, as well as the grand barracks built by Louis XV for his Swiss guards with its triple-pavilion design.[58] The bridge at Courbevoie **(34)**, discussed above, had legendary status, as it was completed in 1611 after the near-drowning of Henri IV and Marie de' Medici on a ferry from Courbevoie to Neuilly several years earlier. The original wooden bridge was replaced by an iron one spanning Courbevoie and La Grande Jatte in the 1870s, by which time a port had been established around it,[59] with small factories sprouting up there in subsequent years. Commercial industry, including a distillery that produced eau-de-vie and a linen factory, made Courbevoie its home.[60] It was also renowned for its pharmacies and perfumeries, with more than forty recorded in 1870, and for its laundry services. Taken together, La Grande Jatte, Levallois, and Courbevoie represented the less industrialized and more natural areas outside of Paris.

This rich fabric of interconnected communities lining the banks of the Seine—leisurely Asnières, industrial Clichy, the gay Grande Jatte, and the more reserved Levallois and Courbevoie—stimulated these five artists' creativity. Restaurants, sailing and boating, fishing, factories and new industries, the range of visual signifiers of these suburbs was vast, and it is notable that these artists concentrated their sights on select motifs. They seem to have shied away from the bourgeois activities that could also be found in Paris—the balls and feasts at Asnières, for example—and focused on the distinctive elements of the landscape: the factories' cranes and smokestacks; the bridges, embankments, and sailboats adorning the glittering Seine, with its dynamic reflections and intense hues; the open green spaces populated by figures promenading and relaxing; the modest edifices of the charming restaurants that were clearly not those of Paris. As the art critic Jules François Felix Fleury-Husson, who wrote under the name Champfleury, mused in 1859: "Industry mixed with nature has its poetic side: the point is to see it and be inspired."[61] It was this friction caused by the juxtaposition of industry and leisure, set against the everchanging landscape, that so inspired these five artists to explore radically new ways of applying paint to canvas during the 1880s. It was outside of the thriving city, whose prosperity initiated the elevation of these peripheral sites and whose reputation as an artistic center attracted Europe's most probing creative minds, that they could refine their visual vocabulary in order to advance painting to a new level. ■

POSTCARDS ALONG THE SEINE

The postcards in this visual essay represent a walk along the Seine, starting downstream from Clichy to Neuilly, crossing the Ile de la Grande Jatte, and then returning upstream from Courbevoie to Asnières, to end at the Ile de Saint-Ouen. The walk dates some fifteen to twenty years after our artists visited the sites. Painters and photographers alike often chose similar sites and viewpoints for their subjects. Thanks to these images, much insight can be gained on the rapidly changing area around Asnières at the turn of the century.

TEIO MEEDENDORP

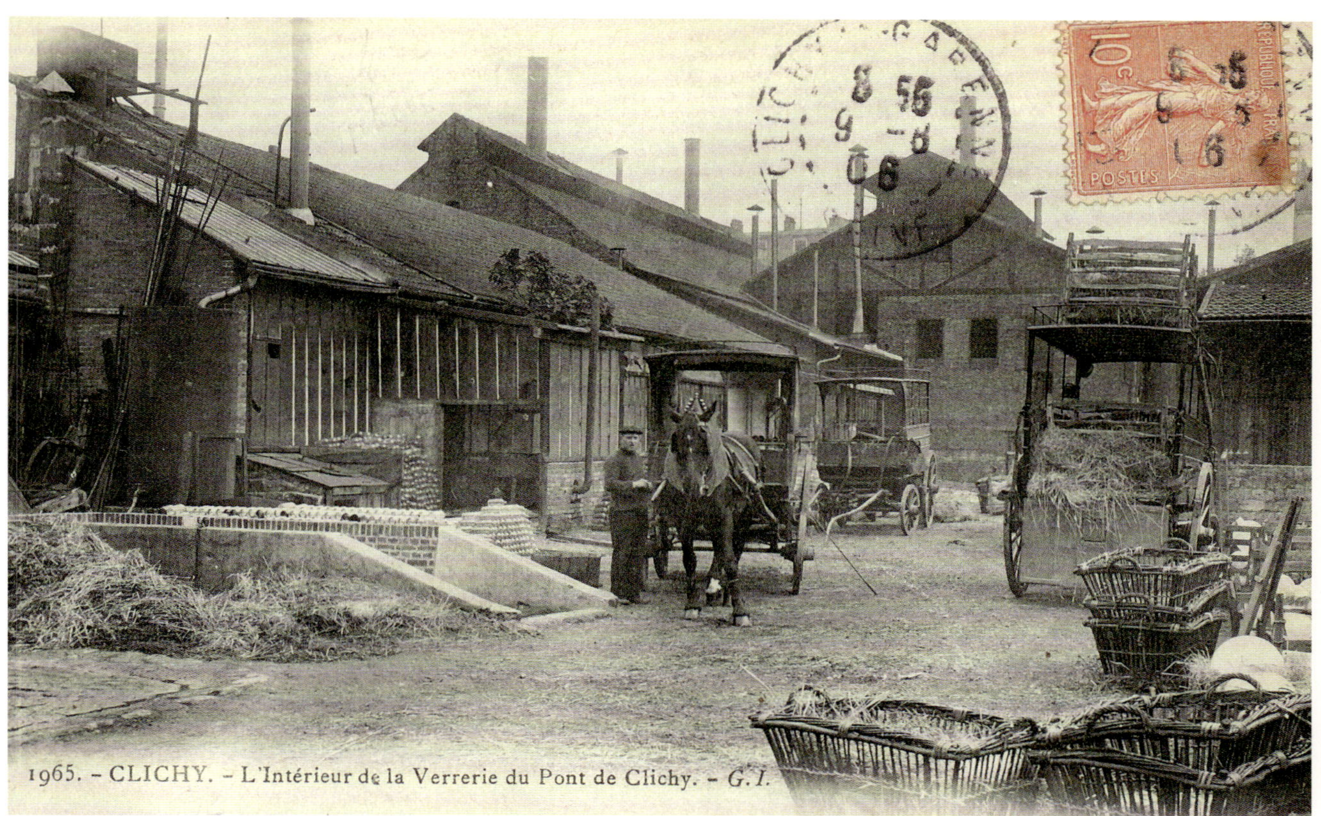

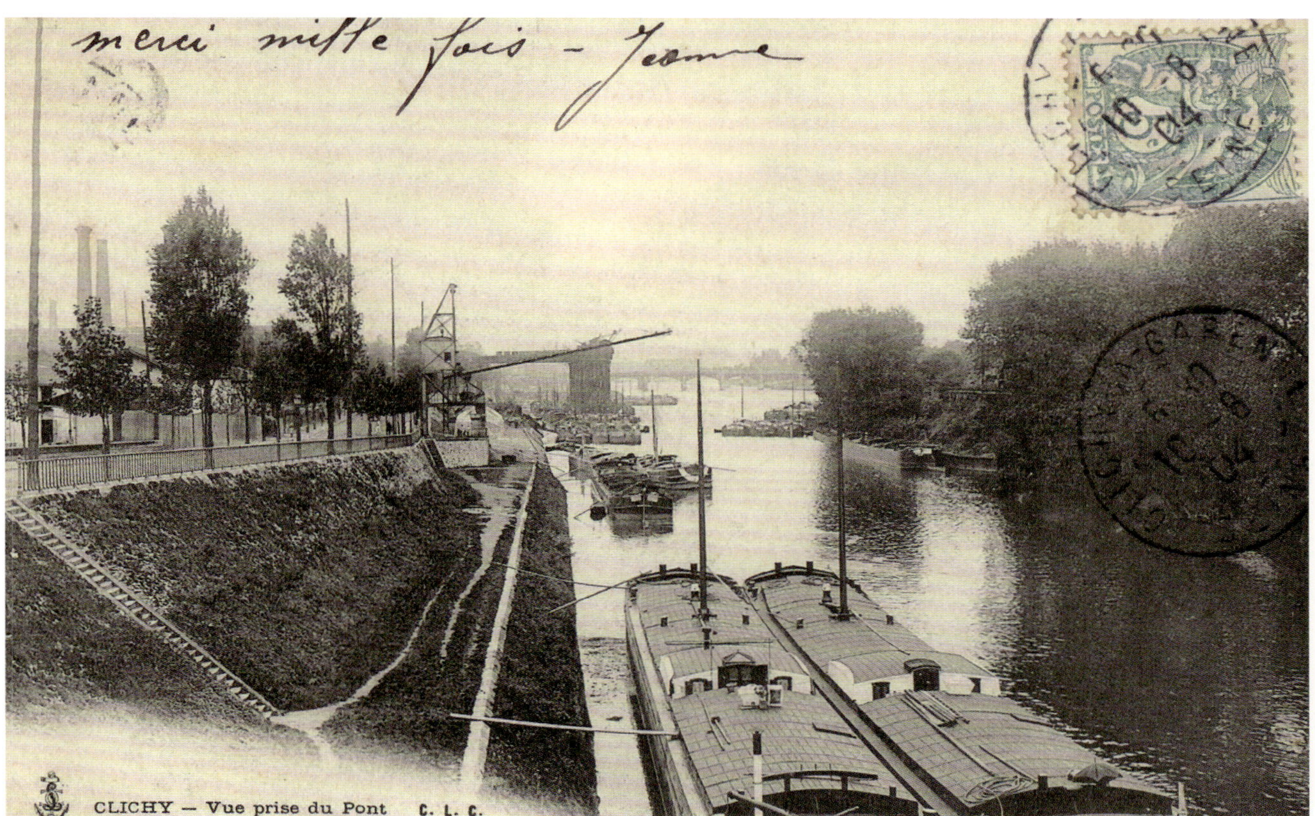

1 Clichy—*Interior of the Verrerie du Pont de Clichy*, c. 1905 (postmarked 1906). This was the inner yard of a glassworks located on the rue du Réservoir in Clichy (now rue Médéric), close to the quai de Clichy and the Pont de Clichy. The scene was painted by Van Gogh from an almost identical viewpoint **(27)**.

2 Clichy—*Quai de Clichy and the Ile Robinson*, c. 1900 (postmarked 1904). The quai de Clichy can be seen on the left with the smokestacks of the gasworks in the distance. Signac painted *Quai de Clichy, Gray Weather* in 1887 from a lower viewpoint **(96)**. The photograph was taken from the Pont de Clichy, which is visible in the painting Van Gogh made on the Ile Robinson looking back **(51)**.

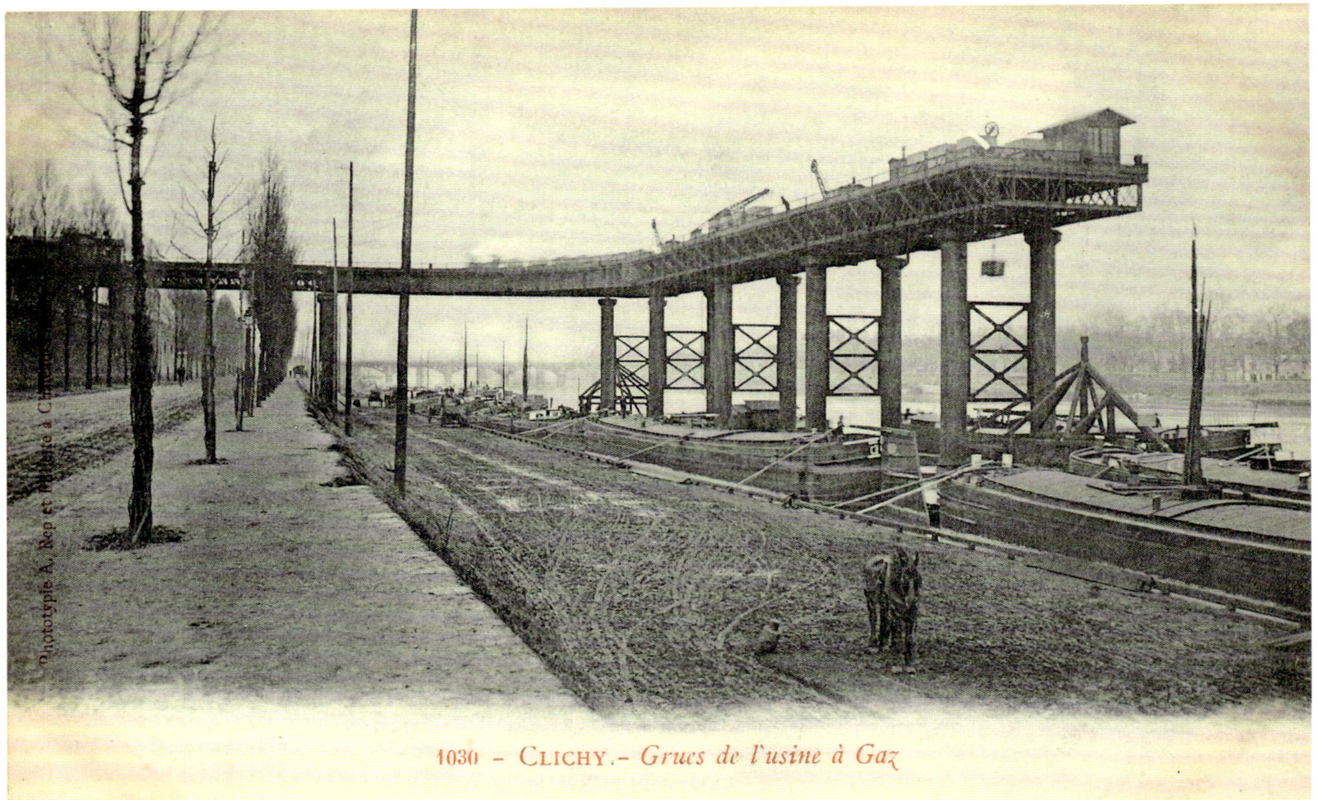

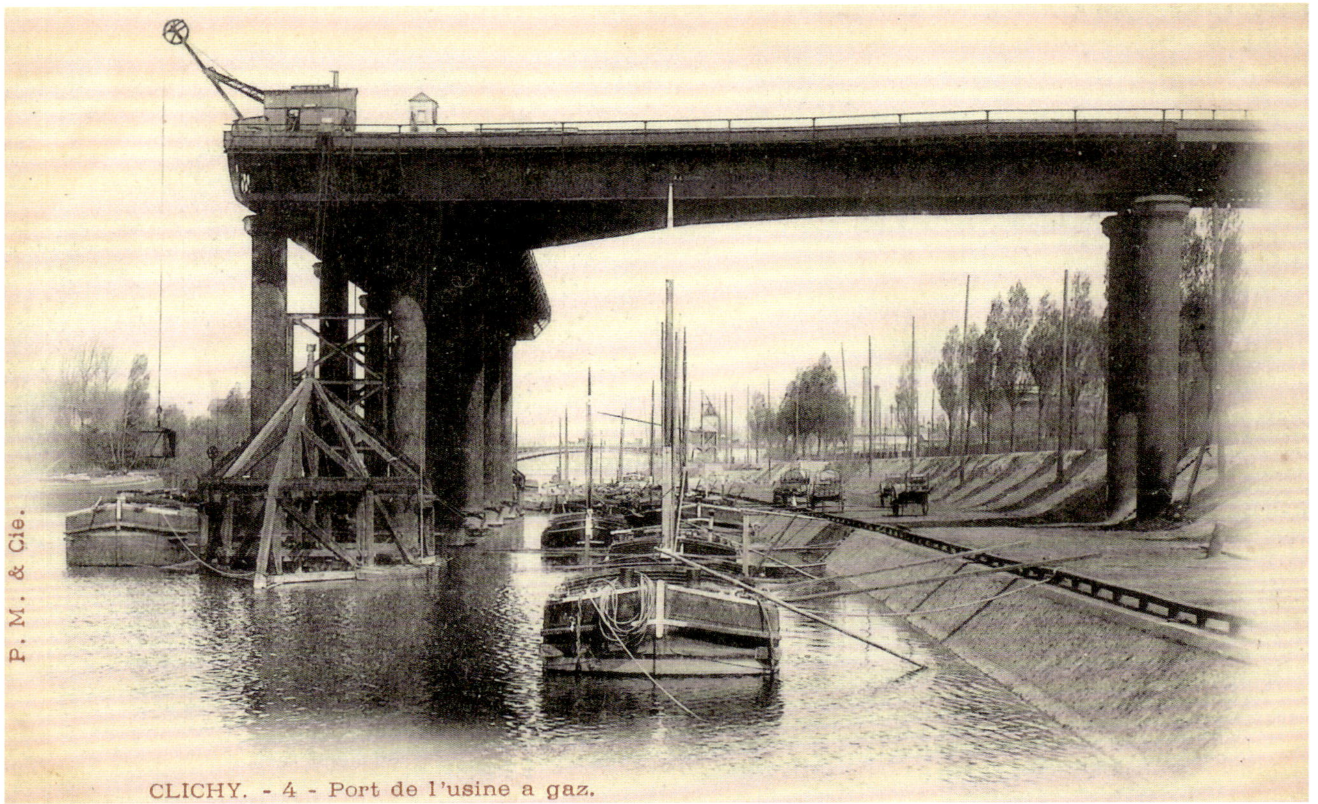

3 Clichy—*Grues de l'usine à Gaz*, c. 1900. Cranes were used to transfer coal from barges on the Seine to elevated railroad carts, after which the coal was transported to the gasworks. From a little further away Signac painted *Quai de Clichy, Gray Weather* **(96)**.

4 Clichy—*Port de l'usine à Gaz*, c. 1900. The quay at Clichy, with the gasworks' crane, and the Pont de Clichy in the distance. This is close to the spot where Bernard painted *Quai de Clichy* **(119)**.

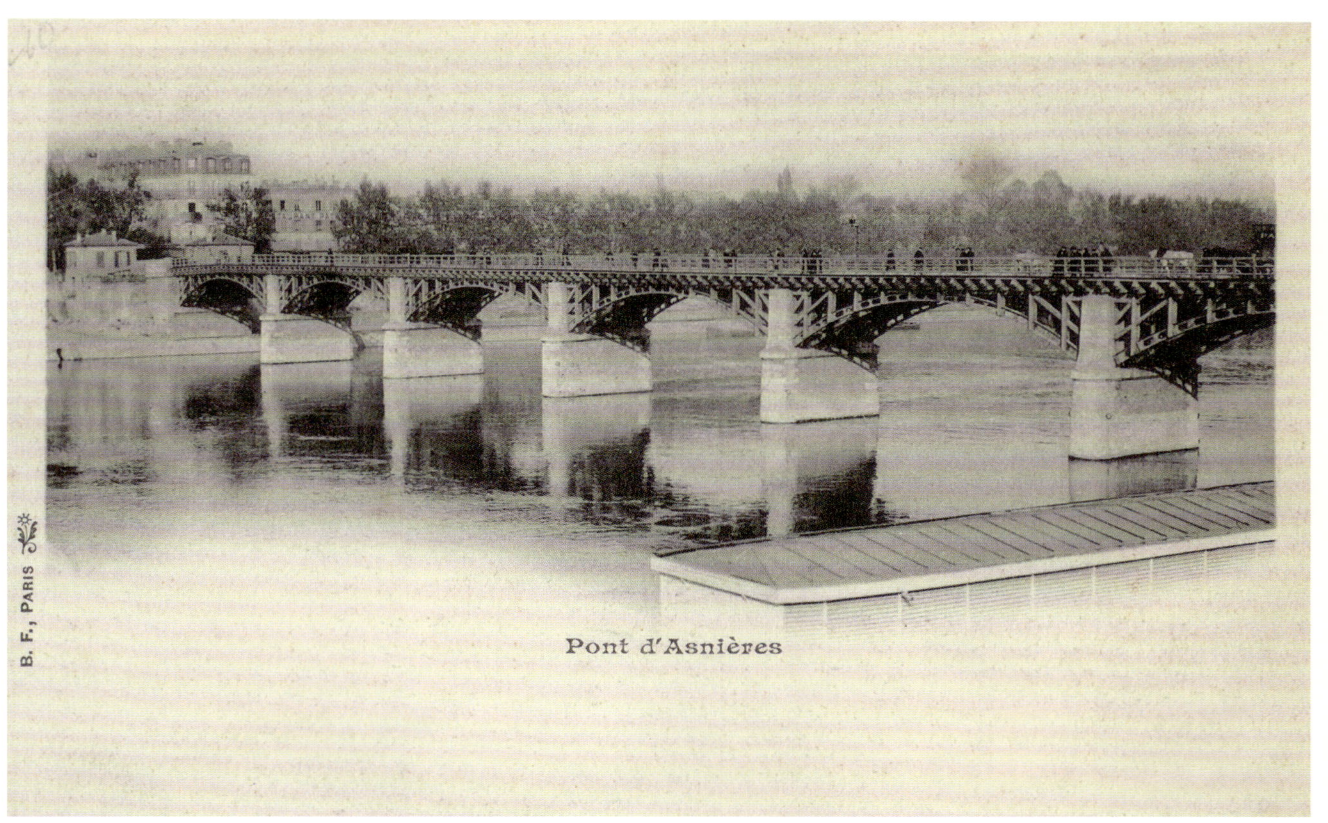

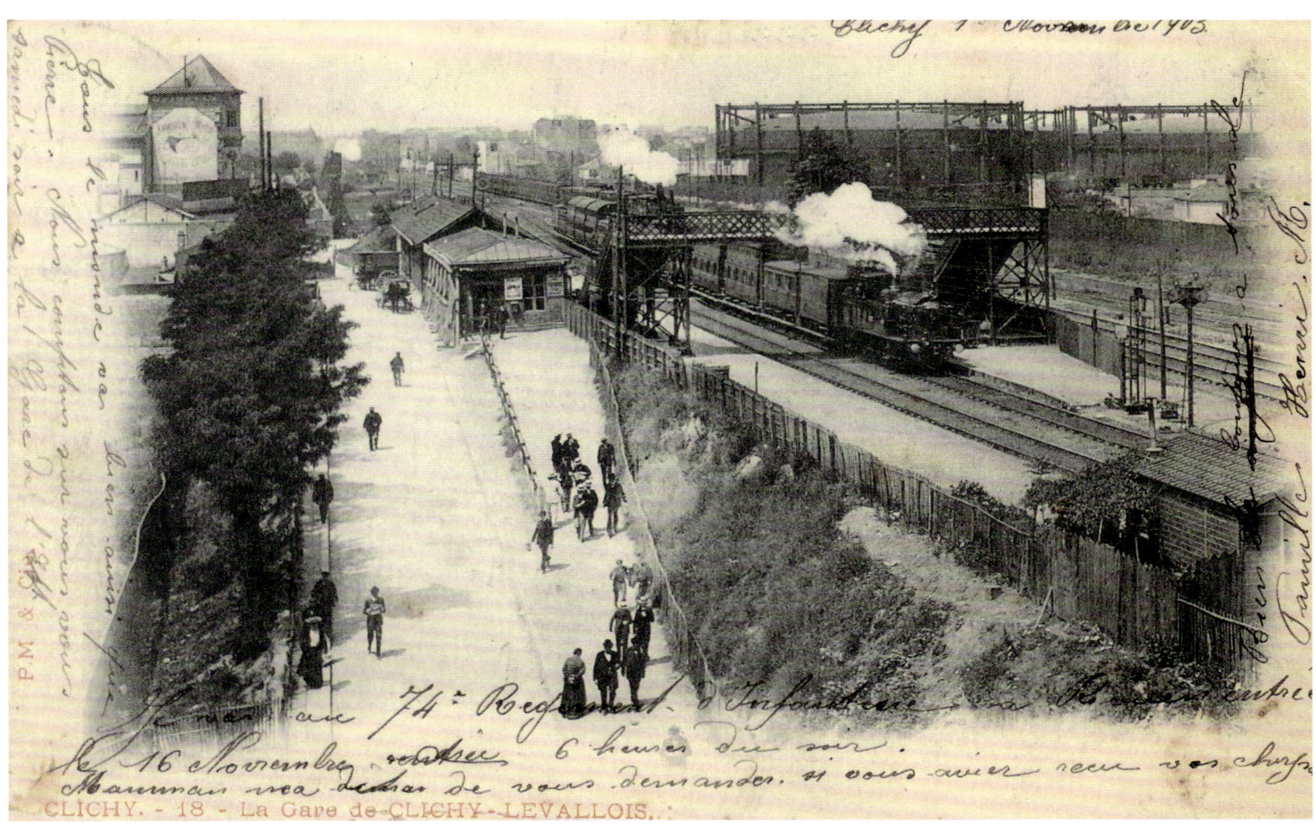

5 Clichy—*Pont d'Asnières*, c. 1900. The old bridge seen here, constructed after the Franco-Prussian War, was replaced by a new bridge after 1904. The second building from the left, just above the second arch of the bridge, is the Restaurant de la Sirène, depicted by Van Gogh **(22,23,49)**; he also painted the bridge from the Asnières side of the river **(1)**.

6 Clichy—*Railroad Station in Clichy-Levallois*, c. 1900. In the right background are the gasometers of the gasworks. The Western Railway **(129)** passes through here to its next stop north over the Seine in Asnières.

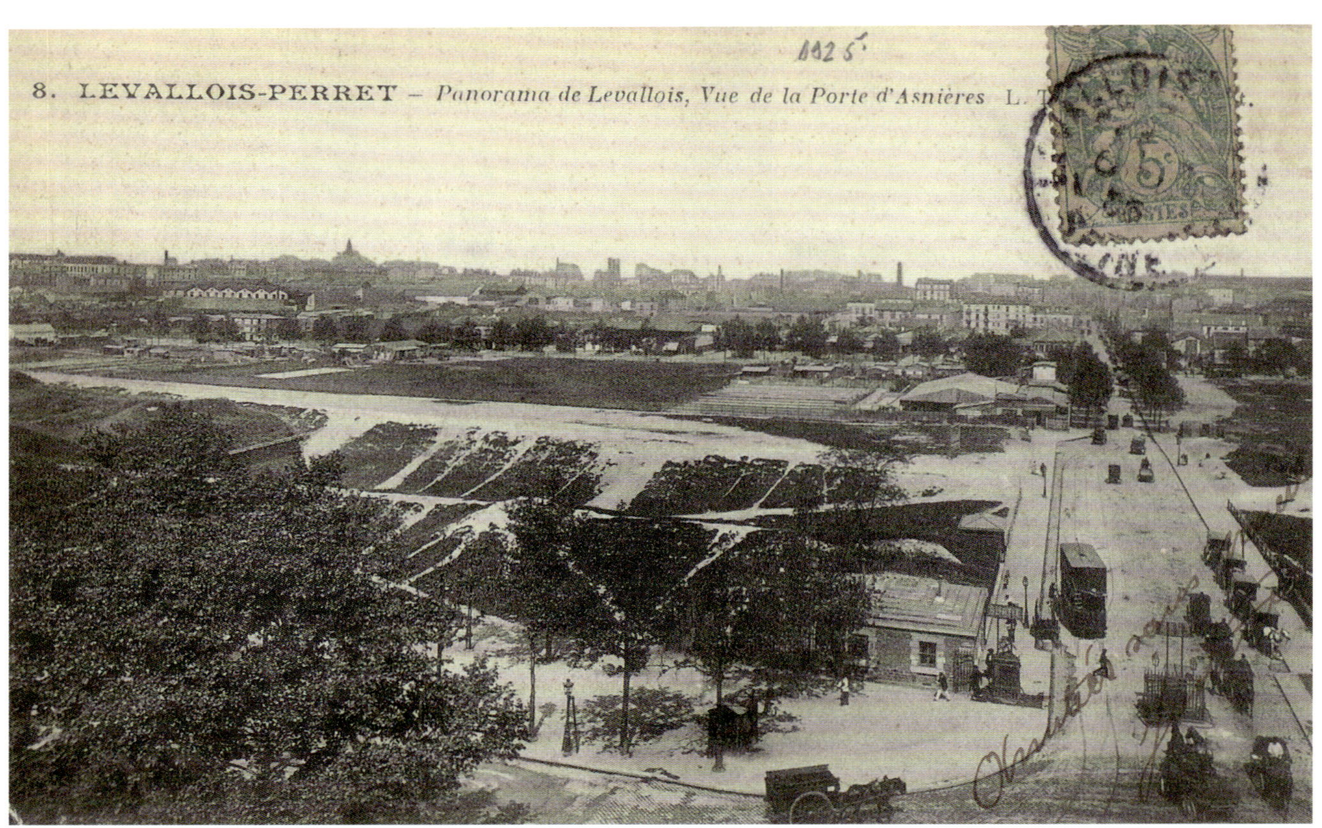

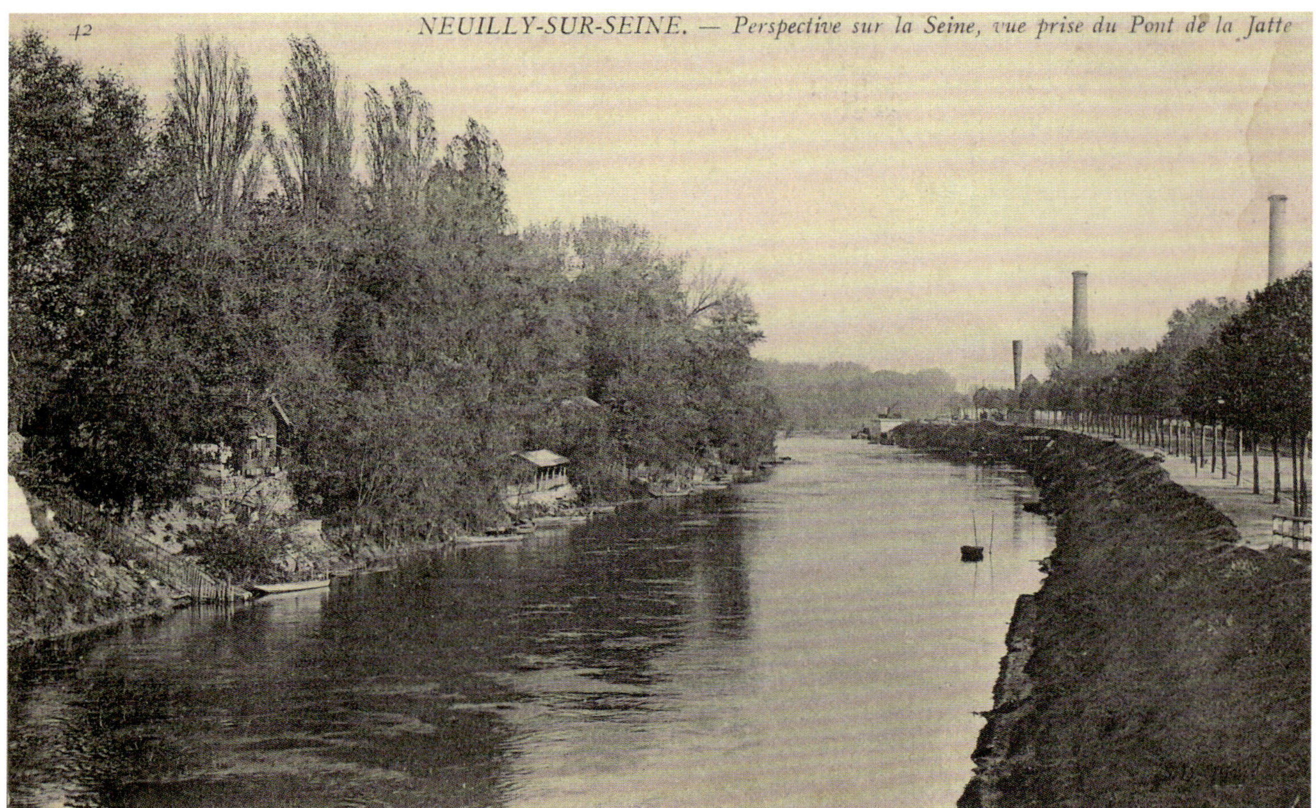

7 Levallois-Perret—*Porte d'Asnières*, c. 1910. This panoramic view to the northwest overlooks Levallois-Perret. In the foreground is the rough hilly terrain of the embankment fortifications interspersed with footpaths. On the right in the distance is the rue Victor Hugo, which leads to the Pont d'Asnières. Angrand painted *The Western Railway at its Exit from Paris* in a similar terrain, about 300 meters to the right, where the train line to Asnières cuts through the fortification wall **(129)**.

8 Neuilly-sur-Seine—*View from the Pont de la Jatte*, c. 1905. To the left we see the island of La Grande Jatte.

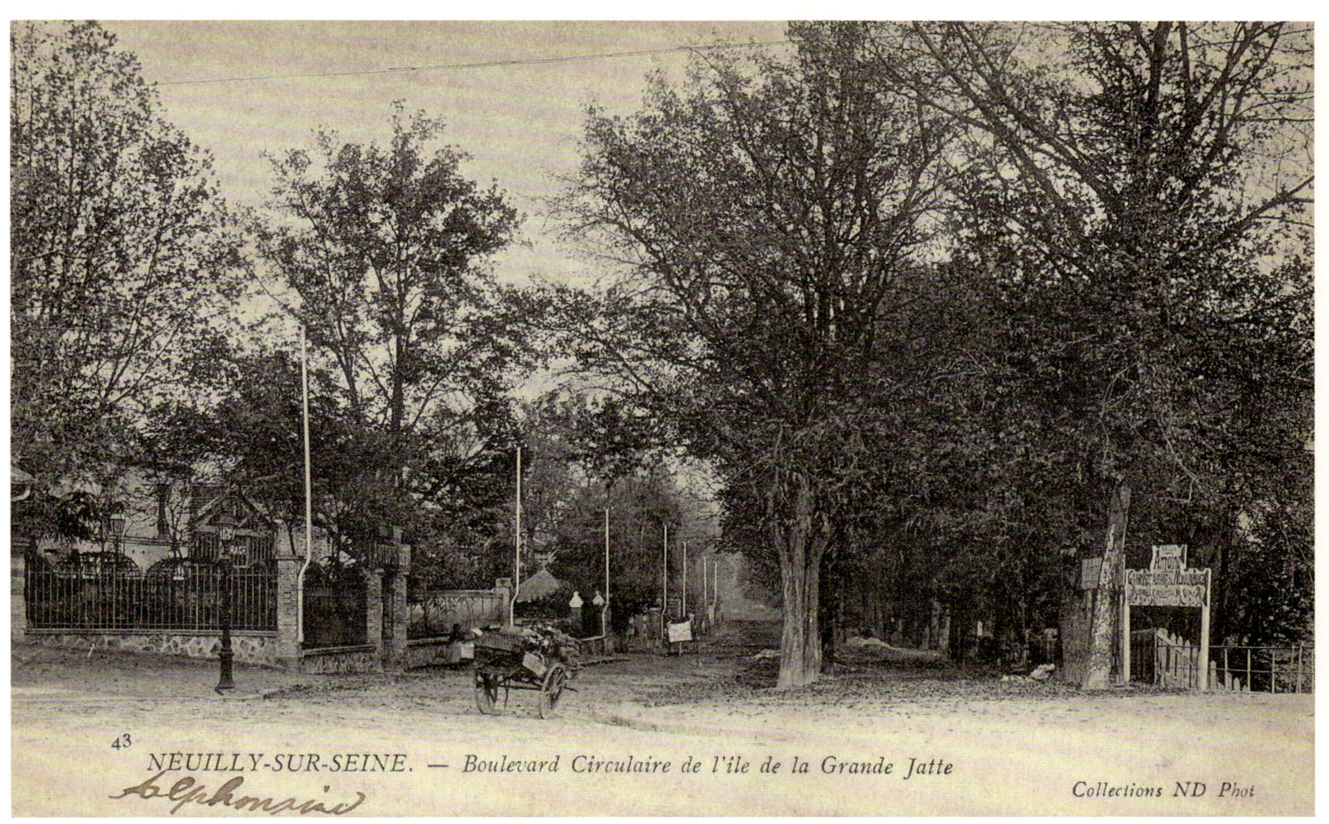

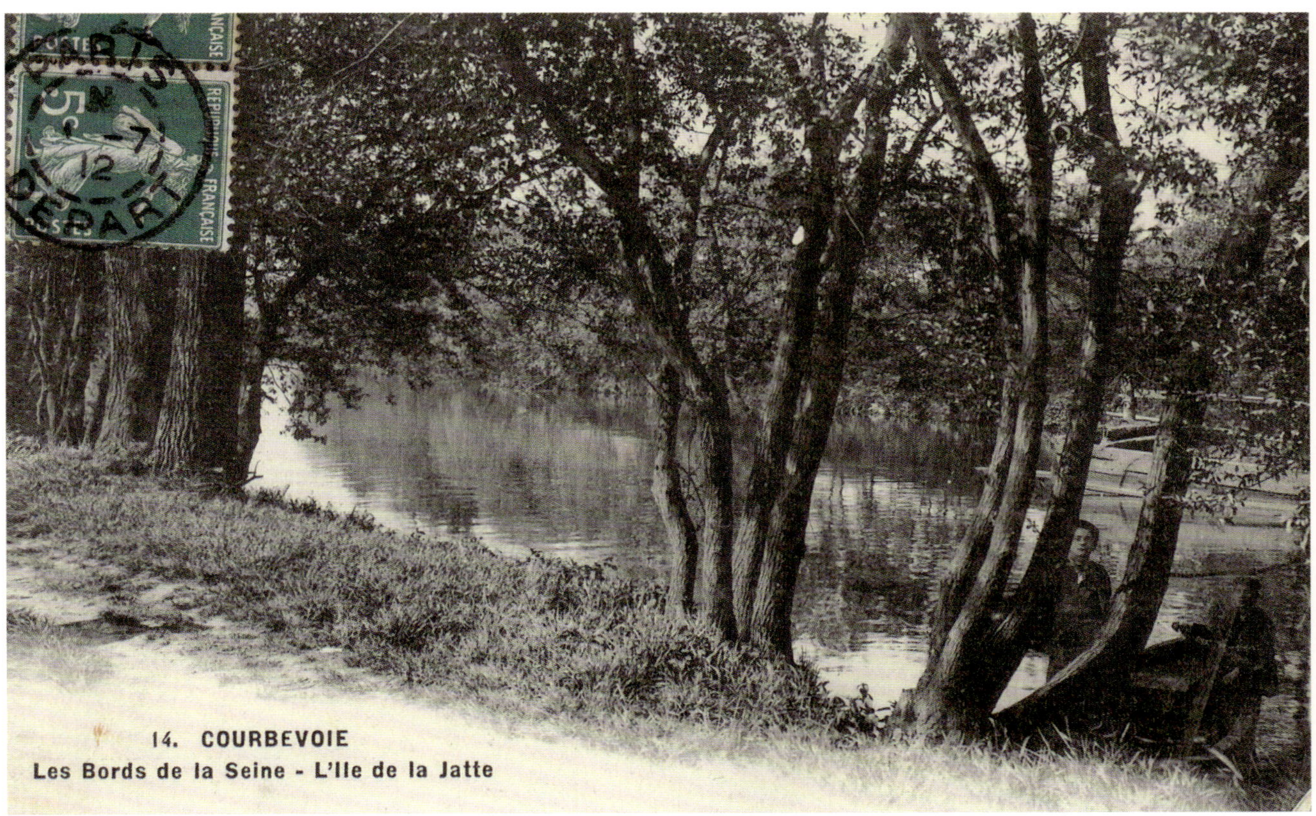

9 Neuilly-sur-Seine—*Boulevard Circulaire on the Ile de la Grande Jatte*, c. 1905. Somewhere along this boulevard, Van Gogh painted an entrance gate, one of the works in his Grande Jatte triptych **(45)**.

10 Courbevoie – *View from the Ile de la Grande Jatte*, c. 1910 (postmarked 1912).

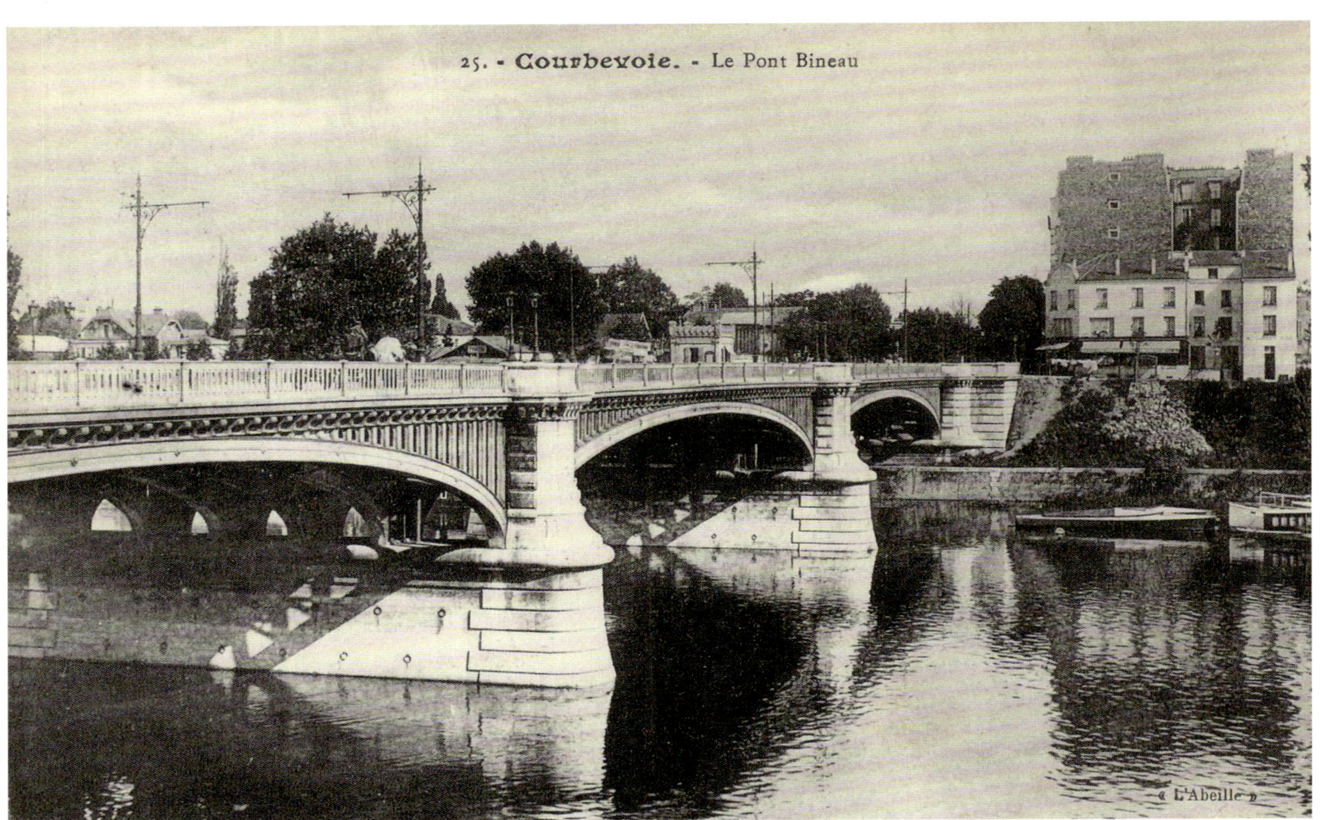

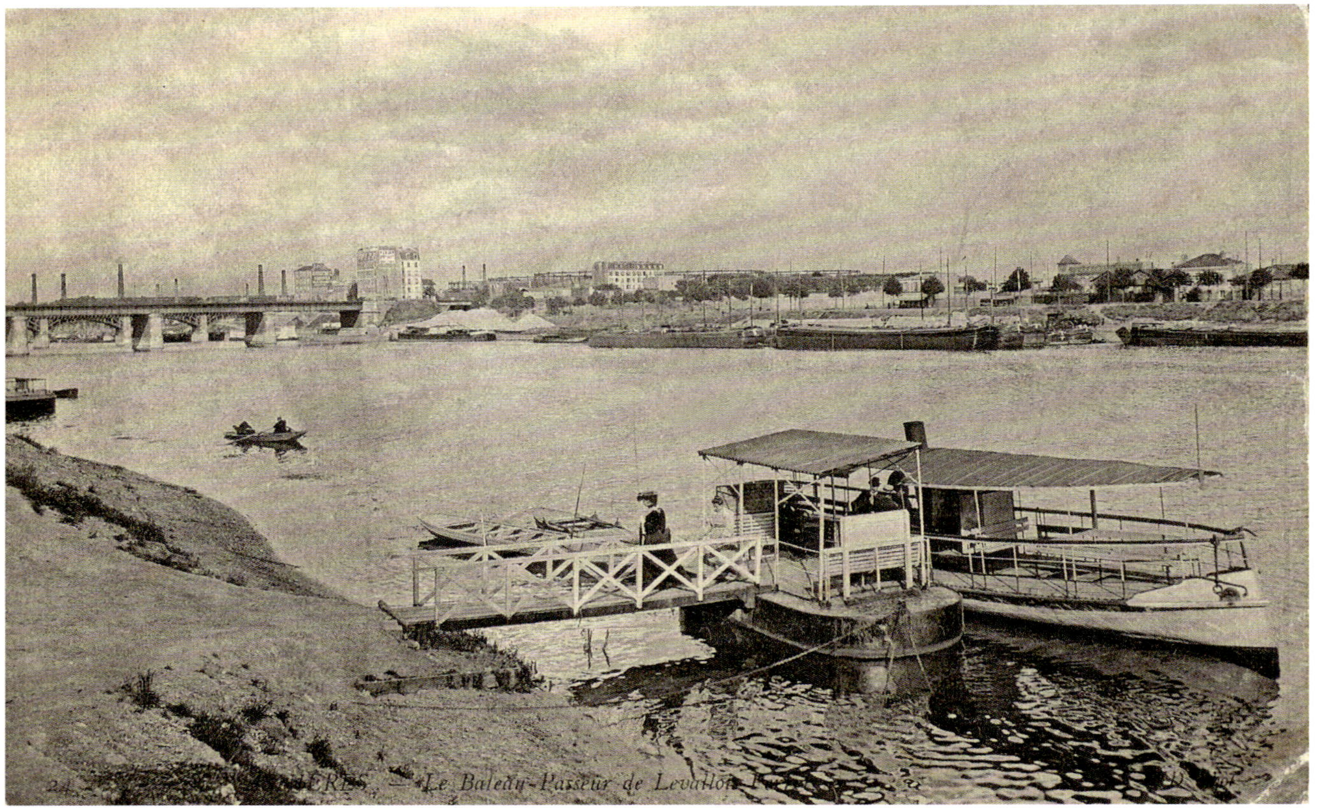

11 Courbevoie—*Pont Bineau, Linking La Grande Jatte with Courbevoie*, c. 1910. Van Gogh painted this view **(34)**, and it can be seen in the distance in several of Seurat's views from La Grande Jatte **(5,61,79,80)**.

12 Courbevoie—*The Ferry ("Bateau-Passeur") Across the Seine to Levallois-Perret*, before 1904. Signac painted this jetty, the "Ponton de la Félicité," from the water **(152)**. The *Félicité* was a well-known steamer used for trips along the Seine.

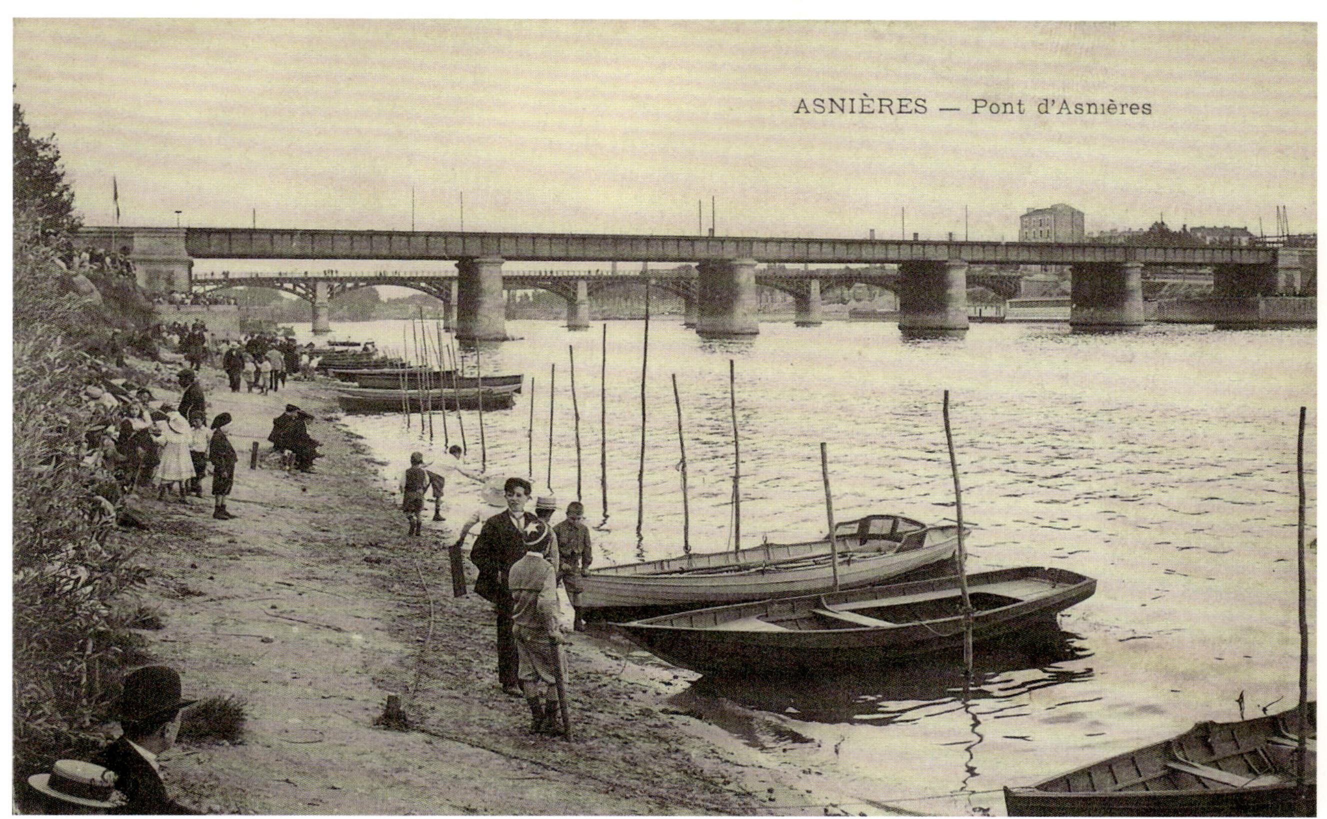

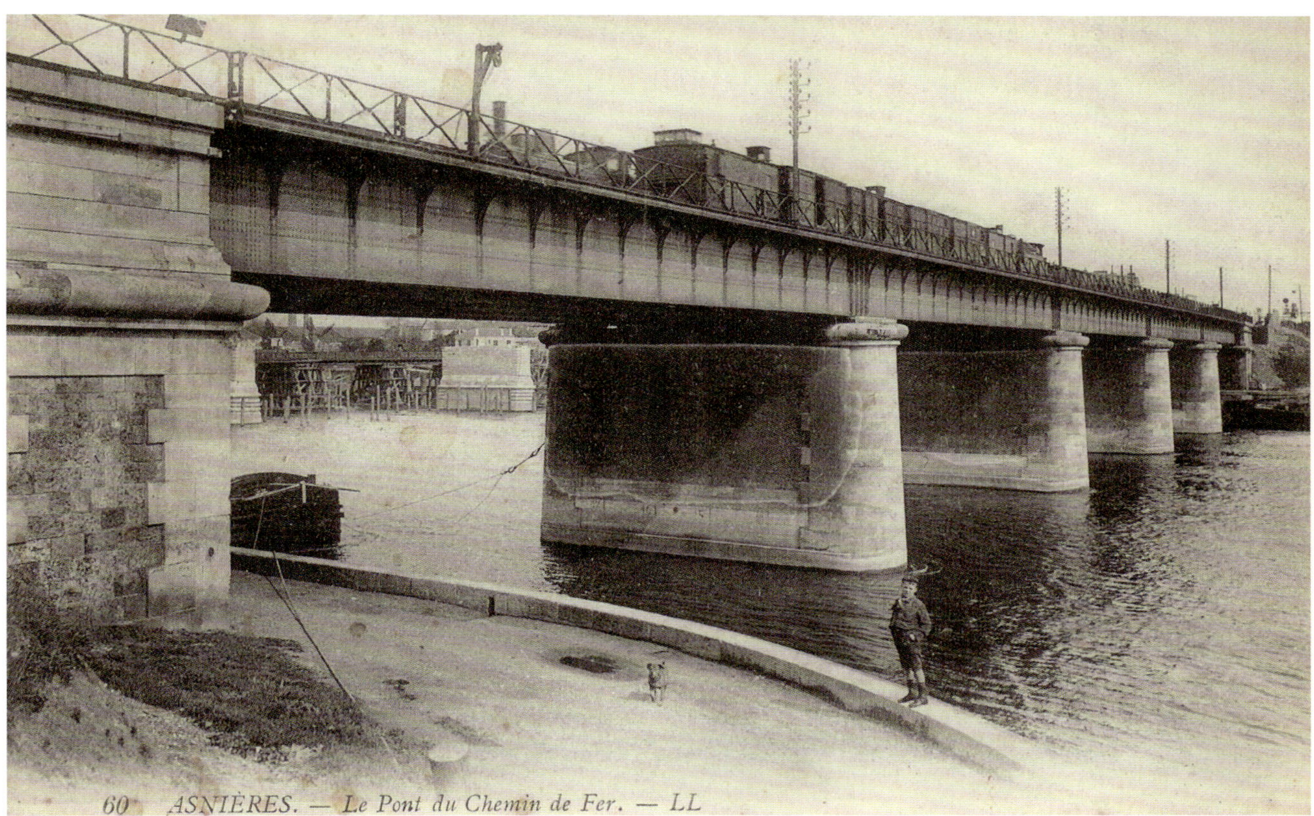

13 Asnières—*Along the Bank of the Seine with the Pont du Chemin de Fer and Pont d'Asnières in the Background*, c. 1900. Signac painted this view from a boat on the river **(99)**, while Van Gogh painted his moored boats from the opposite side, close to the railroad bridge **(50)**.

14 Asnières—*Pont du Chemin de Fer*, c. 1905. Van Gogh painted the bridge from almost exactly this vantage point **(48)**, Bernard stood a little further back **(121)**, and Signac looked away from the bridge, picturing the rounded part of the bank **(149)**.

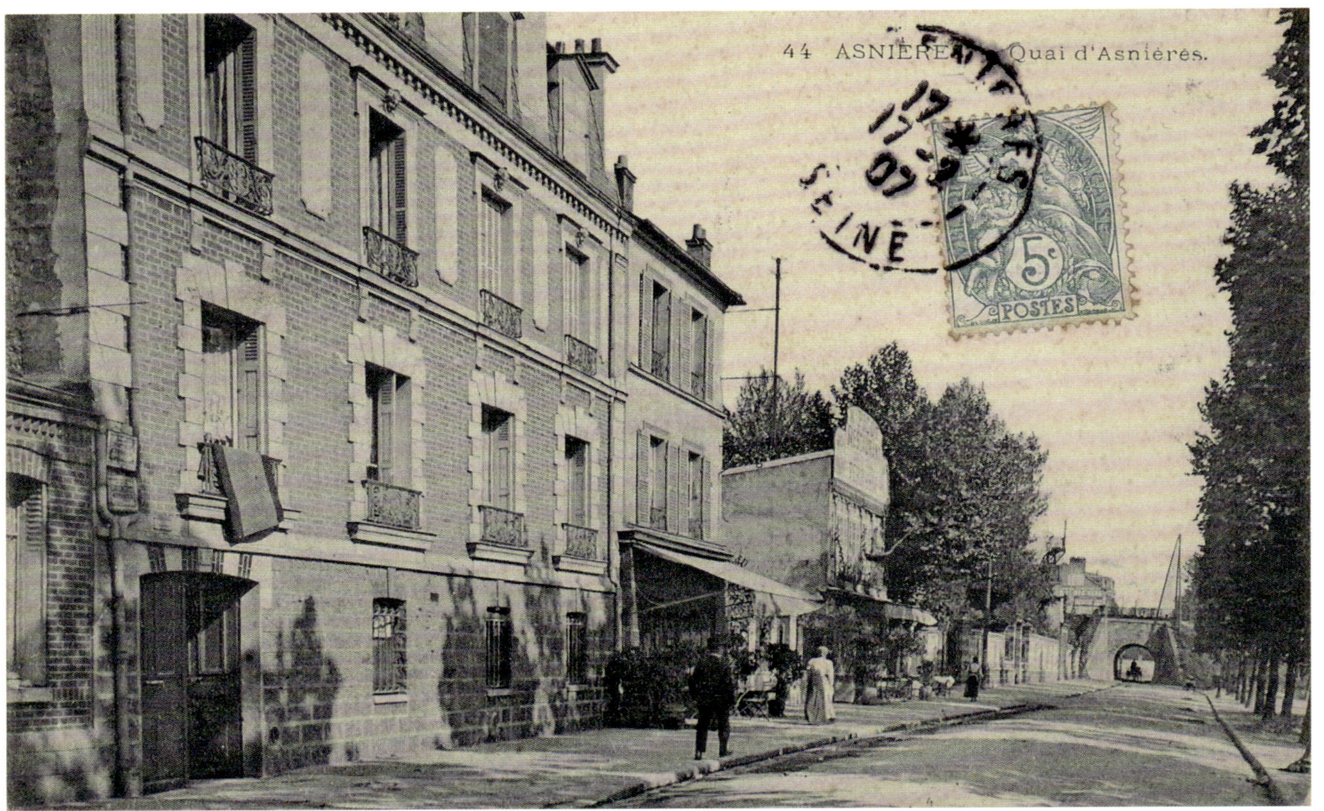

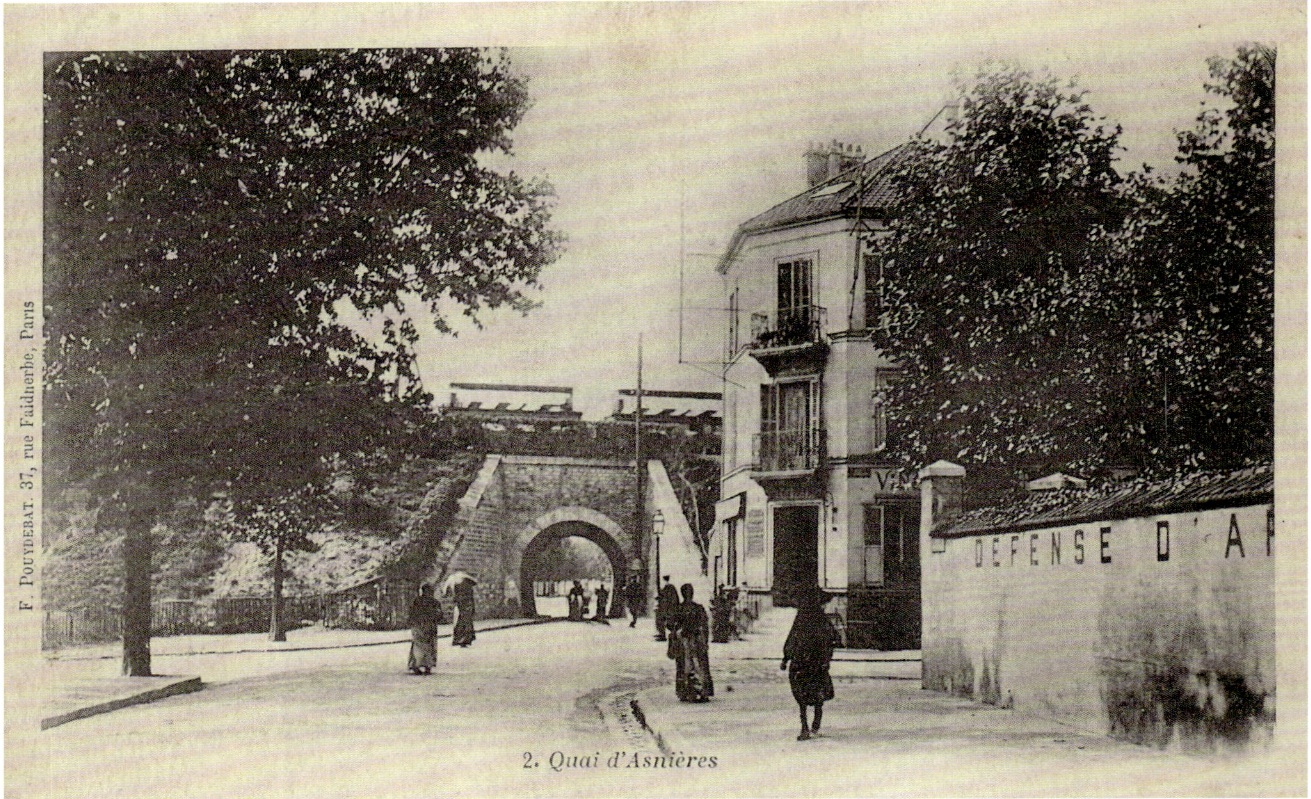

15 Asnières—*Quai d'Asnières*, c. 1905 (postmarked 1907). The railroad underpass to the far right is close to the Pont du Chemin de Fer, painted by Van Gogh **(54)**.

16 Asnières—*Quai d'Asnières*, c. 1905. The chimneys of the building to the right are visible in Van Gogh's view of this underpass, which he painted from the other side **(54)**.

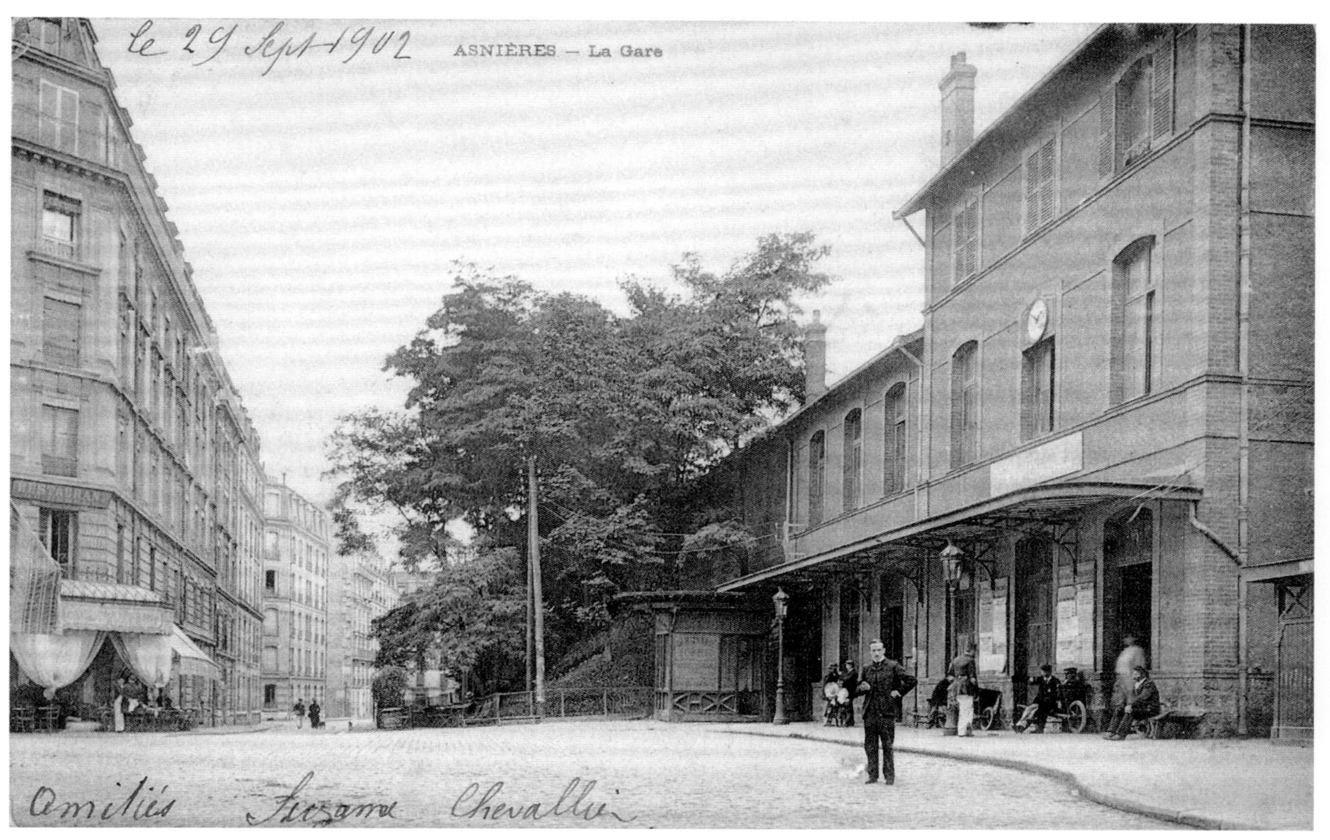

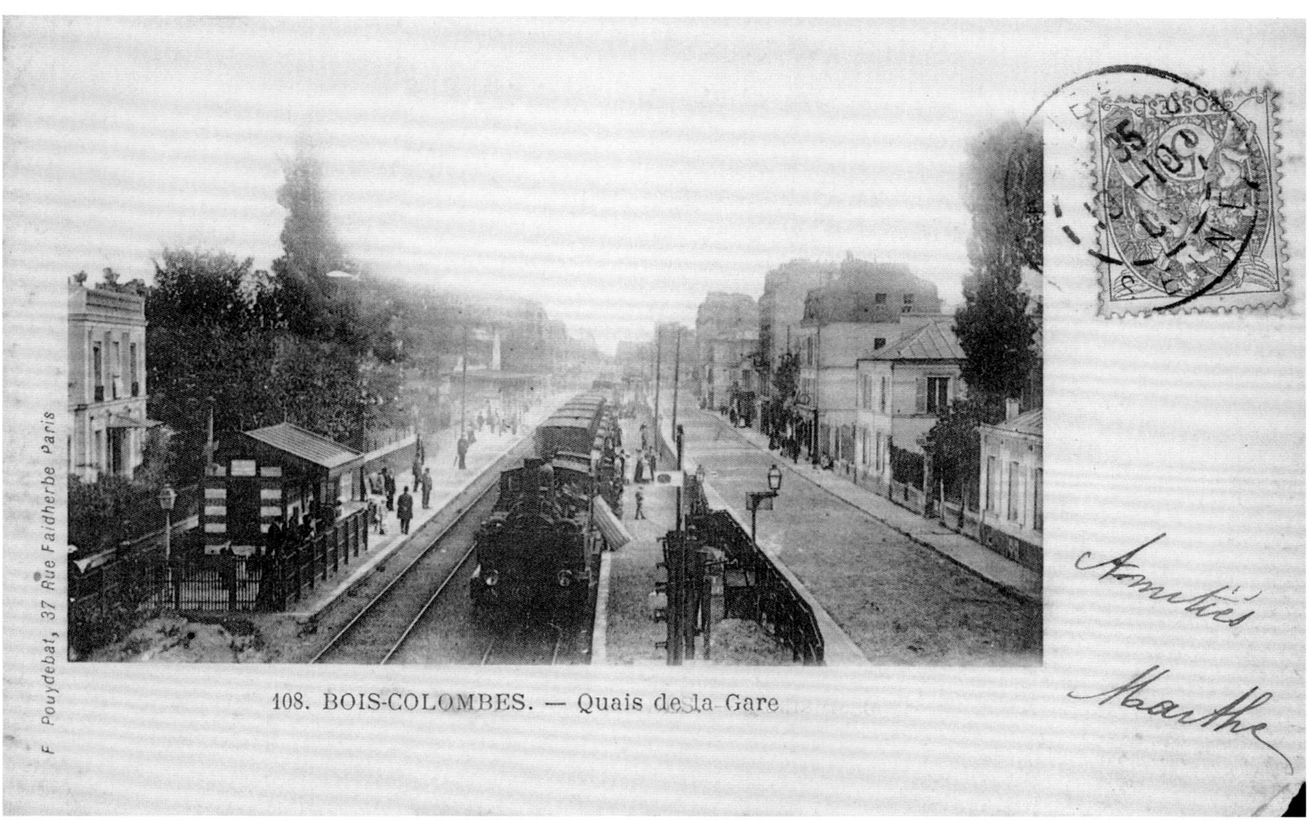

17 Asnières—*Rue de la Station*, c. 1900 (postmarked 1902). Signac painted *Rue de la station* **(108)** near this spot.

18 Bois-Colombes—*Railroad Station*, c. 1900 (postmarked 1903). Signac made several paintings at the railroad **(85,86,87)**.

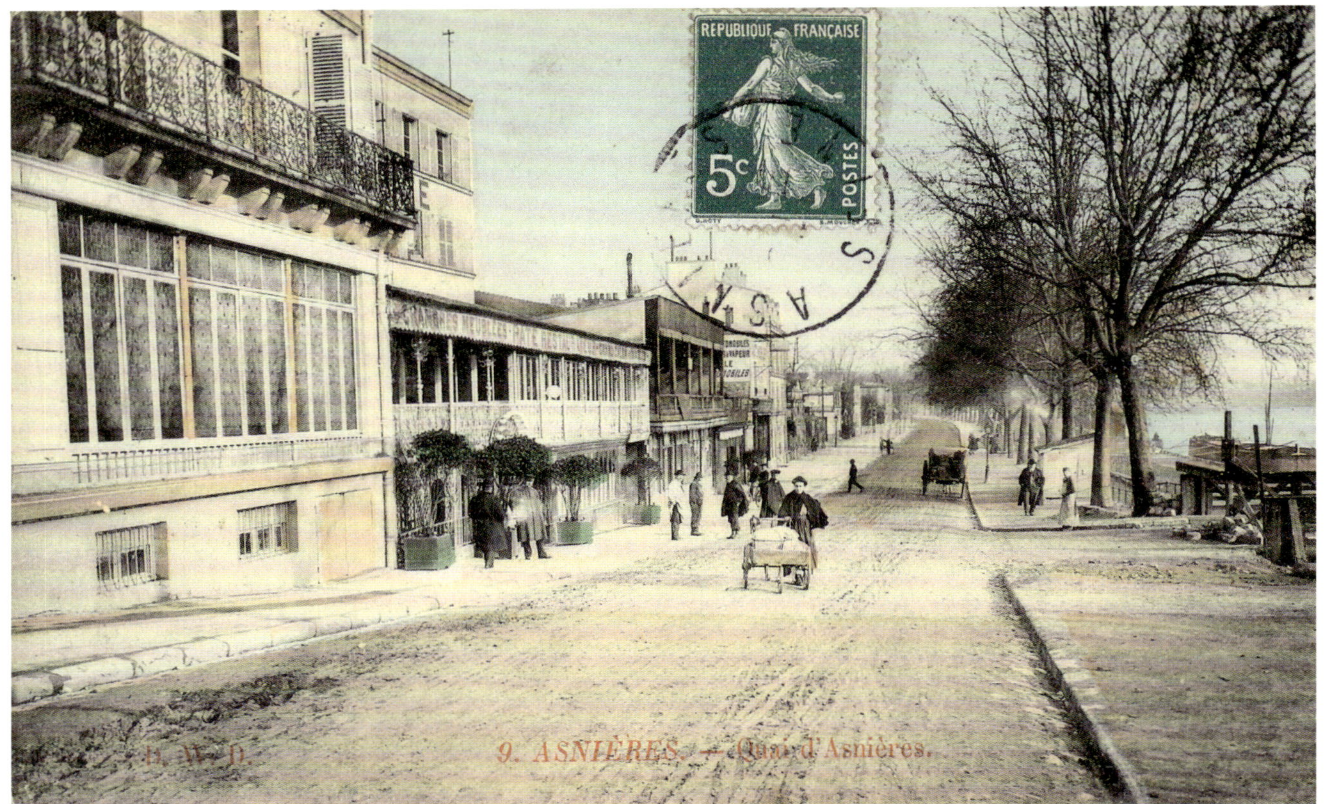

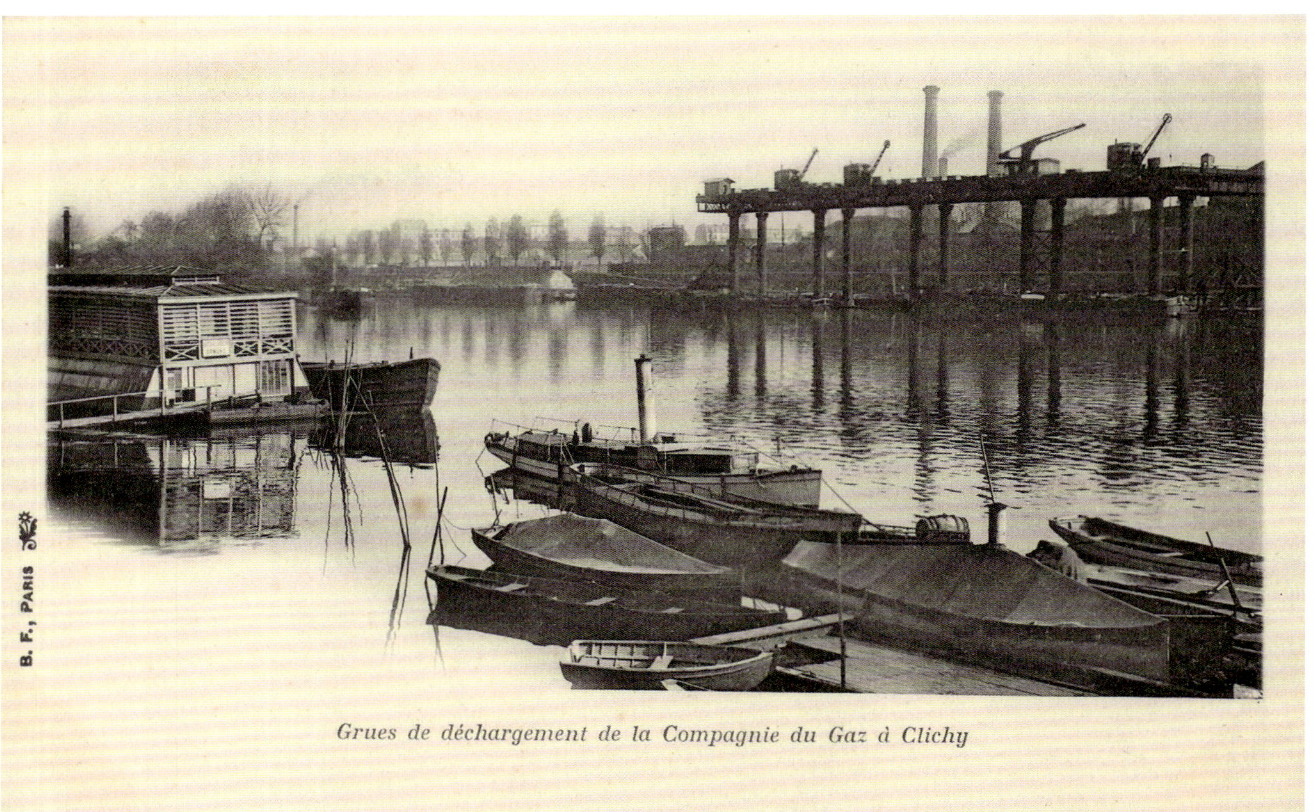

19 Asnières—*Quai d'Asnières*, c. 1905. This quay is close to the Pont d'Asnières, looking downstream. On the left is the former Restaurant de la Sirène, which Van Gogh painted several times **(22,23,49)**.

20 Asnières—*Port d'Asnières*, c. 1900. This photograph captures the elevated cranes at Clichy from across the water, with a laundry boat on the left. Signac produced several paintings and a drawing in this area **(82,83,84)**.

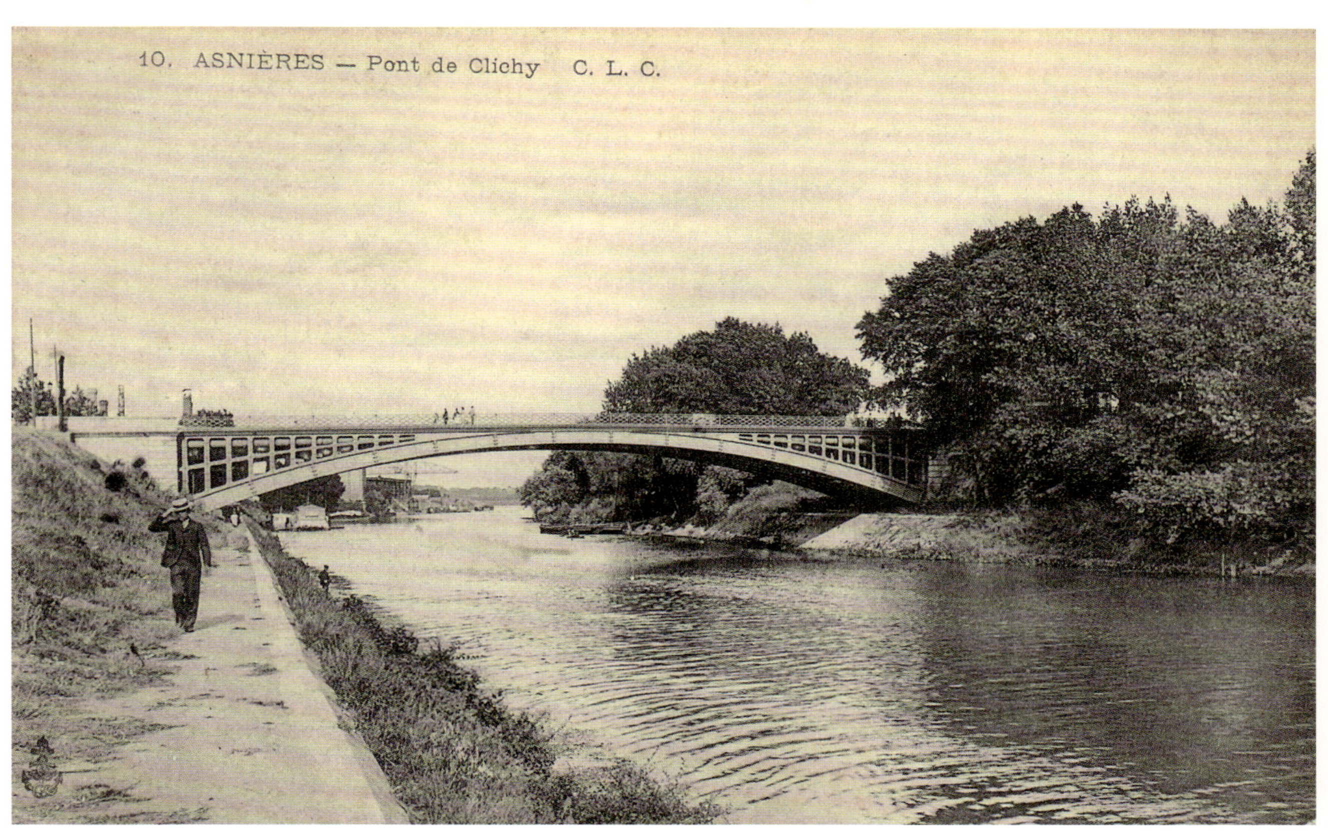

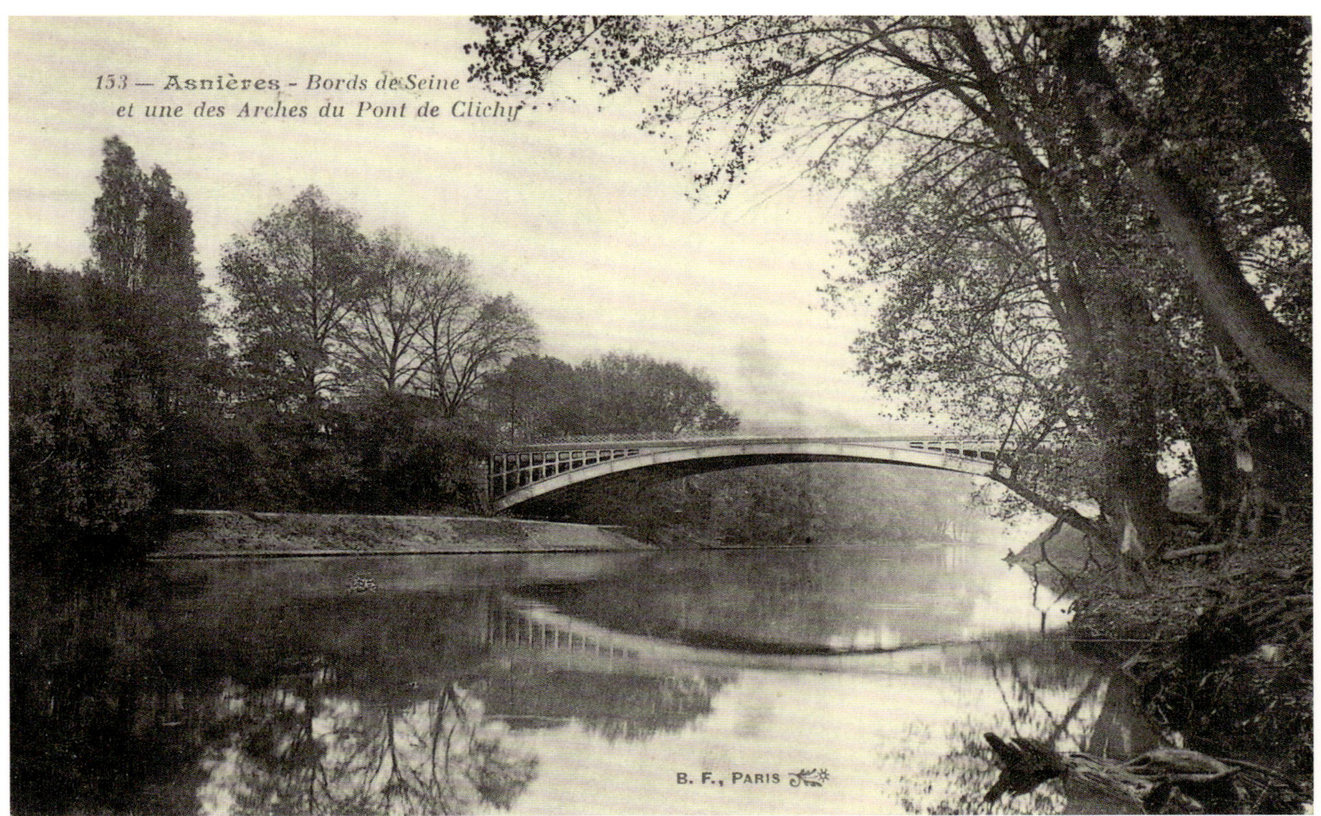

21 Asnières—*Pont de Clichy*, c. 1905. The Clichy bridge consists of three parts. This is the first part from Asnières on the left to the Ile des Ravageurs on the right. It is close to the spot where Van Gogh painted *Pont de Clichy* **(2)**.

22 Asnières—*Pont de Clichy*, c. 1905. The middle arch of the Pont de Clichy, seen from the Ile des Ravageurs with the Ile Robinson on the left, was depicted by Van Gogh **(53)**.

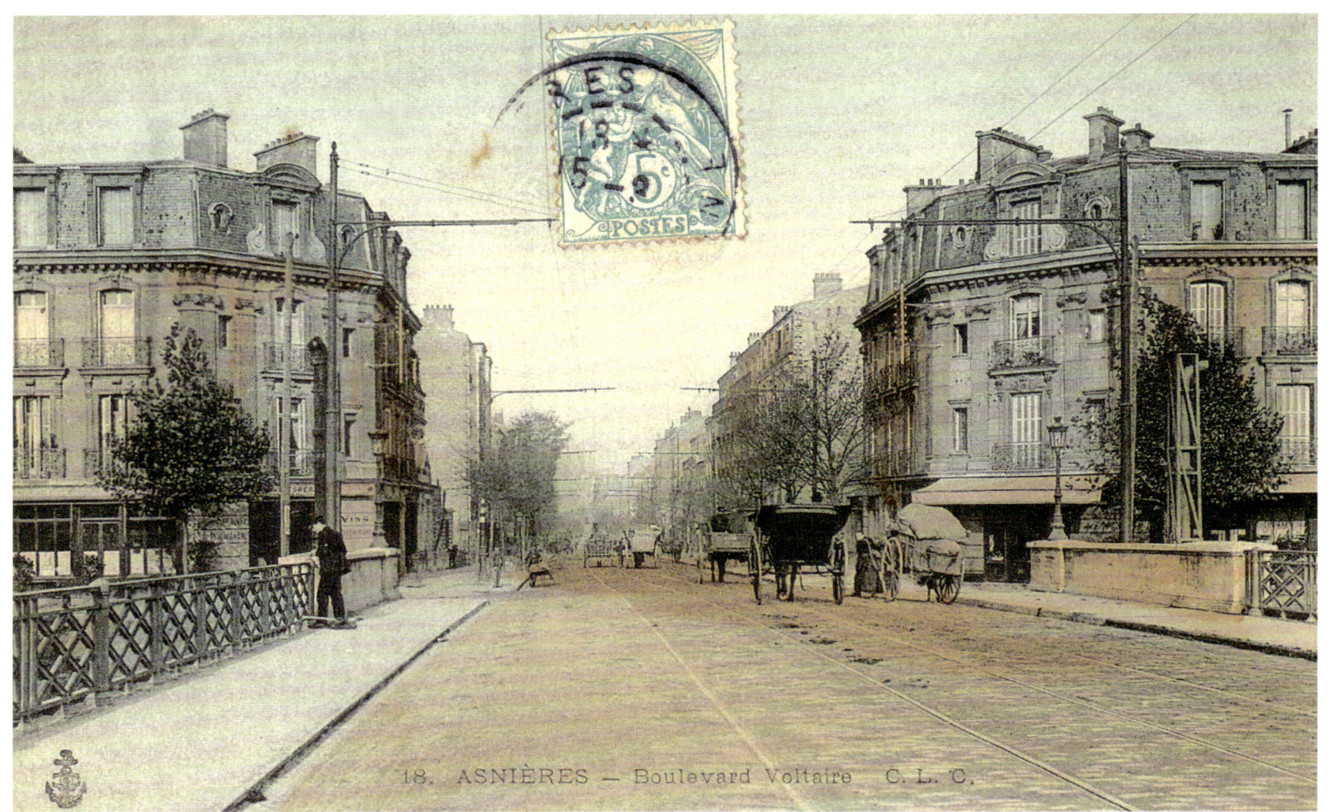

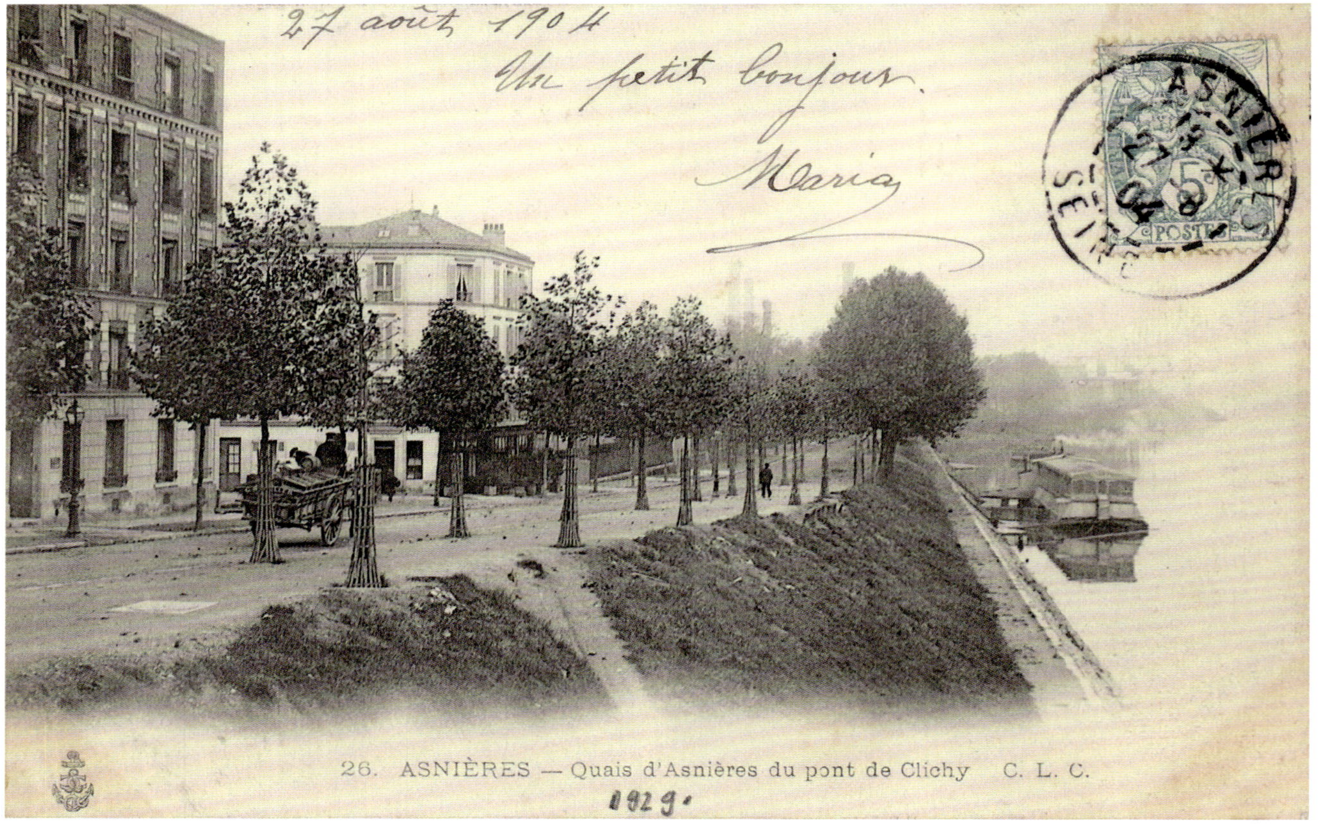

23 Asnières—*Boulevard Voltaire*, c. 1905. This view from the Pont de Clichy shows two buildings on the corners of the quai d'Asnières and boulevard Voltaire that Van Gogh depicted from a vantage point on the Ile des Ravageurs **(3)**.

24 Asnières—*Quai d'Asnières, Seen from Pont de Clichy*, c. 1900 (postmarked 1904). Van Gogh painted the laundry boat **(35)** that lay moored more or less opposite the Rispal restaurant, hidden here behind the treetops but visible in the painting by Signac, from a nearby viewpoint **(36)**.

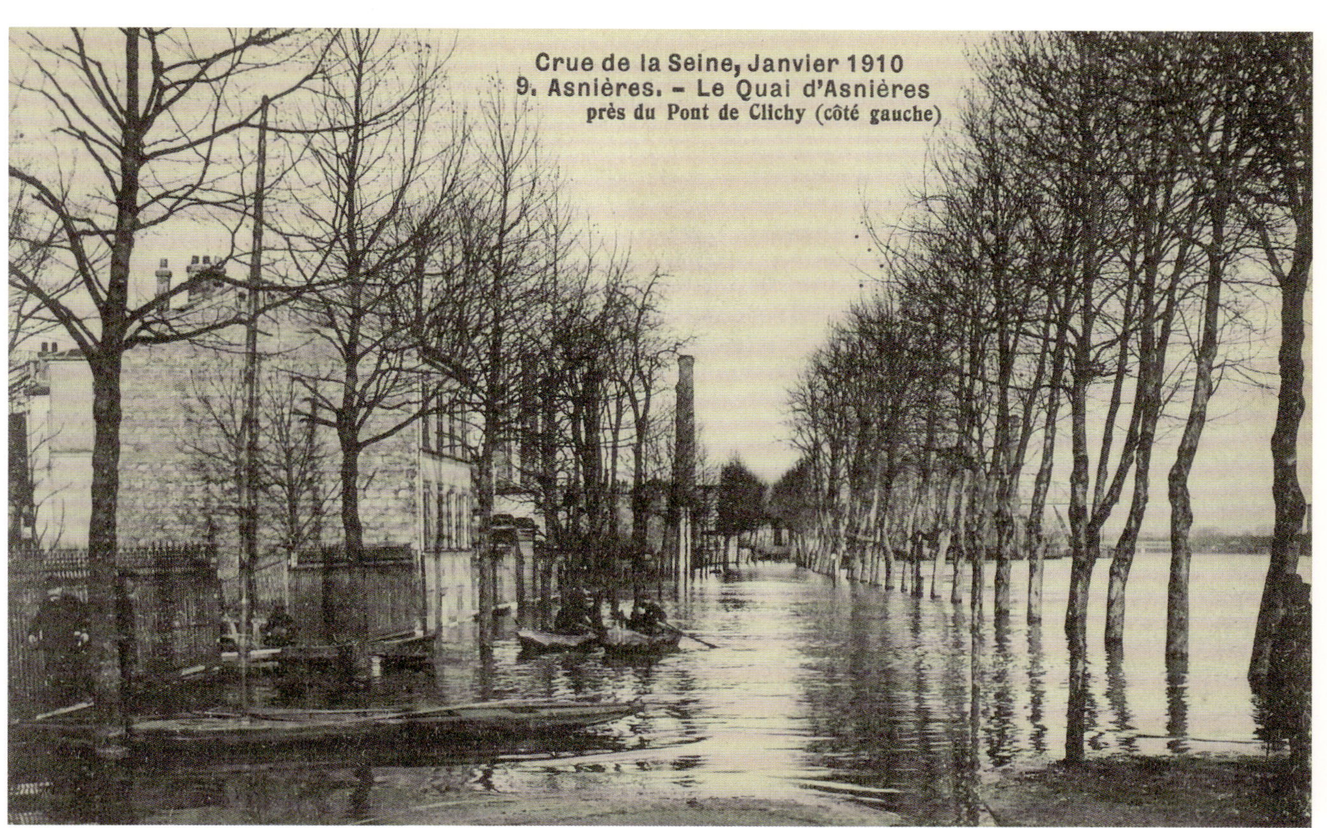

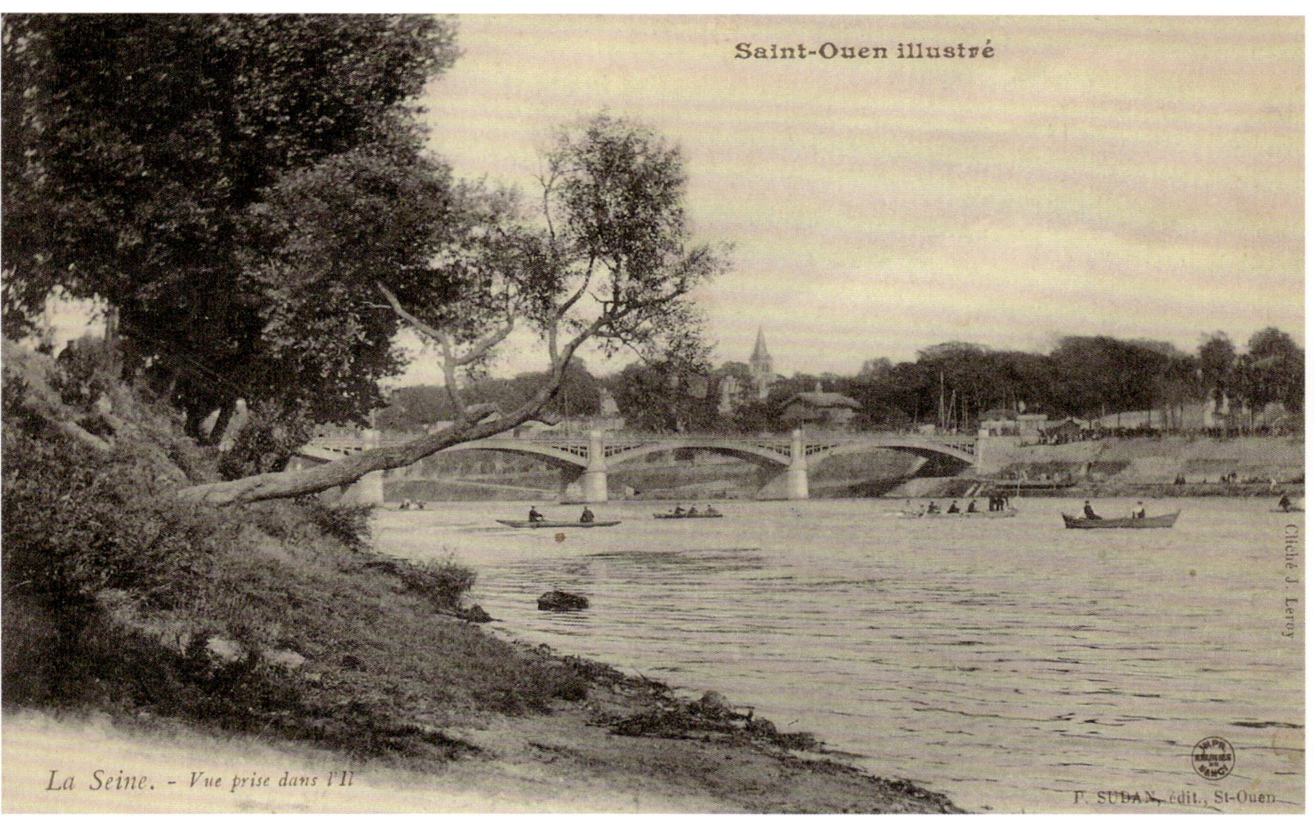

25 Asnières—*Quai d'Asnières During the Inundation of January 1910*, 1910. The building of the former Rispal restaurant on the left was painted by Signac and Van Gogh **(36,38)**.

26 Saint-Ouen—*Ile de Saint-Ouen*, c. 1905. Saint-Ouen is further upstream next to Clichy. This site is close to the spot where Bernard painted his *View of Saint-Ouen* **(110)**.

Map of Asnières

1 Verrerie du Pont de Clichy

2 Quai de Clichy and the Ile Robinson

3 Gas factory cranes

4 Port de l'usine à Gaz

5 Pont d'Asnières

6 Railroad station in Clichy-Levallois

7 Porte d'Asnières at Levallois-Perret

8 View from the Pont de la Jatte

9 Boulevard Circulaire on the Ile de la Grande Jatte

10 View from the Ile de la Grande Jatte

11 Pont Bineau, linking La Grande Jatte with Courbevoie

12 The Ferry ("Bateau-Passeur") across the Seine to Levallois-Perret

13 Along the bank of the Seine with the Pont du Chemin de Fer and Pont d'Asnières in the background

14 Pont du Chemin de Fer

15 Quai d'Asnières

16 Quai d'Asnières

17 Rue de la Station, Asnières

18 Railroad station, Bois-Colombes

19 Quai d'Asnières

20 The Port of Asnières

21 Pont de Clichy

22 Pont de Clichy

23 Boulevard Voltaire

24 Quai d'Asnières, seen from Pont de Clichy

25 Quai d'Asnières during the inundation of January 1910

26 Ile de Saint-Ouen

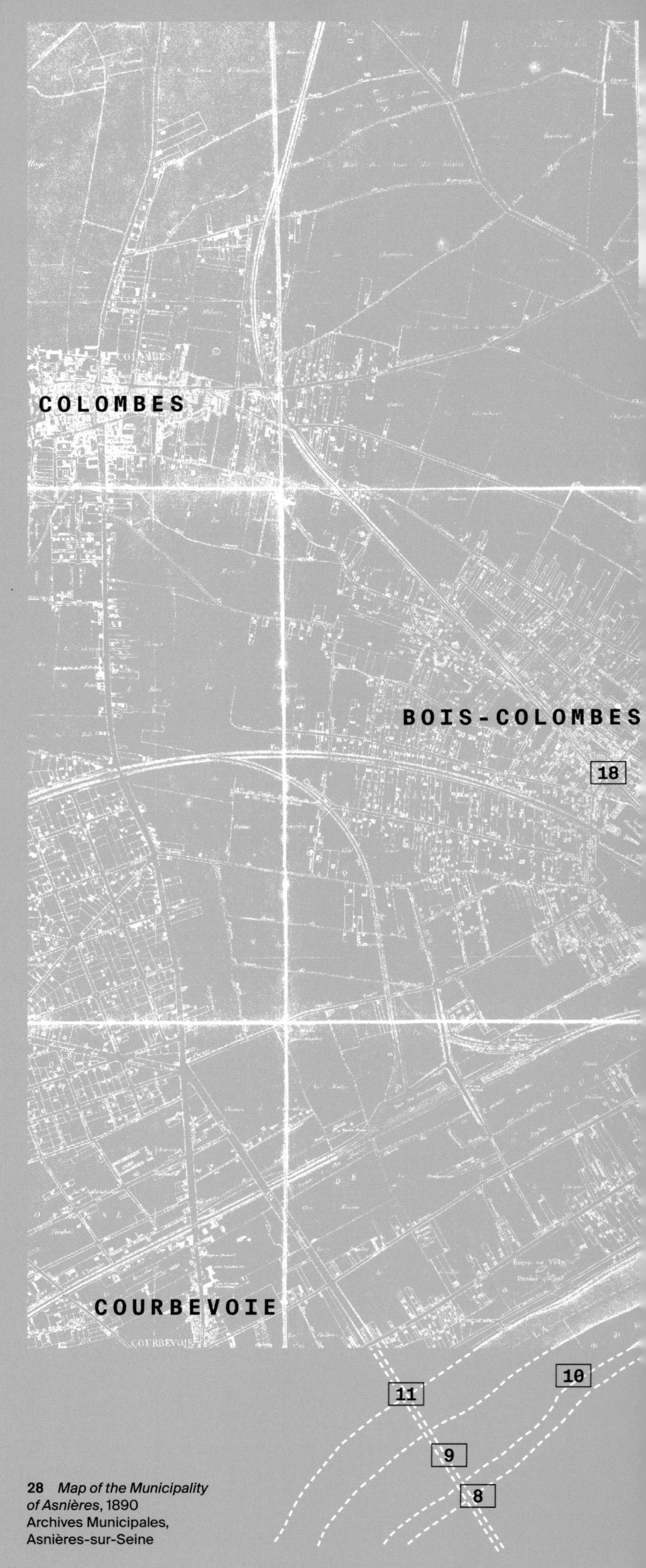

28 *Map of the Municipality of Asnières*, 1890
Archives Municipales, Asnières-sur-Seine

GENNEVILLIERS
26
Seine
25
23
21 24 22
ASNIÈRES
2
1
20
17
19
3
16
14
4
15
5
CLICHY
13
12
6

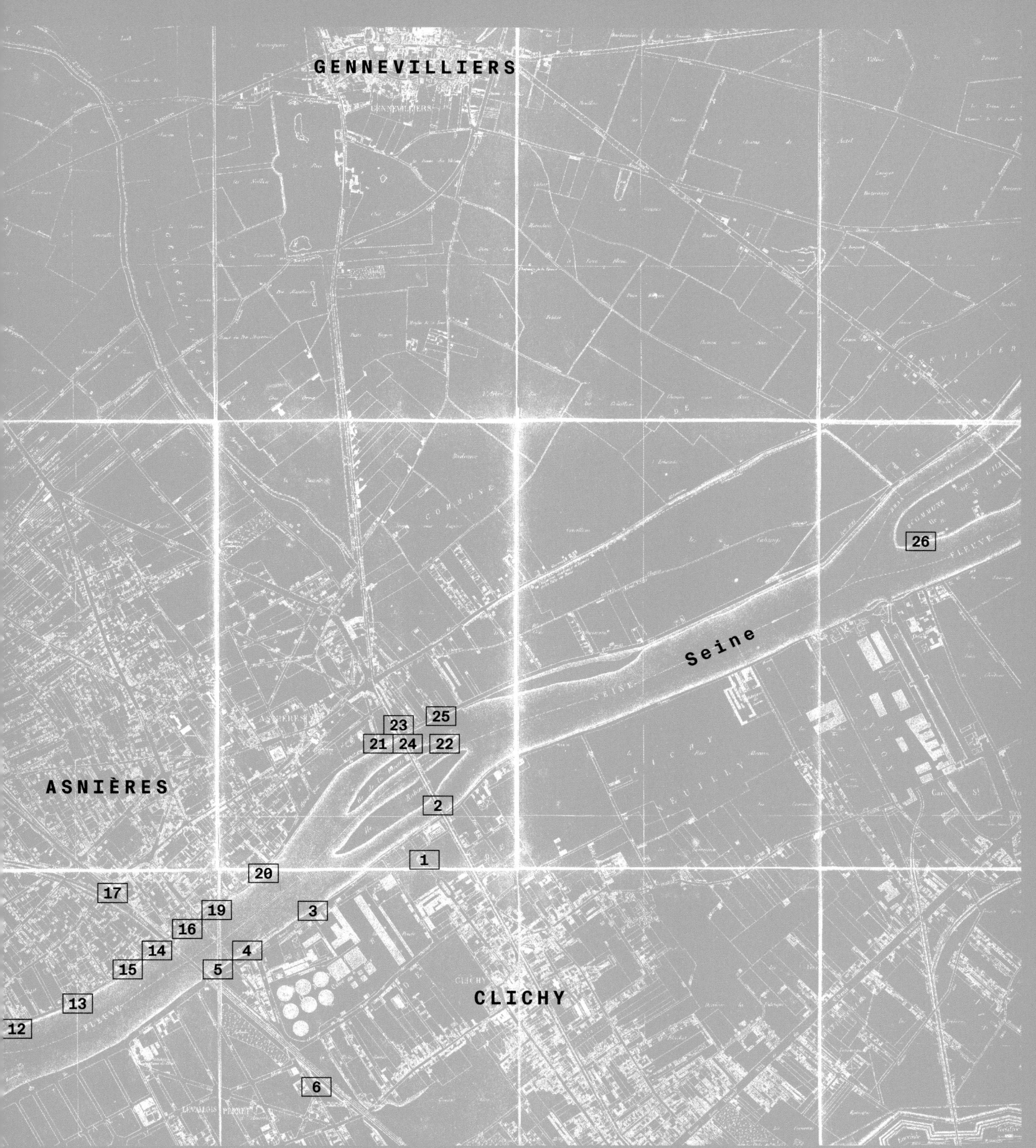

7

VAN GOGH'S PAINTING CAMPAIGN IN ASNIÈRES

BREGJE GERRITSE

Vincent van Gogh **(29)** was formally introduced to modern French art during his time in Paris from late February 1886 to February 1888. His immediate response was ambivalent, but he gradually came to embrace the new direction, which would contribute significantly to his development as a painter. The time he spent in Asnières, a village on the opposite bank of the Seine just northwest of Paris, was especially formative in a number of ways. Between early May and the end of July 1887, he walked the three miles from his home in Montmartre, a northern district in Paris characterized by the eponymous hill, almost every day, carrying his painter's gear with him. He viewed this period as a "painting campaign," in which he aimed to discover new motifs and to experiment intensively with style and color.[1] This essay is the first to study the forty or so pieces Van Gogh completed in and around Asnières as an autonomous group and compares them with the work of four contemporaries who painted at the same spots. Geographical research and examination of historical photographs and postcards have enabled more precise locations to be established for the paintings,[2] while additional information has also been discovered about Van Gogh's time in Asnières and its impact on the works he produced there—as well as his wider oeuvre.[3]

Van Gogh had been toying with the idea of going to Paris for months before he actually boarded a train for the city in 1886. Eager to improve his technique, he immediately enrolled at the studio of the history painter Fernand Cormon—who was renowned for his free style of teaching. He set to work on academic drawing and figure studies.[4] Upon his arrival in Paris Vincent moved in with his brother, Theo, who had been working as an art dealer for several years and rented an apartment on rue Laval, just below the foot of the hill of Montmartre. Moving to Paris placed Van Gogh at the epicenter of modern painting: in a little over a decade, the Impressionists had gained a foothold in the French capital with their highly colorful pictures of modern life. Painters like Claude Monet, Pierre-Auguste Renoir, and Alfred Sisley represented reality—including a great many impressions of the Seine—with a loose touch that was very different from traditional, academic painting. They positioned themselves against the style and subjects of Salon art, abandoning the dark palette of the Barbizon painters and the Hague School, which Van Gogh so admired. A new generation then arose in the 1880s that reacted in turn against the Impressionists, which resulted in surprising stylistic innovations. These artists applied unmixed, fresh colors to the canvas using an entirely new technique of dots and dashes, creating a color effect in which the viewer's eye "blended" the touches of paint optically.

Theo had been following these developments closely, but it was only now that Vincent had the opportunity to see the most modern paintings in the flesh. In 1886, he visited two important exhibitions at which this new generation of artists presented themselves to the public. At the eighth and final Impressionist show in May, he saw works by Georges Seurat and Paul Signac for the first time, along with established names like Monet and Edgar Degas. Later that summer, Van Gogh visited the Salon des

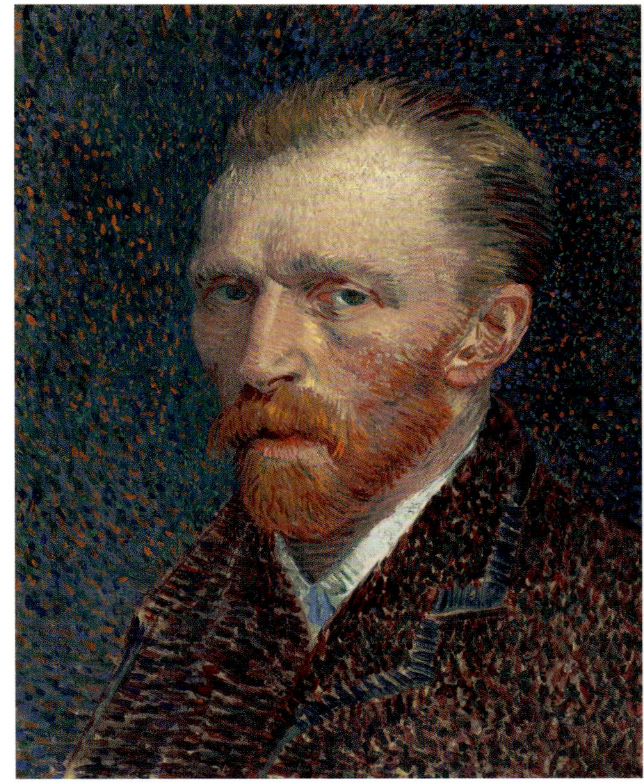

29 (cat.) Vincent van Gogh
Self-Portrait, 1887
Oil on artist's board, mounted on cradled panel, 41×32.5 cm
The Art Institute of Chicago
Joseph Winterbotham Collection

Indépendants—an important annual exhibition for innovative, avant-garde painting and a counterpart to the official Salon. The first edition was organized in 1884 by Seurat, Signac, and Charles Angrand, among others.[5] At the Indépendants in September 1886, Seurat's and Signac's works caught the eye of the art critic Félix Fénéon, who dubbed their new stippling technique "néo-impressionnisme."[6] That same month, Van Gogh wrote to a former fellow student: "In Antwerp I did not even know what the Impressionists were, now I have seen them and though *not* being one of the club, yet I have much admired certain Impressionist pictures—DEGAS, nude figure—Claude Monet, landscape."[7]

An Innovative Palette

The work Van Gogh produced during his first year in Paris mostly referenced Adolphe Monticelli's free impastoed style, which he employed in dozens of floral still lifes over the summer and in more varied work in the fall, including city parks, the windmills of Montmartre, portraits, and several more still lifes.[8] As convinced as ever of the strength of the Barbizon painters and the Hague School, Van Gogh painted tonally after their example, mixing his colors to create muted shades. However, in the latter part of the year, he began to produce more emphatically colorful works, probably in the hope that such canvases would do better on the art market.

In early June 1886, Vincent and Theo moved to an apartment on rue Lepic in Montmartre, where Van Gogh was able to set up a studio in one of the rooms. He sourced his art supplies from the store run by Julien "Père" Tanguy, where he had increasingly frequent contact with other artists and their work from the fall onward, and where he met Signac and the then eighteen-year-old Emile Bernard.[9] The latter, who became a close friend, recalled that the Dutchman "practically lived there."[10] Van Gogh also saw work by Angrand at Tanguy's store, but as far as we know he only met the artist himself once.[11] Van Gogh was a regular café-goer, along with Bernard, as well as fellow artists Henri de Toulouse-Lautrec and Louis Anquetin, whom he had met at Cormon's studio.[12] After more than six months in Paris, he was disappointed not to have sold a single work, although he had been able to connect with like-minded artists.

Van Gogh set to work with renewed enthusiasm at the beginning of the new year. He experimented more extensively with the new styles, abandoned tonal painting and accustomed himself "to a color other than gray."[13] Whether this was primarily an artistic or a commercial consideration we can only guess, but it gradually dawned on him that Hague School painters like "Israëls and Mauve, who didn't use whole colors, who always worked in gray, do not, with the greatest respect and love, satisfy the present-day longing for color."[14] Between February and the end of April, Van Gogh's application of paint grew lighter, his touch became looser and more refined, and he worked with thinned oil paint following Toulouse-Lautrec's example. Van Gogh then decided to produce work along the lines of Seurat and Signac, in which stippling in complementary colors conveyed the perception of color and light.[15] Van Gogh tentatively applied this technique around the end of March, combining it with thinned oil paint in works such as *Self-Portrait* and *View from Theo's Apartment* **(29,150)**.[16] In late April or early May, just before he left for his first painting excursion to Asnières, he made a more systematic exploration of Divisionism, doing so now in the open air.[17] He painted two works with a substantial *pointillé* element

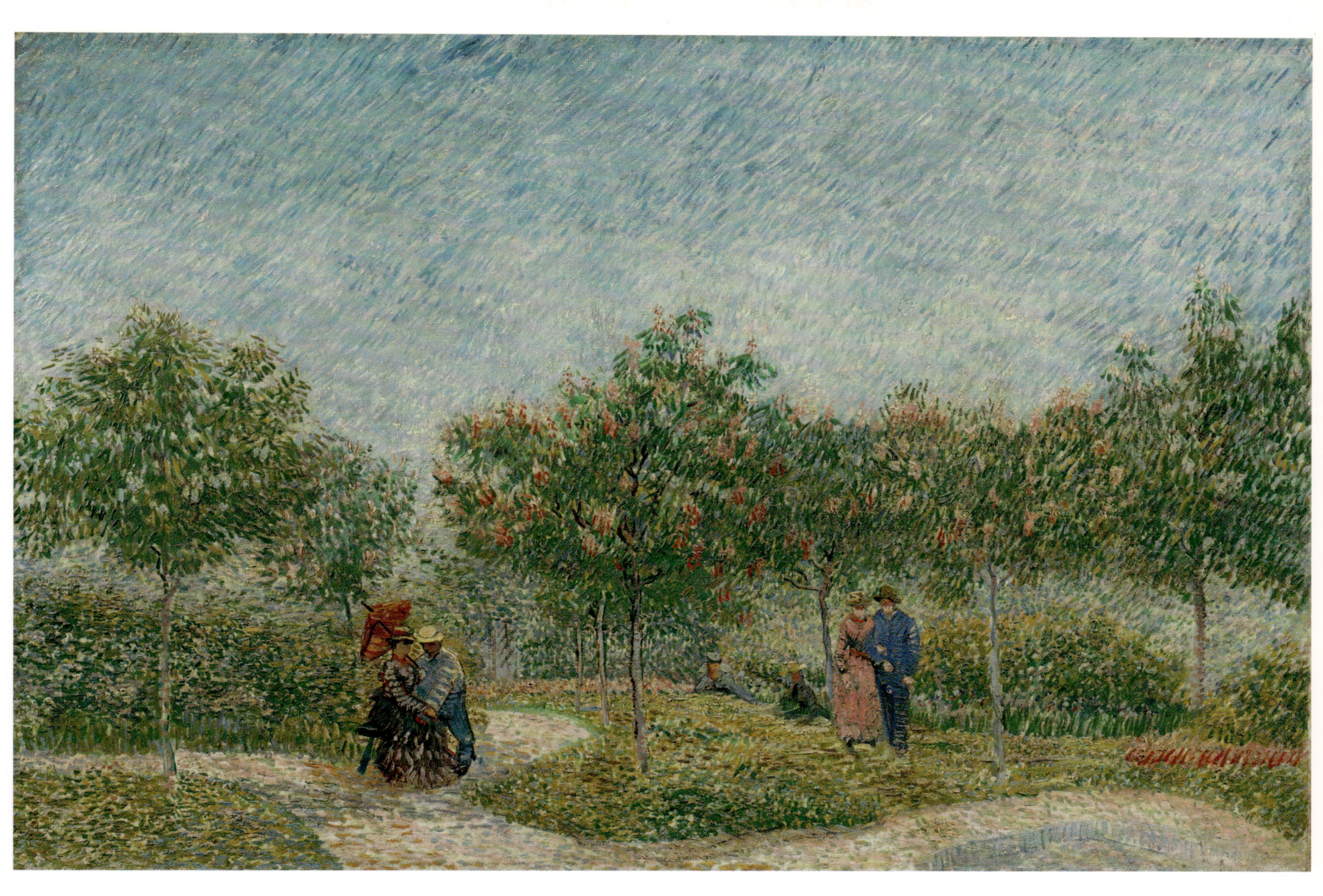

30 Vincent van Gogh
Garden with Courting Couples: Square Saint-Pierre, 1887
Oil on canvas, 75 × 113 cm
Van Gogh Museum, Amsterdam (Vincent van Gogh Foundation)

in a park in Montmartre **(30)**,[18] while his third work in the Neo-Impressionist style, *Outskirts of Paris: Road with Peasant Shouldering a Spade*, was painted outside the city—probably during one of his first reconnoiters of the area northwest of Montmartre **(31)**. The latter features Van Gogh's stock motif of a landscape with a rural worker, but now in an entirely new style. He painted a sunny meadow positioned in front of a row of blossoming chestnut trees, with a peasant with a spade crossing in front of it. The Pointillist dots are applied across almost the entire canvas, with particular attention given to the trees and sky. Of the works he made on the outskirts of Paris, this is one of the largest.[19] He often preferred smaller formats from this time on, probably because they were easier to carry.[20] Despite Van Gogh's fascination with the color effects of juxtaposed dots and dashes of unblended paint, he did not take these experiments any further once he had completed his three ambitious stippled canvases. For his part, Bernard had already rejected the style, although he stated in 1886 that "I did various views of Asnières using the process."[21] Van Gogh remained positive about it—"Signac and the others who are doing pointillism often make very beautiful things with it"[22]—but in the end it was not really a technique that suited him.[23]

Idyll by the Seine

By May 1887, Van Gogh had been living in Paris for more than a year. As a country boy by upbringing, city life could be tough for him at times. Finding himself in need of fresh air and frustrated by his deteriorating relationship with his brother, he planned to travel south to escape the city and paint on location. This was something Theo had been anticipating: in a letter to his mother in late February 1887 he complained that "he's [Vincent's] still here and doesn't seem to be planning to go away in the spring as he had originally planned to do."[24] By the end of April, however, the brothers seem to have patched things up: "we have made

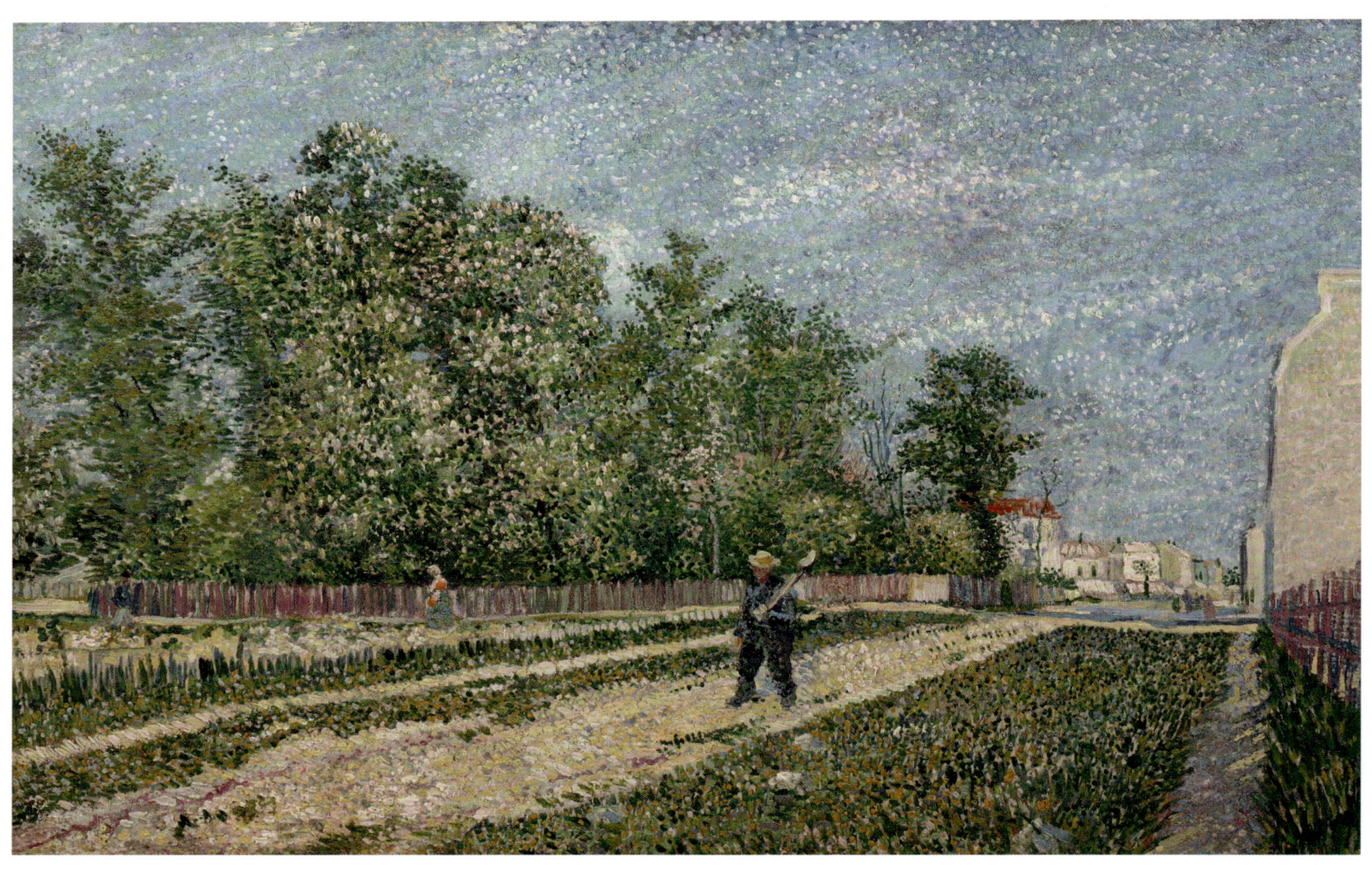

31 (cat.) Vincent van Gogh
Outskirts of Paris: Road with Peasant Shouldering a Spade, 1887
Oil on canvas, 47×71.6 cm
Private collection, Larry Ellison

peace," Theo wrote to their sister Willemien.[25] Something else—most likely a purely artistic impulse—must therefore have prompted Van Gogh's decision to embark on a "painting campaign" in Asnières.

Van Gogh's interest in Divisionist works and in shifting his working terrain to Asnières at the beginning of May 1887 was likely fired by the third exhibition of the Société des Artistes Indépendants, which ran from March 26 to May 3.[26] Neo-Impressionist paintings executed around Asnières were amply represented there, giving Van Gogh the opportunity to see Seurat's works featuring the Pont de Courbevoie, Signac's paintings and drawings with the "Ponton de la Félicité" and the gasometers at Clichy, and Angrand's canvas painted at La Grande Jatte **(79,152, 91)**.[27] Such works had not appealed to him when he saw them a year earlier, but his reaction now was very different.[28] He clearly drew inspiration in this period from both the stylistic innovation and the geographical location.[29] Van Gogh himself did not show at the Indépendants for the first time until 1888; up to that point he had not taken part in any exhibition, group or solo, official or unofficial.[30] He must have realized that without visibility there would be no possibility of selling his works.[31] After visiting the exhibition, he must also have hoped that he, too, would be able to avail himself of the opportunities Seurat, Signac, and Angrand had found on the banks of the Seine northwest of Paris.

For all their innovative style, the Neo-Impressionists were in fact following the example of the Impressionists, who had popularized scenes of the Seine in the 1870s. Painters like Monet and Renoir had taken the train from Paris to spots further downstream, such as Argenteuil, Louveciennes, and Chatou. Their colorful "impressions" captured river views and leisure activities on the Seine itself and along its quays. They also occasionally depicted the latest industrial architecture.[32] A new generation of artists now sought similar motifs, which they found at a different location an hour's walk from Paris, on the opposite bank of the Seine in and around Asnières.[33] The construction of a railroad bridge over the river in 1837 had turned the place into a popular destination for Parisian day-trippers. It was a place of contrasts: the somber factory buildings of Clichy and Levallois were clearly visible from the Asnières waterfront, with its restaurants and terraces, and from neighboring Courbevoie, home to thriving boating activities and Sunday entertainments.

It is not entirely coincidental that so many modern artists ended up working around Asnières. Seurat and Angrand, meanwhile, lived and worked in Montmartre, around the boulevard de Clichy, as did Van Gogh, from where it was a relatively short walk to various idyllic spots.[34] Signac, for instance, already lived in Asnières, having moved there with his mother in 1880 at the age of sixteen after the death of his father. His very first paintings date from the following year, and were mostly executed locally.[35] Emile Bernard was also sixteen when he moved from Paris to Asnières with his family in 1884.[36] The two painters met in March 1886 at an exhibition of Bernard's work in Asnières, where Bernard visited Signac's studio.[37] Seurat also painted the Asnières area early on, for example his studies for a large canvas with bathers in 1883 **(63,64,65)**. He met Signac and Angrand at the first Indépendants exhibition in 1884, where he showed his monumental *Bathers at Asnières* **(66)**.[38] The three became good friends—unusually so for Seurat, who was not a gregarious type.[39] Only four years later did Seurat and Van Gogh meet in Paris in the fall of 1887, but this did not result in a close friendship. As the Frenchman recalled: "I was less intimately acquainted with Van Gogh."[40] Angrand painted on the Ile des Ravageurs near Asnières, and around Saint-Ouen and Clichy, no doubt influenced by Seurat. He worked with the latter in Courbevoie, which resulted in two impressive paintings with the same motif **(134,135)**.[41] In other words, Van Gogh's decision to paint near Asnières was in line with what might be called a trend among Parisian avant-garde painters at the time. The area had plenty of appeal, as the writer Jacques-Emile Blanche later concluded: "It was the fashion to go and sketch around the fortifications, the factories at Suresnes, and the island of La Grande Jatte."[42]

"My campaign in Asnières last spring"

It is hard to pin down precisely when Van Gogh produced his first works in and around Asnières, but there are several clues. In addition to the previously quoted reference to "Asnières last spring," Van Gogh told his sister he had been working there "this summer."[43] Experts previously assumed that he was active in Asnières from mid-May to the end of July, but it seems more likely that he was there somewhat earlier. Although his letters do not reveal much, we can glean a little more through his contact with Signac during this period. Signac told Van Gogh's biographer Gustave Coquiot: "Yes, I knew Van Gogh from Père Tanguy's. I met him on other occasions at Asnières and Saint-Ouen; we painted on the banks of the river; lunched at the *guinguette* [a small café], and returned to Paris on foot, along the avenues of Saint-Ouen and Clichy. Van Gogh wore a blue zinc worker's smock and had painted dots of color on the sleeves. He stuck right by me, shouting, gesticulating, and brandishing his large size-30 canvas, so that he spread wet paint onto himself and the passers-by."[44]

Signac left for the south of France on May 23, 1887, so his collaboration with Van Gogh must have occurred before that date.[45] An important reason for dating Van Gogh's campaign in Asnières to mid-May is that Van Gogh told his brother in a letter that "when I started working at Asnières I had lots of canvases and Tanguy was very good to me."[46] He had an agreement with the supplier in which he traded finished paintings for materials, including canvases. Previously, when he ran short of supports, Van Gogh had painted over earlier canvases from his time in Nuenen, in the south of the Netherlands. His arrangement with Tanguy enabled him to paint on fresh supports. No canvases had been previously identified as reused from the beginning of the Asnières period. Ella Hendriks and Louis van Tilborgh concluded that Van Gogh continued to reuse canvases until the middle of May, as overpainted works have been identified and dated to the early weeks of that month. A work has recently been discovered, however, that was painted over an earlier painting in Asnières in May **(38)**. Van Gogh's use of the word "printemps" and Signac's account suggest that he might already have been working in Asnières shortly before his arrangement with Tanguy—by late April, perhaps, but certainly from the beginning of May.[47] The end of the campaign, meanwhile, has been dated, based on the assumption that he would not have worked in both Montmartre and Asnières simultaneously, because he was accustomed to working in one location at a time. The ambitious Montmartre works from the summer were painted in late July and August.[48] We can thus conclude with reasonable certainty that it was during the months of May, June, and July that Van Gogh experimented with new motifs and styles in and around Asnières. Like his fellow painters, he also worked in neighboring Courbevoie, in industrial Clichy, with Levallois-Perret and Saint-Ouen on either side, and on the river islands of La Grande Jatte, the Ile des Ravageurs, and the Ile Robinson.

As far as we know, Van Gogh produced some forty works in the course of his three-month campaign, meaning that he completed a study or a painting more or less every two days. The drawings and paintings depict the bridges, quays, restaurants, islands, and landscapes from the Asnières area. Unfortunately, our view of the Asnières works is incomplete. Several canvases from the period have been lost because Van Gogh later painted over them. *Trees* (Van Gogh Museum, Amsterdam, F 307), for example, was very likely painted over a canvas of the Seine.[49] It is possible that future technical research could uncover additional, currently unknown Asnières works. A drawing with a sailboat, meanwhile, appears to be a study for a painting that is now unknown or which he never actually executed **(32)**. Van Gogh meticulously noted the colors in pencil for various elements: "vert bleu" for the water, "jaune" for the quayside, "celeste-orange" next to the boat, "cobalt" for the boat itself, and "violet" for the reflection of the vessel in the Seine.[50]

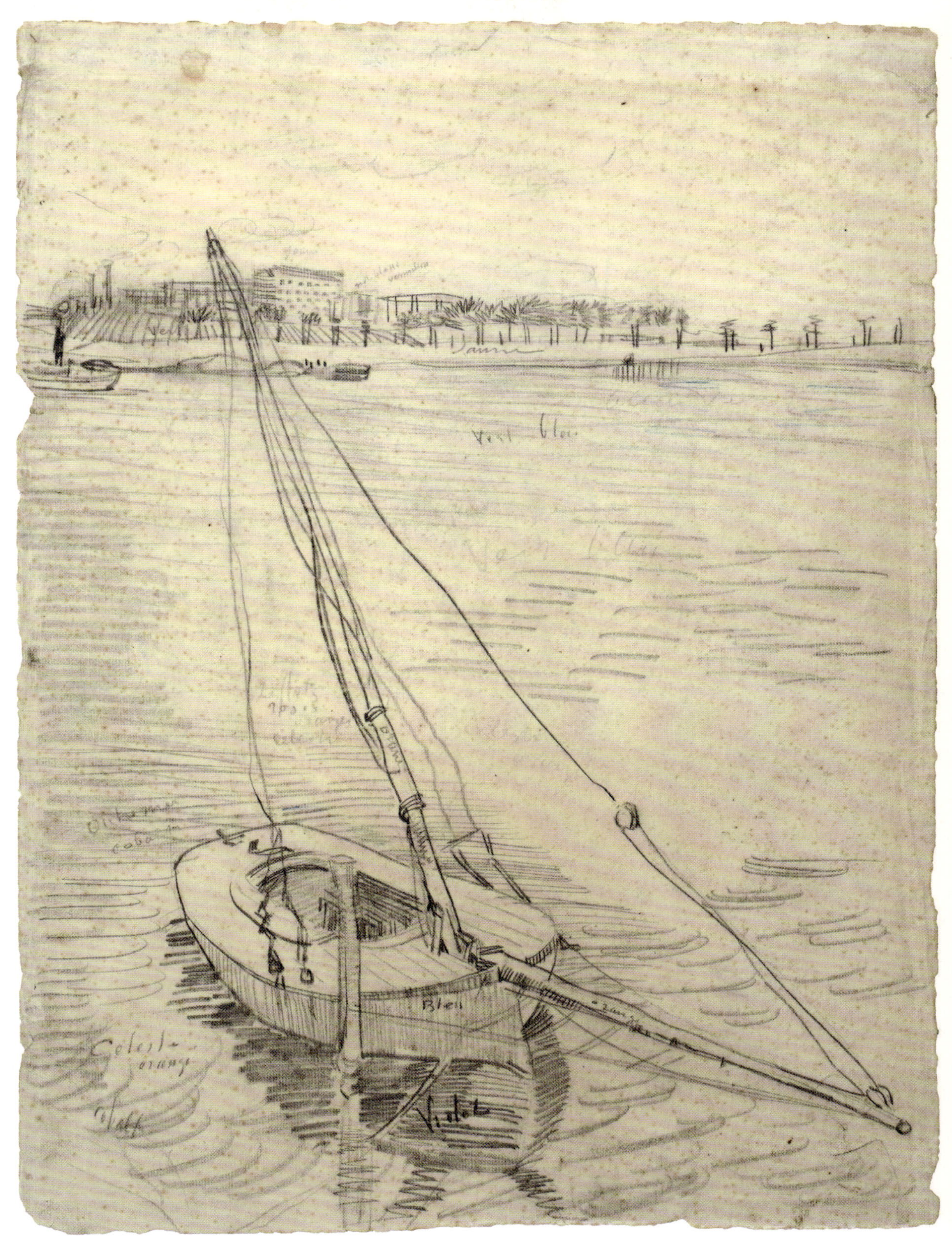

32 (cat.) Vincent van Gogh
Sailing Boat on the Seine at Asnières, 1887
Pencil and chalk on paper, 53.8×39.5 cm
Van Gogh Museum, Amsterdam (Vincent van Gogh Foundation)

Because of the short time frame and the paucity of evidence, few works can be dated with any greater precision within those three months, although several conveniently sized studies suggest the exploration of a new location. Van Gogh had seen Seurat's painting of the Pont Bineau—the bridge linking Courbevoie to the island of La Grande Jatte—at the Indépendants **(79)**, and he then adopted the same bridge as his own subject. The painting is notable for its graphic brushwork, made up of vertical strokes. With small blocks and dashes in bright colors, he offers his own interpretation of the Neo-Impressionist style **(34)**.[51] He painted *Bank of the Seine* in a similar fashion **(33)**. The avant-garde artists had shown Van Gogh a new direction: "And when I painted landscape in Asnières this summer I saw more color in it than before."[52]

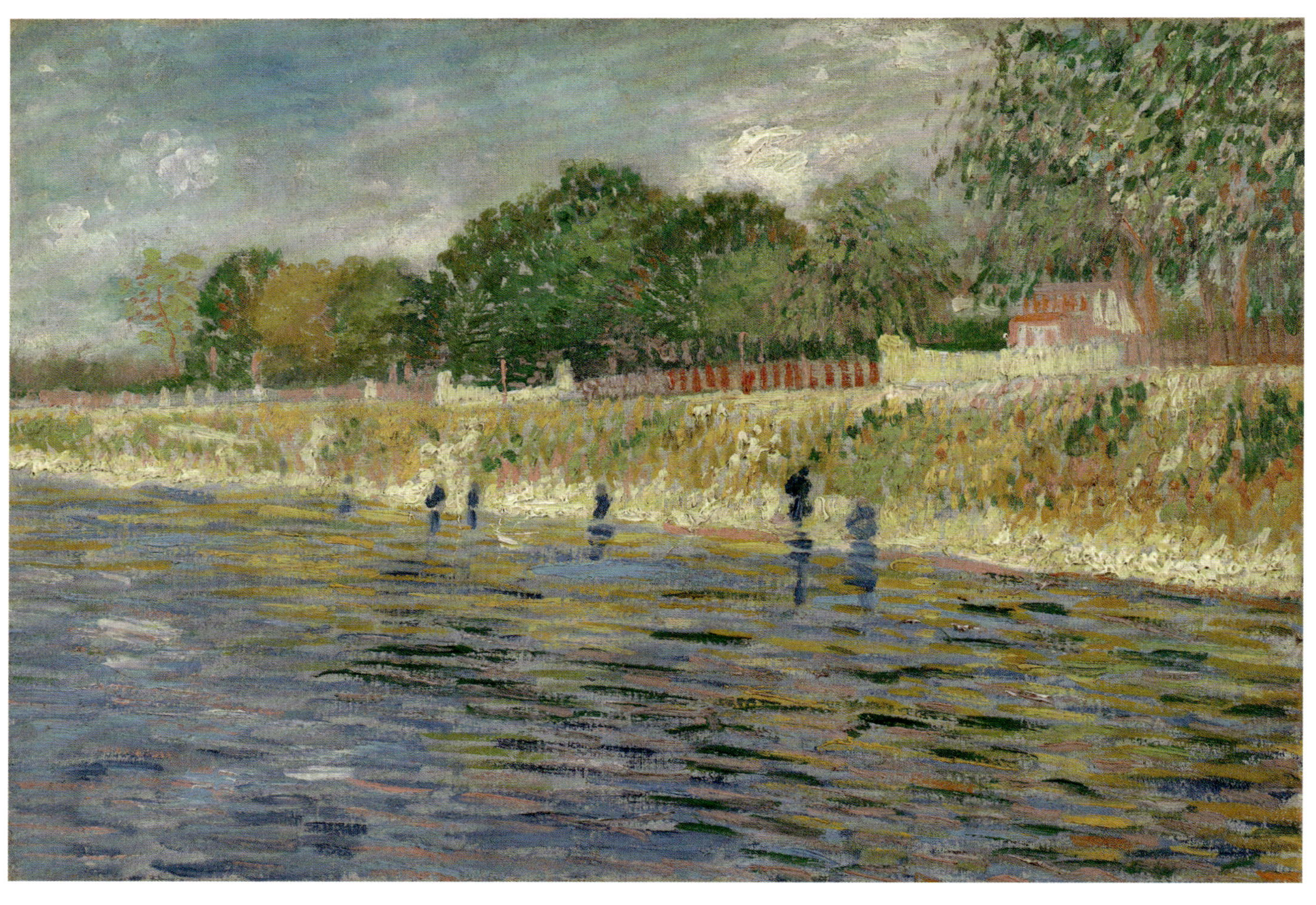

33 (cat.) Vincent van Gogh
Bank of the Seine, 1887
Oil on canvas, 32×46 cm
Van Gogh Museum, Amsterdam (Vincent van Gogh Foundation)

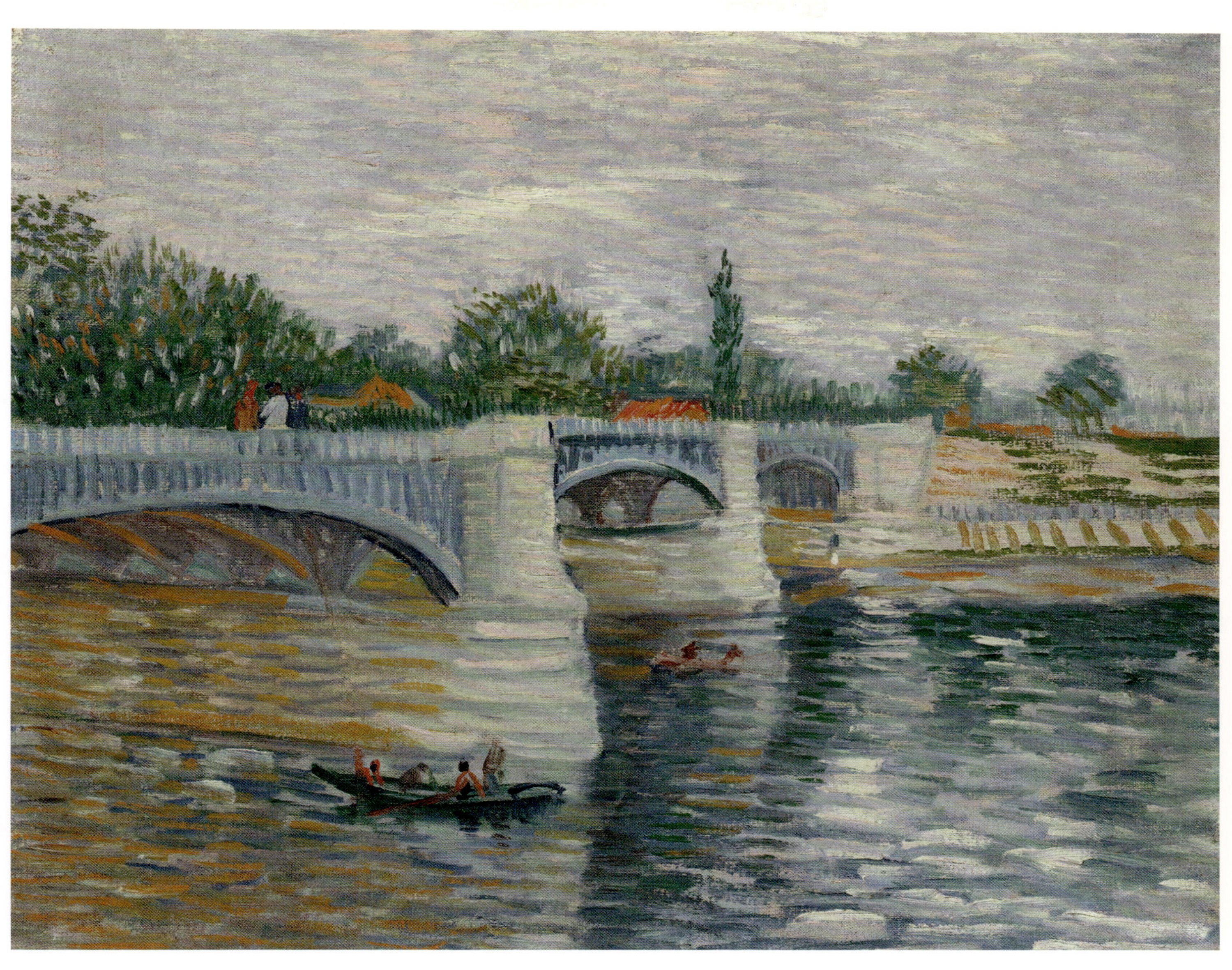

34 (cat.) Vincent van Gogh
The Bridge at Courbevoie, 1887
Oil on canvas, 32.1×40.5 cm
Van Gogh Museum, Amsterdam (Vincent van Gogh Foundation)

Landscapes and Entertainment

Van Gogh painted three small works in precisely the same horizontal format of approximately 19 by 27 cm: *Exterior of a Restaurant in Asnières* **(37)**, *The Laundry Boat on the Seine at Asnières* **(35)**, and *Kingfisher by the Waterside* (1887, Van Gogh Museum, Amsterdam).[53] He might well have had in mind Seurat's *croquetons*—rapid oil sketches—that had been shown at exhibitions.[54] Seurat was known for making these sketchy little paintings on wooden boards measuring around 16 by 25 cm, producing more than seventy at the time.[55] Van Gogh painted *The Laundry Boat on the Seine at Asnières* on a small scale, even though the vessel was actually more than forty meters in length. The boat had been taken over by a couple called Lebreton in 1885 and was moored a hundred and fifty meters from the Pont de Clichy on the quai d'Asnières.[56] The work is executed in loose, impastoed strokes, with bright red accents in the complementary green of the grass and in the boat that stand out from an otherwise somewhat muted palette. Van Gogh, working *en plein air*, used elongated vertical touches to capture the reflection of the floating laundry boat on the water. As in many of his paintings, two figures are visible, although they are laid down so sketchily that the human presence is almost indiscernible. Signac too had depicted the Lebretons' laundry boat two years earlier, viewed from the Pont de Clichy **(36)**. Van Gogh used the same small format for his painting of a restaurant facade **(37)**. The palette must originally have looked fresher, with a bright orange foreground. This vibrant palette is no longer visible, however, because of discoloration over time. Given the matching planters by the door, there is a chance that this is the Restaurant de la Sirène, located right next to the Pont d'Asnières, which Van Gogh must have passed many times coming from Paris. He depicted the restaurant in three other works: two larger format paintings and a drawing **(22,23,49)**.[57]

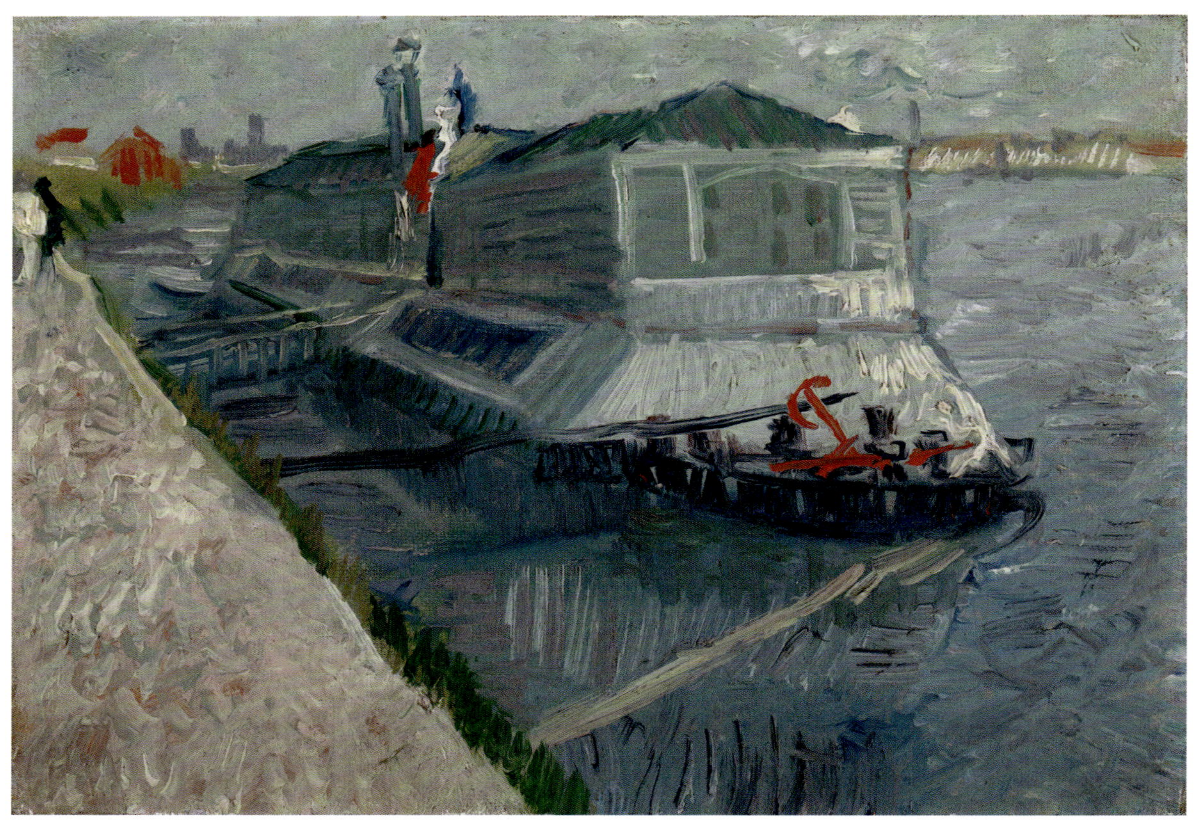

35 (cat.) Vincent van Gogh
The Laundry Boat on the Seine at Asnières, 1887
Oil on canvas, 19.1 × 27 cm
Virginia Museum of Fine Arts, Richmond
Collection of Mr. and Mrs. Paul Mellon

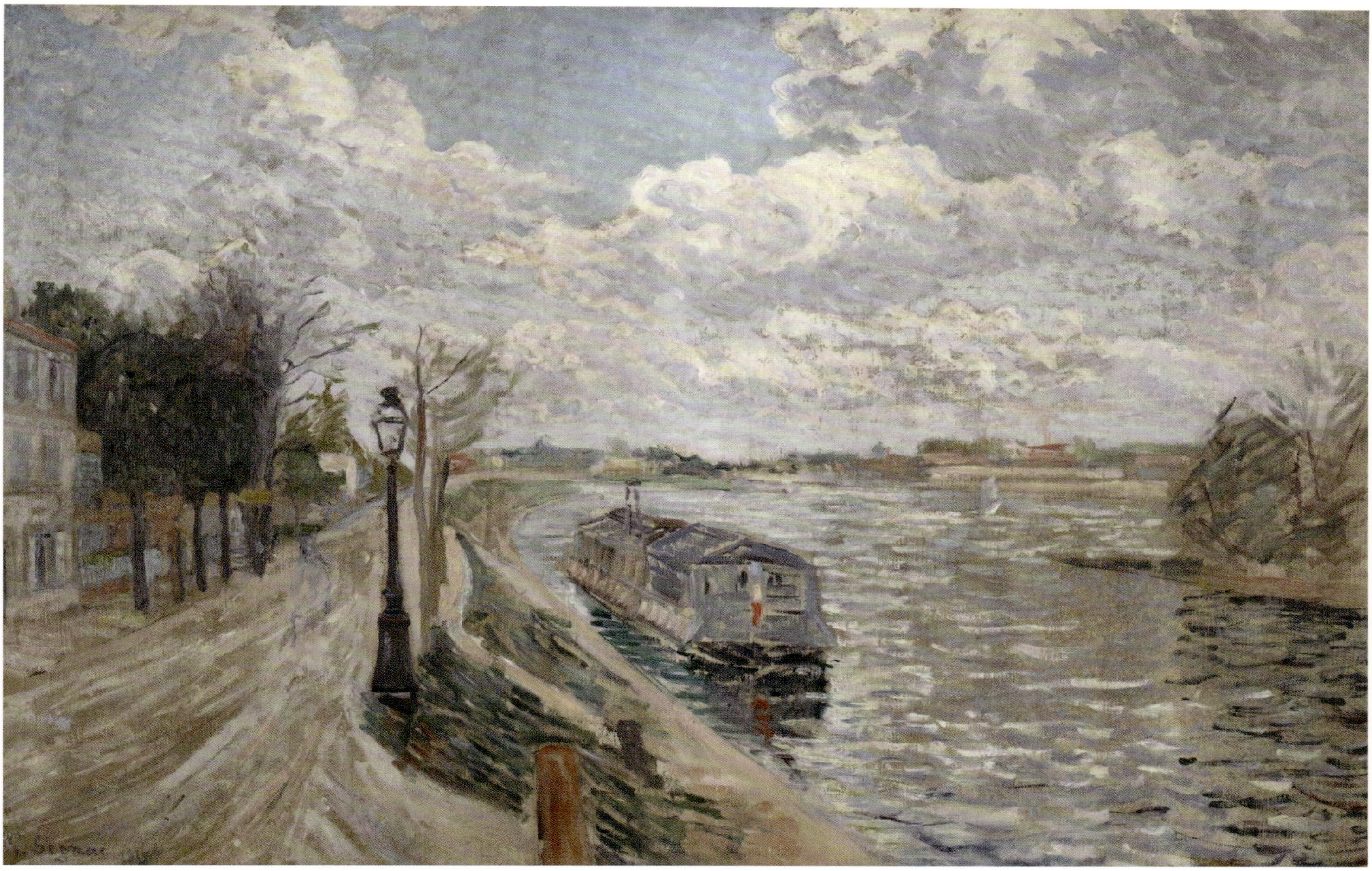

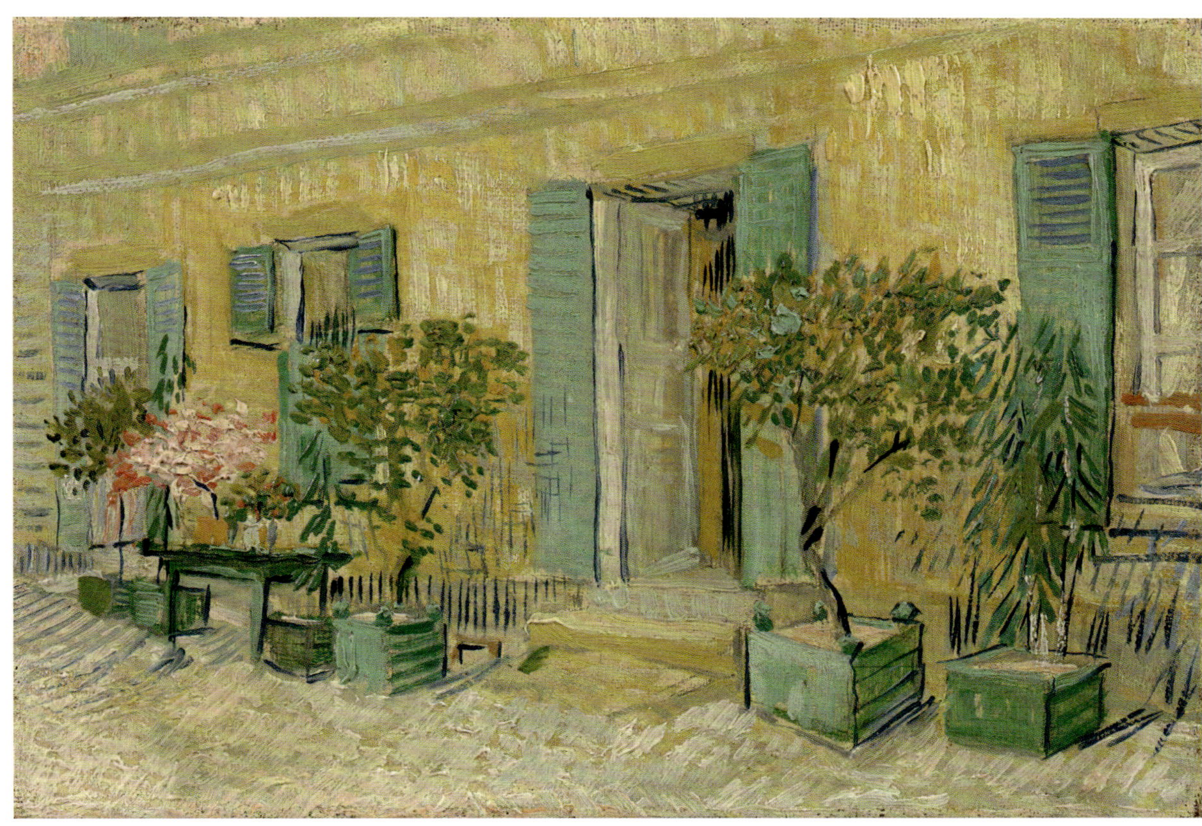

36 (cat.) Paul Signac
Quai de Saint-Ouen, 1885
Oil on canvas, 60 × 92 cm
Private collection

37 (cat.) Vincent van Gogh
Exterior of a Restaurant in Asnières, 1887
Oil on canvas, 18.8 × 27 cm
Van Gogh Museum, Amsterdam (Vincent van Gogh Foundation)

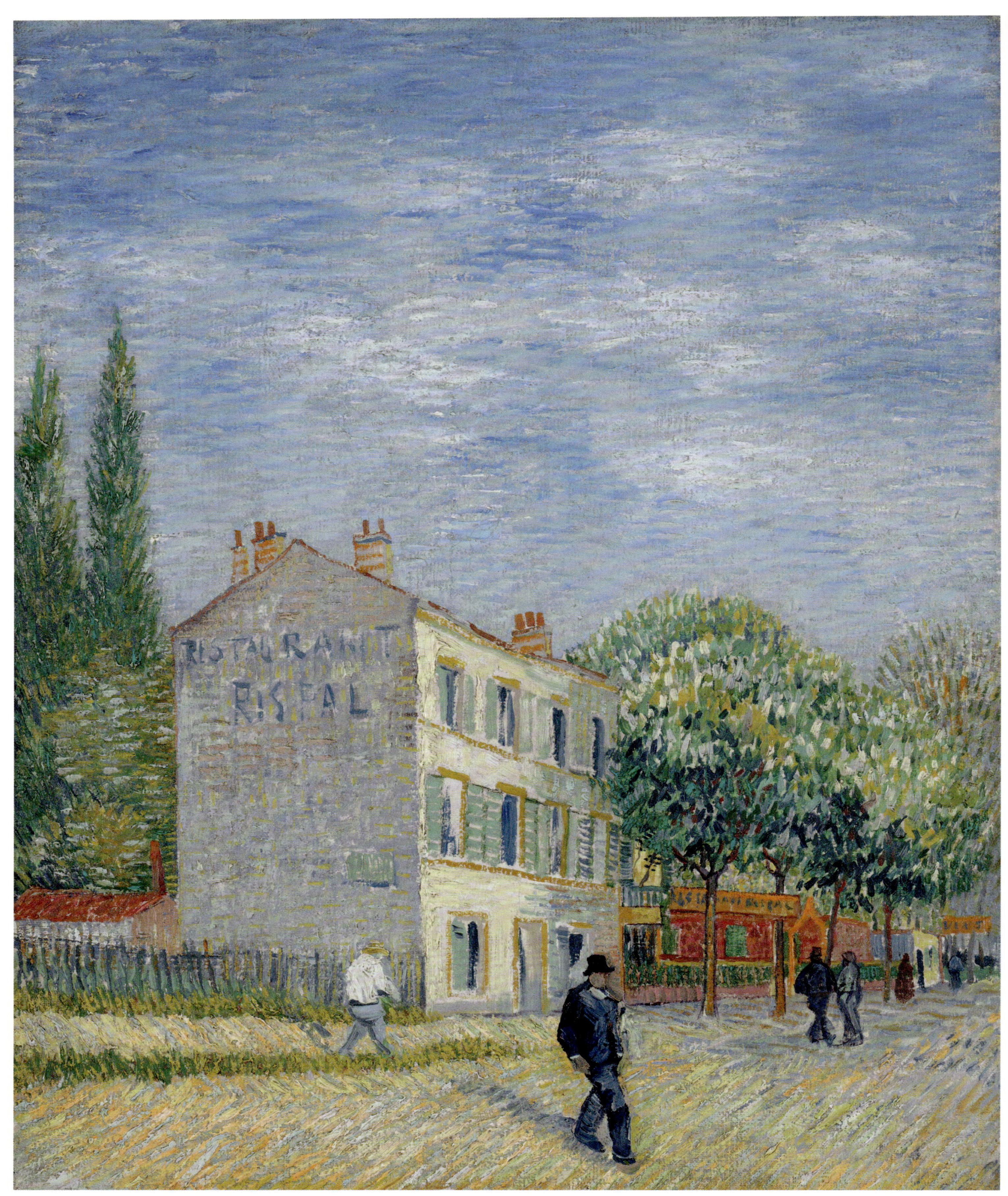

38 (cat.) Vincent van Gogh
Restaurant Rispal at Asnières, 1887
Oil on canvas, 73.3 × 60 cm
The Nelson-Atkins Museum of Art, Kansas City, Missouri
Gift of Henry W. and Marion H. Bloch, 2015.13.10

Van Gogh's largest Asnières painting also features a restaurant, the Rispal at 117 quai de Seine, behind the Pont de Clichy **(38)**.[58] The building is positioned prominently in the scene, surrounded by green trees in blossom. The artist achieves a complementary contrast by using red in the facades further along, as well as in a small building lower right. Various figures walk along the street. As we will see, there was a third restaurant, run by "Père" Perruchot, that Van Gogh must have known well, and a fourth can be identified in a photograph of Van Gogh and Bernard **(113)**, as well as in four works by Bernard **(109,111,112,114)**.[59] The front of the latter is shown in the photograph inscribed with the words "VINS RESTAURANT." It can now be identified for the first time as the premises of the Courbevoie wine merchant Huybert Tericeux, located at 6 quai de Seine.[60]

Van Gogh also painted a spontaneous view of *Bank of the Seine with Boats* **(39)**. Working from the edge of the opposite bank, he depicted a red sloop with an unobtrusive small red rowboat in front of it. Bright touches alternate in a colorful pattern that conveys the reflection in the water. The precise location cannot be determined, but the work must have been painted at a very narrow point in the river, such as that around the two islands between Clichy and Asnières or the narrower "Bras de Neuilly" of the Seine, close to the island of La Grande Jatte. Van Gogh would have been looking from one of the islands toward the village opposite.

Another location he painted several times is linked to a noteworthy encounter he had in Asnières. Three canvases include two identical buildings constructed in the late

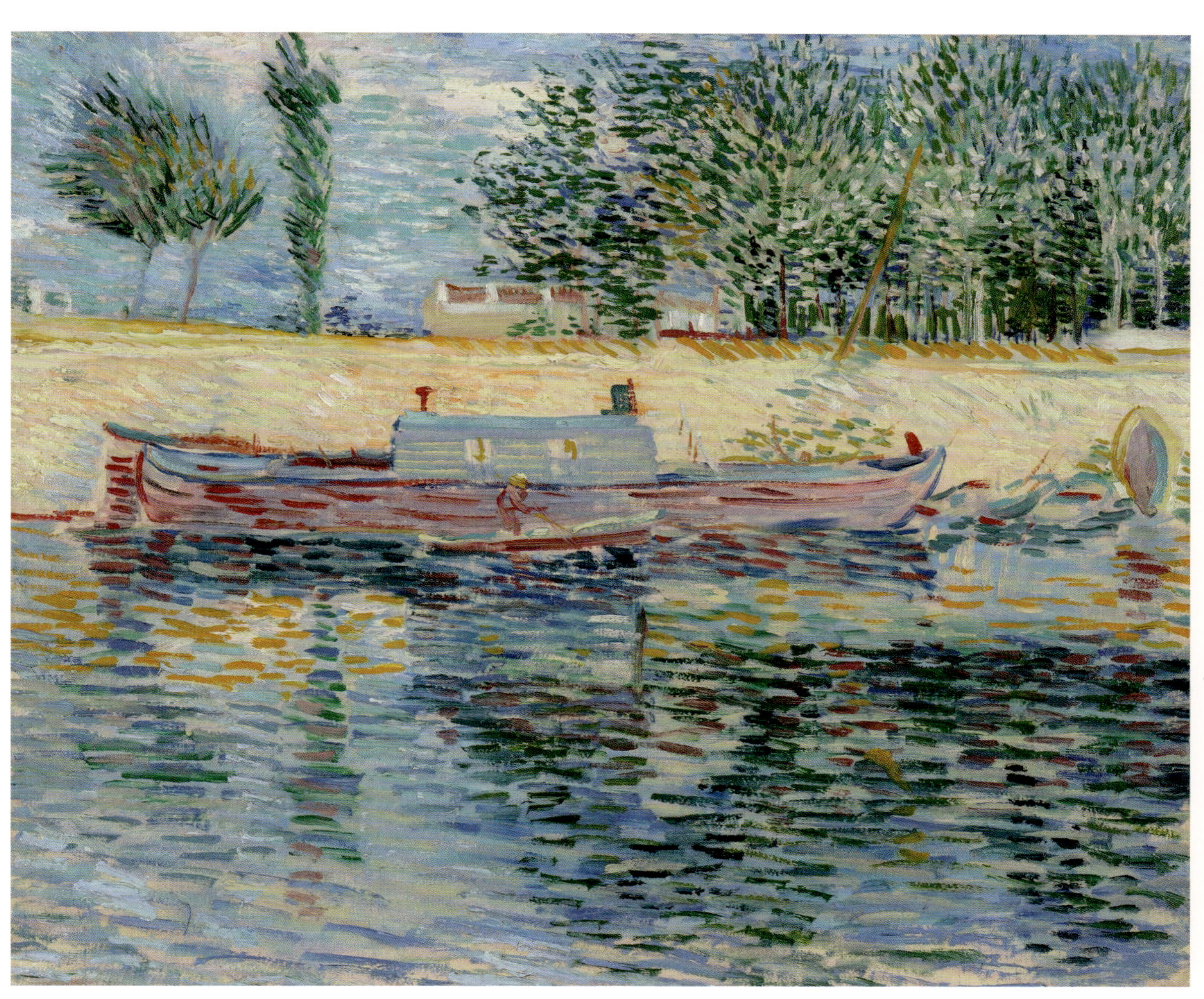

39 (cat.) Vincent van Gogh
Bank of the Seine with Boats, 1887
Oil on canvas, 48 × 55 cm
Private collection

1850s on either side of boulevard Voltaire, which led to the Pont de Clichy. Van Gogh experimented freely in each work with diagonals and perspective, portraying it from a different angle in each instance **(2,3,4)**. The woman who lived in this building seems to have known the Dutchman well, as suggested by a letter from Vincent to Theo dated May 20, 1888: "Tuesday, [Christian Mourier-Petersen] will give you 2 small paintings—nothing much—that I'd like to give to Mme the Countess De la Boissière at Asnières. She stays in boulevard Voltaire, on the first floor of the first house at the end of the Clichy bridge. *Père* Perruchot's restaurant is on the ground floor. Would you take them to her personally on my behalf, saying I had hopes of seeing her again this spring and that even here I haven't forgotten her; I gave them 2 small ones last year as well, her and her daughter. I'd have hope that you wouldn't regret making these ladies' acquaintance. After all, they're *a family.* The countess is far from young but she's first of all a countess, then *a lady*, the daughter ditto."[61]

Countess Clara Le Vaillant de La Boissière—whose full name we know thanks to Ronald Pickvance—kept an apartment on the first floor above Marcellin Perruchot's restaurant at 1 boulevard de Clichy.[62] Pickvance suggests that the two might have had a relationship, but this seems implausible, although it is possible that Van Gogh occasionally left his painting materials at the apartment or even spent the night there.[63]

In the Wake of the Impressionists

Van Gogh's compositions grew more modern over time and made increasing use of elements from the Japanese prints he had begun to collect in the winter of 1886–87.[64] In *Bank with Trees*, for instance, he opted for a dramatic close-up of the riverbank, probably on the northern edge of the Ile des Ravageurs on the Asnières side **(4)**. The two distinctive buildings on boulevard Voltaire described above are painted in the background.[65] Van Gogh had noted in the work of the Impressionists that a white ground layer instilled a canvas with more light and brightness, and so he began increasingly to use the same device.[66] Monet, whose work Theo had recently shown at his branch of the art dealers Boussod, Valadon et Cie, must have been one such example, and Monet's style can be detected in the use of a light primer and airy brushstrokes in Van Gogh's *By the Seine* **(40)**. The open character of the study ensures that the white ground layer, which is still visible in many places, has maximum effect.[67] The rendering of the linden trees in this painting with all sorts of elongated, almost stippled strokes in different shades of green, yellow, and pink is strongly reminiscent of paintings that have been firmly dated to May, such as *Horse Chestnut Tree in Blossom* (1887, Van Gogh Museum, Amsterdam) and the previously discussed *Outskirts of Paris: Road with Peasant Shouldering a Spade* **(31)**.

As noted already, the area around Asnières offered plenty of variety for painters. In addition to charming landscapes, the river with its boats and bridges, and the quays with their cafés and restaurants, there were large industrial buildings nearby, with a thicket of chimney stacks and plumes of smoke showing the way. Unlike the Impressionists, who occasionally depicted the onerous labor that accompanied the rise of industry, Van Gogh, Bernard, Seurat, Signac, and Angrand frequently ignored this aspect.[68] To them, paintings of gasometers and factories were interesting modern subjects that contrasted with the landscape. But their gaze did not extend beyond the architecture, with the exception of a few paintings by Bernard and Seurat. Writing about Signac's gasometers, Bogomila Welsh-Ovcharov noted that they were purely "silhouetted architectural subjects" that lent themselves to his Divisionist studies **(88)**.[69] The same might be said of Van Gogh's *Factories at Clichy*, in which he painted a panorama of industrial buildings with smoking chimneys against a blue sky **(41)**.[70] The canvas's lower half is filled with colorful grassland made up of elongated green and

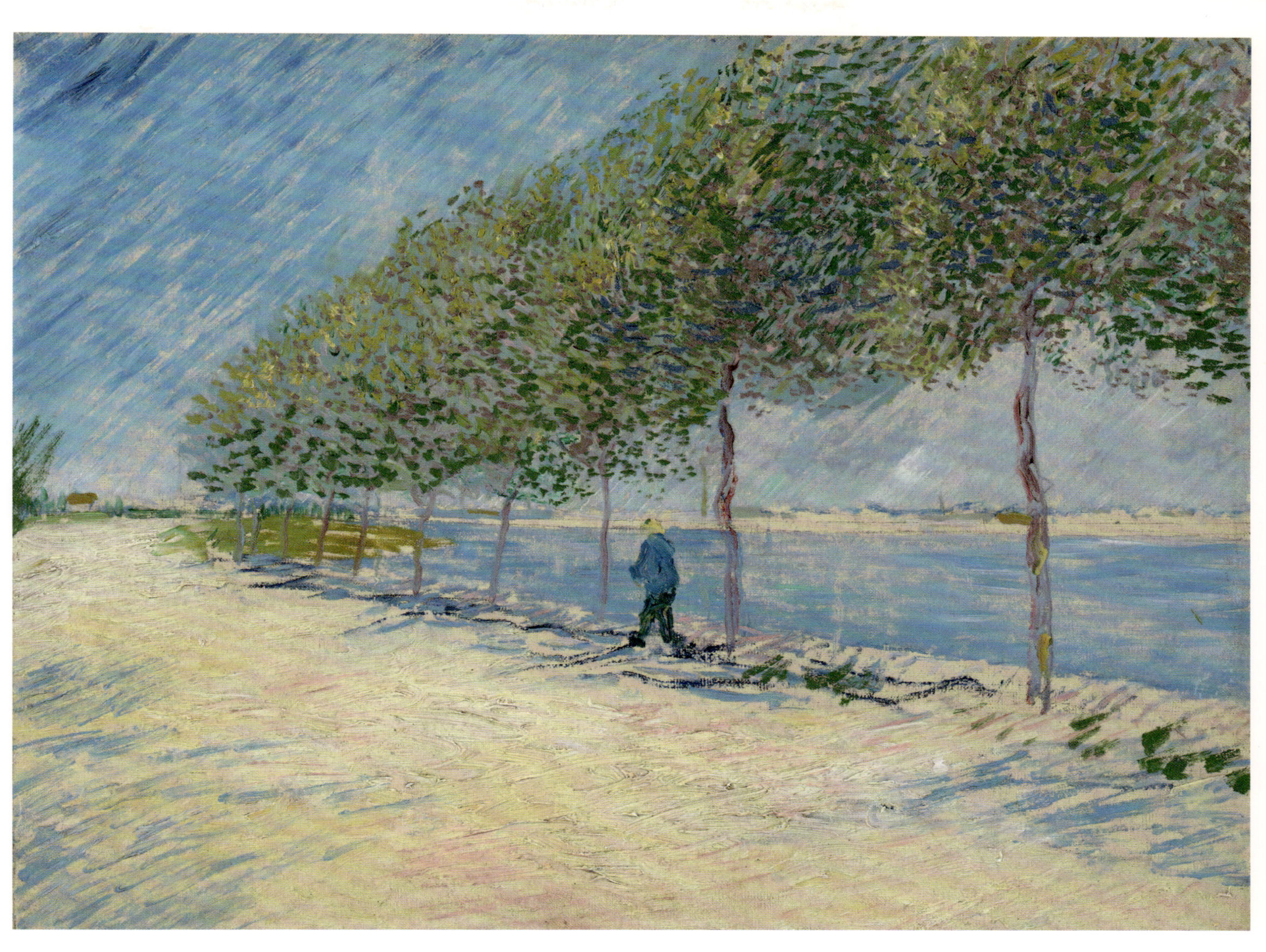

40 (cat.) Vincent van Gogh
By the Seine, 1887
Oil on canvas, 49.4 × 65.3 cm
Van Gogh Museum, Amsterdam (Vincent van Gogh Foundation)

yellow strokes of varying thickness. There is no sign of any workers, and the two small figures that Van Gogh includes in the picture appear as though they are out for a pleasant walk. He seems not to have been interested in representing blue-collar life at this point, although he was a big admirer of Jean-François Raffaëlli, who lived in Asnières and painted "the ragpickers of Paris *in their own small quarter*."[71] Raffaëlli's paintings of the city's underbelly included realistic images of impoverished ragpickers and workers **(43)**, similar to the laborers and peasants that Van Gogh had previously depicted in the Netherlands. He revisited the subject exceptionally in the painting *On the Outskirts of Paris*, which probably dates from the fall of 1886 **(42)**. It shows the waste ground between the city walls and the outlying villages that Van Gogh crossed on his way to Asnières.[72]

The campaign during the spring and summer of 1887 was Van Gogh's first step toward getting out into nature each spring to experiment with new motifs. With the reawakening of the natural world, blossoms and flowers became motifs that he looked forward to every winter, as witnessed by paintings made around Asnières, such as *Poppies in a Wheatfield* (1887; Israel Museum, Jerusalem), *Corner of a Garden on the Ile des Ravageurs*, and *Grass with Butterflies* **(44)**. Bernard wrote: "A springtime poetry emanated from these fragments captured with the tip of a brush, stolen as it were from the fleeting hours. I savored their charm, all the more so as I lived in these places at the time and they were made in keeping with the soul I sensed there."[73]

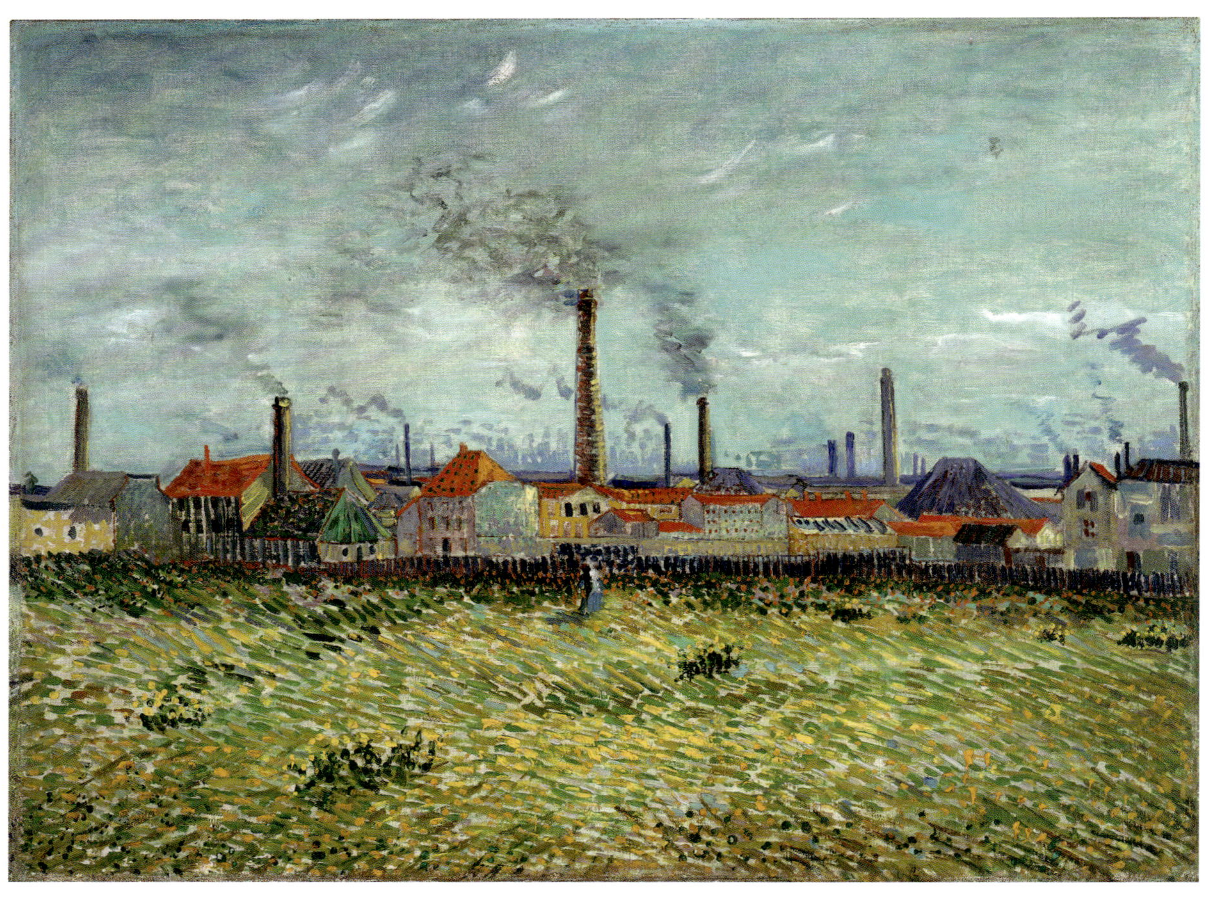

41 (cat.) Vincent van Gogh
Factories at Clichy, 1887
Oil on canvas, 53.7×72.7 cm
Saint Louis Art Museum, Missouri
Funds given by Mrs. Mark C. Steinberg by exchange

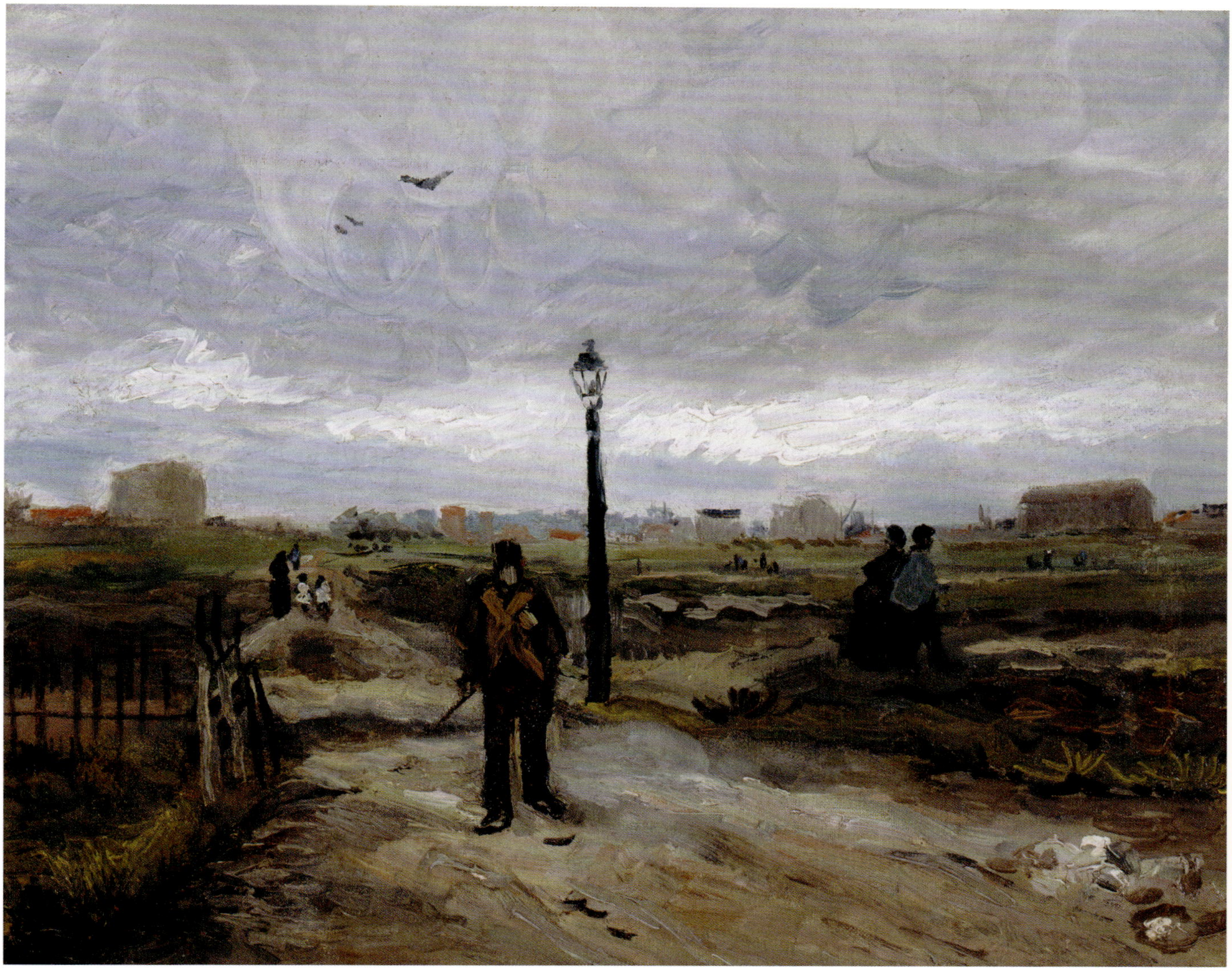

42 (cat.) Vincent van Gogh
On the Outskirts of Paris, 1886
Oil on canvas, 45.7×54.6 cm
Private collection in loving memory of Frank and Marie Wangeman

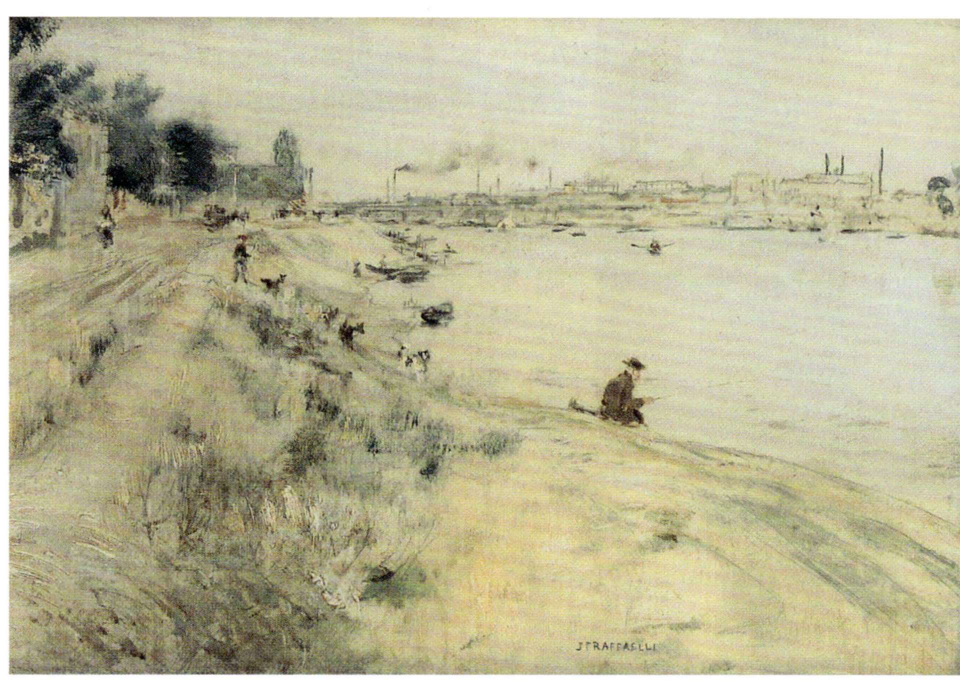

43 Jean-François Raffaëlli
Fisherman on the Banks of the Seine, undated
Oil on canvas, 26×36 cm
Private collection

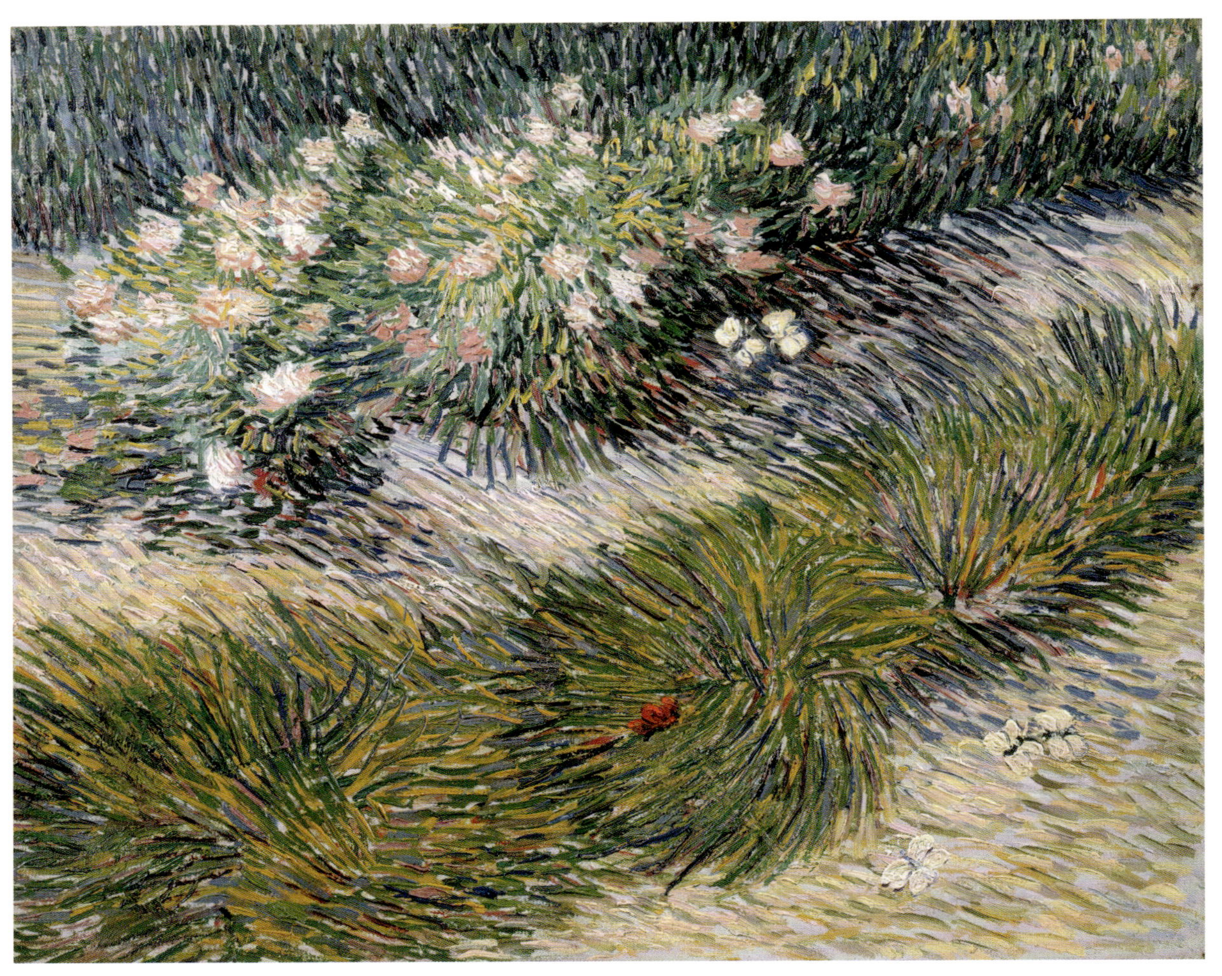

44 Vincent van Gogh
Grass with Butterflies, 1887
Oil on canvas, 50.4 × 61.4 cm
Private collection

Three Sets of Triptychs as an Artistic Peak

The artistic pinnacle of Van Gogh's time in Asnières was achieved in the three sets of triptychs he completed there. Together, these nine paintings—now scattered across different institutional and private collections—represent the entirety of his working terrain. Viewed on the map **(28)** from left to right, they are *La Grande Jatte* **(45,46,47)**, *Riverbank in Asnières* **(48,49,50)**, and *Riverbank in Clichy* **(51,52,53)**. That the canvases in question should be viewed as three triptychs is confirmed by an unpublished inventory drawn up in 1890 of Vincent's paintings at Theo and his wife Jo's apartment in Paris.[74] Reexamination and comparison of the canvas sizes combined with earlier technical analysis of the supports and the red-painted edges allowed a definitive identification to be made of the triptychs.[75]

La Grande Jatte Triptych

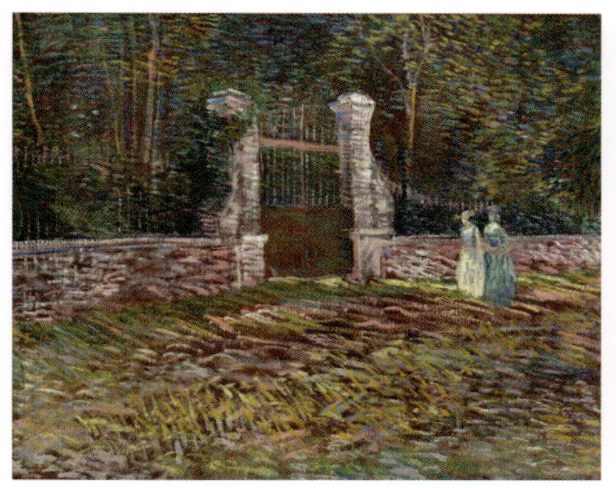
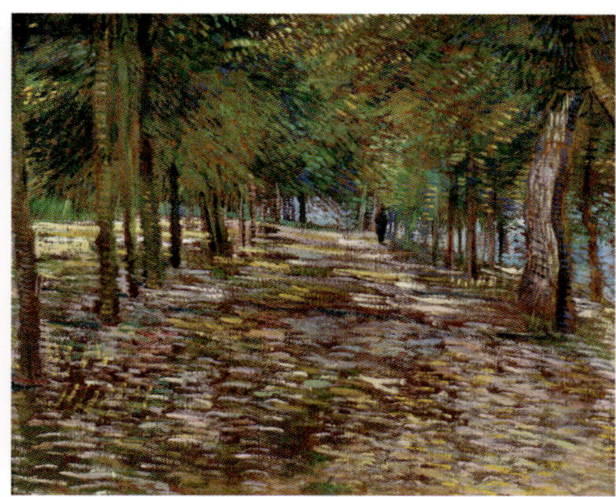
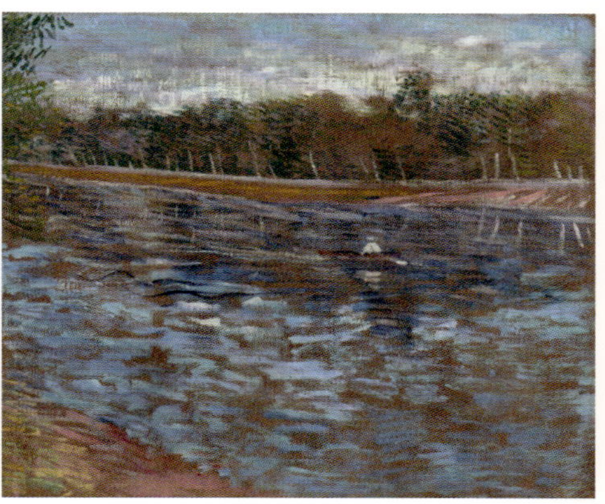

Riverbank in Asnières Triptych

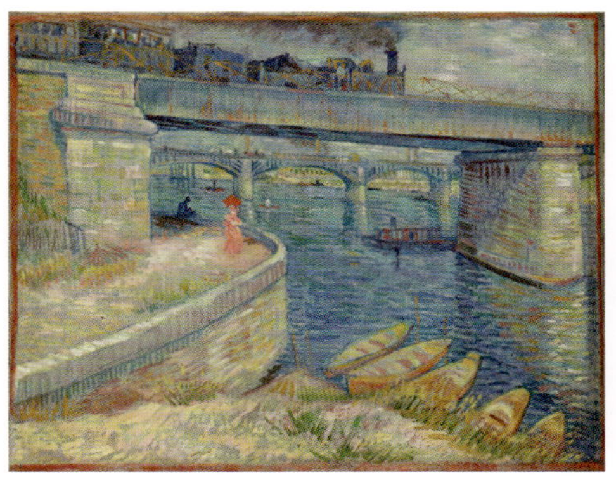
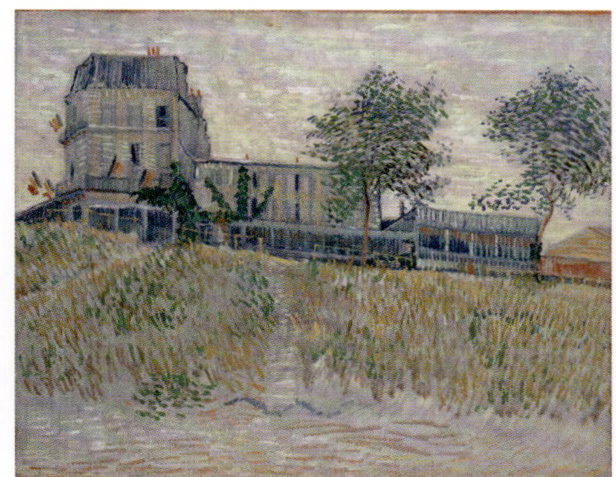
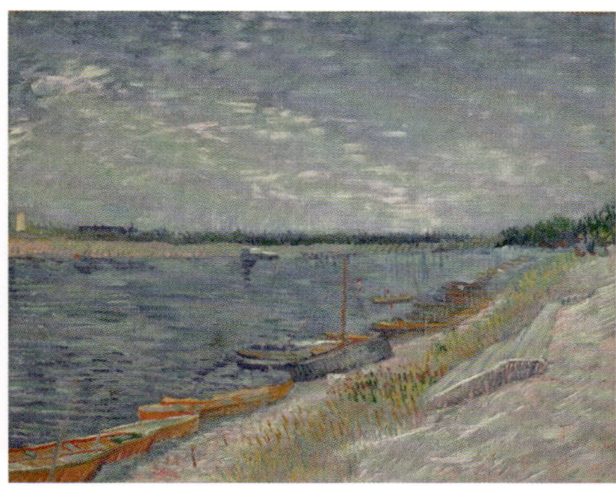

Riverbank in Clichy Triptych

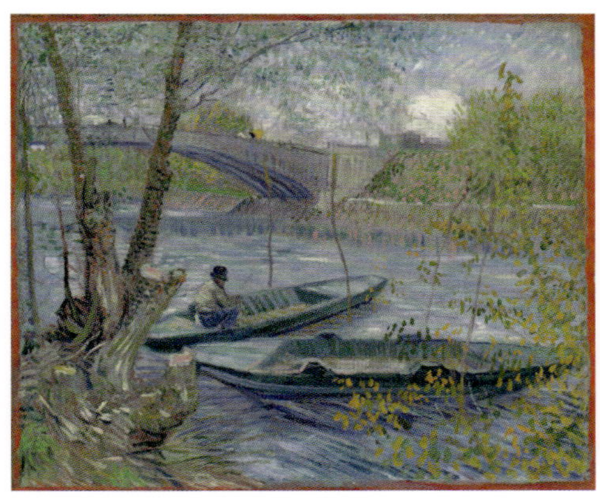
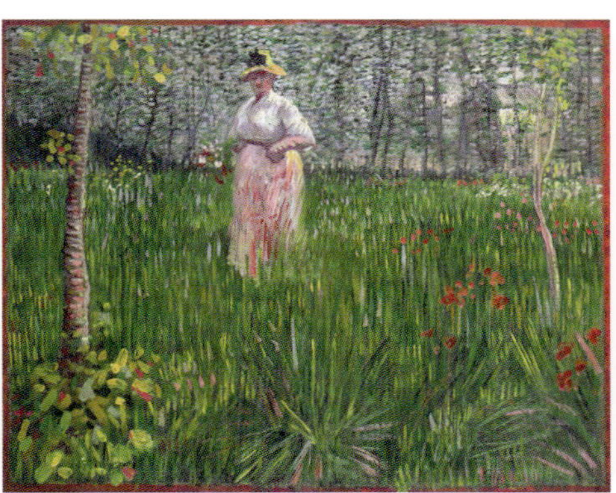
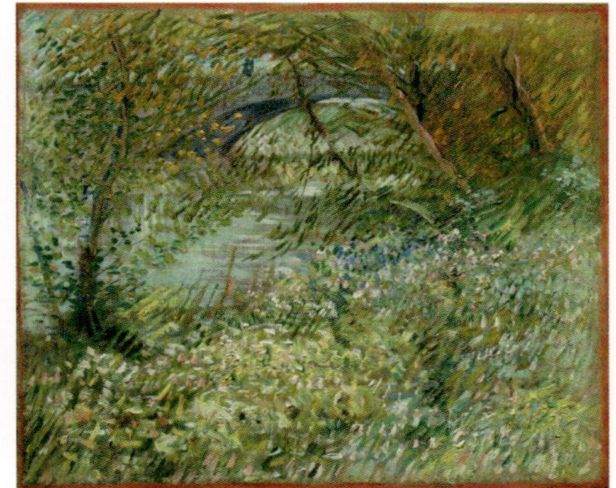

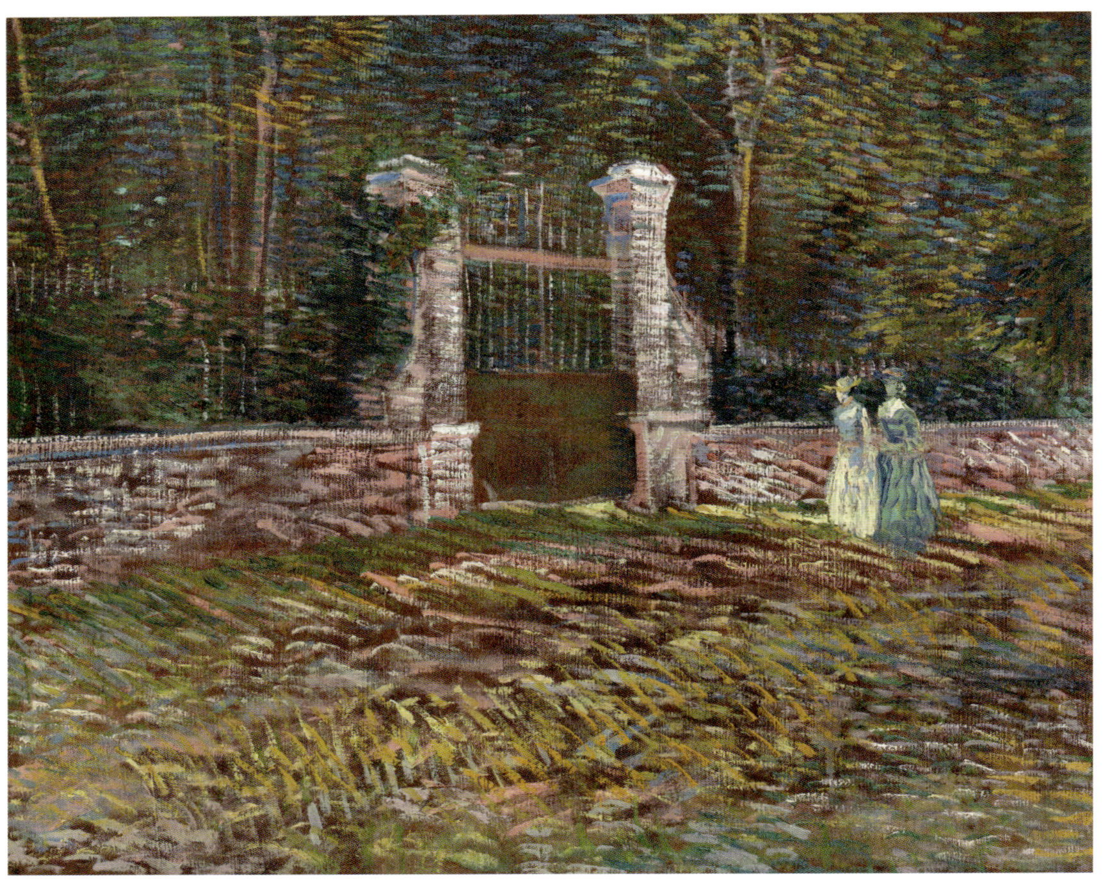

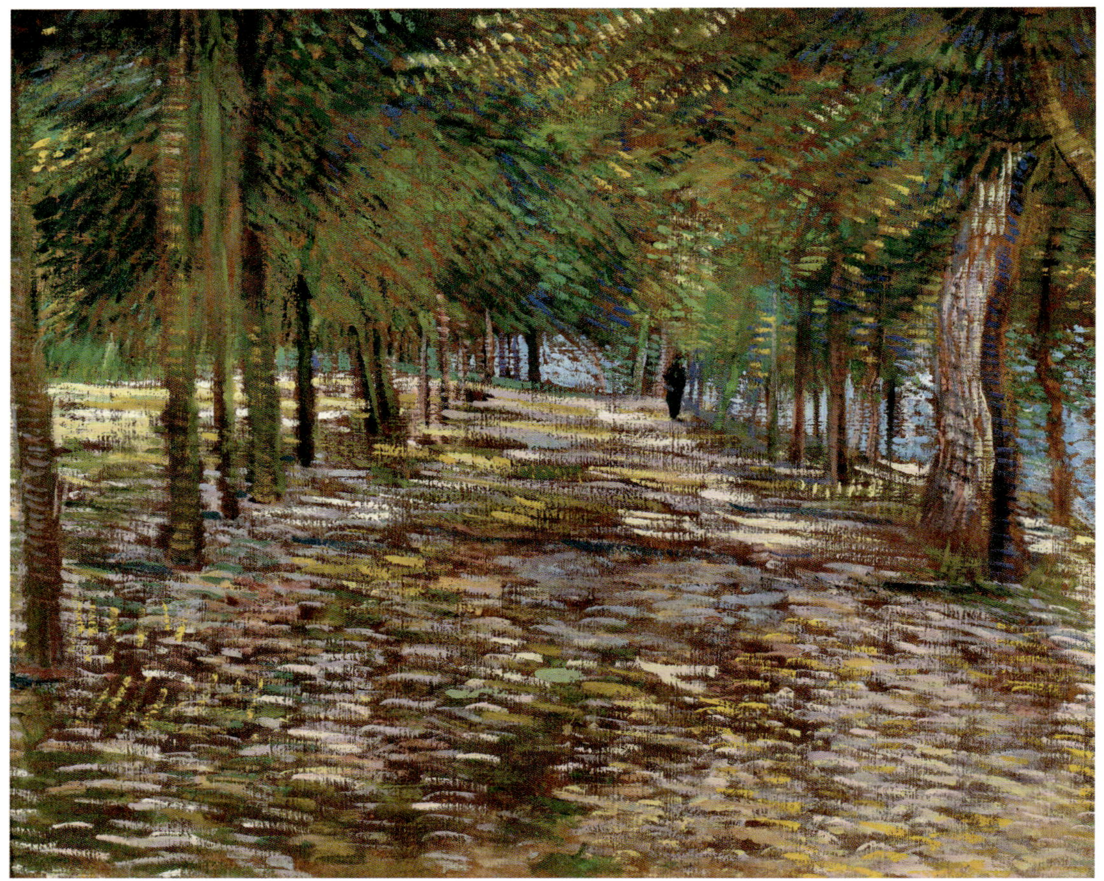

45 (cat.) Vincent van Gogh
Gate on the Ile de la Grande Jatte, 1887
Oil on canvas, 54.6 × 66.8 cm
Bequest of Ignace Hellenberg, Paris, to the State of Israel, In memory of his parents Sigmund and Betty Hellenberg. On permanent loan to The Israel Museum, Jerusalem, from the Administrator General of the State of Israel

46 (cat.) Vincent van Gogh
Lane on the Ile de la Grande Jatte, 1887
Oil on canvas, 55 × 67 cm
Private collection

The Grande Jatte triptych looks a little dark today, probably due to discoloration of the canvas. All the same, the ensemble must originally have been open and bright **(45,46,47)**. It is notable for its sketchy character and, of the three triptychs, it possibly forms the most homogeneous whole, thanks to the consistency of palette and brushwork.[76] The Asnières triptych, meanwhile, brought Van Gogh closer than ever to Impressionism **(48,49,50)**. He experimented in it with different points of view and chose appealing, readily salable motifs. The pictures combine boats moored on the river; a complex, exciting composition of quays, bridges, and a train; and a cheerful restaurant—all three painted with a free hand in the same fresh palette. They are very different from the way Bernard rendered the same motif at the end of 1887, from what must have been almost exactly the same spot as Van Gogh. While the Dutch artist was still pursuing Impressionism, his French colleague had left it far behind, building his composition instead with powerful lines and expanses of color in muted tones in the style that came to be known

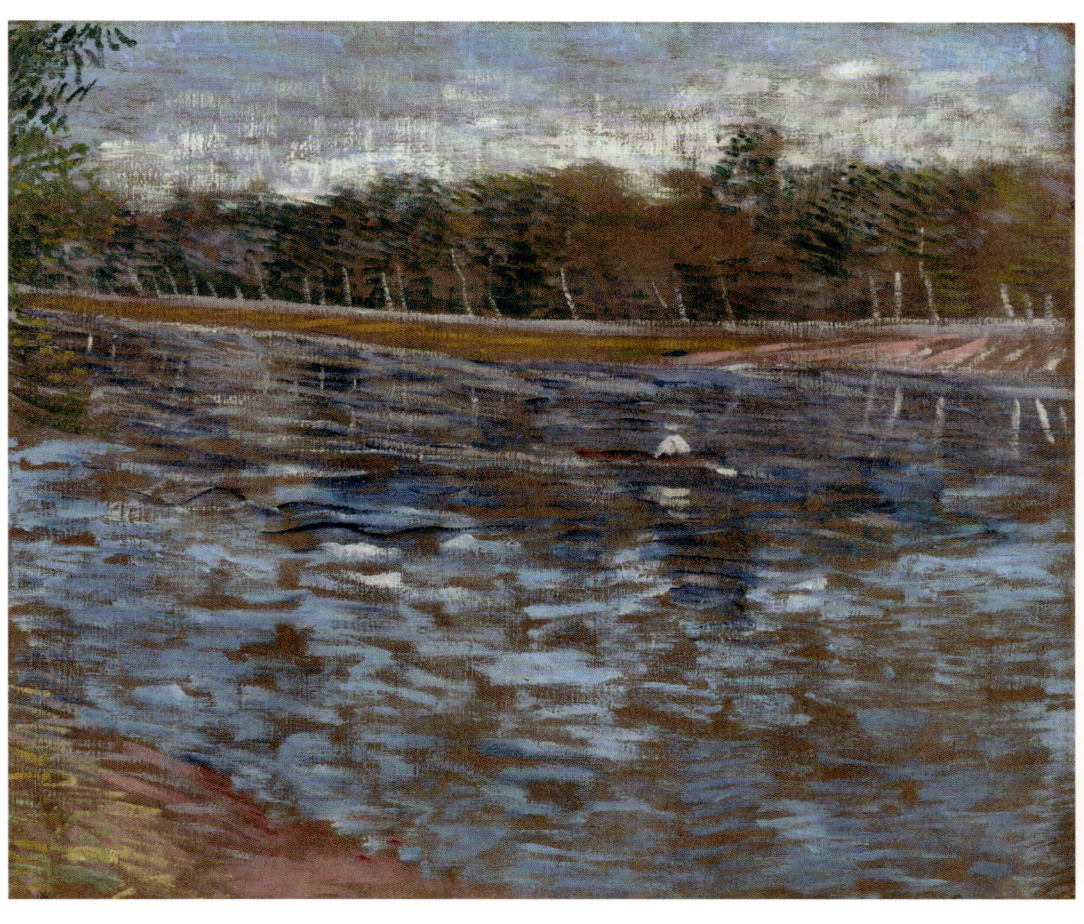

47 (cat.) Vincent van Gogh
Seine with a Rowboat, 1887
Oil on canvas, 55×65 cm
Private collection

as Cloisonnism **(121)**. The Clichy triptych, lastly, in which Van Gogh intensified the colors even more, focuses entirely on nature **(51,52,53)**, with lush vegetation dominating all three canvases. Very exceptionally, the central work includes a worked-up figure: a woman in a yellow hat, holding a bunch of freshly picked flowers. She emerges from the grass, the latter laid down with green-yellow vertical brushstrokes and with bright yellow and red impastoed touches for the flowers. It is an idyllic scene of country life far from the busy city. The two other canvases contain typical Impressionist motifs such as the angler on the river, with overhanging trees and a bridge in the background. It was Asnières paintings like this that prompted Louis van Tilborgh to write that Van Gogh "now allowed himself to be influenced in his brushwork not so much by art as by *nature*."[77]

The Asnières and Clichy triptychs differ from Van Gogh's other work because of the red-painted edges, which were not meant to indicate that the canvases belonged together, but rather served a practical purpose.

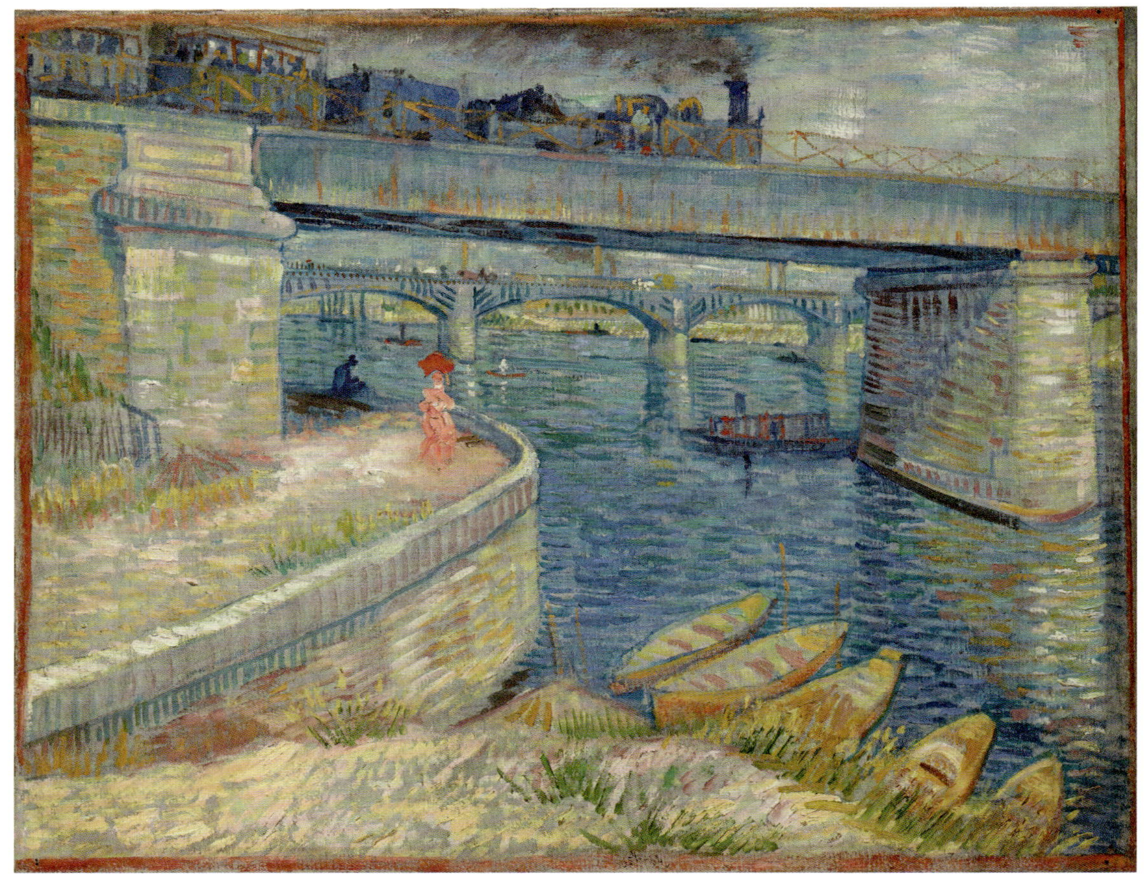

48 (cat.) Vincent van Gogh
Bridges Across the Seine at Asnières, 1887
Oil on canvas, 53.5 × 67 cm
Emil Bührle Collection, on long-term loan at the Kunsthaus Zürich

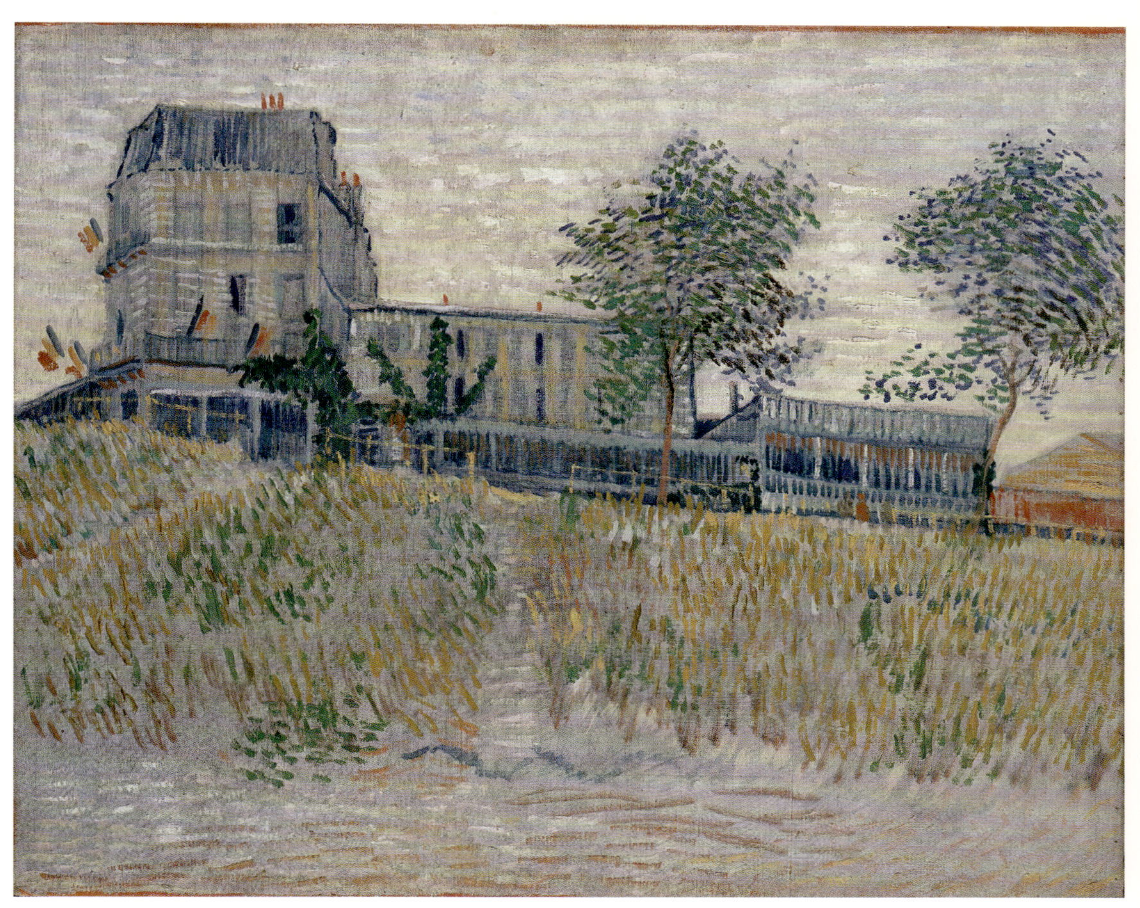

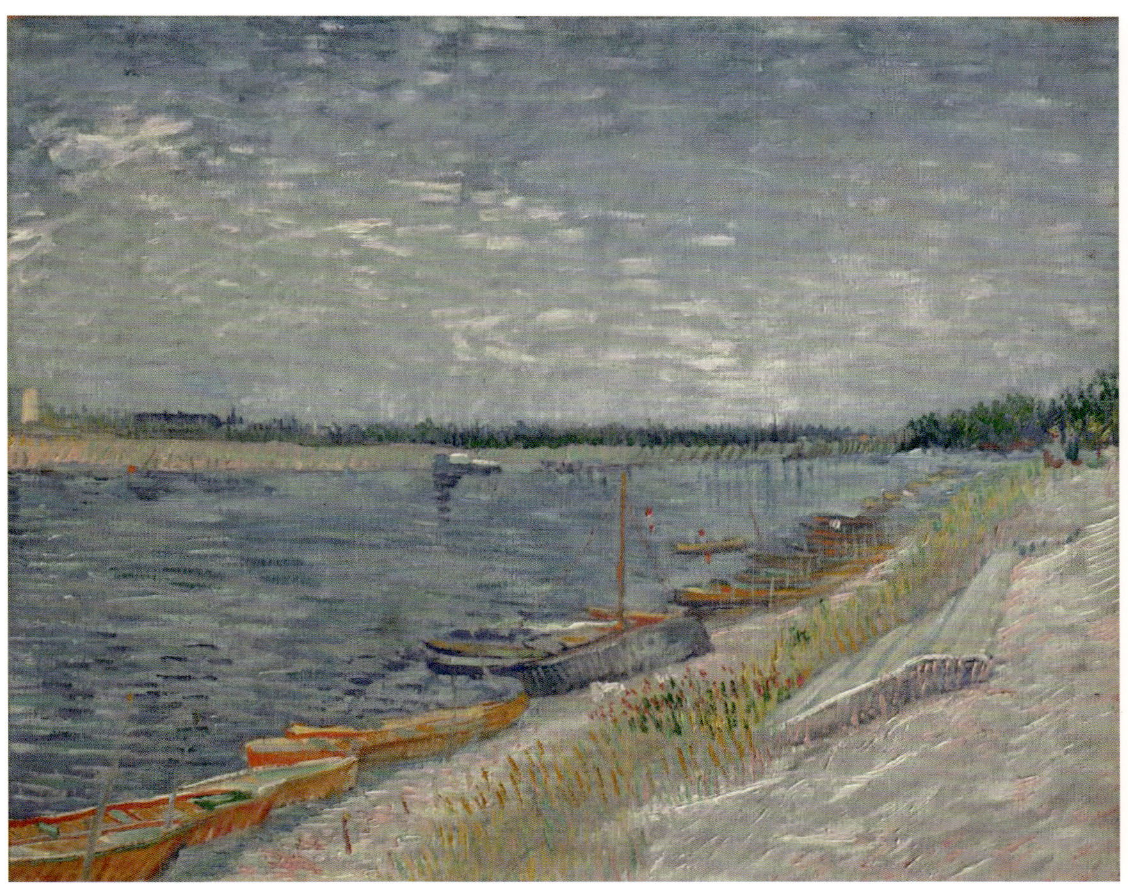

49 (cat.) Vincent van Gogh
Restaurant de la Sirène, Asnières, 1887
Oil on canvas, 52×64.4 cm
The Ashmolean Museum, University of Oxford. Bequeathed by Dr Erich Alport, 1972

50 Vincent van Gogh
View of the Seine with Rowboats, 1887
Oil on canvas, 52×65 cm
Private collection

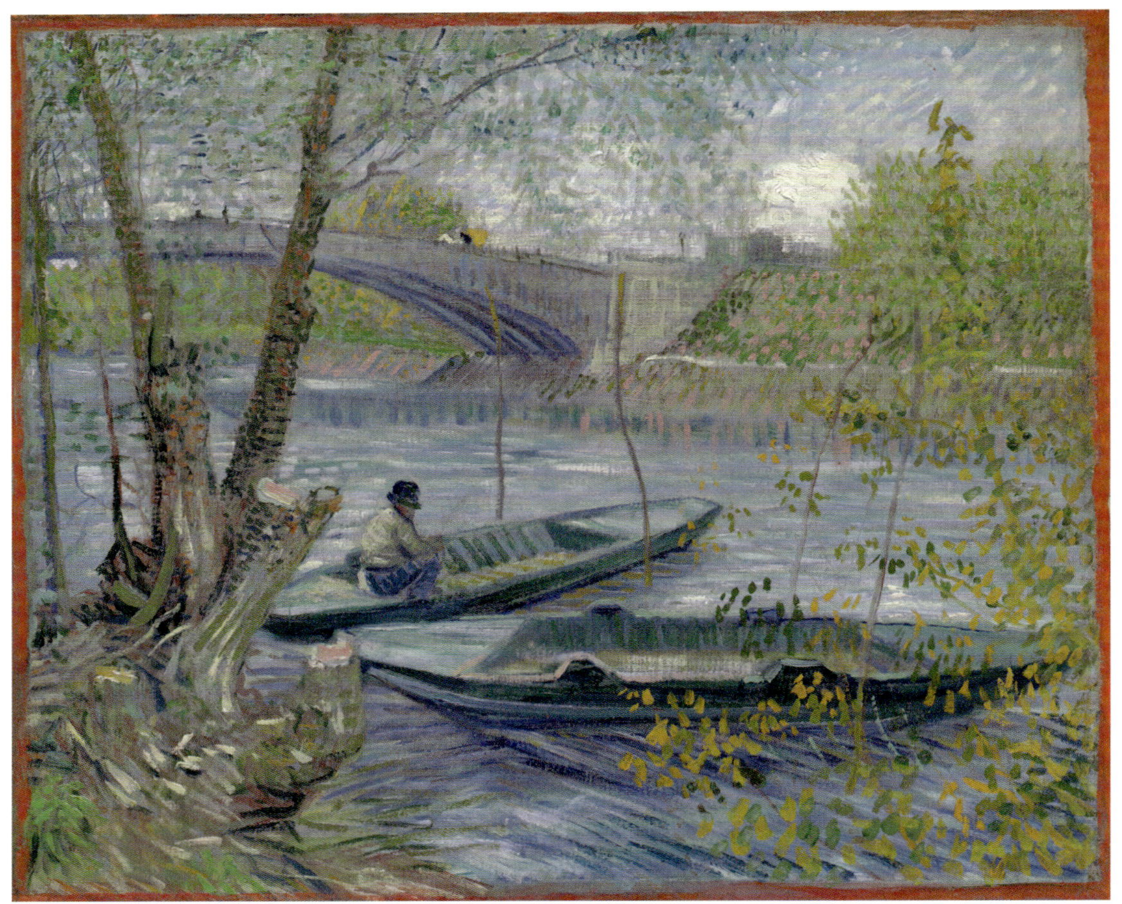

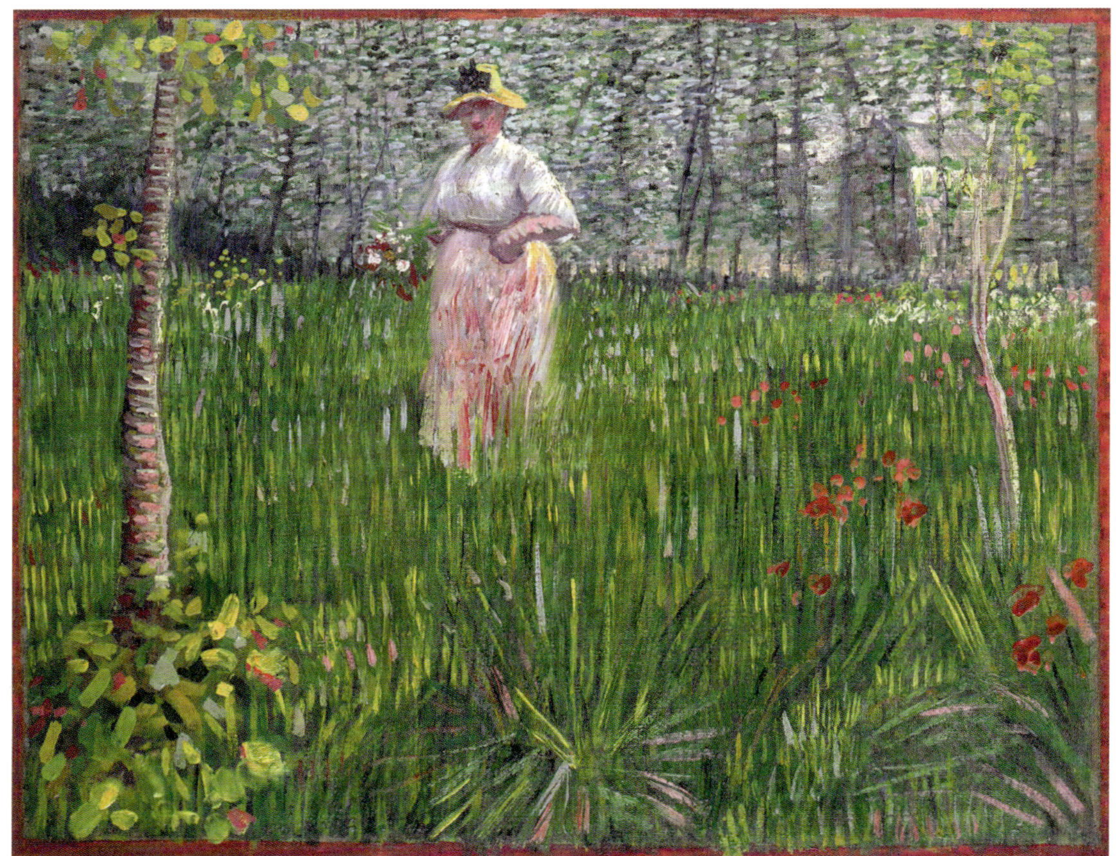

51 (cat.) Vincent van Gogh
Fishing in Spring, the Pont de Clichy (Asnières), 1887
Oil on canvas, 50.5 × 60 cm
The Art Institute of Chicago
Gift of Charles Deering McCormick, Brooks McCormick, and the Estate of Roger McCormick

52 (cat.) Vincent van Gogh
A Woman Walking in a Garden, 1887
Oil on canvas, 48 × 60 cm
Private collection

Research shows that each of these triptychs was made from a long piece of canvas, which Van Gogh only split into three parts after painting. The location of each artwork on the overall stretch of canvas has since been established (see illustrations on p. 85).[78] Van Gogh marked out three rectangles with red paint on the canvas, which must have measured over a meter and a half in length. Bernard recalled this method clearly: "With a large canvas slung on his back, he set off on his journey. He then split it up into so many compartments, depending on the subjects. When evening came, he brought it back, filled up, like a little mobile museum, in which all the emotions of his day were captured. Stretches of the Seine full of boats, islands with blue swings, smart restaurants with multicolored awnings, oleanders, corners of abandoned parks, and properties for sale."[79] The fact that the red edge was repainted after completion might indicate that Van Gogh exhibited these works or at least planned to do so, since, in the absence of picture frames, he sometimes painted the edges of his canvases instead.[80]

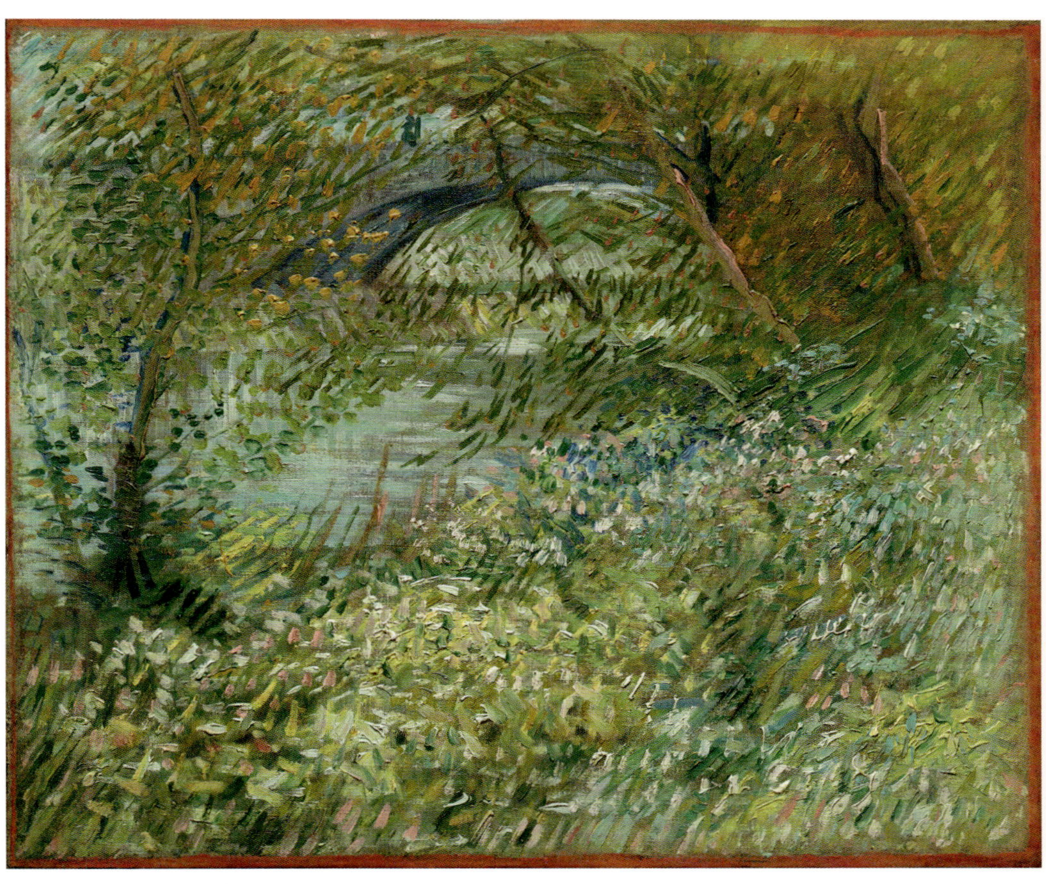

53 (cat.) Vincent van Gogh
River Bank in Springtime, 1887
Oil on canvas, 48.9 × 58.1 cm
Dallas Museum of Art
Gift of Mr. and Mrs. Eugene McDermott in memory of Arthur Berger

Group Exhibitions and Sales Opportunities

It is not entirely clear why Van Gogh decided to return to working in Montmartre toward the end of July 1887, although we do know that he painted outdoors in Asnières once more before leaving Paris. This was in the fall of 1887, when he depicted the railroad viaduct in *Roadway with Underpass at Asnières (Le viaduc)* with an impastoed touch and a palette of muted autumnal colors **(54)**. He no doubt painted it during one of his visits to Bernard's studio in his parents' garden, where the two painters worked together several times during the fall.[81]

After the productive months he spent at Asnières, Van Gogh began to look for opportunities to sell his work. He took the initiative around November or December 1887 to organize an unofficial exhibition featuring his paintings and those by his friends. Etienne-Lucien Martin, proprietor of the Grand Bouillon-Restaurant du Chalet, at 43 avenue de Clichy, gave Van Gogh and his colleagues permission to hang over a hundred works, including contributions from Anquetin, Toulouse-Lautrec, and Arnold Koning.[82] Bernard showed two Cloisonnist works, one of which was *Two Women on the Asnières Footbridge* **(120)**, while Van Gogh was represented by landscapes from his Asnières period and still lifes. The Pointillists Signac and Seurat let the opportunity pass, although they did visit the exhibition, as did Paul Gauguin, Armand Guillaumin, and Camille Pissarro.[83]

Signac and Seurat showed their work from late November 1887 in the rehearsal room of the Théâtre Libre at 96 rue Blanche, where Van Gogh also hung a painting. Signac exhibited *The Banks of the Seine, Asnières*, **(149)** which had also hung at the Indépendants that same year, while Van Gogh showed his Divisionist *Garden with Courting Couples: Square Saint-Pierre* **(30)**.[84]

Van Gogh clearly retained his enthusiasm for his Asnières works and considered them suitable for the art trade, as we see in the spring of 1888 when Theo was about to send a number of works by Impressionist artists to Boussod & Valadon's Dutch branch.[85] Theo suggested to Vincent to add a work of his own to the consignment, for

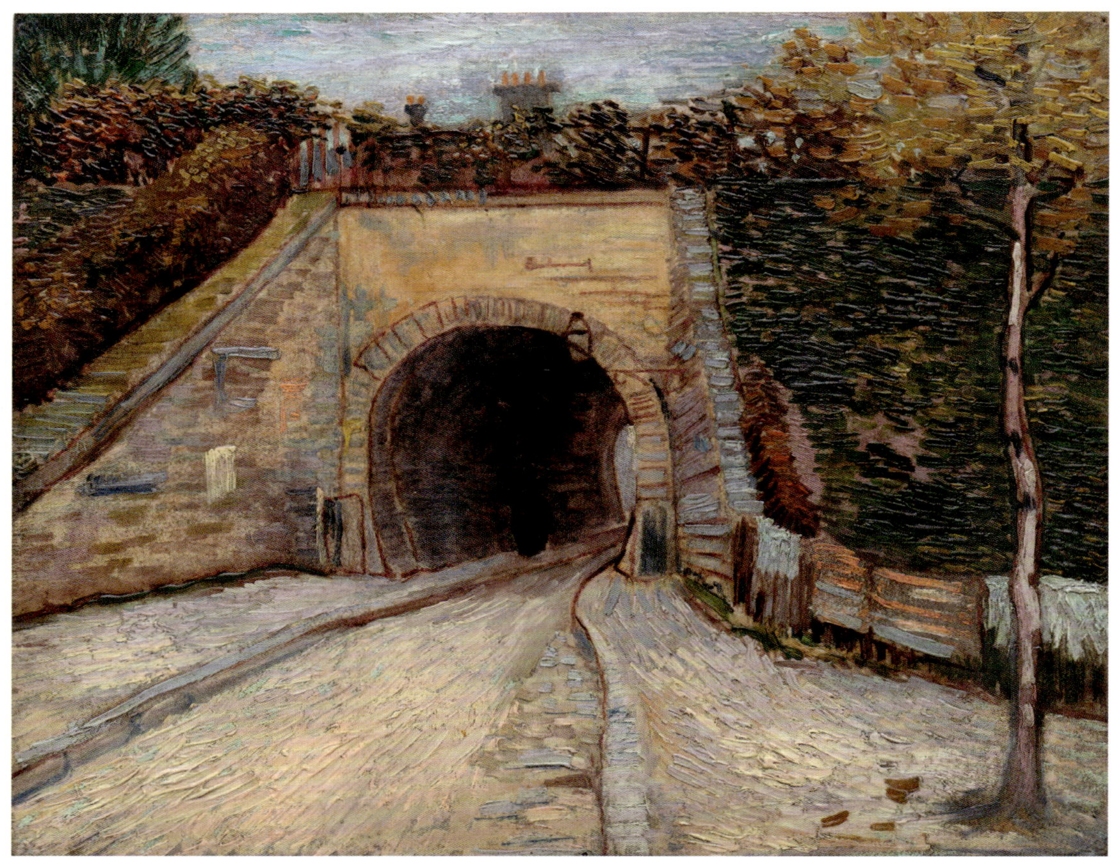

54 (cat.) Vincent van Gogh
Roadway with Underpass (Le viaduc), Asnières, 1887
Oil on cardboard, 32.7×41 cm
Solomon R. Guggenheim Museum, New York
Thannhauser Collection, Gift, Justin K. Thannhauser, 1978

which Vincent considered three medium-sized studies from Asnières: "the Clichy bridge with the yellow sky and two houses reflected in the water? That one, or the butterflies or the field of poppies might do."[86] The final choice was *The Seine with the Pont de Clichy* **(3)** and, to be on the safe side, he also sent a sketch of it in a letter **(55)**.[87] This work, in which he captured the reflections on the water with a loose brush and light palette of numerous white and yellow tones, was very much in keeping with the Impressionist style.[88]

A Pivotal Artistic Period

The three months Van Gogh spent in 1887 in and around Asnières on the river Seine, to the northwest of Paris, were greatly influential to his artistic development. His initial desire to form a group with other artists living and working around the boulevard de Clichy did not come about, but in artistic terms Van Gogh certainly moved among the avant-garde artists of his time.[89] As Bernard put it: "This light . . . soon awakened like a nascent dawn in views of Asnières, La Grande Jatte and the banks of the Seine, which were already joyfully pleasant. This was Van Gogh's prelude to the symphonies of his future palette, he was trying out his instruments. . . . Gray canvases suddenly gave way to 'stippled' studies."[90]

In terms of motif and style, Van Gogh sought to connect with the Impressionists and Neo-Impressionists, while incorporating elements from Japanese prints in his compositions. These experiments enabled him to develop a style of his own, which would culminate in Arles, for which he set off in February 1888. Throughout his Paris period, the peasant life that had featured so strongly in his earlier work gave way to motifs drawn from modern French life, which he felt would be better suited to the art market.[91] It is clear from his letter to Theo from Arles in April 1888 that what he had done in Asnières was the preamble to his southern-French work: "I can assure you that what I'm making here is better than my campaign in Asnières last spring."[92] In Asnières he took decisive steps toward the colorful, loose style that he would develop further in the south of France. When Van Gogh eventually returned to nature in Arles, he was seized by the same energy and productivity that had marked his campaign along the banks of the Seine. ■

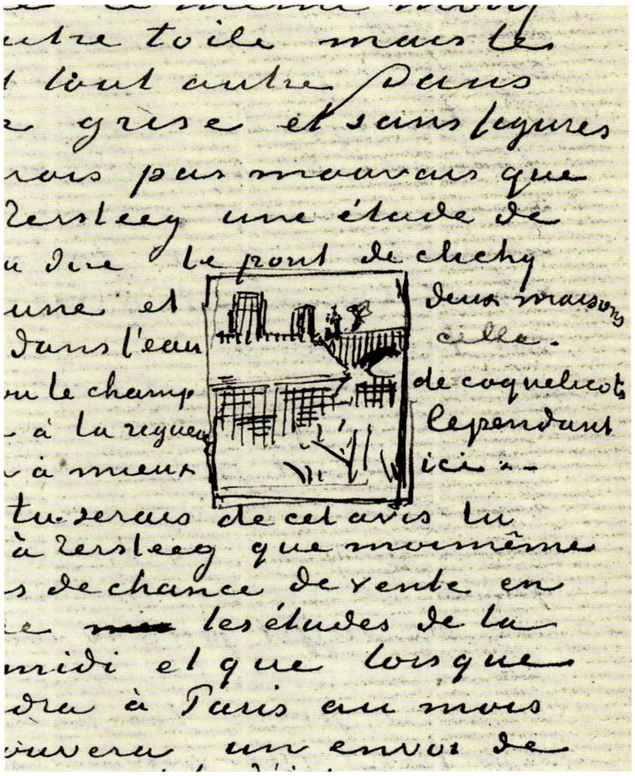

55 Vincent van Gogh
Detail of a letter to Theo van Gogh with sketch of *The Seine with the Pont de Clichy*, c. March 25, 1888
Pen and ink on paper, 26.4 × 20.3 cm (full sheet)
Van Gogh Museum, Amsterdam (Vincent van Gogh Foundation)

SEURAT AT ASNIÈRES: CHROMATICS AND CARICATURE, MELANCHOLY AND MODERNITY

RICHARD THOMSON

It might be said that the suburbs of Paris, and specifically the area around Asnières, launched Georges Seurat's career as one of the most groundbreaking artists of the late nineteenth century. The locality's importance for the development of his radical painting was both various and fundamental. It gave focus: where to paint—not just generic suburban Paris but specific locations. It offered choice: what to paint—a range of possible subjects and motifs was available for selection. It stimulated experiment: how to paint—the choice of medium, the honing of drawing form, the generation of new techniques, and the development of theory. Asnières, therefore, was the arena where Seurat graduated from tyro to his generation's creative maestro.

Painting in the Paris suburbs was far from exceptional. Today we think of the Impressionists in the 1870s, Claude Monet working at Argenteuil or Alfred Sisley at Louveciennes and Marly, but they were hardly pioneers. At the Paris Salon in 1881, for example, thirty paintings had titles that named precise locales in the suburbs, such as Gabriel Guttinguer's *Petit Bras de la Seine, à l'île de la Jatte*, and no doubt there were others titled more generically.[1] Finding landscape subjects not far outside the ring of fortifications encircling Paris, being able to choose from a range of motifs along the river from the modern and industrial to the semi-rural and tree-lined, appealed to artists, and specifying locales may have appealed to potential buyers, themselves acquainted with such vicinities. In addition the highly varied suburban communities proffered a wide range of social experience, from the lively recreational ambiance generated by the resident or visiting bourgeoisie to the squalid conditions of the working-class industrial suburbs. This spectrum had a substantial presence in the Naturalist literature that dominated French writing during the 1870s and 1880s. Thus Edmond and Jules de Goncourts' *Renée Mauperin* (1864) begins with a scene of genteel swimming in the Seine near the Ile Saint-Denis; in Alphonse Daudet's *Fromont jeune et Risler aîné* (1874) the upwardly mobile Fromonts buy a riverside chalet at Asnières; Joris-Karl Huysmans's *Croquis parisiens* (1880) includes a piece on the view from the northern fortifications over the rundown working-class communities; and Guy de Maupassant's short stories published in newspapers such as *Le Gaulois* and *Gil Blas* frequently covered boating and leisure-seeking themes. Seurat had an appetite for such writing, Edmond Aman-Jean remembering how avidly he read the Goncourts as a young painter and Paul Signac that he took his expression "croqueton" (small oil sketch) from their writing.[2]

Such a set of associations—at once commonplace yet complex—clustered around the Parisian suburbs would necessarily draw Seurat into a creative context and eventually a like-minded community. It involved choices, not only the practical painter's particular selection of a visually pleasing motif but also of style, of iconography, of site, and staffage. These would gradually lead Seurat toward an increasingly diverse and engaged representation of the suburbs, centered on Asnières and its vicinity. Not only did he have to develop how to select subjects and the means to paint them, he also had to assess, select, or reject possibilities that he found did not correspond to his developing vision. One of these was the association of the industrial suburbs and melancholy, typified by Huysmans writing in 1880 about a landscape of Gennevilliers exhibited by Jean-François Raffaëlli at that year's fifth Impressionist exhibition, in which "factory chimneys vomited gusts of black smoke" evoking the "melancholic grandeur" of such sites.[3] In 1887 Raffaëlli, with Huysmans and other writers, set up a dinner club, the *dîners de banlieue*, for those who appreciated "the sadness of desolate landscapes"; the group included young literary men such as Henri Fèvre and Jean Ajalbert, both of whom had written about Seurat's work at the eighth Impressionist exhibition the previous year.[4] Certainly writers of Seurat's generation might accept the equation of the poorer suburbs and melancholy, Jules Laforgue writing in 1881 to his fellow poet Gustave Kahn: "when I have spleen, I go into the sad suburbs . . . and contemplate pictures after . . . Raphaëlli [sic]."[5] But this was only one reading of the suburbs, and there were others, not least the chic and ostentatious. More sociological texts recorded Asnières as a place of variety and, above all, constant change. The local writer Edmé Périer, writing in 1890, took issue with Louis Barron's account of the vicinity in *Les Environs de Paris*, published as recently as 1886; Asnières was less rowdy and sporty, and more residential, than Barron's description of it as "the national pleasure port, the holy town of boating."[6]

Seurat was born in 1859, the son of a bailiff with an apartment on the boulevard de Magenta in Paris's 10th arrondissement: a comfortable middle-class background.[7] He attended the Ecole des Beaux-Arts, a student in the atelier of Henri Lehmann, himself a former pupil of Jean-Auguste-Dominique Ingres, entering in March 1878. But by November the following year he had left to undertake his military service, which he completed twelve months later. The year 1881 saw him branching out beyond the tight remit of his academic training, taking notes on paintings by Eugène Delacroix at a Hôtel Drouot sale, making a free copy of Pierre Puvis de Chavannes's *Pauvre Pêcheur* on view at that year's Salon, and purchasing a copy of Ogden Rood's *Théorie scientifique des couleurs*, the translation of his *Modern Chromatics* (1879).[8] Here was a young painter looking for new options in the application of paint, a greater economy of drawing and composition, and a more systematic treatment of color.

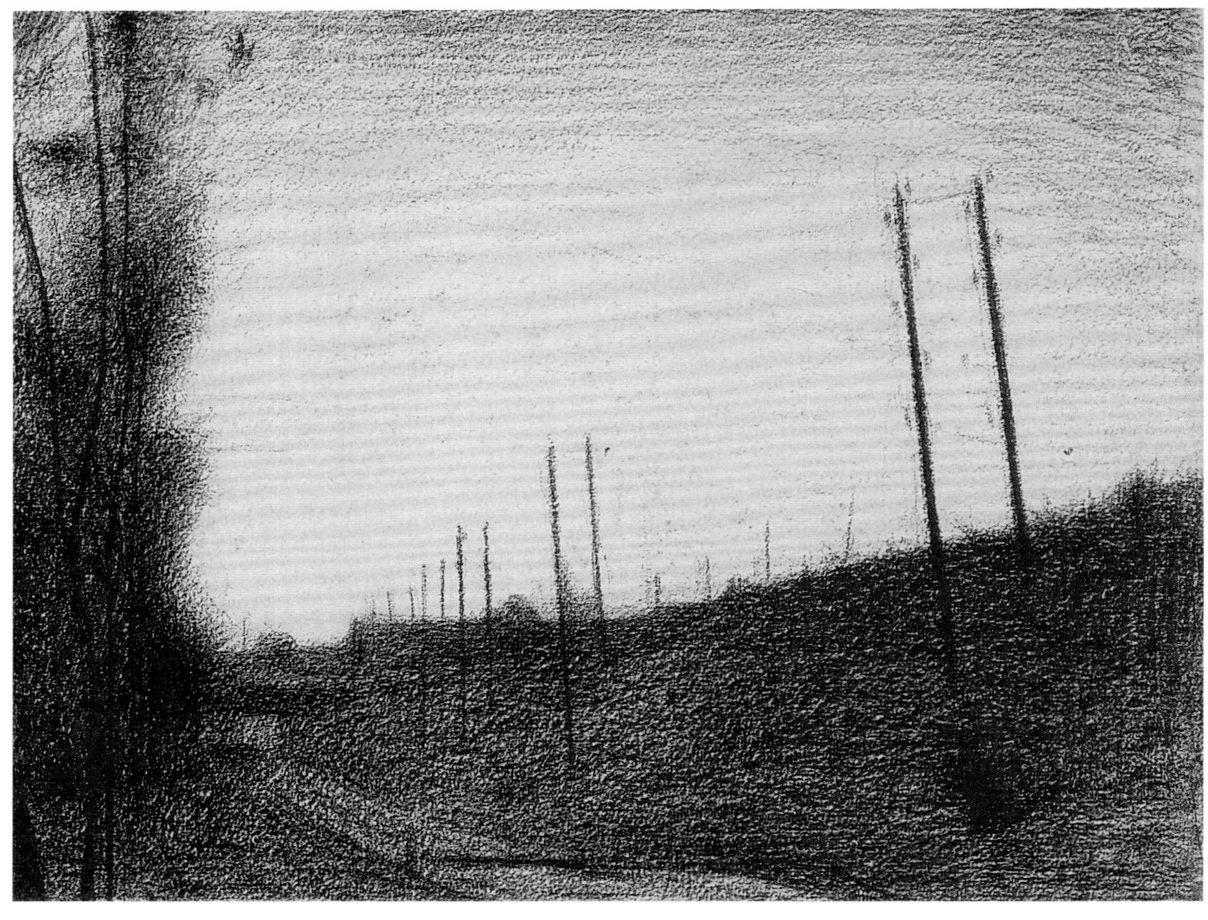

56 Georges Seurat
Railway Tracks, 1881–82
Conté crayon on paper, 24.2 × 31.6 cm
André Bromberg Collection

Seurat began to discover the suburbs to the northwest of Paris around 1881. That year his friend Aman-Jean, whom he had met while a fellow student in Lehmann's studio at the Ecole des Beaux-Arts, started renting a studio on rue de l'Arbalète near the Val-de-Grâce, where Seurat sometimes worked with him. The two painters would take the *bateau-mouche* from this base southeast of the city center to the island of La Grande Jatte on the Seine in the northwest suburbs.[9] Such excursions, initially perhaps as much for pleasure as for work, introduced Seurat to a different range of possibilities in the orbit of the city, hitherto offered by the market gardens of the more outlying Le Raincy, on the eastern outskirts of the city where his family owned another property. Seurat seems to have been attuned to the melancholy interpretation of the suburbs to some degree. In his early drawing *Railway Tracks* **(56)** the subject is inexplicit, disguised. The parapet with the unseen tracks above disappears sharply into distant space, paralleled by the road and the telegraph poles, the regularity of which asserts their dominance over the natural verticals of the marginal trees. Sharp perspective provides a sense of pace. Although Seurat did not become friends with Jean Ajalbert until the mid-1880s, the painter and the writer brought up in Levallois-Perret, just across the Seine from Asnières, shared not only the themes of the suburbs but also the inclination to find new means of expression, whether pictorial or literary. One might compare *Railway Tracks* to Ajalbert's poem "Pointe-Sèche," published in his collection *Sur le vif* in 1886. His description offers a similar aesthetic, responding to industrialization's dreary domination of the natural environment:

> *Les fils du télégraphe, à travers l'air épais,*
> *Découpent, deux par deux, des tranches parallèlles, . . .*
>
> The telegraph lines, through the thick air,
> Slice, two by two, parallel tracks, . . . [10]

A single canvas did the same. *Banlieue (Suburb)* **(57)** represents not gabled houses but the single sloping roofs of industrial buildings; not a church steeple to give height but a factory smokestack. Seurat's motif is not a village—a conventional, time-honored subject of landscape—but modern manufacturing; it is not a meadow in the foreground, but dead ground available for development. Therefore this is a liminal landscape, no longer dealing with the long continuities of agricultural life but the pressing requirements of modernization.

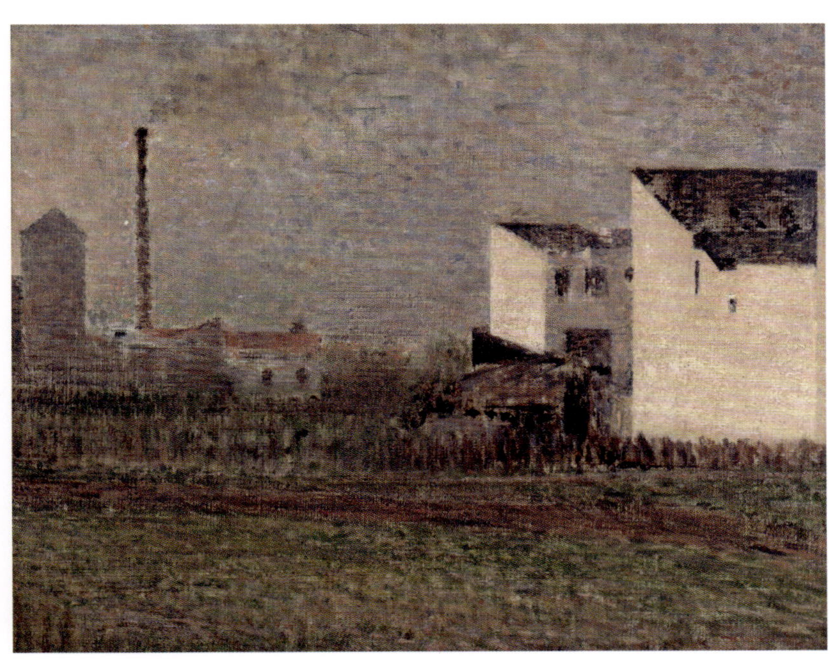

57 Georges Seurat
Suburb (Banlieue), 1882
Oil on canvas, 32.2×41 cm
Musée d'art moderne, Troyes

In the early years of the decade both Seurat's drawing and painting styles—the Conté crayon and the highly simplified, broken touch—were experimental, in development, not unlike the subjects that he chose. Seurat was such a radical artist because his instincts were reductive. On leaving the Ecole des Beaux-Arts he set about returning to the fundamental principles of drawing and painting. His drawings sought light and shade, density and void; his early paintings masses of color and simplified motifs. This propensity for simplification led him away from the naturalism, the detailed description of material actuality, which dominated contemporary French art in the work of painters like Alfred Roll and Jules Bastien-Lepage. Seurat interested himself in books about the nature of artistic style, such as Charles Blanc's *Grammaire des Arts du Dessin* (1867) and David Sutter's *Philosophie des Beaux-Arts* (1858), and in recent discoveries about color theory, notably the work of Michel Eugène Chevreul and the American Ogden Rood. He also looked attentively at paintings, studying their chromatics. On February 23, 1881, he had the opportunity to scrutinize Eugène Delacroix's *Fanatics of Tangier* (1836–38; Minneapolis Institute of Art), his notes recording "the blue of the sky and the orange white of the walls and the gray orange of the clouds."[11] Such analyses bore practical fruit, and similar color effects can be found in the simplified, dabbed touch of *Banlieue*. Stimulus to consider color effects may—curious as it might seem—also have come from Seurat's literary tastes. As already mentioned, the Goncourts' *Renée Mauperin* opens with the heroine swimming in the Seine a few miles downstream from Asnières. Their description brings out the jumbled nature of the suburbs, the close proximity of factories and countryside, the silence of the river broken by the industrial racket of foundries and steam engines. It also notices color and its complementary contrasts: violet clouds, an orange handkerchief, green shutters, red shop-signs.[12] These were succinct observations about motifs and chromatics, from which a young painter could take tips, even if he could not emulate noise.

At Le Raincy Seurat painted rural subjects—workers in the fields, crops, and farmhouses—in simple compositional arrangements featuring strong horizontal planes and sometimes plunging perspectives. His *croquetons*, painted on small rectangular wooden panels about 15 by 25 cm, were dabbed in semi-schematic touches responding to natural textures only in the most generalized way—lighter and more open for grass or foliage, denser for wall or shadow—and recording local color with a gentle use of complementary contrast. In 1882 Seurat began renting a studio in the rue de Chabrol near the Gare du Nord, which he probably retained until 1886.[13] Now based in northern Paris he was within walking distance of omnibuses and suburban trains, which gave him easy access to the banks of the Seine around Asnières. The shift from rural to suburban motifs introduced greater sociability into Seurat's small paintings. Their subjects could be very normal, typical, and not emphatically modern. For example, he painted men fishing. *Les Pêcheurs à la ligne (The Anglers)* **(58)**, probably

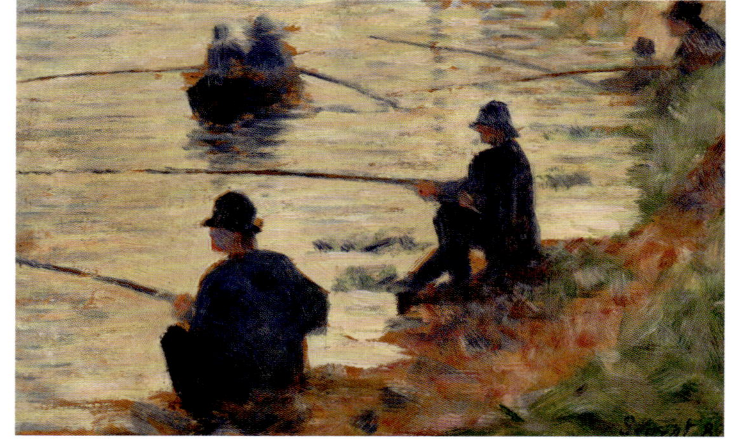

58 Georges Seurat
The Anglers, Study for La Grande Jatte, 1883
Oil on canvas, 16.2 × 24.8 cm
Musée d'art moderne, Troyes
Gift Pierre and Denise Lévy, 1975

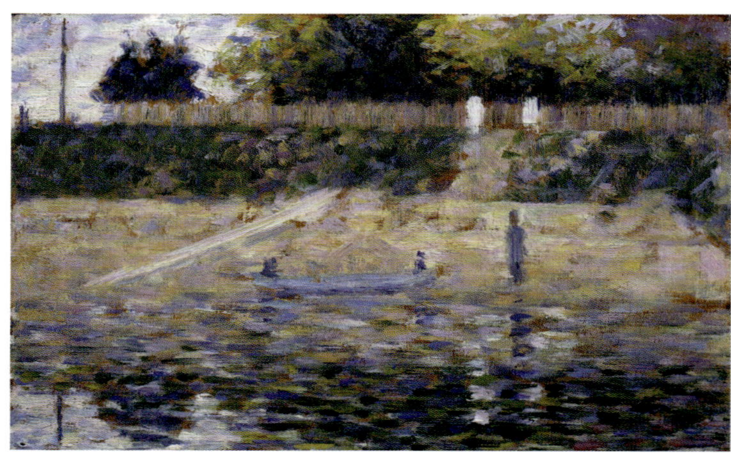

59 Georges Seurat
Boat by the Riverbank, c. 1883
Oil on panel, 15 × 24 cm
The Courtauld, London (Samuel Courtauld Trust)

made in 1883, includes no horizon. The adventurous view down on the anglers from higher on the riverbank makes the reflective surface of the water important, although Seurat's use of a silvery blue is still conventional. The perspective of bank and boat subtly suggests diagonal movement into space. The figures are rendered as simple silhouettes, their activity obvious. Indeed, Seurat remained happy with this *croqueton*, exhibiting it at the 1886 Impressionist exhibition. There the critic for *La République française* called it "the jewel of the exhibition"; its means were simple but just right.[14] Another painting probably from 1883, *Boat by the Riverbank* **(59)**, represented a step toward very ordered design. The composition is structured: the view seems straight across the river, the stretch of water, the moored boat, the sloping bank, and far fence apparently forming a pattern of regular horizontal bands. And yet closer inspection appears to show that Seurat cleverly brought the right of the composition slightly closer than the left, thus obviating the precise regularity of the horizontal. That emphasis is also mitigated by the verticals of the standing figure by the boat, the white gateposts, and the pole to upper left, as well as the diagonal ramp, which gives access to the waterside from the bank. Seurat clustered his warmer colors—notably the pale muddy river edge and its reflection in the Seine—toward the center of his *croqueton*, banded above and below by the varied greens and shadowy blues of the foliage and its reflections. Here, simple subjects were structured into an increasing sense of formal and chromatic order. Yet Seurat continued to be responsive to naturalistic observation, such as the textures of trees, their branches, and leaves. He used a scrappy touch and simple local colors, some bright greens in the upper passages and a drab blue in the sky, and still remained loyal to earth tones. Another painting of an angler, the Yale *Pêcheur (A Fisherman)* **(60)**, used the subtle perspectives of the moored boats and the corner of the island to the right against the arcing vertical of the man standing in his boat. Here the color began to be more experimental than *Banlieue*: violets were added to natural greens, as Seurat played with a harmony of secondaries, and his touch became more controlled, so suggesting a date of 1884.

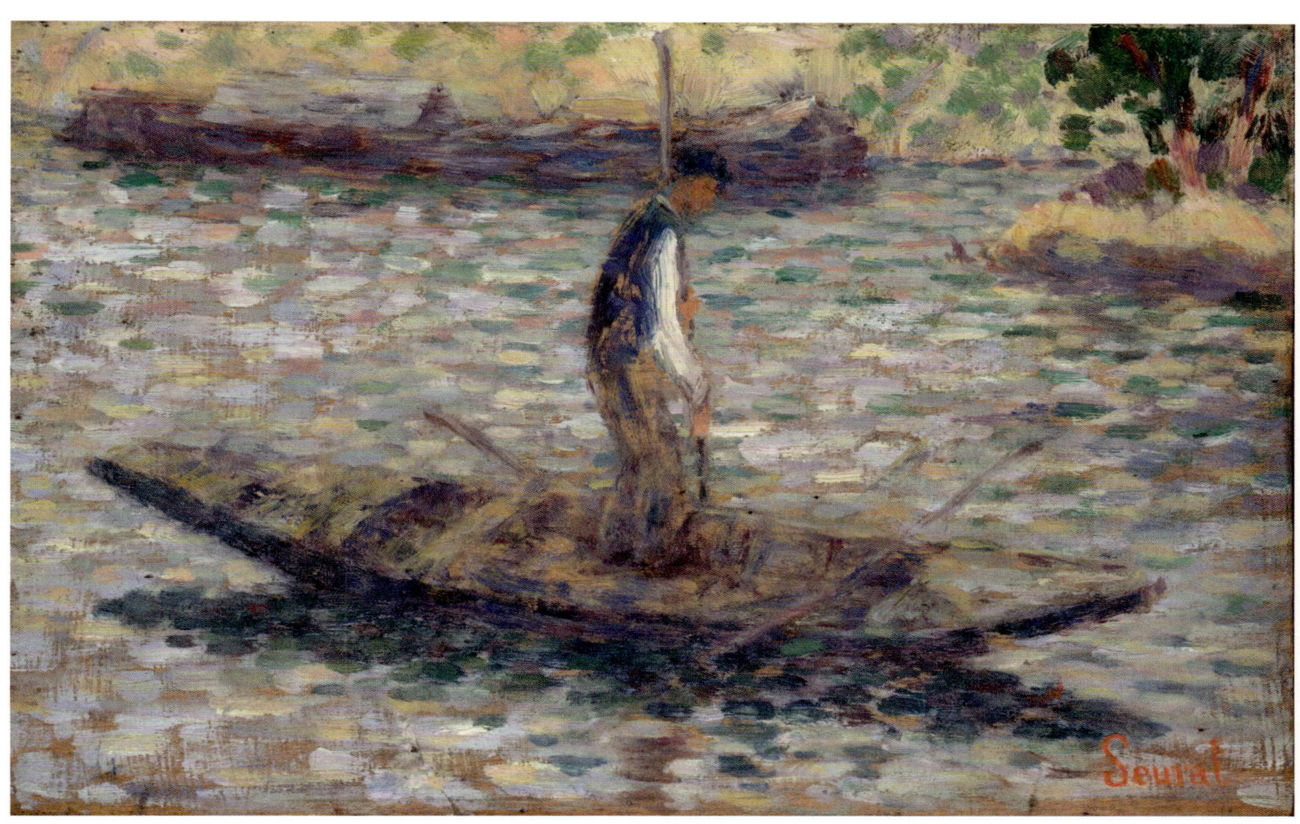

60 Georges Seurat
A Fisherman, c. 1884
Oil on panel, 33.5 × 42.7 cm
Yale University Art Gallery, New Haven
Bequest of Edith Malvina K. Wetmore

It seems that Seurat was actively painting on La Grande Jatte before he started to work on his major canvas of that name. There are oil sketches, which appear to have been painted on the island and bear no relation to either the subject or the composition of the large-scale painting that was to develop between 1884 and 1886. *Une Périssoire (A Canoe)* **(62)** takes the sporting subject of a sculling boat on the Seine. It is glimpsed through trees on the edge of the island. In the background substantial residential buildings are visible on the left bank of the river—the Courbevoie/Asnières side—and through the trees the Pont Bineau, which carried the boulevard of the same name across the middle of La Grande Jatte. The Courtauld *Man Painting a Boat* **(61)** seems to have been painted from a similar spot, though slightly further from the bridge, which can be discerned through the foliage with a figure walking across it. Behind the bourgeois in his boater, busy painting the blue hull of his boat, is a white wooden structure, probably a boat house. All three of these oil sketches, made during the summer months of 1883 and 1884, represent Asnières as a place for boating, whether competitive sport or leisure sailing: the lively preserve, in other words, of the comfortable middle classes.

By 1883 Seurat had decided to make Asnières the subject of his first major exhibition painting: *Une Baignade, Asnières (Bathers at Asnières)* **(66)**. Fourteen *croquetons* and some eight drawings show not only the development of the composition, its chromatics, and brushwork, but also of the staffage.[15] From his vantage on the left bank of the Seine looking slightly northeast, Seurat included the angled riverbank and broad river in the foreground, with the tip of La Grande Jatte on the right, and lined the far horizon with Levallois-Perret's local bridges and distant factories, which he bracketed by tall trees. Choosing a summer's day allowed a bright palette and natural contrast, such as that between the blue Seine and the ochre-orange mud of the bank, brushed in his loose *balayé* (crisscross) stroke. The figures necessitated more selection. The Edinburgh oil sketch clearly depicts the working class, showing an *ouvrier* (worker) resting and another washing a draft horse in the river **(63)**. The London panel has the same composition and represents the same spot, with the bank trodden down to allow horses access to the water **(64)**. But there are no animals, and human presence is suggested by a pile of clothes left on the bank by a swimmer who is not shown; the working riverbank here becomes a place of leisure. Already prefigured in Chicago's final compositional study,

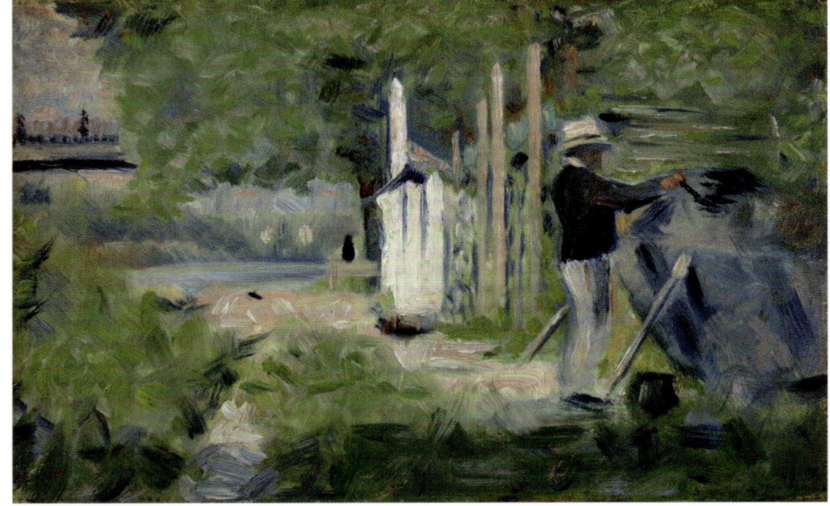

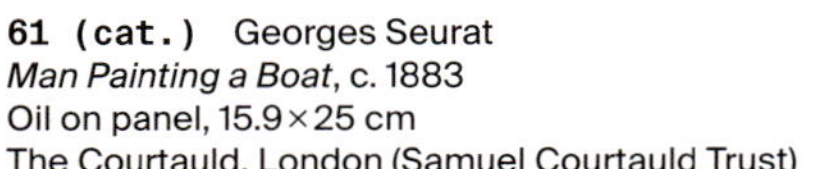

61 (cat.) Georges Seurat
Man Painting a Boat, c. 1883
Oil on panel, 15.9 × 25 cm
The Courtauld, London (Samuel Courtauld Trust)

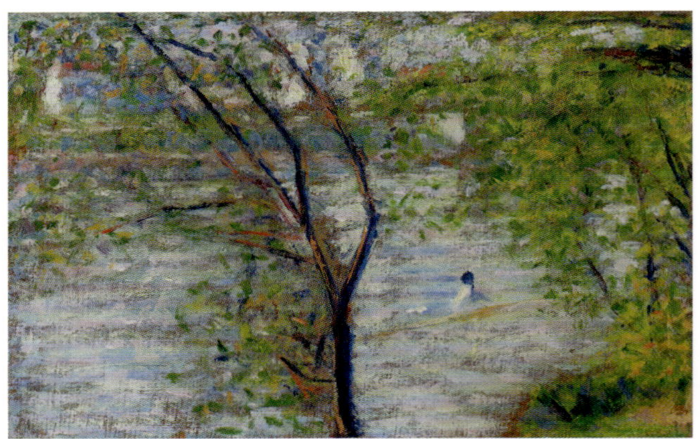

62 Georges Seurat
A Canoe, c. 1883–84
Oil on cradled panel, 15.6 × 25 cm
Private collection

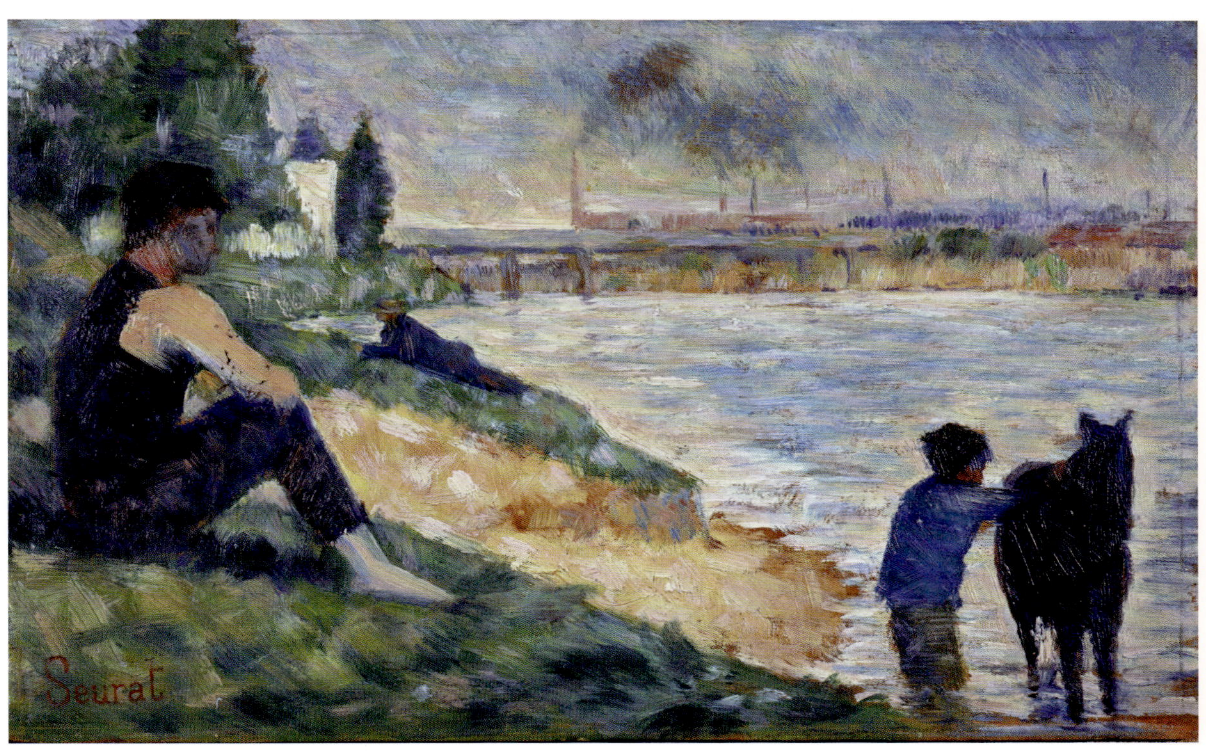

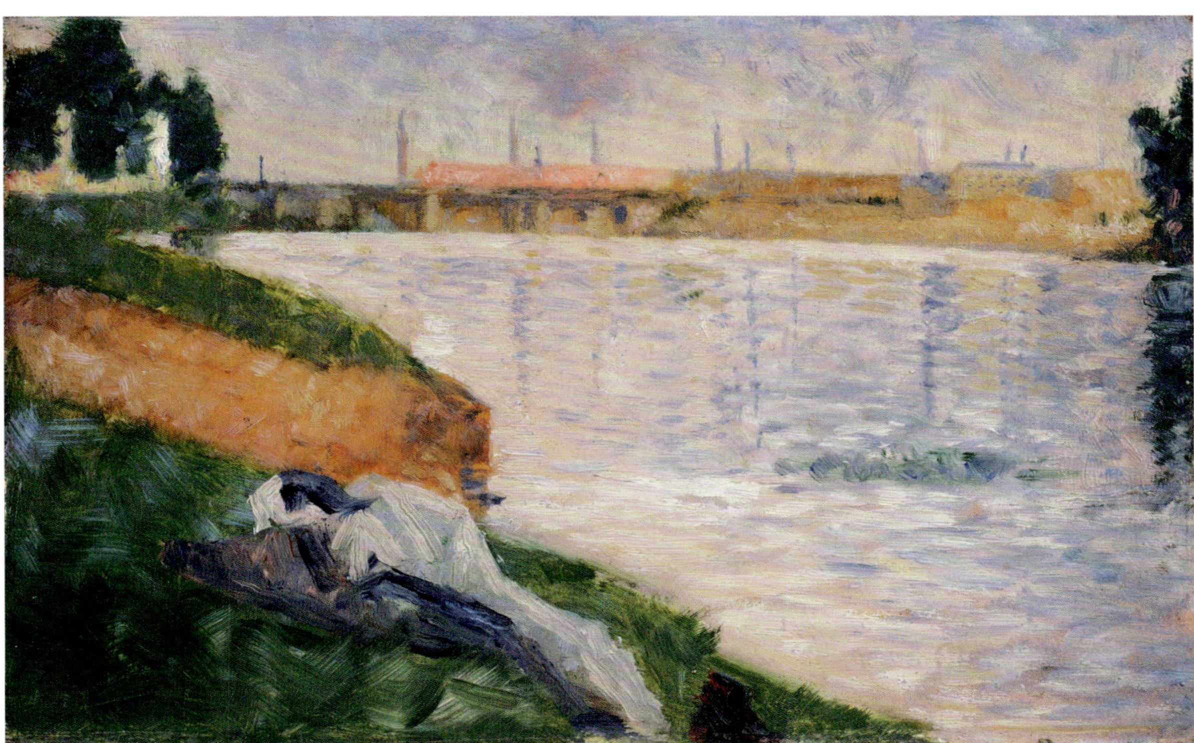

63 (cat.) Georges Seurat
Study for "Une Baignade," c. 1883
Oil on panel, 15.9×25 cm
National Galleries of Scotland, Edinburgh
Presented by Sir Alexander Maitland in memory of his wife Rosalind 1960

64 (cat.) Georges Seurat
Clothes on the Grass, 1883
Oil on panel, 16.2×24.8 cm
Tate, London
Presented by Alex Reid and Lefevre 1926

the completed painting *Une Baignade, Asnières* has a specific site: the two bridges, one for the railroad and the other for the road, the view toward industrialized Levallois-Perret, and to the rear left the wall of a riverside villa **(65, 66)**. The large canvas, two meters by three, portrays a range of male figures, but the boaters, bowlers, and elastic-sided boots, and the sculling and sailing on the water, show the comfortably employed, not the poorest workers. This matched the population of Asnières, by the mid-1880s increasingly a dormitory suburb with manufacturing.[16] One could argue that Seurat made assumptions about his viewers' knowledge of the area, taking for granted that they could read such a suburban scene, even if they could not place it exactly. A suburban view might typically encapsulate both the industrial and the residential. In one of his "croquis parisiens"—*Vue des remparts du Nord-Paris*—Huysmans wrote that "the eternal rule" is the combination of "sumptuous buildings" and "great ironworks and blast furnaces."[17]

Une Baignade does not make such a striking contrast, but for 1884 it was modern in color, simplicity, and subject. However, the jury of the official Salon that year rejected it, perhaps because of its bright chromatics and broad touch, the isolated character of its figures, or its substantial size for an unprepossessing subject. As a student Seurat had imbibed Blanc's *Grammaire des Arts du Dessin*, in which the story of Nicolas Poussin watching washerwomen on the banks of the Tiber and transforming them into *The Finding of Moses* **(67)** is upheld as an exemplar of the artist's metamorphosis of observation of mundane reality into aesthetic ideal.[18] Seurat would have known Poussin's composition from the Louvre, and *Une Baignade* echoes its design: to lower right a male figure waist-deep in the river and to lower left a reclining male figure seen from behind, with the horizon accented by tall trees, blocky buildings, and spanning bridges. The subject of Poussin's creative transformation had been represented by Léon Bénouville in a painting shown at the Salon of 1857. So *Une Baignade* is at once an aggrandized distillation of Seurat's recent painterly progress with touch and color, and a discreet development of academic theory, a composition consciously inherited from past art, with specific associations.[19] Yet these were not entirely without an Asnières connection. If, as seems likely, Seurat knew the Bénouville via reproduction, it was probably one printed by Goupil at the company's Asnières works in 1859 **(68)**.

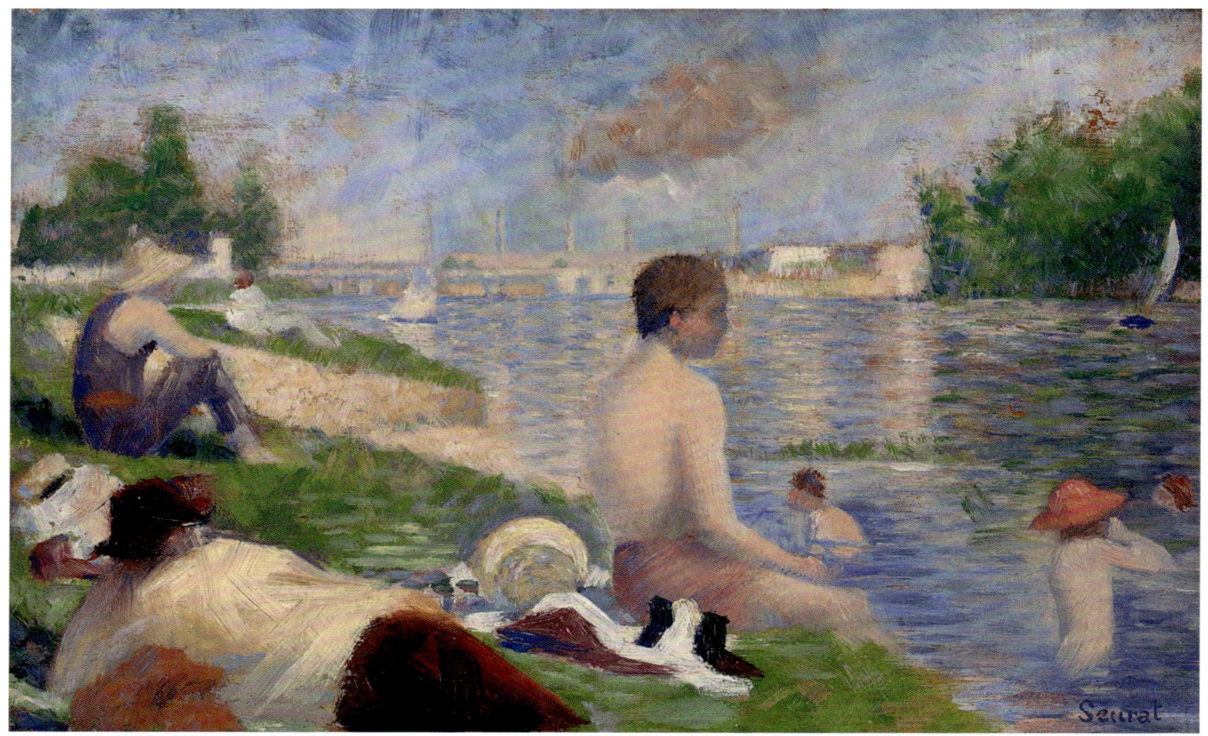

65 (cat.) Georges Seurat
Final Study for "Bathers at Asnières," 1883
Oil on panel, 15.8 × 25.1 cm
The Art Institute of Chicago
Gift of the Adele R. Levy Fund, Inc.

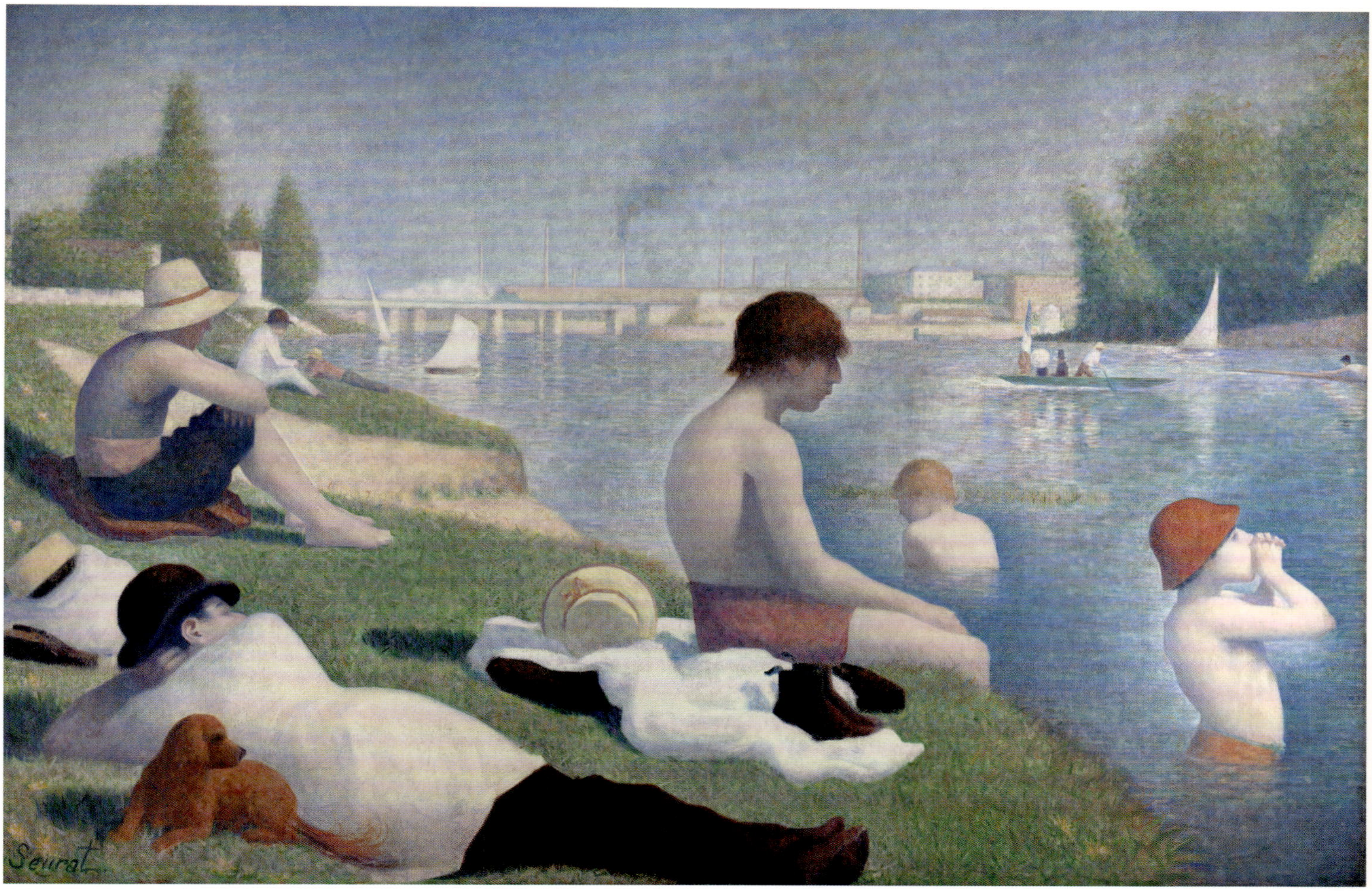

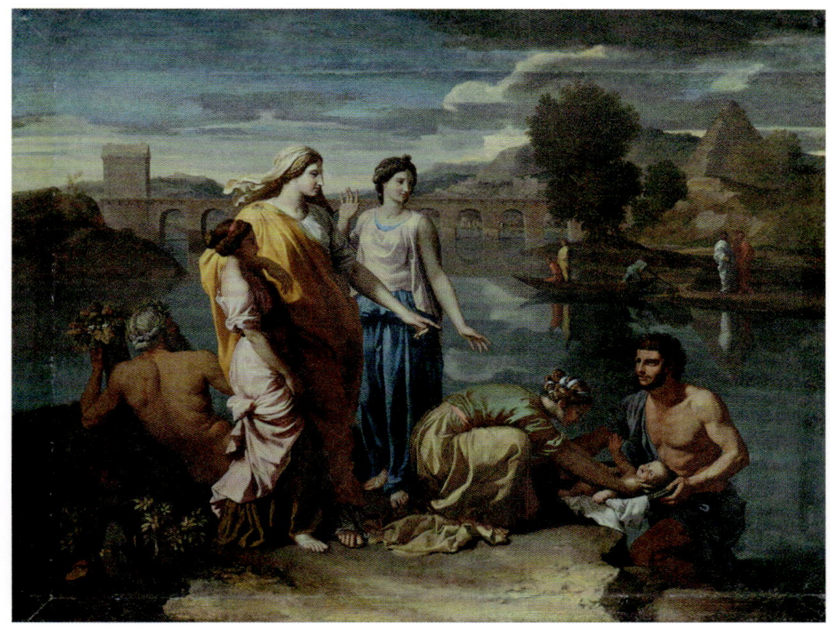

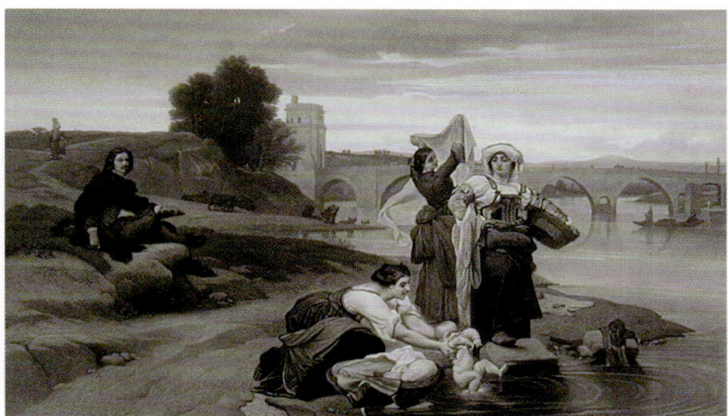

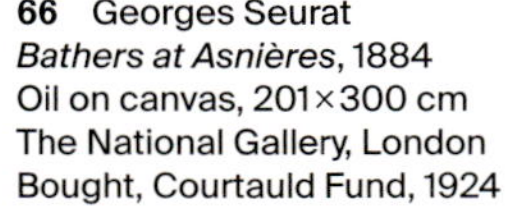

66 Georges Seurat
Bathers at Asnières, 1884
Oil on canvas, 201×300 cm
The National Gallery, London
Bought, Courtauld Fund, 1924

67 Nicolas Poussin
The Finding of Moses, 1638
Oil on canvas, 93.5×121 cm
Musée du Louvre, Paris

68 Emile Pierre Pichard, after Léon Bénouville
Nicolas Poussin (sur les bords du Tibre à Rome), 1859
Etching on paper, mixed techniques, 58×86 cm
Private collection

With *La Seine à Courbevoie (The Seine at Courbevoie)* **(69)**, painted in 1885 with the planning of what would become *La Grande-Jatte* under way, Seurat was striving for something different from *Une Baignade* **(66)**. This is not, after all, a *croqueton* but a finished canvas, significant enough to be exhibited at the eighth Impressionist exhibition the following year. It has an overall coherent touch, not yet the dot, but fairly consistent flecked or dabbed brushwork across the canvas, while still allowing difference between the irregularity of the foliage of the trees and the flat reflections on the waters of the Seine. Seurat made conscious play between natural and man-made shapes, not just contrasting the irregular growth of the trees and their foliage with the geometric roofs and embankment in the distance, but also the play of natural curves—the branches—and the crafted ones: the sail of the dinghy and the shape of women's fashion of the mid-1880s.

When *Une Baignade, Asnières* was rejected from the 1884 Salon but exhibited at the newly formed Salon des Indépendants later that year, Seurat immediately began work on another 2- by 3-meter canvas. Probably ready for exhibition by the spring of 1885, Seurat continued to rework the picture until he had the opportunity to show it at the eighth Impressionist exhibition in May 1886. Titled *Un Dimanche à la Grande-Jatte (1884) (A Sunday on La Grande Jatte—1884)*, the painting was initially handled in a crisscross stroke, over which was later but not consistently applied a more dotted touch; it was literally a progressive development of Seurat's drawing and painting technique **(70)**.[20] A sheet such as *Woman Walking with a Parasol* shows Seurat's figurative drawing style as he began the project and makes a notable contrast with the later *Seated Woman with a Parasol*, which is more starkly simplified, or more "synthetic" in the current avant-garde jargon **(71,72)**.[21]

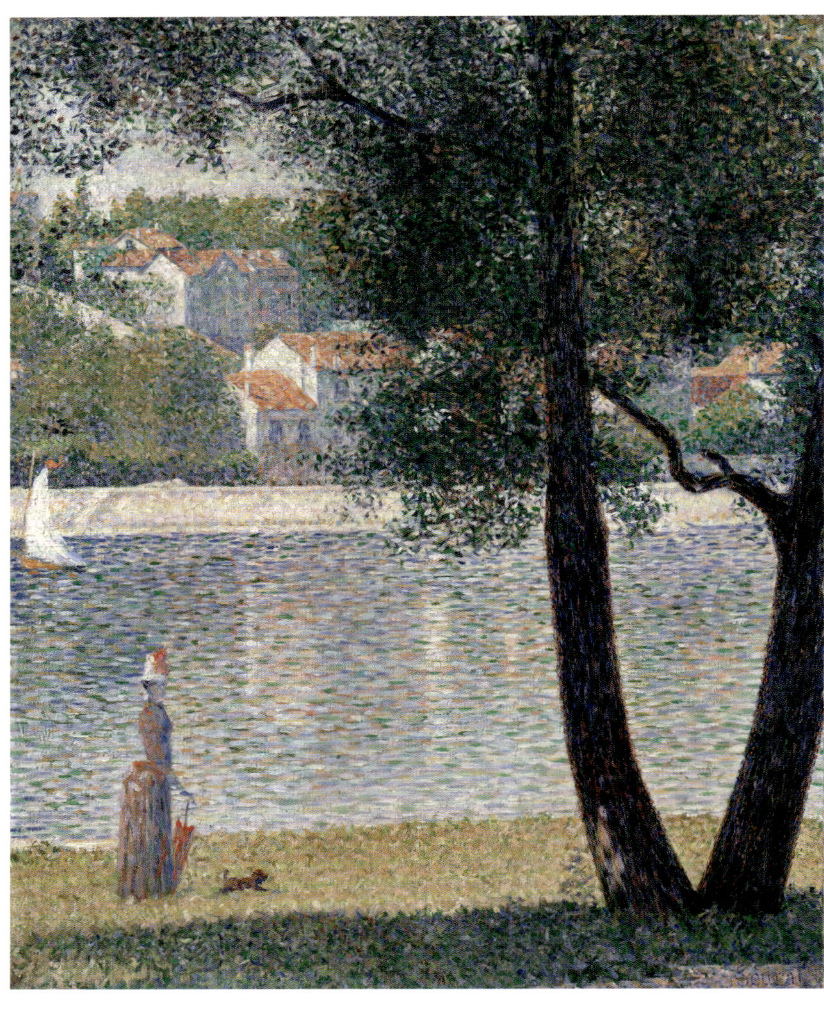

69 (cat.) Georges Seurat
The Seine at Courbevoie, 1885
Oil on canvas, 81.4 × 65.2 cm
Private collection

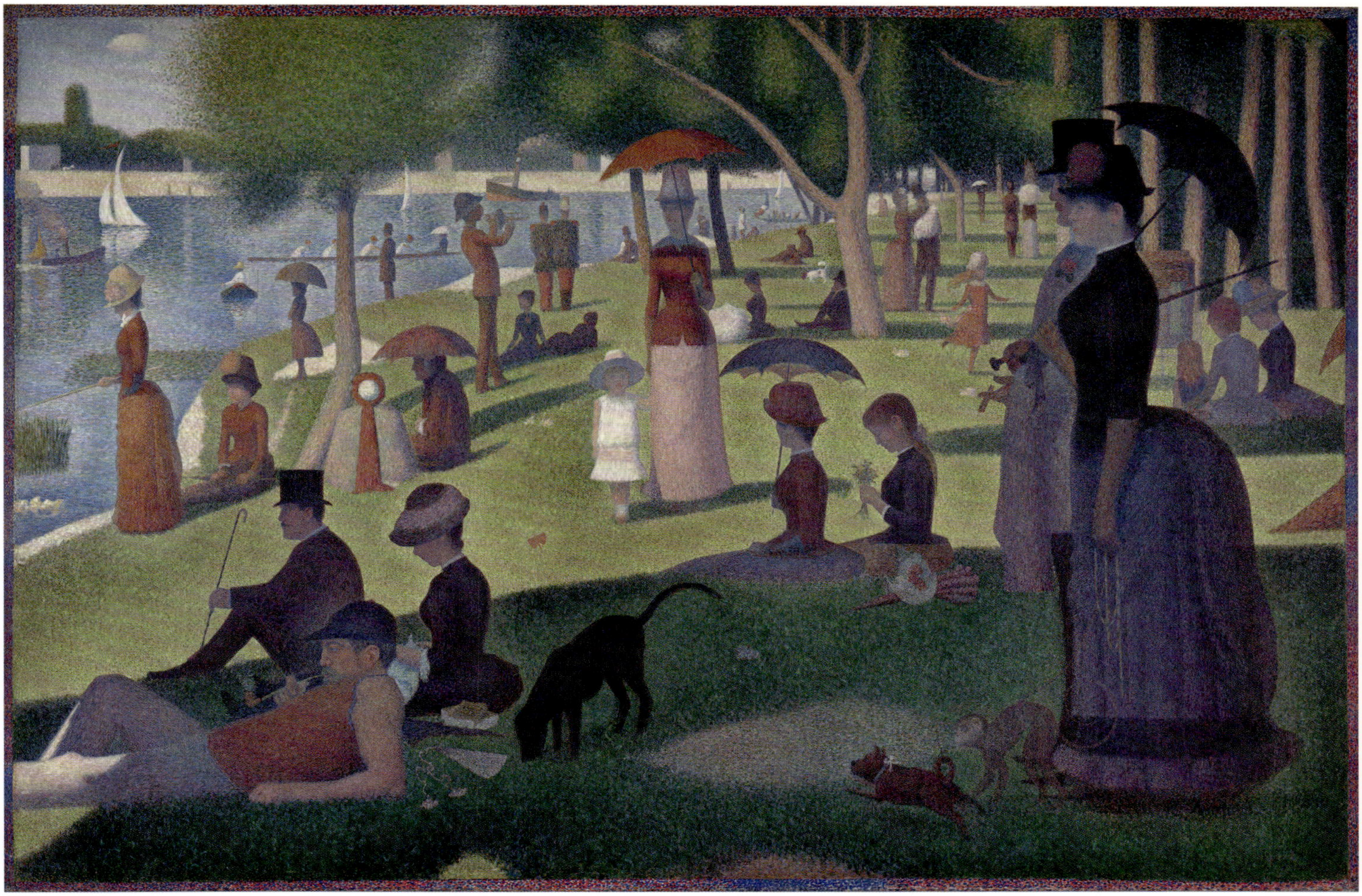

70 Georges Seurat
A Sunday on La Grande Jatte—1884, 1884–86
Oil on canvas, 207.5 × 308.1 cm
The Art Institute of Chicago
Helen Birch Bartlett Memorial Collection

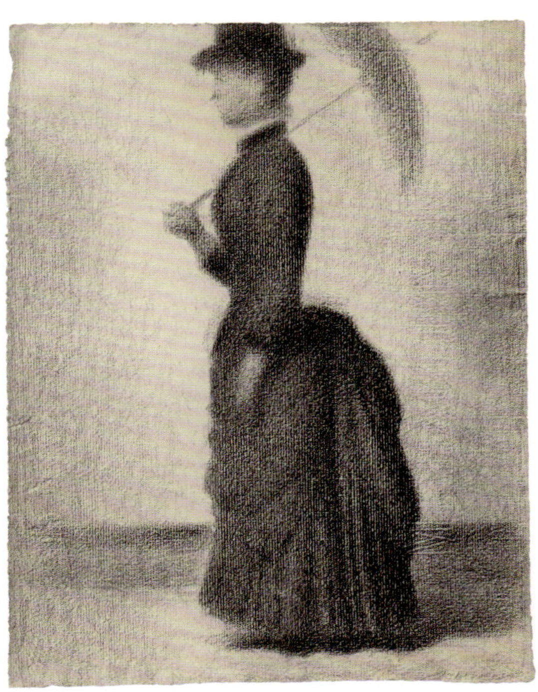

71 (cat.) Georges Seurat
Woman Walking with a Parasol (Study for La Grande Jatte), 1884
Conté crayon on cream laid paper, 31.7 × 24.1 cm
The Art Institute of Chicago
Bequest of Abby Aldrich Rockefeller

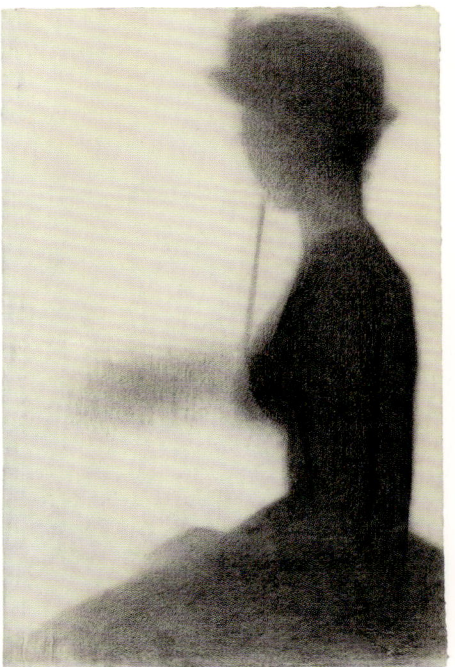

72 (cat.) Georges Seurat
Seated Woman with a Parasol (Study for La Grande Jatte), 1884–85
Black Conté crayon on ivory laid paper, 48 × 31.5 cm
The Art Institute of Chicago
Bequest of Abby Aldrich Rockefeller

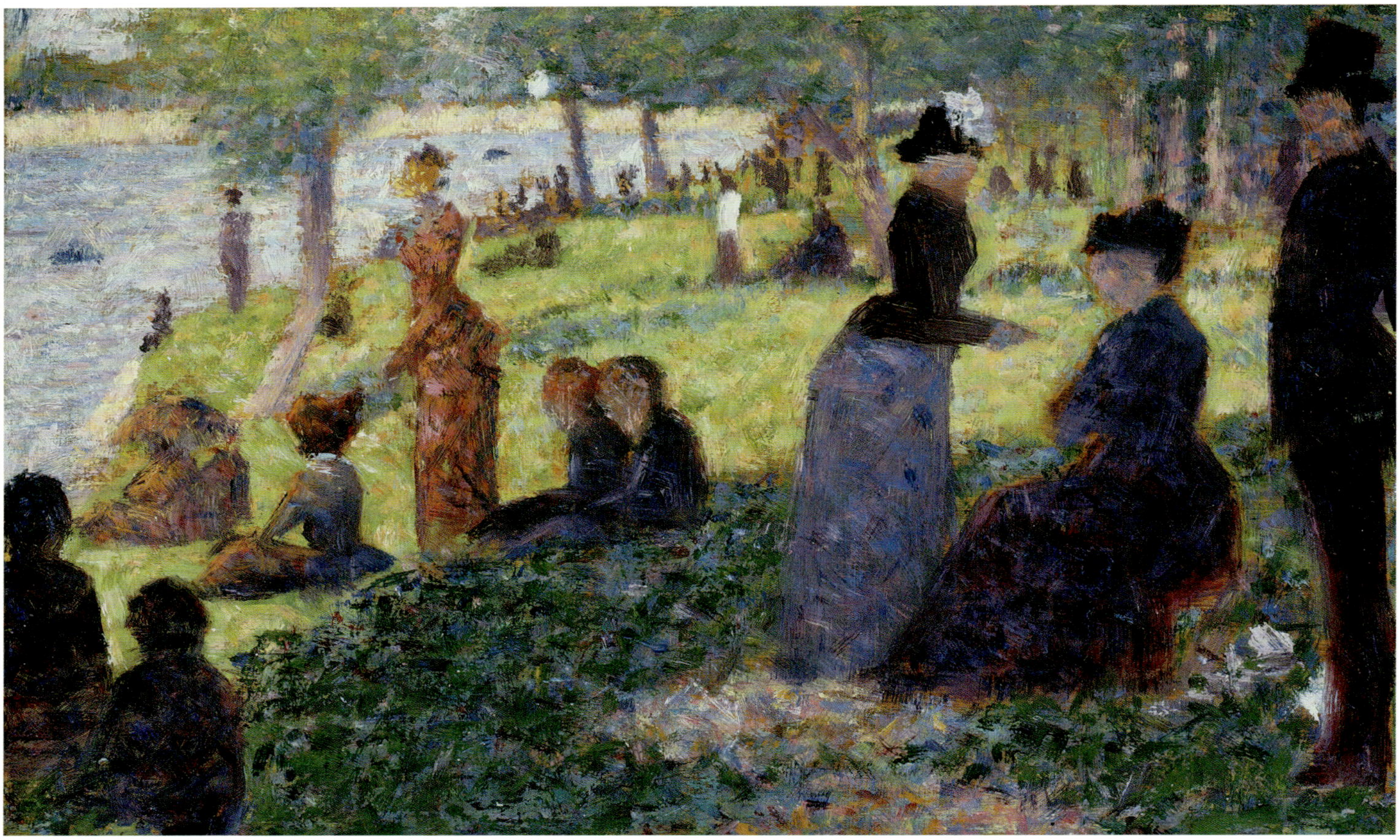

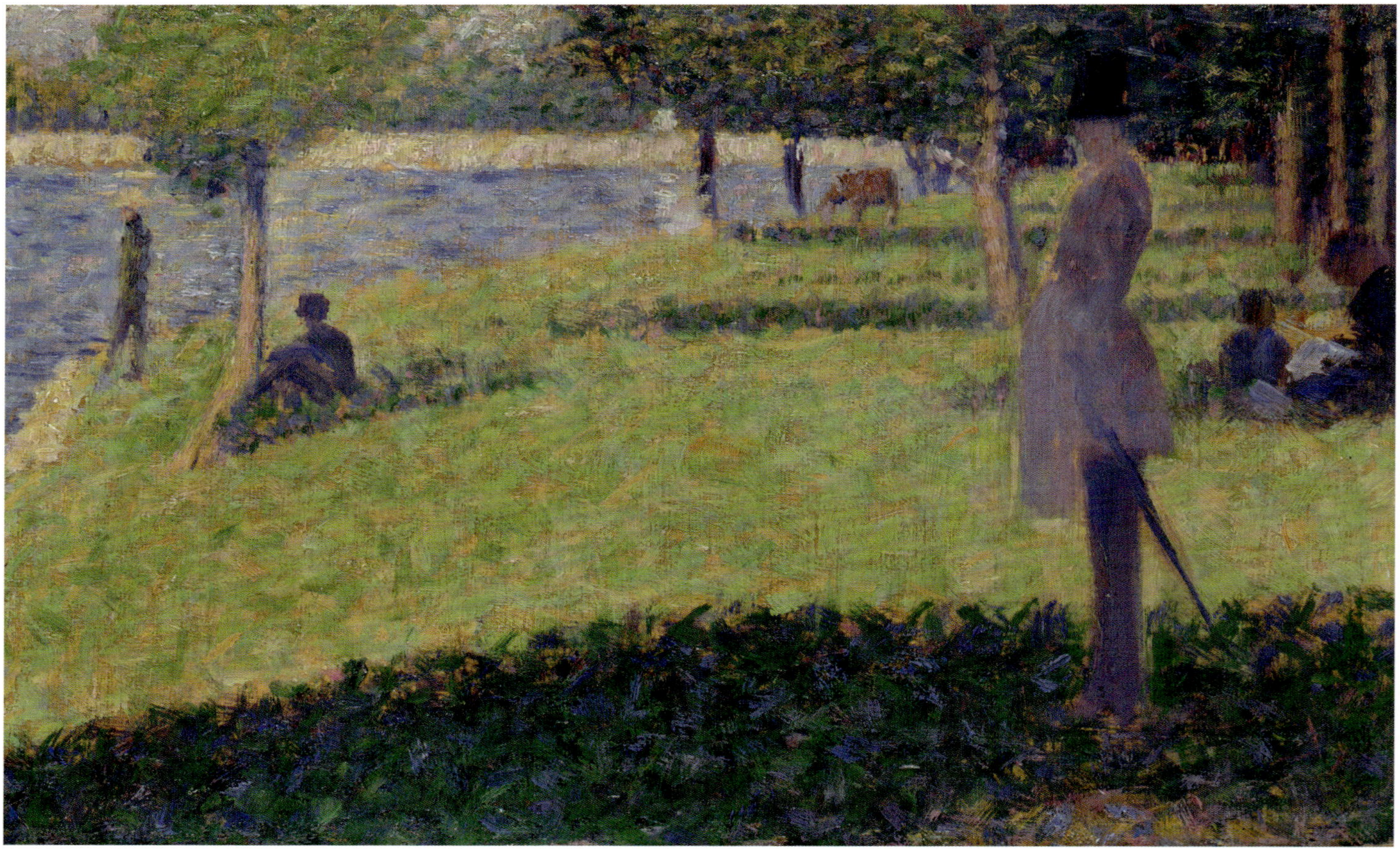

73 (cat.) Georges Seurat
Oil Sketch for "La Grande Jatte," 1884
Oil on panel, 15.5 × 24.3 cm
The Art Institute of Chicago
Gift of Mary and Leigh Block

74 (cat.) Georges Seurat
Study for "La Grande Jatte," 1884–85
Oil on panel, 17.5 × 26 cm
The National Gallery, London
Presented by Heinz Berggruen, 1995

A similar process seems to apply to his preliminary *croquetons*, and it might be argued that the multifigure preparatory panel in the Art Institute's collection, with its looser and less structured handling of paint, predates the more disciplined brushwork, distribution of color, and simplification of the figures in the London oil study **(73,74)**. Just as Seurat was increasingly systematizing his chromatics—keeping true to the greens that are the local color of grass but enlivening them with dabbed or dotted accents of yellow to register the play of sunlight and of red, the color opposite of green, to sharpen their contrast—so in parallel his drawing became more synthetic and, with it, the composition more controlled. Both the Conté drawings and *croquetons* for *La Grande-Jatte* are consistent in their ordered horizontal and planar orientation, the structuring of the composition across the field of vision, its dominant regularity broken by a few incidents such as the approaching mother and child and the running girl.

Something of that sense of order, and in particular the overlapping figures of the couple on the right, may owe to Seurat's study of the *Ergastines (Weavers)*, a fragment of the fifth-century BCE sculptor Phidias's Parthenon Frieze in the Louvre's collection **(75)**. But that conventional academic model was given a modern edge, to which critics reviewing the 1886 exhibition responded. A number of them referred to the flat and simplified treatment of the *Grande-Jatte*'s figures in terms of toys like wooden dolls, lead soldiers, or puppets.[22] Several, such as Marcel Fouquier in *Le XIXe Siècle*, wrote about it as a joke.[23] Others linked the stiff figures to the starchy, corseted clothes then fashionable, to what Paul Adam in *La Revue contemporaine* called "the sound of the modern, the recollection of our stiff costumes, stuck to the body, the restraint of gestures, the British cant everybody imitates."[24] Writing in *La Revue moderne* Ajalbert concurred, describing "the tight-fitting dresses falling straight, the shaping corsets, the hugging jackets," and also using, as others did, the avant-garde artists' recently adopted term, borrowed from science and meaning simplification: "synthèse."[25]

As these writers implicitly recognized, such pared-down drawing reducing the human figure to a schematic and even comic type was the territory of the mass-produced imagery of advertisements and notably of caricature. On July 29, 1881, the Third Republic had passed a law granting

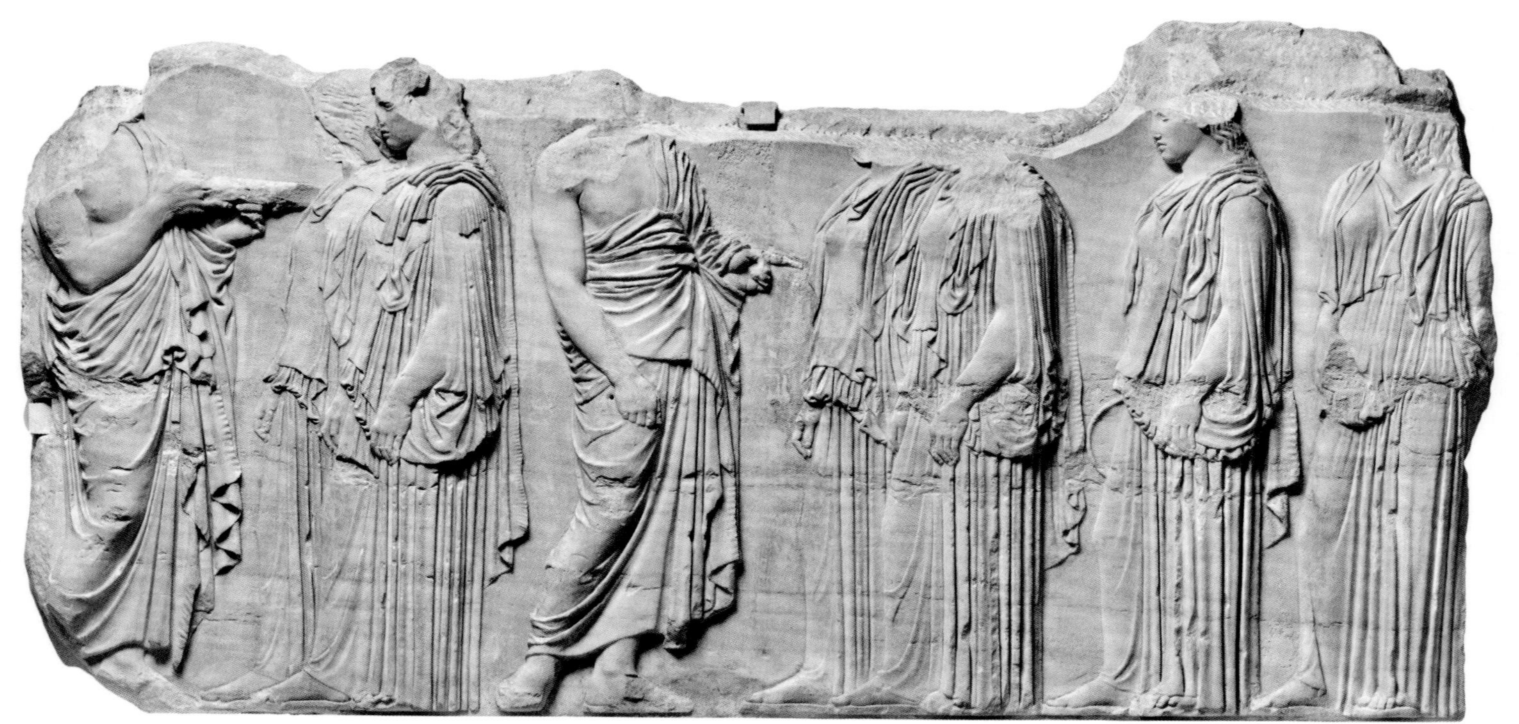

75 Phidias
Ergastines (Weavers), slab VII, from the East Frieze of the Parthenon, c. 447–432 BCE
Marble, 101×207 cm
Musée du Louvre, Paris

liberty to the press. Consequences of the freedom of expression were the rapid emergence of caricatural periodicals such as *Le Courrier français*, which used modern printing technologies to illustrate its pages. The main couple in *La Grande-Jatte* recall not just the adjacent pair in the *Ergastines*, but find their synthetic parallels in graphics promoting department stores and the reductive caricatures published by artists such as Alfred Grévin, Ferdinand Lunel, and Henri Gray **(76,77)**. This radical mentality—making fun of the pomposities and pretentions of the dominant bourgeois culture—also spawned cabarets, the most celebrated being Le Chat Noir in Montmartre, founded in 1881, which hosted satirical singers and comic poets and had its own illustrated journal.[26] An early participant in the pranks of the Chat Noir was Paul Signac, and in 1888 Seurat was listed as a visitor.[27] Perhaps there was an Asnières connection here: the extrovert Signac, who had moved with his parents to that suburb in 1880, encouraging his friend to attend the Chat Noir. Another suburban link could be the awareness of how the riverbank crowd might be caricatured, which seems to have been shared by Seurat and Ajalbert, native of Levallois-Perret, whose slim volume of verse *Sur le vif* was published early in 1886, before *La Grande-Jatte* was on view, and included such poems as "Chromolithographie":

> *Votre chapeau, tressé d'une paille vulgaire,*
> *Couvrait mal vos cheveux, et plus d'un frison fou*
> *S'égarait sur vos yeux de pervenche fleurie.*
> *La gloire de vos seins chantait dans le corset . . .*
>
> Your hat, woven of vulgar straw,
> Covered your hair badly, and more than one crazy curl
> Strayed over your flowery periwinkle eyes.
> The glory of your breasts sang in the corset . . . [28]

Here was a similar parodying use of types and tone, which suggests how Seurat's radical painting was in tune not just with the widespread caricatural imagery but also with Ajalbert's verse as a way of playfully envisaging brassy suburban posturing. Painted in a radical new technique—to be christened "néo-impressionnisme" by the end of 1886—and phrasing its figures in harmony with the current comical mentality, *La Grande-Jatte* exploited the Asnières locality and its well-known associations to make an assertively avant-garde statement. It was entirely at odds with the

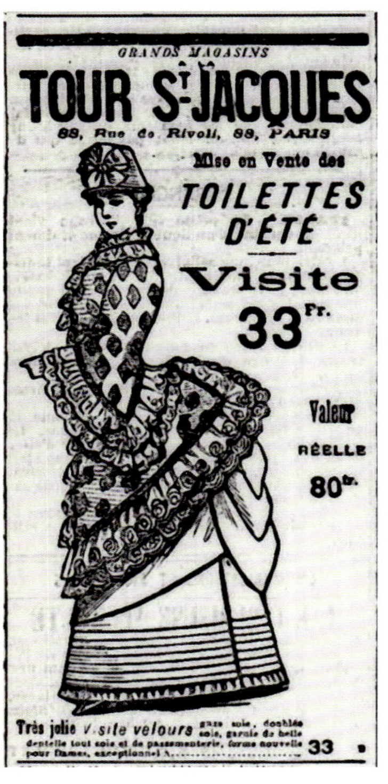

76 "Tour St. Jacques. Toilettes d'Eté," *La Petite République française*, April 20, 1885, p. 4 (detail)

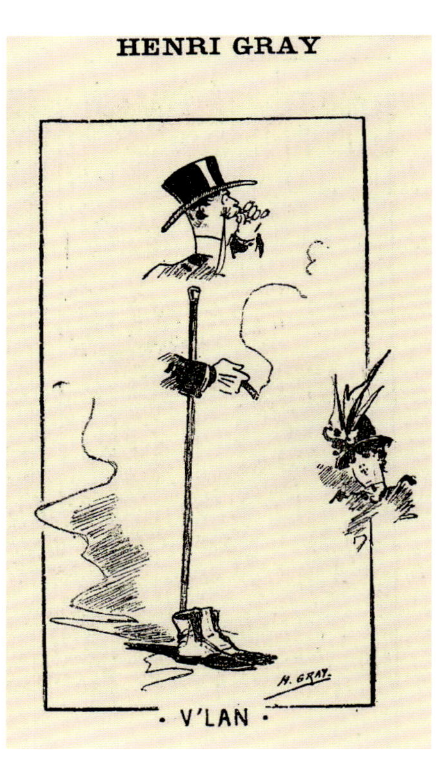

77 Henri Gray "V'lan," *Exposition des arts incohérents, Catalogue illustré,* Paris, 1883, p. viii

dominant naturalism of the paintings of the suburbs that were so common at the Salons, canvases such as Joseph Caraud's *La Pêcheuse (The Fisherwoman)* **(78)**, with its fussy detailing of fingers and pleats, bonnet and picnic basket.

Having exhibited *La Grande-Jatte* in the spring of 1886, over the following two years Seurat completed three canvases on the Asnières-Courbevoie stretch of the Seine, all landscape paintings of conventional size but featuring his newly developed Neo-Impressionist chromatics and brushwork. These were the last paintings Seurat would make in the Asnières locality, and they discreetly attest his complicated loyalties. *Le Pont de Courbevoie (The Bridge at Courbevoie)* **(79)**, exhibited at the Salon des Indépendants in March 1887, by which time it belonged to the art critic Arsène Alexandre, uses a motif explored first in a drawing, which includes only a single figure **(80)**. The finished canvas has three, but all separated, isolated. The painting seems to adopt the common notion of the suburbs as sites of melancholy, independently evoking the "tristesse" of "paysages désolés," about which Raffaëlli had written that January. But *Le Pont de Courbevoie* goes further by distilling melancholic emotion in the logic of its structure and the muted chromatic harmony of violet and green, two subdued secondaries. Seurat may also have been aware of the emerging ideas of the psychophysicist Charles Henry, whose notion that diagonal lines below the horizontal are "inhibitory" or sad corresponds to the shadows on the riverbank.[29] The painting thus registers as Symbolist, embracing the new aesthetic emerging with the publication of Jean Moréas's manifesto in 1886, which dismissed descriptive naturalism in favor of suggestion and evocation.[30] Seurat's landscape gives a sense of order through man-made verticals, horizontals, and arches, in which the vagaries of nature—the leafy branches to the left, the smoke carried by the wind in the distance—play a limited role, and the dead tree in the foreground seems a metaphor for the rigid, lonely men on the riverbank beyond it.

By contrast, Seurat made a gift of *Temps Gris, Grande-Jatte (Gray Weather, Grande Jatte)* to Alexandre Séon, an old friend from the Ecole des Beaux-Arts where they had both been enrolled on the same day in March 1878 **(81)**. Séon had been commissioned in February 1885 to paint a cycle of mural decorations for the *salle des mariages* of the *mairie* (town hall) of Courbevoie. Two of these mural panels, *La Fête* and *Le Travail*, were exhibited at the Salon of 1886, and the four compositions for the ceiling, *Les Saisons*, were installed in 1889.[31] It is possible that Seurat's gift was in celebration of that achievement.

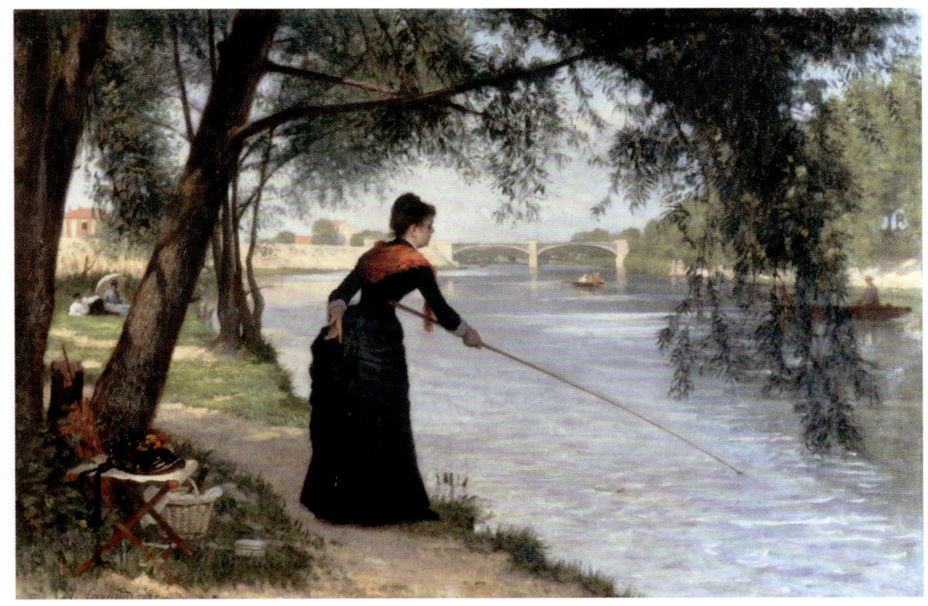

78 Joseph Caraud
The Fisherwoman, 1884
Oil on canvas, 49.5×73.7 cm
Private collection

For his part, Séon dedicated a drawing of a female nude from *L'Eté*, one of the *mairie*'s ceiling panels, to his old colleague. Seurat did not paint decorations for public buildings and, indeed, never seems to have entered a competition to do so, while Séon did not paint in a Neo-Impressionist dot and preferred his own ideas about the symbolism of tones to the use of complementary colors. Nevertheless, the two artists remained in contact, and their exchange of work witnesses not only an interest in each other's practice but also their shared commitment to Courbevoie. The composition of *Temps Gris, Grande-Jatte*, which seems to have been painted without either a preliminary drawing or *croqueton*, is similar to *Pont de Courbevoie*. In both, the bridge or far bank provides a stabilizing horizontal in the upper half of the canvas, counter-pointing the sloping bank. However, *Temps Gris* appears less schematic, its surface not dogmatically dotted, its rippling riverside and consistent screens of foliage more descriptively naturalistic than the more stylized *Pont*, its well-worn path and moored pleasure steamer suggesting sociability, even if no figures are included.

La Seine à La Grande-Jatte, printemps (The Seine at La Grande Jatte , Spring), made in 1888 and another of Seurat's few full-scale landscape canvases of the suburbs painted in a mature Neo-Impressionist style, differs from the two canvases just discussed because it was preceded by a *croqueton*, which it closely followed, as well as in its bright, springtime chromatics **(135,136)**. Clustering its diagonals below the firm band of the far embankment, it shows Seurat's confidence in painting reflected light; indeed, the reflections of the far parapet and houses act as a structural element in the design, as well as introducing some warm tones into the generally cool central band. He rendered the surface of the Seine in dots alone, its blues modulated with some greens and pale violet, with the freer handling of the foliage heightened in orange and pink. The view of villas rather than factories and the sporting character of the sailing dinghy and the sculling boat gives the canvas a different character to its two predecessors, a sunny return to the smaller boating motifs that had preceded *Une Baignade*. But it is close to the motif that Charles Angrand painted in company with Seurat **(134)**, a fraternal collabo-

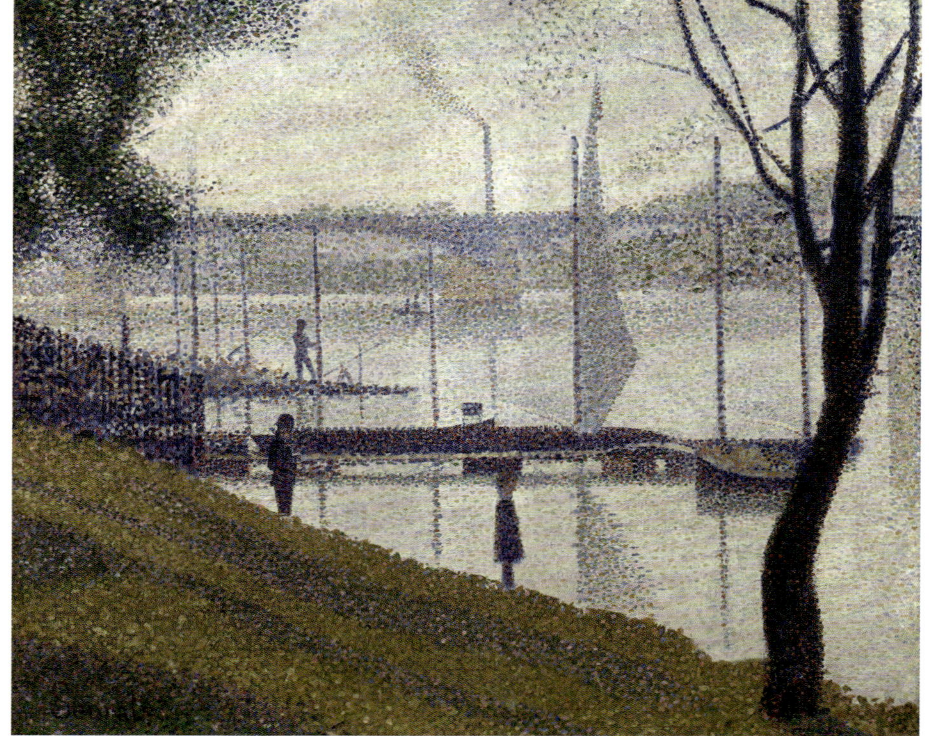

79 Georges Seurat
The Bridge at Courbevoie, 1886–87
Oil on canvas, 46.4×55.3 cm
The Courtauld, London (Samuel Courtauld Trust)

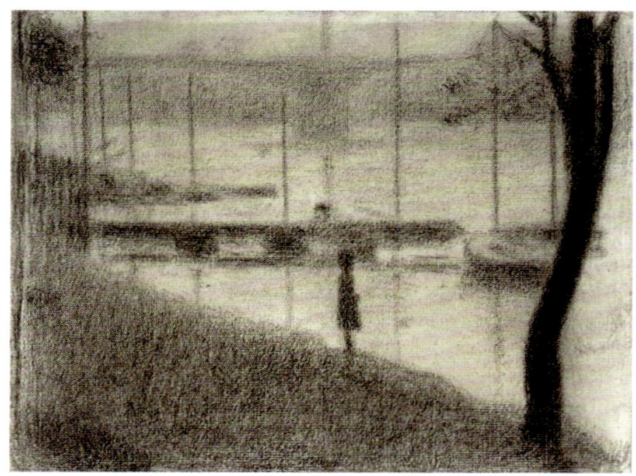

80 Georges Seurat
Pont de Courbevoie, 1886–87
Conté crayon on paper, 24.1×30.5 cm
Private collection

ration between two of the *néo* avant-garde, which Seurat acknowledged by giving his friend the *croqueton* **(136)**.[32]

Seurat's progress toward *Une Baignade* and then *La Grande-Jatte* shows a distinct development, his emergence as a pioneering avant-garde figure in the short years prior to his premature death in 1891. The former had its associations with his academic training's awareness of past art and heralded his reaction to it. The latter was a more radical confrontation of stylistic convention and experimental touch, color, drawing, and caricature. But both major paintings used the suburbs around Asnières with their changing and multi-faceted character not merely as their subject, but also as the society that stimulated Seurat's simultaneous response to nature and modern suburban environs, provoking his evolution as a painter. If his work—*croquetons*, large compositions, and Neo-Impressionist landscapes—operate on the cusp of the caricatural and celebratory, attentive to nature and conscious of style, then they echo the ambiance of Asnières. ■

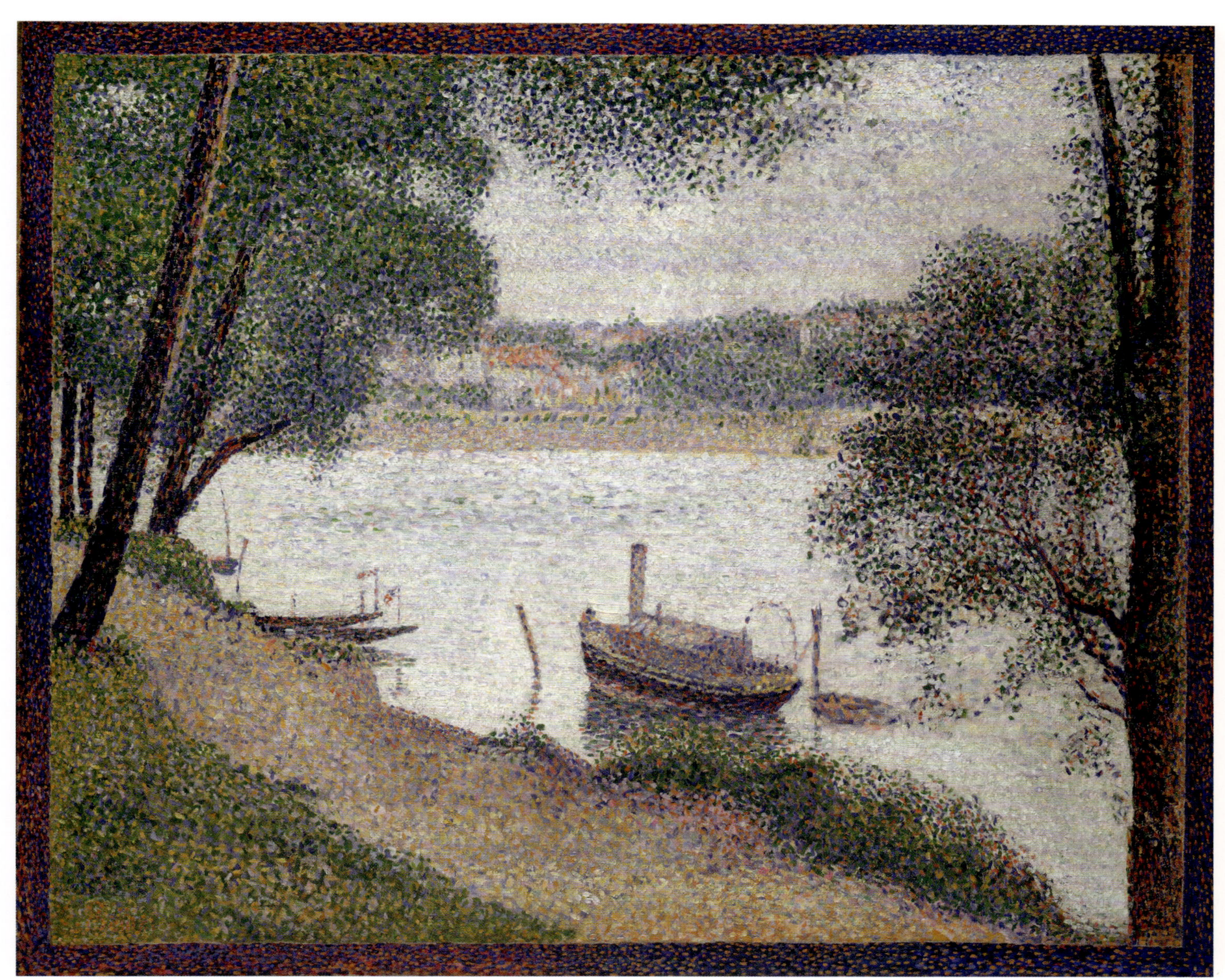

81 Georges Seurat
Gray Weather, Grande Jatte, c. 1886–88
Oil on canvas, 70.5 × 86.4 cm
The Metropolitan Museum of Art, New York
The Walter H. and Leonore Annenberg Collection, Gift of Walter H. and Leonore Annenberg, 2002, Bequest of Walter H. Annenberg, 2002

SIGNAC IN ASNIÈRES: THE FORMATIVE YEARS

CHARLOTTE HELLMAN

The Birthplace of a Vocation

On March 17, 1880, Jules Signac, the strict father of the sixteen-year-old Paul Signac, succumbed suddenly to tuberculosis. For the budding artist, the premature death of his father marked a decisive turning point in several ways. Admittedly, the young man had never had any desire to take control of the prosperous family saddlery firm Sellerie Signac, but this twist of fate definitively set him on a different course. The family firm was liquidated, meaning that the Signac family now had the independent means to support themselves. Paul's mother, Héloïse, decided to leave their luxurious home on avenue Frochot in Paris to move with her son and father-in-law to the small town of Asnières, to their new address of 42 bis rue de Paris (now rue Maurice-Bokanowski). In Asnières, Signac hosted frequent visits from his Parisian friends—including promising young writers like Paul Alexis and John-Antoine Nau (future winner of the first Prix Goncourt)—under the benevolent gaze of his grandfather, "the amiable old man who was so welcoming to your [Signac's] friends, and a reader of the late *Le Cri*."[1]

Asnières at the time was in the process of becoming a wealthy residential neighborhood, but was nevertheless close to that area where the working classes would come to enjoy their free time on Sundays, which would soon be immortalized by Seurat in his first large painting *Bathers at Asnières* **(66)**. By now, the carefree boaters featured in works by Pierre-Auguste Renoir and Claude Monet had given way to scenes of walkers and bathers, in which we can detect a slightly more melancholy air, with the silhouettes of the factories in the background and on the opposite bank. As leisure developed so did the city and its suburbs, which had been going through an industrial transition over the past fifteen years or so. Factories with smoking chimneys, gasometers, and cranes were now well-established elements of this landscape.

Whether a sign of fate or an accident of timing—Paul Signac's biography is peppered with happy coincidences—the year that he moved was the same year that the young man discovered the artist who would seal his vocation. The exhibition of Monet's works held in June 1880 at the premises of *La Vie moderne*, the journal founded in 1879 and devoted to all branches of the artistic avant-garde, was a life-changing event that led to a revelation: he would be a painter, it was decided![2] Signac wrote to Monet asking him for advice and was able to set up his easel *en plein air*, close to the Seine. His very first canvases date from late 1881 and early 1882, and his preferred subjects were the Seine at Asnières and views of Port-en-Bessin, in Normandy. All this was very reminiscent of Monet—Signac even included a haystack as a touching tribute to Monet's first series of paintings in one of his paintings. He went on to break off his studies (despite having made a brilliant start in high school) and was soon dividing his time between Montmartre, where he rented a room, and the family home in Asnières. From the windows of this quiet family house, he was able to see the smokestacks of Clichy. There was a stark contrast in the landscape from one bank of the river to the other, between carefree enjoyment—from boating for the better-off to simple walks for the rest—and the world of work deriving from the new technological and industrial transformations. This marked dichotomy clearly stimulated the budding artist's creative impulse. In an aerial photograph taken in 1885 by the Commandant Fribourg **(19)**, the banks on the Asnières side, dotted with houses and their gardens, face those of Clichy with their factories, gasometers, and coal cranes.[3] Further up, we can also see where the Asnières docks had been built for pleasure boats and the end of the famous island of La Grande Jatte.

Initially, Signac discovered the joys of boating, the pastime of an independently wealthy young man who had already bought himself a *périssoire*, a type of sculling boat, which he christened *Manet-Zola-Wagner*, thereby ostentatiously signaling his embrace of the avant-garde. Signac certainly was a "bourgeois bohemian" even before the term was coined. While his financial resources and free time meant he could take part in the new "advent of leisure"—which marked a sea change in the final twenty years of the nineteenth century—his thinking was definitely that of an artist resolutely committed to progressive ideas and the rejection of social conventions.[4] However, Asnières was first and foremost a place where the passionate young Impressionist experimented with painting and boating, as illustrated by his highly energetic and colorful *Asnières Study (Laundry Boat)* **(82)**.

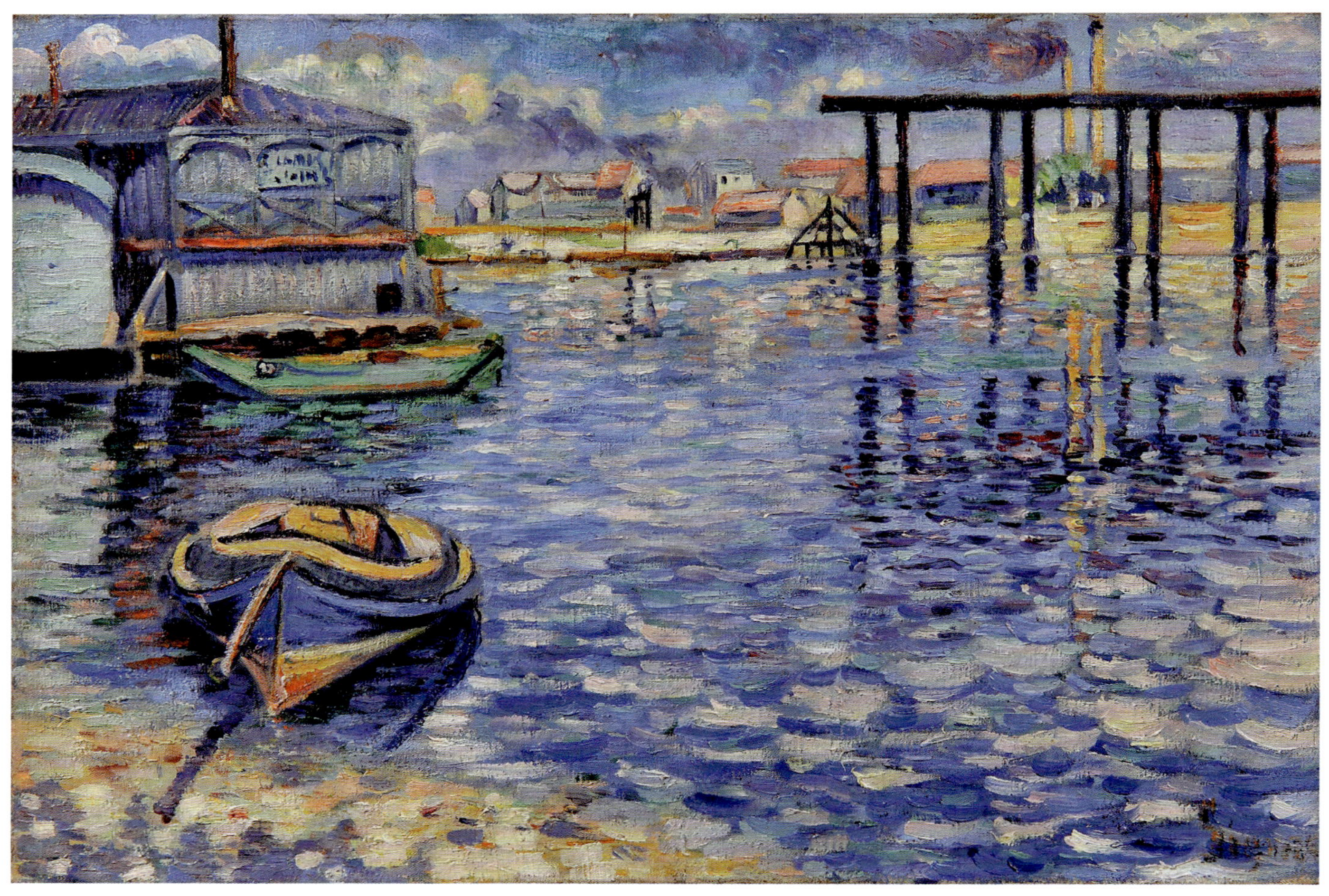

82 (cat.) Paul Signac
Asnières Study (Laundry Boat), 1882
Oil on canvas, 38.6 × 56 cm
Uehara Museum of Art, Shimoda

Signac's literary education—at one point he had even intended to become a writer—certainly stimulated his interest in this new place of residence: Signac was a passionate reader of Emile Zola and Joris-Karl Huysmans, who described life in the small towns on the outskirts of the city like Asnières and Courbevoie.[5] Meanwhile, the term "La vie Moderne" (modern life), borrowed from Charles Baudelaire, was already rife with implications in itself.[6] In addition to the avant-garde art movements championed by the journal of the same name, it also referred to the new ethos of movement that was setting the pace for city-dwellers' working lives and leisure time, as imposed by railroad stations, boats, and factories. Progress, for this young man with a thirst for discovery, equated in large part to movement, by train, boat, and later by car, which corresponded well to the restless temperament of an artist who would go on to become a great traveler.

From that point onward, Signac traveled frequently back and forth between his studios near the place Clichy (initially in the rue de Steinkerque from 1882, then after 1886 in the boulevard de Clichy, near Seurat's studio) and the family home in Asnières. These journeys took him via the Gare Saint-Lazare, the railroad station that had already become an emblem of modernity depicted by the Impressionist painters: Manet (*The Railway*, 1873; National Gallery of Art, Washington), Caillebotte (*The Pont de l'Europe*, 1876; Musée Petit Palais, Geneva), and of course Monet **(17)**, an enduring object of his admiration. In 1886, it was also painted by Charles Angrand **(129)**. Signac's first pencil sketches from 1885 observe this "contemporary cathedral" at the point when it was about to undergo major expansion works. He used a format of sketchbook that could comfortably slip into his pocket and would do so throughout his life. Arriving in Asnières by train, he continued to work in the same sketchbook, capturing the landscape in front of him, both bucolic and industrial, between the branches of a tree in springtime and the smoking chimneys of the factories that were emerging around the *environs* of Paris, a city in the throes of transformation **(83)**. To the left in this drawing can be seen one of the public bathing establishments installed on boats

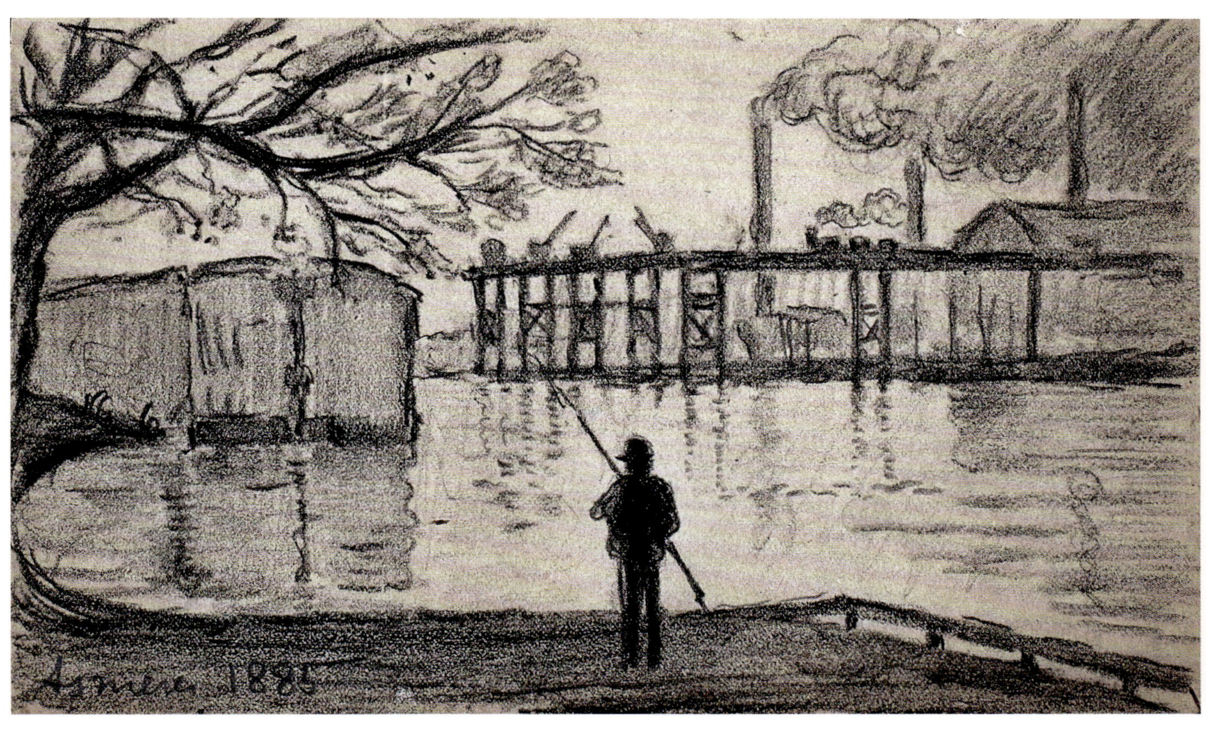

83 Paul Signac
Asnières, the Baths and the Cranes of the Gasworks, 1885
Page from a sketchbook, graphite crayon on paper, 11.8 × 19.5 cm
Archives Signac, Paris

moored at the quays, which he went on to feature in several of his paintings **(84, 36)**. Thanks to a pump fed by the river water, these new establishments offered hot baths in a cabin set over the water. Gradually, these bathing facilities used initially by the working classes were supplemented by sport and leisure infrastructures with pontoons and refreshment stalls.

The very polished sketches Signac made of the Gare Saint-Lazare illustrate his desire to paint his own version of the station, but he ultimately opted instead for the station at the Bois-Colombes railroad junction in Asnières **(85)**. It shows the beginnings of the modern suburb, which was encroaching into the countryside, bathed in late winter light. The following year in the same location, *The Junction at Bois-Colombes (Opus no. 130)* **(86)**, Signac's first Neo-Impressionist work, showed the arrival of spring and concurrently the arrival of separate strokes on the canvas. The approach is more timid but nevertheless present in *Snow, Bois-Colombes* **(87)**, painted the same year. This return to a compelling landscape is a practice that Signac had introduced at this point in his career, and these two paintings have been reunited for the first time in this exhibition.

For Signac, 1885 was a year of transition toward what would be termed "Neo-Impressionism" by the critic Félix Fénéon in 1886. After Seurat's *A Sunday on La Grande Jatte—1884*, the crystallization of the movement under the auspices of its convert and advocate Signac corresponded to a change in his art: he definitively abandoned the fluid, vigorous style of his earlier works in favor of a more controlled technique that was increasingly precise in style. In terms of the Asnières landscapes with their stark contrasts, this transition to the "neo" technique distanced him once and for all from any inclination—if one had ever existed—toward sentimentalism or reflection upon the potential ravages of contemporary industry.

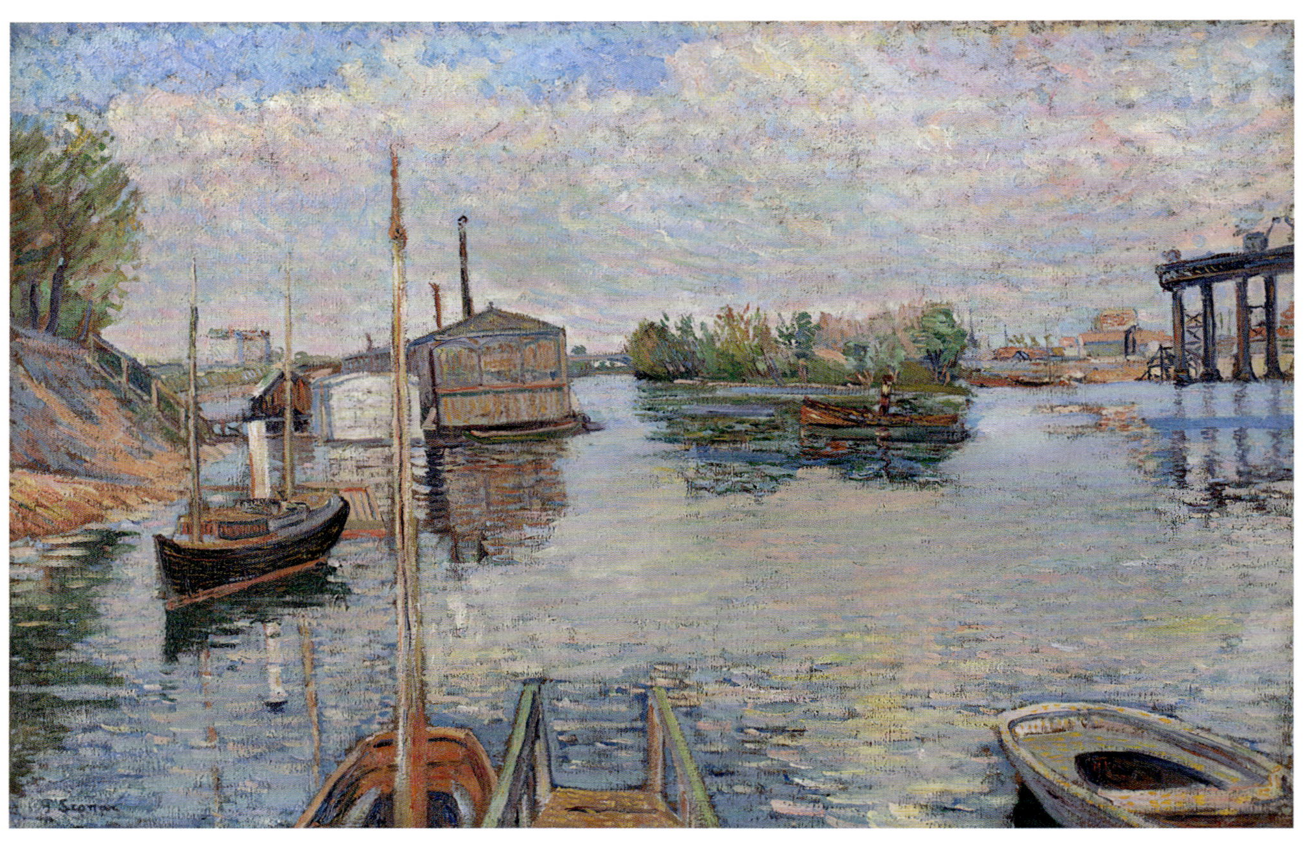

84 Paul Signac
Boats, Bathing Pontoon (Opus no. 96) (recto), 1885
Oil on canvas, 59.5 × 91.7 cm
Private collection

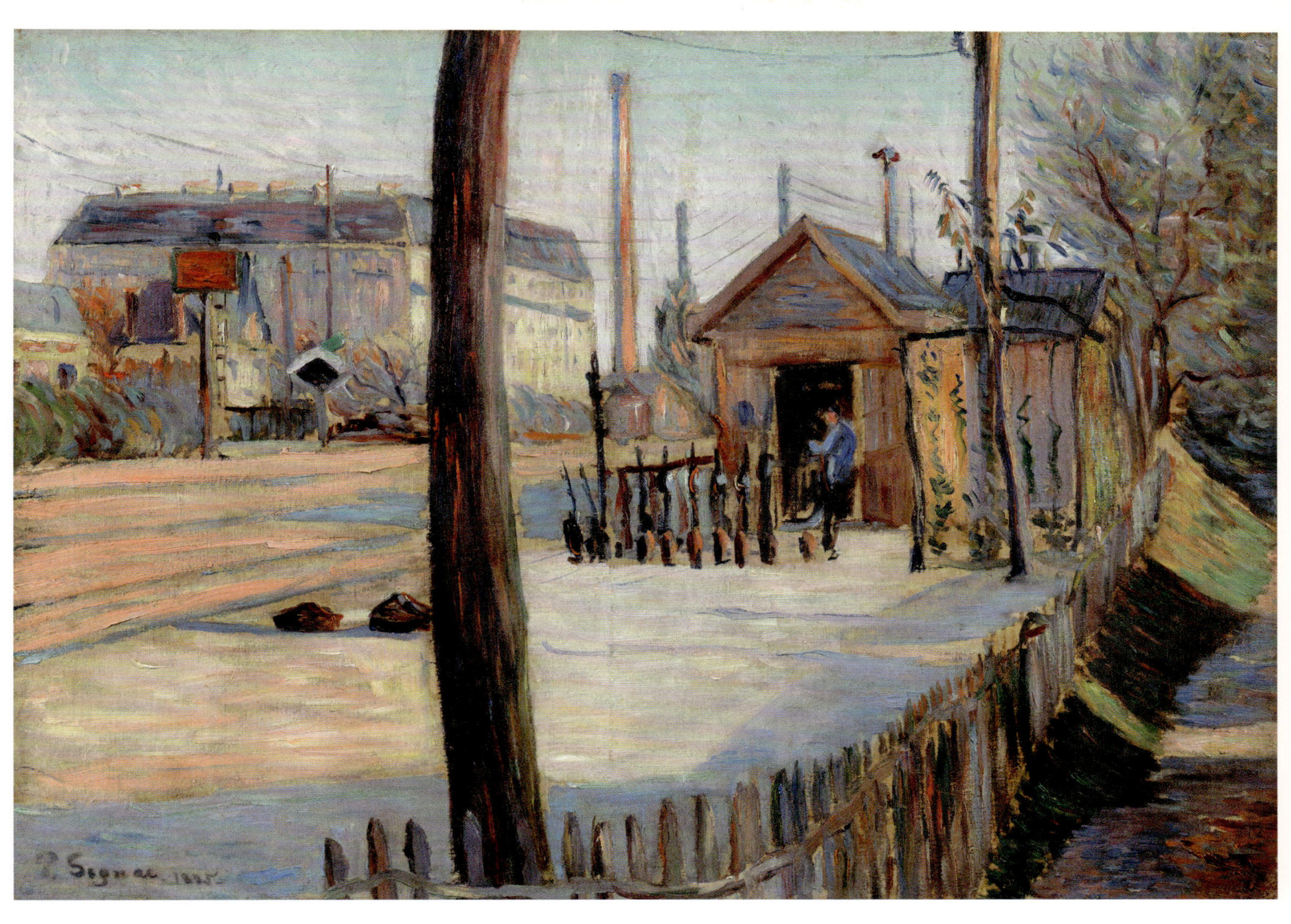

85 (cat.) Paul Signac
Railway Junction near Bois-Colombes, 1885–86
Oil on canvas, 46.5 × 65.5 cm
Van Gogh Museum, Amsterdam

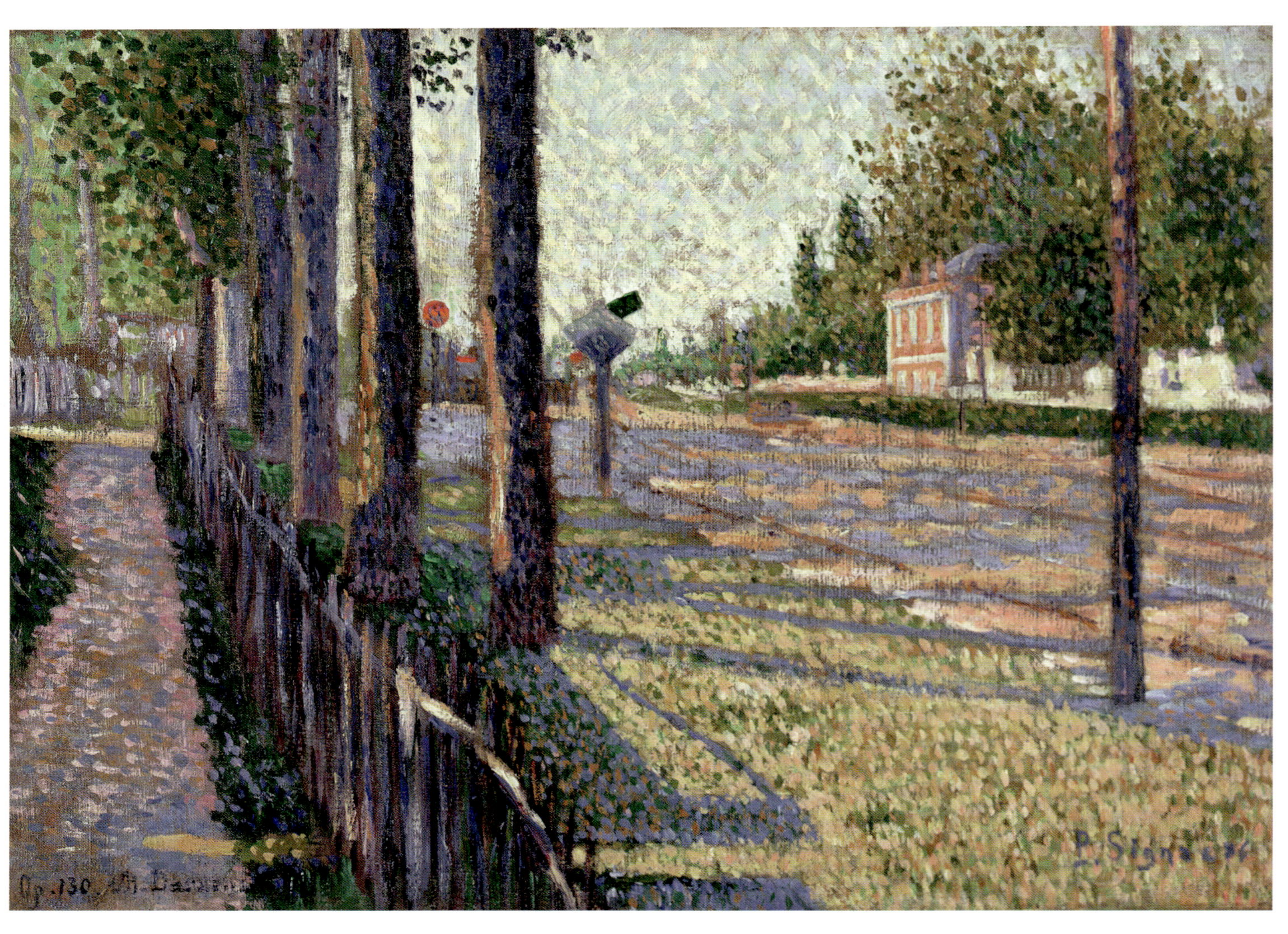

86 (cat.) Paul Signac
The Junction at Bois-Colombes (Opus no. 130), 1886
Oil on canvas, 33 × 47 cm
Leeds Art Gallery, Leeds Museums and Galleries

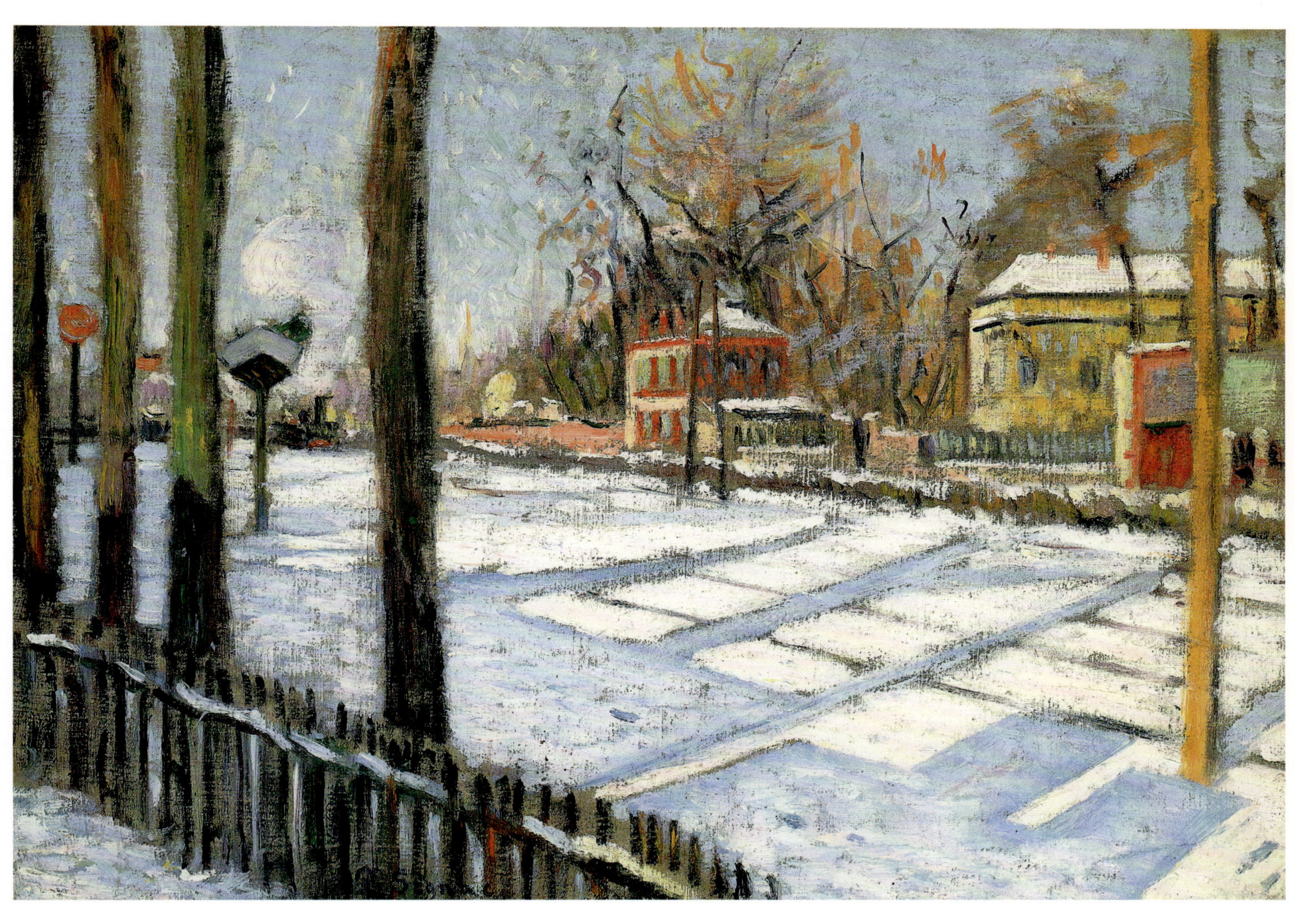

87 (cat.) Paul Signac
Snow, Bois-Colombes, 1886
Oil on canvas, 34.3 × 45.7 cm
Private collection

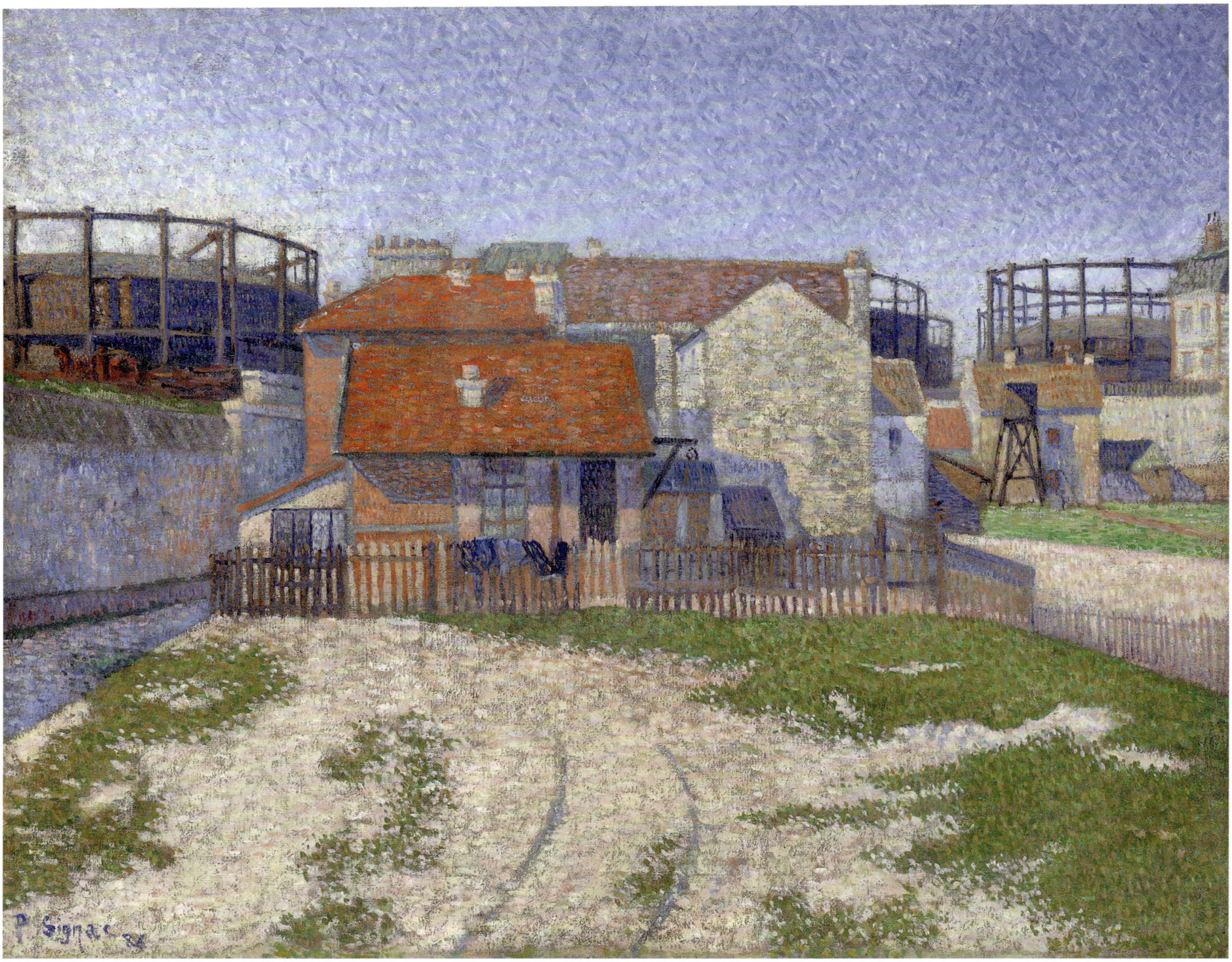

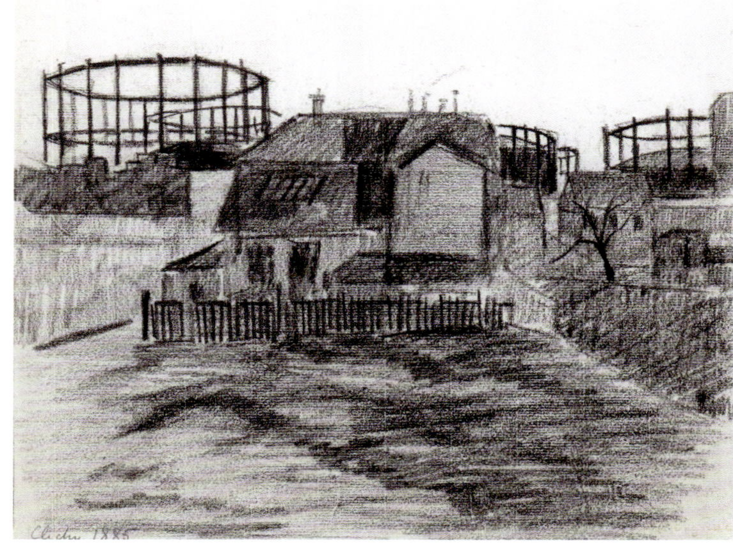

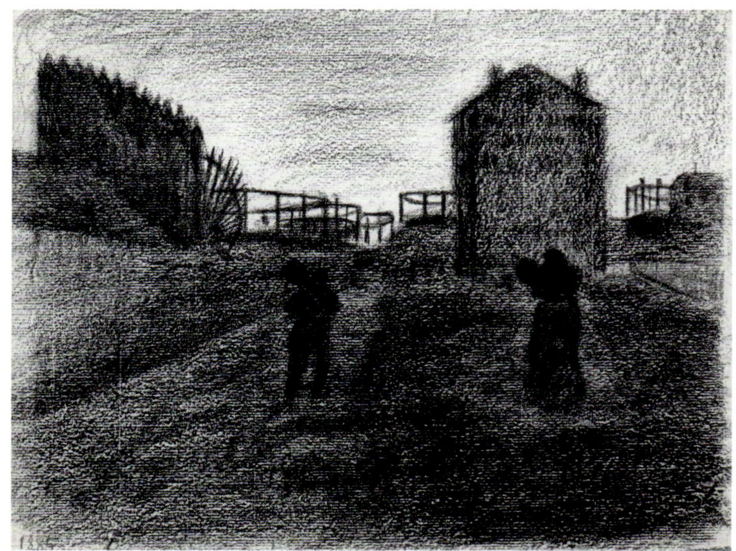

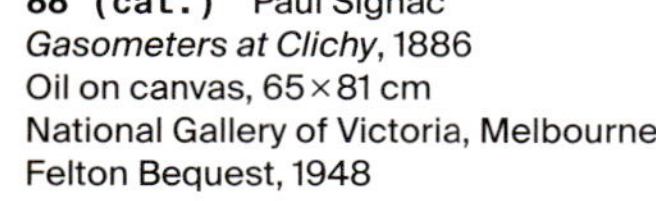

88 (cat.) Paul Signac
Gasometers at Clichy, 1886
Oil on canvas, 65 × 81 cm
National Gallery of Victoria, Melbourne
Felton Bequest, 1948

89 (cat.) Paul Signac
Gasometers, Clichy, 1885
Conté crayon on paper, 23 × 29.5 cm
Private collection

90 (cat.) Paul Signac
Passage du Puits-Bertin (Clichy), 1887
Conté crayon on paper, 24 × 31 cm
Private collection

In his sunlit *Gasometers at Clichy* **(88)**—which he also captured in an impressive Conté crayon drawing **(89)**—the effect seems less politically engaged than descriptive: the painting does not try to induce compassion or social commentary, but rather it presents a serene depiction of modern reality. The scientifically inspired Neo-Impressionist technique creates this impression of objectivity and detachment, freezing forms and colors in states of immobility, in accordance with Signac's objectives. Like many of his generation, he was a believer in the virtues of progress, convinced that science would save humanity from uncertainties. Similarly, his drawings of the passage du Puits-Bertin **(25,90,91)** present this area behind the gasometers "wedged in" between the railroad and factories, where nature has been abandoned, without descending into miserabilism. Finally, the gasometers reappear merely in the background in his highly luminous work *Clipper (Opus no. 155)* **(92)**. The natural setting in these paintings, whether gloomy or joyous depending on the level of sunshine, is by definition indifferent to the living conditions that we can only roughly discern. Everything takes place as if the treatment of the subject rather than the subject itself lay at the heart of his intent. In this way, the artist partially resolved the dilemma of political engagement in his works. Later, in 1891, he published an article on the subject in his friend Jean Grave's anarchist journal *La Révolte*, in which he formulated the idea that artistic innovation, rather than propaganda images, could constitute the counterpart to revolution in politics: "Justice in sociology, harmony in art: the same thing."[7] This was exactly his approach in these Neo-Impressionist paintings from 1886 to 1887.

Creative Perambulations

Signac sometimes traveled to Asnières on foot, and very often he was not alone: the banks of the river also formed the backdrop for friendships that helped the artist to gain self-knowledge. He walked, talked, and worked there, first with Georges Seurat in 1885 and 1886 and then in May 1887 with Vincent van Gogh, two painters who would pass away a few years later. These pioneers were followed by others, including Emile Bernard and Charles Angrand, whose art Signac increasingly came to admire. Since 1884, Bernard had also lived with his parents in Asnières, and that was where the two painters met in 1886, according to Bernard. We can clearly see here how walking could have been the trigger or at the very least a stimulant for the creative process, in the same vein as the meditative walking (*meditatio*) of the Greek philosophers. Certainly, you would not say the

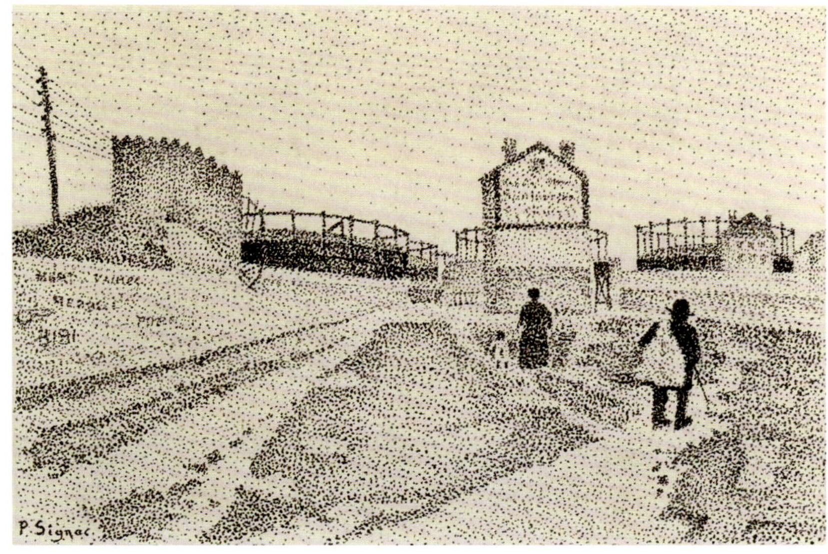

91 (cat.) Paul Signac
Passage du Puits-Bertin (Clichy), 1887
Black ink on paper, 16×25 cm
Musée du Louvre, Paris, fonds du musée d'Orsay

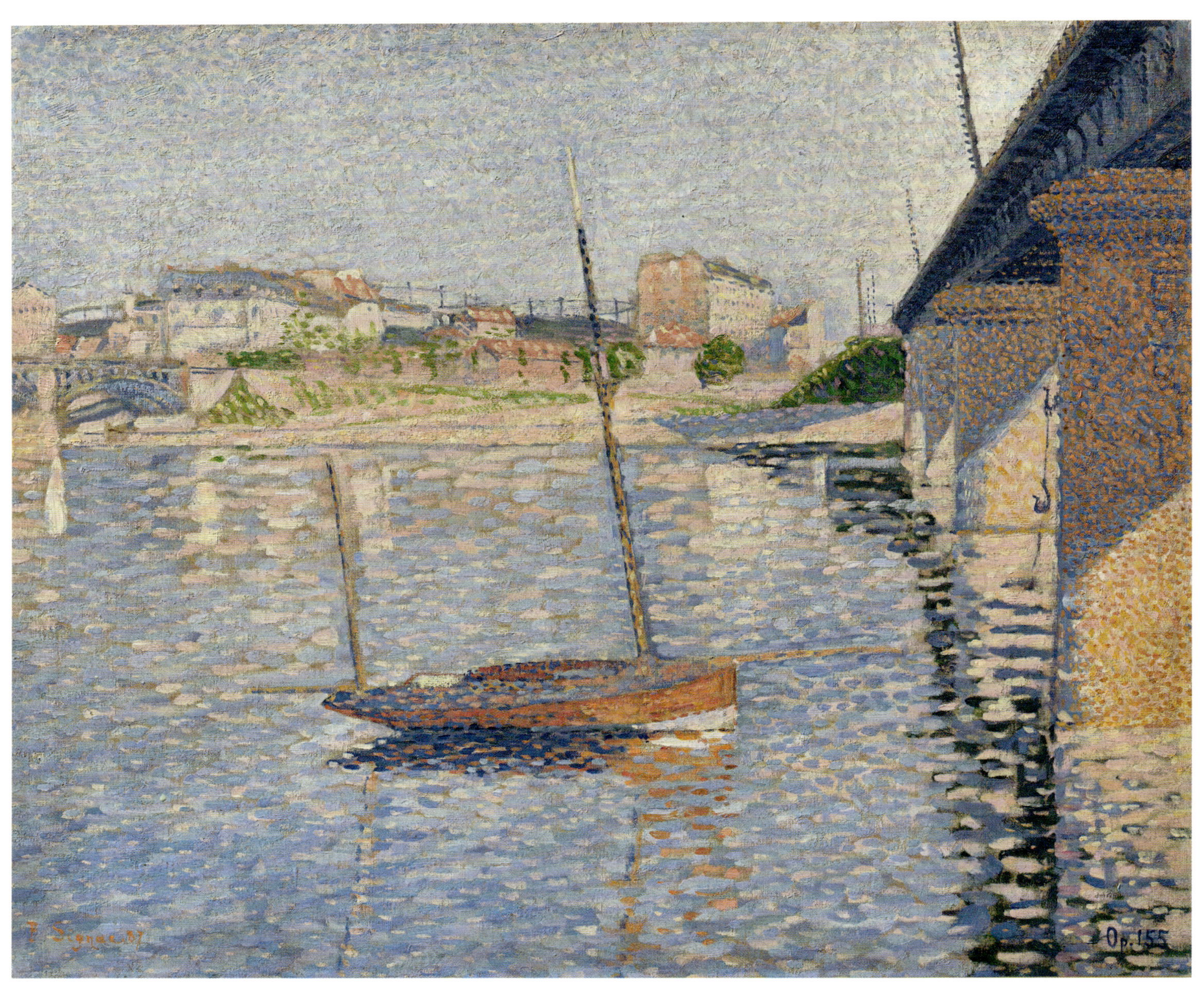

92 (cat.) Paul Signac
Clipper (Opus no. 155), 1887
Oil on canvas, 46 × 55 cm
Hasso Plattner Collection

same things standing in a studio as walking along, all the more so in a landscape you were preparing to capture in a drawing or painting. Signac later described these formative walks: "Yes, I knew Van Gogh from Père Tanguy's. I met him on other occasions at Asnières and Saint-Ouen; we painted on the banks of the river, lunched at the *guinguette* [a small café], and returned to Paris on foot, along the avenues of Saint-Ouen and Clichy. Van Gogh wore a blue zinc worker's smock and had painted dots of color on the sleeves. He stuck right by me, shouting, gesticulating, and brandishing his large, size-30 canvas, so that he spread wet paint onto himself and the passers-by."[8]

These animated walks with Van Gogh must have taken place in spring 1887, before Signac left for the south of France on May 23 of that year. We can imagine that the time he spent there with Georges Seurat was very different and probably calmer. He had met Seurat at the first exhibition of the Société des Artistes Indépendants in 1884. On that occasion, Signac was deeply shocked by Seurat's *Bathers at Asnières*: the painting depicted a location he knew well by that point, but the treatment was revolutionary in terms of its scale and meticulous composition, which exuded a cool calm very different to his own spontaneous Impressionist works. While the encounter did not lead to an immediate change in his painting, Seurat's influence was notable in the technique of his drawings, as can be seen in *The Ile de la Grande Jatte* **(93)**. He was already in the habit of drawing but followed the older painter's lead in experimenting with the Conté crayon technique, which he mastered, like Seurat, creating a delicate tissue of light and shade that would constitute a less widely known aspect of his work. In this drawing, there is a double reference to Seurat, because he combines the choice of both technique and subject. Did they work together *en plein air* at the same time, Seurat on his preparatory studies and Signac on this drawing? Subtly rendering the play of light and shadows

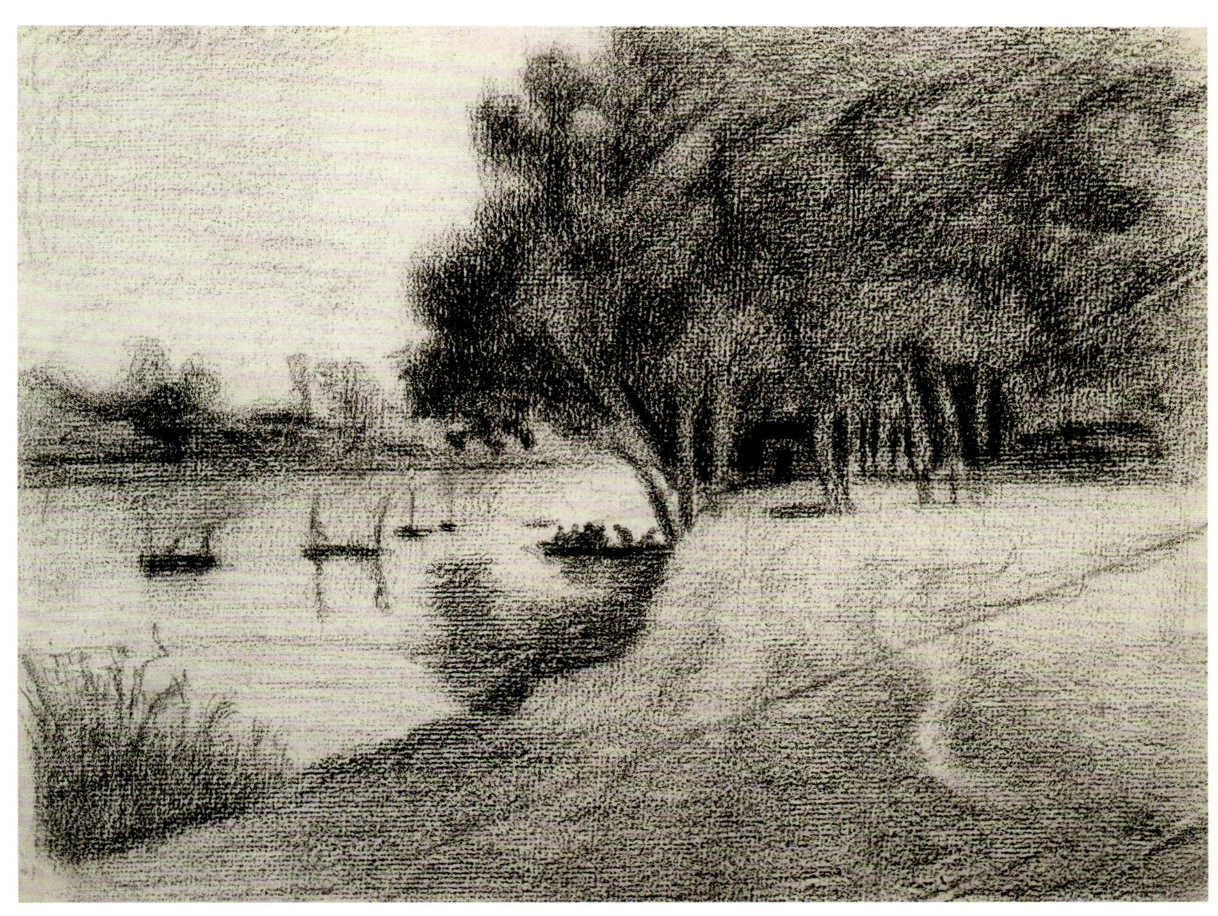

93 Paul Signac
The Ile de la Grande Jatte, c. 1885
Conté crayon on paper, 23×30 cm
Private collection

on the grass would have required direct observation. And this luminous composition was already a significant departure from Signac's more vigorous style up to that point.

In this regard, the comparison of two drawings by the two artists, Signac's work predating Seurat's, also enlightens us as to the circularity of the respective influences, which emerges firstly in the choice of materials (Conté crayon on a thick paper called Michallet, which allowed the artists to play with the grain and depth of the shadows) and their choice of drawing *en plein air*: Seurat, *Regatta (Two Sailboats)* and Signac, *Regatta on the Seine* **(94,95)**.

Signac painted in Asnières for almost the last time in 1888. The following year, he moved to 20 avenue de Clichy in Paris, where his studio also gave him the ability to host other artists. When his grandfather died in June 1889, Héloïse Signac also decided to return to Paris, moving to the boulevard Pereire, in the 17th arrondissement. With this development there was no longer any need for him to return to Asnières. Having already depicted different aspects of the quay at Clichy from the pedestrian side, looking downstream and then upstream **(96,98)**, in *Bow of the Tub (Opus no. 176)* **(97)** and *Stern of the Tub (Opus no. 175)* **(99)**, Signac adopted the perspective of the boatman viewing the landscape from his boat in a series of two "diptychs." This new approach marked a turning point in his work: gradually, the industrial zone with its bridges and cranes—still visible here—gave way to references to the world of boating.

A Return to Asnières for an Official Project

In 1900, Signac was back in Asnières, a place that held so many memories for him, to work on a major project: the competition for the decoration of the reception room in the Asnières town hall. Having become the undisputed leader of Neo-Impressionism, a renowned and celebrated artist in spite of the acerbic criticism from certain quarters, he had become a key figure in the art world, and since he had started spending half the year in Saint-Tropez, under the southern French sun, his brushstrokes had become broader, his tones warmer, and his paintings more flamboyant. He was playing an increasingly active role in the Salon des Indépendants,[9] which he cofounded in 1884, having had a major hand in its slogan: "No jury, no prizes!" At first sight, his participation in an official, regulated competition, launched by the Seine department "for the artistic decoration of the reception room of the town hall of Asnières," might seem surprising. But one has to remember that Signac's temperament was rebellious but equally competitive: he was a great sportsman who won numerous sailing regattas. He also saw it as an opportunity for a twofold return to his source: to the old haunts of his adolescence, and above all to what Félix Fénéon had perceived in his evolution toward "an art of great decorative development that sacrifices the anecdotal to the arabesque, nomenclature to synthesis, the fleeting to the permanent . . . and endows nature, which had ultimately grown weary of its precarious reality, with an authentic reality."[10] Beyond his desire for synthesis and harmony in his work, he had long been interested in decorative art in the strict sense. He had

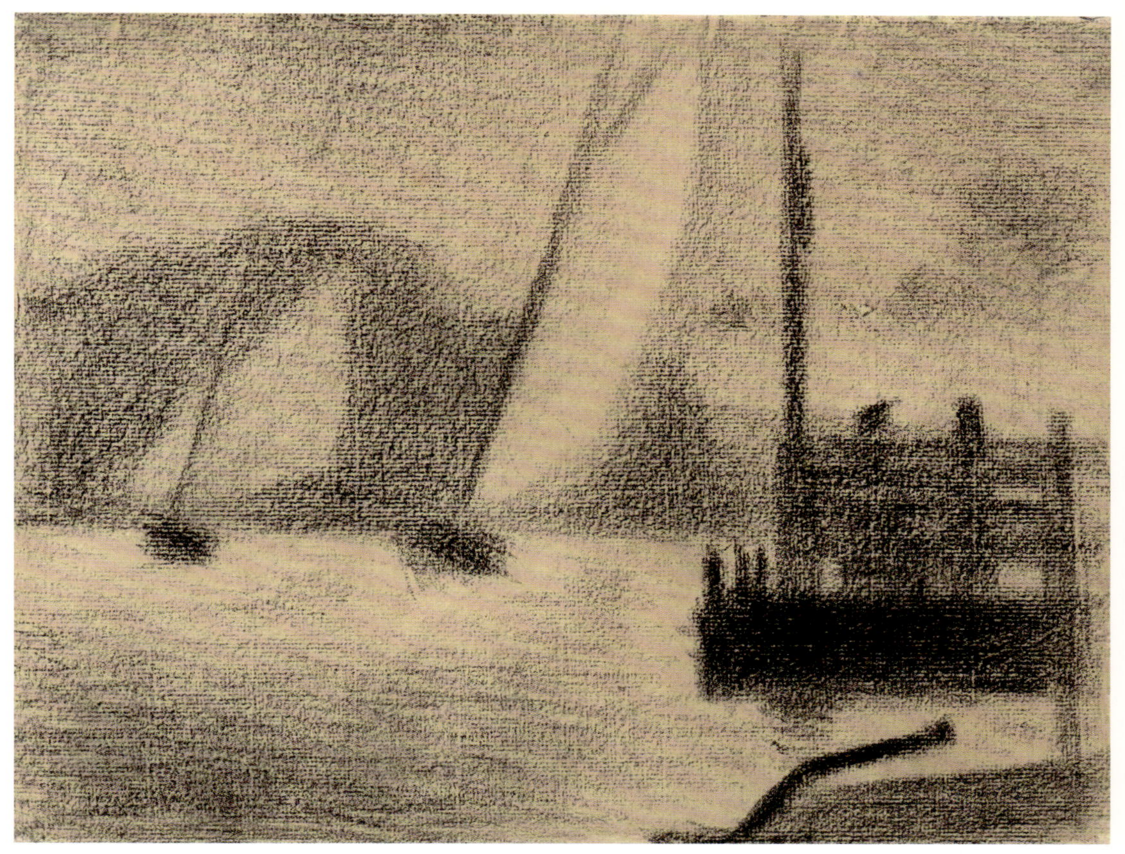

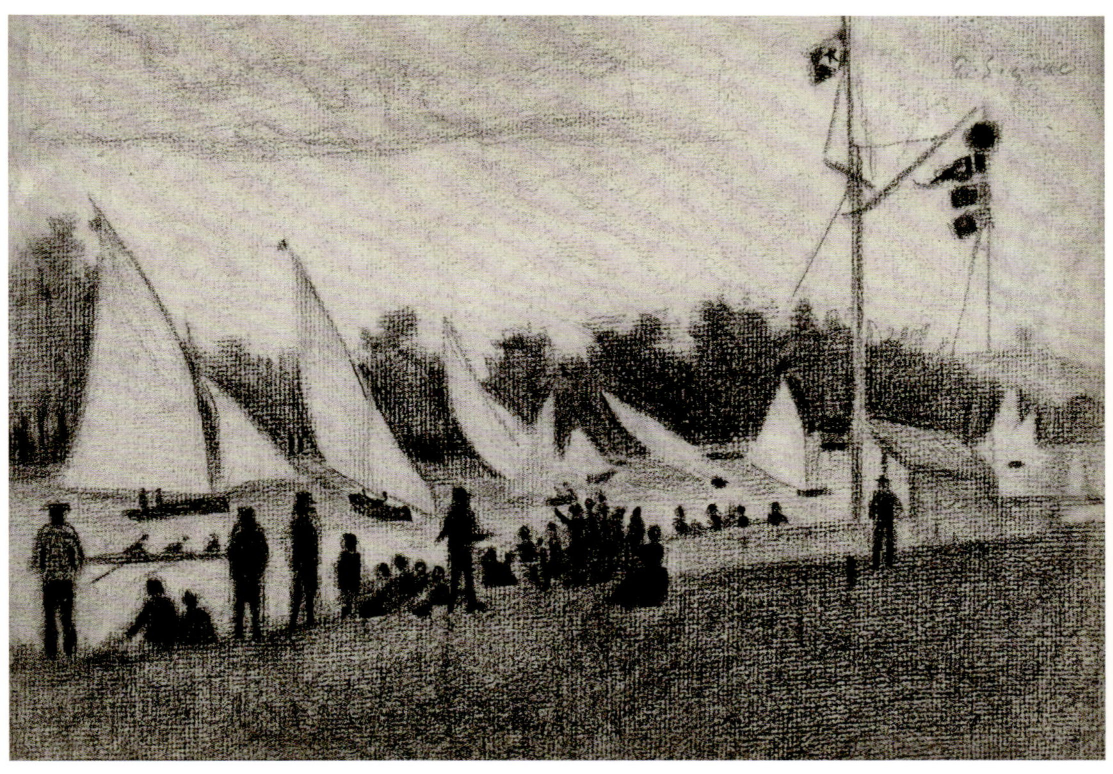

94 (cat.) Georges Seurat
Regatta (Two Sailboats), c. 1890
Conté crayon on paper, 23 × 30.5 cm
Private collection

95 (cat.) Paul Signac
Regatta on the Seine, c. 1885–86
Conté crayon on paper, 21.7 × 31.2 cm
Musée d'Orsay, Paris

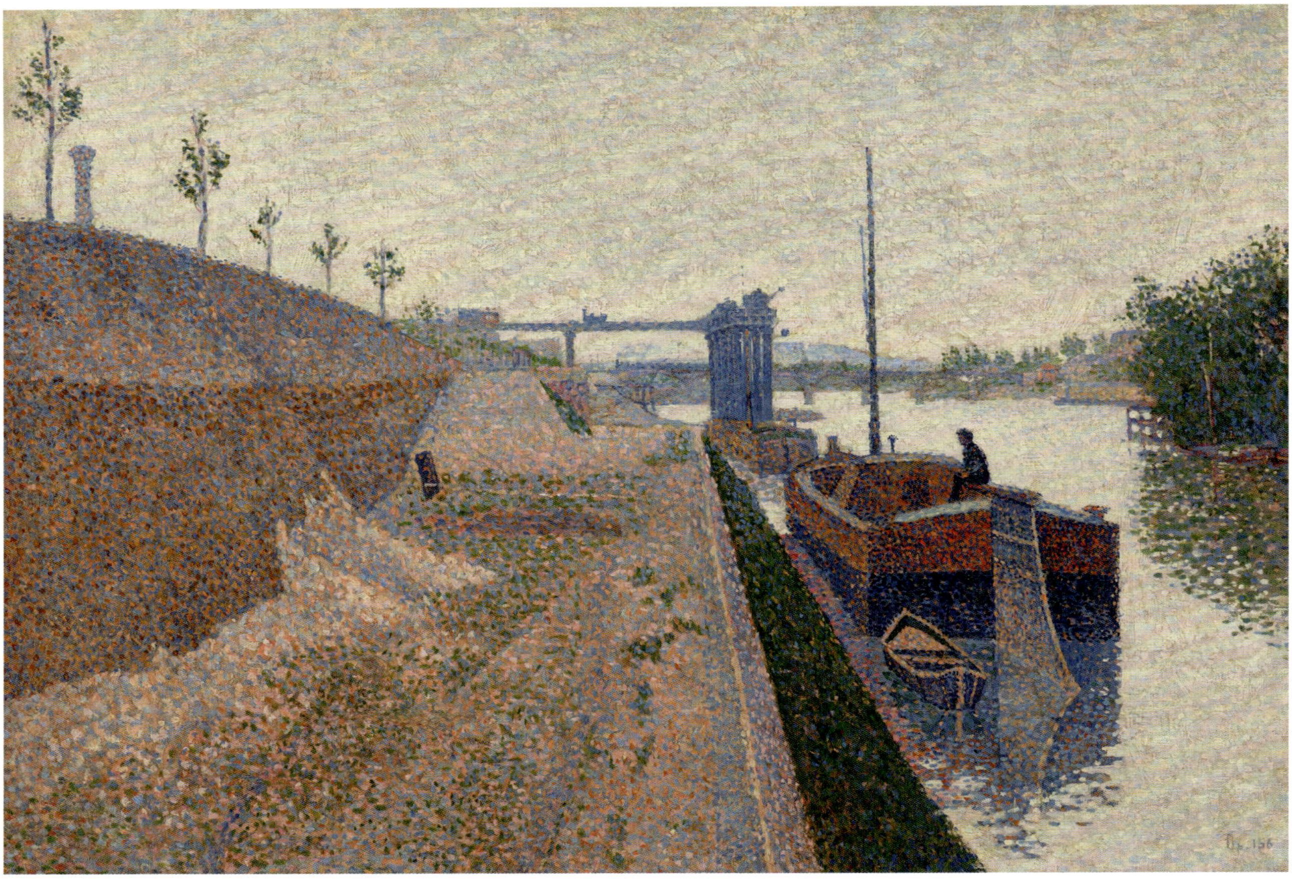

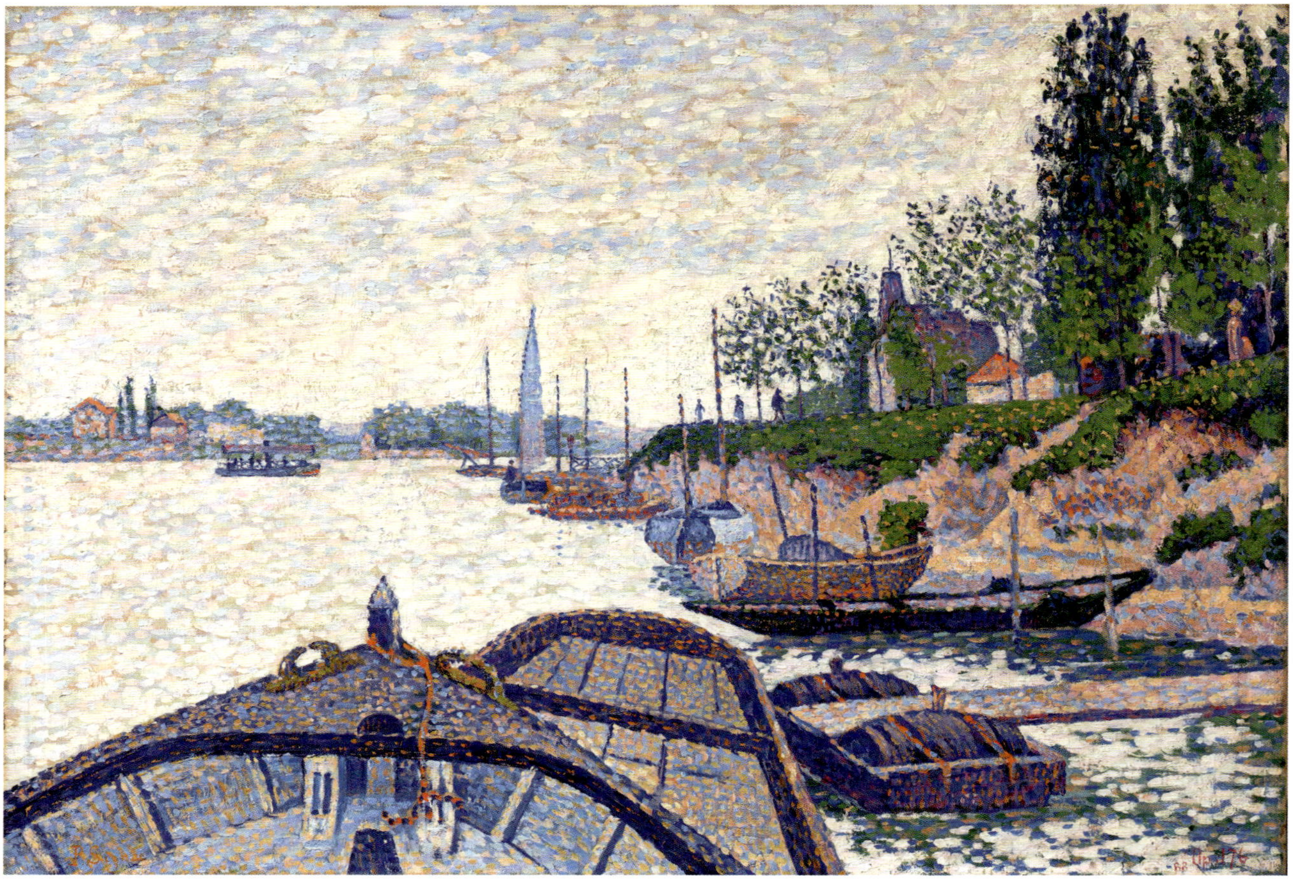

96 (cat.) Paul Signac
Quai de Clichy, Gray Weather, 1887
Oil on canvas, 46×65.5 cm
Private collection

97 (cat.) Paul Signac
Bow of the Tub (Opus no. 176), 1888
Oil on canvas, 45×65 cm
Private collection

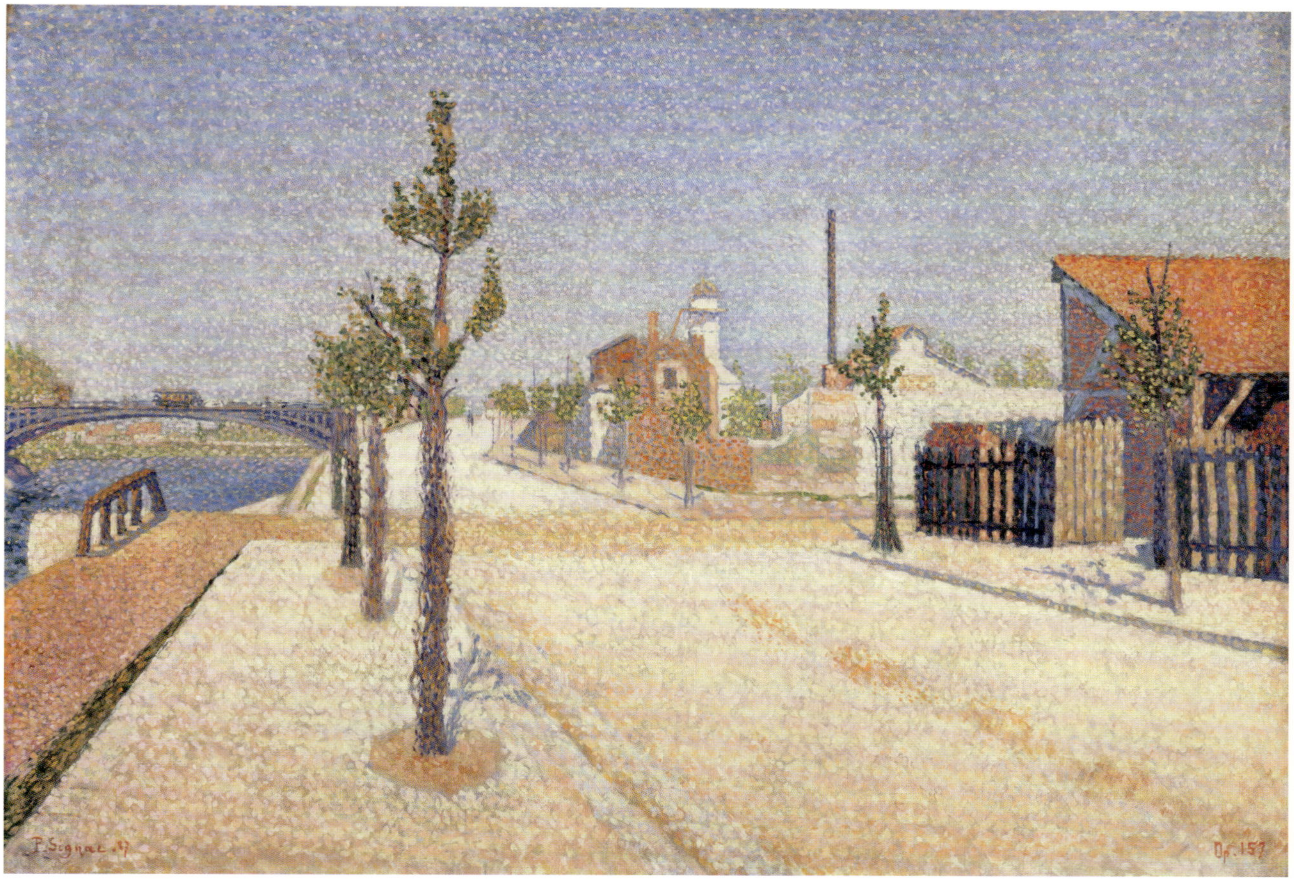

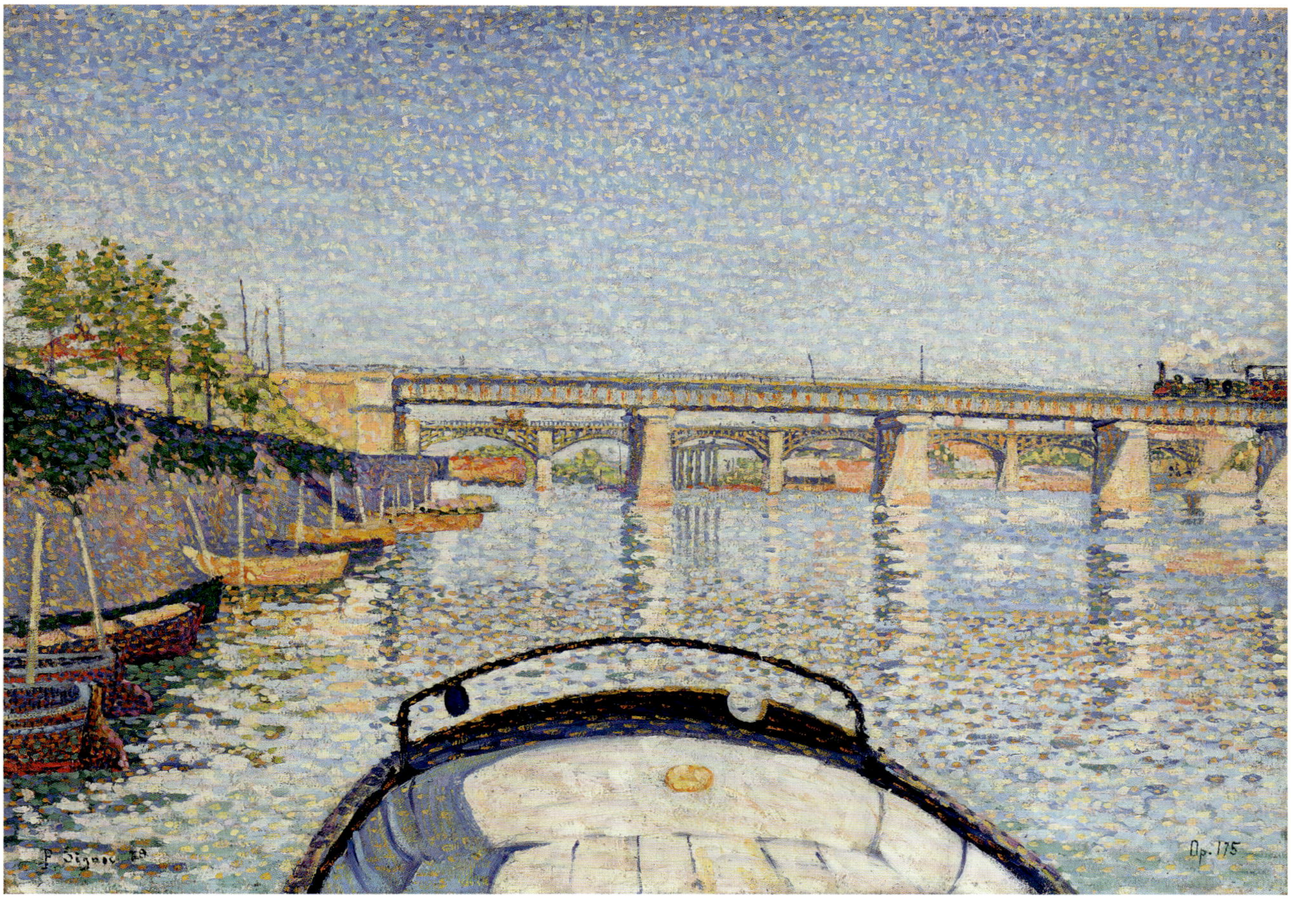

98 (cat.) Paul Signac
Quai de Clichy, (Opus no. 157), 1887
Oil on canvas, 46.4 × 65.4 cm
The Baltimore Museum of Art
Gift of Frederick H. Gottlieb

99 Paul Signac
Stern of the Tub (Opus no. 175), 1888
Oil on canvas, 46 × 65 cm
Private collection

written an article devoted to Hector Guimard's famous Castel Béranger, the building where he lived in Paris,[11] and had already produced several large decorative works, including *In the Time of Harmony*, his famous large fresco measuring 3 by 4 meters for the Maison du Peuple in Brussels.[12]

A total of 114 candidates (including Henri Rousseau, the young Raoul Dufy, and Othon Friesz) worked on designs. With no great hope, he set to work,[13] initially frustrated by the small format he was required to present—sketches at ⅒ of life size for a room measuring 22 by 11 meters: "It is very difficult to indicate the contrasts and gradations that will take on so much importance on the walls. How will the Jury be able to see what would be successful *in situ* in these sketches? . . . at life size, what kind of surprise will this arrangement hold in store?"[14] He was also asked to take account of the color scheme of the room ("pink, green, and white, with no gold or brown"),[15] which he took to be an advantage: "so I have the choice of binary and ternary harmonies, and related lines."[16] He ultimately proposed four panels, once again showing both banks of the Seine: the Asnières side and the left bank featuring boating activities, and on the Clichy side, on the right bank, industrial activities. The railroad bridge linked the two sides of the river **(100,101)**. He made the decision not to include a depiction of night life, although he had clearly had the idea in the past, as is illustrated by his pen and ink design for a fan, in which the boatmen of the daytime alongside the factory smokestacks stand in counterpart to the audience at a cabaret show **(102)**.

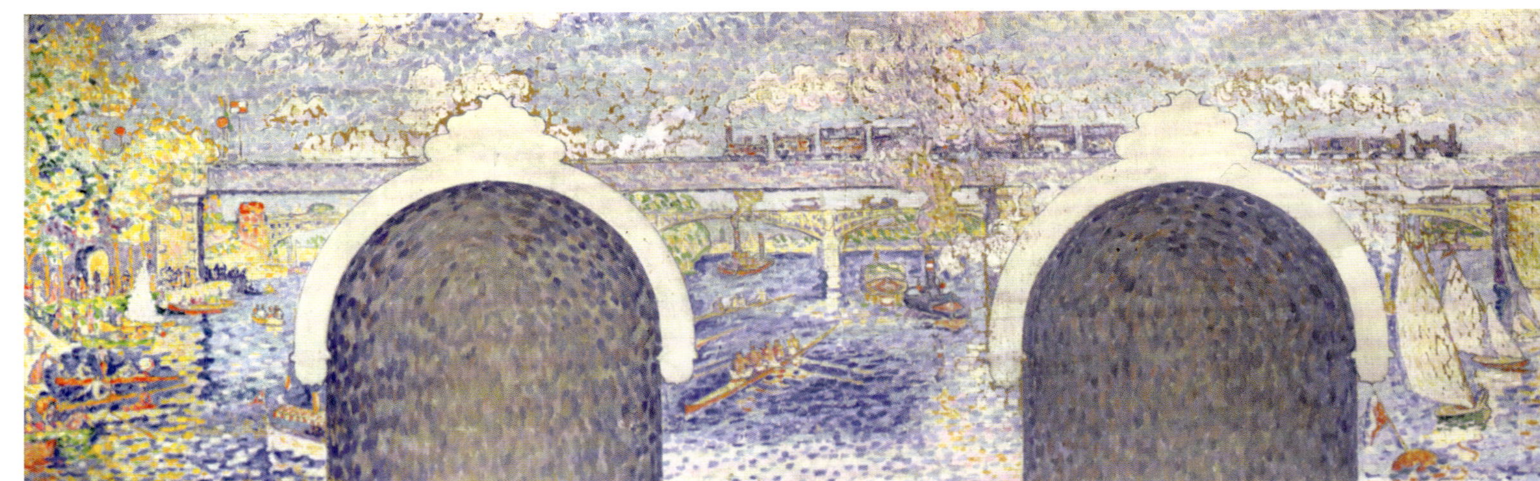

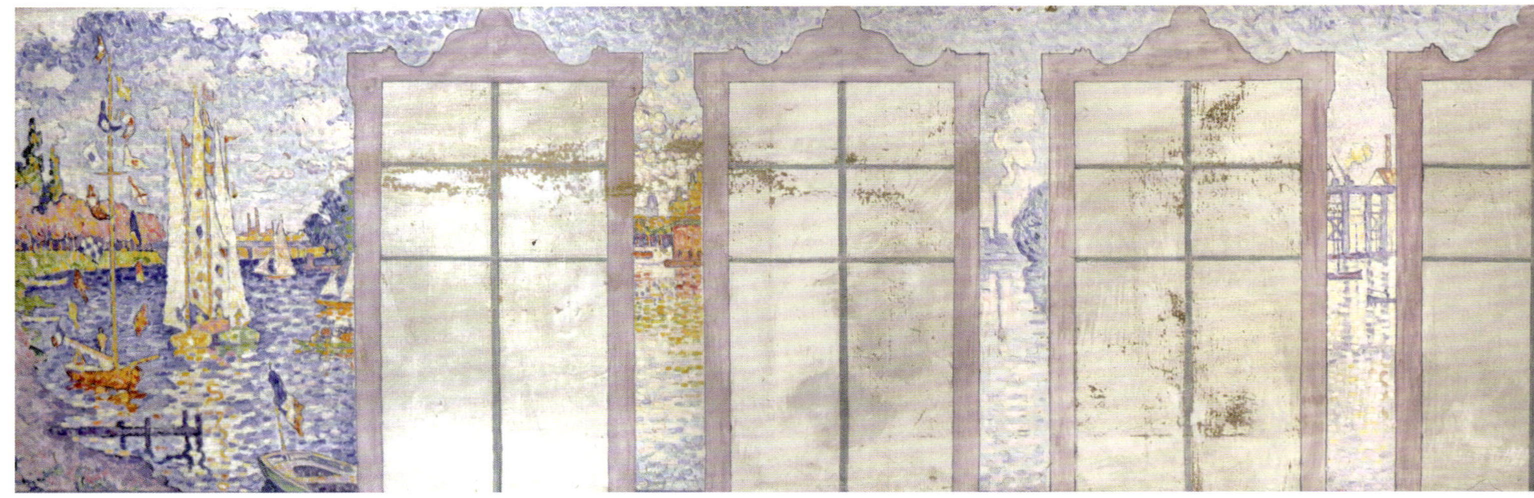

100 (cat.) Paul Signac
Sketch of the Central Panel, Design for the Decoration of the Reception Room of the Town Hall of Asnières, 1900
Oil on canvas, 49 × 224 cm
Private collection

101 (cat.) Paul Signac
Sketch of the Five Windows, Design for the Decoration of the Reception Room of the Town Hall of Asnières, 1900
Oil on canvas, 49 × 224 cm
Private collection

Signac engaged with the challenge of decoration directly, taking into account the technical difficulties posed by the reception room: the mass of moving water and the bustle of boating activities seem to invade the large vaults and the five windows almost naturally. Unlike Signac's previous large decorative panels—*In the Time of Harmony* dating from 1895 and *The Wrecker* dating from 1898[17]—with their politically motivated messages, his perspective here was apparently neutral. Between the factories, symbolizing work, and the sailboats, symbols of leisure, the image to be offered up to the town hall's users and visitors was no utopian golden age but a very real setting with human inhabitants. But, as he had expected, his design was not selected. The winner was Henri Bouvet (1859–1945), an artist from Marseilles, whose very bland sketch of a peaceful landscape enlivened only by a passing barge, in contrast to the profusion of activities proposed by Signac, was probably better suited to the bureaucrats. The Symbolist poet Emile Verhaeren deplored the decision: "The number of competitors was enormous. Just one painter, Paul Signac, had been at pains to arrange the subjects according to the lines and spaces of the room. His work was honest, intelligent, artistic."[18] This new setback, which the critic Gustave Coquiot described in lively and furious terms,[19] almost coincided with the architect Victor Horta's definitive rejection of the famous mural *In the Time of Harmony*, signaling the end of Signac's large-scale mural decorations,[20] as well as the chapter of his life linked to Asnières, a place imbued with memories of family, art, and friends. ■

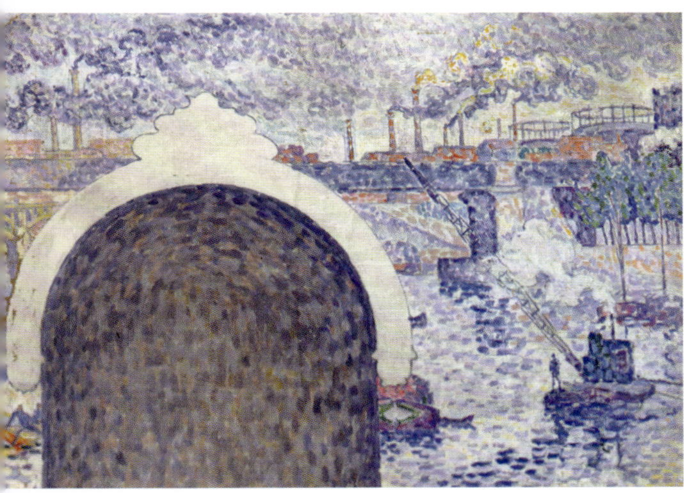

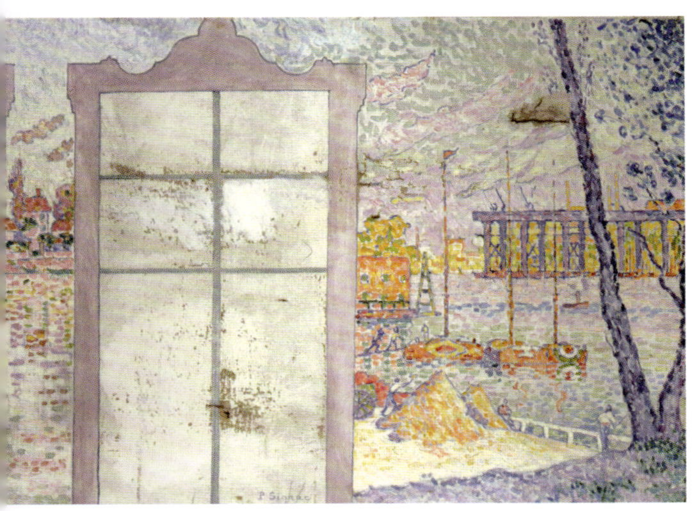

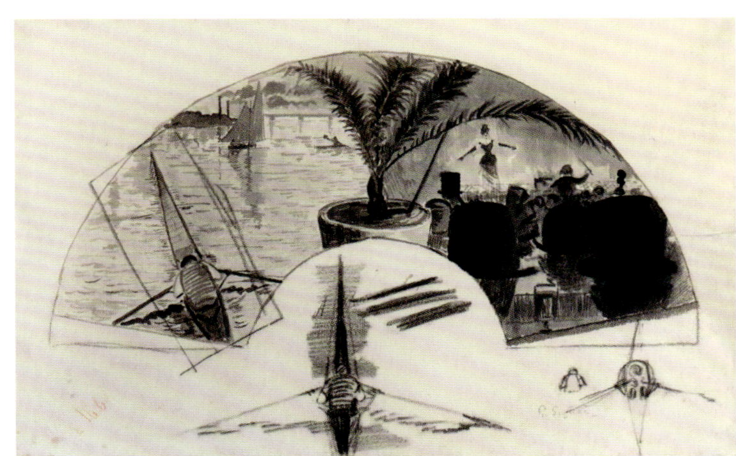

102 Paul Signac
Asnières by Day and Night, c. 1885–1900
Design for a fan, wash and black ink pen, 30 × 48 cm
Archives Signac, Paris

BERNARD AND ASNIÈRES: BACKDROP FOR A STORMY BEGINNING

JOOST VAN DER HOEVEN

Emile Bernard was sixteen in 1884 when his parents traded their apartment on boulevard Voltaire in Paris for a small house on rue Saint-Denis, halfway between Asnières and Courbevoie.[1] Madeleine, his younger sister, was in poor health, so the family took their doctor's advice and moved out of the city to escape the polluted air and urban clamor.[2] Seeking peace and clean air in a place barely half a mile from the heavy industry of Clichy might seem less than logical, but the river Seine lay between them and the pollution, and was viewed at the time as a hard boundary between city and "nature."[3] Being so close to the capital was also a big advantage for Bernard's father, who worked in Paris.

Shortly after they moved, Bernard informed his parents that he wanted to be an artist, a long-cherished ambition, now stoked by the inspiration afforded by his new home in Asnières.[4] The town's paradoxical combination of industry and countryside unleashed such an urge to create that he was unwilling to wait until he had finished high school.[5] Bernard loved the vibrant entertainment and leisure activities along the river, but was fascinated at the same time by the factories on the far bank and the workers who toiled there for long hours every day.[6] In the years that followed, Asnières and the surrounding area became the backdrop for his stormy development as a painter. Bernard began to spend his summers in Brittany from 1886 onward, but still returned to his parents' home for the rest of the year.

The early years of Bernard's artistic career were marked by ambition, experiment, and innovation. He discovered the work of several avant-garde artists, including Claude Monet, Henri de Toulouse-Lautrec, and Georges Seurat, and drew inspiration freely from all the new painting styles that crossed his path. Bernard was quick to recognize that the artists in these circles were trying to distinguish themselves through a style of their own, and so he too set out to find his personal signature. It helps explain the immense variety in style and technique of the now famous paintings he produced in and around Asnières. This essay focuses on the different ways Bernard depicted the place he lived, how these styles succeeded one another, and which interests and examples played a part.

Bernard's early artistic development was quite erratic, making it challenging to answer these questions unequivocally. His painting style and technique varied from one work to another, and he occasionally reverted to an approach he had abandoned several months earlier. This makes it difficult to track his development as an artist precisely. Furthermore, later in life he often backdated his work, presumably with a view to retrospectively burnish his innovatory credentials. It is often hard to determine, therefore, whether a painting really was finished in the year he inscribed on the canvas. In addition to the dating issue, we have only an incomplete view of the works that Bernard produced in Asnières. He drew up lists of his paintings at various moments in his life, in which he included several currently unlocated works said to have been produced there.[7] We are dealing, in other words, with a body of work that is both incomplete and difficult to date.

On the other hand, the older Bernard wrote a great many articles and memoirs, in which he discusses the early stages of his career.[8] The most extensive of these is the unpublished *L'Aventure de ma vie* (The Adventure of My Life), which dates from around 1939. He also collected many of his early sketches in an album titled *L'Enfance d'un peintre* (A Painter's Childhood, now at the Kunsthalle in Bremen, Germany). These documents need to be treated with caution, however, given Bernard's propensity for rewriting his own history: he liked to play up his part in the development of modern painting, while omitting nuances and inconvenient facts. The sources nevertheless offer a vivid picture of the young and ambitious artist who set about capturing his surroundings in Asnières with an abundance of inspiration and experimentation.

An Inspiring Retreat

Asnières, where the Bernard family moved in 1884, grew into a town with a population of 15,200 by 1886, its rapid expansion fueled by the appeal of the countryside combined with a fast rail link to Paris.[9] Throughout the week, its streets and the quays along the Seine were quiet. Anglers waited patiently for fish to bite, while factory workers from Clichy passed by. Come Sunday, however, Asnières awoke from its torpor. Canoes, rowboats, and sailboats were launched on the river, turning the town into a "national marina," as Louis Barron called it in his 1886 travel guide *Les Environs de Paris*.[10] Parisians flocked there in their free time, creating a cheery and colorful chaos of entertainment and leisure on the water, and along the quayside. The nearby island of La Grande Jatte was another popular attraction, and there was dancing every Sunday at an open-air ball, "the splendor of which rivals the luxury of the Elysée Montmartre," Barron wrote, referring to a celebrated ballroom in the capital.[11] It did not escape the author's notice that all this took place against a backdrop of heavy industry on the far side of the river, which he described as forming "a stark contrast."[12]

The moment he arrived in Asnières, Bernard took his sketchbook and began to explore his new surroundings. A small street running from the family home led him straight to the bank of the Seine, where he found exactly what his budding artist's eye yearned for.[13] He later recalled in *L'Aventure de ma vie*: "There was always some beautiful, sparkling sail wafting an elegant boat across the blue or green water; or else a procession of barges towed by tugboats, or oarsmen showing off their bare arms as they rhythmically propelled their long, slender craft, in which a woman with a parasol always sat at the tiller. There was an indescribable joy, an indescribable youth in the air at such moments."[14] He visited La Grande Jatte on Sundays to enjoy the festivity and bustle and on weekdays for the peace and quiet.[15] There are several sketches in the album

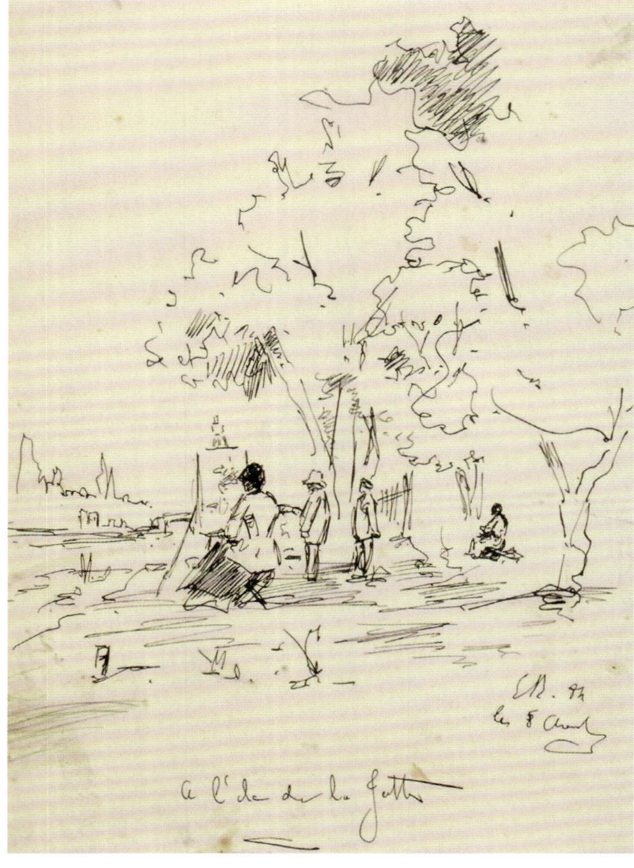

103 Emile Bernard
At the Ile de la Jatte, from the album *L'Enfance d'un peintre*, 1884
Pen and ink on paper, 31.2×19.7 cm
Kunsthalle Bremen—Der Kunstverein in Bremen

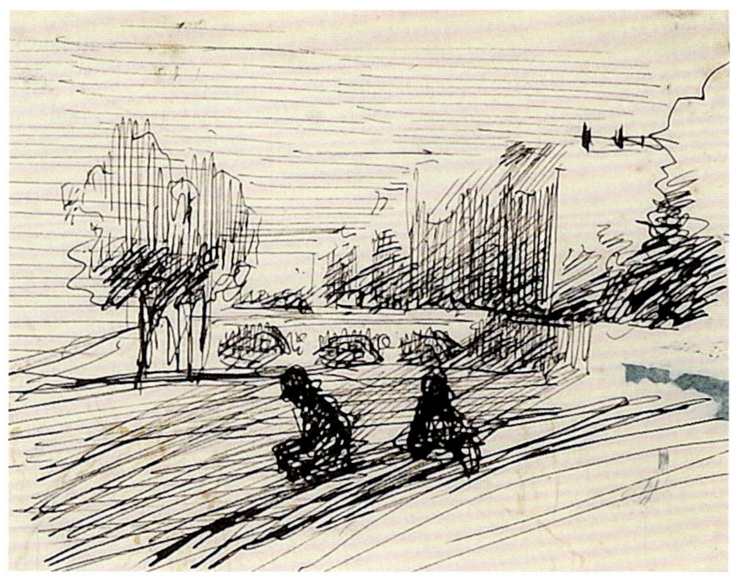

104 Emile Bernard
Sketch of Figures by the Seine, from the album *L'Enfance d'un peintre*, c. 1885
Pen and ink on paper, 7.8×9.7 cm
Kunsthalle Bremen—Der Kunstverein in Bremen

L'Enfance d'un peintre that he must have made during this period, including the pen drawing *At the Ile de la Jatte* **(103)**. Bernard drew the island as a quiet and wooded retreat, with a few hikers enjoying the silence and an artist painting a view of the river.

However, Bernard did not see himself as the kind of artist who painted pretty pictures from the banks of the river at La Grande Jatte. While he loved to visit, he was keen to extend his artistic gaze beyond the green island. It is clear from his album of sketches that he paid special attention to the people he saw in Asnières, and not only the day-trippers who spent their Sundays there. There are drawings of down-at-the-heels figures, for instance, wandering aimlessly through the streets or staring blankly at the river **(104,105)**. They testify to a gaze colored by Naturalist art and literature, in which there is often a sentimental engagement with the poorer in society—something Bernard undoubtedly picked up from novels set in the underbelly of Paris by the likes of Emile Zola, which he had read avidly. He also diligently copied the prints of Gustave Doré, Georges Bellenger, Honoré Daumier, and similar artists, whose illustrations frequently depicted the theme of poverty, as, for instance, in Daumier's *Le Pêcheur acharné ou il ne faut pas disputer des goûts* (The Desperate Fisherman, or There is no Accounting for Taste) **(106)**.[16]

Bernard's early sketches likewise recall the work of Jean-François Raffaëlli, who also worked extensively in the Asnières area, where he had lived since 1879. Like Daumier, Raffaëlli depicted ragpickers and vagrants, but he placed these "portrait-types of common people," as he called them, specifically in the dismal wastelands around Asnières, often with the factories of Clichy in the background.[17]

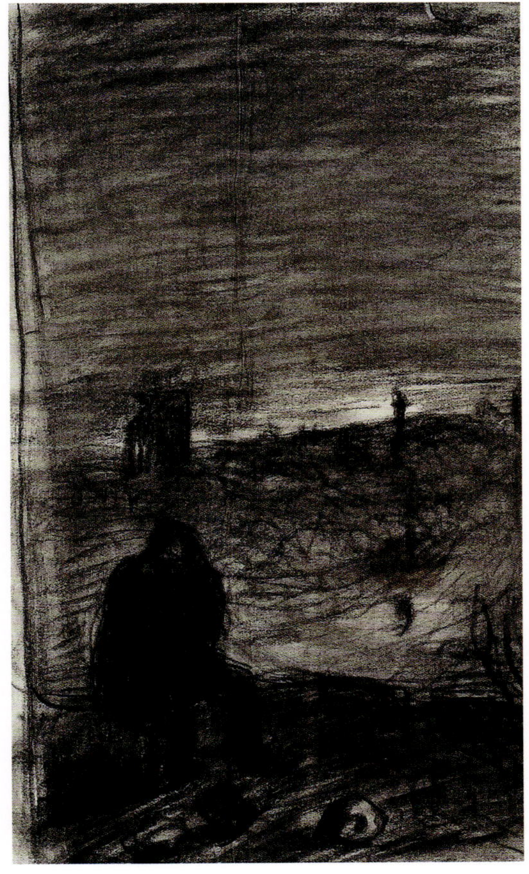

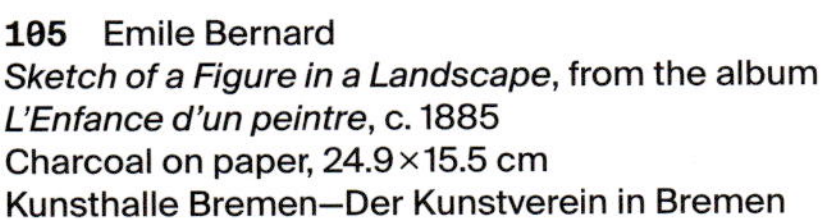

105 Emile Bernard
Sketch of a Figure in a Landscape, from the album *L'Enfance d'un peintre*, c. 1885
Charcoal on paper, 24.9×15.5 cm
Kunsthalle Bremen—Der Kunstverein in Bremen

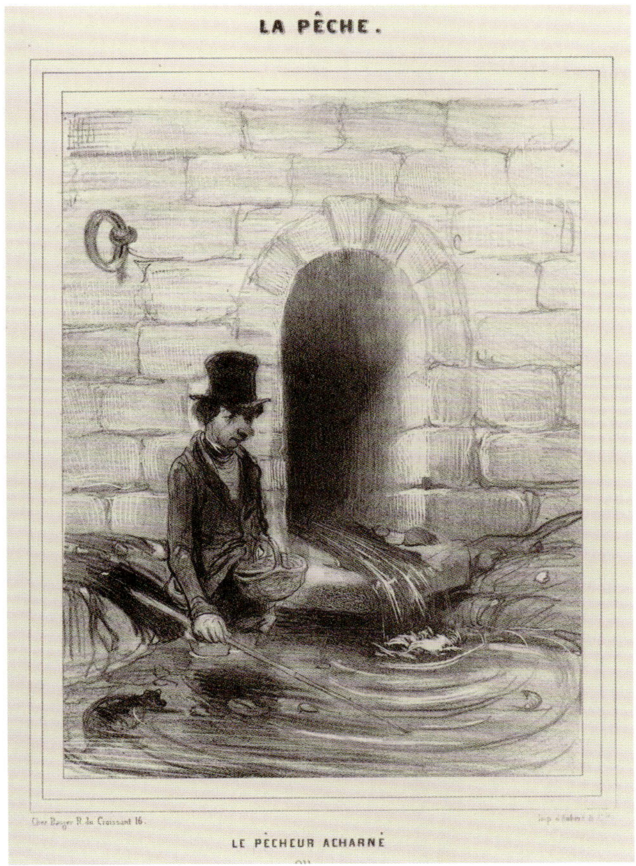

106 Honoré Daumier
"The Desperate Fisherman, or There is no Accounting for Taste," reproduced in *La Caricature* 2, no. 31, August 1, 1840
Bibliothèque Nationale de France, Paris

Raffaëlli had a high-profile solo exhibition in the spring of 1884 on rue de l'Opéra in Paris, which featured twenty-three of his "portraits-types," including *Chiffonnier allumant sa pipe* (Ragpicker Lighting his Pipe) **(107)**.[18] Given his interest in Naturalist art, Bernard is likely to have visited the exhibition. Raffaëlli's work, along with that of Doré and Daumier, might have colored Bernard's first explorations of Asnières, influencing him to focus not only on the Sunday entertainment but also on the underprivileged workers and ragpickers who were a common sight on the streets during the week.

Learning to Paint Among the Avant-Garde

Asnières proved so inspiring that, as noted earlier, Bernard decided within a few months of moving there that he wanted to turn his favorite pastime into a profession and idealistically quit high school straight away, having always attended only with the greatest reluctance. Writing in *L'Aventure de ma vie*, he described the heated argument that ensued when he informed his parents of his choice. Bernard's father had pictured his son's future very differently. There was an explosive fight, after which the would-be artist locked himself

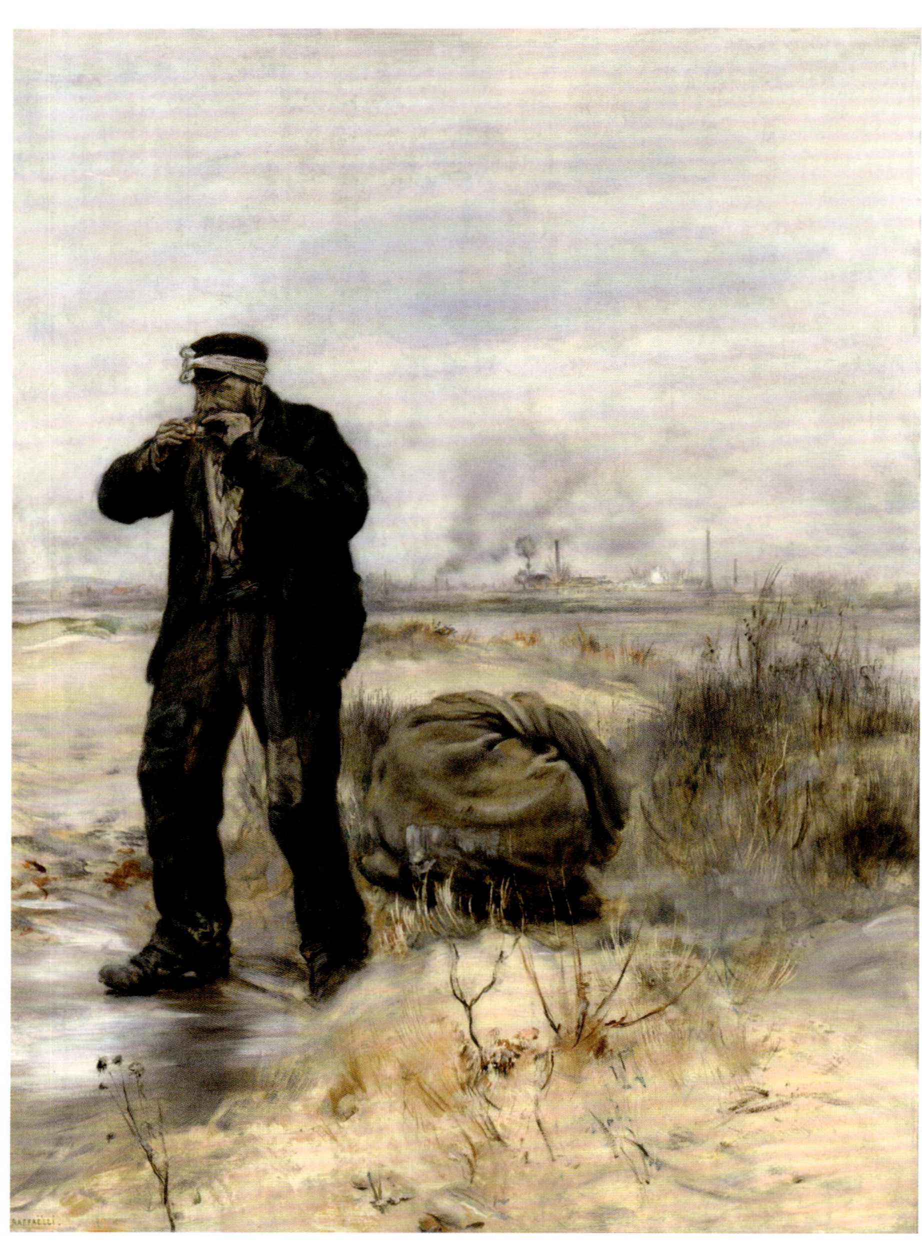

107 Jean-François Raffaëlli
Ragpicker Lighting his Pipe, 1884
Oil on canvas, 77.2 × 48.2 cm
Musée d'art de Nantes

in his room for days on end.[19] The standoff continued until Michel de Wylie, an artist who lived nearby, saw the young Bernard's drawings and told his parents that their son was very talented. His vote of confidence was evidently enough to persuade them to change their minds. De Wylie arranged an apprenticeship, beginning in September 1884, with the academic artist Fernand Cormon.[20] The latter's traditional style was reassuring to Bernard's parents, but they failed to realize that his studio was also a breeding ground for the avant-garde.[21]

Cormon's studio was located in Montmartre, an hour's walk from Asnières, with just over thirty pupils, of whom the sixteen-year-old Bernard was by far the youngest.[22] The others mostly paid him little attention, but a group of three artists—Henri de Toulouse-Lautrec, Louis Anquetin, and Paul Tampier—welcomed the new boy.[23] It is clear from everything Bernard later wrote about his time with Cormon that getting to know these artists was ultimately the most valuable aspect of his apprenticeship. The trio introduced him to the world of modern art, taking him to exhibitions and galleries where Bernard got to know the work of artists such as Gustave Courbet, Edouard Manet, and Claude Monet—the previous generation of modernists, who were steadily growing in popularity by the 1880s.[24] Cormon's pupils viewed them with a mixture of admiration and rivalry. The bright colors and the loose, personal painting style of Impressionists like Monet were a great inspiration, but they were also eager to distinguish themselves from their older counterparts. Many of the young artists tried to make the Impressionist technique their own, before moving on in a no less personal manner.

An avid discussion was going on beyond the walls of the studio about how modern painting should develop. Bernard learned a great deal in his new milieu about the importance of painting style and use of color, and how to deploy them to distinguish oneself as an artist. His view of Asnières as a setting for his art undoubtedly shifted in response: it was no longer enough to draw typical local figures, the painterly style in which he captured Asnières now became at least as important. This recognition was confirmed at the winter salon of the Société des Artistes Indépendants at the end of 1884, to which his new friends are sure to have taken him.[25] The show included work by the young painters Paul Signac and Georges Seurat, who were also keen to build on Impressionism and, like Bernard, often worked in the Asnières area. Bernard might even have bumped into them there already. Seurat exhibited nine swiftly brushed oil sketches and a study for his large painting *Bathers at Asnières* **(66)**. For his part, Signac was represented by paintings of subjects such as the Clichy gasworks and the station square in Asnières **(88, 108)**.[26]

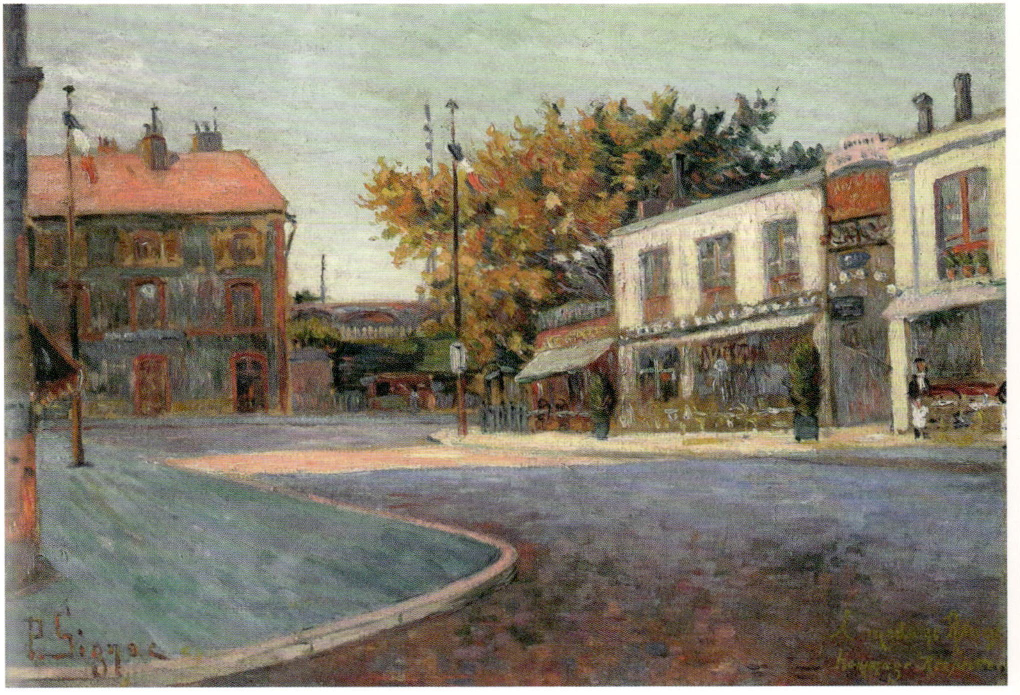

108 (cat.) Paul Signac
Rue de la Station, Asnières, 1884
Oil on canvas, 32 × 46 cm
Private collection

Experimentation and Engagement

Bernard saw the works by Signac and Seurat as marvelous examples of how to use Asnières as a setting for modern painting. Although not yet executed in the Pointillist technique for which the two artists would become famous, they depicted Asnières using a personal style derived from Impressionism. Signac excelled in dynamic brushwork with unexpected color combinations, while Seurat's woolly, soft touch lent a tranquility to his bathing scene. Despite the bright colors and distinctive application of paint, both artists' works also convey Asnières's characteristic tension between countryside and heavy industry. Seurat achieved this by placing the factories of Clichy in the background of his bathers, while two of Signac's paintings contrast the industrial plants with Asnières's quiet weekday streets. They had no eye, however, for the ragpickers or workers that Bernard continued to highlight.

Bernard responded with two small canvases that bring together the same Impressionist elements found in early works by Seurat and Signac: *View of Saint-Ouen* **(110)** and *Banks of the Seine at Asnières* **(109)**. Like Seurat's bathers, each offers a view of the Seine with tall factory chimneys in the background. To paint the first work, Bernard positioned himself on the bank of the Ile de Saint-Ouen, a short distance downstream from Asnières, and looked toward the industrial buildings in Saint-Ouen itself with the Pont de Gennevilliers in front of them. His dynamic brushwork echoed the examples of Signac and the more established Impressionists. The tone of the painting is predominantly blue-purple, but Bernard added several contrasting orange roofs in keeping with the color theory of complementary contrasts that was popular among the Impressionists. He paid close attention to the reflection of the buildings in the water and ingeniously indicated that of the smokestacks by scratching lines in the wet paint with the end of his brush.

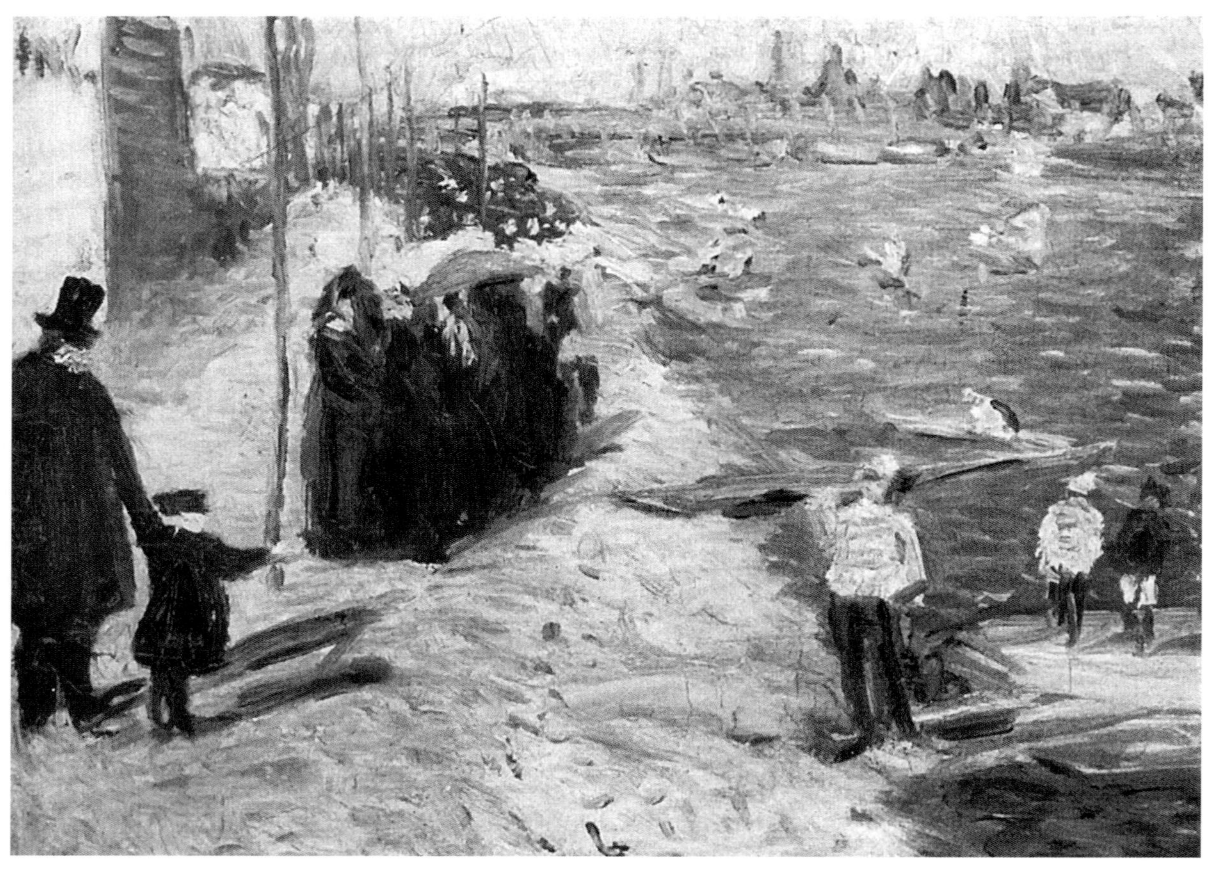

109 Emile Bernard
Banks of the Seine at Asnières, 1885
Oil on canvas, 31×40 cm
Private collection

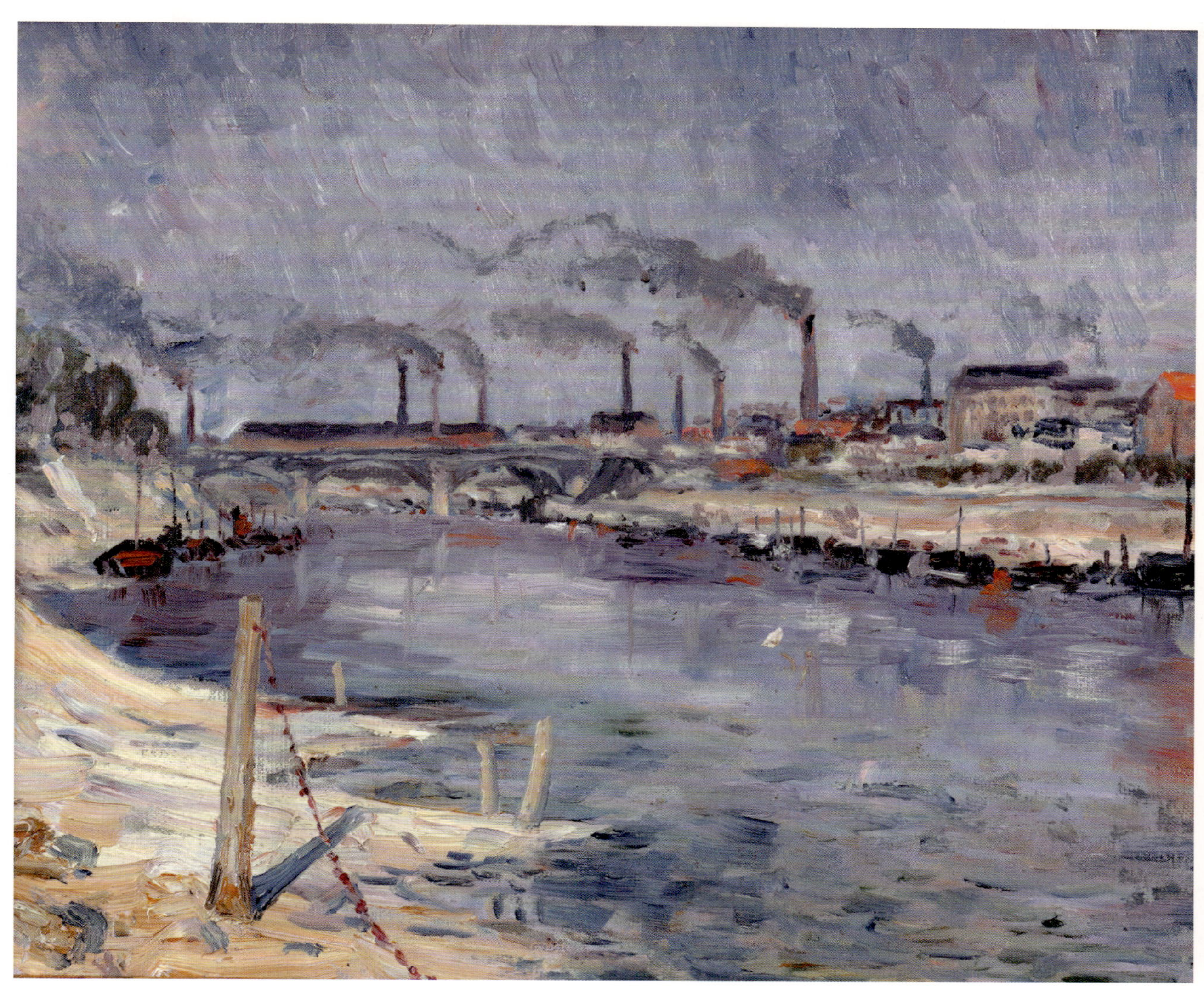

110 (cat.) Emile Bernard
View of Saint-Ouen, 1885
Oil on canvas, 33 × 41 cm
Private collection

Bernard painted *Banks of the Seine at Asnières* closer to home: the factories in the background here are those of Clichy. The composition and painting style are similar to *View of Saint-Ouen*, but now with added figures in the foreground, part of the Sunday bustle around a rowing race on the Seine. It was a theme that plainly continued to fascinate him, as he made at least three large sketches of it in 1885 and 1886 **(111,112,114)**. All the sketches are located on the quayside at Courbevoie, where the Seine bends gently to the left. The two more worked-up drawings, *Boats on the Seine at Asnières* and *The Regatta*, show a group of people in their Sunday clothes sitting around a table with a small tree on the left. The company in both drawings is located partially out of frame, showing that Bernard had noted the abrupt cropping that was particularly common in work by the Impressionists Gustave Caillebotte and Edgar Degas. He directed his gaze a little more toward the quay in *The Regatta*, bringing into view a building on which the artist has clearly written "VINS RESTAURANT" in pencil. This identifies the location as the same place where a famous photograph was taken of Bernard sitting at a table opposite a man viewed from behind, thought to be Vincent van Gogh **(113)**.[27] The number of studies he made here suggests that Bernard was preparing an ambitious painting along the lines of Seurat's *Bathers at Asnières* and *A Sunday on La Grande Jatte—1884* **(66,70)**. Perhaps the photograph with Van Gogh also had something to do with this campaign—Bernard might have had it taken as additional study material alongside his many sketches.[28] Whatever the case, no such completed work has been identified.[29]

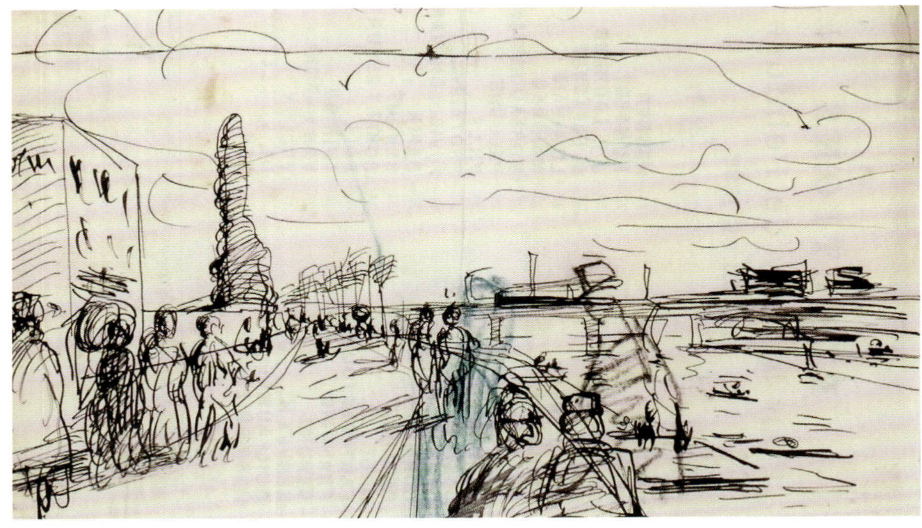

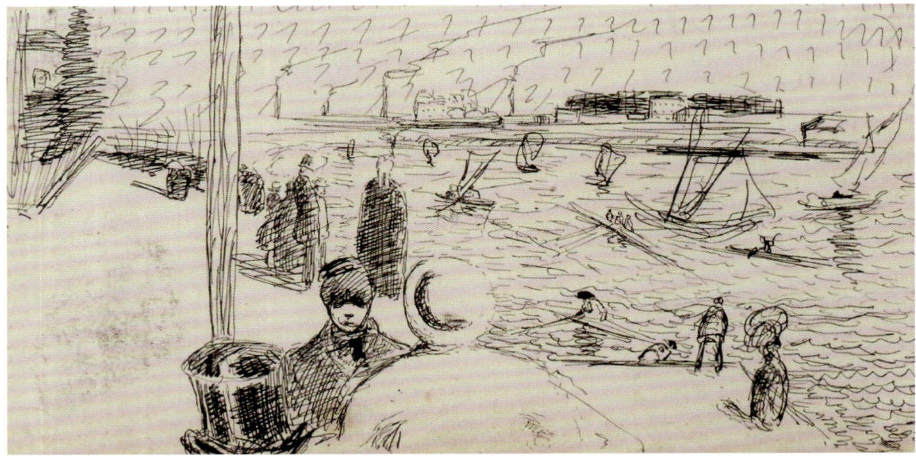

111 Emile Bernard
On the Quay of the Seine at Asnières,
from the album *L'Enfance d'un peintre*, c. 1886
Pen and ink, and black and colored chalk
on paper, 16 × 25.2 cm
Kunsthalle Bremen—Der Kunstverein in Bremen

112 (cat.) Emile Bernard
Boats on the Seine at Asnières, c. 1886
Pen and ink on paper, 15.7 × 31.1 cm
Kunsthalle Bremen—Der Kunstverein in Bremen

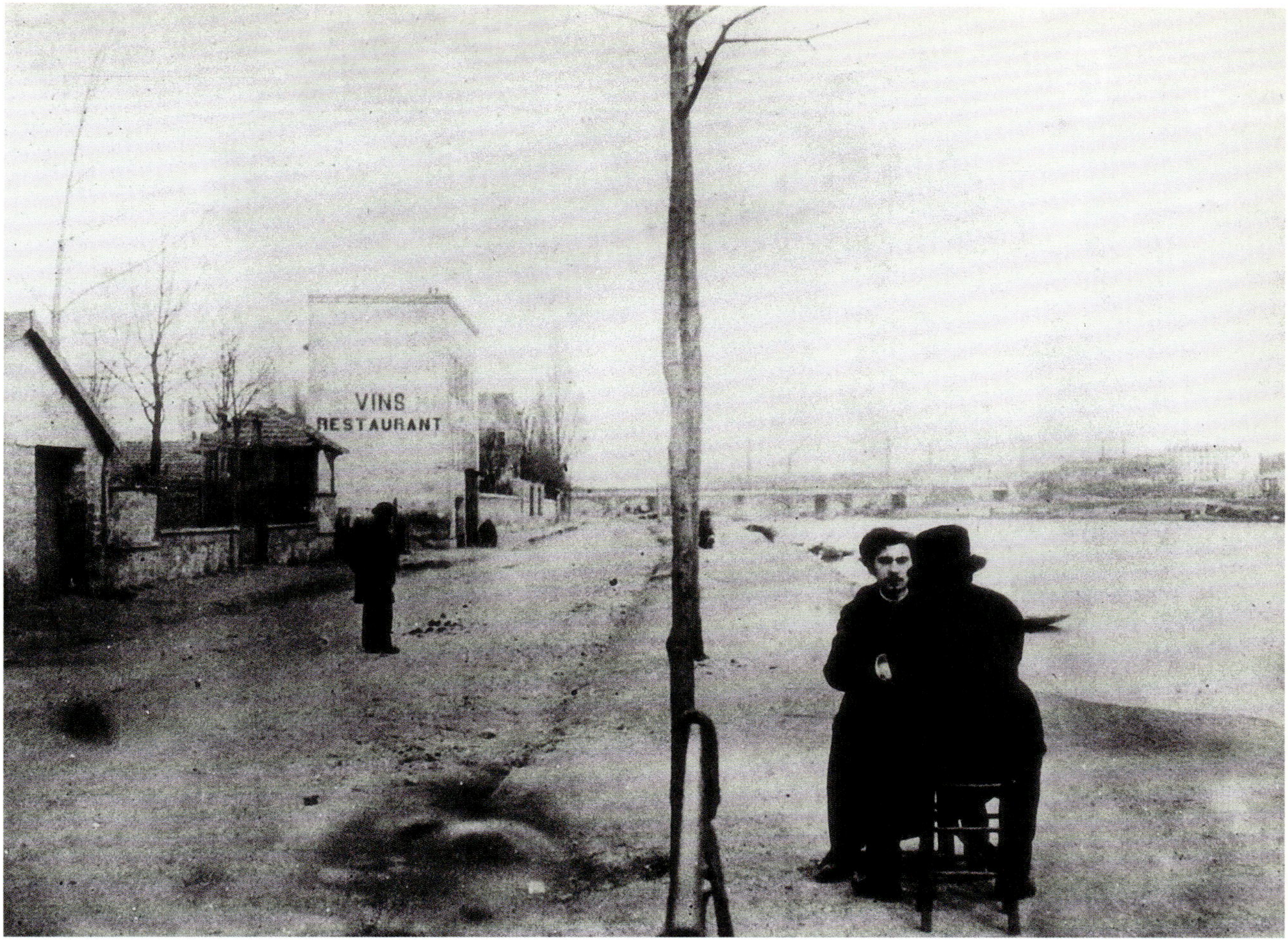

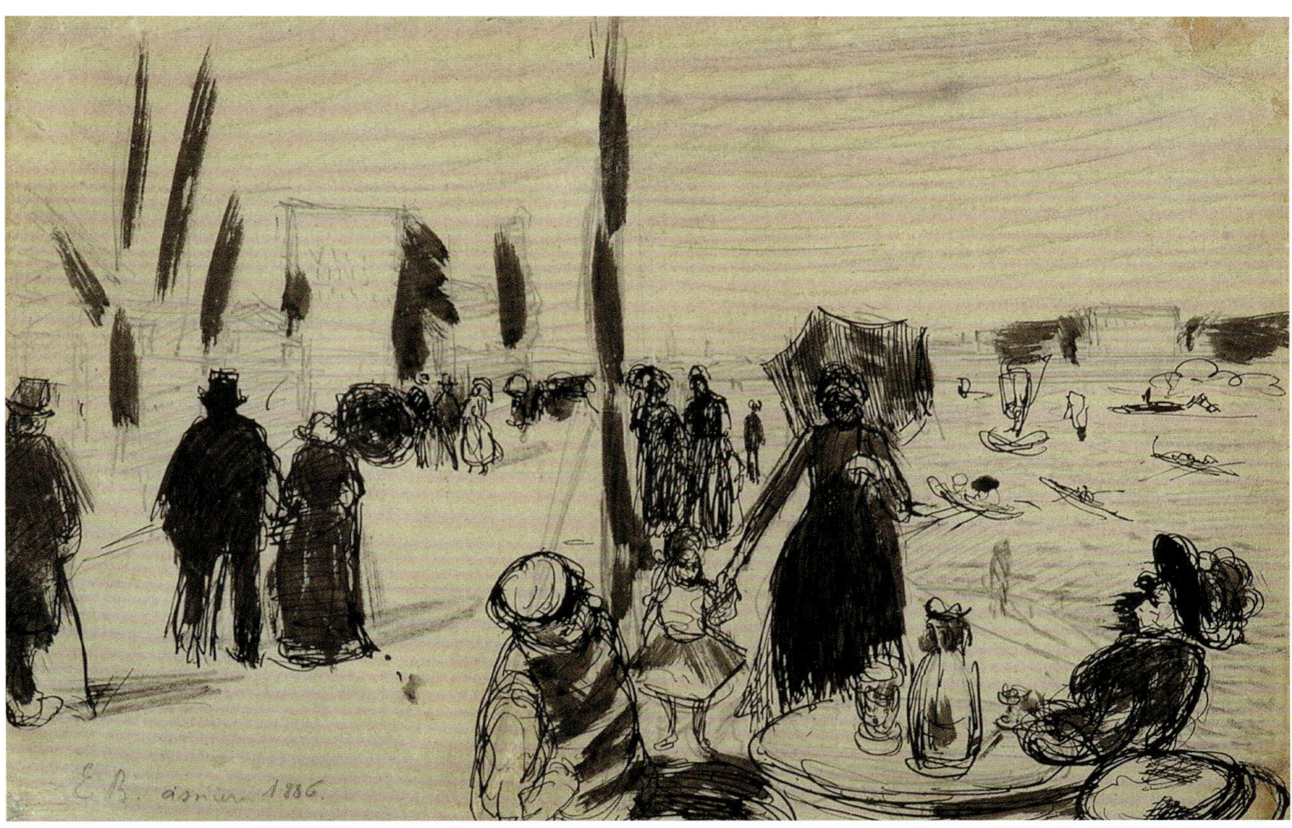

113 Emile Bernard and Vincent van Gogh in Courbevoie, c. 1886-87
Photograph, 13.2×16 cm
Private collection

114 (cat.) Emile Bernard
The Regatta, c. 1886
Pencil, pen, and brush and ink on paper, 19×30 cm
Private collection

Aside from *View of Saint-Ouen* and *Banks of the Seine at Asnières*, the artist's only painting made around Asnières that can be dated to 1885 with any certainty is *Large Landscape from My Window* **(115)**. As the title suggests, Bernard set up this large canvas by his window and painted the less-than-picturesque landscape he saw, neatly capturing Asnières's mismatched buildings, about which many complained. The wall he walked along to reach the Seine is visible in the lower part of the picture.[30] Compared to the other paintings from 1885, this one is a little timid because of the many orange and brown autumnal tones. Bernard nevertheless introduced an element of tension to the canvas by contrasting these tones with a purple sky and through his rapid, loose brushwork. In this way, he showed his desire once again to capture Asnières in a modern Impressionist style, albeit somewhat conservatively.[31]

Fisherman and Boat **(116)**, which Bernard might have completed in the winter of 1885–86, is more radical in both composition and painting style. Rather than a river view or landscape, he filled the entire picture plane with the freely and dynamically painted water of the Seine. The only point of reference is the quay, which juts very slightly into the image. Bernard used orange tones, which contrast nicely with the blue-green water, to paint a rowboat and beyond it the silhouette of an angler who sits somewhat dejectedly with drooping shoulders. The artist's rendering of this figure recalls his sketches of the down-at-the-heels types he drew in and around Asnières, many of which also consist of a dark silhouette.[32] In this canvas, Bernard thus combined his affinity for people from the lower levels of society with his experiments with modern painting techniques.

Flirting with Dots

While Bernard and his fellows experimented widely with their painting style and technique, in the studio they had to stick to Cormon's prescriptions for academic drawing and painting from casts of antique sculptures and life models. Modern painting was something for their spare time.[33] Bernard held out for eighteen months before breaking the rules and painting with unblended shades of green and red in the studio itself. What ensued when Corman arrived is recalled in the memoirs of Archibald Standish Hartrick, a British fellow pupil: “On asking the youth what he was doing, Bernard replied, ‘that he saw it that way.’ Thereupon Cormon announced that if that was the case he had better go and see things that way somewhere else.”[34]

Bernard was suspended, triggering a personal crisis and another argument with his parents. After prolonged deliberation, he decided in April 1886 to go hiking from

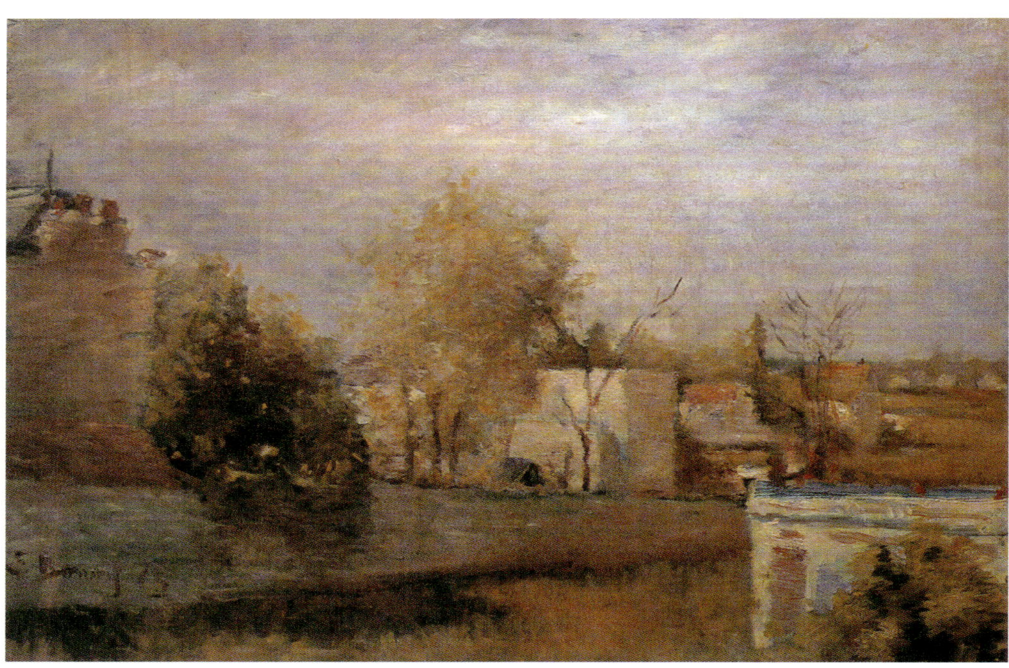

115 Emile Bernard
Large Landscape from My Window, 1885
Oil on canvas, 54 × 81 cm
Private collection

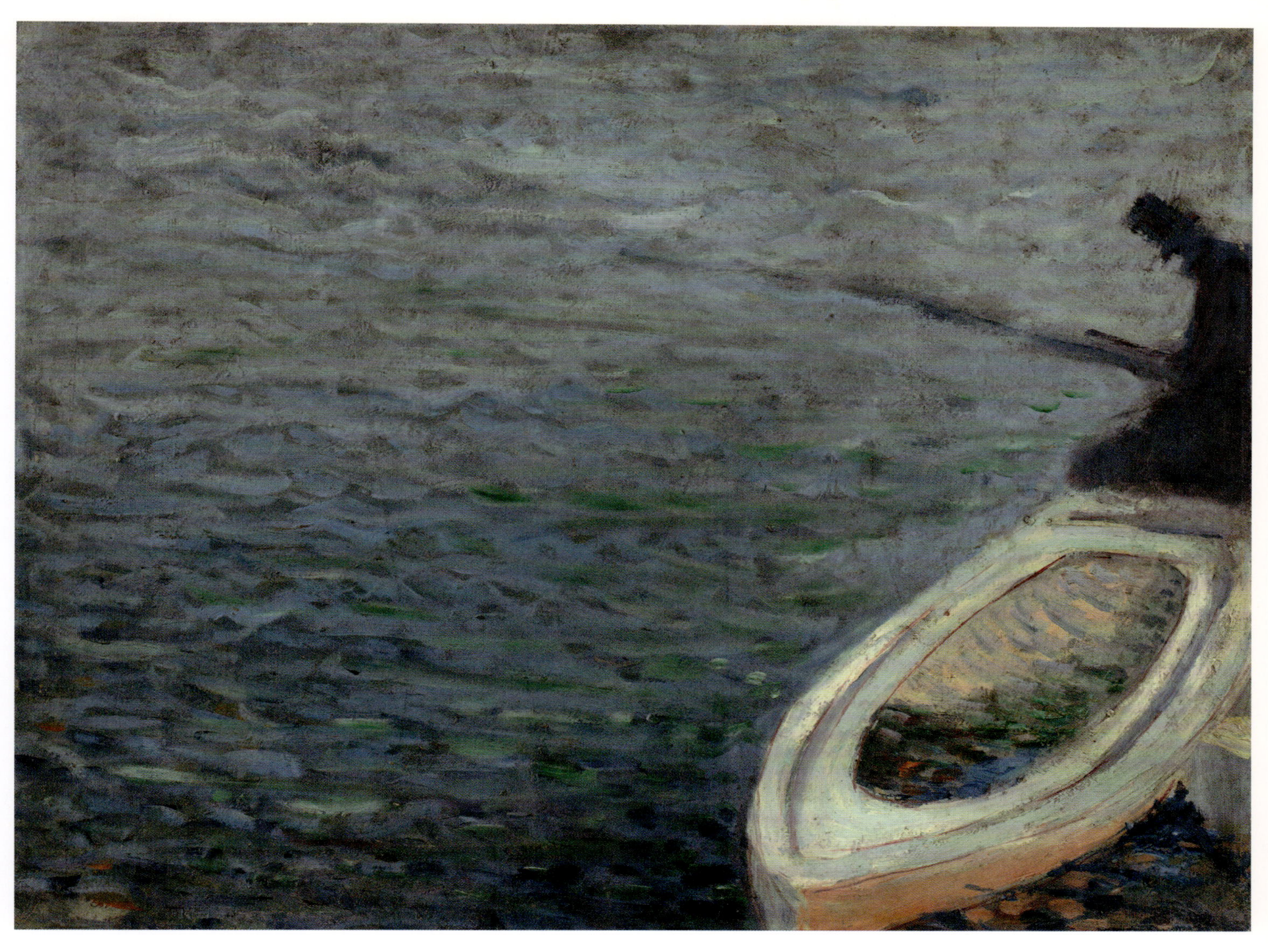

116 (cat.) Emile Bernard
Fisherman and Boat, 1885–86
Oil on canvas, 39 × 51.5 cm
Van Gogh Museum, Amsterdam (Vincent van Gogh Foundation)

village to village in Brittany in search of freedom and his identity as an artist.[35] His *voyage à pied* lasted until September and ended at the artists' village of Pont-Aven.[36] In the years that followed, he would return to the Breton countryside every summer, while spending the intervening period at his parents' home in Asnières.

Bernard's absence meant that he missed one of that year's most seminal events for the Parisian avant-garde—the eighth and final Impressionist exhibition, at which Seurat and Signac caused a furor with their radically new Pointillist paintings. With these canvases, which included numerous views of Asnières and the surrounding area, they achieved what so many had aspired to: freeing themselves from the influence of the Impressionists by developing a style of their own. The letters Bernard wrote from Brittany show that he regretted missing the exhibition.[37] All the same, the news about Pointillism seems to have gotten through, as several of his Pont-Aven paintings from 1886

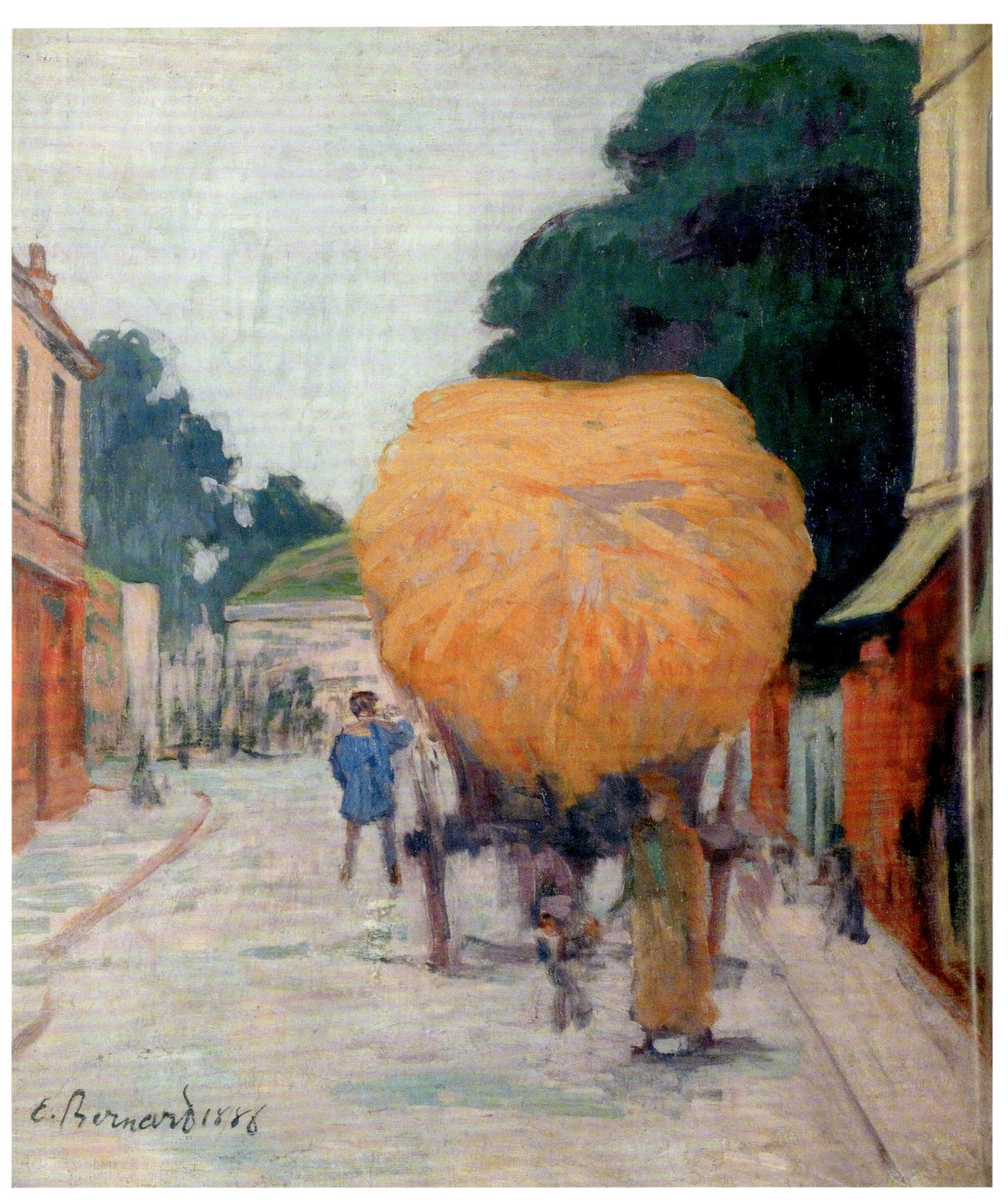

117 Emile Bernard
Haywagon, Asnières, 1886
Oil on canvas, 46 × 33 cm
Private collection

show clear evidence of stippling.[38] Other painters in the Breton village, among them Emile Schuffenecker and Henri Delavallée, had also adopted the technique, and Bernard might have picked it up from them.[39] Either way, his Pointillist paintings from Pont-Aven heralded a brief flirtation with the style that would last until early 1887.

Bernard was not entirely faithful to the Pointillist approach: he also painted works in this period like *Haywagon, Asnières* **(117)**, which used broader and longer brushstrokes and, as a result, appears more Impressionist in style.[40] The atmospheric *Little Evening Effect on the Seine, Asnières* **(118)** also dates from the fall of 1886, even though it is not painted in a strictly Pointillist technique. It shows the quai d'Asnières at dusk, with passages of short strokes alternating with sections painted in flat color. All the same, the other views of Asnières that Bernard painted that fall must have utilized stippling, since he wrote in retrospect: "I did various views of Asnières using the process [Pointillism] and I showed them . . . at a small exhibition of painters from the outskirts of Paris that was held in Asnières."[41]

Strangely enough, all of the Pointillist works that Bernard painted in Asnières are unknown today. He might subsequently have reused or destroyed any such canvases, as he no longer wished to be associated with the style, having rejected Neo-Impressionism not long after the group exhibition in Asnières. Bernard wrote in his memoirs that this rejection occurred after he and Anquetin had seen Signac's Pointillist works in his studio in early March 1887, probably including *The Dining Room, Opus no. 152* (1886–87; Kröller-Müller Museum, Otterlo).[42] Signac had invited him to visit following the exhibition. Their revulsion at what they saw was apparently so intense that he and Anquetin decided to close their Pointillist chapter with immediate effect.[43] Henceforth they would paint in a style they felt to be as far removed from Neo-Impressionism as possible, replacing the visual spectacle of luminous dots with flat, even fields of color and distinct outlines.[44] This style of painting came to be known as "Cloisonnism," a term coined by the art critic Edouard Dujardin in 1888.[45]

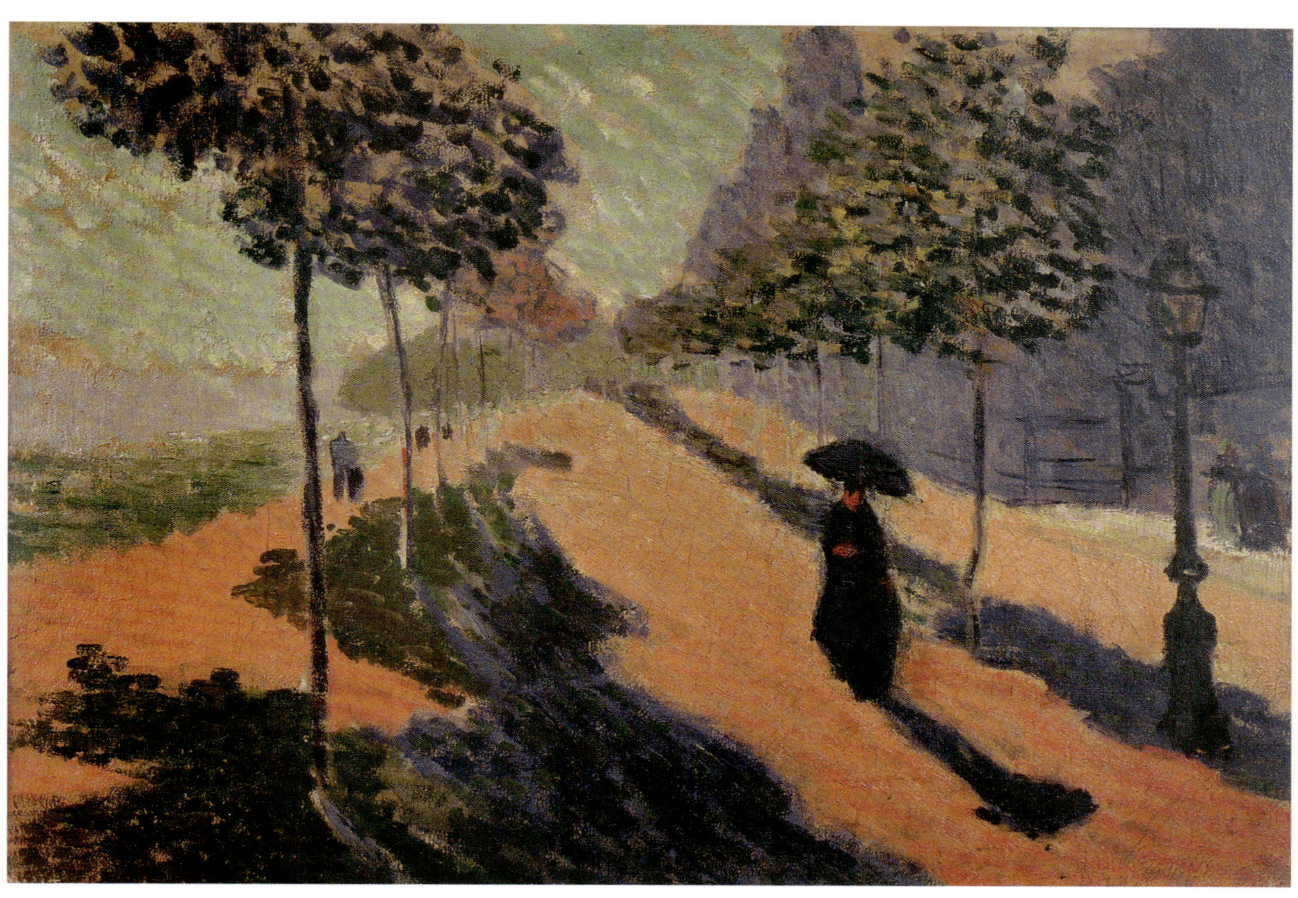

118 Emile Bernard
Little Evening Effect on the Seine, Asnières, 1886
Oil on canvas, 37×54 cm
Private collection

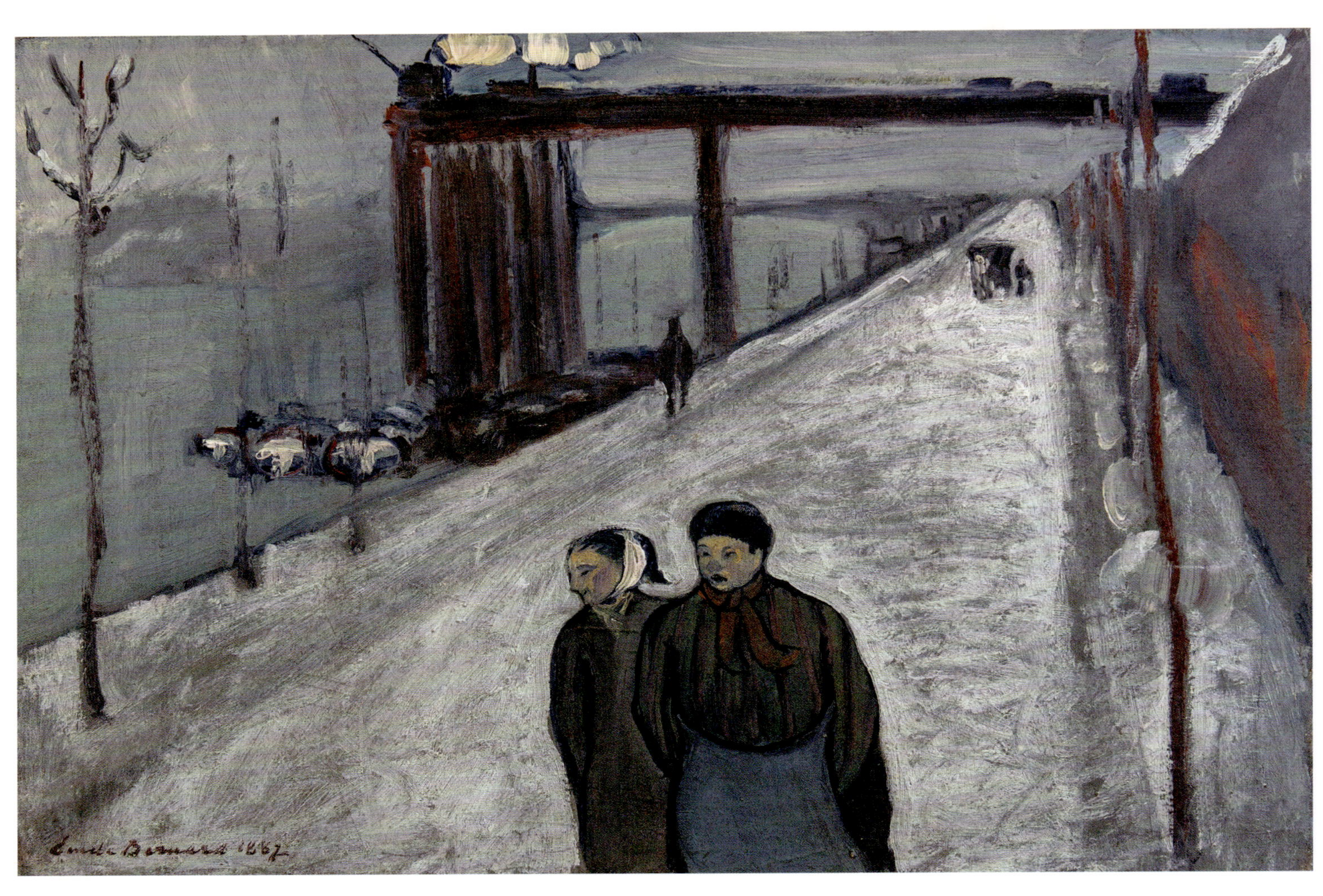

119 (cat.) Emile Bernard
Quai de Clichy on the Seine, 1887
Oil on canvas, 39×59 cm
Musée d'Orsay, Paris, on loan to the Musée départmental du Prieuré, Saint-Germain-en-Laye, bequest of Pierre Farcy, 1989

It could have been shortly after visiting Signac's studio that Bernard painted his first Cloisonnist work, *Quai de Clichy* **(119)**.[46] Despite the revolution in his painting style, he still chose the familiar subject of the Clichy gasworks, near Asnières. The canvas shows the quayside, at which barges carrying raw materials for the plant were unloaded. By choosing a subject that Signac also painted frequently, Bernard emphasized the diametric opposition of his new style to that of his rival **(96)**. The two female factory workers or ragpickers he placed in the foreground, meanwhile, demonstrate his undiminished commitment to the less fortunate. Once again, therefore, Asnières and the people Bernard observed there provided the setting for a new development in his artistic practice. In the space of three years, the artist had first adopted and then abandoned both the loose Impressionist brush and the orderly stippling of Pointillism. He now painted the quayside and the water flowing past it as monochrome expanses, while reducing the gasworks to a geometric pattern of lines and setting down stylized figures with clear outlines. He later wrote of this approach: "The spectacle must be simplified to draw out its meaning."[47]

Van Gogh and Cloisonnism

Bernard and Anquetin drew inspiration for their new painting style from medieval stained-glass windows and tapestries, as well as from Japanese printmaking—art forms where lines and blocks of color feature prominently.[48] Another artist friend of theirs, Vincent van Gogh, had a great deal to do with the Japanese influence. Just as Bernard and Anquetin were exchanging Pointillism for Cloisonnism, Van Gogh organized an exhibition of his Japanese print collection at Le Tambourin, a café where he was a regular.[49] Van Gogh himself reported the marked influence of the exhibition on his two French colleagues.[50]

Van Gogh and Bernard had met in 1886, first at Cormon's studio and later at Julien Tanguy's art supplies store.[51] They quickly became good friends and discussed at length their many sources of inspiration and how these might be given a place in modern painting. Japanese prints were one such source, but so was Asnières. Van Gogh painted there too between May and July of 1887, and many of the locations in Bernard's paintings and drawings also appear in his work. Bernard might have even suggested that he paint there, and the previously mentioned photograph could have been taken during one of the Dutchman's first trips. Oddly enough, though, there is no evidence that the two artists ever worked side by side on the banks of the Seine. Van Gogh's Asnières paintings mostly date from the summer of 1887, by which time Bernard had decamped to Brittany.[52]

The two artists nevertheless worked together a good deal in Asnières, but rather than outdoors, they did so at the home of Bernard's parents, who had moved to a larger house at 5 avenue de Beaulieu, near the Asnières train station, at the beginning of 1887.[53] While Bernard was away in Brittany, they had a wooden studio built for him in their new garden, where Van Gogh frequently came to work with his friend following the latter's return.[54] Fall 1887 was an especially inspiring period for Bernard, due in part to these frequent artistic interactions with his Dutch companion. Three paintings by him of Asnières are known from this period: *The House of Emile Bernard's Parents at Asnières*, *Two Women on the Asnières Footbridge,* and *Iron Bridges at Asnières* **(6,120,121)**. All three are highlights of his Cloisonnist period and are clearly inspired by Japanese printmaking, for which he shared Van Gogh's immense admiration.[55] The paintings show how far he could go in simplifying his subject into flat expanses of color and emphasizing strong outlines.

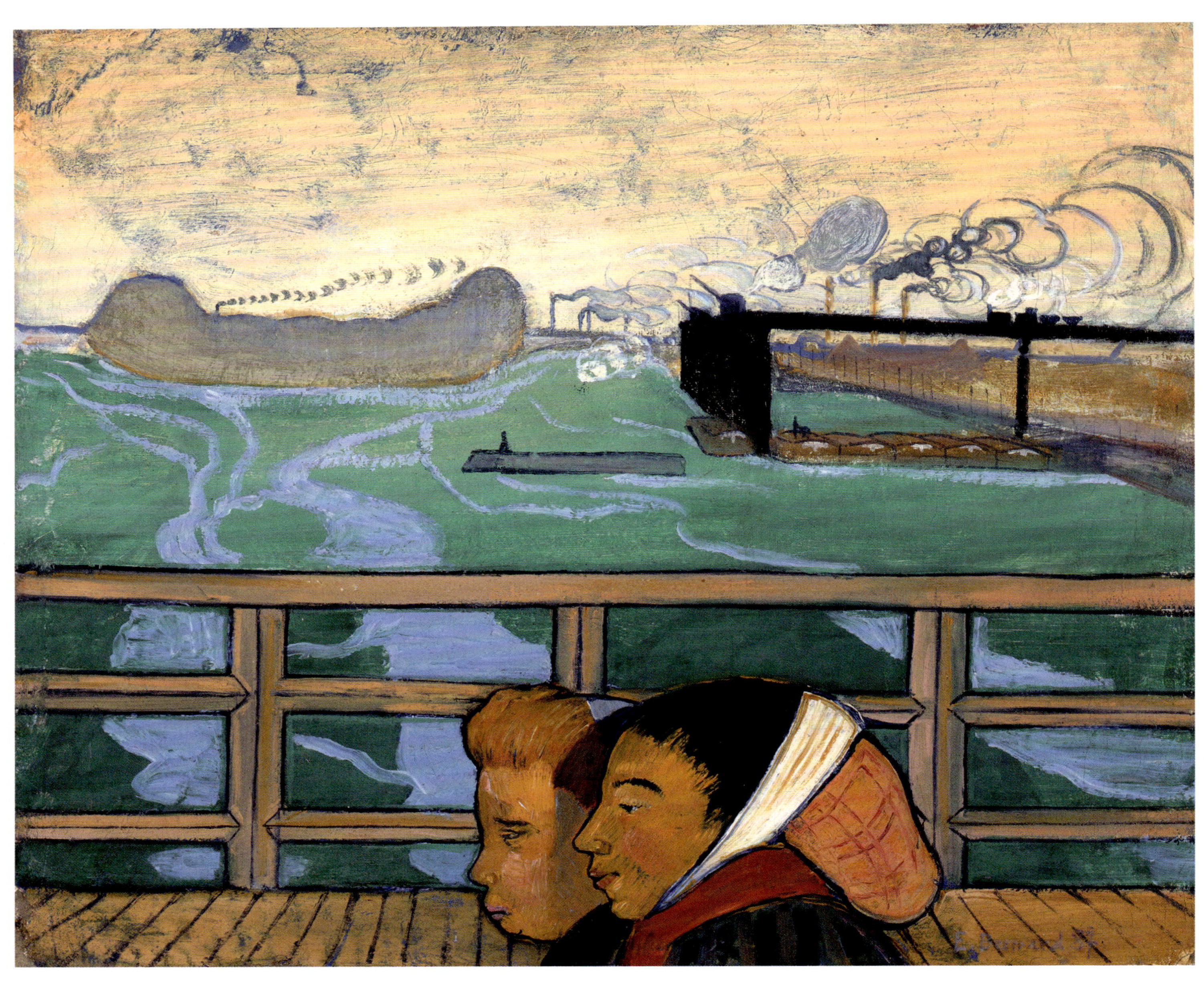

120 (cat.) Emile Bernard
Two Women on the Asnières Footbridge, 1887
Oil on canvas, 38 × 46.5 cm
Musée des Beaux-Arts, Brest métropole

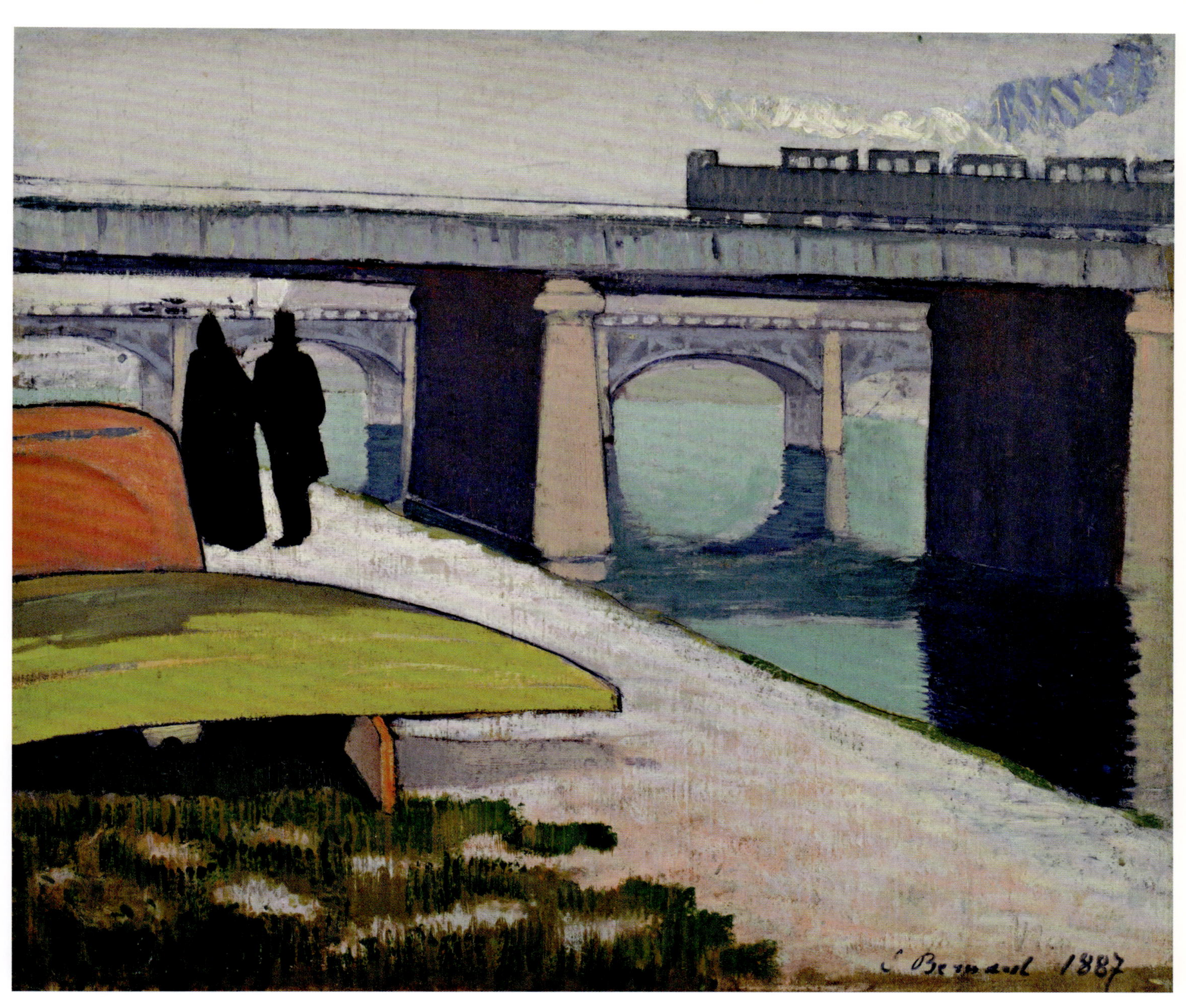

121 (cat.) Emile Bernard
Iron Bridges at Asnières, 1887
Oil on canvas, 45.9 × 54.2 cm
The Museum of Modern Art, New York
Grace Rainey Rogers Fund, 1962

The House of Emile Bernard's Parents at Asnières shows his parents' home in a highly abstracted style and from an unexpected bird's-eye perspective. The house is reduced to a heavily outlined geometric box among stripped-down trees. Bernard placed the signal for a railroad crossing firmly in the foreground, radically breaking up the composition. He did something similar in *Two Women on the Asnières Footbridge*, where the heads of the women (working-class once again) are positioned in the front, centrally, and closely cropped. The foreground of the composition is dominated by the stylized railing—painted in a provocatively naive manner—of the bridge the women are crossing. In the background, meanwhile, the Clichy gasworks are clearly identifiable, with a schematic view of Ile Robinson on the left. Bernard painted the plumes of smoke given off by the distant chimneys as simple, tightly drawn circles, in sharp contrast with the woolly, loosely brushed way he captured the same pollution two years earlier in *View of Saint-Ouen* **(110)**. The bridge *Two Women on the Asnières Footbridge* was painted from can also be seen in the distance in the iconic *Iron Bridges at Asnières*, but it is partially obscured there by the railroad bridge in the middle ground. Van Gogh had painted precisely the same view earlier that year, but in an even looser style **(48)**.
In Bernard's work, a couple of ragpickers walk along the quayside, depicted by the artist as dark silhouettes, as in his drawings and in the painting *Fisherman and Boat* **(116)**. They pass by two brightly colored rowboats, referencing the genteel recreation that took place here

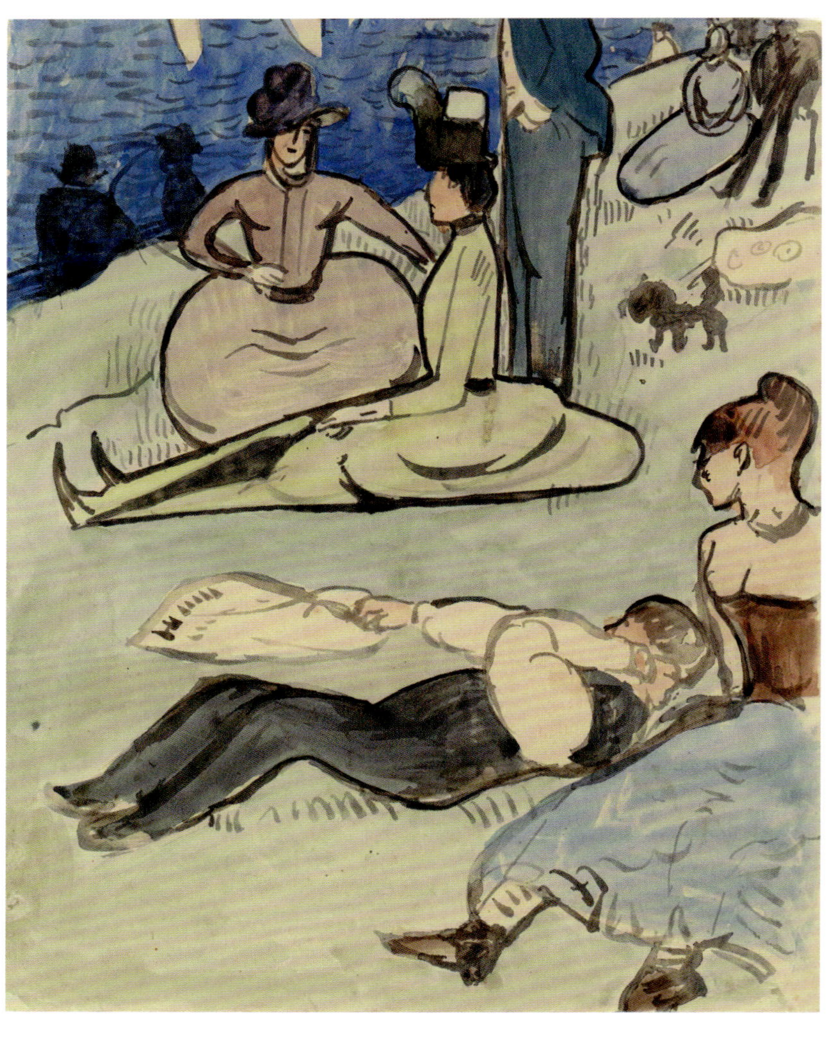

122 (cat.) Emile Bernard
Figures on the Riverbank, 1888
Reed pen and brush and ink and watercolor on paper, 32×26 cm
Van Gogh Museum, Amsterdam (Vincent van Gogh Foundation)

on Sundays. In this way, Bernard subtly alluded once again to his town's social contrasts and showed that his modern paintings of Asnières were more than simply a matter of style. *Iron Bridges at Asnières* unites the different elements that interested him about the place, while his simplified painting style enabled him to capture their essence.

Bernard's Cloisonnist paintings of Asnières placed him in direct opposition to the Pointillists. His continuing inclusion of politically engaged elements distanced him from them even further, given the almost total lack of awareness in their work of the social extremes in Asnières. The difference was exacerbated in late 1887, when Bernard refused to exhibit alongside Signac, following an invitation from Van Gogh to participate in an exhibition of work by the so-called "Painters of the Petit Boulevard." Van Gogh, who was less dogmatic about the niceties of the various painting styles, sought unsuccessfully to mediate in the escalating conflict between Bernard and Signac.[56] In the end, Bernard was the only one of the pair to take part, showing two of his Cloisonnist paintings, including *Two Women on the Asnières Footbridge* **(120)**.[57]

Asnières and Beyond

Bernard seems to have played up his hostility toward the Pointillists, both in 1887 and in his later articles and memoirs, in order to stand out and to emphasize his own originality and individuality. In doing so, he focused on Signac and less so on Seurat, whose monumental *A Sunday on La Grande Jatte—1884* actually interested him a great deal. This is apparent, for instance, from two drawings he sent to Van Gogh in Arles in 1888: *Figures on the Riverbank* and *Idyll at Asnières* **(122,123)**.[58] Like Seurat's painting, they depict the area's leisure activities. Although the

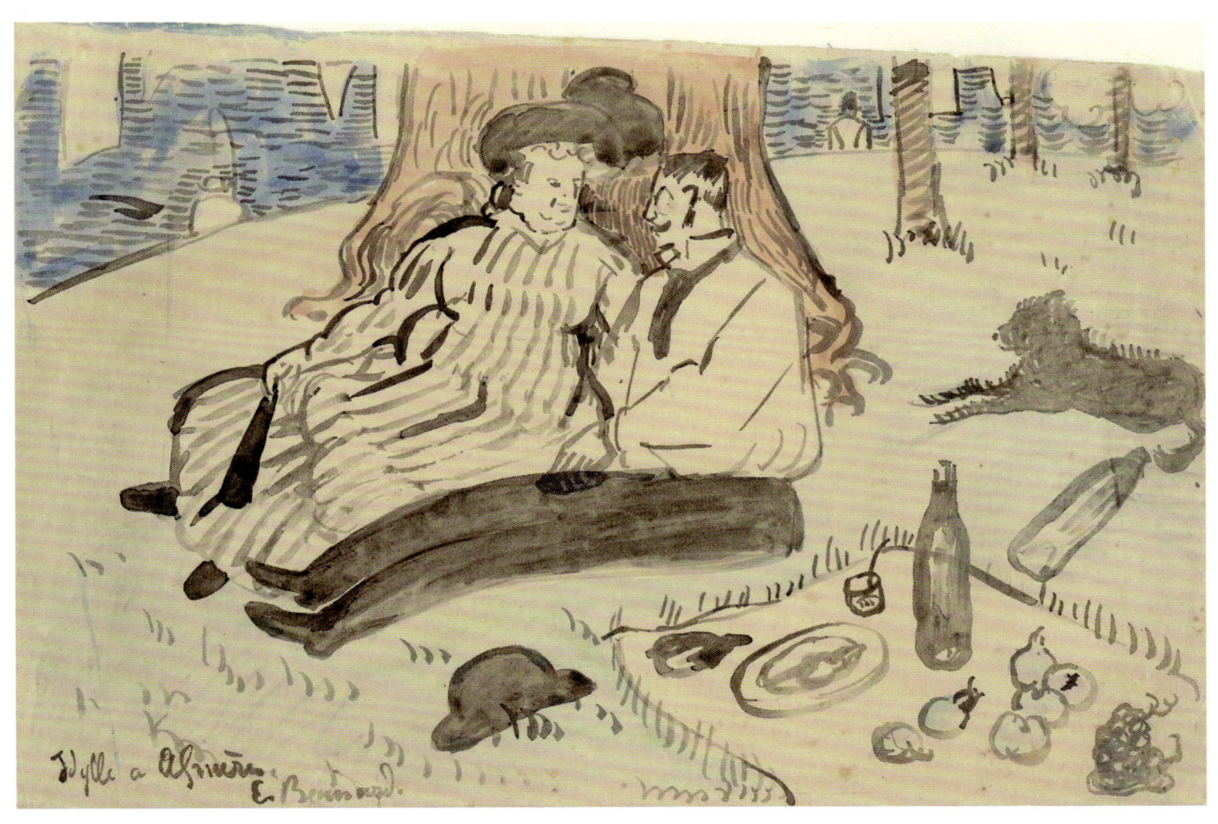

123 (cat.) Emile Bernard
Idyll at Asnières (Idylle à Asnières), 1888
Brush and ink and watercolor on paper, 27.5 × 40.4 cm
Van Gogh Museum, Amsterdam (Vincent van Gogh Foundation)

composition of both drawings is similar to that of *A Sunday on La Grande Jatte—1884*, it is above all in the rendering of the figures that Bernard betrayed his debt to Seurat. The Pointillists' archaic, static forms must have appealed to him, as Bernard's figures have the same appearance. The seated woman in yellow in *Figures on the Riverbank* seems to have been lifted verbatim from *La Grande Jatte*. Bernard substituted Seurat's dots for his own hard lines and blocks of color, yet the shape of the figures undeniably inspired him.

Seurat's influence is equally plain in the painting *La Grande Jatte in Spring* **(124)**. Bernard dated the work 1890, by which point he had already abandoned strict Cloisonnism and was working instead in short parallel brushstrokes, inspired by Paul Cézanne.[59] The painting shows that Bernard continued to choose Asnières and its surroundings as subjects for his art after the winter of 1887–88. He still returned to his parents' home every year, with new paintings resulting each time, including *Garden in Bloom at Asnières* **(125)**. This went on until 1893, when Bernard quit Paris, the center of modern art, and moved to Cairo for more than a decade. He never lived with his parents again and, when they both died in 1911, Bernard lost his *pied-à-terre* in Asnières. But he often thought back to his former home in later life, as his many writings testify. Asnières would always be the place where the stormy first years of his artistic career had unfolded and a location that provided the backdrop for a rapid succession of painting styles. ■

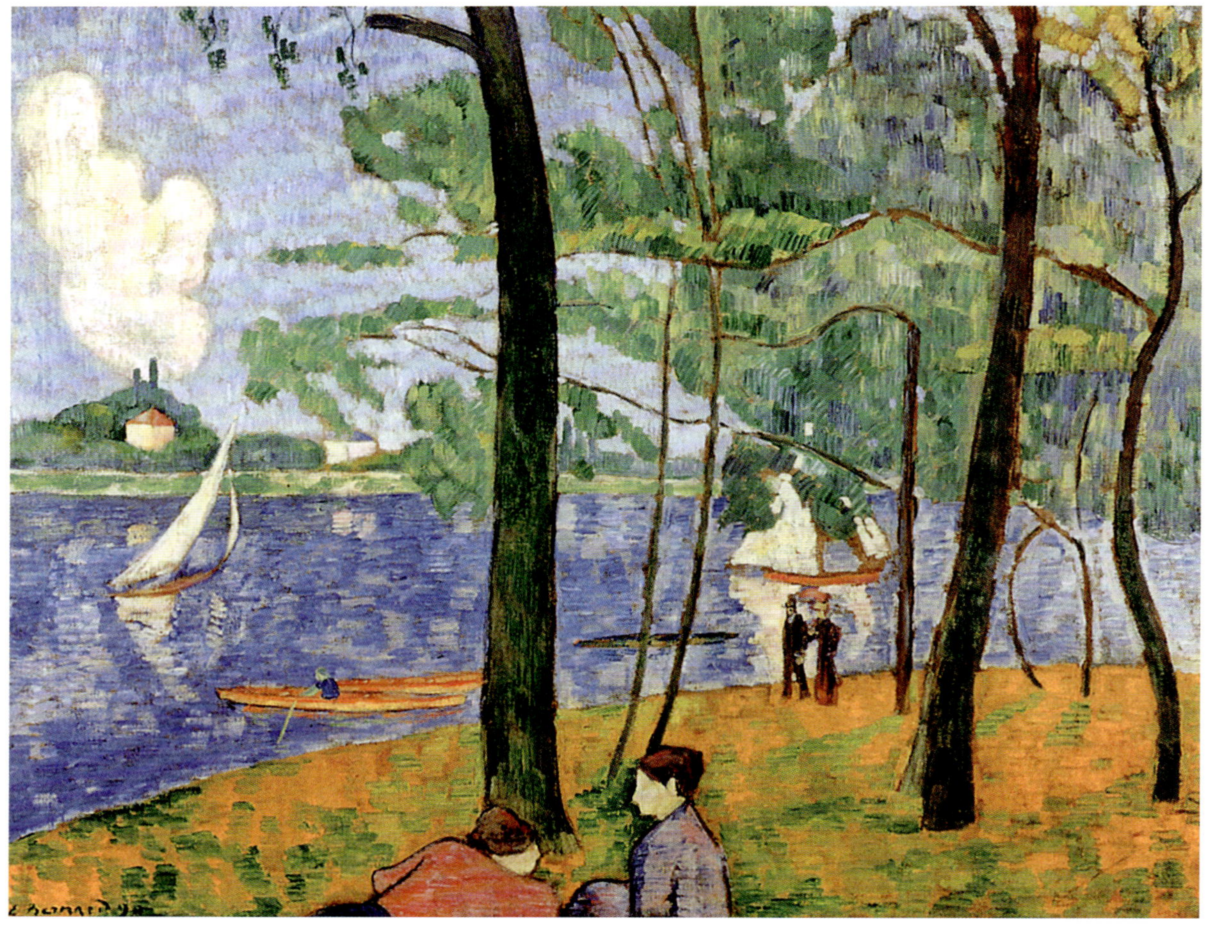

124 Emile Bernard
La Grande Jatte in Spring, 1890
Oil on canvas, 70 × 90 cm
Private collection

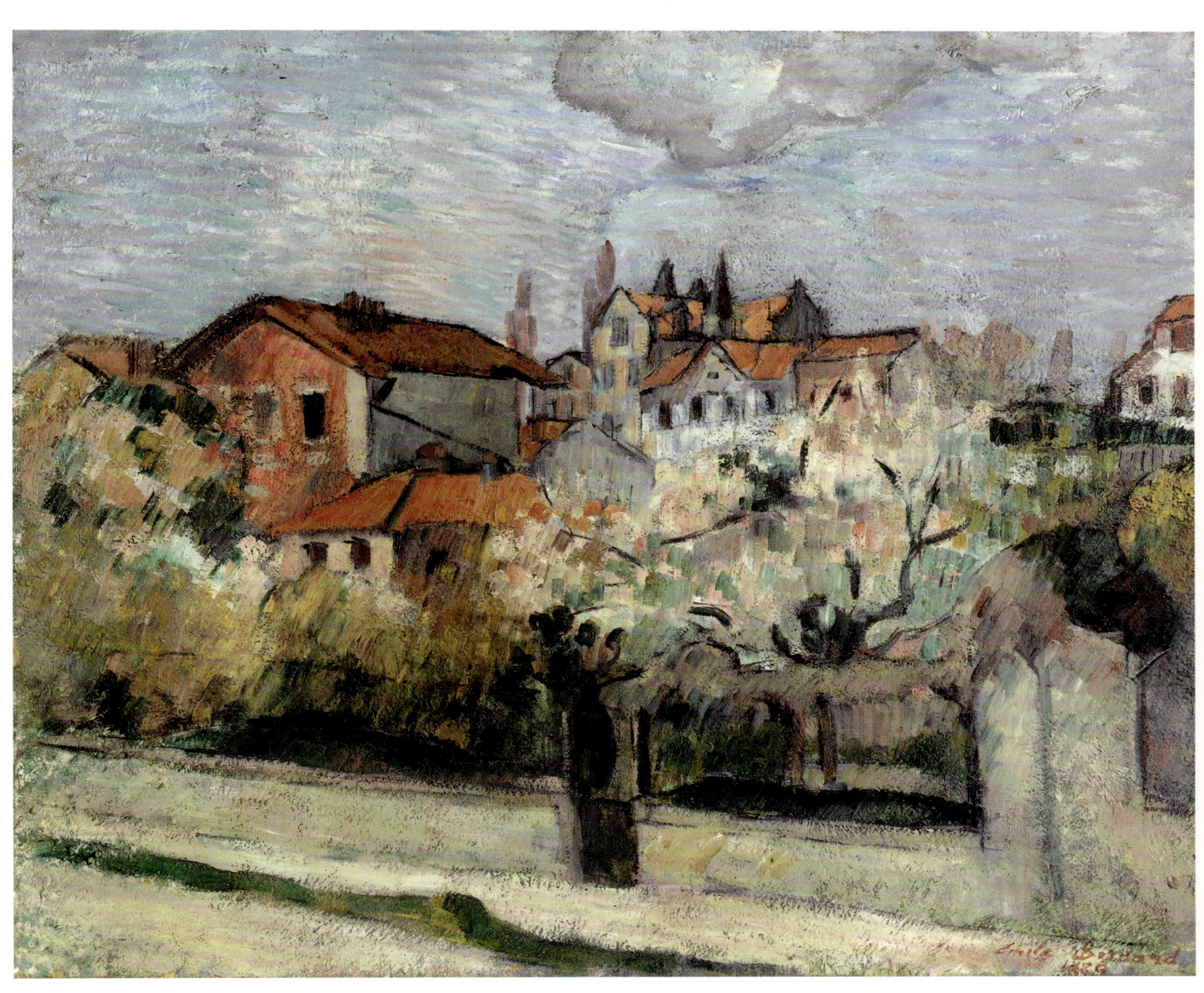

125 (cat.) Emile Bernard
Garden in Bloom at Asnières, 1889
Oil on canvas, 54.3 × 64.1 cm
Collection of Andrew S. Teufel

ANGRAND: EXPRESSIVE HARMONIES FROM SAINT-OUEN AND ASNIÈRES TO COURBEVOIE

FRANÇOIS LESPINASSE

Charles Angrand is one of the least well-known painters in this catalogue, largely because his output included fewer than one hundred paintings. Of these works, six were painted in the suburbs of Paris around Asnières and the Seine between 1885 and 1889, and three at unknown locations. During his lifetime, there were no monographic exhibitions of his paintings, and only one, in Paris in 1925, that brought together twenty-five works in pastel—Angrand's preferred medium during his final years. Furthermore, recent exhibitions have occurred outside of the art-historical center of Paris, with all publications on the artist remaining in his native French. Who was this rare artist, whose work is nevertheless held by leading museums around the world? And what role did his works produced along the Seine play in his oeuvre?

Angrand was born on April 19, 1854, in Criquetot-sur-Ouville, a village in the Pays de Caux region of Normandy, located halfway between the chalky cliffs on the Channel coast and the meanders of the Seine.[1] His father had been the village schoolteacher since 1849 and wanted his son to follow him into the profession. His sister Maria, born in 1852, and Paul, his brother born in 1868, both became educators. After his initial studies, he moved to Rouen, where he was a brilliant student at the teacher training college. He was subsequently appointed to two teaching roles, *répétiteur*, then *maître répétiteur*, at the Lycée Corneille in Rouen in October 1873. In 1875 he went to Paris for the first time to see the retrospective exhibition devoted to Jean-Baptiste-Camille Corot at the Ecole des Beaux-Arts. This was an important trip, sparking his desire to become a painter. Angrand studied at Rouen's Académie de Peinture et de Dessin under the direction of Gustave Morin, and at the Lycée Corneille with Philippe Zacharie. Thanks to this conventional training, he acquired a very solid foundation in academic painting and competed for prizes with his friend Charles Frechon.[2] But his attraction to *plein-air* painting, which ultimately drew him to the suburbs northwest of Paris, was stronger. This essay outlines his biography and his accomplishments across his career while exploring the importance of these suburbs in his artistic development.

Paris and the Salons

In October 1882 Angrand moved to Paris and began the new school year teaching at the Collège Chaptal, at 45 boulevard des Batignolles, which was close to the Gare Saint-Lazare but also the place Clichy, the Café d'Athènes, the Café Guerbois, and Le Chat Noir, some of the capital's artistic and literary landmarks. Angrand devoted all of his free time to painting, remaining at the Collège for fourteen years before returning to live with his mother in the Pays de Caux after she was widowed. Several of his colleagues bought his paintings and drawings, and over those years, he developed into an exceptionally talented artist.

He was tempted by the Salon, the exhibition that attracted artists in large numbers, but he saw his submissions refused in 1883 and 1884. Angrand then turned to the Salon des Jeunes Artistes, attending the meetings at the Café Pygmalion, at 6 boulevard Sébastopol. He exhibited at the second exhibition in December 1883, at the Panorama de Reichshoffen on rue Saint-Honoré—the famous building designed by Charles Garnier to host a painting spanning 360 degrees, which had been transformed into a circus and exhibition hall—and at the Arts Incohérents exhibition at the Galerie Vivienne.[3] Soon after he started playing an active role in the creation of the Salon des Artistes Indépendants, spending time with Georges Seurat, Albert Dubois-Pillet, and Paul Signac at meetings in the Café Marengo. As a result, he became a part of the Parisian avant-garde, with a preference for *plein-air* painting.

Angrand offered his works to the art dealer Paul Durand-Ruel, without success, but received a friendlier reception from Georges Thomas at 43 boulevard Malsherbes; from the art supplies dealer Julien "Père" Tanguy; and also, thanks to his school colleague Jean Le Fustec, at the Galerie Vivienne.[4] He wrote eagerly to his parents about his paintings *Flowers* and *Railway Station*: "They are now at the Galerie Vivienne at the office of *Le Journal des Artistes*. The director of the *Journal* is the friend, or rather the workmate, of a teacher at the school—and this morning he spoke to him about me. He is not buying the paintings but will be pleased to show them—and act as my intermediary should anyone ask for them."[5]

He was one of 402 artists who took part in the first Salon des Artistes Indépendants held from May 15 to July 1, 1884, showing the paintings *In Normandy* (1883; Galerie Bailly, Geneva) and *The Housewife* (current location unknown). But difficulties ensued when around forty members of the group, including one of the founders, Odilon Redon, decided to distance themselves from the rest of the artists. Dubois-Pillet took charge of operations and the Société des Artistes Indépendants was founded on June 11, 1884. The statutes were submitted and registered three days later, and Angrand became a founding member by default.

The first *Exposition de la Société des Artistes Indépendants* was held from December 10, 1884, to January 30, 1885, at the Pavillon de la Ville de Paris (on the Cours-la-Reine, near the Champs-Elysées). Among the 139 exhibitors, Angrand had two paintings on show: *In the Garden* **(126)** and *In the Farmyard (Feeding the Chickens)* **(132)**. He chose a rural subject for these two paintings because, without fail, he spent every school vacation at the family home in Criquetot-sur-Ouville, depicting scenes of his beloved Normandy countryside and, more specifically, the Pays de Caux. His eye would soon shift to a distinctly suburban landscape, partially due to his connections with Paris's most innovative artists.

Discovering the Suburbs

A few weeks before Easter in 1885, Angrand wrote to his parents: "I am taking advantage every day of the fact that the barometer is consistently set fair to take the air on the fortifications. . . . Perhaps I will bring my easel up there—I like the look of the Porte d'Asnières."[6] Having returned to Paris after the summer vacation, during which he twice painted his mother sewing in the family home, he once again wrote to his parents: "I was painting a landscape

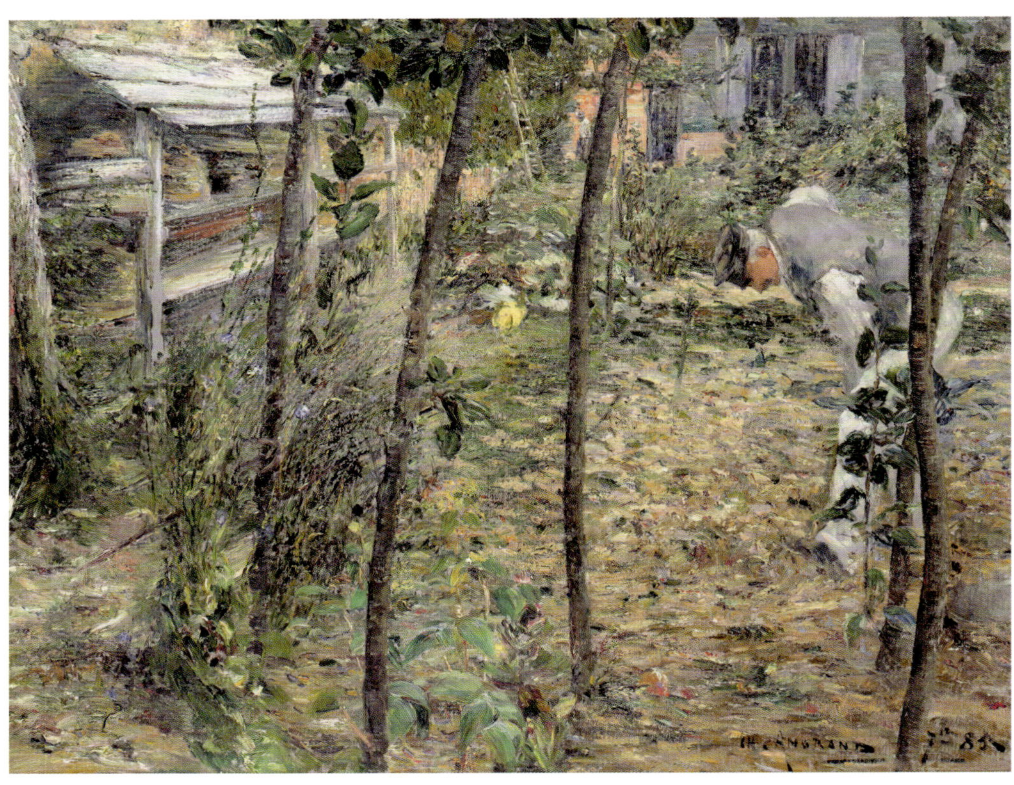

126 Charles Angrand
In the Garden, 1885
Oil on canvas, 73 × 92 cm
Musée des Beaux-Arts, Rouen

at the Pont de Clichy at the end of the Ile des Ravageurs. That (incidentally) is where I have been going for a fortnight to study the fall—and to see the dead leaves falling, falling, as the song goes. Anyway, I found the temperature mild there, even though the wind was coming off the river. Of course, the illusion didn't go as far as to convince me that the smokestacks of Asnières in front of me were minarets."[7]

His first painting at this location produced a new approach to landscape: messy but highly organized, given the rhythm produced by the verticals of the bushes and the pattern of light and shade across the scene that creates a sense of depth **(127)**. A high horizon and a dark figure enliven the landscape. The foreground, dominated by blond tones, and the distant green bank evoke the cheerful landscape outside of the city, while the robust brushstrokes lend the scene an intense energy. It is an early painting such as this that may have helped the artist to formulate his own definition of a painting: "A painting must be above all a composition, in other words an organization by the mind of the lines, forms, and colors to create an expressive harmony."[8] The expressiveness of this scene epitomizes the transition from late summer to early fall, as the leaves start to drop.

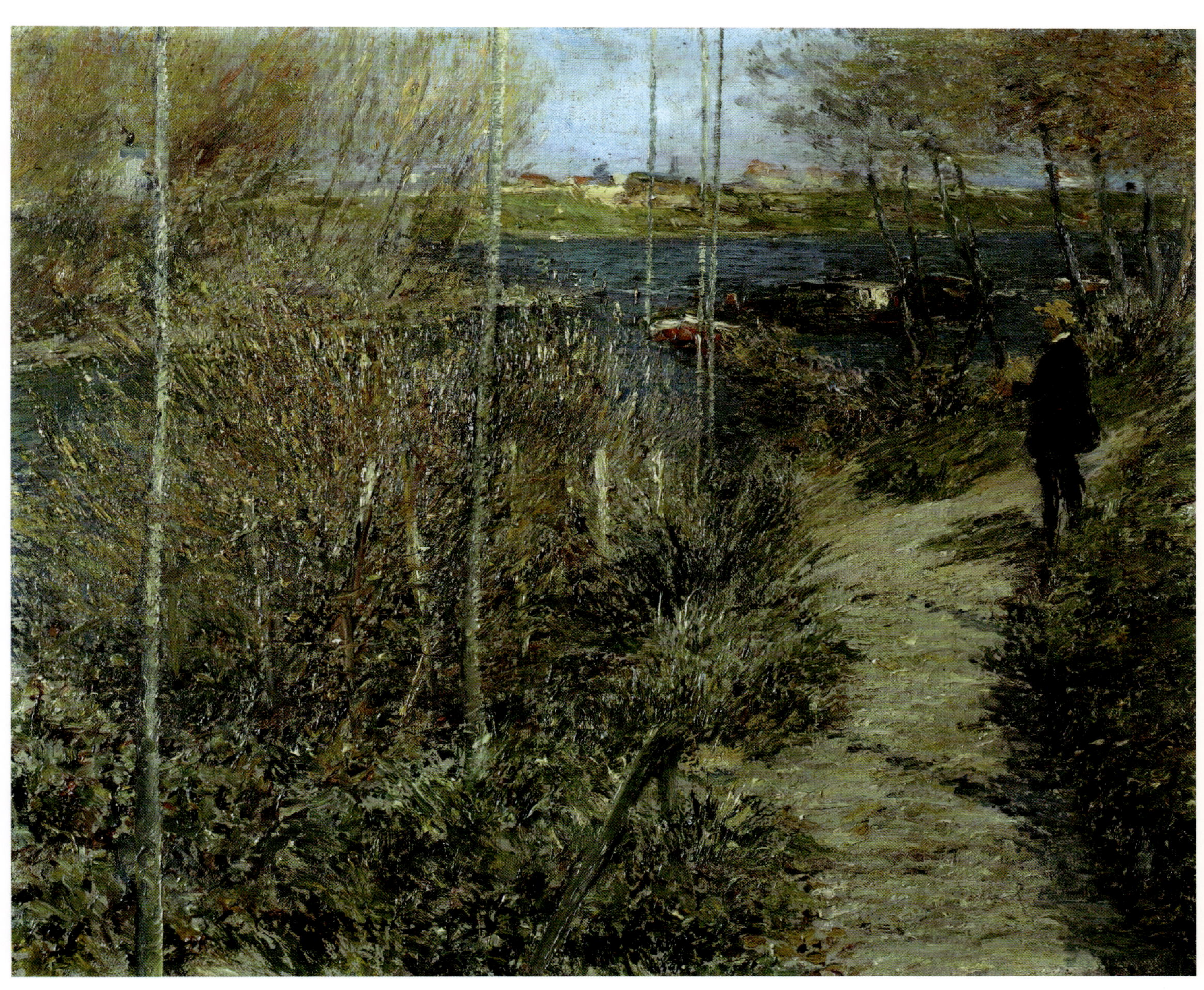

127 Charles Angrand
On the Ile des Ravageurs, 1885
Oil on canvas, 46 × 55 cm
Private collection

The next year witnessed a period of vibrant activity in Paris, the capital of the arts, and Angrand had a front-row seat. On February 28, Vincent van Gogh arrived in time for the eighth and final exhibition of the Impressionist group that was held from May 15 to June 15, with the participation of Seurat, Signac, and Lucien Pissarro through the intercession of Camille Pissarro. Seurat, the inventor of Divisionism, exhibited the exhibition's flagship work, *A Sunday on La Grande Jatte—1884*, which Angrand had seen in his studio **(70)**. The critic Félix Fénéon met Seurat at the exhibition, and became the spokesman for the Neo-Impressionist movement, of which Angrand would become an important member.[9]

Before the school vacation, he painted a view of *The Seine at Saint-Ouen, Morning* **(128)** with an unusual construction that cleverly divided up the composition, devoting three quarters to the river and a quarter to the horizon for the sky. The expanse of water here possesses what Pissarro later described as "its essential character," which the older artist urged the painter to try to convey "by any means whatsoever, without bothering about technique . . . paint what you observe and feel."[10] In other words this artist who was more used to depicting rural landscapes, farmyards with animals, and work in the fields had taken on an extremely delicate challenge of capturing the constantly moving waters of the Seine. In this modest format, he managed to convey the notion of a vast expanse, using visible brushstrokes of blues, oranges, and whites while also harnessing the color of the canvas below to create a compelling and subtly dynamic river surface through almost monochromatic means. The boats to the right and the little red-roofed house attract our attention without disturbing the serene atmosphere of the landscape, which is essentially comprised of the river and the sky.

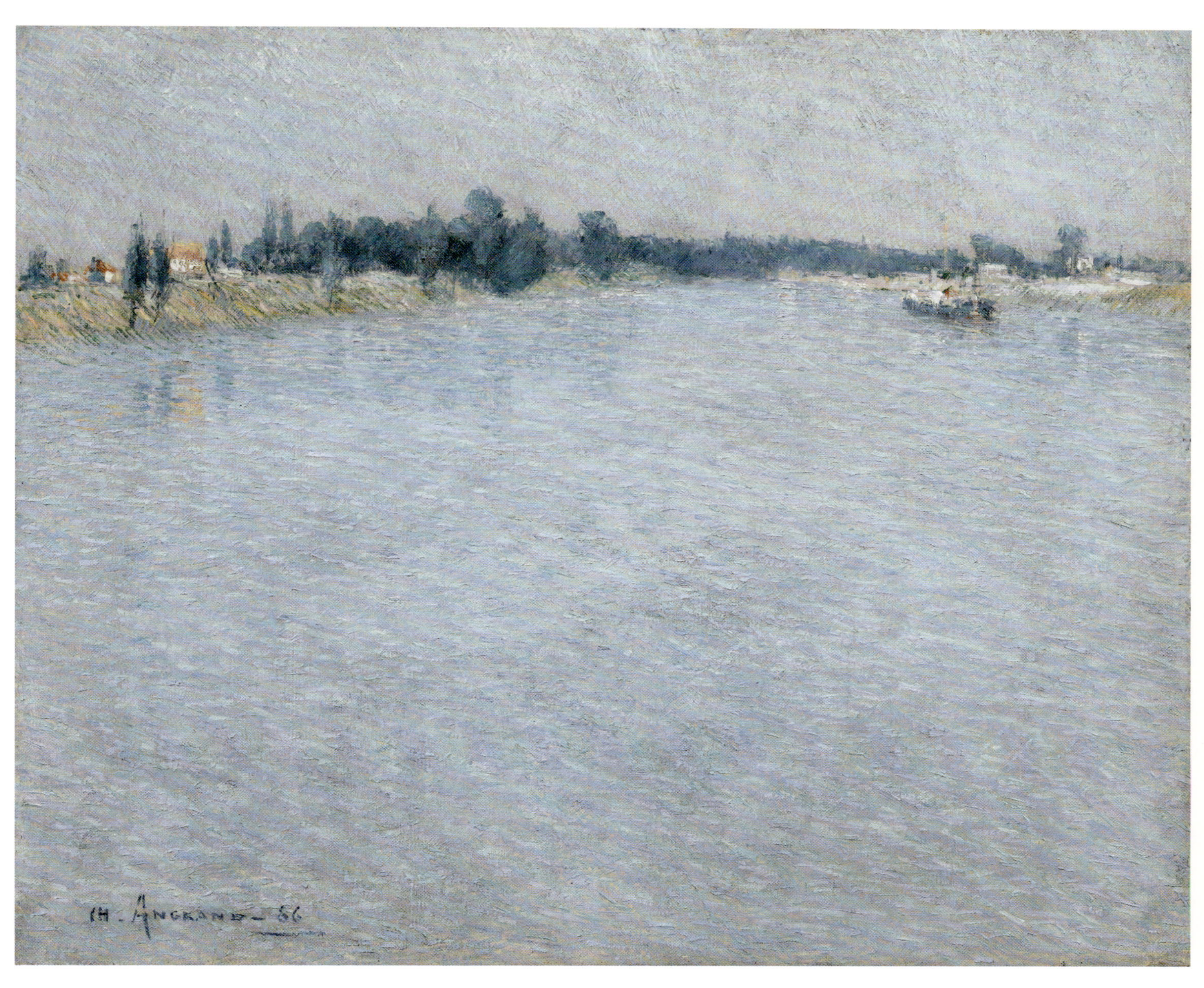

128 (cat.) Charles Angrand
The Seine at Saint-Ouen, Morning, 1886
Oil on canvas, 46×55.4 cm
Van Gogh Museum, Amsterdam (purchased with support from the VriendenLoterij)

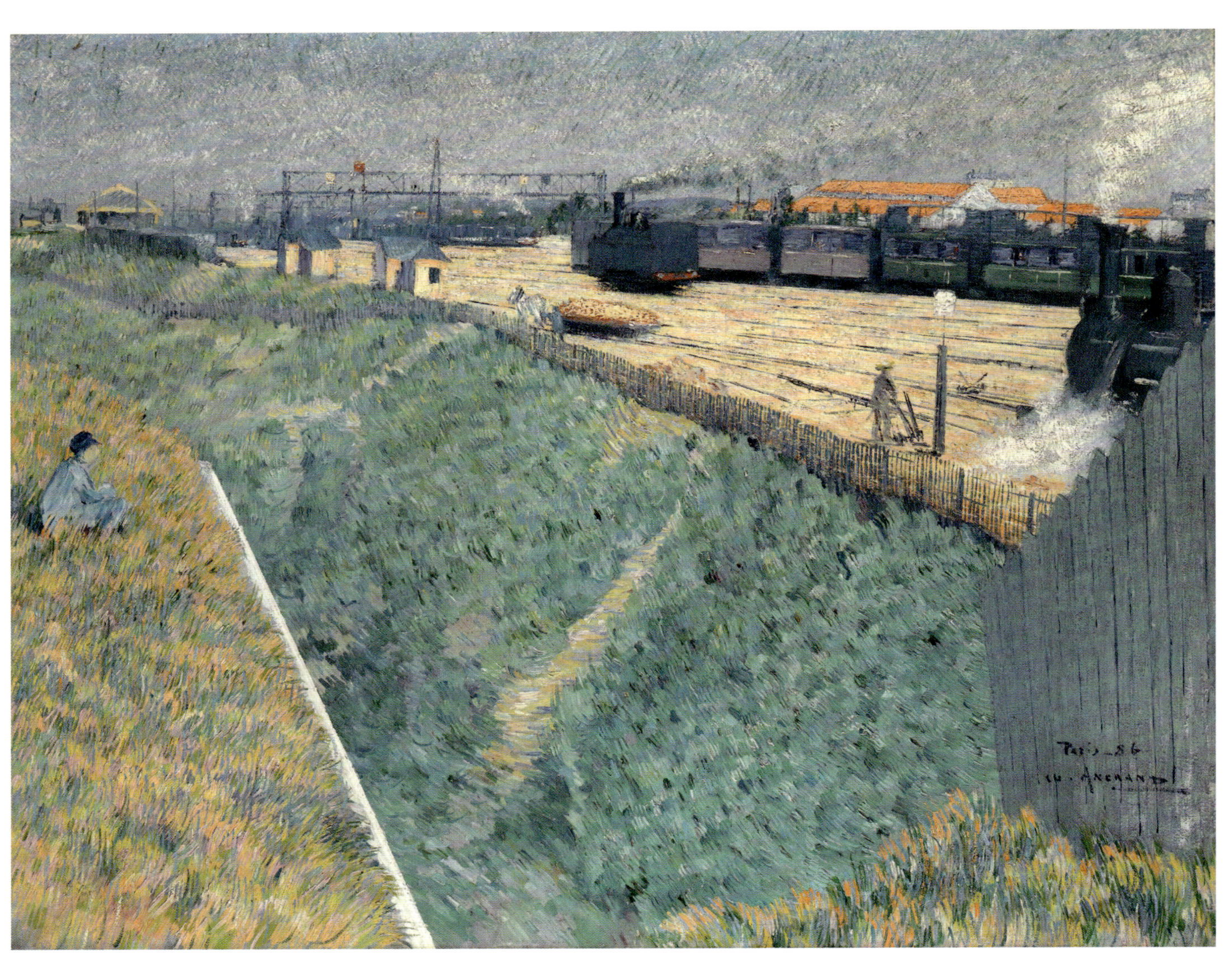

129 Charles Angrand
The Western Railway at its Exit from Paris (View from the Fortifications), 1886
Oil on canvas, 73×92 cm
Private collection

July 1886 was an active month for Angrand. Before returning to the Pays de Caux, he embarked upon two size-30 canvases (roughly 70 by 90 cm): *Waste Ground at Clichy* and *The Western Railway at its Exit from Paris (View from the Fortifications)* **(129)**, writing to his parents: "Previously, I visited Clichy, where I was drawn to the uneven waste ground. I made a painting, with exuberant colors as always—in which yellows of every shade bake in the sun. These last two paintings are the largest I have painted since spring . . . I plan to send them to our exhibition, which I will not see—because it will open on August 20 and end on September 20." This overgrown terrain was close to other structures, yet empty and uninhabited. He went on to say that "Le Fustec will be happy, I believe, to take care of presenting my paintings and to pick them up at the appointed time."[11] In mid-July, he told his parents: "at his [brother Paul's] request I told him that I had painted a size-30 canvas on the waste ground at Clichy—a canvas that is with [the art dealer Alphonse] Bouvret—and that I was currently working on the viewpoint of the western train line leaving Paris . . . ," adding that "I am writing to you between two sessions working on the western line—see opposite. As it is not far—half an hour away—I go in the morning, come back for lunch at midday and go back at around two o'clock. The painting is more or less finished now . . ."[12]

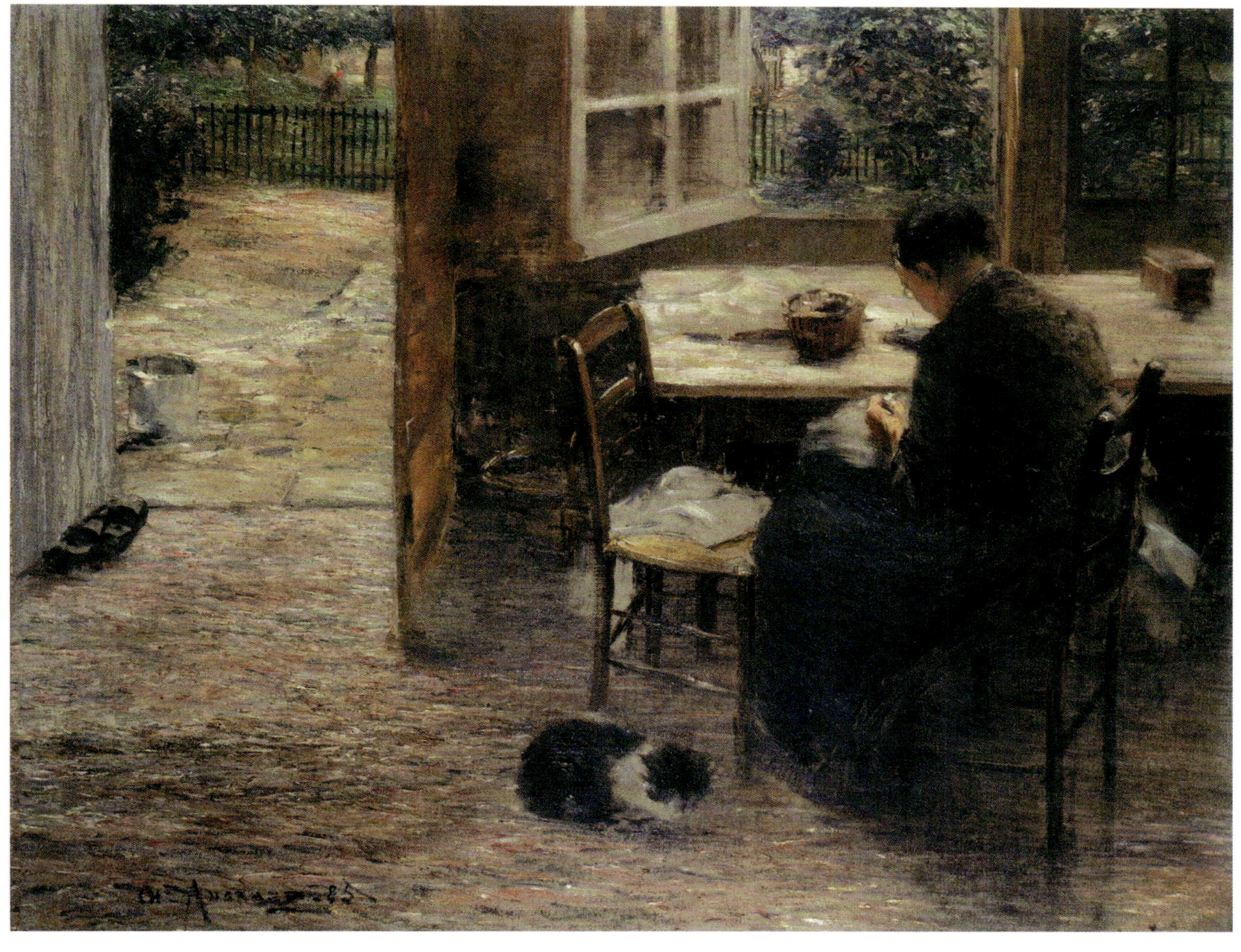

130 Charles Angrand
Woman Sewing (Normandy), 1885
Oil on canvas, 72 x 91 cm
Private collection

These valuable letters describe the period during which Angrand produced two very important works in his limited output. The Gare Saint-Lazare was less than half a mile from the Collège Chaptal. The station was a well-known artistic subject thanks to Claude Monet's paintings and served the 142-mile Paris-Rouen-Le Havre line built between 1843 and 1847. Angrand rode the train for 14 years on his journeys to and from the family home for every school vacation. The painting is structured by a high horizon line and oblique lines running to the left, with a proliferation of vegetation turned yellow by the summer sun. The rough and energetic treatment of the grass is striking, as it was in *Waste Ground*, recalling the approach used in his 1883 work *The Reapers* **(131)** and *On the Ile des Ravageurs* **(127)**. The technique must have interested Van Gogh, who painted with similar vivid yellows the following summer. These technical developments illustrate the artistic revolution that was in full swing.

At the end of the school year, after the distribution of prizes to students, Angrand returned to Criquetot-sur-Ouville. He used the months of August and September to paint his first Divisionist work, *Corner of a Farm*.[13] During this period, the second exhibition of the Indépendants was held in a barracks building in the Tuileries courtyard. The artist's friend Jean Le Fustec brought six of his colleague's paintings to the exhibition: no. 15 *Woman Sewing (Normandy)* **(130)**; no. 16 *The Western Railway at its Exit from Paris (View from the Fortifications)* **(129)**; no. 17 *Manure (Normandy)* (1885; Musée de Tournai); no. 18 *The Seine at Saint-Ouen, Morning* **(128)**; no. 19 *Waste Ground at Clichy*; and no. 20 *On the Ile des Ravageurs* **(127)**. One of them was painted a stone's throw from the Gare Saint-Lazare, which served Asnières, and three others in the immediate vicinity of Saint-Ouen, Clichy, and the Ile des Ravageurs.

Angrand's submissions were favorably received by the Parisian press, including a review by Félix Fénéon, written in his distinctive prose: "Mr Charles Angrand, who exhibited for the first time in 1883, did not adopt the impersonal and seemingly abstract quality of the dissidents of Impressionism: his brush, with its skillful violence, ingeniously works and grinds his thick, plastic paint, configuring it into reliefs, scratching, scraping, engraving and forming it into scales. He is attracted mainly by scenes of rural life in Normandy and the immediate vicinity of Paris: his *Waste Ground at Clichy* (1886), *The Western Railway at its Exit from Paris (View from the Fortifications)* (1886), are characterized by their tastefulness, their rough melancholy, and a tendency toward somber tones."[14]

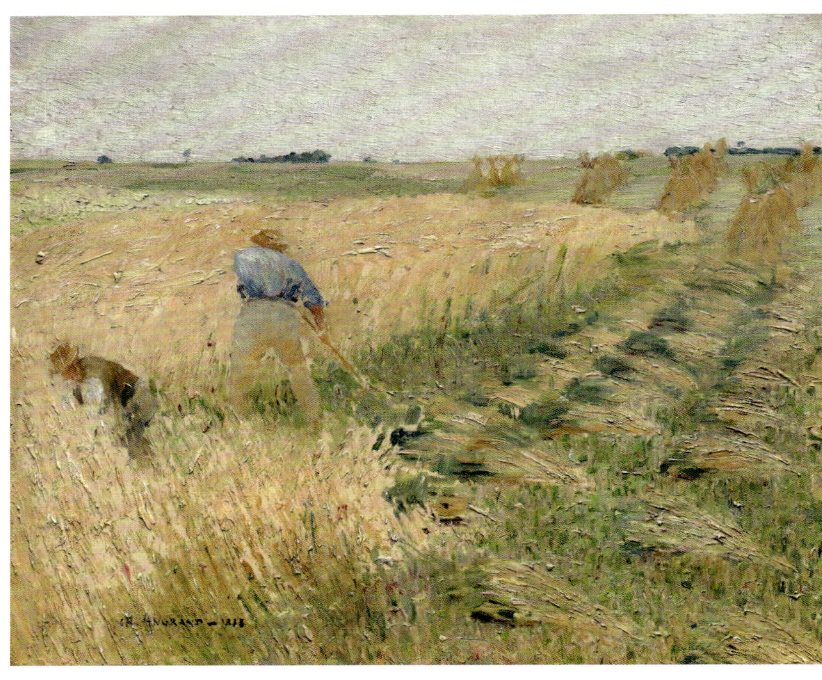

131 Charles Angrand
The Reapers, 1883
Oil on canvas, 46×55 cm
Private collection

Jean Le Fustec's lines in the *Journal des Artistes* are also worth citing because of his detailed observations of Angrand's qualities as a painter: "We are left with Angrand. At first sight, this artist's works leave you with the opinion that they were painted in front of nature. Whether you take the Normandy landscape or the Parisian landscape, the impression is the same. . . . There is a striking truth to the *Waste Ground at Clichy*, with its thin grass burnt in the sun. *The Western Railway at its Exit from Paris* is very powerfully rendered, although the sky is of a questionable shade. The *grisaille* of *The Seine at Saint-Ouen* has a great luminous quality, with a finesse of tone and execution that are truly remarkable. . . . In short, Angrand creates works of art while submitting his palette and brush to observation. . . . But we find an aspect of progress in his work that was observed from the first day, and which, we are convinced, will persist as long as this artist creates genuine Impressionist works while remaining true to observation."[15]

On September 19, Fénéon used the term "Neo-Impressionist" for the first time in his article for *L'Art moderne*, and Angrand went on to benefit from the full extent of the remarkable critic's attention and goodwill. In late October, Angrand met Van Gogh in a café opposite the Collège Chaptal. The Dutch artist wrote to Angrand in a letter dated October 25, 1886: "Dear Sir, I've spoken to Mr. Boggs about the meeting I had with you and if you would like to do an exchange with him be bold about it, because you'll see fine things at his place and he'll be very pleased to make your acquaintance. I also propose myself for an exchange. I happen to have 2 views of the Moulin de la Galette that I could spare. . . . At Tanguy's I had another look at your young girl with hens, that's just the study I'd like to exchange with you. Enclosed, one of my brother's cards, if you didn't find him there you could always go up and look at the paintings."[16] The painting Van Gogh had his eye on was Angrand's *In the Farmyard (Feeding the Chickens)* **(132)**, but the exchange did not take place.

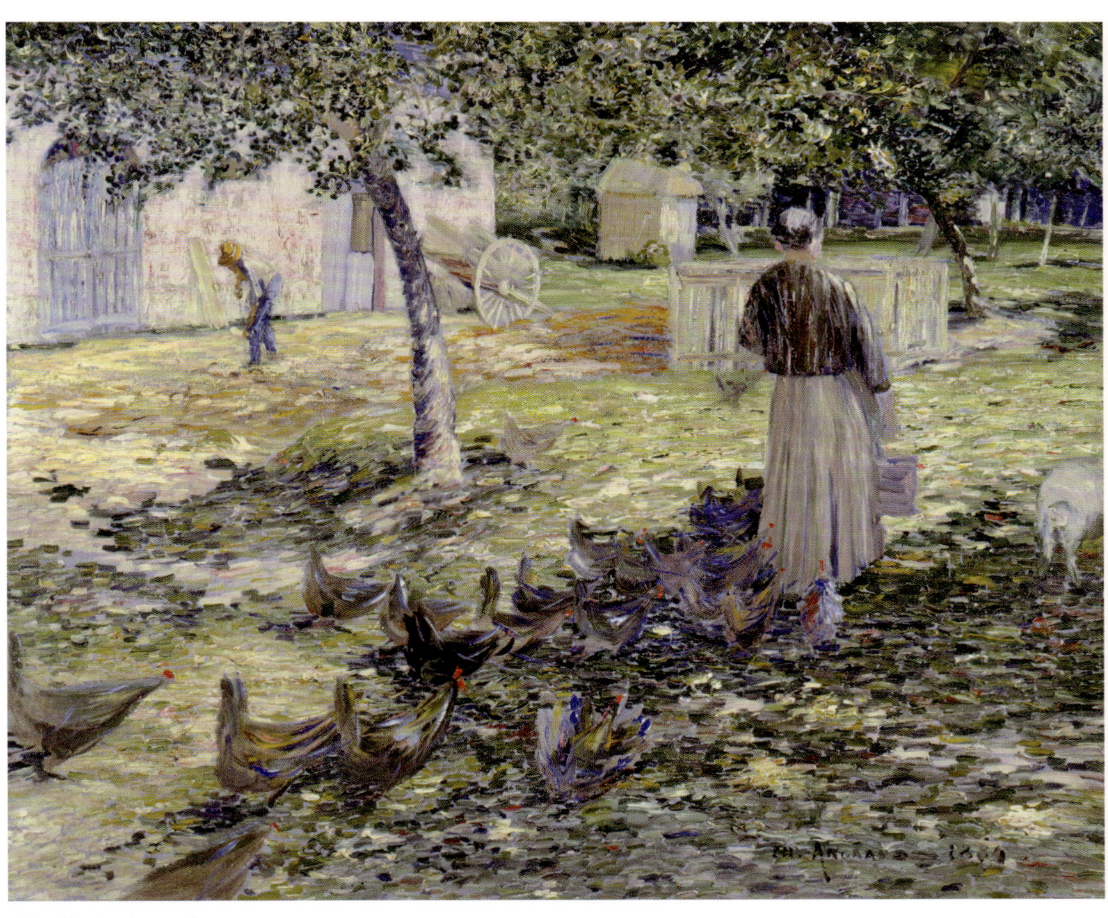

132 Charles Angrand
In the Farmyard (Feeding the Chickens), 1884
Oil on canvas, 53.8 × 65 cm
Ny Carlsberg Glyptotek, Copenhagen, on loan from the National Gallery of Denmark, Copenhagen

Embracing Divisionism

In December, having fully adopted Seurat's method, Angrand set to work on *The Accident*, which he completed in late January 1887 **(133)**. It is one of his finest paintings. On February 28 of the same year, Emile Bernard wrote to his mother: "Going back to Tanguy's, still in front of my paintings, I met a gentleman by the name of Angrand, also an Impressionist and very well known since the last exhibition of the Artistes Indépendants. He also congratulated me."[17] By this time Angrand had attained a respected profile as a painter, and his reputation was boosted a little further by the glowing article written by Le Fustec in the May 8 issue of the *Journal des Artistes*.[18] He spent the summer in Criquetot-sur-Ouville. At the end of the year, he exhibited nine paintings at Georges Petit's gallery in the *Exposition des 33*.

In 1888 Angrand took part in the Salon des Indépendants and the exhibition at the offices of *La Revue Indépendante*. He visited the Salon "twice to get my eye in and to lift my imagination,"[19] but above all spent his time in Paris with his friend Seurat. Angrand's unpublished family correspondence is a useful source for the painting that resulted from their time together **(134)**, which has been shown alongside Seurat's work for the first time in this exhibition **(135)**. It was executed at the same place and the same time during the summer of 1888 as was Seurat's canvas. Angrand was one of the few artists who frequented Seurat's studio and, importantly, painted alongside him as well. He described it to his parents mid-July: "In light of the fine weather I could not resist a trip to La Grande Jatte. . . . Now that the days are favorable, I am taking advantage. I leave at half past 12 for La Jatte and only return at 7 o'clock or later. It's quite exhausting because of the heat, to regularly travel

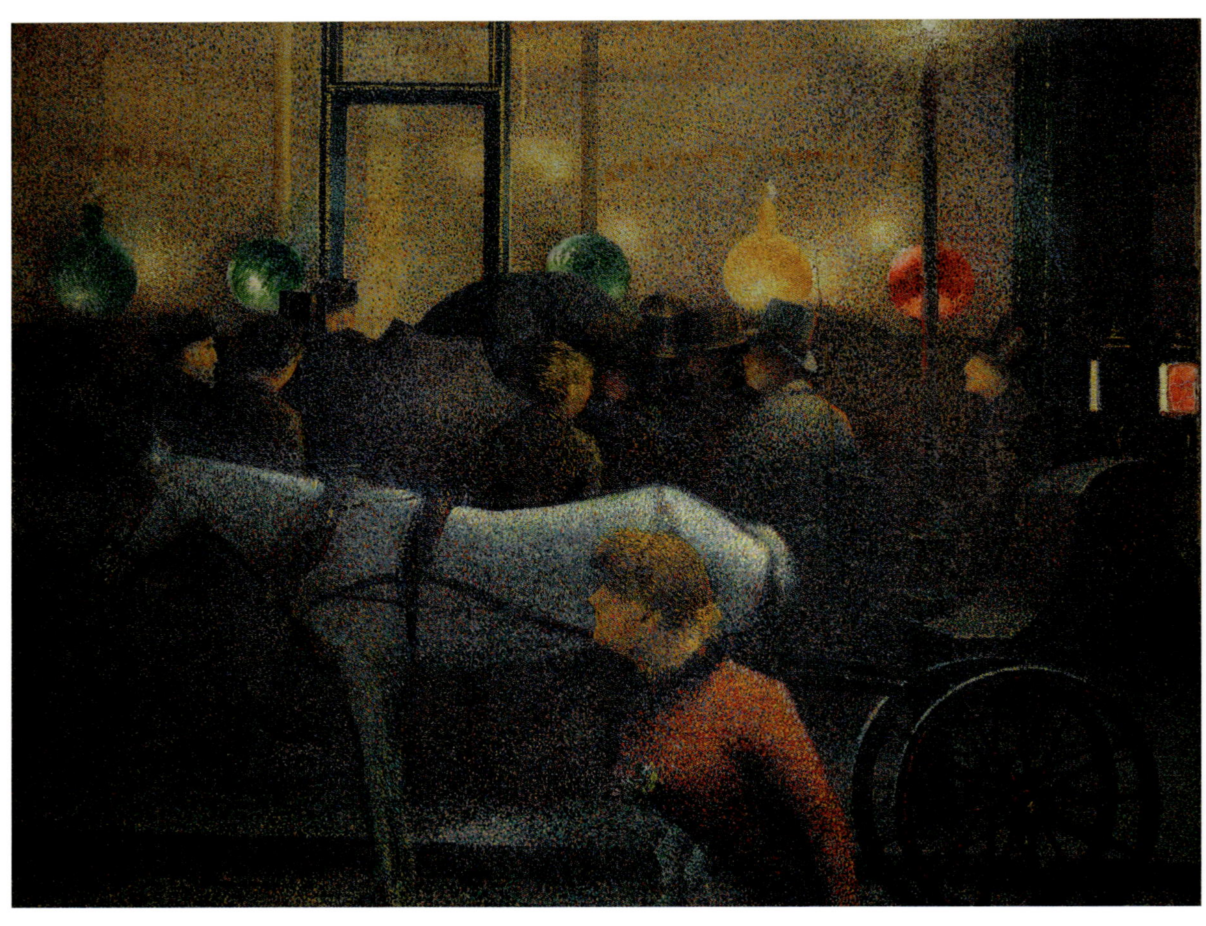

133 Charles Angrand
The Accident, 1886–87
Oil on canvas, 50.6 × 64 cm
Private collection

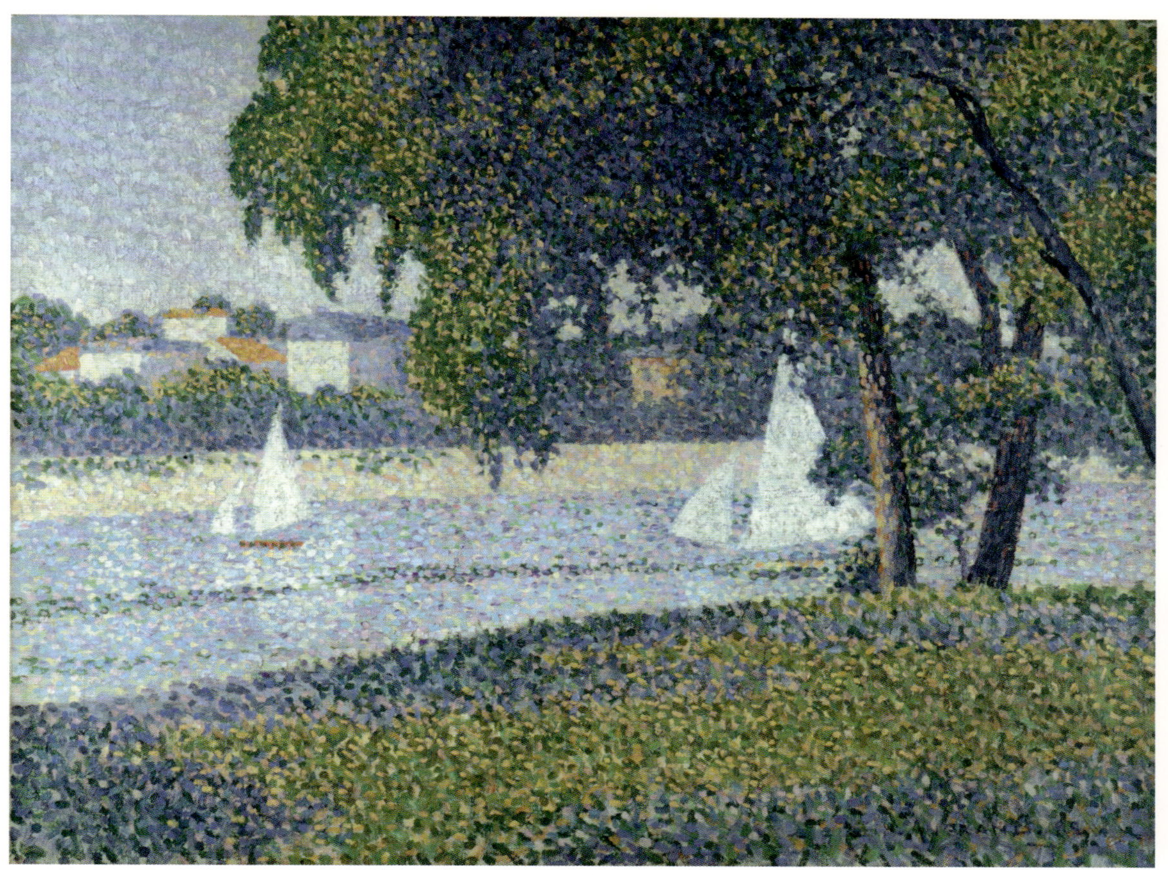

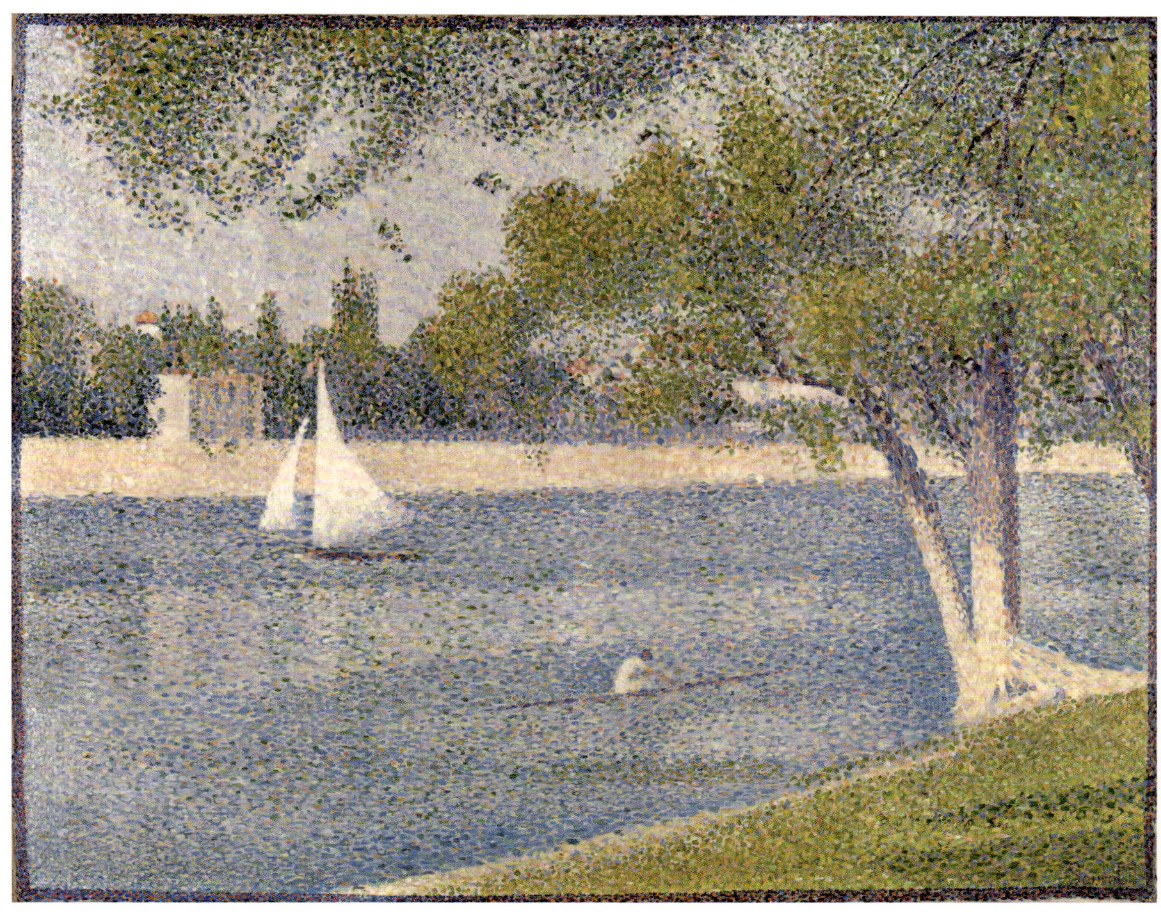

134 (cat.) Charles Angrand
The Seine at Courbevoie: La Grande Jatte, 1888
Oil on canvas, 50 × 60 cm
Private collection

135 (cat.) Georges Seurat
The Seine at La Grande Jatte, 1888
Oil on canvas, 65 × 82 cm
Royal Museums of Fine Arts, Brussels

6 kilometers [4 miles] to my location and the same again to get back. But at least I can enjoy some tranquility there and I'm in the company of Seurat, who also makes the journey on a daily basis."[20]

Later, in a letter to Madame Lucie Cousturier, he added: "Once we had finished our sessions, we would go back across the branch of the Seine in a small ferry called *L'Artilleur*, before returning via Courbevoie and the rue de Lévis. [Seurat] pointed out to me—one detail among a hundred in our conversations along the way—the purple halo of the young trees that had just been planted along the boulevard."[21] Indeed, this halo of dark purple is echoed in the dense shadows of the tree crowns that cast similarly powerful shadows on the grass. Employing heftier dots than Seurat does in his view, Angrand here heightened the contrast between light and shade and eliminated the human presence to create a highly stylized scene of suburban leisure. His interpretation of Pointillism flattens the space, turning it into a tapestry of substantial *points* compared to Seurat's more delicate rendering of the view.

On January 19, 1889, Fénéon wrote in *La Cravache* about Angrand's works in the exhibition of *La Revue indépendante,* noting his embrace of the Pointillist technique: "Around [18]86 this painter adopted the system of scientific division of color tone and stopped serving up his harmonious color mixtures and tricks of the brush in favor of uniform Neo-Impressionist execution. M. Angrand's skill in choosing his subjects is clearly perceptible in *On La Grande Jatte* and in the paintings that accompany it."[22]

In early April, Angrand began a new painting of the Seine, *The Seine at Dawn* **(137)**, telling his friend and colleague at Chaptal, Maurice Dezerville, in mid-June 1889: "With the exception of a walk or two in the rue de Rome, I am devoting the good hours of the day to work . . . a morning melody of white and sacred verses. In prose, I would present it very simply as a stretch of river from which the characteristic mist of the dawn of a fine day is rising. Three months of effort have already accumulated as much as succeeded each other in this work—I can notify you in advance of its calm and serene beauty."[23]

Firsthand observation of the river, atmosphere, and sky resulted in an ethereal terrain under Angrand's astute eye. The serenity of this painting—the golden glow surrounding the rowboat that dissipates into a luminous mist, the untroubled surface of the water, the blues, greens, and yellows that coalesce into a "symphony in gray"—belies the industry that marks the distant landscape with its smokestacks.

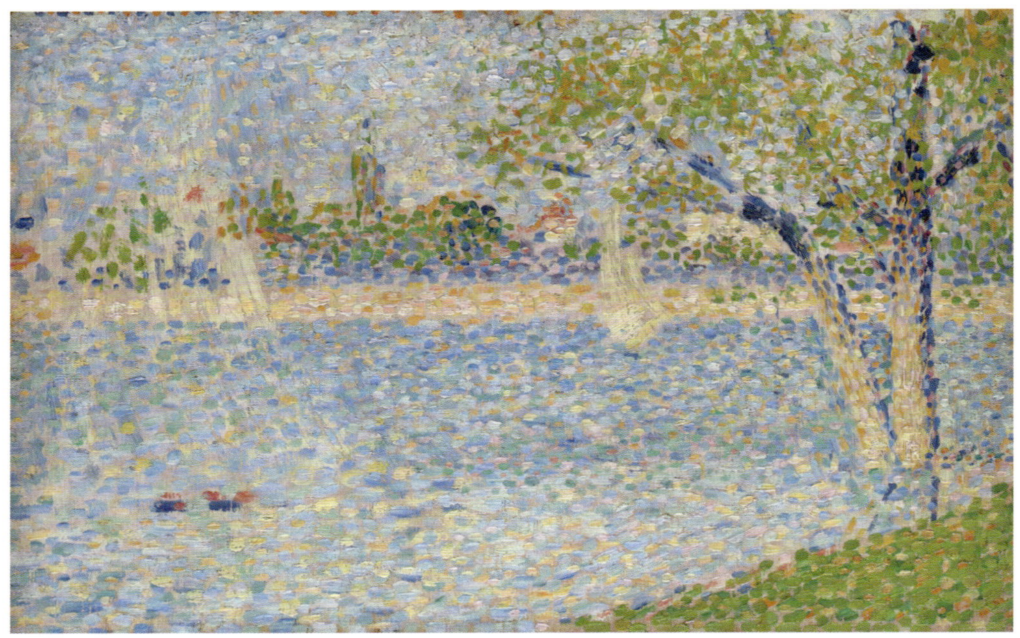

136 (cat.) Georges Seurat
The Seine Seen from La Grande Jatte, 1888
Oil on panel, 15.7×25 cm
The National Gallery, London
Presented by Heinz Berggruen, 1995

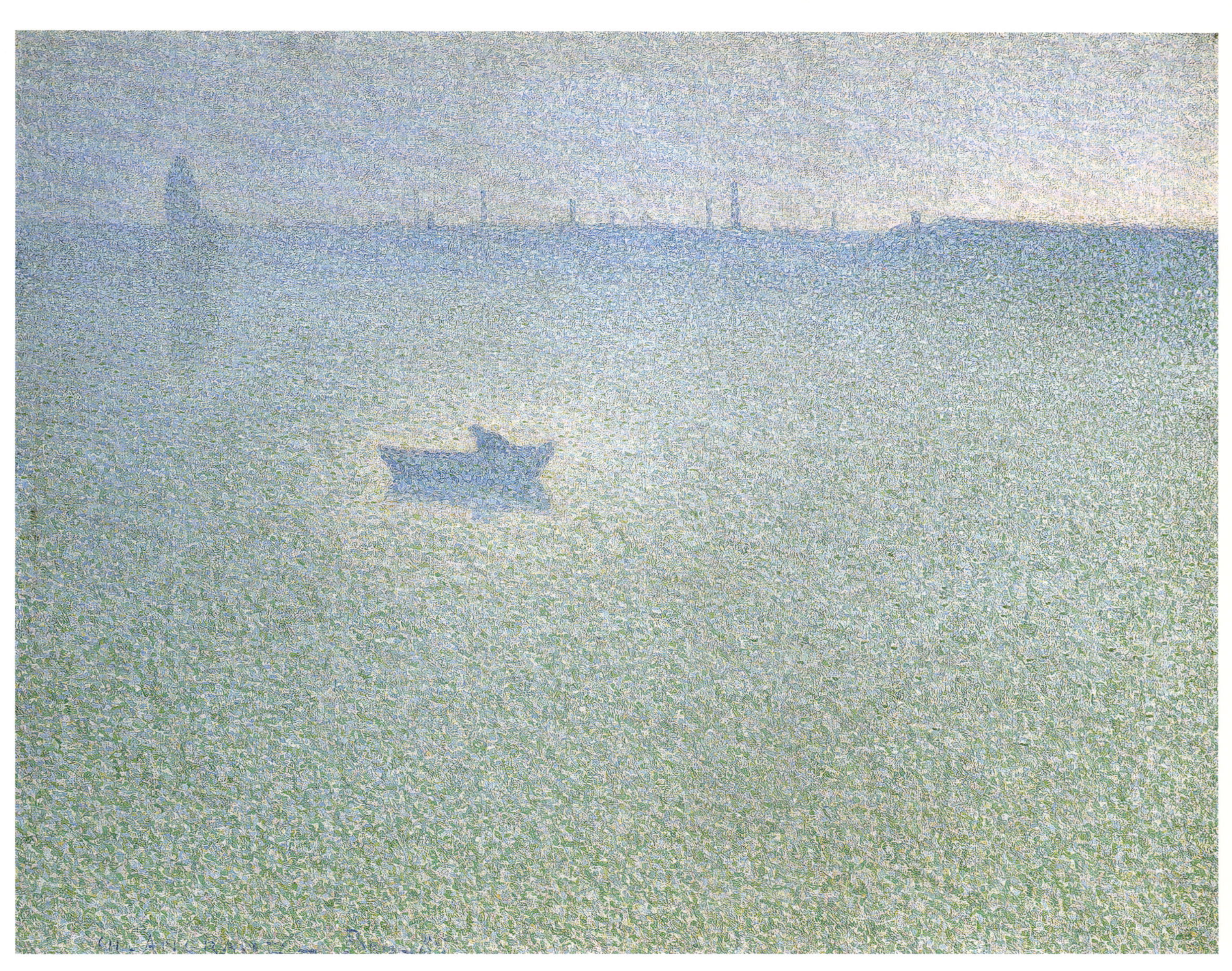

137 (cat.) Charles Angrand
The Seine at Dawn, 1889
Oil on canvas, 61×81 cm
Association des Amis du Petit Palais, Geneva

Angrand decided to enter this Divisionist masterpiece in the Competition of the Société des Amis des arts de Rouen, which was held at Rouen's Musée des Beaux-Arts from October 15 to November 15, 1889. The painting marked the end of his activity in Asnières and the surrounding area. In 1890, he took part in the Salon des Indépendants, and in 1891, he sent work to the exhibition held by Les Vingt in Brussels, then attended the private view of the Salon des Indépendants alongside Seurat, who showed his work *The Circus*, in which Angrand appears **(155)**. After Seurat's death on March 29, Angrand, who was in Criquetot-sur-Ouville at the time, wrote an emotional letter to Signac lamenting the loss of his friend and fellow artist.[24]

Abandoning Painting

For reasons unknown to us, Angrand abandoned oil painting and turned his attention to black-and-white works in Conté crayon, producing some sublime drawings: *Self-Portrait* (1892; Metropolitan Museum of Art, New York), *Housewife* (1892), *Woman Sewing* (1892), *The Lamp*, *The Young Calves* (1894), *Farmyard*, *The Child and the Cat*, *The Outhouse in the Snow*, *The Annunciation to the Shepherds* (1894), and *My Mother* **(138)**. As Fénéon wrote, "this was the series of those great drawings that slip from black to white by means of slow swells of impeccable gradations. In this luminous mist, the animals, objects, and people of the

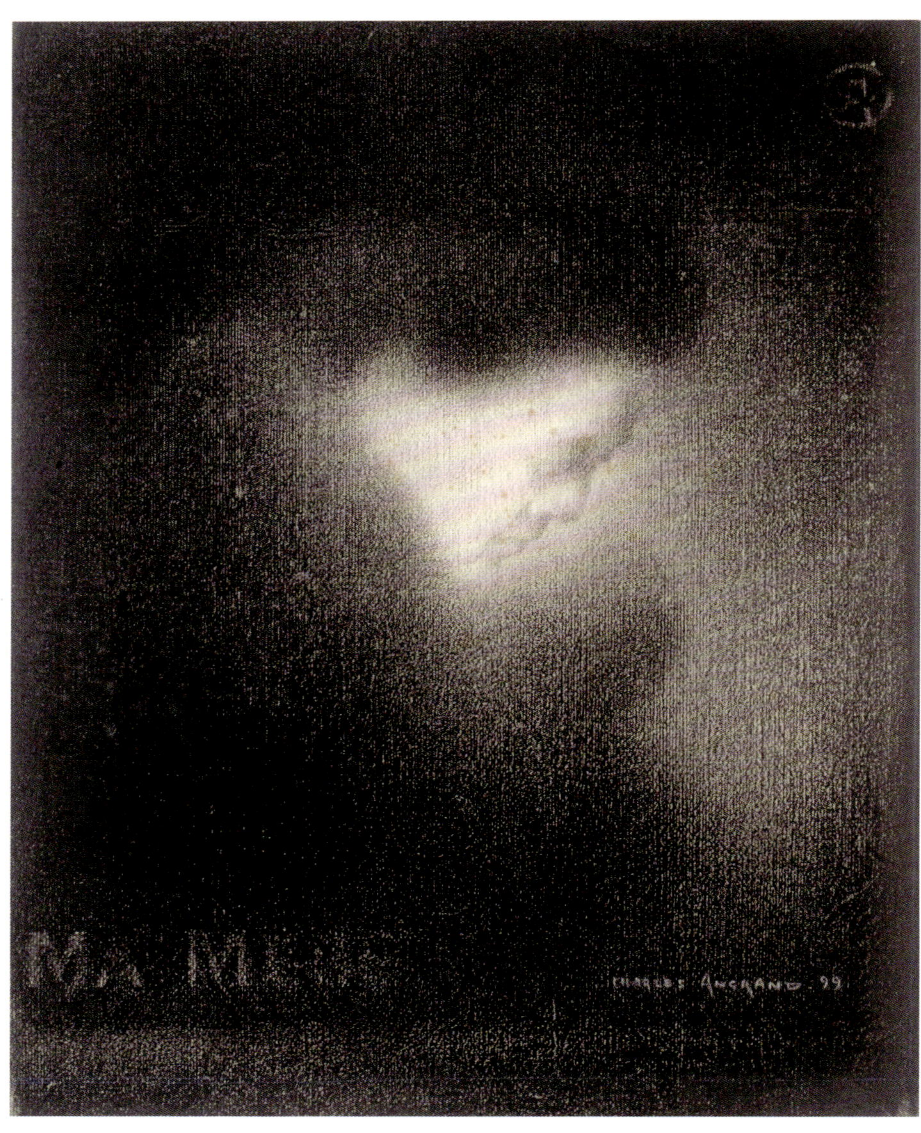

138 Charles Angrand
My Mother, 1899
Conté crayon on paper, 66×48 cm
Musée du Louvre, Paris, fonds du musée d'Orsay

country appear in the guise of simple forms that summed up the discoveries of the observer without retaining a trace of anything anecdotal."[25]

On May 26, 1896, Angrand's father died. After fourteen years in Paris, he decided to leave the capital to live with his mother, but continued to write letters: "the assiduous correspondence he maintained with all three [Henri-Edmond Cross, Maximilien Luce, and Signac] is a mine of documents for a history of Impressionism. In this history he would occupy a greater role than he did in journalists' reports," wrote Fénéon.[26]

Encouraged by Signac, Angrand took part in the major collective exhibition at Durand-Ruel's gallery from March 10 to 31, 1899, presenting six drawings but not selling any of them. After the turn of the century, he began again to send works to the Salon des Indépendants, which he visited, as well as the Salon d'Automne, leaving the Normandy countryside and meeting up with his faithful painter friends Luce and Signac, as well as his colleagues from the Collège Chaptal, Pottier and Mautouchet **(139)**.

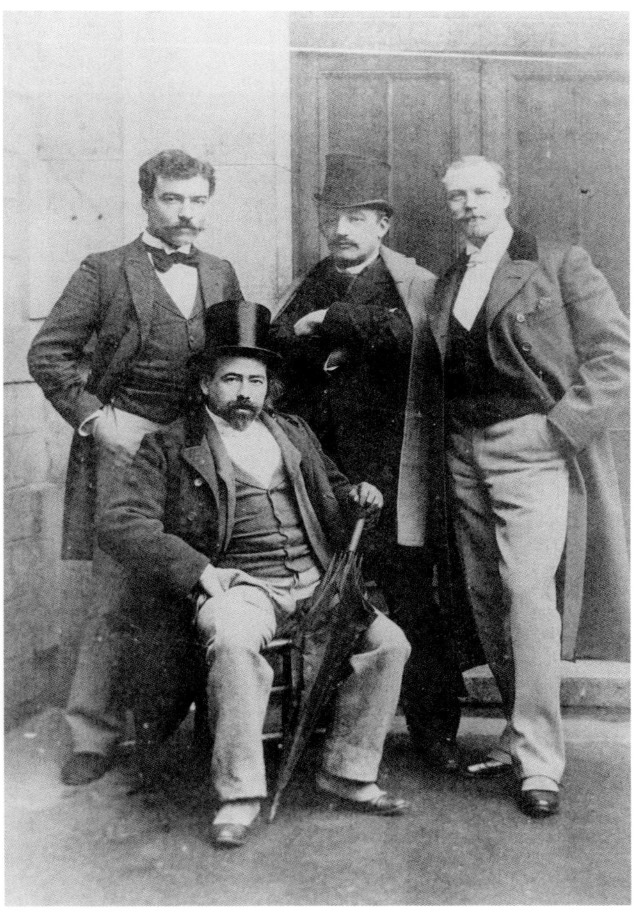

139 Charles Angrand (seated) and his friends at the Collège Chaptal, c. 1896
Photograph
Private collection

Angrand returned to oil painting between 1906 and 1908, and exhibited at the Salon des Indépendants in 1908 with *On the Threshold* (1908; private collection), which some consider his greatest work. In 1913, he made a definitive switch to pastels for the rest of his life. He returned to the Salon des Indépendants in 1914 for the thirtieth exhibition with two pastel works. In 1919, he was represented by three pastel works at the Salon des Artistes Rouennais, and the following year at the Salon des Indépendants, after a five-year gap, by six pastels.[27] His friends Luce and Signac encouraged him to present a collection of his pastel works, but he still hesitated. In early 1922, the first signs of a long illness appeared, and he underwent an operation. He sent work to the Salon des Indépendants and the Salon des Artistes Rouennais in 1923 and 1924. In 1925, from March 2 to April 9, he held his only monographic exhibition of twenty-five pastel works at the Galerie L. Dru, 11 rue Montaigne in Paris. In early 1926, his health slowly worsened and he used his remaining strength to prepare his panel for the *Trente ans d'Art Indépendant* retrospective and the thirty-seventh Salon, which opened on February 20 and March 20, respectively, but was too weak to attend. He died on April 1, 1926, in Rouen and was laid to rest at the city's Cimetière Monumental, accompanied by André Léveillé, Maximilien Luce, representing the Indépendants, and his nephew Pierre.

Between 1882 and 1896, Angrand lived in Paris during the school year. Each time he returned to his beloved Normandy, he produced rural scenes, showing farmers and villagers at work and the lives of animals. But in Paris, he also brilliantly captured scenes of the Seine at Saint-Ouen and Asnières to Courbevoie and urban views, all of which were based on his *plein-air* experiences in and around this dynamic city. He employed increasingly fragmented brush-strokes, in keeping with the avant-garde techniques of the artists with whom he had connected. He used the stimuli of the suburban environment and these innovative artistic practices to achieve "an expressive harmony" in each work.[28] The paintings presented in this exhibition provide the most perfect illustration of that principle. ■

CHRONOLOGY: A DECADE OF ARTISTIC EXPERIMENTATION IN THE PARISIAN SUBURBS

JENA K. CARVANA

1880

Following eighteen months of training at the Ecole des Beaux-Arts and a year of military service, Georges Seurat (1859–1891) begins producing paintings and drawings as an independent artist.[1]

The young Paul Signac (1863–1935) moves to Asnières with his family. Although he lacks formal training, he decides to become a painter, later writing: "My family wanted me to be an architect, but I preferred to draw on the banks of the Seine rather than in a studio at the Ecole des Beaux-Arts."[2]

1881

Seurat begins to explore the suburbs to the northwest of Paris. Together with his friend and fellow painter, Edmond Aman-Jean (1858–1936), he takes the *bateau-mouche* to the island of La Grande Jatte on the Seine.

1882

Signac rents his first studio in Paris on rue de Steinkerque (in Montmartre). Throughout April and May, he paints several small studies of the Seine at Asnières **(140)**.

In the fall, Charles Angrand (1854–1926) leaves his position at the Lycée Corneille secondary school in Rouen, a city in northern France, to teach mathematics at the Collège Chaptal in Paris. He lives in a small room at 47 boulevard des Batignolles, located near the Café de la Nouvelle Athènes and Le Chat Noir, popular artist hangouts.[3]

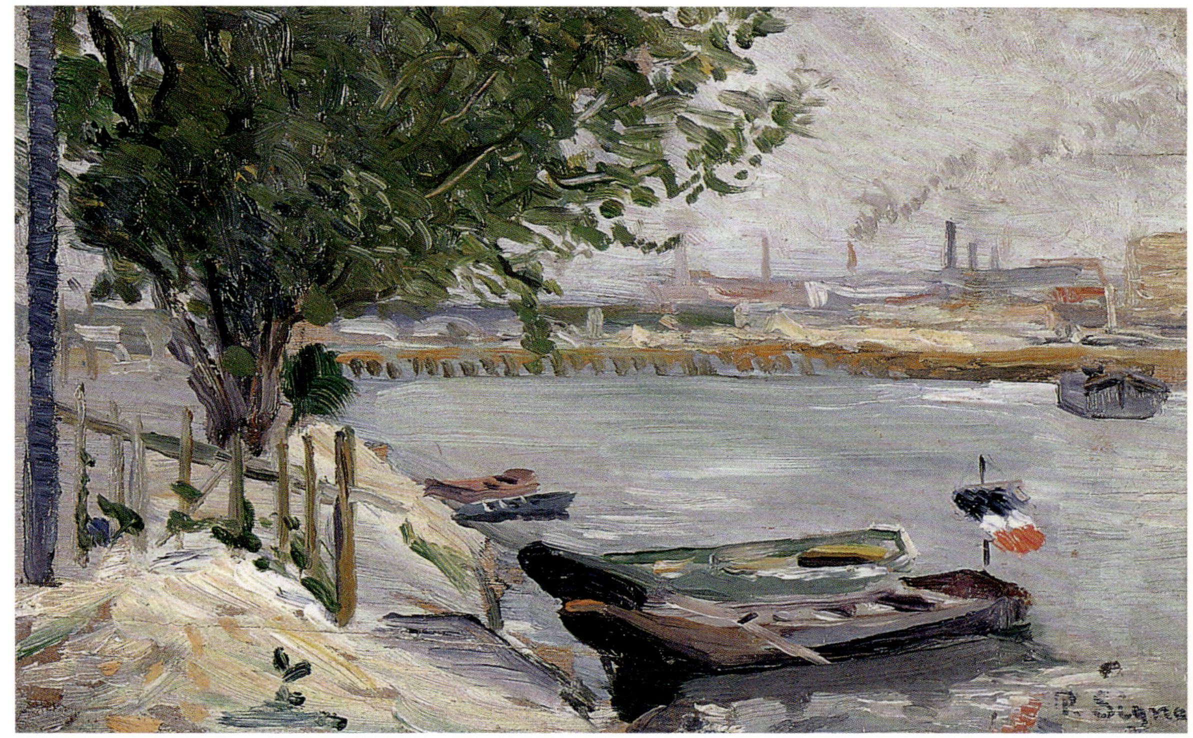

140 (cat.) Paul Signac
Asnières Study (The Ferryman's Boat), 1882
Oil on panel, 14 × 23 cm
Private collection

1883

Seurat works at Asnières and begins a series of preliminary sketches in Conté crayon and oil (*croquetons*) **(141)** in preparation for his first large-scale work, *Bathers at Asnières* **(66)**.

Signac meets Julien "Père" Tanguy (1825–1894), whose art supplies shop at 14 rue Clauzel serves as a popular meeting place for artists **(142)**. He paints in Paris, Asnières, and Courbevoie throughout the fall and winter **(13)**.

1884

Angrand meets Seurat, who had previously purchased one of Angrand's paintings. He visits Seurat's studio, where the artist is in the process of finishing *Bathers at Asnières*.[4] Angrand would become one of Seurat's few close friends, the two meeting regularly and often painting together.

SPRING 1884

Seurat submits *Bathers at Asnières* to the Paris Salon, but it is rejected by the committee. Signac's and Angrand's submissions are also declined. Angrand writes of his rejection in April: "Again refused: they [the Salon jury] are consistent in their exclusivism. . . . A group of independent artists met to decide on a private exhibition. . . . This group of independents has nothing in common with the Impressionists."[5]

This private exhibition, the Salon des Artistes Indépendants, is held May 15 to July 1 in Paris. Angrand, Signac, and Seurat—who only displays *Bathers at Asnières*—present for the first time alongside other artists in a group that would come to be known as the Neo-Impressionists. Seurat and Signac form a close friendship.

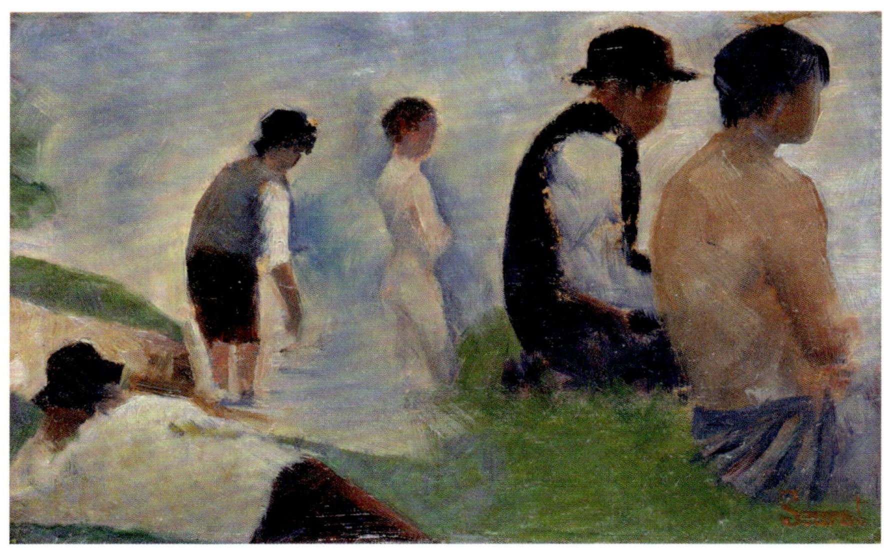

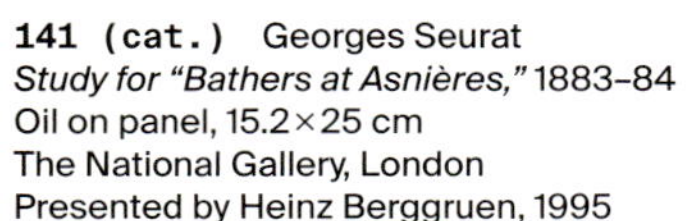

141 (cat.) Georges Seurat
Study for "Bathers at Asnières," 1883–84
Oil on panel, 15.2 × 25 cm
The National Gallery, London
Presented by Heinz Berggruen, 1995

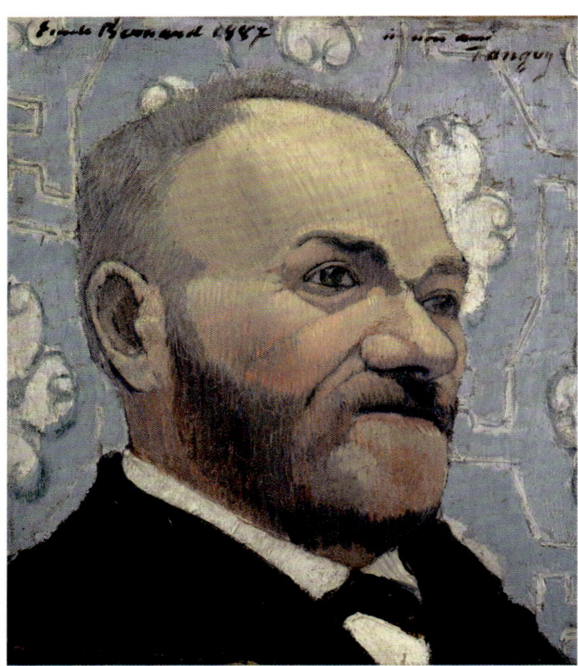

142 Emile Bernard,
Portrait of Père Tanguy, 1887
Oil on canvas, 35.9 × 30.8 cm
Kunstmuseum Basel

SUMMER 1884

Sixteen-year-old Emile Bernard (1868–1941) moves from Paris into a house located between Asnières and Courbevoie with his parents and younger sister. He decorates his room with murals and, although his parents oppose his interest in art, by September he enrolls in the studio of painter Fernand Cormon (1845–1924). There, he meets fellow artists Henri de Toulouse-Lautrec (1864–1901) and Louis Anquetin (1861–1932), among others **(143)**.

After completing a series of preparatory sketches and oil studies **(144,145, 146,147,148)**, Seurat begins working on his next large-scale project, *A Sunday on La Grande Jatte—1884* **(70)**. He paints in small, horizontal brushstrokes indicative of the style of the Impressionists.[6]

In July, the Société des Artistes Indépendants is established with Angrand, Seurat, and Signac among the founding members. Unlike the Paris Salon, the Société does not have an admission jury to select works for the annual exhibitions or restrictions on the number of works submitted, giving artists the opportunity to present their art freely to the public.

WINTER 1884

The first *Exposition de la Société des Artistes Indépendants* opens on December 10 at the Pavillon de la Ville de Paris, Champs-Elysées. Angrand exhibits two paintings while Seurat presents a study for *La Grande Jatte*, as well as nine *croquetons*. Signac exhibits four paintings, including *Coal Crane, Clichy* **(26)**, and *Rue de la Station, Asnières* **(108)**.[7]

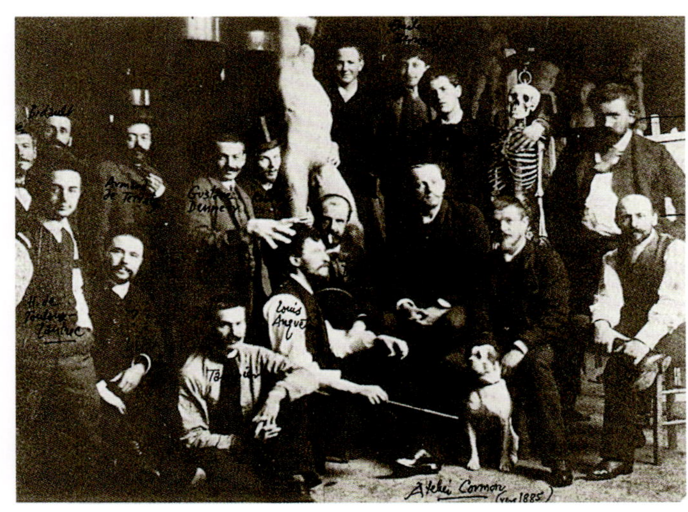

143 Photograph of Cormon's studio, c. 1885. Bernard stands at the back, second right from the nude model. Anquetin sits in the middle, facing to the right. Toulouse-Lautrec, without a beard, stands in the left foreground.

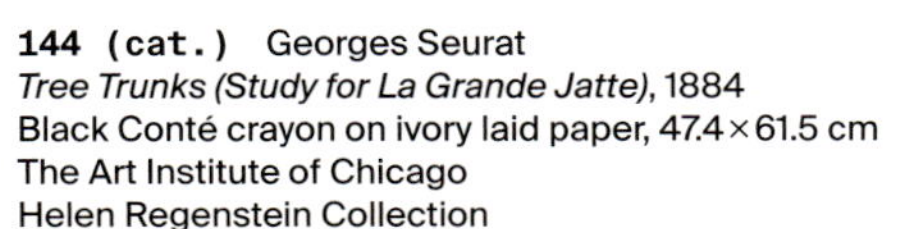

144 (cat.) Georges Seurat
Tree Trunks (Study for La Grande Jatte), 1884
Black Conté crayon on ivory laid paper, 47.4 × 61.5 cm
The Art Institute of Chicago
Helen Regenstein Collection

1885

Toulouse-Lautrec and Anquetin introduce Bernard to Tanguy's shop.

FALL 1885

Charles Henry (1859–1926) publishes "Introduction à une ésthetique scientifique." In the essay, he theorizes that an artist's application of form, line, and color can produce a pleasing (or displeasing) response in the viewer. Henry's writings, along with those of chemist and color theorist Michel Eugène Chevreul (1786–1889), among others, were highly influential to avant-garde artists, especially Seurat.[8]

In October, Seurat begins reworking *A Sunday on La Grande Jatte—1884* based on his studies of color theory and optical mixing. He adds small dots of unmixed colors over the existing paint. A form of Divisionism (in which the artist applies pure, unmixed colors next to each other in consistent brushstrokes or dashes), this technique, called Pointillism, refers to the application of paint in small dots.

Angrand, who left Paris in May, returns to the city and begins working along the banks of the river Seine. The first painting he makes there is *On the Ile des Ravageurs* **(127)**.[9]

1886

Signac moves into a new studio at 130 boulevard de Clichy.

EARLY 1886

Vincent van Gogh (1853–1890) leaves Antwerp for Paris. Upon his arrival on February 28, he lives with his art-dealer brother, Theo (1857–1891), at 25 rue Laval.[10]

SPRING 1886

Van Gogh enrolls at Cormon's studio in early March.

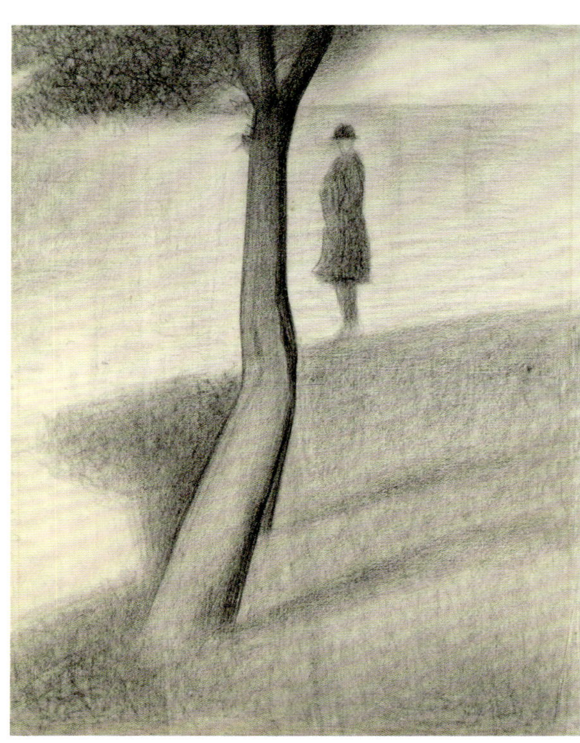

145 (cat.) Georges Seurat
Strolling Man next to a Tree on a Bank (Study for La Grande Jatte), 1884–85
Black chalk on paper, 61.5 × 47.5 cm
Von der Heydt-Museum, Wuppertal

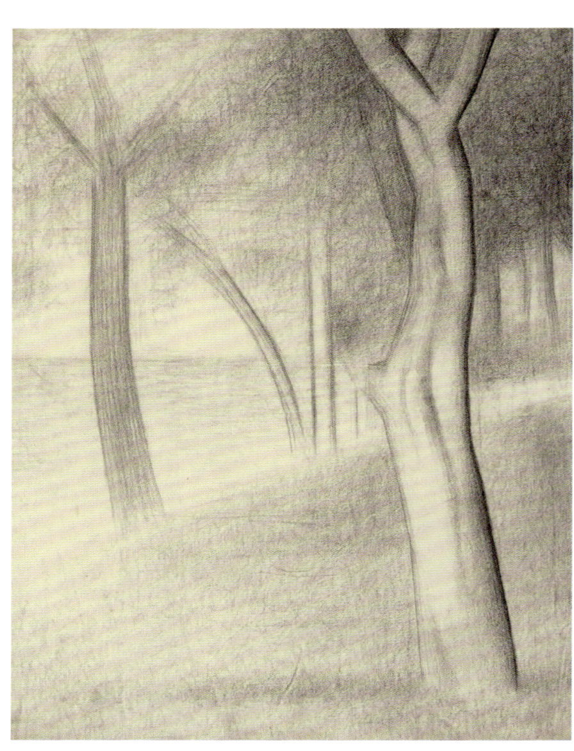

146 (cat.) Georges Seurat
Trees (Study for La Grande Jatte), 1884
Black Conté crayon on white laid paper, laid down on cream board, 62 × 47.5 cm
The Art Institute of Chicago
Helen Regenstein Collection

In late March or early April, Cormon dismisses Bernard from his studio for painting a background in streaks of vermilion and *vert veronese* (a bright green) rather than gray-brown. Bernard and Van Gogh must have met each other around this time, but would not establish a friendship until the fall.[11] On April 6, Bernard travels around the northwest of France where he meets artists Paul Gauguin (1848–1903) and Emile Schuffenecker (1851–1934), who introduces him to Divisionism.

Inspired by Seurat's Pointillist works, Signac begins work on his first Divisionist paintings, including *Gasometers at Clichy* **(88)**.[12] Although he would always identify Seurat as the originator of the technique, Signac—the more charismatic of the two artists—would play a key role in the dissemination and popularization of Neo-Impressionism among artists and critics.

In May, Seurat moves his studio to 128 bis boulevard de Clichy, Montmartre, next door to Signac's studio.

The final exhibition of the Impressionists, the *8e Exposition de peinture*, is held from May 15 to June 15. Seurat and Signac are invited to participate in the exhibition through the intercession of Camille Pissarro (1830–1903). Seurat submits nine works, including three paintings focusing on the Seine: *The Seine at Courbevoie* **(69)**, *The Anglers, Study for La Grande Jatte* **(58)**, and the recently reworked *Sunday on La Grande Jatte—1884* **(70)**. Although his smaller works receive positive reviews from critics, the *Grande Jatte* is met with polarized reactions. Signac presents eighteen paintings and drawings, seven of which take Asnières and Clichy as their subject: *The Banks of the Seine, Asnières* **(149)**, *Gasometers at Clichy* **(88)**, *The Junction at Bois-Colombes (Opus no. 130)* **(86)**, *Snow, Boulevard de Clichy* (1886; Minneapolis Institute of Art), *Passage du Puits-Bertin, Clichy* (1886; current location unknown), *The Watering Place, Asnières* (1885; current location unknown) and a drawing of the Ile des Ravageurs (current location unknown).

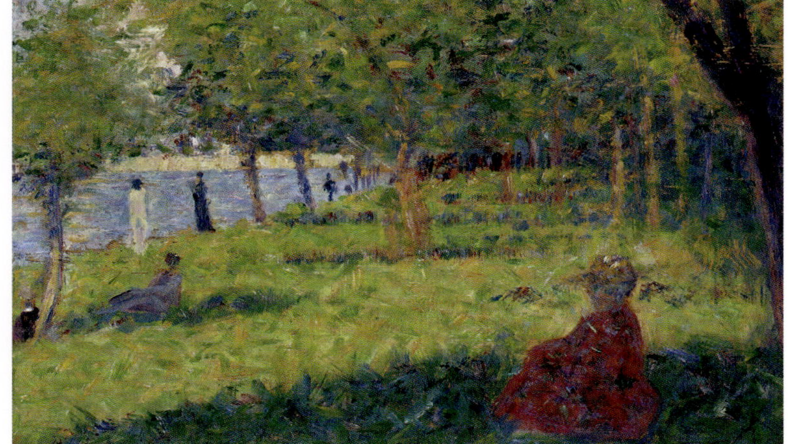

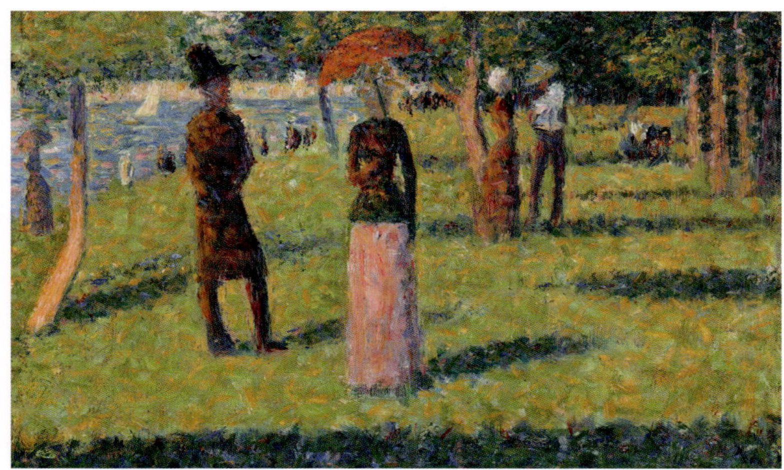

147 (cat.) Georges Seurat
Seated Women (Study for La Grande Jatte), 1884–85
Oil on panel, 15.6 × 25 cm
Private collection

148 (cat.) Georges Seurat
Landscape and Figures (The Pink Skirt), 1884
Oil on cradled panel, 15.2 × 24.9 cm
Private collection

Van Gogh attends the exhibition, one of many he would visit while acquainting himself with the Parisian art scene. Inspired, he produces still lifes and landscapes in which he begins experimenting with expressive brushstrokes and a brighter, more diverse color palette.[13]

SUMMER 1886

In June, Vincent and Theo move into a larger apartment at 54 rue Lepic, Montmartre, where Vincent has his own studio **(150)**. He leaves Cormon's atelier.

That same month, Signac leaves to spend the summer painting in Les Andelys, a village on the river Seine near Giverny.

The second *Exposition de la Société des Artistes Indépendants* is held at the rue des Tuileries Bâtiment B in Paris from August 21 to September 21. Angrand exhibits six works, of which four were painted near Asnières **(127,128,129)**. Seurat and Signac each present ten works, several of which were painted around Asnières and Courbevoie **(69,70,88,149)**. Van Gogh attends, as does Bernard upon his return to Paris in the fall.

FALL 1886

In the September 19 issue of *L'Art moderne*, Félix Fénéon coins the term "Neo-Impressionism" and proclaims the style as the successor to Impressionism.[14]

Bernard takes his new Breton work to Tanguy's shop, where Van Gogh has become a regular, and the artists become good friends and later exchange several canvases. During this time, Bernard begins to experiment with Divisionism, creating several views of Asnières.

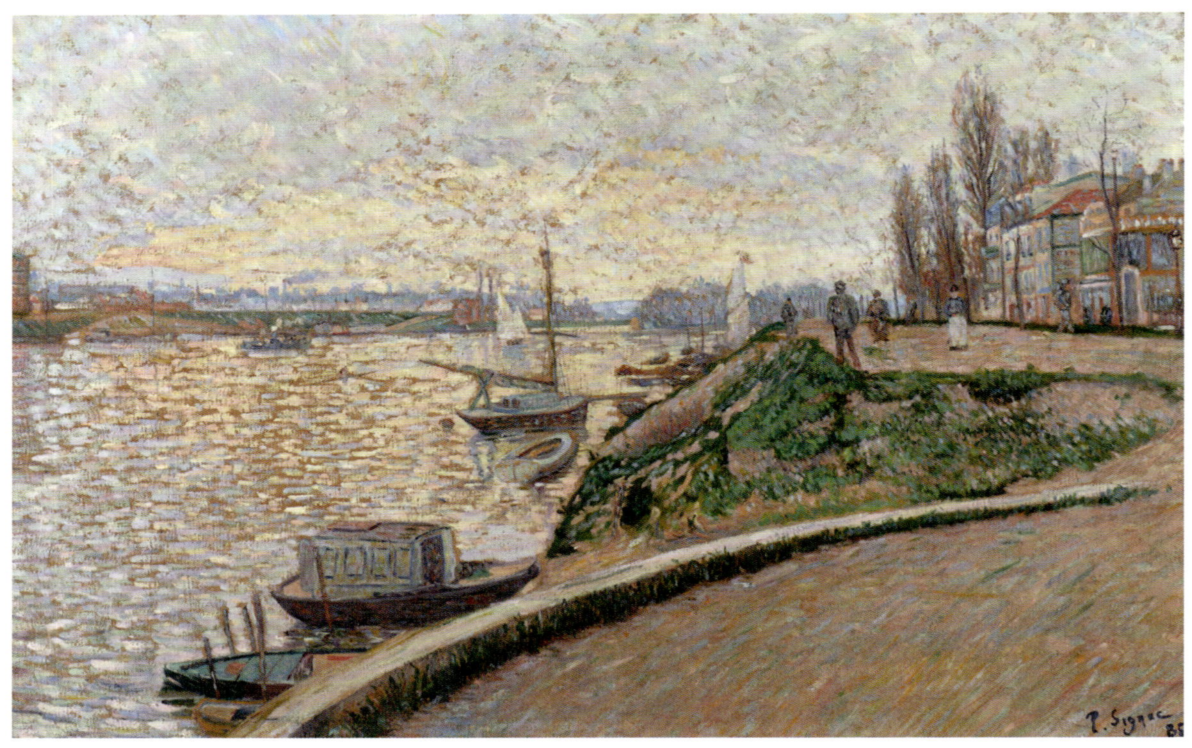

149 (cat.) Paul Signac
The Banks of the Seine, Asnières, 1885
Oil on canvas, 60.2×92.2 cm
The Museum of Modern Art, Saitama

1887

Signac attends gatherings at the Café de la Nouvelle Athènes with Seurat and Pissarro.

Angrand meets Van Gogh at Tanguy's shop in October. After the meeting, he receives a letter from Van Gogh, dated October 25, proposing an exchange of paintings. The exchange of Angrand's *In the Farmyard (Feeding the Chickens)* **(132)** for one of Van Gogh's paintings does not take place.[15]

EARLY 1887

Artists meet at Tanguy's shop early in the year: Angrand meets Bernard before the latter leaves to work outside of Paris.[16] Signac and Van Gogh also meet here.

Signac experiments with Pointillism in works on paper, creating three versions of his 1885 painting *Passage du Puits-Bertin (Clichy)* (current location unknown) to demonstrate that the style is suitable for print **(25, 90, 91)**. The final version is printed in the February 12, 1887 issue of *La Vie moderne* **(151)**.

Van Gogh organizes an exhibition of his collection of Japanese prints at the café Le Tambourin, 62 boulevard de Clichy, sometime in February or March.

SPRING 1887

In March, Bernard displays Divisionist studies at a small exhibition in Asnières, where he meets Signac.[17] Bernard visits Signac's studio with Anquetin on March 12 but, unimpressed with the artist's works, he decides to abandon Divisionism in order to develop a more abstract and imaginative way of painting.[18]

Van Gogh takes Anquetin and Bernard to see the shop of art dealer Siegfried "Samuel" Bing (1838–1905) to teach them about Japanese prints. He exhibits paintings at Le Tambourin.

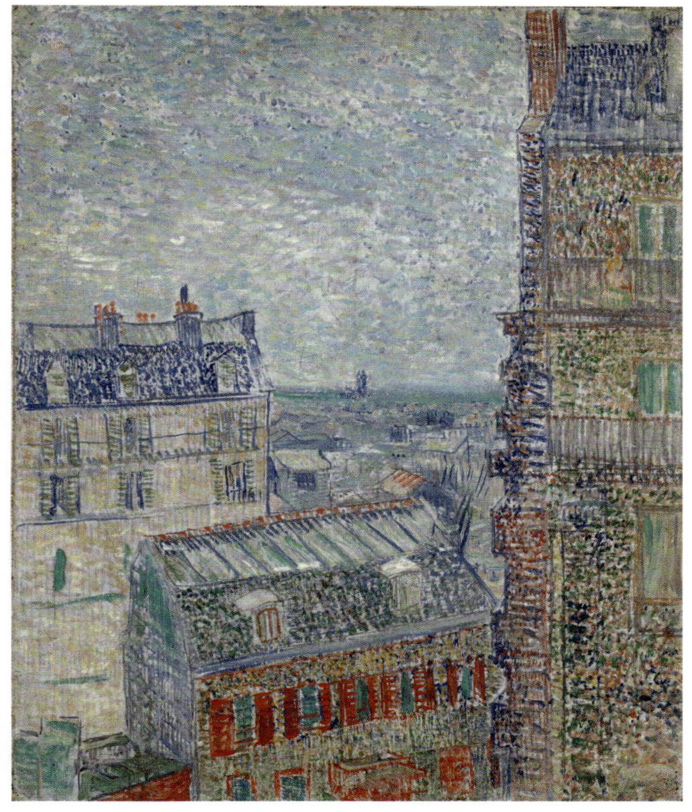

150 Vincent van Gogh
View from Theo's Apartment, 1887
Oil on canvas, 45.9 × 38.1 cm
Van Gogh Museum, Amsterdam (Vincent van Gogh Foundation)

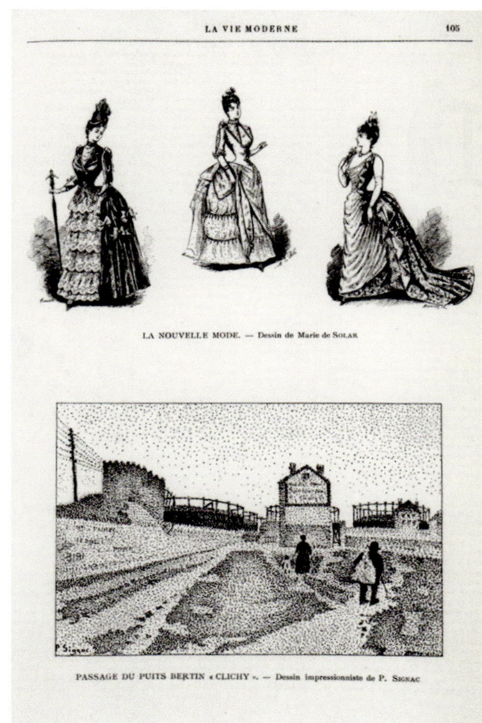

LA VIE MODERNE 105

LA NOUVELLE MODE. — Dessin de Marie de Solar

P. Signac

PASSAGE DU PUITS BERTIN « CLICHY ». — Dessin impressionniste de P. Signac

151 Paul Signac
"Passage du Puits Bertin 'Clichy,'" *La Vie moderne*, February 12, 1887, p. 105

Seurat, Signac, and Angrand participate in the third *Exposition de la Société des Artistes Indépendants* from March 26 to May 3. Angrand exhibits his first Divisionist painting, *The Accident* **(133)** as well as *Flooding at La Grande Jatte* (current location unknown). Seurat presents *The Bridge at Courbevoie* **(79)** with nine other paintings and twelve sketches. Signac submits *The "Ponton de la Félicité" at Asnières (Opus no. 143)* **(152)**, *Snow, Boulevard de Clichy, Paris* (1886; Minneapolis Institute of Art), *The North Pier (Boulevard de Clichy)* (1886; current location unknown), and his drawing *Passage du Puits-Bertin (Clichy)* **(91)**, along with several paintings produced in Les Andelys.

Bernard leaves for Britany on April 13, traveling to Pont-Aven and returning to Paris in October.

In early May, Van Gogh decides to start working in Asnières and Clichy, a campaign that would last three months. Signac meets him on one of his excursions and encourages him to experiment with Divisionism. Signac later writes of this time: "we painted on the banks of the river, lunched at the *guinguette* [a small café], and returned to Paris on foot, along the avenues of Saint-Ouen and Clichy. Van Gogh wore a blue zinc worker's smock and had painted dots of color on the sleeves" **(2,96)**.[19]

Signac travels south on May 23, a trip that would last through the fall. He first visits Auvergne in Central France, then Collioure—his first contact with the Mediterranean and southern France.

SUMMER 1887

Angrand returns to his family home in Criquetot-sur-Ouville, in Normandy, where he spends his summers.

In July, Van Gogh moves his painting activities back to Paris, working mostly in Montmartre. He hangs works in a window display at Tanguy's shop.[20]

Seurat publishes drawings in the *Revue indépendante* in August.

FALL 1887

Bernard returns to Paris in September. While he was away, his family moved to a larger house at 5 avenue de Beaulieu, Asnières. His grandmother, who now lives with the family, has a studio built for him in the garden. Van Gogh visits often, and the two artists paint portraits of Tanguy. During one visit, Van Gogh leaves abruptly after an argument with Bernard's father, who "refused to go along with [Van Gogh's] advice concerning [Bernard's] future."[21]

Throughout November and December, Bernard works with Anquetin to develop what would later be known as Cloisonnism, a style defined by its use of flat areas of color, bold forms, and dark outlines. He draws inspiration from the bridges across the Seine at Asnières for his first fully Cloisonnist work, *Iron Bridges at Asnières* **(121)**.[22]

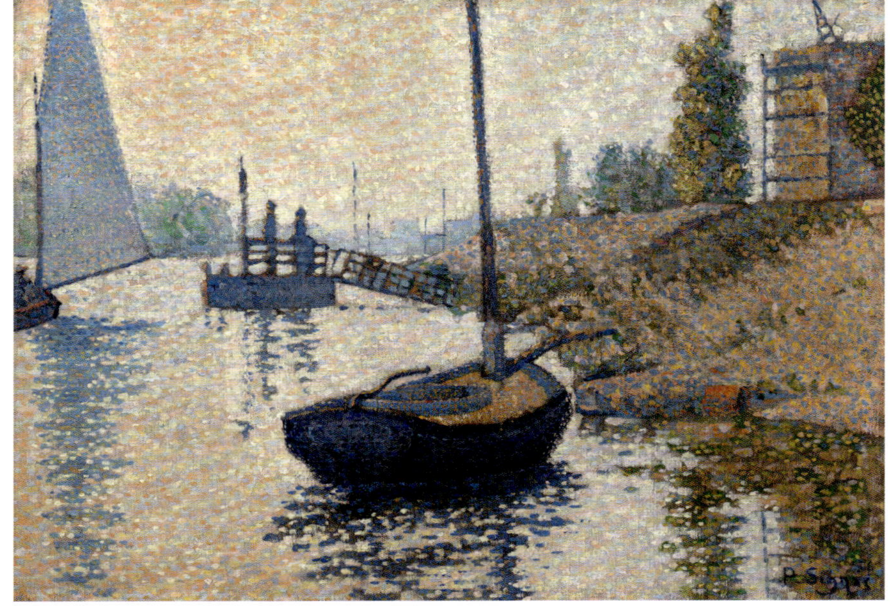

152 (cat.) Paul Signac
The "Ponton de la Félicité" at Asnières (Opus no. 143), 1886
Oil on canvas, 33.4 × 46.7 cm
Van Gogh Museum, Amsterdam (purchased with support from the VriendenLoterij, the Rembrandt Association, with the additional support from its Themafonds Impressionisme/Claude Monet Fonds, Het Liesbeth van Dorp Fonds and Themafonds 19de-eeuwse Schilderkunst, the Mondriaan Fund, and the members of The Yellow House)

1888

An exhibition organized by Van Gogh opens in the late fall or early winter at the Restaurant du Chalet at 43 avenue de Clichy. Van Gogh and Bernard present their recent Asnières works, including *Two Women on the Asnières Footbridge* **(120)**. Bernard, who had originally refused to participate in the exhibition if Signac was included, sells his first painting during the show.[23] Seurat attends the exhibition and meets Van Gogh there.

Beginning in late November, Seurat, Signac, and Van Gogh hang works at the Théâtre Libre, including Van Gogh's *Garden with Courting Couples: Square Saint-Pierre* **(30)**.

WINTER 1887

Angrand exhibits nine paintings at the first *Exposition des 33*, held from December 1887 to January 1888 at Galerie Georges Petit. Of the selection, three works depict areas on the outskirts of Paris: *The Seine at Saint-Ouen, Morning* **(128)**, *Waste Ground at Clichy*, and *Flooding at La Grande Jatte* (1887; current location unknown). Gustave Kahn (1859–1936) reviews the exhibition in January, noting that the "picturesque touch and the happy choice of motif demonstrate that [Angrand] was close to easy triumph, without the sincerity of his aesthetics."[24]

EARLY 1888

A small exhibition is held in the offices of the *Revue indépendante* at 11 rue de la Chaussée-d'Antin in January. Signac exhibits *Gasometers at Clichy* **(88)**, while Seurat and Angrand, who is back from Normandy, display two paintings each.[25]

On February 19, Vincent and Theo visit Seurat's studio before Vincent leaves for Arles in southern France. This marks the end of his two-year stay in Paris, during which time he painted over 190 works.[26]

SPRING 1888

Angrand and Seurat paint together on La Grande Jatte and produce similar views of the Seine **(134, 135)**.[27]

Bernard receives his first letter from Van Gogh in Arles, beginning a correspondence that will continue until the end of 1889 **(153)**.

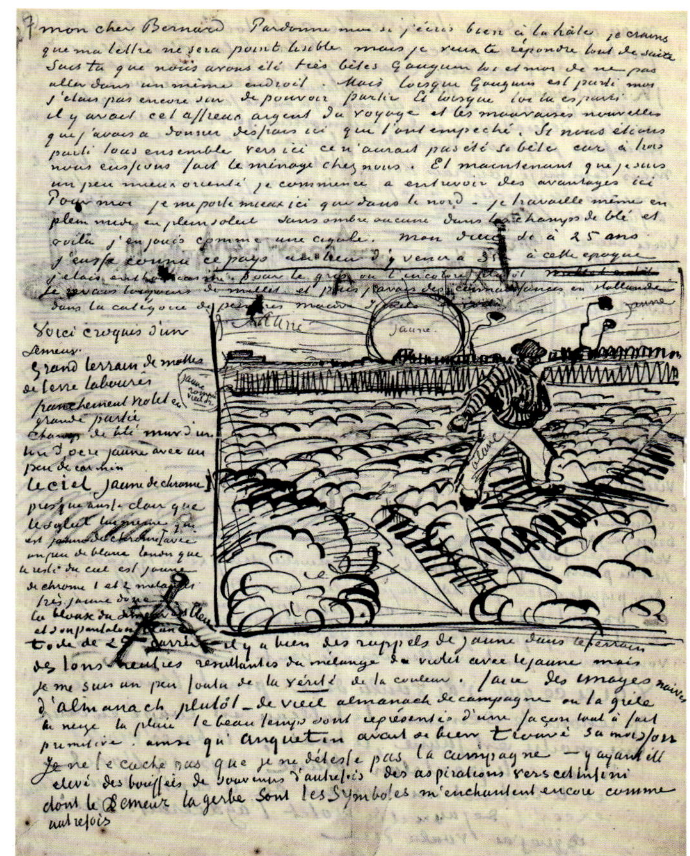

7 mon cher Bernard Pardonne moi si j'écris bien à la hâte je crains que ma lettre ne sera point lisible mais je veux te répondre tout de suite.
Sais tu que nous avons été très bêtes Gauguin toi et moi de ne pas aller dans un même endroit. Mais lorsque Gauguin est parti moi j'étais pas encore sûr de pouvoir partir Et lorsque toi tu es parti il y avait cet affreux argent du voyage et les mauvaises nouvelles que j'avais a donner des frais ici qui l'ont empeché. Si nous étions parti tous ensemble vers ici ce n'aurait pas été si bête car à trois nous eussions fait le ménage chez nous. Et maintenant que je suis un peu mieux orienté je commence a entrevoir des avantages ici
Pour moi je me porte mieux ici que dans le nord - je travaille même en plein midi en plein soleil sans ombre aucune dans les champs de blé et voilà j'en jouis comme une cigale. mon dieu si à 25 ans j'eusse connu ce pays [illegible]
[illegible]

Voici croquis d'un semeur.
grand terrain de mottes de terre labourées franchement violet en grande partie
champ de blé mur d'un ton d'ocre jaune avec un peu de carmin
le ciel jaune de chrome presque aussi clair que le soleil lui même qui est jaune de chrome [avec] un peu de blanc tandis que le reste du ciel est jaune de chrome 1 et 2 melangés très jaune donc.
la blouse du semeur est bleu et son pantalon blanc
toile de 25 carrée il y a bien des rappels de jaune dans le terrain des tons neutres resultants du mélange du violet avec le jaune mais je me suis un peu foutu de la vérité de la couleur. faire des images naïves d'almanach plutôt – de vieil almanach de campagne où la grêle la neige la pluie le beau temps sont représentés d'une façon tout à fait primitive. ainsi qu'Anquetin avait si bien trouvé sa moisson.
Je ne te cache pas que je ne déteste pas la campagne – y ayant été élevé des bouffées de souvenirs d'autrefois des aspirations vers cet infini dont le Semeur la gerbe sont les symboles m'enchantent encore comme autrefois

153 Vincent van Gogh
Letter to Emile Bernard with Sketch of Sower with Setting Sun, c. June 19, 1888
Pen and ink on paper, 26.8 × 20.5 cm
The Morgan Library & Museum, New York
Thaw Collection, given in honor of Charles E. Pierce, Jr., 2007

In March, Theo van Gogh purchases Seurat's drawing *Eden Concert* (1886–87; Van Gogh Museum, Amsterdam) at a Hôtel Drouot auction. Van Gogh writes to congratulate Theo on the purchase and asks his brother to arrange a painting exchange between himself and Seurat.

The fourth *Exposition de la Société des Artistes Indépendants*, held March 22 to May 3, opens at the Pavillon de la Ville de Paris, Champs-Elysées. Signac displays his last two paintings made on the outskirts of Paris, both focusing on the quai de Clichy (**96,98**). Angrand exhibits three works, including *La Seine* (possibly **128** or **137**), while Seurat shows ten and is criticized by Fénéon for his use of painted frames. Van Gogh participates for the first time with three paintings.

Bernard travels to Saint-Briac-sur-Mer in Brittany in April, returning to Paris on November 10.

SUMMER 1888

Seurat works in Port-en-Bessin on the Normandy coast. Signac spends the summer in Brittany.

FALL 1888

Signac illustrates Charles Henry's *Cercle chromatique*, first as a watercolor and then as a lithograph. This illustration demonstrates the juxtaposition of complementary colors utilized to create simultaneous contrast (**154**).

WINTER 1888

After an argument with Gauguin, with whom Van Gogh had been living and working in Arles since October, Van Gogh cuts off his ear on December 23 and is hospitalized the next day.

Sometime between 1888 and 1889, Seurat begins adding a painted border, composed of red and blue dots, to *Sunday on La Grande Jatte—1884*.

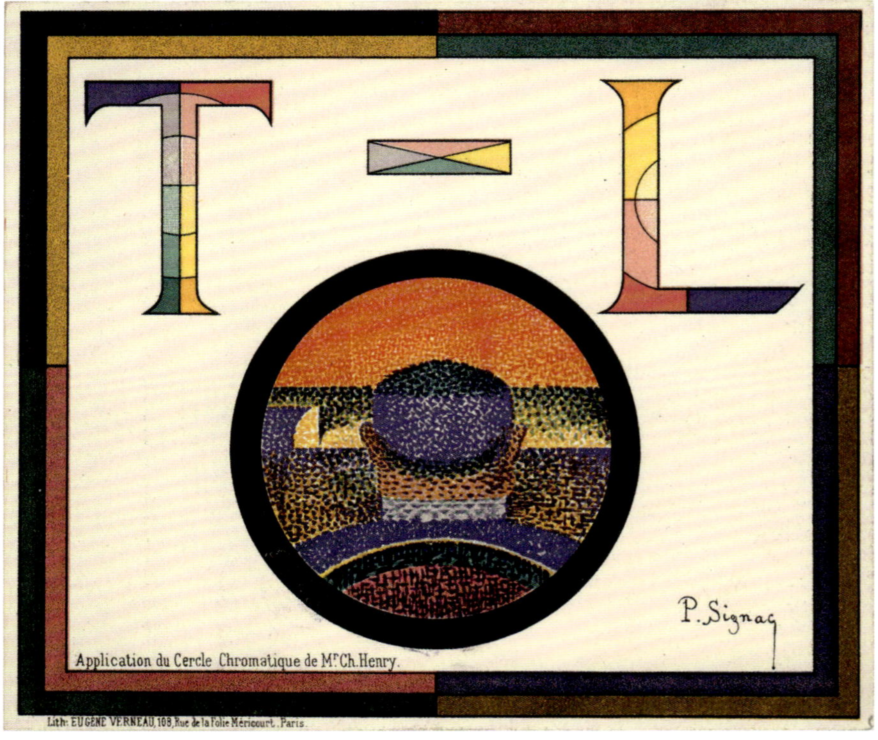

154 Paul Signac
Application of Charles Henry's Chromatic Circle; Théâtre-Libre playbill of January 31, 1889, 1889
Color lithograph on heavy wove paper, 15.5 × 18 cm
The Metropolitan Museum of Art, New York
Purchase, Reba and Dave Williams Gift, 1990

1889

EARLY 1889

Angrand exhibits at the second *Exposition de la Société des 33* at Galerie Georges Petit in January. Among his nine works on display are *La Seine* (possibly **137**), *The Seine at Courbevoie: La Grande Jatte* **(134)**, *On the Riverbank* (current location unknown), and *Corner of an Island* (current location unknown).

Signac leases an apartment and studio at 20 avenue du Clichy, where he holds weekly gatherings he calls "Mondays" until 1892. Angrand and Seurat are among the regular attendees.[28]

Van Gogh spends the beginning of the year in the hospital in Arles.

SPRING 1889

Signac stops in Arles on March 23 to visit Van Gogh on his way to Cassis, on the French Mediterranean coast, where he will live and work until June.

Bernard works at Asnières and displays his recent Breton paintings at Tanguy's shop.[29]

SUMMER 1889

In June, *L'Exposition de peintures du groupe impressionniste et synthétiste* is held at the Café des Arts, a site chosen specifically for its proximity to the *Exposition Universelle*. Bernard, who helped Gauguin arrange the exhibition, exhibits twenty-three works, including *Two Women on the Asnières Footbridge* **(120)**.

Although Van Gogh was invited to participate in the show, Theo declines on his behalf. Theo describes the exhibition to Van Gogh, who had admitted himself to an asylum at Saint-Rémy in May, and Van Gogh agrees with his brother's decision.[30]

In August, Bernard leaves for Saint-Briac-sur-Mer, his father having forbidden him from joining Gauguin at Pont-Aven.[31] He returns to Paris in September.

FALL 1889

The fifth *Exposition de la Société des Artistes Indépendants* opens at the Salle de la Société d'Horticulture at 84 rue de Grenelle-Saint-Germain from September 3 to October 4. Seurat, Signac, and Van Gogh submit paintings to the exhibition, but do not include works painted in the area around Asnières.

Bernard visits Theo in Paris to see Van Gogh's paintings of Arles and Saint-Rémy. He sends photographs of his religious compositions to Van Gogh, who criticizes them and beseeches him to return to his earlier style.[32]

Seurat moves his studio to 39 passage de l'Elysée des Beaux-Arts, Montmartre.[33]

WINTER 1889

Bernard moves to Lille to live with his grandmother because his parents no longer tolerate his desire to be a painter.

Seurat displays paintings in the windows at Tanguy's shop.

1890

EARLY 1890

Drawing upon information provided by Bernard and Theo, Gabriel-Albert Aurier publishes the article “Les Isolés—Vincent van Gogh” in the first issue of the Symbolist journal *Mercure de France* in January.

At the end of January, Signac travels to Saint-Briac and Herblay.

SPRING 1890

Angrand, Van Gogh, Signac, and Seurat exhibit in the sixth *Exposition de la Société des Artistes Indépendants*, held from March 20 to April 27, at the Pavillon de la Ville de Paris, Champs-Elysées. Seurat shows *The Seine at La Grande Jatte* **(135)** and *Gray Weather, Grande Jatte* **(81)** with eight other works. Angrand includes *The Seine at Courbevoie: La Grande Jatte* **(134)** among his seven works on display.

Van Gogh leaves Saint-Rémy on May 16, stopping briefly in Paris before continuing on to Auvers-sur-Oise.

SUMMER 1890

Contention arises among the Neo-Impressionists when Seurat criticizes Fénéon’s biographic essay on Signac in the journal *Les Hommes d’aujourd’hui* for not mentioning Seurat as the founder of Neo-Impressionism. He writes a letter to Fénéon to correct the text.[34]

Seurat leaves for Gravelines, near Calais in the north of France, in late June.

Van Gogh spends July 6 at Theo’s apartment in Paris, where he is visited by friends before he returns to Auvers that evening. On July 27, Van Gogh shoots himself and dies two days later with Theo at his side.

Bernard learns of Van Gogh’s death and attends the funeral in Auvers on July 30 with Tanguy, among others. In August, Bernard loses his parents’ financial support and prepares to sell his paintings by lottery.

FALL 1890

Bernard and Theo hang a small memorial exhibition of Van Gogh’s works at Theo’s apartment in Paris. Van Gogh’s paintings are also on view at Tanguy’s shop from September onward.

Seurat begins work on *The Circus* **(155)**. He includes Angrand among the spectators in the front row.

1891

SPRING 1891

The seventh *Exposition de la Société des Artistes Indépendants* runs from March 20 to April 27. Bernard shows with the group for the first time along with Angrand, Seurat, and Signac. Signac helps to organize a retrospective of ten works by Van Gogh at the exhibition. A review in *L'Echo de Paris* laments, "one is taken with great sadness to think that this painter, so magnificently gifted, so thrilling, so instinctive, so visionary of an artist, is no more."[35]

Seurat falls ill on March 26 and dies three days later of a sudden illness at the age of thirty-one. His funeral is held at Saint-Vincent-de-Paul on March 31.

Camille Pissarro attends Seurat's funeral and writes to his son, Lucien: "I saw Signac who was deeply moved by this great misfortune. I believe you are right, *pointillism* is finished. But I think it will have consequences which later on will be of the utmost importance for art. Seurat really added something."[36]

Angrand is in Criquetot-sur-Ouville when Signac informs him of Seurat's death; he is deeply saddened by this unexpected passing. Angrand abandons color and turns to black-and-white charcoal and *pierre noir* (black chalk) drawings.

In May, Signac, Fénéon, and artist Maximilien Luce (1858–1941) produce an inventory of Seurat's studio, marking the end of a revolutionary movement in painting. ■

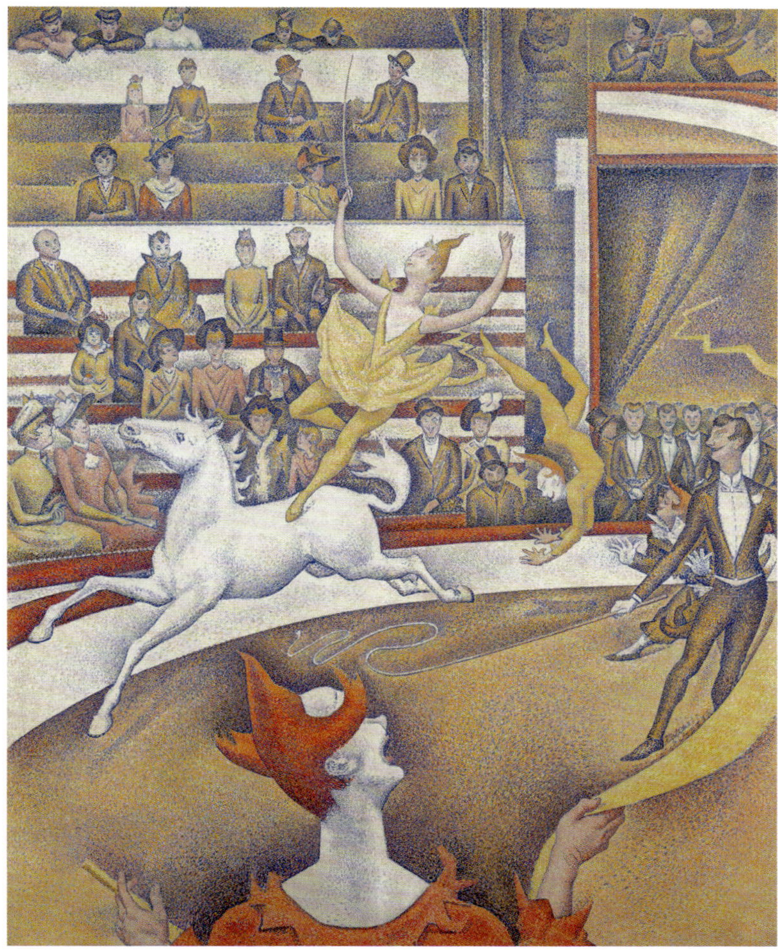

155 Georges Seurat
The Circus, 1891
Oil on canvas, 186 × 152 cm
Musée d'Orsay, Paris

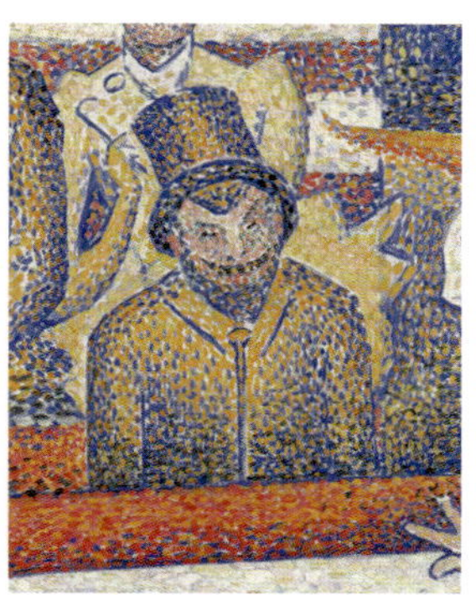

Georges Seurat
The Circus, detail with portrait of Charles Angrand

Artists' Biographies

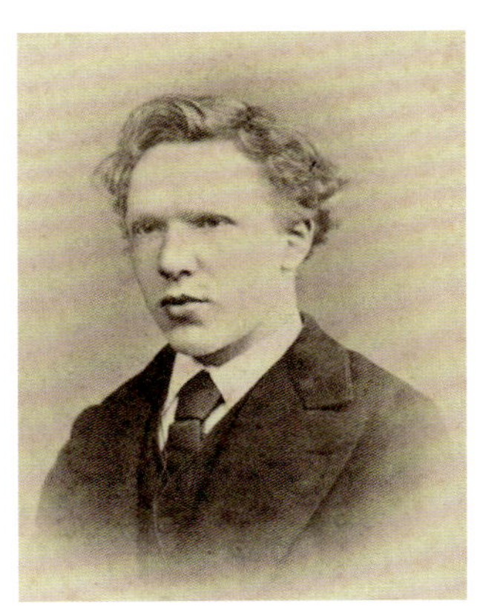

VINCENT VAN GOGH

(1853-1890)

Vincent van Gogh grew up the son of a Protestant minister in the southern Dutch province of Brabant, the eldest of six brothers and sisters. At the age of twenty-seven, he decided to follow his brother Theo's advice and become an artist. Van Gogh initially focused on drawing in The Hague, where he also took his first painting lessons. After moving back to rural Brabant in 1883, he painted numerous weavers and farm workers. In 1886 he traveled to Paris, where he encountered modern painting. His brushwork grew freer and his colors steadily more intense under the influence of the Impressionists and others. After two years in the capital, he set off for the southern French town of Arles, where the bright light and colorful landscape would be a powerful inspiration for paintings such as *Sunflowers* and *The Bedroom*. A quarrel with Paul Gauguin, who stayed with him for two months in Arles, led Van Gogh to cut off his ear in late 1888. In May 1889, he was voluntarily committed to a psychiatric hospital in Saint-Rémy-de-Provence. Despite persistent mental-health problems, he produced a large number of paintings in the institution's garden and its mountainous surroundings. Van Gogh moved back north to Auvers-sur-Oise near Paris in early 1890, where he spent several immensely productive months. He died there on July 29 at the age of thirty-seven, two days after shooting himself in the chest.

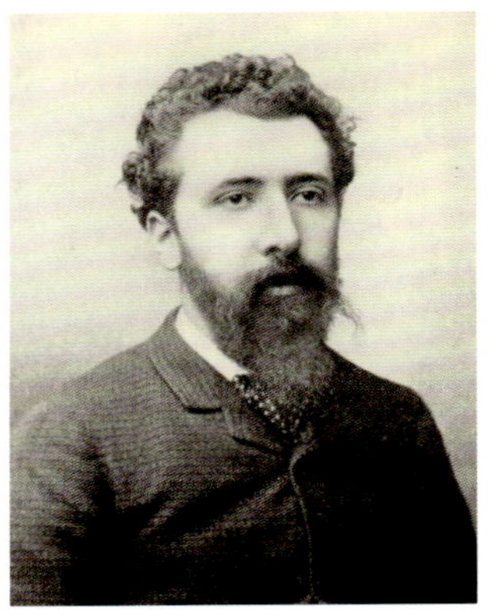

GEORGES SEURAT

(1859-1891)

Born in Paris in 1859 to a bourgeois family, Georges Seurat studied briefly at the Ecole des Beaux-Arts under Henri Lehmann (1878–79). Following a year's military service he began his independent career as an artist in 1881. Seurat gradually developed a simplified black-and-white drawing style and experimented with paintings of controlled touch using modern chromatic knowledge. This highly personal style was first manifested in *Bathers at Asnières*, which was rejected from the 1884 Salon but shown at the first Salon des Indépendants that year. *A Sunday on La Grande Jatte—1884* followed, displayed at the eighth Impressionist exhibition in 1886 and pioneering a new style, with a broken, dotted touch and active use of complementary colors, which became known as Neo-Impressionism. This drew other artists, such as Paul Signac and Charles Angrand, to adopt his technique. Seurat's career developed with a pattern of large figurative canvases exhibited at the Indépendants—*Poseuses* and *Parade de cirque* (1888), *Chahut* (1890), and *Cirque* (1891)—with themes increasingly drawn from urban entertainment, a cultivated caricatural edge, and exaggerated arabesques and chromatics. Seurat varied this output with marines painted during summer campaigns on the northern French coast, at Grandcamp (1885), Honfleur (1886), Port-en-Bessin (1888), Le Crotoy (1889), and Gravelines (1890). An introverted personality, Seurat relied on his work to assert his leadership of the avant-garde and colleagues such as the painter Signac and critic Félix Fénéon to promote his innovative authority. He died of a sudden illness in March 1891.

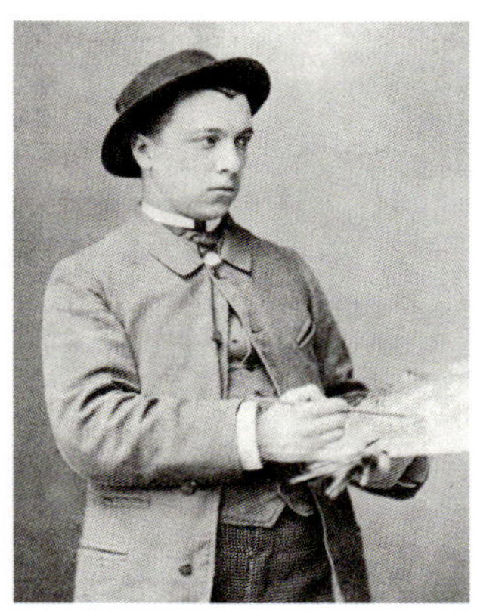

PAUL SIGNAC
(1863–1935)

Born into a bourgeois but progressive environment, Paul Signac was at first almost as tempted by literature as he was by painting. From the age of twenty, he began to acquire Impressionist paintings, and this taste for the art of others—starting with his contemporaries Paul Cézanne, Camille Pissarro, Edgar Degas, and later the Fauves and the Nabis—would never leave him. His first steps as a painter were inspired by Claude Monet and Armand Guillaumin. In the town of Asnières, where his family settled after the death of his father in 1880, he discovered boating and painted his first large canvases, worked with Van Gogh, and above all, converted to Neo-Impressionism after meeting Georges Seurat. Following the sudden death of the latter in 1891, Signac found himself at the head of this innovative movement, which he would vigorously defend and whose recognition he would champion through his theoretical writings and his energy as much as through his pictorial production. As head of the Salon des Indépendants for nearly thirty years (1908–34), he expounded and theorized as much as he painted, and in turn became a mentor and champion for many artists of the following generations.

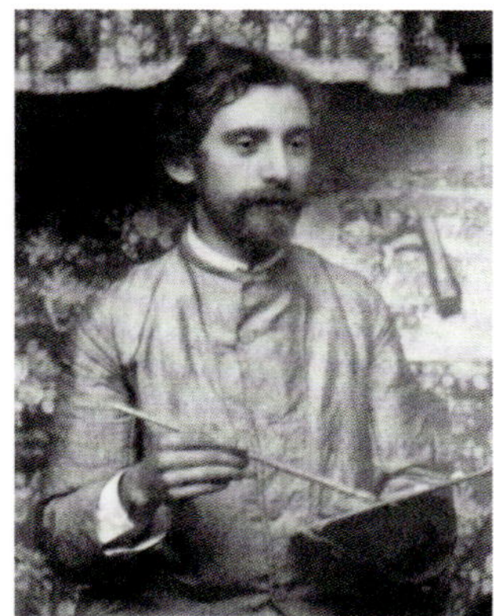

EMILE BERNARD
(1868–1941)

Emile Bernard was sixteen in 1884 when he began his career as a painter in Fernand Cormon's studio in Paris. He worked there alongside Henri de Toulouse-Lautrec and Louis Anquetin, who introduced him to the world of modern art. Bernard spent two years experimenting with the painting styles of the Impressionists and Neo-Impressionists before he and Anquetin replaced the short strokes or dots with blocks of flat color and solid outlines. Friends such as Vincent van Gogh and Paul Gauguin were impressed and inspired by their radically innovative style. Although esteemed for his talent and experimentation, Bernard eventually turned his back on modern painting, due primarily to a lack of appreciation and several spiritual crises. He departed in 1893 for Egypt, where he painted in an increasingly traditional style, only returning to France eleven years later. After traveling to Marseilles and Aix-en-Provence, Bernard moved into a studio on the quai Bourbon, Paris, in 1912 and continued to work there until his death in 1941. Apart from his main occupation as a painter, Bernard was also a prolific art writer. From 1890 onward, he published numerous articles on Van Gogh, Gauguin, Paul Cézanne, and Odilon Redon, among others. His writings also include many autobiographical notes, in which he both recounted and embellished his role in the development of modern art. Toward the end of his life he gathered all his memoirs in the unpublished manuscript *L'Aventure de ma vie*.

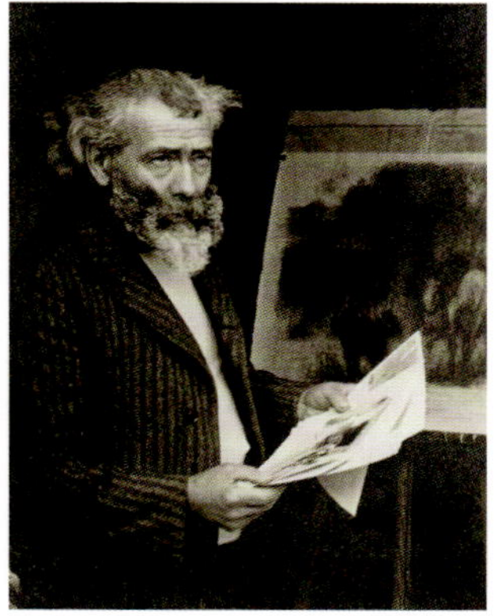

CHARLES ANGRAND
(1854–1926)

Charles Angrand was born in Normandy in Criquetot-sur-Ouville on April 19, 1854. After graduating from the teacher training college in Rouen, he took up a teaching post at the city's Lycée Corneille and attended classes at the Academy of Painting and Drawing. Drawn to Impressionism, he decided to become a painter. He first exhibited his work in 1878 in Rouen, before moving to a new teaching position at the Collège Chaptal in Paris in October 1882. He unsuccessfully submitted work to the Salon before helping to launch the Société des Artistes Indépendants in 1884, exhibiting regularly with the group until 1926. In Paris, Angrand became friends with Georges Seurat, Paul Signac, Henri-Edmond Cross, and Maximilien Luce. He adopted Seurat's Pointillist method and in 1891 began to work with Conté crayon. He returned to Normandy in 1896, and in March 1899 he contributed six drawings to a flagship exhibition at the Durand-Ruel gallery. Between 1906 and 1908 he made a brief return to oil painting, then worked on charcoal drawings that he exhibited at the Salon des Indépendants, before finally adopting a pastel technique in 1913. That year he spent time in Dieppe, then in 1914 moved permanently to Rouen, where he also sent pastel works to the Salon des Artistes Rouennais. His only solo exhibition was held at the Galerie L. Dru in Paris in March–April 1925. He died in Rouen on April 1, 1926.

Notes

"Aggressive, Industrial, and Bourgeois All at the Same Time": The Cultural Landscape of Asnières in the 1880s

1 B.-R. 1856, p. 27, as translated in Tucker 1982, p. 18.

2 In a letter to Emile Bernard of June 26, 1888 [632], Van Gogh referred to the journey between Paris and Asnières as being "*flat*" [emphasis is the artist's]. Paul Signac records that he and Van Gogh "returned on foot" from the suburbs; see Coquiot 1923, p. 140.

3 Vincent van Gogh to Theo van Gogh, Antwerp, on or about January 2, 1886 [551].

4 See, among others, Pinkney 1958; De Moncan and Heurteux 2002.

5 See Clark 1999, p. 37; Merriman 1991, p. 80.

6 Edinburgh 1994, p. 27.

7 Toronto 2019, p. 120; Rubin 2008, p. 92.

8 Jouan 1976, pp. 65–66.

9 Joanne 1881, p. xxxii. Joanne also details access via tram and omnibus, two cheaper modes of public transport.

10 Jouan 1976, p. 66.

11 Advertisement for De La Bédollière 1861 bound in with publication at the Bibliothèque nationale in Paris.

12 "Before the creation of the railroad, nature did not throb; it was a Sleeping Beauty, a cold statue, a vegetable, a jellyfish; even the sky seemed immobile. The railroad animated everything, mobilized everything. The sky became an active infinity, nature an energized beauty." From Gastineau 1863, as translated in Tucker 1982, pp. 81–82.

13 "Et la vie de la rivière, l'activité des quais, cette humanité dont le flot débouchait des rues, roulait sur les ponts, venait de tous les bords de l'immense cuve, fumait là en une onde visible, en un frisson qui tremblait dans le soleil. Un vent léger soufflait, un vol de petits nuages roses traversait très haut l'azur pâlissant, tandis qu'on entendait une palpitation énorme et lente, cette âme de Paris épandue autour de son berceau." See Zola 1886, p. 283.

14 Védry 2015, p. 28.

15 Gandy 1999, p. 29. See also Védry 2015, p. 75.

16 Védry 2015, pp. 83–86. See also Agief 1888.

17 Gandy 1999, p. 36.

18 See, for example: Clark 1999; Herbert 1988, pp. 1–32; Rubin 2008.

19 Barron 1886, p. 39.

20 Dulaure 1858, p. 8.

21 Herbert 1988, pp. 198–99.

22 "Sa proximité de la capitale, et la facilité des moyens de transport, en font un des environs de Paris les plus fréquentés." As quoted in Lehaguez 1864, p. 37.

23 Herbert 1988, p. 242.

24 Joanne 1881, p. 2. The original pedestrian bridge was built in 1826, and its later iterations were replaced in 1904 by a bridge with four spans. See Védry 2015, p. 72. The tollhouses charged travelers only until 1880. See Jouan 1976, p. 63.

25 The railroad bridge was destroyed in 1848, during the abdication of Louis-Philippe, and in 1870, to forestall the invading Prussians. See Jouan 1976, pp. 69, 89.

26 Gaillard 1992, p. 78.

27 Joanne 1881, p. 2.

28 Barron 1886, p. 38.

29 De La Bédollière 1861, p. 135.

30 Ibid.

31 "Asnières fut mis à la mode par les canotiers parisiens; mais l'on peut dire aussi que les canotiers parisiens furent mis à la mode par Asnières." Ibid.

32 Ibid., p. 376.

33 "Les gentilles canotières / Aim'nt l'amour et le bal / Elles fréquentent Asnières, / Suresn's, Bougival," as quoted in Lucenet 2005, p. 99.

34 Both were mentioned in Adolphe Joanne's 1881 guidebook. See Joanne 1881, p. 643.

35 Jouan 1976, p. 76.

36 Barron 1886, p. 38.

37 There were about forty within and beyond Paris by 1900. See Védry 2015, p. 29.

38 As translated in Giverny 2010, p. 17.

39 As translated in Rubin 2008, p. 87.

40 Gaillard 1992, p. 94.

41 These two islands were filled in in 1975. See Védry 2015, p. 79.

42 Société historique et archéologique 1974, p. 68.

43 Dulaure mentions that this is prized among the highest quality in the world. See Dulaure 1858, p. 4.

44 Gaillard 1992, p. 68.

45 De La Bédollière 1861, p. 138.

46 Société historique et archéologique 1974, p. 70.

47 Gaillard 1992, p. 72.

48 These cranes were eliminated in 1950. See Védry 2015, p. 74.

49 Ibid., p. 72.

50 Gaillard 1992, p. 62.

51 Ibid., pp. 62–64.

52 De La Bédollière 1861, p. 138.

53 *Gazette de Neuilly et de Courbevoie*, March 23, 1884.

54 "le travail est impraticable les dimanches et jours de fête à cause de l'affluence des promeneurs que je n'aime pas avoir dans le dos quand je travaille." As quoted in Lucenet 2005, p. 94.

55 Ibid., p. 86.

56 Départment de la Seine 1903, pp. 132–35.

57 Joanne 1881, p. 4.

58 Ibid.

59 Bourgeois 1996, vol. 1, p. 104.

60 Merriman 1991, p. 42.

61 Rubin 2008, p. 96.

Van Gogh's Painting Campaign in Asnières

1 Van Gogh himself referred to "my campaign in Asnières last spring": Vincent van Gogh to Theo van Gogh, Arles, about April 3, 1888 [592]. Van Gogh was used to thinking in terms of campaigns, in the course of which he would concentrate for a set period on a particular place or motif. He did so several times in his career, in the hope of producing salable and artistically successful paintings.

Another campaign, for instance, occurred during the spring of 1888, when he made several series of paintings of orchards in Arles.

2 Geographical research was carried out in collaboration with Teio Meedendorp. See also his essay, pp. 50–65.

3 Three publications shed light on this period: Welsh-Ovcharov 1976; Martigny 2000; Hendriks and Van Tilborgh 2011.

4 Bernard 1903 in Rivière 1994, pp. 63–64; Van Tilborgh 2007, pp. 54–56, 65, n. 19; Paris 1988, p. 17.

5 Unlike the official state-sponsored Salon, for which works were selected by a jury, the Indépendants invited artists to participate, making this *the* place for innovative artists to show in Paris. Thomson 2001, pp. 73, 76.

6 Fénéon 1886a. The art critics Joris-Karl Huysmans and Gustave Kahn published glowing articles about the Neo-Impressionist movement in April 1887. See Huysmans 1887; Kahn 1887; Paris 1886.

7 Vincent van Gogh to Horace Mann Livens, Paris, September or October 1886 [569].

8 Hendriks and Van Tilborgh 2011, pp. 40, 51, n. 4, 51, 69.

9 Like Van Gogh, Bernard studied under Cormon, but he had already set off on foot for Brittany on April 6, 1886: "I met Vincent van Gogh for the first time at Cormon's studio; . . . Then at Tanguy's, . . . we swiftly became friends." ("J'ai rencontré Vincent van Gogh pour la première fois à l'atelier Cormon ; . . . Puis chez Tanguy, . . . vite nous fûmes amis.") Bernard 1890 in Rivière 1994, p. 26; Signac later said: "Yes, I knew Van Gogh from Père Tanguy's." ("Oui, j'ai connu Van Gogh chez le père Tanguy.") Coquiot 1923, p. 140; Van Tilborgh 2007, p. 56; Bernard entered Cormon's studio at the age of sixteen in September 1884. Leeman 2013, pp. 31–32, 49.

10 Bernard 1908 in Rivière 1994, p. 167.

11 Van Gogh suggested that he and Angrand exchange paintings. In return for a painting by Angrand hanging at Tanguy's, he offered "2 views of the Moulin de la Galette that I could spare," but the exchange did not proceed [570]; Welsh-Ovcharov 1988, p. 17; Pontoise 2006, p. 20.

12 Bernard 1903 in Rivière 1994, pp. 63–64; Van Tilborgh 2007, pp. 54–56, 65, n. 19; Welsh-Ovcharov 1988, p. 17.

13 Vincent van Gogh to Willemien van Gogh, Paris, late October 1887 [574].

14 Vincent van Gogh to Willemien van Gogh, Arles, between 16 and 20 June 1888 [626].

15 Hendriks and Van Tilborgh 2011, pp. 44–45, 66, 70, 72–73.

16 Ibid., pp. 349-50.

17 According to Bernard, "[Van Gogh] tried out a free form of divisionism on Signac's advice." Bernard 1924: ". . . sur les conseils de Signac, [Van Gogh] s'essayait à un *divisionnisme* libre." Quoted in Hendriks and Van Tilborgh 2011, p. 74, n. 98; see also Bernard 1911, p. 22.

18 It was long supposed that *Square Saint-Pierre at Sunset*, *Garden with Courting Couples: Square Saint-Pierre* **(30)**, and *Square Saint-Pierre* (1887, Yale University Art Gallery, New Haven) were painted at the Voyer d'Argenson Park in Asnières, having been so identified by Pierre Leprohon. The same went for two works from the Grand Jatte triptych **(45,46)** and *Corner of a Garden*. This is contradicted, however, not only by the description of one of the works in an 1890 inventory as "Petit jardin à Montmartre," but also by the fact that the park in Asnières must still have been private property in Van Gogh's time. Hendriks and Van Tilborgh 2011, pp. 366, n. 1, 368, n. 11.

19 Pickvance suggested that the man with the spade might be the painter with his gear and that the female figure, whom the artist later painted over, was his model. This seems implausible, however. Martigny 2000, p. 297.

20 The painting under consideration measures 48×73 cm. Only two works painted in Asnières are larger than this, namely *View of the Pont d'Asnières*, 54.3×73.3 cm **(1)** and *Restaurant Rispal at Asnières*, 73.3×60 cm **(38)**. Only toward the end of July 1887, when Van Gogh began to work closer to home once more among the gardens at Montmartre, did he revert to larger canvases, such as his *Kitchen Gardens on Montmartre* (Stedelijk Museum, Amsterdam), which measures 113.5×146 cm, and *Montmartre: Behind the Moulin de la Galette* (Van Gogh Museum, Amsterdam), 81×100 cm.

21 "Je fis diverses vues d'Asnières par ce procédé." Bernard 1952 in Rivière 1994, p. 318; Hendriks and Van Tilborgh 2011, p. 75; Toronto/Amsterdam 1981, p. 31.

22 Vincent van Gogh to Emile Bernard, Paris, about December 1887 [575].

23 Hendriks and Van Tilborgh 2011, p. 78; Toronto/Amsterdam 1981, pp. 33–35.

24 Letter from Theo van Gogh to his mother Anna Cornelia van Gogh-Carbentus, Paris, February 28, 1887, Van Gogh Museum, Amsterdam (b906). In Hendriks and Van Tilborgh 2011, p. 73, n. 86, 87. Andries Bonger, Theo's future brother-in-law, wrote to his parents in December 1886: "[Theo] has now decided to separate from Vincent; living together is impossible." ("Hij [Theo] is nu besloten van Vincent te scheiden; samen wonen is niet mogelijk"). Letter from Andries Bonger to his parents H. C. Bonger and H. L. Bonger-Weissman, Paris, December 31, 1886, Van Gogh Museum, Amsterdam (b1867).

25 "We hebben vrede gemaakt, want het diende nergens toe om op die manier voort te gaan" b 911. Hendriks and Van Tilborgh 2011, p. 77, n. 117.

26 Hendriks and Van Tilborgh 2011, p. 78.

27 Lobstein 2003, vol. 1, p. 107, vol. 3, pp. 1582, 1591–92.

28 In 1886, Seurat's *A Sunday on La Grande Jatte—1884* and *The Seine at Courbevoie* were exhibited at both the eighth and final Impressionist exhibition and the second exhibition of the Indépendants **(70,69)**. The same shows included Signac's first Divisionist works from March and April that year, such as *The Gasometers, Clichy*, *The Junction at Bois-Colombes (Opus no. 130)*, and *The Banks of the Seine, Asnières* **(86,88,149)**. Another example was his *Passage du Puits-Bertin, Clichy*, known today purely from the Divisionist drawings of the same motif **(25,90,91)**. If we compare the Indépendants in 1886 and 1887 in terms of works painted in and around Asnières by Signac, Seurat, and Angrand, we find nine more of them in the first exhibition. Lobstein 2003, vol. 1, p. 107, vol. 3, pp. 1582, 1591–92; Paris 1886, pp. 16–17.

29 Van Gogh had previously lived in Paris as a young employee of Goupil art dealers between October and December 1874 and again from March 1875 to January 1876. He probably knew Asnières already as Goupil had a photography studio and printing shop there, which he might well have visited. See Paris 1988, p. 11, for a description of the urban development of Montmartre and Asnières between 1876 and 1886. The printing shop was located on the route de Courbevoie from 1869 onward; Amsterdam/Paris 1999, pp. 124, 125; Nonne 2000, p. 51; Nonne 1988, p. 332; see also Bordeaux/Albi 1997.

30 Van Gogh was able to exhibit at the Indépendants for the first time in 1888. Three of his paintings were included. Other contributors included Seurat, Signac, and Angrand. Letter 589, n. 13. See also letter 582, n. 9.

31 The only place where Van Gogh had previously exhibited was Agostina Segatori's café Le Tambourin, where he was allowed to hang his work in the spring of 1887. The "exhibition" did not generate any sales. Worse than that, in July the imminent bankruptcy of the café led to the seizure of all Van Gogh paintings that were still there. Hendriks and Van Tilborgh 2011, pp. 67, 301, 377.

32 See also Herbert 1988.

33 Thomson 2001, p. 88; House 2001, p. 165; Martigny 2000, p. 294.

34 Signac shared a house with his mother and grandfather at 42 bis rue de Paris in Asnières from 1880 and at 20 avenue de Clichy from 1889. He kept a studio in Paris from 1882 onward, first on rue de Steinkerque and from 1886 at 130 boulevard de Clichy. Seurat had a studio at 128 bis boulevard de Clichy from 1887, and Angrand lived at 45 boulevard des Batignolles. Emile Bernard's family relocated in 1884 from Paris to Asnières, where they moved to 5 avenue de Beaulieu in February 1887. Toronto/Amsterdam 1981, p. 26; Welsh-Ovcharov 1976, pp. 247–48; Leeman 2013, pp. 28, 30; Cachin 2000, p. 350; Paris 1988, pp. 13, 36–37. Pickvance rightly noted that the distance from rue Lepic where Van Gogh lived to Asnières was not much further than that from the Yellow House in Arles to Montmajour. We know, moreover, that Van Gogh did not shy away from walking long distances: see Martigny 2000, p. 142.

35 In addition to his Paris studio, Signac probably had another at his parents' house at 42 bis rue de Paris in Asnières. Cachin 2000, pp. 146–47; Welsh-Ovcharov 1976, p. 30.

36 Cachin 2000, pp. 344–45; Leeman 2013, p. 30.

37 "I did various views of Asnières using the [Divisionist] process and I showed them with a study after the *Unknown Woman* at a small exhibition of painters from the outskirts of Paris that was held in Asnières. Mr. Paul Signac immediately came to my parents' wishing to speak to me. I had no idea what the gentleman could want of me. He explained that he had seen my attempts at 'Divisionism,' and that he and Georges Seurat had invented it. Upon hearing this, I was delighted to meet him, and he took me to see his paintings." ("Je fis diverses vue[s] d'Asnières par ce procédé et je les exposai avec une étude d'après la *Femme inconnue* dans une petite exhibition de peintres de la banlieue qui s'était organisée à Asnières. Aussitôt se présenta chez mes parents M. Paul Signac, désireux de me parler. Je ne pouvais savoir ce que me voulait ce monsieur. Il m'expliqua qu'il avait vu mes essais de 'divisionnisme' et qu'il en était l'inventeur avec Georges Seurat. Je fus, là-dessus, très heureux de faire sa connaissance et il me conduisit voir ses tableaux.") Bernard 1952 in Rivière 1994, p. 318.

38 Although doubt is expressed in many publications as to where Signac and Seurat first met, there is a letter from Signac to Seurat's biographer Coquiot, which states: "Bills were posted around Paris in the spring of 1884: Groupe des Artistes Indépendants.... The exhibitors then attended a meeting chaired by Redon.... It was there that I made the acquaintance of my neighbor: his name was Seurat." ("Au printemps de 1884 des affiches furent collées sur les murs de Paris: Groupe des Artistes Indépendants.... Les exposants firent alors une réunion présidée par Redon.... C'est là que je fis la connaissance de mon voisin : il s'appelait Seurat.") Coquiot 1924, pp. 140–41.

39 Lespinasse F. 2006, p. 17; Lespinasse A. 2006, p. 49; Cachin 2000, pp. 348–49, 357.

40 "je connaissais moins intimement Van Gogh." Vincent and Theo visited this founder of Neo-Impressionism's studio just before Van Gogh departed for Arles in 1888. The Dutch artist was a great admirer of Seurat, but they knew each other only superficially; letter from Georges Seurat to Maurice Beaubourg, August 28, 1890, in Stein 1986, p. 90; Herbert 2004, pp. 50, 54.

41 Lespinasse F. 1981, p. 28; Pontoise 2006, pp. 17, 19.

42 "La mode fut d'aller faire des croquis sur les fortifications, aux usines de Suresnes, à l'Ile de la Grande Jatte." Blanche 1928, p. 37. Quoted in Lespinasse F. 1981, p. 27.

43 Vincent van Gogh to Willemien van Gogh, Paris, late October 1887 [574].

44 "Oui, j'ai connu Van Gogh chez le père Tanguy. Je le rencontrai d'autres fois à Asnières et à Saint-Ouen ; on peignait sur les berges ; on déjeunait à la guinguette et on revenait à pied à Paris, par les avenues de Saint-Ouen et de Clichy. Van Gogh, vêtu d'une cotte bleue de zingueur, avait peint sur les manches des petits points de couleur. Collé tout près de moi, il criait, il gesticulait, brandissant sa grande toile de 30 toute fraîche : et il en polychromait lui-même et les passants." Coquiot 1923, p. 140; Welsh-Ovcharov 1976, pp. 29–30. The "large" canvas cannot, incidentally, have been a size 30 as Signac says, as that standard format measures 70×90 cm, while the biggest known work from Asnières is *Restaurant Rispal at Asnières*, which is 73.3×60 cm **(38)**, see also note 20; Lucien Pissarro recalled something very similar about Van Gogh a little later: "My father and I met him one day on rue Lepic. He was coming back with some canvases from Asnières, where he had been painting. He was dressed in blue canvas, a smock like a zinc worker, and he insisted on showing my father his studies. This involved him propping them up against the wall by the roadside, to the astonishment of the passers-by." ("Un jour mon père et moi l'avons rencontré dans la rue Lepic, il revenait d'Asnières avec des toiles, revenant du motif – il était vêtu de toile bleue, un bourgeron comme un zingueurs – et il a insisté pour montrer ses études à mon père – pour le faire il les a accoté au mur de la rue au grand ébahissement des passants.") Camille Pissarro left for Eragny on May 21. Letter from Lucien Pissarro to Paul Gachet, January 26, 1928, b886, in Stein 1986, pp. 88–89; Bailly-Herzberg 1986, no. 421, p. 171; Cachin 2000, pp. 180–81.

45 We know that Signac was working in Asnières at the beginning of May from a letter written by Camille Pissarro to his son Lucien, in which he states that he went there with Signac on May 8 1887. Letter from Camille to Lucien Pissarro, no. 421, in Bailly-Herzberg 1986, p. 161; Toronto/Amsterdam 1981, p. 102.

46 Vincent van Gogh to Theo van Gogh, Paris, between about July 17 and 19, 1887 [571].

47 Mme Tanguy put an end to the deal in mid-July, after which Van Gogh reverted to painting over old canvases. This is the case, for instance, with a series of forest views done at that time (F 307, F 308, F 309a). It is important to note that not every canvas has been examined. The discovery that *Restaurant Rispal at Asnières* **(38)** was painted over an earlier work was made in the course of the Weave Matching Project by Don Johnson, William Sethares et al., Van Gogh Museum, Amsterdam/Rice University, Houston/University of Wisconsin 2022; Hendriks and Van Tilborgh 2011, pp. 46, 49.

48 The works he produced in Montmartre feature sunflowers, which would have been in bloom at the end of July. Vincent was forbidden from painting on the streets in August 1887, although it is not clear why this was. Hendriks and Van Tilborgh 2011, pp. 39, 45–46, 48, 82, n. 127; Martigny 2000, p. 144. Letters 571 and 574.

49 Hendriks and Van Tilborgh 2011, p. 413.

50 Vellekoop and Van Heugten 2001, pp. 278–82. During his time in Arles, Van Gogh prepared another painting with a drawing containing color notes. Both the painting itself and a watercolor version of it are known, F 413 and F 1428. Pickvance suggested that he might have given the sailboat picture to the countess, but no evidence for this has been found. Martigny 2000, p. 144.

51 Hendriks and Van Tilborgh 2011, p. 399.

52 Vincent van Gogh to Willemien van Gogh, Paris, late October 1887 [574].

53 This latter work is the only one of the three where the edges of the stretcher were subsequently painted red. Its format, however, is 19×27 cm. Hendriks and Van Tilborgh 2011, pp. 448–50.

54 For the sake of convenience, Van Gogh opted for the standard *haute paysage 3* format, which he only used for two other works: the vertically oriented portraits F 208 and F 215c from one year earlier. Seurat had exhibited nine *croquetons* at the Indépendants in 1884, and he showed *croquetons* at later exhibitions too. Lobstein 2003, vol. 3, p. 1582.

55 Paris/New York 1991, p. 103.

56 "Le bateau-lavoir stationnant sur la rive gauche de la Seine à Asnières à 150 m en aval du Pont de Clichy," in Martigny 2000, p. 295. Archives Municipales, Asnières.

57 Hendriks and Van Tilborgh reproduced the postcard of the restaurant but did not identify the painting as such. Hendriks and Van Tilborgh 2011, pp. 387, 389–90.

58 See also Gray 2022.

59 Martigny 2000, p. 295.

60 Given the view of the bridges, this must have been the quai de Seine in Courbevoie. The Courbevoie population register has a single entry for this quayside in 1886, that of the "marchand de vin" Huybert Tericeux. A family of five is recorded as living at number 6: grandfather, daughter, daughter-in-law, and two children. Daughter-in-law Anna (age thirty-three) was also registered as a wine merchant. *Dénombrement 1886, liste nominative des habitants de la commune de Courbevoie*, Département de la Seine 1886, Archives départementales de Hauts de Seine, p. 233.

61 Vincent van Gogh to Theo van Gogh, Arles, about May 20, 1888 [611].

62 Ronald Pickvance was the first to identify the "comtesse." Martigny 2000, pp. 143–44; see also p. 146, n. 17. Although Van Gogh stated that the countess was "far from young," she was thirty in 1887 and was married, with a twelve-year-old daughter. The way Vincent describes her to Theo suggests he had not told his brother about her previously. The 1889 *Annuaire* records that Marcellin Perruchot—"M[archan]d de vin" of Asnières—was declared bankrupt on October 31, 1889, indicating that in the preceding years he had indeed been active as a wine merchant. His wife had died in 1884 at the age of forty-seven, and her obituary confirms the address 1 boulevard Voltaire. *Archives Commerciales de la France* 1889, p. 1543; *Le Phare* 1884, unpaginated.

63 We do not know whether Theo actually delivered the works. An indication that the countess possessed at least some works by Van Gogh is provided by a 1929 memorandum of sale for five paintings by him at the Charpentier Gallery in Paris. The provenance described there (in German) bears strong similarities with the Le Vaillant de La Boissière family: "[of] a family from Asnières with whom Van Gogh lived and which he gave to them" ("einer Familie aus Asnières, bei der Van Gogh wohnte und die er dieser schenkte"). The detail "with whom Van Gogh lived" is interesting, as it suggests that a close relationship existed between the countess and the painter. Hendriks and Van Tilborgh 2011, p. 24, n. 20; see Holtmann et al. 2006, p. 48; according to De la Faille 1970, it might be these Paris works at any rate: F 239 and F 365v.

64 Van Tilborgh 2018, pp. 41–65; Hendriks and Van Tilborgh 2011, p. 73.

65 F 303, F 302.

66 Hendriks and Van Tilborgh 2011, p. 391.

67 Ibid., pp. 65–66, 73, 395, 397.

68 Shields 2019, pp. 15, 19–25; Hunter 2019, pp. 62–70.

69 Toronto/Amsterdam 1981, p. 102.

70 The only other industrial buildings that Van Gogh painted were the glassworks at Clichy **(27)**.

71 Vincent van Gogh to Theo van Gogh, Nuenen, about July 14, 1885 [515]. Raffaëlli decided in 1879 to move from Paris to Asnières, where he had more motifs to paint. He continued to live there until 1889.

72 Theo sold a work by Raffaëlli for the first time in 1886, and Van Gogh must also have known his paintings well although he never met the artist himself as far as we know. His brother sent him an illustrated exhibition catalogue of the artist's work in July 1885, see letter 512. The "Caractères de banlieue" theme ran to no fewer than twenty-two paintings with titles like *Le paysage de Saint-Ouen, La route de Courbevoie, Le quai de Levallois,* and *Quai de Seine, à Asnières, Le pont de Clichy*—all places where Van Gogh himself would work two years later. Raffaëlli 1884, pp. 16–17; see also Amsterdam/Paris 1999, pp. 104–6.

73 "Une poésie printanière émanait de ces morceaux enlevés à bout de brosse et comme dérobés aux heures fugitives. J'en goutais le charme, d'autant plus que j'habitais alors ces lieux, qu'ils étaient rendus selon l'âme que j'y sentais." Bernard wrote these words in response to the triptychs: see below. Bernard 1911, p. 12.

74 Jo's brother, Andries Bonger, drew up the list after Theo's death. "La grande Jatte (triptyque)," "Bord de la Seine à Asnières," "Bord de la Seine à Clichy." Bonger list nos. 70, 81, 82; Hendriks et al. 2013, p. 168. Jo Bonger also mentioned the triptychs in her preface to the 1958 edition of the letters: "With spring everything improved. Vincent could work in the open air again and painted much at Asnières, where he painted the beautiful triptych of 'l'Isle [sic] de la Grande Jatte,' the borders of the Seine with their gay, bright restaurants, the little boats on the river, the parks and the gardens, all sparkling with light and color." Van Gogh-Bonger 1958, p. xlii.

75 Hendriks and Van Tilborgh (2011) still felt that the identification could not be made firmly (p. 387), while Pickvance (Martigny 2000) and Welsh-Ovcharov (1988) also made earlier attempts. It was Welsh-Ovcharov who proposed the Grande Jatte triptych. Definitive identification was made possible by Nina Zimmer, supplemented by material and technical research in the context of the Van Gogh Studio Practice Project (2013) by Hendriks et al. for the Clichy and Asnières triptychs. Hendriks et al. were unwilling to express a definitive opinion on the Clichy and Asnières triptychs they studied, as two of the six works (F 300, F 368) were missing. It appears possible, nevertheless, based on earlier research combined with the dimensions of the works they identified. The canvases from the Grande Jatte triptych, which Welsh-Ovcharov identified, are the largest at approx. 55×66 cm. Those making up the Asnières triptych measure approx. 52×65 cm, while the dimensions of the Clichy triptych paintings are the smallest at approx. 50×60 cm. Two very precise notes of dimensions made by the painter himself on the Asnières triptych—65.5×52 cm and 65×54 cm—show that he intended the sizes to correspond closely. The notes were found on F 301 and F 312. *The Restaurant de la Sirène at Asnières* **(22)** is very similar in size at 54×65.5 cm to the other works in the Grande Jatte triptych, but it lacks a red edge, confirming that it does not belong with that group. See below for the significance of the red edges. There are no other works so similar in dimensions, which means we can now speak of a definitive identification; Zimmer 2009, pp. 102–5; Hendriks et al. 2013, pp. 168–72.

76 Zimmer 2009, p. 104.

77 Hendriks and Van Tilborgh 2011, p. 79.

78 It is apparent in one of the works from the Asnières triptych that Van Gogh worked wet-on-wet in the red border, telling us that he must have painted the edge at an early stage. Weave-matching performed on four paintings has revealed that the Asnières and Clichy triptychs were each done on a single long length of canvas. It can be seen in the case of the Asnières triptych that *Bridges Across the Seine at Asnières* **(48)** was stretched on three sides and must hence have been positioned on the left of the canvas. *Restaurant de la Sirène, Asnières* **(49)** was only stretched at the top and bottom, indicating that it came from the middle section. Van Gogh seems to have worked in a similar way for the Clichy triptych, where the two examined paintings apparently formed the outermost elements of the triptych. Hendriks et al. 2013, pp. 170–72; for the drawing of the Restaurant de la Sirène **(23)** see Vellekoop and Van Heugten 2001, pp. 283–85.

79 "Une grande toile installée sur son dos, il se mettait en route, puis il la divisait en autant de cases, au hasard des motifs; le soir il la rapportait pleine, et c'était comme un petit musée ambulant, ou toutes les émotions de sa journée étaient captées. Il y avait des bouts de Seine pleins de bateaux, des îles aux balançoires bleues, des restaurants pimpants aux stores multicolores, aux lauriers roses ; des coins de parc abandonnés ou des propriétés à vendre." Bernard 1911, pp. 11–12. Bernard also wrote: "He was soon spending his days in Asnières. He went there on foot from Paris with a huge canvas which he divided up into compartments. It was so big that passers-by took him to be a sign-carrier." ("Bientôt il passe ses journées à Asnières : il y vient à pied de Paris, avec une toile énorme, qu'il divise en compartiments ; une toile si grande que les passants le regardent comme un porteur d'enseignes," Bernard 1926 in Rivière 1994, p. 250. Quoted in Hendriks et al. 2013, p. 172.

80 *Kingfisher by the Waterside* and *Lane in Square Saint-Pierre* are works that probably had their edges painted red for an exhibition. The latter painting is displayed on the wall in *Interior of a Restaurant* (Kröller-Müller Museum, Otterlo, F 342) without a frame and with a painted red edge visible. Jooren 2013, pp. 302–4.

81 Bernard was not in Asnières at the time of Van Gogh's painting campaign, as he had left for Brittany on April 13 and would return only in October. Leeman 2013, pp. 30, 67, 72, 79; Welsh-Ovcharov 1976, pp. 32–33; Bernard later recalled: "Vincent often came to see me at the wooden studio built in my parents' garden in Asnières. It was there that we did Tanguy's portrait together." ("Vincent venait souvent me voir à l'atelier de bois construit dans le jardin de mes parents à Asnières. C'est là, que nous fîmes ensemble le portrait de Tanguy.") Bernard 1911, p. 12; Tanguy's portrait is F 364.

82 Louis Anquetin and Henri de Toulouse-Lautrec were French artists working at the studio of Fernand Cormon, which is how they met Vincent van Gogh. Arnold Koning was a Dutch painter working in Paris between September 1887 and May 1888 who knew Vincent and Theo well.

83 Hendriks and Van Tilborgh 2011, p. 513; Paris 1988, pp. 19–20, p. 27, n. 32; Toronto/Amsterdam 1981, pp. 28–31. Letter 575, nn. 7, 9. Van Gogh did not sell anything, but he did exchange a work with Gauguin; see letter 576, n. 2 and letter 640: "For the 2nd exhibition at the showroom on boul. de Clichy, I have fewer regrets about the time and effort. Bernard having sold his first painting there, Anquetin having sold a study there, and I having made the exchange with Gauguin, we all got something." See also Bernard 1924 in Rivière 1994, p. 241; Bernard 1903 in Rivière 1994, p. 65.

84 See letter 592, n. 17; Cachin 2000, p. 354; Paris 1988, p. 34. Seurat, Signac, and Angrand were among the participants in a joint exhibition at the offfices of *La Revue Indépendante* in January and February 1888. Van Gogh is likely to have visited before leaving for Arles, but he did not take part.

85 The branch manager in The Hague, Hermanus Tersteeg, took the works on a sale-or-return basis. See letter 592.

86 They are likely to have been *Poppies in a Wheatfield* (1887, Israel Museum, Jerusalem) and *Grass with Butterflies* **(44)**. Vincent van Gogh to Theo van Gogh, Arles, about March 25, 1888 [589], see nn. 4, 10, 11.

87 Letter 626.

88 Martigny 2000, pp. 143, 146, n. 15.

89 In a letter from Arles Van Gogh expressed his wish to form an association of artists of the "Petit Boulevard", as he called them. This was a younger generation of artists among whom he counted Bernard, Signac, Seurat, Angrand, and himself. Letter 584, n. 6.

90 "Cette lumière . . . s'éveille bientôt comme une naissante aurore, dans les vues déjà joyeusement aimables d'Asnières, de la Grande-Jatte et des bords de Seine. Van Gogh prélude aux symphonies de sa palette future et essaie ses instruments. . . . Tout à coup, aux toiles grises succèdent des études 'pointillées.'" Bernard 1924 in Rivière 1994, p. 246.

91 He resumed his focus on peasant life after arriving in Arles. Hendriks and Van Tilborgh 2011, p. 67.

92 Vincent van Gogh to Theo van Gogh, Arles, about April 3, 1888 [592].

Seurat at Asnières: Chromatics and Caricature, Melancholy and Modernity

Seurat's original French titles have been foregrounded in this text. The English titles are given in parentheses at the first mention of the work.

1 Paris 1881, no. 1082. See also nos. 76, 99, 200, 242, 271, 301, 472, 630, 892, 898, 1030, 1082, 1128, 1191, 1246–47, 1357, 1442, 1621, 1656, 1705, 1722, 1760, 1950, 1982, 2082, 2124, 2312, 2328.

2 Coquiot 1924, p. 29; Rich 1935, p. 16, n. 4.

3 "des tuyaux d'usines vomissent des bouillons de fumée noire . . . la mélancolique grandeur." Huysmans 2006, p. 171.

4 "tristesse les paysages désolés." Letter from

Jean-François Raffaëlli to Léon Hennique, about January 10, 1887, in Heintz 1962, p. 364.

5 "quand j'ai le spleen, je vais dans les banlieues tristes . . . contempler des tableaux d'après . . . Raphaëlli." Letter from Jules Laforgue to Gustave Kahn, February 1881, in Laforgue 1941, letter IV, p. 35.

6 "port national d'agrément, ville sainte du canotage." Périer 1890, p. 61; Barron 1886, p. 38.

7 Distel 1991, p. 399.

8 Ibid., pp. 399–401.

9 Paris 1970, p. 14.

10 Ajalbert 1891, p. 188.

11 "le bleu du ciel et l'orangé blanc des murailles et le gris orange des nuages." Hauke 1961, vol. 2, DH386, p. 53.

12 De Goncourt 1864, pp. 7–8.

13 Distel 1991, p. 401.

14 "le bijou de l'exposition." Anonymous 1886.

15 Leighton 1997.

16 Périer 1890, p. 11.

17 "l'immuable loi . . . bâtisses somptueuses . . . hauts-fourneaux et grandes forges." Huysmans 1880, p. 69.

18 Blanc 1867, p. 10.

19 Thomson 1997, p. 87; Thomson 2021, pp. 117–18.

20 For a full technical and historical study of the painting, see Chicago 2004.

21 Thomson 1985, pp. 97–108; Thomson 1989, pp. 188–96.

22 Fèvre 1886; X 1886.

23 Fouquier 1886; Fèvre 1886, p. 149; "Labruyère" 1886.

24 "le son du moderne, le rappel de nos costumes étriqués, collés au corps, la réserve des gestes, le cant britannique par tous imité." Adam 1886, p. 550.

25 "Les robes moulantes et tombant droit, les corsages ajustés, les vestons collants." Ajalbert 1886, p. 392; Hermel 1886.

26 Thomson 2012, pp. 143–64.

27 Virmaître 1888, p. 64.

28 Ajalbert 1891, p. 173.

29 Herbert 1991, pp. 391–93.

30 Moréas 1886, pp. 1–2.

31 Jumeau-Lafond 2015, pp. 30, 36–38.

32 Coquiot 1924, pp. 39–40.

Signac in Asnières: The Formative Years

1 "Cet aimable vieillard si accueillant pour vos amis, et lecteur de feu *le Cri*." Letter from Paul Alexis to Paul Signac, June 28, 1889, Archives Signac. This reference to *Le Cri du peuple*, the former newspaper of the Paris commune, is a reminder of the sympathy Signac's family had for the people's cause in spite of their privileged status.

2 "What was behind my decision to paint? It was Monet . . . nothing seemed simpler to me . . . I had no idea at that point!" ("Qu'est ce qui m'a poussé à faire de la peinture ? C'est Monet . . . rien ne me paraissait plus facile . . . je ne me rendais pas compte à cette époque-là!") Kunstler 1935.

3 Commandant Fribourg was a battalion commander in the French army's engineering corps and the head of photography in the army's geographic service. He took this photograph from a hot-air balloon in 1885.

4 The phrase "the advent of leisure" is the translation of the title of a book exploring the phenomenon: Corbin 1995.

5 See, in particular, Zola 1878.

6 Charles Baudelaire's essay, *Le Peintre de la vie moderne*, was first published in *Le Figaro* in 1863.

7 It is a mistake, wrote Signac in this article in defense of artistic freedom, to suppose that only propagandist art can be political. "Pure aesthetes, revolutionary in temperament . . . take a pickax to the old social edifice that is breaking apart. . . . Justice in sociology, harmony in art: the same thing" ("Les purs esthètes, révolutionnaires par tempérament . . . portent un coup de pioche au vieil édifice social en train de craquer. . . . Justice en sociologie, harmonie en art: même chose."), Signac 1891, cited in Herbert, Rougerie, and Rougerie 1961.

8 "Oui, j'ai connu Van Gogh chez le père Tanguy. Je le rencontrai d'autres fois à Asnières et à Saint-Ouen; on peignait sur les berges; on déjeunait à la guinguette, et on revenait à pied à Paris, par les avenues de Saint-Ouen et de Clichy. Van Gogh, vêtu d'une cotte bleue de zingueur, avait peint sur les manches des petits points de couleur. Collé tout près de moi, il criait, il gesticulait, brandissant sa grande toile de 30 toute fraîche: et il en polychromait lui-même et les passants." Coquiot 1923, p. 140.

9 First held in 1884, the Salon des Indépendants had led to the creation of the society of the same name, founded by Seurat, Angrand, Dubois-Pillet, and Signac: "based on the suppression of admission juries, the society of independent artists has the goal of allowing artists to freely present their works for the judgement of the Public." ("basée sur la suppression des Jurys d'admission, la société des artistes Indépendants a pour but de permettre aux artistes de présenter librement leurs œuvres au jugement du Public.") Signac served on the placement committee several times and took on the presidency of the society in 1908, energetically occupying the role until his resignation in 1934.

10 "un art à grand développement décoratif qui sacrifie l'anecdote à l'arabesque, la nomenclature à la synthèse, le fugace au permanent, . . . et confère à la nature, que lassait à la fin sa réalité précaire, une authentique réalité." Fénéon 1890.

11 Signac 1899.

12 Paul Signac, *Au temps d'harmonie* (1895; Montreuil Town Hall).

13 "It is without any hope, very sincerely, that I am participating in this competition. But does one have the right to complain of having no walls to decorate, if one does nothing to obtain any? It will firstly be a good lesson in composition, and then another good lesson to compare my design to those of the others." ("C'est sans aucun espoir, bien sincèrement, que je fais ce concours. Mais a-t-on le droit de se plaindre de n'avoir pas de murailles à décorer, si on ne fait rien pour en obtenir ? Ce sera d'abord une bonne leçon de composition, et puis une autre bonne leçon de comparer mon projet à ceux des autres.") Paul Signac, November 11, 1900. See Hellman 2021, p. 471.

14 "Il est bien difficile d'indiquer les contrastes et les dégradés qui prendront tant d'importance sur les murailles. Comment le Jury pourra-t-il voir sur ces esquisses, ce qui ferait bien en place réelle? . . . en grandeur d'exécution, quelle surprise cet arrangement réservera-t-il?" Ibid.

15 "rose, verte et blanche, sans or, sans brun." Letter from Paul Signac to Félix Fénéon, November 1900, Archives Signac.

16 "J'ai donc le choix des harmonies binaires et ternaires et des lignes en rapport." Ibid.

17 *Le Démolisseur* (1897–99; Musée d'Orsay, Paris).

18 "Le nombre de concurrents était énorme. Un seul peintre, Paul Signac, s'était évertué à ordonner les thèmes selon les lignes et les espaces de la salle. Son travail était probe intelligent, artiste." Verhaeren 1901.

19 "Stupid jury, outrageous like all juries! And the decoration of the town hall was naturally entrusted to one those base, squalid types who have made all the town halls of Paris hideous and repugnant . . . ! And Paul Signac, meanwhile, with his fresh, delicate, brilliant sketches, introduced the joy of living, the joy of working, the joy of loving. He celebrated everything that helps us to bear the burden of sorrows down here." ("Jury stupide, effarant comme tous les jurys! Et la décoration de la Mairie fut naturellement accordée à un de ces bas bourbeux, qui ont fait de toutes les mairies de Paris de hideux et repoussants immeubles . . . ! Et Paul Signac, lui, par ses fraîches, délicates, brillantes esquisses, apportait la joie de vivre, la joie de travailler, la joie d'aimer. Il chantait tout ce qui nous aide à porter ici-bas le fardeau des douleurs.") Coquiot 1921.

20 Ironically, this monumental painting ended up decorating the communist town hall in Montreuil after Signac's death in 1935.

Bernard and Asnières: Backdrop for a Stormy Beginning

1 Leeman 2013, p. 50, n. 33.

2 Bernard c. 1939-a, p. 19.

3 Martigny 2000, p. 141.

4 In his memoir, *L'Aventure de ma vie*, Bernard recalled a conversation with his father about his future in 1886, who wanted him to finish his studies. Emile had other ideas: "'so what do you want to do?' he said to me . . . 'I want to be a painter,' I replied." ("Alors que veux-tu faire me dit-il . . . 'Je veux être peintre' répondis-je.'")

5 Bernard c. 1939-a, p. 38.

6 Ibid., pp. 36–37.

7 Currently unknown works feature in two lists that Bernard drew up in 1893 and 1901, both of which are now in the Bibliothèque de l'INHA, BCMN Ms 374. Examples include no. 27 in the 1893 list: *Neige à Courbevoie*, 1885; and no. 88 in the 1901 list: *Maisons dans les arbres à Asnières*, 1888. Or "a large canvas with a boating party" ("une grande toile de canotiers") that he probably completed in 1886, of which a sketch is now unfortunately all that remains. The composition consists of oarsmen in a rowboat with a large figure viewed from the back in the foreground, no doubt inspired by the many paintings Gustave Caillebotte made of the same theme. See Bremen 2015, p. 78.

8 See Rivière 1994.

9 Martigny 2000, p. 140; Herbert 1988, pp. 198–99.

10 "port national d'agrément." Barron 1886, p. 38.

11 "dont la splendeur rivalise avec le luxe de l'Elysée Montmartre." Ibid., p. 30.

12 "un contraste violent." Ibid.

13 Bernard c. 1939-a, p. 36: "We lived right by the Seine, so I only had to walk down a road bordered by a wall and pass the lovely trees in a garden to reach the riverbank." ("Nous étions sur la hauteur qui domine la Seine, ainsi je n'avais qu'a [sic] descendre une rue bordée d'un grand mur et laissant passer les beaux arbres d'un jardin, pour être sur la berge.")

14 "Il y avait toujours quelque belle voile éblouissante qui faisait glisser sur l'eau bleue ou verte un élégant bateau, ou lieu, c'étaient des défilés de péniches tirées par un remorqueur ou des canotiers étalant leurs bras nus et faisant filer en rhytme [sic] leurs longues et minces embarcations, où tenait toujours au gouvernail une femme avec une ombrelle. Il flottait alors dans l'air je ne sais quelle joie, je ne sais quelle jeunesse." Ibid., pp. 36–37.

15 Ibid., p. 37.

16 See Ibid., pp. 17, 19, 23–24.

17 "Portraits-types de gens du bas peuple" was the name Jean-François Raffaëlli used for his paintings of figures from the lower social classes. See Anonymous 1884, p. 7.

18 See ibid., pp. 7–9.

19 Bernard c. 1939-a, p. 39.

20 Ibid., p. 40. The starting date is found in a letter to Bernard from his sister Madeleine, dated September 26, 1884, transcribed in *L'Aventure de ma vie* between pages 40 and 41.

21 Bernard 1932 in Rivière 1994, p. 261: "Indeed, from the moment I entered the studio, a wind of rebellion had blown upon the theories of the house. It came, they said, from 'the Durand Ruel boutique,' of which Anquetin and Lautrec were frequent visitors." ("Justement, dès mon entrée à l'atelier, un vent de révolte avait soufflé sur les théories du lieu. Il venait, disait-on, de 'la boutique à Durand Ruel' où Anquetin et Lautrec faisaient de fréquentes visites.")

22 Bernard 1952 in Rivière 1994, p. 317.

23 Bernard 1932 in Rivière 1994, p. 261.

24 Bernard 1952 in Rivière 1994, pp. 315–16.

25 This second exhibition of Les Indépendants opened on December 10, 1884. More information can be found in Lobstein 2003.

26 Ibid., pp. 1582, 1591. The work is identified in Dorra and Rewald 1959 (p. 100) as *Étude finale pour "Une baignade à Asnières,"* 1883–84, The Art Institute of Chicago. See Cachin 2000, nos. 79 and 80 for Signac's works.

27 Bernard's son, Michel Ange Bernard-Fort, wrote on the back of the photograph, which is now privately owned: "Emile Bernard conversing with Vincent van Gogh on the quay by the Seine at Asnières." ("Emile Bernard en conversation avec Vincent van Gogh sur les quais de la Seine à Asnières.")

28 Bernard often had photographs taken, including pictures of the murals in his studio in Saint-Briac in 1888. The following year, he commissioned photographs of six paintings, which he then sent to Van Gogh. See Vincent van Gogh to Emile Bernard, Saint-Rémy-de-Provence, about November 26, 1889 [822].

29 The possible existence of this work was previously suggested in Toronto/Amsterdam 1981, p. 263.

30 Bernard c. 1939-a, p. 39.

31 Bernard himself must have liked the work, because when Julien Tanguy visited him just over a year later, he still had it in his possession and gave it to him to sell in his store. Emile Bernard to his mother and grandmother, February 1887, Bibliothèque de l'INHA, BCMN Ms 374: "I gave him [Tanguy] quite a few canvases to take with him, including the big one I did from my window, which I thought very good." ("Je lui ai donné à emporter bon nombre de toiles entre autres la grande faite par ma fenêtre qu'il a trouvé très belle.") Bernard later painted the same view again, but now in a completely different style. See Luthi and Israël 2014, no. 2, *Paysage*. The work is wrongly dated in that catalogue to 1883.

32 Bernard might have been inspired in this regard by the shadow theater as seen at Le Chat Noir, which he probably visited with Anquetin and Toulouse-Lautrec, both of whom were regulars. See Destremau 1994, pp. 85–87.

33 Gauzi 1954, p. 22: "The influence of the Impressionists in Cormon's studio remained discreet. Pupils who were susceptible to it contented themselves with drawing and limited their experiments to studies made at home, without their master's knowledge." ("À l'atelier Cormon l'influence des impressionnistes restait discrète; les élèves qui la subissaient se contentaient de dessiner, réservant leurs recherches pour des études exécutés chez eux, à l'insu du patron.") Quoted in Destremau 1996, p. 179.

34 Hartrick 1939, p. 42.

35 Bernard c. 1939-a, pp. 48–49.

36 See Emile Bernard to his parents, early September 1886, in McWilliam 2012, no. 18.

37 Letter from Emile Bernard to his parents, May 22, 1886, in Harscoët-Maire 1997, pp. 116–17.

38 They are *Août, verger à Pont-Aven,* 1886, Musée des Beaux-Arts, Quimper, and *Two Breton Women in a Meadow*, 1886, Van Gogh Museum, Amsterdam.

39 See Leeman 2013, pp. 59–60; Le Paul 1987, p. 107.

40 Bernard himself dated the canvas to 1886 and located it in Asnières in an inscription on the stretcher (see Christie's, Paris, December 1, 2006, lot 62). Although the accuracy of Bernard's own dating cannot be guaranteed, it seems correct in this instance. The use of color and the restrained touch resemble the first series of paintings dating from his journey through Brittany. It cannot have been made before then, as the trees were not in such full leaf when he left on April 6, nor would there have yet been any hay in early spring. In other words, the work must have been painted in late September or in October 1886, immediately after he returned from Brittany.

41 "Je fis diverses vue d'Asnières par ce procédé [pointillisme] et je les exposai . . . dans une petite exhibition de peintres de la banlieue qui s'était organisée à Asnières." Bernard 1952 in Rivière 1994, p. 318.

42 Ibid: "I saw large landscapes there that were very luminous but rather lifeless; interiors in which all the figures struck me as wooden." ("J'y regardai de grands paysages très lumineux, mais peu vivants; des intérieurs dont tous les personnages me parurent en bois.") The date of early March is found in a letter from Camille Pissarro to Lucien Pissarro, March 13, 1887, in Bailly-Herzberg 1986, pp. 139–40: "Signac's painting is very good, that will be a surprise. Anquetin and Bernard came to see it yesterday and did not breathe a word in front of the canvas, which represents very real progress; they are a difficult pair, those gentlemen." ("Le tableau de Signac est très bien, ce sera une surprise. Anquetin et Bernard ont été hier le voir ils n'ont soufflé un mot devant cette toile qui dénote un progrès très réel ; ils sont bien difficiles ces messieurs.")

43 Bernard 1952 in Rivière 1994, p. 318.

44 Bernard c. 1939-a, pp. 66–67: "I concluded that while this process was good for the vibrant rendering of light, it impoverished the color, and I immediately threw myself into the opposite theory." ("J'en conclus que si ce procédé était bon pour la production vibrante de la lumière, il dépouillait la couleur, et je me jetai aussitôt dans la théorie contraire.")

45 Dujardin 1888, pp. 487–92.

46 There was still snow on the ground when the work was painted. Temperatures fell below zero in March 1887 for a week beginning on the thirteenth. This was the only prolonged period of frost that year until the end of December. By then, however, Bernard had begun to execute his Cloisonnist paintings in a tidier manner. Anonymous 1888, p. 141.

47 "Il faut simplifier le spectacle pour en tirer le sens." Bernard 1919 in Rivière 1994, p. 201.

48 Ibid. for the medieval influences. On Japanese printmaking as a source of inspiration: Bernard 1903 in Rivière 1994, p. 63.

49 Letter 640, n. 5; see also Uhlenbeck and Van Tilborgh 2018.

50 Vincent van Gogh to Theo van Gogh, Arles, July 15, 1888 [640]: "The exhibition of Japanese prints that I had at the Tambourin had quite an influence on Anquetin and Bernard, but it was such a disaster." ("L'exposition de crépons que j'ai eu au Tambourin a influencé Anquetin et Bernard joliment mais cela a été un tel désastre.")

51 Bernard 1890 in Rivière 1994, p. 26.

52 The first paintings that Van Gogh did in Asnières date from late April or early May 1887. Bernard had left for Brittany on April 13 that year. See Leeman 2013, p. 72.

53 Ibid., p. 71.

54 Letter from Emile Bernard to his parents, September 3, Pont-Aven, 1887, McWilliam 2012, no. 25: "I am very happy that the studio has been completed. Many thanks for the huge sacrifices father has made for me." ("Je suis très heureux que l'atelier soit achevé. Bien des remerciements pour les grands sacrifices que père fait pour moi."); Bernard 1911, p. 12.

55 Ibid., p. 14: "We were, it must be said, avid

admirers of Japanese prints." ("Nous étions, il faut l'avouer, des fervents des images japonaises.")

56 See Vincent van Gogh to Emile Bernard, Paris, about December 1887 [575].

57 Bernard 1901: "At a popular restaurant on avenue de Clichy, an exhibition . . . where he, Vincent, is showing fifty or a hundred canvases, landscapes, flowers, portraits; where I am exhibiting 'My Grandmother' and 'Ragpickers at the Pont de Clichy.'" ("Dans un restaurant populaire de l'avenue de Clichy, une exposition . . . où lui, Vincent, met cinquante ou cent toiles, paysages, fleurs, portraits, où j'expose 'Ma grand'-mère' et 'Les chiffonnières du pont de Clichy.'") The latter work is likely to have been one of his recent canvases, *Two Women on the Asnières Footbridge (Vue du Pont d'Asnières)* (**120**) or *Iron Bridges at Asnières* (**121**). His reference to "chiffonnières"—the feminine plural of "ragpickers"—means that it must have been *Two Women on the Asnières Footbridge*, which shows two women.

58 Vincent van Gogh to Emile Bernard, Arles, between September 27 and October 1, 1888 [690].

59 See *Tableaux modernes, sculptures: Vente, Enghien-Les-Bains, Hôtel des ventes*, November 21, 1990, lot 5.

Angrand: Expressive Harmonies from Saint-Ouen and Asnières to Courbevoie

1 See Angrand 1965; New York 1968; Sutter 1970; Welsh-Ovcharov 1971; Lespinasse F. 1982; Paris 1988; Lespinasse F. 1988; Lespinasse F. 2006; Lespinasse A. 2006.

2 Charles Frechon (1856–1929). See Lespinasse F. 1980; Lespinasse F. 2004; Rouen 2008.

3 Alphonse Bouvret (1831–1898) was the founder of the Théâtre Lyrique at the Galerie Vivienne, executor of the comtesse de Caen's will, director of the *Journal des Artistes,* and an art lover. The Galerie Vivienne, which opened in 1823 and where Bouvret also lived, was located in the 2nd arrondissement (district) close to the Palais Royal. Les Arts Incohérents was an artistic, anti-establishment movement, which organized ten exhibitions in Paris between 1882 and 1893, as well as exhibitions in Rouen, Nantes, Besançon, and Nancy. Angrand participated in 1883 and 1884 (Paris and Rouen), and 1889 (Paris). See Charpin 1990 and Naldi 2022.

4 Jean Le Fustec (1855–1910) was a colleague at the Collège Chaptal, a journalist at *Le Magasin Pittoresque*, a critic at the *Journal des Artistes*, and a Breton cultural and political activist who became the first Grand Druid in 1900. He owned three paintings by Charles Angrand.

5 "Elles sont maintenant Galerie Vivienne au bureau du Journal des Artistes. Le directeur du Journal est l'ami, le camarade plutôt, d'un maître du collège – et ce matin, lui avait parlé de moi. Il n'achète pas, mais se fera un plaisir de les faire voir – et de me servir d'intermédiaire dans le cas où quelqu'un les demanderait." Letter from Charles Angrand to his parents, spring 1883. Family letters: 281 letters to the artist's parents, his brother Paul (1868–1924), his sister Maria (1852–1921), and his nephew Pierre (1906–1990). Not published in Lespinasse F. 1988. Archives Angrand.

6 "je profite chaque jour de cette immuable sérénité du baromètre pour prendre le grand air sur les fortifications. . . . Peut-être vais-je y transporter mon chevalet – La porte d'Asnières me fait de l'œil." Letter from Charles Angrand to his parents, mid-March 1885, Archives Angrand; for more information on the Parisian fortifications see Thomson 1987.

7 "Je prenais un paysage au pont de Clichy dans le bout de l'île des Ravageurs. C'est soit dit (entre parenthèse) là que je vais depuis quinze jours étudier l'automne – et voir tomber – tomber les feuilles mortes, comme dit la chanson. Eh bien, j'ai trouvé la température douce, quoique le vent me vient du large. Certes l'illusion n'allait pas jusqu'à me faire prendre les cheminées d'Asnières que j'avais en face de moi pour des minarets." Letter from Charles Angrand to his parents, fall 1885, Archives Angrand.

8 "Le tableau doit être avant tout une composition, c'est à dire une organisation par l'esprit, des lignes, formes, couleurs en vue d'une harmonie expressive." Charles Angrand, Cahier 39, Archives Angrand; these notebooks (in *cahier d'école*, or school notebook format) were used by the artist during his numerous visits to the municipal library in Rouen.

9 Félix Fénéon (1861–1943). See Halperin 1970; Paris/New York 2019.

10 "Peignez le caractère essentiel des choses, essayez de le transmettre par n'importe quel moyen, sans vous soucier de la technique . . . peignez ce que vous observez et sentez." Letter from Camille Pissarro to Louis Le Bail, 1896, in Howard 1997, p. 201.

11 "Précédemment, j'étais allé à Clichy. Il y a là des terrains vagues, accidentés qui m'avaient séduit. J'ai fait un tableau exubérant de couleurs comme toujours – où des jaunes de toutes nuances se chauffent au soleil. Ces deux dernières toiles sont les plus importantes que j'ai faites depuis le printemps. . . . Je destine ces derniers sujets à notre exposition que je ne verrai pas – car elle ouvrira le 20 août pour se terminer le 20 septembre. Le Fustec voudra bien, je crois se charger de présenter mes toiles et aussi de les relever en temps et heure." Letter from Charles Angrand to his parents, July 1886, Archives Angrand.

12 "Sur sa demande [à Paul] je lui ai dit que j'avais fait une toile de 30 dans les terrains vagues de Clichy – toile qui est chez Bouvret et qu'actuellement je prenais le point de vue de la ligne de l'ouest sortant de Paris. . . . C'est entre deux séances de – la ligne de l'ouest – voir ci-contre que je vous écris. Comme ce n'est pas loin – une demi heure de trajet- j'y vais le matin, rentre dîner à midi et retourne vers deux heures. La toile est à peu près achevée maintenant . . ." Letter from Charles Angrand to his parents, mid-July 1886, Archives Angrand.

13 *Coin de ferme*, 1886 (current location unknown).

14 "M. Charles Angrand. Celui-ci, qui exposait pour la première fois en 1883, n'a pas adopté la facture impersonnelle et comme abstraite des dissidents de l'impressionnisme : sa brosse, d'une violence rusée, travaille et triture ingénieusement une pâte épaisse et plastique, la configure en reliefs, l'érafle, l'écorche, la guilloche et la papelonne. Le requièrent surtout les scènes de la vie agreste normande, et les environs immédiats de Paris: ses *Terrains vagues à Clichy* (1886), sa *Ligne de l'ouest à sa sortie de Paris, vue prise des fortifications* (1886), se particularisent par leur sapidité, leur mélancolie rude, une tendance aux tons graves." Fénéon 1886b in Halperin 1970, p. 44.

15 "Reste Angrand. A première vue, les œuvres de cet artiste vous imposent l'opinion qu'elles ont été faites devant la nature. Que vous preniez le paysage normand ou le paysage parisien, l'impression est la même. . . . Les terrains vagues à Clichy, avec leurs herbes maigres et brûlées de soleil sont d'une vérité frappante. La ligne de l'ouest à sa sortie de Paris est très puissamment rendue, quoique son ciel soit d'un ton discutable. La Seine à Saint-Ouen est une grisaille toute lumineuse, et d'une finesse de ton et d'exécution vraiment remarquables. . . . En somme Angrand fait œuvre d'artiste en soumettant sa palette et son pinceau à l'observation. . . . Mais il y a chez lui un progrès qui a été constaté dès le premier jour, et qui, nous en sommes convaincu, persistera tant que cet artiste fera œuvre d'impressionniste véritable en se maintenant dans l'observation." Le Fustec 1886.

16 Vincent van Gogh to Charles Angrand, Paris, October 25, 1886 [570]; in Paris 1988, p. 60.

17 "Retournant chez Tanguy, j'ai fait la connaissance encore devant mes toiles d'un nommé Angrand, c'est aussi un impressionniste fort connu depuis la dernière exposition des indépendants. Il m'a également félicité." Letter from Emile Bernard to his mother and grandmother, February 28, 1887, private collection.

18 Le Fustec 1887, pp. 139–40.

19 "deux fois pour me faire l'oeil et m'élever l'imagination." Charles Angrand, Cahier 39, Archives Angrand.

20 "Devant le beau temps je n'ai pu résister à aller à la Grande Jatte. . . . Maintenant que les journées sont favorables, j'en profite. Je pars à midi ½ pour la Jatte et n'en reviens que vers 7 heures et plus tard. C'est assez éreintant par la chaleur qu'il fait, de faire ainsi régulièrement 6 km pour gagner le motif et autant pour revenir. Mais au moins j'y jouis de tranquillité et j'y suis en compagnie de Seurat qui lui aussi fait journellement le voyage . . ." Letter from Charles Angrand to his parents, July 1888, Archives Angrand.

21 "Les séances finies, nous repassions le bras de Seine dans un petit bac L'Artilleur, puis nous rentrions par Courbevoie et la rue de Lévis. Il me faisait observer – détail entre cent de nos entretiens de route – l'auréole pourpre des jeunes arbres qu'on venait de planter sur le boulevard . . ." Letter from Charles Angrand to Lucie Cousturier, July 4, 1912, Saint-Laurent-en-Caux, Archives Angrand; Lucie Cousturier (1876–1925) was a painter and writer. See Lanfranchi 2008.

22 "Quand vers [18]86 ce peintre adopte le système de la division scientifique du ton et annula dans l'uniforme facture néo-impressionniste ses ragoûts de pâte et ses ruses de brosses. L'habileté de M. Angrand à choisir ses thèmes est bien sensible dans cet A la Grande Jatte et dans les tableaux qui l'accompagnent." Fénéon 1889.

23 "Exception faite pour une promenade ou deux rue de Rome, je consacre les bonnes heures de la journée au travail . . . une mélodie matinales aux strophes blanches et sacrées. En prose, je vous la présenterais tout simplement sous les espèces d'un bout de fleuve d'où s'essore la brume caractéristique d'une belle journée qui s'éveille. Trois mois d'effort se sont déjà accumulés autant que succédés sur cette œuvre – dont je vous notifie d'avance le calme et la sereine beauté." Letter from Charles Angrand to Maurice Dezerville, Paris, mid-June 1889, private archives; Maurice Dezerville (1864–1927) was a colleague at the Collège Chaptal, a notary's clerk, then an attorney in Dijon.

24 Letter from Charles Angrand to Paul Signac, April 1891, Lespinasse F. 1988, p. 43 (Archives Signac).

25 "Et ce fut la série de ces grands dessins qui glissent du noir au blanc par lentes houles impeccablement dégradées. Dans cette brume lumineuse les bêtes, les choses, les gens de la campagne apparaissent selon des formes simples qui résumaient les trouvailles de l'observateur sans garder trace de rien d'anecdotique." Fénéon 1926 in Halperin 1970, p. 481.

26 "la correspondance assidue qu'il entretint avec tous trois [Henri-Edmond Cross, Maximilien Luce et Signac] est une mine de documents pour une histoire de l'impressionnisme. Dans cette histoire il occuperait plus de place qu'il n'en occupa dans l'actualité." Fénéon 1926 in Halperin 1970, p. 481. For Henri-Edmond Cross, see Sutter 1970; Compin 1964. For Maximilien Luce, see Bouin-Luce and Bazetoux 1986. For Paul Signac, see Cachin 2000; Paris 2021.

27 See Sanchez et al. 2014.

28 Charles Angrand, Cahier 39, Archives Angrand.

Chronology: A Decade of Artistic Experimentation in the Parisian Suburbs

1 Adapted from Lynn DuBard's extensive chronology in Saint Louis/Frankfurt 2001, pp. 201–38.

2 "Ma famille voulait faire de moi un architecte, mais je préférais dessiner sur les bords de la Seine que dans un atelier de l'Ecole des beaux-arts". Kunstler 1935; quoted and translated in Leighton 2001, p. 4.

3 Clement and Houzé 1999, p. 311.

4 The exact date of their meeting is unknown, but it must have happened sometime in 1884. Angrand writes of the meeting in an unedited and undated letter addressed to his parents, quoted in Pointoise 2006, p. 17. The work that Seurat purchased is also unknown.

5 "Encore refusé: ils sont constants dans leur exclusivisme. . . . Un groupe d'artists indépendants s'est réuni pour décider une exposition privée . . . Ce groupe d'indépendants n'a rien de commun avec les impressionnistes." Quoted in Pointoise 2006, p. 17.

6 See Chicago 2004 for an in-depth look at the *Grande Jatte*.

7 For lists of works presented by all artists with the Indépendants, see Monneret 2000; Lobstein 2003, vols. 1 and 3.

8 Henry was a close friend of many Neo-Impressionists, including Signac and Seurat. See Henry 1885.

9 Pointoise 2006, p. 19.

10 Vincent writes to Theo on February 28, 1886 [567], asking him to not be angry at his sudden arrival, and requesting Theo meet him at the Louvre.

11 Paris 2014, p. 230. Bernard would write in 1891 that he met Van Gogh in Cormon's studio. He does not give a date for the meeting, but it likely took place before Bernard left Paris in April.

12 Galitz 2001, p. 300.

13 Van Gogh notes in a letter to the English artist Horace Mann Livens (1862–1936) of September or October 1886 [569] that he was unfamiliar with the Impressionists before arriving in Paris. He goes on to explain his experimentations: "I have made a series of color studies in painting simply flowers. . . . Trying to render intense COLOR and not a gray harmony. . . . I did a dozen landscapes too, frankly *green*, frankly *blue*. And so I am struggling for life and progress in art."

14 Fenéon 1886a, reprinted in Halperin 1970, pp. 52–58.

15 Welsh-Ovcharov 1971, p. 52; see also letter 570 for the request to exchange works.

16 See Lespinasse p. 162 in this volume for Bernard's letter to his mother describing this meeting.

17 The works Bernard presented are unknown.

18 Leeman 2013, p. 68.

19 "on peignait sur les berges; on déjeunait à la guinguette et on revenait à pied à Paris, par les avenues de Saint-Ouen et de Clichy. Van Gogh, vêtu d'une cotte bleue de zingueur, avait peint sur les manches des petits points de couleur." Coquiot 1923, p. 140.

20 The exact works are unknown, but it is likely that Tanguy had either *View of the Seine with Rowboats* **(50)** or *Bank of the Seine with Boats* **(39)**. See Van Gogh's letter to Theo [572] note 5.

21 Bernard notes that, after this incident, Van Gogh refused to return to his studio. Bernard instead visited Vincent and Theo at 54 rue Lepic. Bernard 1911, p. 12; quoted and translated in Stein 1986, p. 92.

22 This term, coined by critic Edouard Dujardin (1861–1949) at the 1888 Indépendants exhibition, was inspired by pieces of enamel with areas of color held together by small metal bands (*cloisons*), a technique perfected in France during the late Medieval and early Renaissance periods.

23 See Van Gogh's letter to Bernard [575], where Van Gogh urges Bernard to respect Signac and other artists for the beauty they are able to achieve with Pointillism. Signac did not take part in the show. The exhibition consisted of works by Van Gogh, Bernard, Anquetin, Toulouse-Lautrec, and Arnold Hendrik Koning (1860–1945).

24 "M. Angrand expose des toiles vielles de trois ans où le pittoresque de la touche et l'heureux choix du motif démontrent que [Angrand] était près du triomphe facile, sans la sincérité de son esthétique." Kahn 1888, p. 149.

25 Galitz 2001, p. 302.

26 Hendriks and Van Tilborgh 2011, pp. 571–77.

27 Herring 1997, p. 153.

28 Ibid.; Pointoise 2006, p. 26.

29 Luthi and Israël 2003, p. 38.

30 See Van Gogh and Theo's letters [779] and [781–82].

31 While Bernard's father did not support his son's artistic career, it is possible that Gauguin was the reason he forbade his son from traveling to Pont-Aven. Gauguin was unpopular among his contemporaries for a variety of reasons that cannot be adequately addressed here. For more on this, see Copenhagen 2020.

32 "I would long to see things of yours again . . . those Breton women walking in a meadow, the arrangement of which is so beautiful, the color so naively distinguished. Ah, you're exchanging that for something—must one say the word—something artificial—something affected." Letter from Vincent van Gogh to Emile Bernard, Arles, about November 26, 1889 [822].

33 Herring 1997, p. 153.

34 Letter from Seurat to Fénéon, June 20, 1890, cited in Herbert 2001, pp. 172–73.

35 "l'on se prend d'une grande tristesse à penser que ce peintre, si magnifiquement doué, que ce si frissonnant, si instinctif, si visionnaire artiste, n'est plus." Mirbeau 1891, p. 1.

36 Pissarro and Rewald 2002, p. 158.

Bibliography

Archives

Archives Angrand

Archives départementales des Hauts-de-Seine, Nanterre

Archives Municipales, Asnières-sur-Seine

Archives Signac, Paris

Letters

The Bernard letters cited in this book can be found in Emile Bernard, *Lettres de Vincent van Gogh à Emile Bernard*, Paris 1911, and Neil McWilliam (ed.), *Emile Bernard – les lettres d'un artiste (1884–1941)*, Dijon 2012.

The Van Gogh letters, letter numbers, and associated notes cited in this book can be found at www.vangoghletters.org and in the six-volume edition: Leo Jansen, Hans Luijten, Nienke Bakker (eds.), *Vincent van Gogh: The Letters. The Complete, Illustrated and Annotated Edition*, Amsterdam/Brussels 2009.

The Signac letters cited in this book can be found in Charlotte Hellman (ed.), *Paul Signac, Journal: 1894–1909*, Paris 2021, and Archives Signac.

Bibliography

Adam 1886
Paul Adam, "Peintres impressionnistes," *La Revue contemporaine*, no. 4 (April–May 1886), pp. 541–51

Agief 1888
Agief, *Oseront-ils empoissonner Paris et la vallée de la Seine?*, Paris 1888

Ajalbert 1886
Jean Ajalbert, "Les Salon des impressionnistes," *La Revue moderne: littéraire, politique et artistique*, no. 30 (June 20, 1886), p. 392

Ajalbert 1891
Jean Ajalbert, *Femmes & Paysages*, Paris 1891

Amsterdam/Paris 1999
Chris Stolwijk and Richard Thomson, *Theo van Gogh, 1857–1891: Art Dealer, Collector and Brother of Vincent*, exh. cat., Amsterdam (Van Gogh Museum) / Paris (Musée d'Orsay) 1999

Angrand 1965
Pierre Angrand, *Naissance des artistes indépendants*, Paris 1965

Anonymous 1884
Anonymous, *Catalogue illustré des oeuvres de Jean-François Raffaelli: exposées 28 bis, avenue de l'Opera suivi d'une étude des mouvements de l'art moderne et du beau caractériste*, Paris 1884

Anonymous 1886
Anonymous, "L'Exposition des impressionnistes," *La République française*, May 17, 1886, p. 3

Anonymous 1888
Anonymous, "L'Année 1887 au point de vue météorologique et la marche normale de la température à Paris," *L'Astronomie*, vol. 7 (April 1888), pp. 137–41

***Archives commerciales de la France* 1889**
"Clôtures de Faillites," *Archives commerciales de la France*, 6th year, no. 98 (December 7, 1889), p. 1543

Bailly-Herzberg 1986
Janine Bailly-Herzberg (ed.), *Correspondance de Camille Pissarro*, vol. 2: *1886–1890*, Paris 1986

Barron 1886
Louis Barron, *Les Environs de Paris*, Paris 1886

Basel 2009
Carel Blotkamp et al., *Vincent van Gogh. Between Earth and Heaven: The Landscapes*, exh. cat., Basel (Kunstmuseum Basel) 2009

De La Bédollière 1861
Emile de La Bédollière, *Histoire des environs du nouveau Paris, illustrés par Gustave Doré*, Paris 1861

Bernard 1890
Emile Bernard, "Vincent van Gogh," *Les Hommes d'aujourd'hui*, no. 390 (1890), in Rivière 1994, pp. 26–28

Bernard 1901
Emile Bernard, "Les Peintres originaux: Vincent van Gogh," *L'Arte*, vol. 11, no. 12 (February 9, 1901), pp. 1–3

Bernard 1903
Emile Bernard, "Notes sur l'école dite de 'Pont-Aven,'" *Mercure de France*, December 1903, in Rivière 1994, pp. 63–66

Bernard 1908
Emile Bernard, "Julien Tanguy dit le 'Père Tanguy,'" *Mercure de France*, December 16, 1908, in Rivière 1994, pp. 163–73

Bernard 1911
Emile Bernard, *Lettres de Vincent van Gogh à Emile Bernard*, Paris 1911

Bernard 1919
Emile Bernard, "Mémoire pour l'histoire du symbolisme pictural de 1890," *Maintenant*, no. 3 (1919), in Rivière 1994, pp. 198–206

Bernard 1924
Emile Bernard, "Souvenirs sur Van Gogh," *L'Amour de l'art*, December 1924, in Rivière 1994, pp. 241–47

Bernard 1926
Emile Bernard, "Vincent van Gogh," 1926, in Rivière 1994, pp. 250–51

Bernard 1932
Emile Bernard, "Louis Anquetin artiste peintre," *Mercure de France*, November 1932, in Rivière 1994, pp. 260–69

Bernard c. 1939-a
Emile Bernard, *L'Aventure de ma vie*, unpublished manuscript, c. 1939-a, Bibliothèque de l'Institut national d'histoire de l'art, BCMN Ms 374

Bernard 1952
Emile Bernard, "Des relations d'Emile Bernard avec Toulouse-Lautrec," manuscript c. 1939-b, posthumously published in *Art Documents*, no. 18 (March 1952), in Rivière 1994, pp. 315–18

Blanc 1867
Charles Blanc, *Grammaire des arts du dessin*, Paris 1867 (4th ed., 1882)

Blanche 1928
Jacques-Emile Blanche, *Propos de peintre*, vol. 4, Paris 1928

Bordeaux/Albi 1997
Sabine du Vignau, *Degas, Boldini, Toulouse-Lautrec: portraits inédits par Michel Manzi*, exh. cat., Bordeaux (Musée Goupil) / Albi (Musée Toulouse-Lautrec) 1997

Bouin-Luce and Bazetoux 1986
Jean Bouin-Luce and Denise Bazetoux, *Maximilien Luce: catalogue raisonné de l'oeuvre peint*, Paris 1986

Bourgeois 1996
Claude Bourgeois, *Courbevoie*, 2 vols., Joué-les-Tours 1996

B.-R. 1856
B.-R., *Le Guide du promeneur aux barrières et dans les environs de Paris . . .*, Paris 1856

Bremen 2015
Dorothee Hansen (ed.), *Emile Bernard: Am Puls der Moderne*, exh. cat., Bremen (Kunsthalle Bremen) 2015

Cachin 2000
Françoise Cachin, *Signac: catalogue raisonné de l'oeuvre peint*, Paris 2000

Charpin 1990
Catherine Charpin, *Les Arts Incohérents (1882–1893)*, Paris 1990

Chevreul 1839
Michel Eugène Chevreul, *De la loi du contraste simultané des couleurs et ses applications,* Paris 1839

Chicago 2004
Robert L. Herbert (ed.), *Seurat and the Making of "La Grande Jatte,"* exh. cat., Chicago (The Art Institute of Chicago) 2004

Clark 1999
T. J. Clark, *The Painting of Modern Life: Paris in the Art of Manet and His Followers*, rev. ed., Princeton 1999

Clement and Houzé 1999
Russell T. Clement and Annick Houzé, *Neo-Impressionist Painters: A Sourcebook on Georges Seurat, Camille Pissarro, Paul Signac, Théo Van Rysselberghe, Henri-Edmond Cross, Charles Angrand, Maximilien Luce, and Albert Dubois-Pillet*, Westport, CT 1999

Compin 1964
Isabelle Compin, *H.E. Cross: catalogue raisonné de l'oeuvre peint*, Paris 1964

Copenhagen 2020
Anna Kærsgaard Gregersen and Anna Manly (eds.), *Paul Gauguin: Why Are You Angry?*, exh. cat., Copenhagen (Ny Carlsberg Glyptotek) 2020

Coquiot 1921
Gustave Coquiot, *Les Indépendants, 1884–1920*, Paris 1921

Coquiot 1923
Gustave Coquiot, *Vincent van Gogh*, Paris 1923

Coquiot 1924
Gustave Coquiot, *Georges Seurat*, Paris 1924

Corbin 1995
Alain Corbin, *L'avènement des loisirs, 1850–1960*, Paris 1995

Départment de la Seine 1903
Départment de la Seine, *Etat des Communes: Levallois-Perret. Notice historique et renseigne-ments administratifs*, Montévrain 1903

Destremau 1994
Frédéric Destremau, *Louis Anquetin et Henri de Toulouse-Lautrec: amitié, environnement, rencontre et résonance*, PhD thesis, Université de Paris IV – Sorbonne 1994

Destremau 1996
Frédéric Destremau, "L'Atelier Cormon (1882–1887)," *Bulletin de la société de l'histoire de l'art français*, 1996, pp. 171–84

Distel 1991
Anne Distel, "Chronology," in Paris/New York 1991, pp. 399–412

Dorn 1990
Roland Dorn, "Emile Bernard and Vincent van Gogh," in MaryAnne Stevens (ed.), *Emile Bernard 1868–1941: A Pioneer of Modern Art*, exh. cat., Mannheim (Städtische Kunsthalle) / Amsterdam (Van Gogh Museum) 1990, pp. 30–47

Dorra and Rewald 1959
Henri Dorra and John Rewald, *Seurat: l'œuvre peint, biographie et catalogue critique*, Paris 1959

DuBard 2001
Lynn DuBard, "Chronology, 1886–1892," in Saint Louis/Frankfurt 2001, pp. 201–38

Dujardin 1888
Edouard Dujardin, "Aux XX et aux indépendants: le cloisonisme," [sic] *La Revue indépendante*, March 1888, pp. 487–92

Dulaure 1858
J.-A. Dulaure, *Histoire physique, civile et morale des environs de Paris . . .*, 2nd ed., vol. 2, book 1, Paris 1858

Edinburgh 1994
Richard Thomson, *Monet to Matisse: Landscape Painting in France, 1874–1914*, exh. cat., Edinburgh (National Gallery of Scotland) 1994

De la Faille 1970
J.-B. de la Faille, *The Works of Vincent van Gogh: His Paintings and Drawings*, Amsterdam 1970

Fénéon 1886a
Félix Fénéon, "L'Impressionnisme aux Tuileries," *L'Art moderne de Bruxelles*, September 19, 1886, pp. 300–2, in Halperin 1970, pp. 52–58

Fénéon 1886b
Felix Fénéon, "Les Impressionnistes en 1886. VIIe exposition de la société des artistes indépen-dants," *La Vogue*, October 1886, in Halperin 1970, pp. 43–45

Fénéon 1889
Félix Fénéon, "Catalogue des 33," *La Cravache*, January 19, 1889

Fénéon 1890
Felix Fénéon, "Signac," *Les Hommes d'aujourd'hui*, no. 373, 1890, unpaginated

Fénéon 1926
Félix Fénéon, "Charles Angrand," *Bulletin de la vie artistique*, April 15, 1926, in Halperin 1970, pp. 481–82

Fèvre 1886
H. Fèvre, "L'Exposition des impressionnistes," *Revue de demain*, May–June 1886, p. 149

Fouquier 1886
Marcel Fouquier, "Les Impressionnistes," *Le XIXe siècle: journal républicain*, May 16, 1886

Gaillard 1992
Marc Gaillard, *Les Belles-heures de Clichy: de Dagobert . . . à aujourd'hui*, Amiens 1992

Galitz 2001
Kathryn Calley Galitz, "Chronology," in Marina Ferretti-Bocquillon et al., *Signac, 1863–1935*, exh. cat., New York (Metropolitan Museum of Art) 2001, pp. 297–323

Gandy 1999
Matthew Gandy, "The Paris Sewers and the Rationalization of Urban Space," *Transactions of the Institute of British Geographers*, vol. 24, no. 1 (1999), pp. 23–44

Gastineau 1863
Benjamin Gastineau, *Histoires des chemins de fers*, Paris 1863

Gauzi 1954
François Gauzi, *Lautrec et son temps*, Paris 1954

Giverny 2010
Marina Ferretti Bocquillon, *Impressionism on the Seine*, exh. cat., Giverny (Musée des Impressionnismes) 2010

Van Gogh-Bonger 1958
Jo van Gogh-Bonger, "Preface," in *The Complete Letters of Vincent van Gogh*, vol. 1, Greenwich 1958, pp. lix–lxvii

De Goncourt 1864
Edmond and Jules de Goncourt, *Renée Mauperin*, Paris 1864

Gray 2022
Meghan L. Gray, "Vincent van Gogh, *Restaurant Rispal at Asnières*, 1887," in Aimee Marcereau DeGalan (ed.), *French Paintings and Pastels, 1600–1945: The Collections of The Nelson-Atkins Museum of Art*, Kansas City 2022, https://doi.org/10.37764/78973.5.736

Halperin 1970
Joan Ungersma Halperin (ed.), *Felix Fénéon: oeuvres plus que complètes*, vol. 1, Geneva 1970

Harscoët-Maire 1997
Laure Harscoët-Maire (ed.), "Lettres d'Emile Bernard (1886): de Cancale à Saint-Briac," in *Le Pays de Dinan*, vol. 17 (1997), pp. 107–83

Hartrick 1939
Archibald Standish Hartrick, *A Painter's Pilgrimage through Fifty Years*, Cambridge 1939

Hauke 1961
César M. de Hauke, *Seurat et son oeuvre*, 2 vols., Paris 1961

Heintz 1962
C. Heintz, "Huysmans et les dîners de banlieue," *Bulletin de la société J.-K. Huysmans*, no. 43 (1962), pp. 361–64

Hellman 2021
Charlotte Hellman (ed.), *Paul Signac, Journal: 1894–1909*, Paris 2021

Hendriks et al. 2013
Ella Hendriks et al. (eds.), "Automated Thread Counting and the Studio Practice Project," in Vellekoop et al. 2013, pp. 156–81

Hendriks and Van Tilborgh 2011
Ella Hendriks and Louis van Tilborgh, *Vincent van Gogh Paintings, Volume 2: Antwerp and Paris 1885–1888*, Amsterdam 2011

Henry 1885
Charles Henry, "Introduction à une esthétique scientifique," *La Revue contemporaine*, August 2, 1885, pp. 441–69, translated as "Introduction to a Scientific Aesthetics," *Art in Translation*, vol. 10, no. 2 (2018), pp. 198–222

Herbert 1988
Robert L. Herbert, *Impressionism: Art, Leisure, and Parisian Society*, New Haven/London 1988

Herbert 1991
Robert L. Herbert, "Appendix L. Charles Henry," in Paris/New York 1991, pp. 391–93

Herbert 2001
Robert L. Herbert, *Seurat: Drawings and Paintings*, New Haven/London 2001

Herbert 2004
Robert L. Herbert, "Before *La Grande Jatte*," in Chicago 2004, pp. 26–67

Herbert, Rougerie, and Rougerie 1961
Robert L. Herbert, Anne-Marie Rougerie, and Jacques Rougerie, "Les Artistes et l'anarchisme d'après les lettres inédites de Pissarro, Signac et autres," *Le Mouvement social*, no. 36 (July–September 1961), pp. 2–19

Hermel 1886
Maurice Hermel, "L'Exposition de peinture de la rue Lafitte," *La France libre*, May 28, 1886, pp. 1–2

Herring 1997
Sarah Herring, "Chronology," in John Leighton and Richard Thomson (eds.), *Seurat and the Bathers*, exh. cat., London (National Gallery) 1997, p. 153

Holtmann et al. 2006
Heinz Holtmann et al., *Thannhauser, Händler, Sammler, Stifter: Sediment, Mitteilungen zur Geschichte des Kunsthandels*, vol. 11, Nuremberg 2006

Homburg 2001
Cornelia Homburg, "Introduction," in Saint Louis/Frankfurt 2001, pp. 13–55

House 2001
John House, "Towards the Modern Landscape," in Saint Louis/Frankfurt 2001, pp. 159–95

Howard 1997
Michael Howard, *Encyclopedia of Impressionism*, San Diego 1997

Hunter 2019
Mary Hunter, "White Collars and Working Bodies in the Age of Industry," in Toronto 2019, pp. 60–71

Huysmans 1880
Joris-Karl Huysmans, *Croquis parisiens*, Paris 1880

Huysmans 1887
Joris-Karl Huysmans, "Chronique d'art: les indépendants," *La Revue indépendante*, April 1887, pp. 51–57

Huysmans 2006
J.-K. Huysmans, "L'Exposition des indépendants en 1880," in Patrice Locmant (ed.), *Ecrits sur l'art, 1867–1905*, Paris 2006, pp. 162–85

Jansen, Luijten, and Bakker 2009
Leo Jansen, Hans Luijten, and Nienke Bakker (eds.), *Vincent van Gogh: The Letters. The Complete, Illustrated and Annotated Edition*, Amsterdam/Brussels 2009

Joanne 1881
Adolphe Joanne, *Les Environs de Paris illustrés*, Paris 1881

Jooren 2013
Marieke Jooren, "Van Gogh's Finishing Touches: Varnish, Signatures, Frames and Painted Borders," in Vellekoop et al. 2013, pp. 290–305

Jouan 1976
Lucienne Jouan, *Asnières-sur-Seine au cours des siècles*, Asnières 1976

Jumeau-Lafond 2015
Jean-David Jumeau-Lafond, "'Attendant les murs': Séon décorateur," in Jean-David Jumeau-Lafond and Guillaume Ambroise, *Alexandre Séon (1855–1917): la beauté idéale*, exh. cat., Quimper (Musée des Beaux-Arts) / Valence (Musée d'Art et d'Archéologie) 2015, pp. 29–45

Kahn 1887
Gustave Kahn, "La Vie artistique," *La Vie moderne*, April 9, 1887, pp. 229–31

Kahn 1888
Gustave Kahn, "Chronique de la litterature et de l'art," *La Revue indépendante*, January 6, 1888, p. 149

Kunstler 1935
Charles Kunstler, "Chez Paul Signac ou l'apothéose du pointillisme," *Le Petit Parisien*, April 4, 1935, p. 4

"Labruyère" 1886
"Labruyère," "Les Impressionnistes. II," *Le Cri du peuple*, May 28, 1886, pp. 1–2

Laforgue 1941
Jules Laforgue, *Lettres à un ami, 1880–1886*, ed. G. Jean-Aubry, Paris 1941

Lanfranchi 2008
Adèle de Lanfranchi, *Lucie Cousturier, 1876–1925*, Paris 2008

Leeman 2013
Fred Leeman, *Emile Bernard (1868–1941)*, Paris 2013

Le Fustec 1886
Jean Le Fustec, “Exposition de la société des artistes indépendants,” *Journal des artistes*, 5th year, no. 35 (August 29, 1886), pp. 290–91

Le Fustec 1887
Jean Le Fustec, “Les Palettes: Ch. Angrand,” *Journal des artistes*, 6th year, no. 18 (May 8, 1887), pp. 139–40

Lehaguez 1864
M. Lehaguez, *Le Nouveau Paris et ses environs: guide de l’étranger . . .*, Paris 1864

Leighton 1997
John Leighton, “The Oil Studies” and “The Drawings for the Bathers,” in John Leighton and Richard Thomson (eds.), *Seurat and the Bathers*, exh. cat., London (National Gallery) 1997, pp. 52–63, 64–67

Leighton 2001
John Leighton, “Out of Seurat’s Shadow: Signac, 1863–1935, An Introduction,” in Marina Ferretti-Bocquillon et al., *Signac, 1863–1935*, exh. cat., New York (Metropolitan Museum of Art) 2001, pp. 3–22

Le Paul 1987
Judy Le Paul, *Gauguin and the Impressionists at Pont-Aven*, New York 1987

Lespinasse A. 2006
Adèle Lespinasse, “Charles Angrand et Georges Seurat,” in Pontoise 2006, pp. 49–102

Lespinasse F. 1980
François Lespinasse, *L’Ecole de Rouen*, Rouen 1980

Lespinasse F. 1981
François Lespinasse, *Charles Angrand, 1865–1926*, Rouen 1981

Lespinasse F. 1982
François Lespinasse, *Charles Angrand, 1854–1926*, Rouen 1982

Lespinasse F. 1988
François Lespinasse (ed.), *Charles Angrand: correspondances 1883–1926*, Rouen 1988

Lespinasse F. 2004
François Lespinasse, *Charles Frechon et Michel Frechon*, Rouen 2004

Lespinasse F. 2006
François Lespinasse, “Charles Angrand, 1854–1926,” in Pontoise 2006, pp. 11–48

Lobstein 2003
Dominique Lobstein, *Dictionnaire des indépendants, 1884–1914*, 3 vols., Dijon 2003

Lucenet 2005
Monique Lucenet, *La Grande Jatte: belle isle en Seine*, Neuilly-sur-Seine 2005

Luthi and Israël 2003
Jean-Jacques Luthi and Armand Israël, *Emile Bernard, fondateur de l’école de Pont-Aven et précurseur de l’art moderne*, Paris 2003

Luthi and Israël 2014
Jean-Jacques Luthi and Armand Israël, *Emile Bernard, sa vie, son oeuvre: catalogue raisonné*, Paris 2014

Martigny 2000
Ronald Pickvance, *Van Gogh*, exh. cat., Martigny (Fondation Pierre Gianadda) 2000

McWilliam 2012
Neil McWilliam (ed.), *Emile Bernard – les lettres d’un artiste (1884–1941)*, Dijon 2012

Merriman 1991
John M. Merriman, *The Margins of City Life: Explorations of the French Urban Frontier, 1815–1851*, New York/Oxford 1991

Mirbeau 1891
Octave Mirbeau “Vincent van Gogh,” *L’Echo de Paris*, March 31, 1891, p. 1

De Moncan and Heurteux 2002
Patrice de Moncan and Claude Heurteux, *Le Paris d’Haussmann*, Paris 2002

Monneret 2000
Jean Monneret, *Catalogue raisonné du Salon des Indépendants, 1884–2000. Les Indépendants dans l’histoire de l’art*, Paris 2000

Moréas 1886
Jean Moréas, “Le Symbolisme,” *Le Figaro, supplément littéraire*, September 18, 1886, pp. 1–2

Naldi 2022
Johann Naldi, *Arts Incohérents – Découvertes et nouvelles perspectives*, Paris 2022

New York 1968
Robert L. Herbert, *Neo-Impressionism*, exh. cat., New York (Solomon R. Guggenheim Museum) 1968

Nonne 1988
Monique Nonne, “Les marchands de van Gogh,” in Paris 1988, pp. 330–47

Nonne 2000
Monique Nonne, “Theo van Gogh. His Clients and Suppliers,” *Van Gogh Museum Journal* 2000, pp. 38–51

Paris 1881
Anonymous, *Salon de 1881. Explication des Ouvrages de Peinture . . .*, Paris 1881

Paris 1886
Anonymous, *Catalogue de la 8e exposition de peinture*, Paris 1886

Paris 1970
François Aman-Jean, *Souvenir d’Aman-Jean (1859–1936)*, exh. cat., Paris (Musée des Arts Décoratifs) 1970

Paris 1988
Bogomila Welsh-Ovcharov, Françoise Cachin et al. (eds.), *Van Gogh à Paris*, exh. cat., Paris (Musée d’Orsay) 1988

Paris 2014
Dorothee Hansen (ed.), *Emile Bernard, 1868–1941*, exh. cat., Paris (Musée de l’Orangerie) 2014

Paris 2021
Marina Ferretti and Charlotte Hellman, *Signac collectionneur*, exh. cat., Paris (Musée d’Orsay) 2021

Paris/New York 1991
Robert L. Herbert et al., *Georges Seurat, 1859–1891*, exh. cat., Paris (Galeries nationales du Grand Palais) / New York (Metropolitan Museum of Art) 1991

Paris/New York 2019
Isabelle Cahn and Philippe Peltier (eds.), *Félix Fénéon: critique, collectionneur, anarchiste*, exh. cat., Paris (Musée du quai Branly / Musée de l’Orangerie) / New York (Museum of Modern Art) 2019

Paulet 1886
Alfred Paulet, “Les Impressionnistes,” *Paris*, June 5, 1886, pp. 1–2

Périer 1890
Edmé Périer, *Notes sur la ville d’Asnières*, Asnières 1890

***Le Phare* 1884**
“Etat-civil,” *Le Phare: journal républicain des cantons de Courbevoie et d’Argenteuil*, 2nd year, no. 81 (July 20, 1884), unpaginated

Pinkney 1958
David H. Pinkney, *Napoleon III and the Rebuilding of Paris*, Princeton 1958

Pissarro and Rewald 2002
Lucien Pissarro and John Rewald (eds.), *Camille Pissarro: Letters to his Son Lucien*, trans. Lionel Abel, Boston 2002

Pontoise 2006
Christophe Duvivier, Adèle Lespinasse, and François Lespinasse, *Charles Angrand: 1854–1926*, exh. cat., Pontoise (Musée de Pontoise) 2006

Raffaëlli 1884
Jean-François Raffaëlli, *Catalogue illustré des œuvres de Jean-François Raffaelli: suivi d’une étude des mouvements de l’art moderne et du beau caractériste*, Paris 1884

Rich 1935
Daniel Catton Rich, *Seurat and the Evolution of "La Grande Jatte,"* Chicago 1935

Rivière 1994
Anne Rivière (ed.), *Emile Bernard: propos sur l'art*, vol. 1, Paris 1994

Rood 1881
Ogden Rood, *Théorie scientifique des couleurs*, Paris 1881

Rouen 2008
Laurent Salomé, Diederik Bakhuys, and François Lespinasse, *Charles Frechon: 1856–1929*, exh. cat., Rouen (Musée des Beaux-Arts) 2008

Rubin 2008
James H. Rubin, *Impressionism and the Modern Landscape: Productivity, Technology, and Urbanization from Manet to Van Gogh*, Berkeley 2008

Rubin 2019
James H. Rubin, "Industry and Labour at the Impressionist Exhibitions," in Toronto 2019, pp. 72–83

Saint Louis/Frankfurt 2001
Cornelia Homburg (ed.), *Vincent van Gogh and the Painters of the Petit Boulevard*, exh. cat., Saint Louis (Saint Louis Art Museum) / Frankfurt (Städel Museum) 2001

Sanchez et al. 2014
Pierre Sanchez, Gérard Bonnin, and François Lespinasse, *Salons et Expositions: Rouen: répertoire des exposants et liste de leurs oeuvres, 1833–1949*, 3 vols., Dijon 2014

Shields 2019
Caroline Shields, "Geographies of Impressionism in the Age of Industry, an Introduction," in Toronto 2019, pp. 12–49

Signac 1891
Paul Signac, "Variétés: impressionnistes et révolutionnaires," *La Révolte, Organe communiste-anarchiste*, June 13–19, 1891, pp. 3–4

Signac 1899
Paul Signac, "L'Art dans l'habitation moderne, le Castel Béranger," *La Revue blanche*, no. 137 (February 15, 1899), pp. 317–19

Société historique et archéologique 1974
Société historique et archéologique, *Clichy-la-Garenne: vingt siècles d'histoire*, La Madeleine 1974

Stein 1986
Susan Alyson Stein (ed.), *Van Gogh: A Retrospective*, New York 1986

Sutter 1970
Jean Sutter, *Les néo-impressionnistes*, Neuchâtel 1970

Thomson 1985
Richard Thomson, *Seurat*, Oxford 1985

Thomson 1987
Richard Thomson, "Van Gogh in Paris: The Fortifications Drawings of 1887," *Jong Holland* 3 (September 1987), pp. 14–25

Thomson 1989
Richard Thomson, "The *Grande-Jatte*: Notes on Drawing and Meaning," *Art Institute of Chicago Museum Studies*, vol. 14, no. 2 (1989), pp. 181–97, 245–46

Thomson 1997
Richard Thomson, "Adapting the Ideal," in John Leighton and Richard Thomson (eds.), *Seurat and the Bathers*, exh. cat., London (National Gallery) 1997, pp. 85–95

Thomson 2001
Richard Thomson, "The Cultural Geography of the Petit Boulevard," in Saint Louis/Frankfurt 2001, pp. 65–108

Thomson 2012
Richard Thomson, *Art of the Actual: Naturalism and Style in Early Third Republic France, 1880–1900*, New Haven/London 2012

Thomson 2021
Richard Thomson, *The Presence of the Past in French Art, 1870–1905: Modernity and Continuity*, New Haven/London 2021

Van Tilborgh 2007
Louis van Tilborgh, "Van Gogh in Cormon's Studio: A Chronological Puzzle," in Chris Stolwijk et al., *Current Issues in 19th-Century Art: Van Gogh Studies 1*, Zwolle/Amsterdam 2007, pp. 52–71

Van Tilborgh 2018
Louis van Tilborgh, "In the Light of Japan: Van Gogh's Quest for Happiness and a Modern Identity," in Louis van Tilborgh et al., *Van Gogh & Japan*, exh. cat., Amsterdam (Van Gogh Museum) 2018, pp. 40–91

Van Tilborgh 2022
Louis van Tilborgh, "Van Gogh's Self-Portraits: Reaching for the Infinite," in Karen Serres et al., *Van Gogh Self-Portraits*, exh. cat., London (The Courtauld) 2022, pp. 37–62

Toronto 2019
Caroline Shields (ed.), *Impressionism in the Age of Industry*, exh. cat., Toronto (Art Gallery of Ontario) 2019

Toronto/Amsterdam 1981
Bogomila Welsh-Ovcharov, *Vincent van Gogh and the Birth of Cloisonism*, exh. cat., Toronto (Art Gallery of Ontario) / Amsterdam (Van Gogh Museum) 1981

Tucker 1982
Paul Hayes Tucker, *Monet at Argenteuil*, New Haven/London 1982

Uhlenbeck and Van Tilborgh 2018
Chris Uhlenbeck and Louis van Tilborgh, *Japanese Prints: The Collection of Vincent van Gogh*, London 2018

Védry 2015
Bernard Védry, *Balade écologique au fil de la Seine en 1900*, Paris 2015

Vellekoop and Van Heugten 2001
Marije Vellekoop and Sjraar van Heugten, *Vincent van Gogh Drawings, Volume 3: Antwerp & Paris, 1885–1888*, Amsterdam 2001

Vellekoop et al. 2013
Marije Vellekoop et al. (eds.), *Van Gogh's Studio Practice*, New Haven/London 2013

Verhaeren 1901
Emile Verhaeren, "L'Art moderne," *Mercure de France*, no. 134 (February 1901), p. 544-47.

Virmaître 1888
Charles Virmaître, *Paris-palette*, Paris 1888

Walther and Metzger 1997
Ingo F. Walther and Rainer Metzger, *Vincent van Gogh: The Complete Paintings* vol. 1: *Etten, April 1881–Paris, February 1888*, Cologne 1997

Welsh-Ovcharov 1971
Bogomila Welsh-Ovcharov, *The Early Works of Charles Angrand and his Contact with Vincent van Gogh*, Utrecht/The Hague 1971

Welsh-Ovcharov 1976
Bogomila Welsh-Ovcharov, *Vincent van Gogh: His Paris Period, 1886–1888*, Utrecht/The Hague 1976

Welsh-Ovcharov 1988
Bogomila Welsh-Ovcharov, "Introduction, adresses et plan, chronologie," in Paris 1988, pp. 10–38

X 1886
X, "Les Artistes Indépendants," *La Liberté*, May 18, 1886

Zimmer 2009
Nina Zimmer, "Serial Van Gogh: Cycles, Groups, Triptychs," in Basel 2009, pp. 96–118

Zola 1878
Emile Zola, *La Banlieue*, 1878, republished in Emile Zola, *Le Capitaine Burle*, Paris 1882

Zola 1886
Emile Zola, *L'Oeuvre*, Paris 1886

List of Exhibited Works

Works marked with an ▫ are only included in the exhibition at The Art Institute of Chicago. Works marked with an • are only included in the exhibition at the Van Gogh Museum.

Exhibited works are indicated in the captions by (cat.).

Charles Angrand

The Seine at Saint-Ouen, Morning, 1886
Oil on canvas, 46×55.4 cm
Van Gogh Museum, Amsterdam (purchased with support from the VriendenLoterij)

The Seine at Courbevoie: La Grande Jatte, 1888
Oil on canvas, 50×60 cm
Private collection

The Seine at Dawn, 1889
Oil on canvas, 61×81 cm
Association des Amis du Petit Palais, Geneva

Emile Bernard

View of Saint-Ouen, 1885
Oil on canvas, 33×41 cm
Private collection

Fisherman and Boat, 1885–86
Oil on canvas, 39×51.5 cm
Van Gogh Museum, Amsterdam (Vincent van Gogh Foundation)

Boats on the Seine at Asnières, c. 1886 •
Pen and ink on paper, 15.7×31.1 cm
Kunsthalle Bremen—Der Kunstverein in Bremen

The Regatta, c. 1886
Pencil, pen, and brush and ink on paper, 19×30 cm
Private collection

Iron Bridges at Asnières, 1887 ▫
Oil on canvas, 45.9×54.2 cm
The Museum of Modern Art, New York
Grace Rainey Rogers Fund, 1962

Quai de Clichy on the Seine, 1887
Oil on canvas, 39×59 cm
Musée d'Orsay, Paris, on loan to the Musée départmental du Prieuré, Saint-Germain-en-Laye, bequest of Pierre Farcy, 1989

Two Women on the Asnières Footbridge, 1887
Oil on canvas, 38×46.5 cm
Musée des Beaux-Arts de Brest métropole

Figures on the Riverbank, 1888
Reed pen and brush and ink and watercolor on paper, 32×26 cm
Van Gogh Museum, Amsterdam (Vincent van Gogh Foundation)

Idyll at Asnières (Idylle à Asnières), 1888
Brush and ink and watercolor on paper, 27.5×40.4 cm
Van Gogh Museum, Amsterdam (Vincent van Gogh Foundation)

Garden in Bloom at Asnières, 1889
Oil on canvas, 54.3×64.1 cm
Collection of Andrew S. Teufel

Vincent van Gogh

On the Outskirts of Paris, 1886
Oil on canvas, 45.7×54.6 cm
Private collection in loving memory of Frank and Marie Wangeman

A Woman Walking in a Garden, 1887
Oil on canvas, 48×60 cm
Private collection

Bank of the Seine, 1887
Oil on canvas, 32×46 cm
Van Gogh Museum, Amsterdam (Vincent van Gogh Foundation)

Bank of the Seine with Boats, 1887
Oil on canvas, 48×55 cm
Private collection

Banks of the Seine with the Pont de Clichy, 1887 •
Oil on canvas, 30.5×39 cm
Private collection

Bank with Trees, 1887 •
Oil on canvas, 37×45.5 cm
P. & N. de Boer Foundation, Amsterdam

Bridges Across the Seine at Asnières, 1887 •
Oil on canvas, 53.5×67 cm
Emil Bührle Collection, on long-term loan at Kunsthaus Zürich

By the Seine, 1887
Oil on canvas, 49.4×65.3 cm
Van Gogh Museum, Amsterdam (Vincent van Gogh Foundation)

Exterior of a Restaurant in Asnières, 1887
Oil on canvas, 18.8×27 cm
Van Gogh Museum, Amsterdam (Vincent van Gogh Foundation)

Factories at Clichy, 1887
Oil on canvas, 53.7×72.7 cm
Saint Louis Art Museum, Missouri
Funds given by Mrs. Mark C. Steinberg by exchange, 579:1958

Fishing in Spring, the Pont de Clichy (Asnières), 1887
Oil on canvas, 50.5×60 cm
The Art Institute of Chicago
Gift of Charles Deering McCormick, Brooks McCormick, and the Estate of Roger McCormick, 1965.1169

Gate in the Paris Ramparts, 1887 ▫
Pencil, pen and ink, watercolor, on paper, 24.1×31.6 cm
Van Gogh Museum, Amsterdam (Vincent van Gogh Foundation)

Gate on the Ile de la Grande Jatte, 1887
Oil on canvas, 54.6×66.8 cm
Bequest of Ignace Hellenberg, Paris, to the State of Israel, In memory of his parents Sigmund and Betty Hellenberg. On permanent loan to The Israel Museum, Jerusalem, from the Administrator General of the State of Israel

Lane on the Ile de la Grande Jatte, 1887
Oil on canvas, 55×67 cm
Private collection

Outskirts of Paris: Road with Peasant Shouldering a Spade, 1887
Oil on canvas, 47×71.6 cm
Private collection, Larry Ellison

Restaurant de la Sirène, Asnières, 1887
Oil on canvas, 52×64.4 cm
The Ashmolean Museum, University of Oxford
Bequeathed by Dr Erich Alport, 1972

Restaurant de la Sirène at Asnières, 1887
Pencil and chalk on paper, 39.8×53.8 cm
Van Gogh Museum, Amsterdam (Vincent van Gogh Foundation)

Restaurant Rispal at Asnières, 1887
Oil on canvas, 73.3×60 cm
The Nelson-Atkins Museum of Art, Kansas City, Missouri
Gift of Henry W. and Marion H. Bloch, 2015.13.10

River Bank in Springtime, 1887
Oil on canvas, 48.9×58.1 cm
Dallas Museum of Art
Gift of Mr. and Mrs. Eugene McDermott in memory of Arthur Berger, 1961.99

Road Running Beside the Paris Ramparts, 1887 •
Pencil, watercolor, chalk, brush and (oil) paint, pen and ink, on paper, 39.7×53.8 cm
Van Gogh Museum, Amsterdam (Vincent van Gogh Foundation)

Roadway with Underpass (Le viaduc), Asnières, 1887
Oil on cardboard, 32.7×41 cm
Solomon R. Guggenheim Museum, New York
Thannhauser Collection, Gift, Justin K. Thannhauser, 1978, 72.2514.17

Sailing Boat on the Seine at Asnières, 1887
Pencil and chalk on paper, 53.8×39.5 cm
Van Gogh Museum, Amsterdam (Vincent van Gogh Foundation)

Seine with a Rowboat, 1887
Oil on canvas, 55×65 cm
Private collection

Self-Portrait, 1887 ▫
Oil on artist's board, mounted on cradled panel, 41×32.5 cm
The Art Institute of Chicago
Joseph Winterbotham Collection, 1954.326

The Bridge at Courbevoie, 1887
Oil on canvas, 32.1×40.5 cm
Van Gogh Museum, Amsterdam (Vincent van Gogh Foundation)

The Fortifications of Paris with Houses, 1887 ▫
Pencil, black chalk, watercolor, and bodycolor on paper, 38.7×53.4 cm
The Whitworth Art Gallery, The University of Manchester

The Laundry Boat on the Seine at Asnières, 1887
Oil on canvas, 19.1×27 cm
Virginia Museum of Fine Arts, Richmond
Collection of Mr. and Mrs. Paul Mellon, 83.25

The Restaurant de la Sirène at Asnières, 1887
Oil on canvas, 54.5×65.5 cm
Musée d'Orsay, Paris, bequest of Joseph Reinach, 1921

View of the Pont d'Asnières, 1887
Oil on canvas, 54.3×73.3 cm
Private collection, Larry Ellison

Georges Seurat

Clothes on the Grass, 1883
Oil on panel, 16.2×24.8 cm
Tate, London
Presented by Alex Reid and Lefevre 1926

Final Study for "Bathers at Asnières," 1883
Oil on panel, 15.8×25.1 cm
The Art Institute of Chicago
Gift of the Adele R. Levy Fund, Inc., 1962.578

Man Painting a Boat, c. 1883
Oil on panel, 15.9×25 cm
The Courtauld, London (Samuel Courtauld Trust)

Study for "Une Baignade," c. 1883
Oil on panel, 15.9×25 cm
National Galleries of Scotland, Edinburgh
Presented by Sir Alexander Maitland in memory of his wife Rosalind 1960

Study for "Bathers at Asnières," 1883–84
Oil on panel, 15.2×25 cm
The National Gallery, London. Presented by Heinz Berggruen, 1995

The Seine at Courbevoie, 1883–84
Oil on panel, 15.5×24.5 cm
Van Gogh Museum, Amsterdam (purchased with support from the Vincent van Gogh Foundation and the Rembrandt Association, with the additional support from the Prins Bernhard Cultuurfonds)

Oil Sketch for "La Grande Jatte," 1884
Oil on panel, 15.5×24.3 cm
The Art Institute of Chicago
Gift of Mary and Leigh Block, 1981.15

Landscape and Figures (The Pink Skirt), 1884
Oil on cradled panel, 15.2×24.9 cm
Private collection

Trees (Study for La Grande Jatte), 1884
Black Conté crayon on white laid paper, laid down on cream board, 62×47.5 cm
The Art Institute of Chicago
Helen Regenstein Collection, 1966.184

Tree Trunks (Study for La Grande Jatte), 1884
Black Conté crayon on ivory laid paper, 47.4×61.5 cm
The Art Institute of Chicago
Helen Regenstein Collection, 1987.184

Woman Walking with a Parasol (Study for La Grande Jatte), 1884 ▫
Conté crayon on cream laid paper, 31.7×24.1 cm
The Art Institute of Chicago
Bequest of Abby Aldrich Rockefeller, 1999.8

Strolling Man next to a Tree on a Bank (Study for La Grande Jatte), 1884–85
Black chalk on paper, 61.5×47.5 cm
Von der Heydt-Museum, Wuppertal

Seated Women (Study for La Grande-Jatte), 1884–85
Oil on panel, 15.6×25 cm
Private collection

Seated Woman with a Parasol (Study for La Grande Jatte), 1884–85 ▫
Black Conté crayon on ivory laid paper, 48×31.5 cm
The Art Institute of Chicago
Bequest of Abby Aldrich Rockefeller, 1999.7

Study for "La Grande Jatte," 1884–85
Oil on panel, 17.5×26 cm
The National Gallery, London. Presented by Heinz Berggruen, 1995

The Seine at Courbevoie, 1885
Oil on canvas, 81.4×65.2 cm
Private collection

The Seine at La Grande Jatte, 1888
Oil on canvas, 65×82 cm
Royal Museums of Fine Arts, Brussels

The Seine Seen from La Grande Jatte, 1888
Oil on panel, 15.7×25 cm
The National Gallery, London. Presented by Heinz Berggruen, 1995

Regatta (Two Sailboats), c. 1890 ▫
Conté crayon on paper, 23×30.5 cm
Private collection

Paul Signac

Asnières Study (Laundry Boat), 1882
Oil on canvas, 38.6×56 cm
Uehara Museum of Art, Shimoda

Asnières Study (The Ferryman's Boat), 1882
Oil on panel, 14×23 cm
Private collection

Road to Gennevilliers, 1883
Oil on canvas, 73.5×92 cm
Musée d'Orsay, Paris, acquired in 1968

Coal Crane, Clichy, 1884
Oil on canvas, 59 × 91.4 cm
Lent by Glasgow Life (Glasgow Museums) on behalf of Glasgow City Council. Presented by the Trustees of the Hamilton Bequest, 1946

Rue de la Station, Asnières, 1884
Oil on canvas, 32 × 46 cm
Private collection

The Festival at Asnières, 1884
Oil on canvas, 26.7 × 45.5 cm
Private collection

Gasometers, Clichy, 1885
Conté crayon on paper, 23 × 29.5 cm
Private collection

Quai de Saint-Ouen, 1885
Oil on canvas, 60.2 × 92.3 cm
Private collection

The Banks of the Seine, Asnières, 1885 ▫
Oil on canvas, 60.2 × 92.2 cm
The Museum of Modern Art, Saitama

Railway Junction near Bois-Colombes, 1885–86
Oil on canvas, 46.5 × 65.5 cm
Van Gogh Museum, Amsterdam

Regatta on the Seine, c. 1885–86 •
Conté crayon on paper, 21.7 × 31.2 cm
Musée d'Orsay, Paris

Gasometers at Clichy, 1886
Oil on canvas, 65 × 81 cm
National Gallery of Victoria, Melbourne
Felton Bequest, 1948

Snow, Bois-Colombes, 1886
Oil on canvas, 34.3 × 45.7 cm
Private collection

The Gas Tanks at Clichy, 1886 ▫
Pen and iron gall ink over graphite on Japan paper on cardboard, 24.5 × 36.6 cm
Lent by The Metropolitan Museum of Art, Harris Brisbane Dick Fund, 1948 (48.10.4)

The Junction at Bois-Colombes (Opus no. 130), 1886
Oil on canvas, 33 × 47 cm
Leeds Art Gallery, Leeds Museums and Galleries

The "Ponton de la Félicité" at Asnières (Opus no. 143), 1886
Oil on canvas, 33.4 × 46.7 cm
Van Gogh Museum, Amsterdam (purchased with support from the VriendenLoterij, the Rembrandt Association, with the additional support from its Themafonds Impressionisme/Claude Monet Fonds, Het Liesbeth van Dorp Fonds and Themafonds 19de-eeuwse Schilderkunst, the Mondriaan Fund, and the members of The Yellow House)

Clipper (Opus no. 155), 1887
Oil on canvas, 46 × 55 cm
Hasso Plattner Collection

Passage du Puits-Bertin (Clichy), 1887 •
Black ink on paper, 16 × 25 cm
Musée du Louvre, Paris, fonds du musée d'Orsay

Passage du Puits-Bertin (Clichy), 1887
Conté crayon on paper, 24 × 31 cm
Private collection

Quai de Clichy, Gray Weather, 1887 •
Oil on canvas, 46 × 65.5 cm
Private collection

Quai de Clichy, (Opus no. 157), 1887
Oil on canvas, 46.4 × 65.4 cm
The Baltimore Museum of Art
Gift of Frederick H. Gottlieb, BMA 1928.6.1

Bow of the Tub (Opus no. 176), 1888 •
Oil on canvas, 45 × 65 cm
Private collection

Sketch of the Central Panel, Design for the Decoration of the Reception Room of the Town Hall of Asnières, 1900
Oil on canvas, 49 × 224 cm
Private collection

Sketch of the Five Windows, Design for the Decoration of the Reception Room of the Town Hall of Asnières, 1900
Oil on canvas, 49 × 224 cm
Private collection

About the Authors

JENA K. CARVANA

Jena K. Carvana is the Curatorial Associate in Painting and Sculpture of Europe at the Art Institute of Chicago, where she has provided research support for the present exhibition and *El Greco: Ambition and Defiance* (2020). She received a master of arts degree in medieval history from the University of Leeds with a thesis on Alfonso VI of León and Castile's treatment of religious minorities following his conquest of Toledo, Spain. Before joining the Art Institute, she held collection and curatorial internships at the Museum of Science and Industry, Chicago; Royal Armories, Leeds; and Museum of Contemporary Art Chicago.

JACQUELYN N. COUTRÉ

Jacquelyn N. Coutré is the Eleanor Wood Prince Associate Curator in Painting and Sculpture of Europe at the Art Institute of Chicago. She received her doctorate from New York University with a dissertation on the late work of Rembrandt's colleague Jan Lievens and has published widely on seventeenth-century Dutch art. She has held curatorial positions at the Metropolitan Museum of Art, the Indianapolis Museum of Art, and the Agnes Etherington Art Centre of Queen's University at Kingston, Ontario. There, she curated a wide range of exhibitions, including *Printmakers at War, 1914–1918* (2018); *Leiden circa 1630: Rembrandt Emerges* (2019), which was accompanied by a catalogue; and *Paul Litherland: B-Side Agnes Etherington* (2020).

BREGJE GERRITSE

Bregje Gerritse is a Researcher at the Van Gogh Museum. She was curator of the exhibition *The Potato Eaters: Mistake or Masterpiece?* (2021–22) and has assisted on several exhibition projects, including *On the Verge of Insanity : Van Gogh and His Illness* (2016) and *Van Gogh & Japan* (2018). She is one of the authors of a forthcoming collection catalogue *Vincent van Gogh: Paintings 3: Arles, Saint-Rémy and Auvers*. She completed a master's degree in museology at the Ecole du Louvre in Paris and is currently a PhD candidate at the University of Amsterdam; her research topic is *The Reception of Vincent van Gogh in Paris 1886–1914: Art Dealers, Collectors, Critics, and Contemporary Artists.*

CHARLOTTE HELLMAN

Charlotte Hellman is the only living descendant of the artist Paul Signac. She is responsible for the Signac Archives Center in Paris (archives-signac.com) and a specialist in his work. She has written numerous articles and two books about Signac, including *Glissez, mortels, les vies amoureuses de Paul Signac* (Philippe Rey, 2019), a biography about Signac's love life. In 2021 she published the full, annotated edition of Paul Signac's *Journal (1894–1909)* (Gallimard). She was co-curator of the exhibition *Signac, the Collector* (Musée d'Orsay, Paris, 2021–22).

JOOST VAN DER HOEVEN

Joost van der Hoeven is a Researcher at the Van Gogh Museum. He is editor and one of the authors of the forthcoming catalogue of paintings and drawings of Van Gogh's contemporaries in the museum's collection, specifically those that were once collected by Vincent and Theo van Gogh. In 2018 he co-curated the exhibition *Gauguin and Laval in Martinique*, and he is both co-editor and one of the authors of a forthcoming scholarly volume on the same topic. In 2020 he published on the critical reception of Impressionism in the Netherlands. He is one of the authors of the exhibition catalogue *Van Gogh in America* (Detroit Institute of Arts, 2022–23).

FRANÇOIS LESPINASSE

François Lespinasse was born in Rouen and has been interested in the painters of the Rouen School since 1976, with a predilection for Charles Angrand. He ran an art gallery in Rouen from 1979 to 2007 and published his first book in 1980 on the painters of the Rouen School. This was followed by a series of monographs on Angrand and other artists. Between 1992 and 2002 he worked for the Wildenstein Institute in Paris on the catalogue of Albert Lebourg and as an expert for the Rouen Court of Appeal. Lespinasse has curated several exhibitions, including *Charles Angrand* (Musée de Pontoise, 2006), *Ecole de Rouen: Les peintres impressionnistes et postimpressionnistes* (Atelier Grognard, Rueil-Malmaison, 2011), and *François Depeaux, collectionneur des Impressionnistes* (Musée des Beaux-Arts, Rouen, 2020).

TEIO MEEDENDORP

Teio Meedendorp is a Senior Researcher at the Van Gogh Museum, which he joined in 2009 to work on the project "Van Gogh's Studio Practice." This research concluded in 2013 with several publications and an exhibition. He is one of the authors working on the forthcoming collection catalogue *Vincent van Gogh: Paintings 3: Arles, Saint-Rémy and Auvers.* He publishes regularly on a wide range of Van Gogh–related subjects, most recently in scholarly exhibition catalogues such as *Van Gogh and the Olive Groves* (2021) and *Van Gogh in Auvers-sur-Oise: His Final Months* (2023). Meedendorp was previously employed at the Kröller-Müller Museum in Otterlo, where he helped compile the collection catalogues for the paintings (2003) and drawings and prints (2007) of Vincent van Gogh.

RICHARD THOMSON

Richard Thomson is Research Professor in the History of Art at the University of Edinburgh, where he was Watson Gordon Professor of Fine Art (1996–2018). He has published widely on late nineteenth-century French art. His work on Seurat includes a monograph (Phaidon, 1985) and two focus exhibitions: *Seurat and The Bathers* (with John Leighton; National Gallery, London, 1997) and *Seurat's Circus Sideshow* (with Susan Stein and Charlotte Hale; Metropolitan Museum of Art, New York, 2017). His most recent book, *The Presence of the Past in French Art, 1870–1905: Modernity and Continuity* (Yale University Press, 2021), discusses Seurat in terms of the classicism of early Third Republic France.

Acknowledgments

First and foremost, we are indebted to Maite van Dijk, former Senior Curator of Paintings at the Van Gogh Museum, since 2021 Director of Museum MORE in Gorssel, who first conceived the idea for this exciting exhibition project focusing on five artists working in Asnières and the surrounding areas in the 1880s. Our team of distinguished authors—Jena K. Carvana, Charlotte Hellman, Joost van der Hoeven, François Lespinasse, Teio Meedendorp, and Richard Thomson—helped deepen the extensive research for the publication and exhibition. With their assistance, we were able to locate and clarify many of the sites represented in the exhibited objects and to further strengthen our understanding of these artists. We are profoundly grateful for the insights of our editorial board, Gloria Groom, Curator and David and Mary Winton Green Curator, Painting and Sculpture of Europe, the Art Institute of Chicago, and Nienke Bakker, Senior Curator of Paintings, Van Gogh Museum.

Many documentation specialists and archival professionals shared their expertise on Paris's northwest suburbs along the Seine. Pascal Deroche opened the doors of the Archives départementales d'Asnières to us. Our inquiries were also graciously received by Xavier Theret at the Centre municipal d'Archives et de Documentation in Levallois; Mélaine Betoule at the Archives municipales in Clichy; Isabelle Stephan at the Service Archives in Courbevoie; and Julien Le Magueresse at the Archives départmentales des Hauts-de-Seine. Their collegiality and generosity were fundamental to this project's success.

The exhibition has been made possible by the support of a large number of institutions and individuals: Alexander Sturgis, Colin Harrison, An Van Camp, Catherine Whistler, Ilenia Scerra, Aisha Burtenshaw, and Christina Gernon, Ashmolean Museum of Art; Christine Dietz, Asma Naeem, Christopher Bedford (formerly), Katy Rothkopf, and Giselle Piqué, The Baltimore Museum of Art; Lukas Gloor, Emil Bührle Collection; Ernst Vegelin van Claerbergen and Karen Serres, The Courtauld; Agustín Arteaga, Nicole Myers, and Tricia M. Earl, Dallas Museum of Art; Denis Weil, Henk van Doornik, Barbara Meltz Kahn, Silvia Rozenberg, Efrat Klein, Adina Kamien, Miryam Alafi, Shlomit Steinberg, Tanya Sirakovich, and Shani Zahavi, Israel Museum; Duncan Dornan, Pippa Stephenson, Vivien Hamilton, Karen Stewart, and Rebecca Quinton, Kelvingrove Art Gallery and Museum; Dorothee Hansen and Tanja Borghardt, Kunsthalle Bremen; John Roles, Nigel Walsh, Sarah Murray, and Emii Alrai, Leeds City Art Galleries; Max Hollein, Emily Foss, Ashley Dunn, and Clara Goldman, Metropolitan Museum of Art; Marie-Aline Charier, Musée départemental du Prieuré, Saint-Germain-en-Laye; Sophie Lessard, Saoussan Sabeh, and Reza Salami, Musée des Beaux-Arts de Brest métropole; Christophe Leribault and Odile Michel, Musée d'Orsay; Matthias Heitbrink, Hasso Plattner Collection; Claude Ghez and Marjorie Klein, Musée Petit Palais, Geneva; Ortrud Westheider, Michael Philipp, Helene von Saldern, Anne Barz (formerly), and Daniel Zamani, Museum Barberini; Glenn Lowry, Lily Goldberg, and Marissa Klein-Kundrath, Museum of Modern Art, New York; Ayuka Sato and Ryoko Gomi, Museum of Modern Art, Saitama; John Leighton, Delphine Charpentier, and Jacqui Austin, National Galleries of Scotland; Gabriele Finaldi, Caroline Campbell (formerly), Richard Dark, Claire Hallinan, and Samantha Saward, National Gallery, London; Tony Ellwood, Henry Blackshaw, Liam Crowe, and Ieva Kanepe, National Gallery of Victoria; Julián Zugazagoitia, Aimee Marcereau DeGalan, and Julie Mattsson, The Nelson-Atkins Museum of Art; Michael Draguet, Valérie Haerden, and Dominique Marechal, Royal Museums of Fine Arts, Brussels; Min Jung Kim, Jamie Sepich, Simon Kelly, Diane Mallow, and Cait Kennedy, Saint Louis Art Museum; Richard Armstrong, Vivien Greene, Tracey Bashkoff, Indira Abiskaroon, David Horowitz, and Carol Nesemann Klebanoff, Solomon R. Guggenheim Museum; Maria Balshaw, Sarah-Jane Stockings, and Dana Mokaddem, Tate; Yoshiko Ohira and Tomonori Tsuchimori, Uehara Museum of Art; Roland Mönig, Alex Nygeres, Michael Taylor, Sylvain Cordier, and Nancy T. Nichols, Virginia Museum of Fine Arts; Beate Eickhoff, Bettina Klecha, and Sarah Breuer, Von der Heydt-Museum; Alistair Hudson, Imogen Holmes-Roe, Gillian Smithson, and Jamilla Briggs, The Whitworth Art Gallery. We also recognize the numerous private collectors who wish to remain anonymous.

In addition, many colleagues graciously facilitated loans: Lucrezia Argyropoulus, Allegra Bettini, Jennifer Biederbeck, Tyler Cann, Carrie Chen, Cyanne Chutkow, Rebekah Cox-Tianga, Deborah Coy, Lucy Economakis, Marina Ferretti, Dorothée Galludec, Leonard Gianadda, Jean-Christophe Giuseppi, Rachel Helfand Giuseppi, Lehka Hileman, Cornelia Homburg, Eik Kahng, Anke Kausch, Brooke Lampley, Funahashi Masanori, Claire McGowan, Cynthia Miller, Robert Miller, Eva Reifert, Mark Scala, Alana Topham, Chelsea Troper, Cecilia Weaver, Alexis Wells, and Joan Wyatt.

We are grateful to both institutions for supporting and devoting resources to an exhibition of this size and scale. At the Van Gogh Museum we thank the Vincent van Gogh Foundation for their unwavering support. We also acknowledge the assistance of the Ministry of Education, Culture, and Science of the Netherlands. The exhibition has been subsidized by the Dutch government: an indemnity grant has been provided by the Cultural Heritage Agency of the Netherlands on behalf of the Minister of Education, Culture, and Science. We recognize our main partners the VriendenLoterij, ASML, and DHL as well as our exhibition partners Van Lanschot Kempen and The Sunflower Circle. This would not have been possible with the outstanding members of our Development team, Marissa Otten, Emma Swaan, Josine Vermei, and Sonia Gunning. At the Art Institute of Chicago, lead support is generously provided by The Kenneth C. Griffin Charitable Fund. Major support is provided by the Shure Charitable Trust, the Jentes Family, the Pepper Family Foundation, Julie and Roger Baskes, The Manitou Fund, and Margot Levin Schiff and the Harold Schiff Foundation. Additional funding is provided by the Jack and Peggy Crowe Fund, the Suzanne and Wesley M. Dixon Exhibition Fund, and The Regenstein Foundation Fund. Members of the Luminary Trust provide annual leadership support for the museum's operations, including exhibition development, conservation and collection care, and educational programming. The Luminary Trust includes an anonymous donor, Karen Gray-Krehbiel and John Krehbiel, Jr., Kenneth C. Griffin, the Harris Family Foundation in memory of Bette and Neison Harris, Josef and Margot Lakonishok, Robert M. and Diane v.S. Levy, Ann and Samuel M. Mencoff, Sylvia Neil and Dan Fischel, Cari and Michael J. Sacks, and the Earl and Brenda Shapiro Foundation.

This ambitious project would have been impossible without the generous encouragement of the staff of both museums and the rewarding collaboration between the two institutions. At the Van Gogh Museum, we particularly appreciate Teio Meedendorp and Louis van Tilborgh for their expertise on Van Gogh. We have received much assistance from Monique Hageman and Juliette van Uhm. At the Art Institute we acknowledge the members of the department of Painting and Sculpture of Europe: Gloria Groom, Zahra Bahia, Emerson Bowyer, Robert Burnier, Deniseya Hall, Rebecca J. Long, Andrea Morgan, Megan True, and Daisy Wong. Colleagues in other curatorial departments have enthusiastically supported this endeavor: Ellenor Alcorn, Christopher Maxwell, Jonathan Tavares, and Kate Heller in Applied Arts of Europe; Jay A. Clarke and Jamie Gabbarelli in Prints and Drawings; Melinda Watt in Textiles; Ashley Arico in Arts of Africa; and Caitlin Haskell in Modern and Contemporary. Megan Hurlbert at the Art Institute and Sander Rutjens at the Van Gogh Museum have been outstanding project managers; their sophisticated skills guaranteed the successful organization and installation of this exhibition.

The conservation departments of each museum have generously contributed much time and goodwill to enable these artworks to be exhibited in pristine condition. At the Van Gogh Museum we recognize René Boitelle, Hannie Diependaal, Ruth Hoppe, Nico Lingbeek, Oda van Maanen, Saskia van Oudheusden, and Kathrin Pilz. At the Art Institute, we thank Allison Langley, Kimberley Muir, Julie Simek, Jann-Nicole Trujillo, Kirk Vuillemot, and Chris Wood for their skillful treatments.

The beautiful presentation of the exhibition benefitted enormously from a vast and talented team at each institution. At the Van Gogh Museum, Christiaan Borstlap from Part of a Bigger Plan created an innovative and inspiring exhibition design. Many thanks are due to Jolein van Kregten and Ann Blokland from the educational department and our graphic designer Franck Nederstigt. At the Art Institute, independent designer Barbara Materia produced an innovative layout. Colleagues in Experience Design facilitated the exhibition presentation, video, and the audio tour: Michael Neault, Gina Giambalvo, Vitalii Emelianov, Kari McCluskey, Devin Davis, Kirill Mazor, Logan A. Chappe, and Alex Quintanilla. Emily Fry and Loren Wright ensured the thoughtfulness and creativity of the interpretive materials.

The logistics of safely packing and transporting such a number of works around the world are incredibly complex. For their expertise in arranging transit, we commend at the Art Institute Cayetana Castillo, Tim Campos, and Joyce Penn in Collections and Loans, and Maria Patijn, Annemieke Bouma-Bouwmans, Mechtild Beckers, and Jolande Roest (formerly) in the Registrar's Office of the Van Gogh Museum. For their care in crating and handling such significant works of art, at the Art Institute we are grateful to Michael Kaysen, Jon Fiersten, and Herbert Metzler in Packing; for the meticulous installation, we thank Leslie Carlson, Matt Alicea, Christine Huck, Dave Ford, Patrick Smith, Ryan Pfeiffer, Acassia Ferreira da Cunha, and Christine Wallers. The Legal and General Counsel specialists at the Art Institute have overseen all documentation with superb proficiency: Heather Costello, Leslie Darling, Troy Klyber, Jennifer Sostaric, Carolyn Boies, and Justine E. Quinn. At the Van Gogh Museum we express our gratitude to Marvin Rot, Hans-Martijn Groeneveld-Nijsen, Anne Steegstra, Ronald van den Haak, and Elsemiek Hofman for their expert art handling and installation, and Edwin Kolster and Domenico Casillo for the exhibition construction. Special praise is due to Heleen van Driel and Maurice Tromp for their beautiful photography and image editing of our artworks. We also recognize the Legal and General Counsel specialists at the Van Gogh Museum, Babette Meerdink-Schenau and Alise Akimova. Jill Bugajski, Autumn Mather, and their staff at Ryerson Library of the Art Institute assisted in our research queries. The publishing team at the Van Gogh Museum expertly took the lead in organizing this catalogue, guided by Anniek Meinders, Heleen Ruijg, Merel Dijkhuizen, and Suzanne Bogman (formerly). In Publishing at the Art Institute, Joseph Mohan, Lisa Meyerowitz, Kit Shields, Lauren Makholm, Ben Bertin, and Isella Sandoval furthered its smooth production. Our Imaging department has ensured that our works look exceptional: Bonnie Rosenberg, Elyse M. Allen, Robert Lifson, and Craig T. Stillwell. We offer our deep appreciation to Kees van den Hoek at THOTH Publishers who oversaw the production of this book and Yale University Press for its distribution. Designer Julian Kleyn brought our manuscript to life with a spectacular design and lithographer Bert van der Horst took care of the beautiful illustrations. Particular thanks are due to our editors: Kate Bell, Lisa Meyerowitz, Kit Shields, Monique den Ouden, and Els Brinkman. David Olsen proofread the final pages. Our highly skilled translators, Ted Alkins, Alan Thawley, Maaike Post, Arjen Mulder, and Hilde Pauwels, facilitated multiple language editions.

The promotion of an exhibition with Van Gogh at its center requires a highly skilled and unified team. At the Art Institute, we would like to thank Shannon Burke, Nora Gainer, Jen Nelson, Kathryn Rahn, and Nadine Schneller in Marketing; we would also like to acknowledge the creative teams at Leo Burnett Worldwide and Spark Foundry for their smart promotional strategies. At Leo Burnett, the team includes Chelsea Berger, Mark Burgess, Emily Doskow, Franki Geib, Gareth Goodall, SeVohn Hunter, Michelle Mahoney, Adriana Meneses, Britt Nolan, Kim Shields, and Andrew Swinand; at Spark Foundry, Miriam Gillan, Tracie Jasper, Alex McCann, Sabrina Pierrard, Ashley Smith, and Stephanie Verbeke shared their expertise. At the Van Gogh Museum, Lisa Brack, Oscar Bouwhuis, Fransje Pansters, Corinne Jongh, Alain van der Horst, and Gideon Querido van Frank oversaw marketing, press, and digital communications.

Finally, the support of such an undertaking required unwavering support at the highest levels. For their ongoing enthusiasm for this project, we are grateful to James Rondeau, President and Eloise W. Martin Director and Emilie E. S. Gordenker, Director. At the Art Institute we also thank Sarah Guernsey, Deputy Director and Senior Vice President of Curatorial Affairs; Hilary Branch, Executive Director of Museum Initiatives and Strategy; Ann Goldstein, Deputy Director and Chair and Curator of Modern and Contemporary Art; Eve Jeffers, Chief Operating Officer; and the executive support team in the director's office: Amanda Block, Claire M. Burdulis, Jennifer R. Cohen, Alexander Jen (formerly), and Maureen T. Ryan. At the Van Gogh Museum: Rob Groot, Managing Director; Willem van Gogh, Advisor to the Board; Marije Vellekoop, Senior Manager Collection and Research; Amanda Vollenweider, Senior Manager Exhibitions, Education and Interpretation; Yvonne Nassar, Senior Manager Marketing and Communications; and the executive support team Hilda Bakker, Senior Management Assistant; Sarah Sprenger, Project Coordinator; Martine Blok, Management Assistant.

This project would not have been possible without the help of the numerous people mentioned above. We recognize the contributions of each and every person, and we have valued their expertise and generous collaboration.

Jacquelyn N. Coutré and Bregje Gerritse

Index

Page numbers in **bold** refer to artworks, page numbers in *italic* refer to images of said persons and page numbers followed by an n refer to endnotes.

Photo Credits

Every effort has been made to trace and credit all known copyright or reproduction right holders; the publishers apologize for any errors or omissions and welcome these being brought to their attention. Copyright of works of visual artists affiliated to a CISAC organization has been arranged with Pictoright in Amsterdam, © c/o Pictoright Amsterdam 2023. Unless otherwise noted, photography of artworks in the collection of the Art Institute of Chicago are by Robert Lifson and Craig Stillwell, with post-production by Hayley Hinsberger and Owen Conway, and are copyrighted by the Art Institute of Chicago.

2001 Christie's Images Limited: 87
2003 Christie's Images Limited: 147
2007 Christie's Images Limited: 99
2008 Christie's Images Limited: 18
2015 Christie's Images Limited: 62
2018 Christie's Images Limited: 84
2020 Christie's Images Limited: 131
akg-images / Cameraphoto: 133
Ashmolean Museum: 49
Christian Baraja SLB: 89, 90
Courtesy of the Barnes Foundation, Merion and Philadelphia, Pennsylvania: 27
Bridgeman Images: 126
The Courtauld: 61, 79
The Courtauld / Bridgeman Images: 59
CSG CIC Glasgow Museums Collection: 26
Dallas Museum of Art: 53
Travis Fullerton © Virginia Museum of Fine Arts: 35
J. Geleyns—Art Photography: 135
Mitro Hood: 98
The Israel Museum Jerusalem by Elie Posner: 45
M. Johnston: 106
Leeds Museums and Galleries, UK / Bridgeman Images: 86
The Metropolitan Museum of Art/Art Resource/Scala, Florence: 25, 154
Jamison Miller: 38
The Morgan Library & Museum, New York: 153
Musée des Beaux-Arts de Brest métropole: 120
Musée d'Orsay, Dist. RMN-Grand Palais / Patrice Schmidt: 155
The Museum of Modern Art, New York/Scala, Florence: 121
The National Gallery, London: 17, 64, 66, 74, 136, 141
Antonia Reeve: 63
RMN-Grand Palais (musée d'Orsay) / Michèle Bellot: 91, 95
RMN-Grand Palais (musée d'Orsay) / Jean-Gilles Berizzi: 138
RMN-Grand Palais / Gérard Blot: 57, 58, 107
RMN-Grand Palais (musée d'Orsay) / Adrien Didierjean: 22, 67
RMN-Grand Palais (musée d'Orsay) / Hervé Lewandowski: 13, 75
Peter Schälchli, Zurich: 96, 97
Schälchli/Schmidt, Zurich: 48
Leonard de Selva / Bridgeman Images: 119
Sotheby's / akg-images: 78
Studio Monique Bernaz, Geneva: 137
The Whitworth, The University of Manchester, photo Michael Pollard: 11
Yale University Art Gallery: 60
Antje Zeis-Loi, Medienzentrum Wuppertal: 145

Illustrations

Cover (paperback edition): Map of Paris, 1886, G.W. Colton. Photo: David Rumsey Map Collection, David Rumsey Map Center, Stanford Libraries
p. 4: Vincent van Gogh, *Bridges Across the Seine at Asnières*, 1887 (fig. 48)
p. 5: Postcard no. 14, p. 57
p. 6: Postcard no. 13, p. 57
p. 7: Paul Signac, *Stern of the Tub (Opus no. 175)*, 1888 (fig. 99)
p. 8: Vincent van Gogh, *River Bank in Springtime*, 1887 (fig. 53)
p. 9: Postcard no. 22, p. 61
p. 10: Charles Angrand, *On the Ile des Ravageurs*, 1885 (fig. 127)
p. 12: Emile Bernard, *Quai de Clichy on the Seine*, 1887 (fig. 119)
p. 13: Postcard no. 4, p. 52
p. 14: Postcard no. P 10, p. 55
p. 15: Georges Seurat, *Seated Women (Study for La Grande Jatte)*, 1884–85 (fig. 147)
p. 16: Paul Signac, *Clipper (Opus no. 155)*, 1887 (detail of fig. 92)
p. 18: Vincent van Gogh, *River Bank in Springtime*, 1887 (detail of fig. 53)
p. 182: Vincent van Gogh, 1873. Van Gogh Museum, Amsterdam (Vincent van Gogh Foundation). Photo Jacobus Marinus Wilhelmus de Louw
p. 182: Georges Seurat, c. 1888. Private collection
p. 183: Paul Signac, c. 1883. Archives Signac, Paris
p. 183: Emile Bernard, c. 1888. Van Gogh Museum (Documentation), Amsterdam
p. 184: Charles Angrand. Private collection

Colophon

This catalogue was published on the occasion of the exhibition:

Van Gogh and the Avant-Garde: The Modern Landscape
The Art Institute of Chicago
May 14, 2023–September 4, 2024

Van Gogh Along the Seine
Van Gogh Museum, Amsterdam
October 13, 2023–January 14, 2024

The exhibition was co-organized by the Van Gogh Museum in Amsterdam and The Art Institute of Chicago.

Catalogue editors
Bregje Gerritse and Jacquelyn N. Coutré

Authors
Bregje Gerritse, Joost van der Hoeven, and Teio Meedendorp (Van Gogh Museum), Jena K. Carvana and Jacquelyn N. Coutré (The Art Institute of Chicago), Charlotte Hellman, François Lespinasse, and Richard Thomson

Editorial Board
Nienke Bakker and Gloria Groom

Publisher
Kees van den Hoek, THOTH Publishers

Publication management
Anniek Meinders, Van Gogh Museum
Sarah Guernsey, The Art Institute of Chicago

Coordination
Heleen Ruijg, Van Gogh Museum
Joseph Mohan and Lisa Meyerowitz, The Art Institute of Chicago

Image editor
Merel Dijkhuizen

Copy-editing
Kate Bell, Lisa Meyerowitz, and Kit Shields

Proofreader
David Olsen

Translation
Ted Alkins, Hilde Pauwels, and Alan Thawley

Design
Julian Kleyn, Studio Berry Slok, Amsterdam

Color separations
Bert van der Horst, BFC Graphics, Amersfoort

Printing and binding
Drukkerij Wilco, Amersfoort

Typeset in Suisse Int'l, Roumald (Erkin Karamemet)
Printed on Condat Périgord 150 g

FSC www.fsc.org MIX Paper from responsible sources FSC® C004472

www.vangoghmuseum.com
www.artic.edu
www.thoth.nl

ISBN 978 90 6868 869 6

Cover illustrations
Front cover: Vincent van Gogh, *Fishing in Spring, the Pont de Clichy (Asnières)*, 1887 (fig. 51)
Back cover: Vincent van Gogh, *Bridges Across the Seine at Asnières*, 1887 (fig. 48),
Georges Seurat, *Final Study for "Bathers at Asnières,"* 1883 (fig. 65)
Paul Signac, *Quai de Clichy, Sunlight* (*Opus no. 157*), 1887 (fig. 98)
Emile Bernard, *Two Women on the Asnières Footbridge*, 1887 (fig. 120)
Charles Angrand, *The Seine at Courbevoie: La Grande Jatte*, 1888 (fig. 134)

The exhibition at the Van Gogh Museum and this book were made possible by the support of:

Main partners

Ministry of Education, Culture and Science

VRIENDENLOTERIJ
- SINDS 1989 -
WIN MEER, BELEEF MEER

ASML

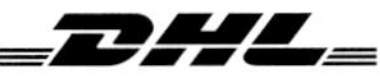

Exhibition partners Van Gogh Museum

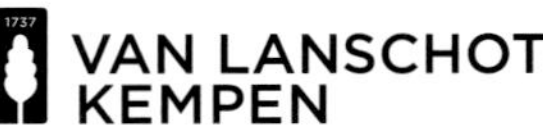

The
Sunflower
Circle

The exhibition has been supported by the Dutch government: an indemnity grant has been provided by the Cultural Heritage Agency of the Netherlands on behalf of the Minister of Education, Culture and Science.

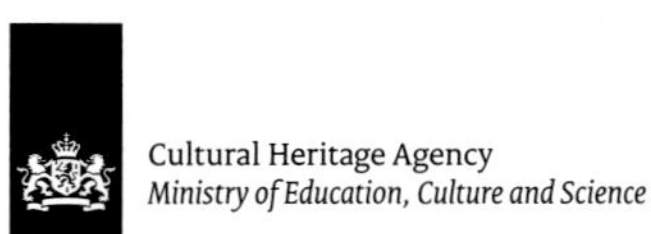